Applying Cultural Anthropology

An Introductory Reader

Second Edition

Aaron Podolefsky
University of Northern Iowa

Peter J. Brown
Emory University

Mayfield Publishing Company
Mountain View, California
London • Toronto

For Paula Brown,
a gifted teacher, mentor, and scholar whose
outstanding work has earned her a secure
place in the history of the anthropological
study of New Guinea and in the hearts of
her many students.

Library of Congress Cataloging-in-Publication Data

Applying cultural anthropology : an introductory reader / [selected
  by] Aaron Podolefsky, Peter J. Brown. — 2nd ed.
      p.   cm.
    Includes index.
    ISBN 1-55934-325-7
    1. Applied anthropology.   I. Podolefsky, Aaron.   II. Brown, Peter
J.
  GN397.5.A68   1993
  301—dc20   93-14433
                                                             CIP

Manufactured in the United States of America
10 9 8 7 6 5 4 3 2

Mayfield Publishing Company
1280 Villa Street
Mountain View, California 94041

Sponsoring editor, Janet M. Beatty; production editor, Lynn Rabin
Bauer; manuscript editor, Dale Anderson; cover designer, Steve
Naegele; cover photograph: David C. Gibson, U.S. Agency for
International Development; manufacturing manager, Martha
Branch. The text was set in 10/12 Palatino by Harrison
Typesetting and printed on 50# Butte des Morts by Banta
Company.

 This book is printed on recycled paper.

To the Student

An introductory course in any discipline is chock-full of new terminology, concepts, and facts. Sometimes students forget that these new ideas and vocabulary are actually intellectual tools that can be put to work for analyzing and solving problems. In preparing this book, we have selected readings that will show you how anthropological concepts, discoveries, and methods can be applied in today's world.

The study of anthropology can help you view the world in a completely different way than you ever had before. You can come to appreciate the great diversity of human cultures and the interrelatedness of economic, sociopolitical, and religious systems. Anthropology can give you a broad perspective on humanity and help you understand other people's beliefs and customs. In doing so, it can help you become a better citizen in an increasingly global society.

The fascinating side of anthropology seems obvious to most educated people, but there is also a lesser known practical side of the discipline. The readings we have selected demonstrate that practical, applied side. Many of the articles are examples of anthropological ideas and research methods in action—as they are used to understand and solve practical problems. We have included career profiles of anthropologists working outside the academic setting to show how they are applying anthropology. We believe that the fundamental lessons of anthropology can be applied to many careers and all areas of human endeavor.

To benefit from the study of anthropology, you need to study effectively. Over the years, we have found that students often read assignments without planning, and this actually makes studying less efficient. Before you read a selection, spend a few moments skimming it to get an idea of what it is about, where it is going, and what you should look for. This kind of preliminary reading is a poor idea for mystery novels, but is essential for academic assignments.

Without this preparation, the article may become a hodgepodge of facts and figures; details may be meaningless because you have missed the big picture. By planning your reading, you can see how the details are relevant to the central themes of an article.

To help you plan your reading, at the beginning of each article we have included questions and a list of glossary terms. By studying these questions in advance, you may gain an idea of what is to come and why the article is important. This will help make the time you spend reading more fruitful. Most of the questions highlight the central themes of the selection or draw your attention to interesting details. Some of the questions, however, do not have straightforward answers—they are food for thought and topics for discussion.

These articles have been selected with you, the student, in mind. We hope they convey our excitement about the anthropological adventure, and we expect that you will find them both enjoyable and thought-provoking.

If you are interested in further reading in applied anthropology, there are several excellent books available, such as *Applied Anthropology: A Practical Guide*, by Erve Chambers; *Applied Anthropology: An Introduction*, by John van Willigen; *Anthropological Praxis: Translating Knowledge into Action*, by Robert M. Wulff and Shirley J. Fiske; *Applied Anthropology in America*, by Elizabeth M. Eddy and William L. Partridge, and *Making Our Research Useful*, by John van Willigen, Barbara Rylko-Bauer, and Anne McElroy. You might also want to look at the journals *Human Organization* and *Practicing Anthropology*, both of which are published by the Society for Applied Anthropology. The National Association of Practicing Anthropologists (NAPA) has also published interesting works on specific fields such as Medical Anthropology.

To the Instructor

Introductory cultural anthropology has become an established part of the college curriculum, and through this course our profession communicates with a large and diverse undergraduate audience. Members of that audience differ in experience, academic concentration, and career aspirations. For those students considering anthropology as a major, we need to provide (among other things) a vision of the future, a view of anthropological work to be done in the public domain as well as within academia. For them, we need to provide some answers to the question, "What can I do with a degree in anthropology?" For students majoring in other areas, such as business, engineering, or psychology, we need to address the question, "How can anthropological insights or research methods help me understand and solve human problems?" If we can provide such a service, we increase the likelihood that students will find creative solutions to the professional problems that await them, and we brighten the future for our anthropology majors by underscoring the usefulness of an anthropological perspective in attempts to solve the practical problems of today's world.

Over the years, we have found that most introductory texts have done little more than include a chapter on applied anthropology at the end of the book. This suggests, at least to students, that most of anthropology has no relevance to their lives. Such treatment also implies that the application of anthropological knowledge is a tangent or afterthought—at best, an additional subject area, such as kinship or politics.

We disagree. We believe that the applications of anthropology cut across and infuse all the discipline's subfields. This reader is a collection of articles that provide examples of both basic and *applied* research in cultural anthropology and anthropological linguistics.

One of our primary goals is to demonstrate some of the ways our discipline is used outside the academic arena. We want anthropology to be seen as a field that is interesting as well as relevant to the real world. Like the public at large, students seem well aware that the subject matter of anthropology is fascinating, but they seem unaware of both the fundamental questions of humanity addressed by anthropologists and the practical applications of the field.

Although people distinguish between basic and applied research, much of anthropology falls into a gray area, having elements of both. Many selections in this reader fall into that gray zone—they are brief ethnographic accounts that contain important implications for understanding and resolving problems. We could have included a large number of articles exemplifying strictly applied research—an evaluation report of agency performance, for example. While this sort of research is fascinating and challenging to do, it is usually not exciting for students to read. We have selected articles that we believe are fascinating for students and convey the dual nature (basic/applied) of social science research.

Any student who completes an introductory course in cultural anthropology should learn that anthropological work, in its broadest sense, may include (or at least contribute to) international business, epidemiology, program evaluation, social impact studies, conflict resolution, organizational analysis, market research, and nutrition research, even though their introductory anthropology texts make no mention of these fields. The selections in this book should help students understand why cultural anthropology is important in today's world, and also make the course more memorable and meaningful.

FEATURES OF THIS EDITION

- We chose the readings in this book to complement the typical course in introductory cultural anthropology. The sequence of articles follows the organization of standard cultural anthropology textbooks, grouped under traditional headings such as culture and communication, rather than headings based on the applied areas such as medical anthropology or the anthropology of development. Had we meant this book to be a reader on applied anthropology, our organization would have been different. While this book could be used in courses on applied anthropology (an earlier edition has been), this was not our intended audience. Also, for this reason, we have not provided extensive discussion of the history or definition of applied anthropology. For students interested in this, there are a number of fine books on the subject. These include *Applied Anthropology: A Practical Guide*, by Erve Chambers; *Applied Anthropology: An Introduction*, by John van Willigen; *Anthropological Praxis: Translating Knowledge into Action*, by Robert M. Wulff and Shirley J. Fiske; *Applied Anthropology in America*, by Elizabeth M. Eddy and William L. Partridge, and *Making Our Research Useful*, by John van Willigen, Barbara Rylko-Bauer, and Anne McElroy.

- To emphasize how anthropology can be put to work in different settings, we have included a number of profiles of anthropologists whose careers involve applying anthropology outside the university setting.

- To help students better understand the subject matter, we have included a number of pedagogical aids: introductions, a list of glossary terms, and guiding questions for each article; a world map that pinpoints the locations of places and peoples discussed in the articles; and, for easy reference, an extensive glossary and index.

- To help busy instructors, we have provided an instructor's manual for this edition that includes for each article a brief summary, glossary terms, and test questions.

- Among the 12 new articles in this edition are several that pertain to gender issues. We've combined two sections, "Sex Roles and Marriage" and "Socialization and Parenting," into one called "Gender and Socialization." In addition to two new articles here (one on changing marriage patterns and population growth among a group of Amazonian Indians and the other on dowry death in India), we've included a new article on male–female mis-

communication in the section "Culture and Communication."

ACKNOWLEDGMENTS

We want to thank the entire staff at Mayfield Publishing Company and especially our editor, Jan Beatty, for her vision, good humor, and tolerance.

We would especially like to thank the following instructors who reviewed our selections for this edition: Jill Brody, Louisiana State University; Tom Fitzgerald, University of North Carolina, Greenville; Nicholas Honorkamp, University of Tennessee, Chattanooga; Danial J. Yakes, Muskegon Community College; and Todd Young, Humboldt State University.

We're also grateful to the many instructors who returned questionnaires about the selections in the first edition that their students found most valuable and enjoyable: Myrdene Anderson, Purdue University; Dean E. Arnold, Wheaton College; Frank Bartell, Community College of Philadelphia; Harold R. Battersby, SUNY College at Geneseo; Jeffrey A. Behm, University of Wisconsin, Oshkosh; Vaughn M. Bryant, Jr., Texas A&M; Peter Castro, Syracuse University; B. Dennis, University of Michigan, Flint; Charles Ellenbaum, College of DuPage; Thomas Fitzgerald, University of North Carolina, Greensboro; Patrick D. Gaffney, University of Notre Dame; Francis B. Harrold, University of Texas, Arlington; David T. Hughes, Wichita State University; B. Joans, San Jose State University; D. Johnson, North Carolina Agricultural and Technical State College; Frank C. Leonhardy, University of Idaho; Janet E. Levy, University of North Carolina, Charlotte; Susan Long, John Carroll University; Ronald R. McIrvin, University of North Carolina, Greensboro; James H. Mielke, University of Kansas; Winifred Mitchell, Mankato State University; S. Moore, Georgia Southern College; R. Mucci, Indiana University Northwest; Phillip D. Neusius, Indiana University of Pennsylvania; Sarah Ward Neusius, Indiana University of Pennsylvania; Catherine J. Sands, Central Washington University; Diane Sank, City College of New York; C. Shelton, La Salle University; B. Siegel, Furman University; N. Stirrat, College of Lake County; James A. Wanner, University of Northern Colorado; Nancy White, University of South Florida, Tampa; and I. Wundram, Oxford College of Emory University.

We would also like to thank the following people who have been so willing to share their viewpoints and efforts in compiling this volume: George Armelagos, Lauren Bailey, Peggy Barlett, Jennifer Erskine, Donna Horne, Mel Konner, Lori Kool, Beth Krueger, Anne Nugent, Judy Robinson, Kristi Seavey, Bradd Shore, and Pat Woelber.

Contents

RITUAL AND CURING

SOCIAL AND CULTURAL CHANGE

Introduction:
Understanding Humans and Human Problems

To the uninitiated, the term *anthropology* conjures up images of mummies' tombs, Indiana Jones, and treks through steaming jungles or over high alpine peaks. Anthropologists agree that their chosen field is exciting, that they have been places and seen things that few experience firsthand, and that they have been deeply and emotionally involved in understanding the human condition. At the same time, however, the vision of anthropology presented by Hollywood has probably done more to obscure the true nature of the profession than it has to enlighten the public about what we really do.

Providing an accurate image of anthropology and anthropological work is both simple and complex. Essentially, anthropology is the study of people, or more properly, of humankind. But, you may say, many disciplines study people: psychology, sociology, history, biology, medicine, and so on. True, but anthropology is different in that it seeks to integrate these separate and narrow views of humanity. To understand ourselves, we need to join these disparate views into a single framework, a process that begins with our biological and evolutionary roots, explores the development of culture through the prehistoric and historical periods, probes the uniquely human ability to develop culture through communication, and examines the diversity of recent and present-day cultures that inhabit the globe.

From this conception of the *holistic* and *comparative* study of humankind emerge what are termed the four fields of anthropology: biological (or physical) anthropology, archaeology, anthropological linguistics, and cultural anthropology. Some universities offer an introductory course that covers all four of these subfields. Other schools cover the subfields in two or three separate introductory courses. Each approach has its advantage. The former may more fully integrate the biocultural and historical dimensions of humanity; the latter allows students to explore each subfield in greater depth. This book introduces you to the field of cultural anthropology and how it is used in today's world.

Another way to divide the discipline—in fact almost any discipline—is into *basic* and *applied* research. These categories are important in this reader because we would like students to appreciate both the basic and applied sides of cultural anthropology. A survey of natural and social scientists and engineers conducted by the U.S. Census Bureau for the National Science Foundation used the following definitions of these fundamental concepts: *Basic research* is study directed toward gaining scientific knowledge primarily for its own sake; *applied research* is study directed toward gaining scientific knowledge in an effort to meet a recognized need.

Anthropology is a discipline concerned primarily with basic research. It asks "big" questions concerning the origins of humankind, the roots of human nature, the development of civilization, and the functions of our major social institutions (such as marriage or religion). Nevertheless, anthropologists have put the methods and skills developed in basic research to use in solving human problems and fulfilling the needs of society. Anthropologists have, for example, worked with medical examiners in the identification of skeletal remains. They have also helped communities preserve their cultural heritage and businesses and government agencies understand the social impacts of programs or development projects.

Although the application of anthropology has a long history, it has, until recent years, remained in the shadows of "pure" or basic research. The last 20 years have seen a change. Anthropologists have moved beyond their traditional roles in universities and museums and now work in a broad range of settings. They are employed in many government agencies, in the private sector, and in a variety of nonresearch capacities (such as administrator, evaluator, or policy analyst).

In response to the growing opportunities for anthropologists outside academia and to the demands of students, an increasing number of master's degree and doctoral programs provide training specifically in the applications of anthropology. This is not to say that the classified ads list jobs titled "anthropologist." Rather, for those interested in anthropology, there are increasing opportunities to find careers that draw on anthropological training and skills. Profiles of people in nonacademic careers (consumer marketing, high-tech industry, and school administration) can be found in this reader. At the same time, studies have shown that there will be increasing job opportunities for anthropologists in universities and colleges during the 1990s and beyond.

Applications of anthropology are found in all four subfields. Anthropological work includes the identification of skeletal remains (forensics); the study of size and fit for the design of clothing, furniture, or airplane cockpits (ergonomics); exploration of the patterns and causes of disease (epidemiology); evaluation of the effectiveness of programs (from Third World development to crime prevention); assessment of community needs; prediction of the social impact of change; analysis of organizations such as businesses or government agencies; market research; and research into health and nutrition, to name but a few.

School administrators, engineers, business leaders, lawyers, medical researchers, and government officials have become aware that the substantive knowledge, the unique perspective, and the research skills of anthropologists are applicable to practical problems—in the United States as well as other countries.

As we explore anthropology, keep in mind the interplay between and interdependence of basic cultural research and the applications of anthropological knowledge and research methods to the solution of human problems.

CULTURAL ANTHROPOLOGY

Cultural anthropology is concerned with the description and analysis of people's lives and traditions. In the past, cultural anthropologists almost always did research in far-off "exotic" societies, but today, we have expanded our research interests to include our own society. Cultural anthropology can add much to both the basic and applied scientific understanding of human behaviors and beliefs. The study and interpretation of other societies—of their traditions, history, and view of the world—is inherently interesting and important because it documents the diversity of human lifestyles. The anthropological approach to understanding other societies also has practical value for addressing contemporary human problems and needs.

The concept of *culture* is central to anthropology. It refers to the patterns of economy, social organization, and belief that are learned and shared by members of a social group. Culture is traditional knowledge that is passed down from one generation to the next. Although generally stable over time, culture is flexible and fluid, changing through borrowing or invention. The influential American anthropologist Franz Boas championed the concept of culture for understanding human diversity; culture, Boas argued, is distinct from biological "race" or language. Anthropologists believe that all cultural lifestyles have intrinsic value and validity. Other societies deserve to be studied and understood without being prejudged using our own narrow (and sometimes intolerant) beliefs and values; this universal tendency to prejudge based on the supposed superiority of one's own group, called *ethnocentrism*, is something everyone should avoid.

Culture is the crowning achievement of human evolution. To understand ourselves is to appreciate cultural diversity. Dependence on culture as our primary mechanism of survival sets humans apart from other members of the animal kingdom. This dependence is responsible for the tremendous evolutionary success of our species, which has grown in population (sometimes to the point of overpopulation) and can inhabit nearly every niche on the planet.

The paradox of culture is that, as we humans learn to accept our own cultural beliefs and values, we unconsciously learn to reject those of other peoples. At birth, we are capable of absorbing any culture and language. We are predisposed to cultural learning, but we are not programmed to adopt a particular culture. As we grow, our parents, our schools, and our society teach us what is right and wrong, good and evil, acceptable and unacceptable. At the subconscious level, we learn the symbolic meanings of behavior and through them interpret the meanings of actions. Beliefs, values, and symbols must be understood within the context of a particular culture. This is the principle of *cultural relativity*.

In addition to the concept of culture, the anthropological approach to the study of human behavior and belief has two essential characteristics: a holistic approach and a comparative framework. The *holistic approach* means that anthropologists see a particular part of culture—for example, politics, economy, or religion—in relation to the larger social system. Individuals are viewed, not in isolation, but as part of an intricate web of social relationships. Although an anthropological study may have a particular focus, the holistic approach means that the broader cultural context is always considered important because the different parts of a cultural system are interrelated. When, for example, the economy or technology changes, other aspects of the culture will change as well.

The *comparative framework* means that explanations or generalizations are informed by cross-cultural research. Questions about humanity cannot be based on information from a single society or a single type of society—like the industrial societies of the United States and Europe. Such a limited framework is simply too narrow for understanding the big picture that basic anthropological research seeks. By studying others within a comparative frame, we can better understand ourselves. If other cultures are a mirror in which we see ourselves, then anthropology is a mirror for humankind.

The broad generalizations about culture and society that we have been talking about are based on detailed knowledge of the world's cultures. To gain this knowledge, anthropologists go to the people. Often accompanied by spouses and children, we pack our bags and travel to far-off lands—to the highlands of New Guinea, the frozen arctic, the savannas of Africa, or the jungles of South America. Increasingly, anthropologists are bringing their research methods and comparative, holistic perspective into the cities and suburbs of America, the American schoolroom, or the corporate jungle. This "research adventure" has become the hallmark of cultural anthropology.

The research methods used by the cultural anthropologist are distinctive because they depend, to a large extent, on the firsthand experiences and interpretations of the field researcher. Cultural anthropologists conduct research in natural settings rather than in laboratories or over the telephone. This method for studying another society is often called *participant observation*, *ethnography*, or *qualitative methods*. The goal of describing, understanding, and explaining another culture is a large task. It is most often accomplished by living in the society for an extended period, by talking with people, and, as much as possible, by experiencing their lives.

The fieldwork experience usually involves a kind of culture shock in which the researcher questions his or her own assumptions about the world. In this way, fieldwork is often a rewarding period of personal growth. In their work, anthropologists expect to find that other people's behavior, even when it seems bizarre when seen from the outside, makes sense when it is viewed from the people's own point of view. This is why anthropological research often means letting people speak for themselves. While doing research, the anthropologist often thinks of herself or himself as a child—as being ignorant or uninformed and needing to be taught by the people being studied. This approach often involves in-depth interviewing with a few key informants and then interpreting (and writing about) that other culture for the researcher's own society. The ethnographic method, pioneered and developed in anthropology, is now being used in a range of applied areas, including marketing, management research, and school evaluation. Although ethnography is an important research style, the selections in this book demonstrate that many different methods are used in anthropology today.

The applications of cultural anthropology are diverse. Internationally, anthropologists are involved in programs of technical assistance and economic aid to Third World nations. These programs address needs in such areas as agriculture and rural development; health, nutrition, and family planning; education; housing and community organizing; transportation and communication; and energy. Anthropologists do many of the same things domestically as well. They evaluate public education, study agricultural extension programs, administer projects, analyze policy (such as U.S. refugee resettlement programs), and research crime and crime prevention, for example.

In the private sector, cultural anthropologists can add a fresh perspective to market research. They analyze office and industrial organization and culture. They create language and cultural training workshops for businesspeople and others who are going overseas. These workshops reduce the likelihood of cross-cultural misunderstanding and the problems of culture shock for the employee and, often more important, for his or her family.

Applied anthropological work can be divided into four categories. In the first group, applied and basic research look very much alike, except that the goal of applied research is more directly linked with a particular problem or need. For example, in Selection 31, Aaron Podolefsky studies the causes of the reemergence of tribal warfare in New Guinea. Such studies provide planners and policymakers with important insights for understanding the problem. This knowledge can lead to the design and implementation of programs that help bring an end to warfare in the region.

In the second category, anthropologists work as researchers for a government agency, corporation, or interest group on a specific task defined by the client as discussed in the selection "Corporate Anthropologists" (Selection 6).

In the third category, anthropologists work as consultants to business and industry or to government agencies that need in-depth cultural knowledge to solve or prevent a problem. In "Problems in Pocatello" (Selection 10), Barbara Joans enters the realm of law to assess the level of misunderstanding between government agents and a group of Native American women. Anthropologists often act as cultural brokers, mediating and translating between groups who are miscommunicating, not because of their words but because of cultural meanings.

Finally, a few anthropologists have developed and administered programs. Gerald F. Murray's work in reforestation in Haiti (Selection 19) exemplifies the development and actual administration of a project in which cultural understanding is a fundamental component. The overwhelming success of this agroforestry project attests to the practical value of cultural understanding for solving human problems.

A great deal of anthropological work remains to be done, though this seems to be a well-kept secret. People have a far easier time focusing on the individual as the level of analysis. When divorce, drug abuse, or suicide affects small numbers of people, we may look to the individual and to psychology for answers. When divorce rates climb to 50 percent of all marriages and the suicide rate increases tenfold, however, we must look beyond the individual to forces that affect society at large. Because we are so immersed in our own culture, we have difficulty seeing it as a powerful force that guides—even controls—our behavior. We begin these readings, therefore, with three selections that convey the hidden, but powerful, nature of culture.

1

Swimming in Cross-Cultural Currents

Conrad Phillip Kottak

Time is understood and interpreted differently in various parts of the world. For us, it is the primary way in which our daily life is organized. Most Americans awake to the buzzing of a precisely set alarm. Following our regular morning rituals, we leave home in the hopes of being on time. The day is punctuated by a series of time periods: breakfast time, break time, lunch time, quitting time, and dinner time. According to our children, snack time comes just before bedtime. Time is money; we often spend time and save time. In many ways time defines our interpretation of behavior. For example, guests who arrive early to a dinner party are inconsiderate (you're still setting the table or, worse yet, getting dressed) whereas guests who arrive on time are appreciated, as are, to a lesser degree, those who arrive appropriately (however that is defined) late. Guests who arrive too late are considered rude. Some people are consistently rude and therefore don't get invited to a lot of dinner parties.

Most of us agree that time is a real, digitally measurable dimension, and of course it is. However, not all cultures consider time as crucially important as we do; in fact, concern with time permeates American culture. A host's response to a tardy guest is neither God-given nor genetically determined. In some cultures, being late is not a concern because being on time is not expected. Americans who travel overseas often have difficulty getting used to other people's habits and perceptions about time. A businesswoman, finding her guest a half-hour late, gets increasingly annoyed. To her, the guest's tardiness reflects a lack of respect for her and her corporation and a lack of concern for the deal she is pursuing. When he does arrive, she is on

the defensive and considerably less friendly than he had expected. When the deal falls through, both wonder what happened and why the other had changed so since their previous encounter. The answer, of course, is that we take very seriously—and often quite unconsciously—the culturally defined, symbolic meanings of social behavior.

As you read this selection, ask yourself the following questions:

☐ *How do Brazil and the United States differ in terms of their cultural attitudes toward time?*

☐ *How are attitudes toward time reflected in the organization of a swim meet?*

☐ *If you were in the business of producing champion swimmers, what changes might you suggest for Brazil?*

☐ *Do you have the gnawing feeling that our way of looking at time is right? Why?*

The following terms discussed in this selection are included in the Glossary at the back of the book:

chiefdom
cross-cultural research
cultural values
institutions
social class
social mobility
social stratification
values

With permission from *Natural History*, no. 5, vol. 94; copyright the American Museum of Natural History, 1985.

Why do athletes from some countries excel at particular sports? Why do certain nations pile up dozens of Olympic medals while others win only a handful or none at all? It isn't simply a matter of being rich or poor, developed or underdeveloped. Cultural values and social conditions also play a role in international sports success. The United States and Brazil, giants of the Western Hemisphere, with populations of about 235 million and 135 million, respectively, offer a good contrast in Olympic success. Both are countries of almost continental proportions; both have people of ethnically diverse backgrounds, with roots in Europe, Africa, Asia, and Native America. Each is the major economic power of its continent. However, in the 1984 Summer Olympics, the United States won 174 medals, while Brazil managed only 8. The contrast was particularly noticeable in swimming, where the United States won 34 medals and Brazil one.

From early August 1983 to late August 1984, I was in Rio de Janeiro to set up a research project on the impact of nationwide commercial television on traditional Brazilian culture. Among other aspects of the project, I was interested in television sports coverage, but I also had a personal connection with swimming because my son is a competitive swimmer. During those thirteen months, I noticed many striking contrasts between Brazilian and American swimming. Since most successful international swimmers begin their training in childhood, a closer look at the cultural values affecting children's swimming may help us understand some of the reasons that the United States excels at that sport and Brazil doesn't.

The most obvious contrasts between competitive swimming in the United States and Brazil have to do with different cultural attitudes toward time, which is valued more highly and calculated more carefully in the United States. Many Brazilians find the American obsession with time to be the outstanding contrast between the two cultures. Brazilians don't make appointments for such punctual times as 1:45 or 2:15, and they react suspiciously to the precision offered by digital watches. As they point out, delays are common in traffic-jammed cities such as Rio de Janeiro; no one arrives, or is expected to arrive, on time.

I have been following children's competitive swimming since my son, an age-group swimmer in the USS (United States Swimming, formerly AAU) program, was 7. (Age-group refers to the organization of most events by age-based categories: 8 and under, 9–10, 11–12, 13–14, and 15–16. Age groups in the United States don't have ages similar to those of everyone else. In the tribal vocabulary, instead of being 6 or 7, one is "8 and under"; my son just turned "13–14.") During a period of six years, I have attended dozens of swimming practices and meets. I have discussed swimming with other parents and coaches, have chaired the swim committee of a local club, and have helped out at swimming meets. USS swim meets, which take place throughout the winter and summer, lead to state and national championships.

A swimmer's objective in a given meet is not just to win but to better his or her time. One's time for any event is always the fastest time yet achieved in that event. At a given meet, swimmers may participate in all events in which they have made certain cutoff times announced at the beginning of the season. There are A meets for swimmers who have achieved A cutoff times, B meets for those whose times are slower, and C events for the slowest. One's time for any event can only get better, never worse.

Within the swimmer's world, time is paramount. Even winners are disappointed if they don't better their times, since a new time means progress compared with other swimmers and a step toward state and national championships—and toward that final goal, Olympic gold and a new world record. I have watched small children sob on discovering that a win did not better their time. On the adult level, a gold-medal-winning American backstroker in the 1984 Summer Olympics reacted similarly when he won the finals without beating his own previously set world record.

Conversation among swimmers could be mistaken for chitchat at a convention of time and motion study experts, so frequent are the references to hundredths of a second. Kids who haven't yet studied long division routinely reel off "19.16s" (nineteen and sixteen-hundredths seconds) and "35.97s." The most common question among American swimmers is probably "What's your time for the 50 free?" Swimmers not only know their own times but also those of their teammates and their fiercest rivals.

It's easy to find out swimmers' times. Just buy a mimeographed program at a meet. This program lists, by numbered event, the name of each swimmer and his or her time for each event. In this way, an American swimmer's times become public knowledge. Parents consult the program as they watch each event, comparing previous best times with those achieved that day. As they monitor their own child's performance, parents also comment favorably to other moms and dads whose children have done well. Parents sit in silent embarrassment or make audible excuses when their children don't match or better their former best times.

American children are motivated to keep on swimming because they know that even if they don't achieve a new time in one event that day, they might better their time in another. Because they are allowed to swim in as many events as they have A times (for an

6

A meet) or B times (for a B meet), most swimmers usually have something to be happy about when they get home.

An American swimming meet closely mirrors the larger society in that most people have good and bad moments, strong and weak performances, and despite disappointments, generally find rewards. Swimming is a particularly appropriate sport for a competitive, achievement-oriented society in which lines of social class are not clearly and rigidly drawn. Status within the American swimmer's world is like the form of social organization that anthropologists call the chiefdom, common a century ago in the Polynesian islands. In the chiefdom, slight gradations in prestige and power, rather than demarcated social classes, meant that everyone had a distinctive social status, just a bit higher or lower than anyone else's. A swimmer's unique status is the end result of a complex scoring process that takes into account a series of constantly changing times in different events. Like a Polynesian, every swimmer has a social status slightly different from everyone else's.

Time, then, is the basis of social status in American swimming. Public recognition of excellent times is, in itself, a potent reward. The more tangible prizes—medals and ribbons—go to only a small number of finalists (normally six, eight, or twelve), but everyone has a best time.

Since precious commodities usually have guardians, the swimmer's world has guardians of time (for example, parents armed with the most modern stopwatches). Even when electronic timing pads are used, each lane always has two human timers. There are also finish judges to determine finish order in close races and, for important meets, winning-lane timers. At the end of each heat, times are written on cards, which are used to determine and list finish order, official times, and winners. The results of each race are posted one by one in the halls of the building (usually a high school) where the meet takes place. By consulting these sheets, parents can compare their children's times with previous bests and with those of other swimmers. In this way the adult members of the society monitor whether their young are keeping up with their peers and whether they are bettering themselves in terms of the values emphasized in American culture, including individual achievement and hard work.

Swimmers' times—these public, precious symbols of achievement—are tended, guarded, enshrined in print, and transmitted from local to state to national levels, where they are used to establish rankings. The most important source of information about times and national rankings is the monthly magazine *Swimming World*. *Swimming World* also publishes results of meets held throughout the country, and sells a popular

T-shirt, proclaiming "I made it in *Swimming World*," an achievement that confers considerable prestige among fellow swimmers. The particularly American character of the swimmer's world just described emerges crystal clear when we consider the same sport in Brazil.

Before enrolling my son in a competitive swim program in Rio de Janeiro in 1983, I accepted the above procedure as part of swimming per se—not as an illustration of distinctive American cultural values. Even though I am accustomed to comparing American institutions and behavior with those of other cultures, I had not thought much about how swim programs might be run differently elsewhere or what the meets might tell me about different values and traditions. But striking differences between Brazilian and American swimming were soon apparent. First, Brazilian swim teams are associated with private, money-making professional clubs, such as the Fluminense Football (soccer) Club, for which my son swam. Most of the soccer clubs that battle for city, state, and national championships have divisions of amateur sports, which manage swimming, gymnastics, and other competitive programs for children.

The clubs are commercial organizations, rather than the high school, college, age-group, and sports-club teams that dominate competitive swimming in the United States. It was as though my son were swimming for the Detroit Tigers. One of the tasks of the vice-president for amateur sports of a Brazilian club is to find rich sponsors, businesses or individuals, national or foreign, for the swim team. The soccer rivalry between such teams as Fluminense, Flamengo, and Vasco spills over into amateur sports. In Rio de Janeiro, swimmers and gymnasts play their own small parts in an ongoing battle for sports supremacy, and the system is similar in other Brazilian cities.

Daily practices are held in the Olympic-sized pools of the different clubs, and the competition is stiffer in a city of eight million than in the Detroit metropolitan area. Many Brazilian national champion age-group swimmers live in Rio, and their times (at least through the early teens) are comparable to those of top American swimmers. Cutoffs are much more stringent, however, and there are fewer meets—which means that swimmers lack opportunities to better their times and to gain experience.

Compared with the United States, Brazilian meets are badly organized. In the United States, meets are planned a year in advance; in Brazil, coaches often don't know until a day or two before the meet where it will be held, and sites are frequently changed at the last minute—for example, from a convenient pool a few blocks away to a suburb requiring an hour's drive. Cariocas (residents of Rio de Janeiro) are accustomed to associating with family and friends, but not with such strangers as the parents of their children's colleagues. There is no tradition of car pooling, and swimmers frequently miss meets because of last-minute changes. For American swimmers, to miss a meet is practically unheard of; mild illnesses or relatives' birthday parties are not acceptable excuses for letting down one's teammates. If one is scheduled to swim a relay, to miss a meet is considered especially unfair to other team members.

American swim meets almost always have relays—freestyle and medley (backstroke, breaststroke, butterfly, and freestyle, or crawl). Brazilian meets, however, rarely include relays; only one of the half dozen meets I attended in Rio had them. Perhaps relays are almost always a part of American meets because they embody key American values so well. The free relay is based on pure speed; it is the fastest of the races because everyone swims the fastest stroke, the crawl, normally called "the free."

The medley relay tests speed through specialization; each of four specialized swimmers tries for a best time to bring his or her team in first. It shows specialized individuals working rapidly together, like an efficient industrial or managerial team. Making the relay through a best time is a valued achievement. In relays, the win is more important than in individual events. Since relay members can change from week to week, swimmers have a less accurate recollection of relay times than personal ones. In these events, swimming celebrates certain American values: winning organization, competition through speed, efficiency, and specialization with other, similar groups. These values have spread out from the American economy to the larger society and are well represented in competitive swimming. In Brazil, the absence of relays helps focus attention on the individual win.

Even more noteworthy, however, than capricious meet planning and the absence of relays is the treatment of time in Brazilian swimming. In the United States, times are recorded electronically, as well as by people with stopwatches, and are publicly posted. In Brazil, however, times are not published in the mimeographed meet program. The swimmers' names and club affiliations are listed for each event, but their times are not. At first I supposed that, as in the United States, names were listed in an order established by prior best times and that the fastest swimmers swam in the last heat. After observing the results of several races in different meets, I learned this was not the case. Swimmers in the first or second heat were as likely to win as those in the last one.

Since times are not listed, parents and swimmers can concentrate only on who wins, not on who betters former times, which means that, rather than several possible winners, each event has only one. Public

recognition of improvement—a key reward and powerful reason to keep on swimming—is missing. Nor are times publicly posted after each race. They are announced by loudspeaker after finish order is determined, beginning with the slowest swimmer and laboriously moving up to the winner—sometimes through twenty or thirty names. In this way parents and swimmers are reminded, not that many swimmers have improved, but that there are twenty times as many losers as winners.

Another feature of the Brazilian meet illustrates different cultural values about time. Where were the many guardians of time? I saw no attentive parents with stopwatches; there were no frantic winning-lane timers. Each lane had a single timer—even when the electronic pads weren't working. And, since timers often chatted as swimmers raced home, times were occasionally lost, an unheard-of occurrence in USS swimming. Times are not gathered, tended, and cherished as in the United States. This is one of many symbolic statements in the swimmer's world of the different values attached to time in the cultures of the two Western giants.

Brazilian coaches do keep track of their swimmers' times, which they use to determine who will swim what events in the next meet. But in contrast to USS swimming, in which kids are normally entered in all races for which they have made cutoff times, in Brazil they are limited to three of four races. This further reduces their opportunities for meet experience.

Why are there so few opportunities to swim competitively in Brazil? One reason is the absence of public school, particularly high school, athletic programs. Another is the reduced level of parental involvement in organizing and running meets, compared with that in the United States. There are simply too few volunteers to provide the needed chances to compete, particularly in a city of eight million where thousands of young people train as swimmers.

The pattern of stiff cutoffs and restricted competition is persistent and has unfortunate consequences for Brazil in international competition. For example, the Brazilian Olympic Committee did not send female swimmers to Los Angeles in 1984 because none had made arbitrarily established cutoffs. This excluded a South American record holder, while swimmers with no better times were attending the Olympics as representatives of other South American countries. The attitude was that only swimmers who had made the cutoffs had any chance to place in Los Angeles. No one imagined that the power of Olympic excitement might spur swimmers to extraordinary efforts. During television coverage of the 1984 South American Championships, held in Rio, I was aghast to hear commentators downgrade chances that any Brazilian other than

Ricardo Prado might win a medal. More than once I heard this comment about a new champion: "He doesn't have a chance to win at Los Angeles because his time isn't good enough"—as though it could never get better.

American coverage, in contrast dotes on unexpected results, showing adherence to an American sports credo: "It's not over till it's over." In Brazil, the credo seems to be "It's over before it's begun."

Winning, of course, is an important American cultural value, and this is particularly true for college and professional team sports like football, basketball, and baseball. Football coaches are fond of making such comments as "Winning isn't a good thing; it's the only thing" and "Show me a good loser and I'll show you a loser." For sports such as running and swimming, however, in which the focus is on the individual, American culture also recognizes and admires moral victories, personal bests, comeback athletes, and Special Olympics, and commends those who run good races without finishing first. In amateur sports, personal improvement can be as important as winning.

· Americans have been told so many times that their culture overemphasizes winning that they may find it hard to believe that Brazilians seem to value winning even more. Prior to the 1984 Summer Olympics, swimmer Ricardo Prado (instead of the eventual Brazilian gold medalist, Joaquim Cruz) was touted by the media as Brazil's most likely gold medal winner (he was a silver medalist). Prado had won 200- and 400-meter individual medley (IM) events in the 1983 Pan American Games and, until 1984, held the world record for the 400 IM. Commenting on his massive press coverage, Prado observed that only winning athletes were noticed in Brazil—only number ones, never number twos. He blasted the press for formerly neglecting his achievements and those of other Brazilian swimmers who were not, or not yet, world record holders.

Perhaps Brazilians value winning so much because it is so rare. In USS swimming, the focus on times means there are always multiple winners. This may be the key to the relationship of swimming to cultural values. In American society, where poverty is less pervasive, resources more abundant, social classes less marked, opportunities for achievement more numerous, and individual social mobility easier than in Brazil, there can be multiple winners. Brazilian society is more stratified; a much smaller middle class and elite group make up at most 30 percent of the population. Brazilian swimming echoes lessons from the large society: victories are scarce and reserved for the few.

But there is another dimension to the relationship between competitive swimming and society. Even in the United States the opportunity to swim competitively is limited, generally to people of the middle class

and above. To swim seriously in America requires money, time, and parental involvement. American children begin swimming competitively for sports clubs or country clubs, which have membership fees. Success in summer swimming may then lead them to join Y or USS programs for winter competition. The United States is an automobile-oriented culture. Cars and parents' time are necessary to drive to practices and meets. During Michigan winters, in order to arrive at distant meets for 8:00 A.M. warmups, my son and I have sometimes spent the night in a motel. Swimmers' parents have money to spend on gas, food, lodging, and club memberships. Children whose parents can afford to belong to clubs are more likely to get interested in swimming in the first place.

In Brazil the situation is somewhat different. Public transportation is better in Brazilian cities than in most parts of the United States. There is less residential segregation of rich and poor, black and white. Given the dense urban populations and that the major soccer clubs—and therefore their swimming pools—are located right in the city, poor kids, including black children, can work out as swimteam members almost as easily as children from middle-class families. As a result, in contrast to the United States, where it is rare to see a black swimmer at a USS meet or in a state championship, swimmers with dark skins and fast times are present at virtually any carioca swimming meet.

Some Americans think that blacks and whites excel in particular sports because of biological and physiological differences but Brazil, which has proportionately as many blacks as the United States, demonstrates that sports abilities reflect culture rather than biology. When blacks have opportunities to do well in swimming, soccer, or tennis, they are physically capable of doing as well as whites. In schools, parks, and city playgrounds in the United States, blacks have access to baseball diamonds, basketball courts, football fields, and tracks. However, because of restricted economic opportunities, black families have traditionally lacked the resources to invest in hockey or ski equipment or join clubs with tennis courts and swimming pools. But as Brazilian swimming demonstrates, when these opportunities are available, blacks do well.

Here then is a different way in which the swimmer's world provides a microcosm of the surrounding culture. Despite the emphasis in the United States on the possibility of rising through hard work and individual achievement, in swimming, as in society, success is easiest for those who are better off to begin with.

What can we conclude about the different cultural models for competitive swimming? Perhaps the more relaxed approach to swimming encountered in Brazil reflects a culture in which there is less emphasis on time, measurement, comparison, and achievement. Brazilians may even experience fewer stresses and be happier because they live in a less competitive, less achievement-oriented society. Whatever the case, one thing is eminently clear: the United States is a better training ground than Brazil for international competitive swimming. As we know from years of Olympic games and a glance at today's world records, the countries that do best at swimming are the United States, East Germany, and the Soviet Union. State support of Soviet and East German swimmers is a powerful incentive for talented young people in those countries.

Other nations that do well in international competition—Australia, Canada, Great Britain, the Netherlands—are more like the United States than Brazil in their cultural backgrounds and current socioeconomic conditions.

Despite pride in country, Brazilian swimmers know that it wasn't accidental that the South American giant could manage only one medal while its North American counterpart was winning thirty-four. Recognizing this, most of the Brazilian men who swam in the 1984 Olympics, including silver-medalist Ricardo Prado, are now training in the United States.

2

Loading the Bases:
How Our Tribe Projects Its Own Image into the National Pastime

Bradd Shore

Culture is a remarkable human invention not only because it allows us to adapt and survive, but also because it requires us to make meaning of the world and our lives. People use cultural concepts and symbolic rituals to construct a view of reality.

Space and time, for example, are two fundamental scientific concepts. Until recently, scientists thought that space and time could be measured in ways that remained constant in all conditions. We now know, thanks to Einstein, that space and time must be understood in relation to motion; they are relative values. The effects of motion, however, are very small and cannot be easily seen unless the observer or the observed moves at speeds that shatter the confines of everyday existence. In other words, properties we know are relative when viewed from a broader perspective seem absolute when viewed from where we normally stand. An interesting analogy can be made between the physics of space and time and the culture of space and time. In the latter, we deal with cultural understandings and interpretations of abstract physical concepts.

This selection provides an insightful view of American culture by interpreting the hidden meanings of baseball. Baseball is both a game and a ritual that appeals to particular cultural notions of space, time, and social relationships. Some of the symbolic meanings in baseball hinge on the structural asymmetries of the game, especially when the lone heroic batter faces the communal efforts of the defense. Bradd Shore does not believe that baseball is just a game; he sees it as a symbolic way of expressing central cultural

ideas and paradoxes. Natives might not agree with the symbolic interpretation here, but they may be too close to their own ritual to analyze it. Interestingly, when games are exported to other societies, like baseball to Japan or cricket to the Trobriand Islands, the meanings and nuances of the cultural forms are changed remarkably.

As you read this selection, ask yourself the following questions:

☐ *Why does baseball seem boring and tedious to some people? What is the meaning of "contingent" time?*

☐ *Why is it permissible for fans to shout derogatory things at the umpire? Why do team managers display anger when they know that the umpire will not change his or her mind?*

☐ *Do you think that the appeal of and fascination with baseball is gender-linked? Why or why not?*

☐ *How do baseball fields project an open and endless image of time and space?*

☐ *What does baseball have to do with the concept of culture?*

The following terms discussed in this selection are included in the Glossary at the back of the book:
institutions
ritual
walkabout

Americans will recall the night of October 25, 1986, not because of any political upheaval, scientific breakthrough or natural cataclysm but because of certain events involving one William Hayward Wilson, known since childhood as Mookie. Thirty years old, five feet ten inches tall and weighing 168 pounds, Mookie Wilson was, at that time, a much cherished outfielder for the New York Mets. His playing record, comfortably better than mediocre, had been spiced with flashes of brilliance. True, he struck out a bit too often, could have drawn a few more walks and had a weak throwing arm. But he was a joy to watch for the wide sweep of his swing and the gleeful abandon with which he scampered around the bases. And he was beloved by fans and players alike for his unfailing good nature.

Thus did Mookie Wilson stand in the batter's box that autumn evening, in the bottom of the tenth inning of the sixth game of the 1986 World Series. Only minutes before, Shea Stadium had been funereal. The visiting Boston Red Sox had opened up a 5–3 lead in the top of the tenth and had retired the first two Mets on outfield flies in the bottom of the inning. With one more out, what had been a glorious season for New York would have ended ignobly, and Boston would have had its first world championship since 1918. On the field several Red Sox flashed grins, while in their clubhouse preparations were being made for the customary champagne-bath celebration. Over on the Mets' side the fiery first baseman Keith Hernandez, the inning's second out, sat sipping beer and dragging on a cigarette, sullenly awaiting the inevitable.

Then it started. In swift succession singles by Gary Carter, Kevin Mitchell and Ray Knight made it 5–4, with runners on first and third, bringing William Hayward Wilson to the plate and the crowd to its feet. Another hit would tie the score; one of Wilson's occasional home runs would win it for New York.

Wilson worked the count to two balls and two strikes against Boston's Bob Stanley, then fouled off two superlative pitches to stay alive. The next delivery followed a sinking trajectory in the direction of Wilson's ankles. Had he been struck by the pitch, he would have been sent to first, loading the bases. But the agile outfielder jumped, twisted and fell to the ground, avoiding the ball, which eluded the grasp of the catcher Rich Gedman and skipped on toward the backstop, allowing Mitchell, the barrel-chested rookie, to score the tying run and, no less important, moving Knight down to second.

Moments later Stanley pitched and Wilson took

one of his enormous swings, spinning off a lazy, squirming hopper toward the gallant Boston first baseman Bill Buckner, playing despite excruciating pain in his legs. With Wilson sprinting desperately toward first, Buckner reached down for the ball to make the kind of routine defensive play he'd executed countless times over the previous seventeen years.

He missed it. The ball squirted through his legs and rolled into right field as Knight ran home with the run that brought the Mets a 6–5 victory and forced the Series to a seventh game. Buckner meanwhile stared off toward the outfield, aware perhaps that in one split second he had tarnished indelibly a distinguished career during which he had made 2,464 base hits and earned a reputation for unsurpassed competitive spirit. In the stands and all over the New York area people danced and screamed and kissed perfect strangers as if they had just heard of the end of a major war. In New England—even though the Series was not yet over—many prepared to spend a long dour winter contemplating yet another Red Sox collapse. (Rightly so, as it turned out, for the Mets again came from behind to win game seven.) And across the nation millions of people would never forget where they were when they saw Mookie Wilson's at bat climax what may well have been the most extraordinary inning of major league baseball ever played.

Well, one could reasonably ask, as many do: So what? Why all the fuss? Baseball is, after all, just a game, a diversion from life's serious business. Maybe. But a more considered view suggests that while it is incontestably a game, our national pastime is also something more. Baseball symbolizes for many Americans a nostalgia for childhood and summer and a lost agrarian age; it engages our passions, shapes our weekends and helps lubricate our casual social relationships; it transcends the control of the clock over our harried lives; and understood as a kind of ritual drama, baseball takes us beyond the uncertainty of play in motion to the enduring forms that make it a cultural institution—confirming the oft-quoted observation by the historian Jacques Barzun, professor emeritus of Columbia University, that "whoever wants to know the heart and mind of America had better learn baseball."

Many attempts have been made to define the elusive fit between baseball and the American character. Most of them have focused on certain general aspects of the game—its leisurely pace, its concern for precision and self-control and its alleged stress on fair play. Few if any observers, however, have analyzed baseball as a pageant linked closely with the American world view, emphasizing the structural patterns that shape baseball time, baseball space and the social relationships choreographed by the rules of the game.

This article is reprinted by permission of *The Sciences* and is from the May/June 1990 issue.

Like the anthropologist who studies an exotic culture, I came to baseball as a kind of outsider, never having been especially interested in the game. I knew its basic rules and had played a few dismal years out in left field as a Little Leaguer. But I had never really understood what made this sport so special. Frankly, I had always found watching baseball pretty dull. So my latter-day appreciation of it is inevitably that of an outside observer—a kind of convert—not that of a player or even an avid fan.

What strikes me most about baseball is that compared with other American field sports is it so consistently asymmetrical. Almost everywhere in the game one finds an endearing oddness instead of the efficient balance of basketball, football or hockey. There is barely an even number associated with baseball: nine players, nine innings, three strikes, three outs and a seventh-inning stretch. A full count is five—three balls and two strikes. Even the apparent symmetry of the diamond is broken by its division into three square bases and the lopsided pentagon that serves as home plate. Charmingly skewed, the game gives us no quarters and no halftimes. Baseball play may be fair, but it is not even.

This asymmetry shapes the odd sense of time in baseball. As many writers have noted, baseball is unique among American field sports in its utter disregard for the clock. Baseball time is controlled by innings and the contingencies of events. A game is over only when the losing team has had at least nine at bats and when a difference between the teams has been generated. The rare exceptions are when umpires call a game, say for darkness or bad weather. Otherwise, the fearful symmetry of a tie score is not allowed. The open-endedness of baseball is guaranteed by the theoretically endless moments of the game. The batter might foul off an infinite number of pitches and thus remain at the plate to dig in and take his cuts for eternity. The team at bat could mount an interminable hitting streak and prolong indefinitely its half of the inning. Or the score might be inextricably deadlocked, sending the contest sprawling into an infinity of extra innings.

Detractors of the game are fond of pointing to its leisurely pace as its most glaring defect. Aficionados rarely deny the charge and instead locate much of the genius of baseball in its alternation of long periods of languor with sudden bursts of action. For the fan the drawling rhythm of the game allows a continuous shift of attention from the public spectacle at hand to more private pursuits: staring at the field, the scoreboard, the sky or the cityscape; discussing the game and arguing over what's to come; eating, drinking and making small talk. For the uninitiated these long breaks account for the tedium of baseball; but for true believers

the resolute pokin
imaginative enga
watching a safe'
This kind of in'
kinesthetic rus
along with C
own body E
percuts. It
more eleg
game—ba
strategy, anecdo
statistics.

The romance of baseball w
defying the clock, is equally apparent ..
subdue the flow of history. For many Americ..
ball encapsulates their own biographies through .
seamless chain of teams that propels youth into age and projects age back to reclaim its lost vitality. From Little League to Babe Ruth League, high school, college, the Minors and the Majors, baseball is an idiom by which the dream of the endless summer is tied up with an individual life history. This may be why it is with a swing of the bat that most old-timers seem to think they can recapture youth. As the San Francisco columnist Herb Caen mused: "Whereas we cannot imagine ourselves executing a two-handed slam-dunk or a 50-yard field goal, we are still certain we have one base hit left in us."

If baseball time is open-ended, it nonetheless maintains its fundamental asymmetry by insistently fixing its beginnings. If the conclusion of a game is contingent on subsequent events, the start is always ritually precise: the national anthem and the umpire's cry "Play ball!" The baseball season may end with a contingent world series, but it begins with a single, sacred act: the presidential toss on opening day, a tradition that dates to 1910 and the beaming, corpulent William Howard Taft. In fact, the opening of the season is itself a reenactment of the birth of professional baseball. Game one of each new National League campaign is always played in Cincinnati, in memory of the Cincinnati Red Stockings, which in 1869 became the first salaried team.

The same need to demarcate its beginnings may well have inspired the invention of the mythical birth of baseball. In 1903 Henry Chadwick, the premier baseball authority in his day, testified in the *Baseball Guide* that the American game was without doubt a natural offspring of the British game rounders. Such heresy riled Albert Goodwill Spalding, a great pitcher of the 1870s who had by then become the nation's leading sporting goods magnate. The influential Spalding called for the formation of a fact-finding committee to determine the true pedigree of baseball. And in 1907

...tified that, Chadwick's compelling ...standing, baseball was a deliberate ...merican creation.

...all nativity story can be traced to the col-...scences of one Abner Graves, a friend of a ...major general named Abner Doubleday. ...claimed to recall how in 1839 Doubleday—...onveniently enough happened also to be ac-...nted with Abraham G. Mills, the fact-finding ...mmittee's chairman—had cleaned up an anarchic ...ame called town ball played by boys in Cooperstown, New York. By mapping out a precise and orderly diamond on a pasture and by codifying the loose rules of the game, this latter-day Justinian was said to have single-handedly given America its national pastime. Like our nation itself, baseball could now lay claim to a fixed domestic origin, a certifiable beginning in an act of deliberate reason—the rationalization of a cow pasture on a summer's day in 1839.

Thus, baseball time juxtaposes the fixed beginning and the open end, the determinate and the contingent, in a characteristic asymmetrical relation. This pattern is paralleled closely by the game's orchestration of space. Baseball is the only American field sport that does not use a symmetrical field, defined by sides and ends. The baseball park defines a tension between an ever narrowing inner point, called home, and an ever widening outer field. The diamond, which includes the home area, is marked out with exacting precision and is the same in every park. The modern baseball diamond consists of a focal plate, located at home, and of three bases (or bags) situated at ninety-foot intervals around the diamond. Exactly sixty feet six inches from home plate is the pitcher's mound, raised no more than fifteen inches above the level of the bases.

Whereas this diamond area is precisely and uniformly measured, there are no rules governing the size or the outer boundaries of the outfield. It is the indeterminacy of the outfield that has given the classic ballparks—Wrigley Field in Chicago, Ebbets Field in Brooklyn, Yankee Stadium in the Bronx, Fenway Park in Boston—their distinctive souls. Moreover, outfields are subject to historical revision: only in baseball can the field be reshaped to accommodate new configurations of talent on the hometeam. There have been more than a few examples of outfield fences' being raised or lowered or moved closer to or farther from home plate. The most notorious instance of such boundary manipulation was the adjustable-height fence concocted by Bill Veeck, Jr., owner of the hapless Saint Louis Browns during the early 1950s. An inveterate showman, Veeck was renowned for the outlandish marketing gimmicks with which he enticed fans into watching his abysmal team. To enhance the Browns' home-field advantage,

he installed an outfield fence that could be raised or lowered depending on who was at bat. The innovation lasted one game, after which a rule forbidding the practice was passed.

Whereas other field sports present focal goals for the object in play at each end of the field, the baseball park extends into the community. In a sense, the batter's goal lies beyond the park itself, on the city streets; in fact, according to ballplayers' slang, to hit a home run is to "go downtown." Through the home run, baseball celebrates the possibility of a heroic action's momentarily overcoming the limits of the contest. The home run is an authentic sacred event—not so much the everyday homer that merely drops into the stands, but the electric smash, announced by the loud crack of a bat, that sails clear of the park, beyond the fielder's futile leap, beyond the reach of the riotous fans, beyond the bounds of the game itself. That is why the royalty of baseball—the likes of Babe Ruth, Hank Aaron, Willie Mays and Mickey Mantle—are nearly always home-run kings.

The spatial open-endedness of baseball differs sharply from the "bowls" associated with football, arenas that surround the players totally, cutting the game space off completely and symmetrically from the surrounding community. The recent introduction of hybrid stadiums suitable for both baseball and football is for baseball purists an unfortunate development. If, traditionally, baseball parks were engagingly idiosyncratic, the modern era surely has encouraged a standardization alien to the game's authentic locale.

The most powerful of the asymmetries of baseball is social: it is the only American field sport that never directly confronts one team with another. Instead, the game pits a team—nine players on the field—against a lone batter and no more than three base runners at one time. Moreover, the team at bat remains out of sight, with members in a dugout awaiting their trips to the plate. Each player has two personas—a reactive defensive identity in which he plays a part in a highly coordinated communal enterprise on the field, and an aggressive offensive persona, in which he faces the opposing team as an individual batter and base runner. Although he functions as part of the communal fielding unit, the pitcher is the only player whose primary roles are aggressive on offense and defense alike.

The social asymmetry is reflected in baseball talk. Take for instance the difference between "playing" and "being." Those in the field merely "play" positions; but the batter "is" at bat, and the pitcher "pitches." Consider the awkwardness of such phrases as "Jose Canseco is playing the batter for the Oakland A's" or "Whitey Ford played pitcher for the Yankees." The more active a role is in baseball, the more the players *are* what they do, whereas "playing" is relegated to more passive, defensive roles. The language of being rather than of playing is also associated with proximity to "home." These speech conventions reflect a world view in which being is linked to an individual activity in a domestic, or home, environment. In contrast, social role playing is linked to an "outer" field.

In other field sports one team tries to move an object from one end of the field, through a hostile set of defenders, to a goal at the opposite end. The object, not the players, makes the score. In baseball it is the runner alone who scores. The ball is controlled largely by the fielders, whose ability to move it around the field works against the runner's interest. The batter, meanwhile, opposes the ball, hoping to knock it free of the fielders' control—out of the park, if possible. When he fails—if the ball is caught in the air or is returned to confront him or one of the base runners—he has made an "out." This essentially hostile relationship between offensive players and the ball is a distinctive characteristic of the game.

The action of baseball, then, can be conceived of as a series of travels by individuals who attempt to leave home and make a circuit through a social field marked with obstacles. It is not getting through the field itself that scores, however, but returning safely home. Baseball is our version of what Australian aborigines call a walkabout—a circular journey into alien territory, with the aim of returning home after making contact with sacred landmarks and braving hazards along the way.

Thus baseball dramatizes a recurrent cultural problem: how to reconcile communal values with a tradition of heroic individualism and privatism. But the power of baseball as a ritual comes from more than a simple opposition between the social and the individual. It derives from the dramatization of the tension between the two and from an attempt to reconcile them symbolically. So baseball can be viewed as several kinds of contest going on simultaneously, each representing a different aspect of the relation between self and society.

On the first and broadest level, baseball is a contest between two teams, a clash that involves some profound social loyalties. The spatial opposition between home and outfield around which the game is organized is mimicked by the opposition between home team and visitors, or outsiders, a contest that provokes powerful community allegiances among fans. The second level of competition in baseball is the contest between the batsman at home plate and his opponents arrayed on the field. It is here that the game most vividly reflects the American dilemma: reconciling ideas of community and fair play with those of privacy and heroic individualism.

At the third level the teams disappear altogether, and baseball becomes a showdown between pitcher and batter, who face off in a mythic shoot-out scenario, each struggling to control the ball and unnerve the other. This dimension of the game has been greatly amplified by the advent of television, which in more ways than one has brought baseball home. By zooming in on the batter and the pitcher, televised baseball blocks out the fielding game for all but a few action-packed moments and is almost exclusively confined to the intimate battle taking place between the mound and the plate.

Finally there is a fourth level, where not only the teams fade from view but also the game, the season and the decade. At this level, through statistics, each player enters into a kind of ongoing universal supergame, beyond time and space, in which each is pitted against every other player who has ever worn a uniform. The lure of the "stats" has been perhaps the most commonly noted distinctive aspect of baseball. As Angell has written, a host of statistics "swarm and hover above the head of every pitcher, every fielder, every batter, every team, recording every play with an accompanying silent shift of digits." Thus Ty Cobb's .367 career batting average (the all-time standard) has merged with his name, his dates of birth and death and the memory of his irascible disposition.

An obsession with batting average, RBI, ERA and such is characteristic of a society at once democratic and individualistic, egalitarian and fiercely competitive, a nation preoccupied with enforcing a vision of community upon a vastly heterogeneous population. What statistics do for baseball, polls and elections do for society at large. As Rousseau noted long ago, in *A Discourse Upon the Origin and Foundation of the Inequality Among Mankind*, in a democracy the general will of the people can never really be general. It can only be manifest through the assertion of numerical superiority—the will of the majority.

Thus it is altogether fitting that stats are an important way in which the spectator can participate in a professional's game. If gradations in players' skills can be translated through statistics into a quantitative hierarchy of value, so too can differences in skill and devotion among fans be ranked through a contest that engages their knowledge of the numbers. This is metabaseball; one can be bored with the actual events of a game—yet relish the ongoing Pythagorean drama of numbers piling up against numbers in the mind's own ballpark.

Children enter early into this cosmic contest through baseball cards. In their incarnations as cards, players can be lifted out of their local team context and placed into the wider marketplace of baseball, their stats compared, their value calculated. When my seven-year-old son, his box of baseball cards tucked under his arm, sets off to close a deal with a boy down the block, he joins the ranks of baseball owners. Through a combination of shrewd business savvy and raw hero worship he connects with the most atomistic dimension of baseball.

The central Christian rite of Communion involves confronting and momentarily overcoming basic theological contradictions: life and death, body and spirit, god and human being. Whether religious or secular, ritual thrives on such paradoxes, crystallizing for the participants a fleeting reconciliation of opposites. As a civic ritual baseball enacts tensions between domestic, private and individual concerns, on the one hand, and social, public and communal concerns, on the other. Americans often use the language of the game metaphorically to represent other activities that involve the problematic nexus of self-interest and social responsibility, and no activity is more frequently so described than sexual behavior. Consider these expressions: "I can't get to first base"; "making a hit with him"; "he struck out with her"; "going all the way"; "I scored last night." Along the same lines American schoolboys commonly liken a sexual interlude to an epic dash around the base paths, in which they achieve more daring levels of physical intimacy with every base—and, with any luck, go all the way.

At first glance one might assume that baseball terminology is applied to all realms of sexual endeavor. Yet "My wife and I went all the way last night" and "I couldn't get to first base with the prostitute" seem jarringly inappropriate. Evidently, the baseball metaphor doesn't apply to sex when sex either is fully domesticated and private or is a fully public and commercial transaction. Baseball lingo is linked to sexual adventurism in dating behavior, in which a male must negotiate a perilous field of play with at least the possibility of coming home to score.

Like all games, baseball has rules to govern the competitive relationships between players. But possibly because it is a game that calls into question issues of individual freedom and social regulation, the attitude toward rules in baseball is notoriously ambivalent. Behind home plate, at the very apex of the infield, stands the embodiment of the rule book: the umpire, whose judgments represent the final authority in the game. But while umpires hold absolute power, managers, coaches and some players regularly treat their decisions as if they are open to protracted, sometimes violent negotiation. Such legendary figures as John McGraw, Leo Durocher and Billy Martin earned

folkloric niches as much for their profane, dirt-kicking, tobacco-spewing debates with arbiters as for their managerial skills. This venerable ritual of challenging authority endures even though umpires rarely change decisions—certainly not in response to abuse by a player or a coach.

This leitmotiv of rebellion extends from the field to the grandstand: In no other American sport is there any counterpart of the traditional cry to kill the ump, a recurring ritual rebellion aimed not only at a particular call but also at the dominion of the rule book itself. In the nineteenth century club owners encouraged their patrons to humiliate the umpires. As Albert Spalding suggested, fans who harassed umpires were merely expressing a democratic right to protest tyranny. In fact, nineteenth-century fans were called cranks, an appropriate sobriquet, given their predilection for razzing and, on occasion, rioting.

The same reckless spirit can be found within the game itself. Spitters and brushback pitches, phantom double plays and the hidden-ball trick: these moments of petty villainy have a revered place in the sport. A reputation for insouciance has followed baseball almost from the start: as Harvey Frommer notes in *Baseball: The First Quarter-Century of the National Pastime*, Cincinnati's Red Stockings—models of Victorian propriety in their daguerreotypes—were loved in the 1860s not just for their on-field adventures but for their rowdy off-field antics.

For the most part the challenge of baseball to social order has always had an endearing tameness about it: it is the schoolboy playing hooky or swiping penny candy from a glass jar at the sweet shop, not the darker sins of elders. The authentic hero of American baseball is not the rapacious Hun but the errant knight—not the man but the Babe. Thus, as Paul Gardner points out in his 1975 book, *Nice Guys Finish Last: Sport and American Life*, George Herman Ruth was the perfect embodiment of the game's ambiguous relation with the idea of order:

> He had come up the hard way. He had reached the top without special training, without a college education; he was a graduate of "the school of hard knocks." He was a big man, with big appetites. He was irreverent and scornful of authority. He liked kids. And he made a lot of money. . . . He drank and he ate enough for two men, ignored the training rules and curfews, yet he played baseball better than anyone else around. . . . Ruth, it seemed, could get away with anything, while Americans chuckled and muttered in envious admiration, "That Babe. . . ."

For its millions of devotees baseball, though obviously a game to be played, is also a ritual to be observed; and ritual, by most definitions, is religion in motion, constituted by activities directed toward the sacred. In his book *The Savage Mind*, the French anthropologist Claude Lévi-Strauss reflects on the relation between games and rituals:

> Games thus appear to have a *disjunctive* effect: they end in the establishment of a difference between individual players or teams. . . . At the end of the game they are distinguished into winners and losers. Ritual, on the other hand, is the exact inverse; it *conjoins*, for it brings about a union . . . between two initially separate groups.

For Lévi-Strauss the crucial difference between games and rituals hinges on the relation between the fixed rules, or structural forms, and the unpredictable events to which they give rise. In games the structure of play is taken for granted and recedes into the background like the bass line in a piece of music: a barely perceptible but deeply resonant grounding on which the melody dances with illusory freedom. Games use the rules to create disequilibrium between players and teams that ostensibly started out as equals. Rituals, on the other hand, bring the shared framework of forms and rules forward into consciousness. A ritual can serve as a kind of public social memory, an enacted recollection of shared experience. It brings us together.

An oft-noted characteristic of games is that they are not for real: they are "just play." All games take place within an agreed-upon "play frame" that suspends to some extent the seriousness of ordinary activity. The play frame is defined by both time and space, so that the suspension of workaday reality is understood to be in effect only within the confines of the park, or game space, and only for as long as the game is in play.

Ritual shares with games this framing of reality. Often, however, a ritual is assumed to be more important than everyday behavior. Whereas games seem to operate on a level just below ordinary business, rituals rise transcendently above it, largely because ritual—particularly religious ritual—is frequently believed to be the repetition of sacred primal events. To devout worshipers, the rites of their faith may fairly be characterized as more real than reality or, at least, part of a higher reality. At the same time, ritual draws much of its power from the interplay of its immutable forms and the possibility that a real event may chance upon the scene. At the edge of performance, ritual flirts with reality: Rites of passage can come unnervingly close to bodily experience, whether for novices in New Guinea or fraternity pledges on college campuses. Real pain, authentic danger and, not infrequently, body mutilation figure prominently in such rites, throwing into doubt their status as performance.

Baseball, it seems, is neither game nor ritual alone but both at once. Our experience of the sport as player or spectator exemplifies what might be called—to use a musical metaphor—the polyphonic mind. That is, a thick, complex texture of conscious experience is made possible by the simultaneous interaction of several layers of knowledge. From our box at the ballpark our immediate attention may be riveted on the flow of the events of the game. But the total experience of baseball includes the embodied awareness of the recurrent forms and traditions of the game, which have a resonance all their own.

The interplay of game, ritual and reality in baseball was brought into sharp relief last fall, when a major earthquake struck before the third game of the World Series between the San Francisco Giants and the Oakland Athletics. There is no more sacred event in American sport than the Series, in which two major league titlists duel for what is a bit jingoistically called the World Championship. Feats accomplished during this festival are transcendent, and those who achieve them are enshrined in myth. When the earthquake struck the Bay Area, game, ritual and reality collided violently. We were jolted, confused by the sight of uniformed players huddling with their wives and children in Candlestick Park, reacting to an all too real intrusion from beyond game space. In the aftermath the reality of leveled buildings and of cars crushed on a freeway bridge seemed at first to render baseball absurdly insignificant. Even at World Series time, it *was* only a game. Or was it? As bodies were being pulled from wreckage, questions of when, where and whether or not the Series should resume were being hotly debated. And when, after what was deemed a respectable interlude, the Giants and the Athletics took to the field, the restoration of baseball, game and ritual, was for many like awakening from a nightmare to look again on the real world.

3

Body Ritual Among the Nacirema

Horace Miner

Generations of anthropologists have traveled the globe, reaching to the far corners of the five continents to discover and describe the many ways of humankind. Anthropologists have gathered a diverse collection of exotic customs, from the mundane to the bizarre. Understanding and appreciating other societies requires us to be culturally relative. But people tend to judge others in terms of their own cultural values in a way that is ethnocentric. This is because people take their cultural beliefs and behaviors for granted; they seem so "natural" that they are seldom questioned. Among the most interesting social customs on record are the rituals of the Nacirema. By viewing Nacirema behaviors as rituals we gain insight into their culture, and into the meaning of the concept of culture. We also gain insight into the problem of ethnocentrism.

Unlike space and time, which were discussed in the two previous selections, ritual is not a cultural interpretation of a physical phenomenon—it is totally cultural. Ritual can be found in all cultures. It can be defined as a set of acts that follow a sequence established by tradition. In Selection 37, for example, we will examine hospital operating room procedure as ritualized behavior.

Throughout the world, ritual reflects the fundamental cultural beliefs and values of a society by giving order to important activities and particular life crises like death and birth. Everyday, mundane rituals, however, are performed unconsciously. In fact most Nacirema people do these things without being aware of their underlying symbolic meanings. Pay particular attention to the quotation at the end of the selection.

As you read this selection, ask yourself the following questions:

☐ How do the Nacirema feel about the human body?

☐ Do you think the charms and magical potions used by the Nacirema really work?

☐ Can you list those aspects of social life in which magic plays an important role?

☐ What are your opinions of the importance of body ritual, and, if you went to live among the Nacirema, would you tell them of your opinions?

The following terms discussed in this selection are included in the Glossary at the back of the book:

clan
culture
ethnocentrism
ritual

The anthropologist has become so familiar with the diversity of ways in which different peoples behave in similar situations that he is not apt to be surprised by even the most exotic customs. In fact, if all of the logically possible combinations of behavior have not been found somewhere in the world, he is apt to suspect that they must be present in some yet undescribed tribe. This point has, in fact, been expressed with respect to clan organization by Murdock (1949:71). In this light, the magical beliefs and practices of the Nacirema present such unusual aspects that it seems desirable to describe them as an example of the extremes to which human behavior can go.

Professor Linton first brought the ritual of the Nacirema to the attention of anthropologists twenty years ago (1936:326), but the culture of this people is still very poorly understood. They are a North American group living in the territory between the Canadian Cree, the Yaqui and Tarahumare of Mexico, and the Carib and Arawak of the Antilles. Little is known of their origin, although tradition states that they came from the east. According to Nacirema mythology, their nation was originated by a culture hero, Notgnihsaw, who is otherwise known for two great feats of strength—the throwing of a piece of wampum across the river Pa-To-Mac and the chopping down of a cherry tree in which the Spirit of Truth resided.

Nacirema culture is characterized by a highly developed market economy which has evolved in a rich natural habitat. While much of the people's time is devoted to economic pursuits, a large part of the fruits of these labors and a considerable portion of the day are spent in ritual activity. The focus of this activity is the human body, the appearance and health of which loom as a dominant concern in the ethos of the people. While such a concern is certainly not unusual, its ceremonial aspects and associated philosophy are unique.

The fundamental belief underlying the whole system appears to be that the human body is ugly and that its natural tendency is to debility and disease. Incarcerated in such a body, man's only hope is to avert these characteristics through the use of the powerful influences of ritual and ceremony. Every household has one or more shrines devoted to this purpose. The more powerful individuals in the society have several shrines in their houses and, in fact, the opulence of a house is often referred to in terms of the number of

such ritual centers it possesses. Most houses are of wattle and daub construction, but the shrine rooms of the more wealthy are walled with stone. Poorer families imitate the rich by applying pottery plaques to their shrine walls.

While each family has at least one such shrine, the rituals associated with it are not family ceremonies but are private and secret. The rites are normally only discussed with children, and then only during the period when they are being initiated into these mysteries. I was able, however, to establish sufficient rapport with the natives to examine these shrines and to have the rituals described to me.

The focal point of the shrine is a box or chest which is built into the wall. In this chest are kept the many charms and magical potions without which no native believes he could live. These preparations are secured from a variety of specialized practitioners. The most powerful of these are the medicine men, whose assistance must be rewarded with substantial gifts. However, the medicine men do not provide the curative potions for their clients, but decide what the ingredients should be and then write them down in an ancient and secret language. This writing is understood only by the medicine men and by the herbalists who, for another gift, provide the required charm.

The charm is not disposed of after it has served its purpose, but is placed in the charm-box of the household shrine. As these magical materials are specific for certain ills, and the real or imagined maladies of the people are many, the charm-box is usually full to overflowing. The magical packets are so numerous that people forget what their purposes were and fear to use them again. While the natives are very vague on this point, we can only assume that the idea in retaining all the old magical materials is that their presence in the charm-box, before which the body rituals are conducted, will in some way protect the worshipper.

Beneath the charm-box is a small font. Each day every member of the family, in succession, enters the shrine room, bows his head before the charm-box, mingles different sorts of holy water in the font, and proceeds with a brief rite of ablution. The holy waters are secured from the Water Temple of the community, where the priests conduct elaborate ceremonies to make the liquid ritually pure.

In the hierarchy of magical practitioners, and below the medicine men in prestige, are specialists whose designation is best translated "holy-mouth-men." The Nacirema have an almost pathological horror of and fascination with the mouth, the condition of which is believed to have a supernatural influence on all social relationships. Were it not for the rituals of the mouth, they believe that their teeth would fall out, their gums bleed, their jaws shrink, their friends desert

---

The author of this article used the term *man* to refer to humanity in general. This term is not used by modern anthropologists because, to many people, it relects an unconscious sexist bias in language and rhetoric. At the time that this article was written, however, the generalized *man* was a common convention in writing. In the interest of historical accuracy we have not changed the wording in this article, but students should be aware that nonsexist terms (*humans, people, Homo sapiens*, and so on) are preferred. — The Editors.

them, and their lovers reject them. They also believe that a strong relationship exists between oral and moral characteristics. For example, there is a ritual ablution of the mouth for children which is supposed to improve their moral fiber.

The daily body ritual performed by everyone includes a mouth-rite. Despite the fact that these people are so punctilious about care of the mouth, this rite involves a practice which strikes the uninitiated stranger as revolting. It was reported to me that the ritual consists of inserting a small bundle of hog hairs into the mouth, along with certain magical powders, and then moving the bundle in a highly formalized series of gestures.

In addition to the private mouth-rite, the people seek out a holy-mouth-man once or twice a year. These practitioners have an impressive set of paraphernalia, consisting of a variety of augers, awls, probes, and prods. The use of these objects in the exorcism of the evils of the mouth involves almost unbelievable ritual torture of the client. The holy-mouth-man opens the client's mouth, and using the above mentioned tools, enlarges any holes which decay may have created in the teeth. Magical materials are put into these holes. If there are no naturally occurring holes in the teeth, large sections of one or more teeth are gouged out so that the supernatural substance can be applied. In the client's view, the purpose of these ministrations is to arrest decay and to draw friends. The extremely sacred and traditional character of the rite is evident in the fact that the natives return to the holy-mouth-men year after year, despite the fact that their teeth continue to decay.

It is to be hoped that, when a thorough study of the Nacirema is made, there will be careful inquiry into the personality structure of these people. One has to but watch the gleam in the eye of a holy-mouth-man as he jabs an awl into an exposed nerve, to suspect that a certain amount of sadism is involved. If this can be established, a very interesting pattern emerges, for most of the population shows definite masochistic tendencies. It was to these that Professor Linton referred in discussing a distinctive part of the daily body ritual which is performed only by men. This part of the rite involves scraping and lacerating the surface of the face with a sharp instrument. Special women's rites are performed only four times during each lunar month, but what they lack in frequency is made up in barbarity. As part of this ceremony, women bake their heads in small ovens for about an hour. The theoretically interesting point is that what seems to be a preponderantly masochistic people have developed sadistic specialists.

The medicine men have an imposing temple, or *latipso*, in every community of any size. The more elaborate ceremonies required to treat very sick patients can only be performed at this temple. These ceremonies involve not only the thaumaturge but a permanent group of vestal maidens who move sedately about the temple chambers in distinctive costume and headdress.

The *latipso* ceremonies are so harsh that it is phenomenal that a fair proportion of the really sick natives who enter the temple ever recover. Small children whose indoctrination is still incomplete have been known to resist attempts to take them to the temple because "that is where you go to die." Despite this fact, sick adults are not only willing but eager to undergo the protracted ritual purification, if they can afford to do so. No matter how ill the supplicant or how grave the emergency, the guardians of many temples will not admit a client if he cannot give a rich gift to the custodian. Even after one has gained admission and survived the ceremonies, the guardians will not permit the neophyte to leave until he makes still another gift.

The supplicant entering the temple is first stripped of all his or her clothes. In every-day life the Nacirema avoids exposure of his body and its natural functions. Bathing and excretory acts are performed only in the secrecy of the household shrine, where they are ritualized as part of the body-rites. Psychological shock results from the fact that body secrecy is suddenly lost upon entry into the *latipso*. A man, whose own wife has never seen him in an excretory act, suddenly finds himself naked and assisted by a vestal maiden while he performs his natural functions into a sacred vessel. This sort of ceremonial treatment is necessitated by the fact that the excreta are used by a diviner to ascertain the course and nature of the client's sickness. Female clients, on the other hand, find their naked bodies are subjected to the scrutiny, manipulation and prodding of the medicine men.

Few supplicants in the temple are well enough to do anything but lie on their hard beds. The daily ceremonies, like the rites of the holy-mouth-men, involve discomfort and torture. With ritual precision, the vestals awaken their miserable charges each dawn and roll them about on their beds of pain while performing ablutions, in the formal movements of which the maidens are highly trained. At other times they insert magic wands in the supplicant's mouth or force him to eat substances which are supposed to be healing. From time to time the medicine men come to their clients and jab magically treated needles into their flesh. The fact that these temple ceremonies may not cure, and may even kill the neophyte, in no way decreases the people's faith in the medicine men.

There remains one other kind of practitioner, known as a "listener." This witch-doctor has the power to exorcise the devils that lodge in the heads of people who have been bewitched. The Nacirema believe that parents bewitch their own children. Mothers are particularly suspected of putting a curse on children while teaching them the secret body rituals. The counter-magic of the witch-doctor is unusual in its lack of ritual. The patient simply tells the "listener" all his troubles and fears, beginning with the earliest difficulties he can remember. The memory displayed by the Nacirema in these exorcism sessions is truly remarkable. It is not uncommon for the patient to bemoan the rejection he felt upon being weaned as a babe, and a few individuals even see their troubles going back to the traumatic effects of their own birth.

In conclusion, mention must be made of certain practices which have their base in native esthetics but which depend upon the pervasive aversion to the natural body and its functions. There are ritual fasts to make fat people thin and ceremonial feasts to make thin people fat. Still other rites are used to make women's breasts larger if they are small, and smaller if they are large. General dissatisfaction with breast shape is symbolized in the fact that the ideal form is virtually outside the range of human variation. A few women afflicted with almost inhuman hypermammary development are so idolized that they make a handsome living by simply going from village to village and permitting the natives to stare at them for a fee.

Reference has already been made to the fact that excretory functions are ritualized, routinized, and relegated to secrecy. Natural reproductive functions are similarly distorted. Intercourse is taboo as a topic and scheduled as an act. Efforts are made to avoid pregnancy by the use of magical materials or by limiting intercourse to certain phases of the moon. Conception is actually very infrequent. When pregnant, women dress so as to hide their condition. Parturition takes place in secret, without friends or relatives to assist, and the majority of women do not nurse their infants.

Our review of the ritual life of the Nacirema has certainly shown them to be a magic-ridden people. It is hard to understand how they have managed to exist so long under the burdens which they have imposed upon themselves. But even such exotic customs as these take on real meaning when they are viewed with the insight provided by Malinowski when he wrote (1948:70):

> Looking from far and above, from our high places of safety in the developed civilization, it is easy to see all the crudity and irrelevance of magic. But without its power and guidance early man could not have mastered his practical difficulties as he has done, nor could man have advanced to the higher stages of civilization.

REFERENCES

Linton, Ralph, 1936, *The Study of Man*. New York, D. Appleton-Century Co.

Malinowski, Bronislaw, 1948, *Magic, Science, and Religion*. Glencoe, The Free Press.

Murdock, George P., 1949, *Social Structure*. New York, The Macmillan Co.

4

Letter from Peri—Manus II

Margaret Mead

Throughout this book you will be reading about a variety of fascinating people and their cultural practices, and you may wonder how the authors learned about them. The answer to this question is not obvious. Social scientists can collect information in a variety of ways: Sociologists often do telephone surveys and psychologists work in laboratory settings; anthropologists do fieldwork.

Fieldwork—long-term, firsthand contact with another culture—is the hallmark of anthropology. From the traditional village to the urban village to the corporate boardroom, anthropologists go to the people. Ethnography is a term that refers to both a product (an ethnography) and a method (doing ethnography). As a method, ethnography is based on detailed personal observation; anthropologists become immersed in the culture while doing what is called participant observation. *Typically, an anthropologist spends a year living in a host community and getting to know the people on a firsthand basis; at the same time, the anthropologist is collecting data. Ethnographers may use both quantitative methods (surveys, cognitive tests, and so forth) and qualitative methods (direct observation, interviews, and so on). Sometimes anthropologists spend a period in one field site and then move on to do research in other areas, but many anthropologists return to the same site over a period of many years. In this selection, Margaret Mead reflects on her long involvement with Peri village (off the northern coast of New Guinea) and how the lives of the villagers have changed.*

As you read this selection, ask yourself the following questions:

☐ *What changes have taken place in the village of Peri over the last 37 years?*

☐ *How do you think Mead feels about the people of Peri?*

☐ *Mead says that fieldworkers are "equipped principally with a way of looking at things." What do you think she means by this?*

☐ *What might be the advantages and disadvantages of doing fieldwork alone or in a group?*

☐ *Different field settings have particular attractions for individuals. How would you like to spend a year in Peri village doing field research?*

The following terms discussed in this selection are included in the Glossary at the back of the book:

ethnography
fieldwork
longitudinal
participant observation
qualitative methods
quantitative methods

May 1966

I am writing in the little house made of rough wood and sago-palm thatch that was built for me by the people of Peri village. The wind brings the sound of waves breaking on the reef, but my house, its back to the sea, looks out on the great square where the public life of the village takes place. At the opposite end of the square is the meetinghouse, and ranged along the sides are the houses of eminent men. Everything is new and paint sparkles on the houses. The handsomest ones are built of corrugated iron; the others are built of traditional materials, with decorative patterns woven into the bamboo.

This is the fourth version of Peri that I have lived in over the last thirty-seven years. The first was the primitive village. When I first came to study the Manus, they were an almost landless sea people and all the houses of Peri were built on stilts in the shallow sea. When I returned twenty-five years later, in 1953, the Manus had moved ashore and the new Peri, located on a small strip of marshy land, was their first attempt to build a "modern" village, designed in accordance with their notions of an American town. By 1964, when I came back on a third field trip, this village had degenerated into a kind of slum, noisy, dilapidated, cramped and overcrowded, because the people of a neighboring village had moved in so that their children too could go to school. Now, a year later, an entirely new village has been built on a spacious tract of land bought with the people's own savings, and here Peri villagers, for so long accustomed only to sea and sand, are planting flowers and vegetables.

For two months everything went along quietly, but now the whole village is humming with activity. Last-minute preparations are in progress for a tremendous celebration at which Peri will entertain some two thousand members of the Paliau movement—all the people who, under the leadership of Paliau Moluat, have taken part in the strenuous and extraordinary effort to create a new way of life. It is the holiday season, and every day more of the adolescents who have been away at school and the young people who have become teachers in faraway parts of New Guinea are returning home to visit their families, see the new village and join in the festivities. Some families have built special rooms for the visitors. In one house there is a real room in which bed, chair and bench, all made by hand, are arranged to make a perfect setting for a schoolboy—the bed neatly made, pictures of the Beatles on the wall, schoolbooks on the table and a schoolbag hung in the window. In another house a few books piled on a suitcase in one corner of a barnlike room are all that signal the return of a school child. But whatever arrangements families have managed to make, the village is alive with delight in the visitors.

The children have come home from modern schools. But some of the young teachers have been working all alone in small bush schools among alien peoples only a few years removed from cannibalism and head-hunting. So the tales circulating in the village are extremely varied. There are descriptions of boarding-school life, stories of examinations and of prizes won in scholarship or sports. But there are also stories about the extraordinary customs of the people in the interior of New Guinea. Listening, I ask myself which is harder for the people of Peri to assimilate and understand—a savage way of life, which in many ways resembles that of their own great-grandfathers but which now has been so enthusiastically abandoned; or the new way of life the Manus have adopted, which belongs to the modern world of the planes that fly overhead and the daily news on the radio. Nowadays this may include news of the Manus themselves. Yesterday morning a newscaster announced: "At the first meeting of the new council in Manus, Mr. Paliau Moluat, member of the House of Assembly, was elected president."

I have come back to Peri on this, my fourth trip to Manus, to witness and record the end of an epoch. The new forms of local self-government, supported by an insistent and originally rebellious leadership, all are legalized. Paliau, the head of what the government once regarded as a subversive movement, now holds elective office and is immersed in work that will shape the future of the Territory of Papua–New Guinea. On a small scale this handful of people living on the coast of an isolated archipelago have enacted the whole drama of moving from the narrow independence of a little warring tribe to participation in the development of an emerging nation.

During the last two months I have been aware of all the different stages of change, as they can be seen simultaneously. On weekdays I see men and women passing by, stripped bare to the waist and holding pandanus hoods over their heads to keep off the rain. On holidays some of the younger women dress in fashionable shifts, bright with splashed flower designs. The oldest men and women, people I have known since 1928, were born into a completely primitive world, ruled over by ghosts, dominated by the fear of disease and death and endlessly preoccupied by the grinding work entailed in meeting their obligations and making the exchanges of shell money and dogs' teeth for oil and turtles, grass skirts and pots. The middle-aged grew up in the period when warfare was ending; as young men they still practiced throwing and dodging the spears they would never use as weapons of war. The next-younger group, in whose childhood the first Christian mission came, lived through the Japanese occupation and reached manhood when the people of the whole south coast were uniting in a small, decisive social revolution. And the youngest group, adolescents and children, are growing up in a world of school and clinic talk. Before them lies the prospect of career choice and the establishment of a new university, the University of Papua–New Guinea, in Port Moresby. These are the first-comers to the new epoch.

Yet, in spite of everything, the Manus have preserved their identity as a people and their integrity as individuals. The shy little boys I knew in the past have grown up into shy, quiet men. The boastfully brash still are brash. The alert-minded are keen and aware. It is as if the changes from savagery to civilization were new colors that had been laid on over the hard, clear outlines of their distinct personalities. At the same time, where once the Manus feared and plotted war, they now hear only echoes of distant battlefields in places of which formerly they were totally unaware. Where once they suffered hunger when storms kept the fishermen at home, they now can buy food for money in the village shops. Where once flight to live precariously among strangers was the outcome of a quarrel, now it is proud ambition that takes the Manus abroad.

One outcome of the chance that brought me to their village to do field work in 1928 is that their history has been chronicled. Unlike most simpler peoples of the world, the Manus can bridge past and present. Here in my house I hang up photographs of all the "big-fellow men belong before," who would otherwise be no more than half-remembered names. Seen from the vantage point of the present, pictures taken ten years ago and thirty-seven years ago have a continuity that overcomes strangeness. Instead of being ashamed of the life that has been abandoned, young people can be proud of an ancestral mode of life that is being preserved for others to know about and is mentioned in speeches made by visitors from the United Nations. Then old pride and new pride merge and the old men, nodding agreement, say: "After all, the Manus people started in Peri."

Each day I go about the ordinary business of field work. I accept the presents of fresh fish and accede to small requests for tobacco, matches, a postage stamp or perhaps four thumbtacks. Whatever I am working at, I listen to the sounds of the village, ready to go quickly to the scene of wailing or shouting or some child's uncharacteristic cry. As I type notes I also watch the passers-by to catch the one person who can answer a question, such as: "Is it really true that the same two women first married Talikat and then later married Ponowan?" Or word comes that two turtles, necessary for the coming feast, have been brought in, and I hurriedly take my camera out of its vacuum case and rush to record the event.

At the same time I think about field work itself. For an anthropologist's life is keyed to field work. Even at home, occupied with other activities, writing up field notes and preparing for the next field trip keeps your mind focused on this aspect of your life. In the past, actual field work has meant living with and studying a primitive people in some remote part of the world. The remoteness has been inevitable, for the peoples anthropologists have studied were primitive because they lived far from the centers of civilization—in the tropics or in the Arctic, in a mountain fastness or on an isolated atoll. Remoteness also has set the style of field work. Cut off from everything else, your attention is wholly concentrated on the lives of the people you are working with, and the effort draws on all your capacities, strength and experience. Now, as the most remote places become known, the conditions of field work are changing. But the need to see and respond as a whole does not change.

I am especially aware of the conditions of field work on this trip because for the first time since my original field trip to Samoa forty years ago I am working alone, without any collaborators in the same or a nearby village. This and the fact that I am using only one camera, a notebook and a pencil—instead of all the complex paraphernalia of the modern field team—throws me back to the very core of field work: one person, all alone, face-to-face with a whole community. Equipped principally with a way of looking at things, the fieldworker is expected somehow to seize on all the essentials of a strange way of life and to bring back a record that will make this comprehensible as a whole to others who very likely never will see this people in their living reality. The role of the fieldworker and the recognition that every people has a culture, the smallest part of which is significant and indicative of the whole, go together. Once the two were matched, our field work helped us to learn more about culture and to train a new generation of anthropologists to make better field studies.

Nevertheless, as I sit here with the light of my pressure lamp casting long shadows on the dark, quiet square, wondering what may happen in the next few hours, I also reflect that field work is one of the most extraordinary tasks we set for young people. Even today it means a special kind of solitude among a people whose every word and gesture is, initially, unexpected and perhaps unintelligible. But beyond this, the fieldworker is required to do consciously something that the young child, filled with boundless energy and curiosity, does without conscious purpose—that is, learn about a whole world. But whereas the child learns as part of growing up and becomes what he learns, the anthropologist must learn the culture without embodying it, in order to become its accurate chronicler.

Whether one learns to receive a gift in both hands or with the right hand only, to touch the gift to one's forehead or to refuse it three times before accepting it, the task is always a double one. One must learn to do something correctly and not to become absorbed in the doing. One must learn what makes people angry but one must not feel insulted oneself. One must live all day in a maze of relationships without being caught in the maze. And above all, one must wait for events to reveal much that must be learned. A storm, an earthquake, a fire, a famine—these are extraordinary conditions that sharply reveal certain aspects of a people's conceptions of life and the universe. But the daily and the recurrent events that subtly shape people's lives are the ones on which the anthropologist must concentrate without being able to foresee what he can learn from them or when any particular event may occur. Equipped as well as possible with his growing knowledge of names and relationships, his experience of expectations and probable outcomes, the fieldworker records, learns—and waits. But it is always an active waiting, a readiness in which all his senses are alert to whatever may happen, expected or unexpected, in the next five minutes—or in an hour, a week, a month from now. The anthropological fieldworker must take a whole community, with all its transmitted tradition, into his mind and, to the extent that he is a whole person, see it whole.

And then my mind turns back to Manus. What is happening here is a kind of paradigm of something that is happening all over the world: grandparents and parents settle for the parts they themselves can play and what must be left to the comprehension of the children. The Manus have taken a direction no one could have foreseen thirty-seven years ago. Yet in the midst of change they are recognizably themselves. Field work provides us with a record of the experiments mankind has made in creating and handing on tradition. Over time it also provides a record of what men can do and become.

5

Crack in Spanish Harlem

Philippe Bourgois

Urban America vibrates with the intensity of a taut drum. The cadence of street life is a constant reminder that things are different here. Suburban folks who meander into some of these inner-city neighborhoods immediately notice the contrasts between these streets and their home towns. Beset by what has been called the "signs of incivility," outsiders are uneasy and often afraid. Outsiders seldom understand the subculture of the inner city, and most don't want to.

Yet, it is in the inner city that many of our most serious social problems are found, including unemployment, homelessness, broken families, poor medical care, and crime. Survival in this milieu, particularly in the drug scene, requires a deep understanding of the subculture. In the same way, effective public policy is more likely to result if policymakers understand the cultural meaning of people's behavior. But how can they achieve such an understanding?

This riveting account reveals how anthropological work can lend an important dimension to our comprehension of a way of life almost as foreign to most of us as is the life of an Amazon Warrior, a !Kung bushman, or a rain forest pygmy.

As you read this selection, ask yourself the following questions:

☐ What is meant by the "culture of resistance," and what effects does this culture have on a community and society?

☐ In what ways is the underground economy like a business?

☐ How is a job in the underground economy different from a legal job in terms of respect and an individual's feeling of self-worth?

☐ What is meant by "the culture of terror," and what is the role of violence in maintaining social status?

☐ What can be learned through ethnographic fieldwork as opposed to questionnaires and surveys?

The following terms discussed in this selection are included in the Glossary at the back of the book:

cultural reproduction
ethnography
ghetto

participant observation
subculture
urban villages

A MUGGING IN SPANISH HARLEM

The heavy-set, white undercover policeman pushed me across the ice-cream counter, spreading my legs and poking me around the groin. As he came dangerously close to the bulge in my right pocket I hissed in his ear 'It's a tape recorder.' He snapped backwards, re-

"Crack in Spanish Harlem: Culture and Economy in the Inner City" by Philippe Bourgois, from *Anthropology Today*, Vol. 5, No. 4, 1989. Royal Anthropological Institute. Reprinted with permission.

leasing his left hand's grip on my neck and whispering a barely audible 'Sorry.' Apparently, he thought he had clumsily intercepted an undercover from another department because before I could get a close look at his face he had left the *bodega* grocery-store cum numbers-joint. Meanwhile, the marijuana sellers stationed in front of the *bodega* that Gato and I had just entered to buy 16-ounce cans of Private Stock (beer), observing that the undercover had been rough with me when he searched through my pants, suddenly felt safe and relieved—finally confident that I was a white drug addict rather than an undercover.

As we hurried to leave this embarrassing scene we were blocked by Bennie, an emaciated teenager high on angel dust who was barging through the door along with two friends to mug us. I ran to the back of the *bodega* but Gato had to stand firmly because this was the corner he worked, and those were his former partners. They dragged him onto the sidewalk surrounding him on all sides, shouting about the money he still owed, and began kicking and hitting him with a baseball bat. I found out later that Gato owed them for his share of the supply of marijuana confiscated in a drug bust last week . . . After we finished telling the story at the crack/*botanica*[1] house where I had been spending most of my evening hours this summer, Chino, who was on duty selling that night with Julio (pronounced Jew-Lee-oh), jumped up excitedly calling out 'what street was that on? Come on, let's go, we can still catch them—How many were they?' I quickly stopped this mobilization for a revenge posse, explaining that it was not worth my time, and that we should just forget about it. Chino looked at me disgustedly sitting back down on the milk crate in front of the *botanica*'s door and turned his face away from me, shrugging his shoulders. Julio, whom I knew better and had become quite close to for a number of weeks last year, jumped up in front of me raising his voice to berate me for being 'pussy.' He also sat back down shortly afterwards feigning exasperated incredulity with the comment 'Man you still think like a *blanquito*.' A half dozen spectators—some of them empty-pocketed ('thirsty!') crack addicts, but most of them sharply dressed teenage drug-free girls competing for Chino's and Julio's attentions—giggled and snickered at me.

CULTURE AND MATERIAL REALITY

The above extract from sanitized fieldwork notes is merely a personalized glimpse of the day-to-day struggle for survival *and for meaning* by the people who stand behind the extraordinary statistics on inner city violent crime in the United States.[2] These are the same Puerto Rican residents of Spanish Harlem, New York City, that Oscar Lewis in *La Vida* declared to be victims of a 'culture of poverty' enmired in a 'self-perpetuating cycle of poverty' (Lewis 1966: 5). The culture of poverty concept has been severely criticized for its internal inconsistencies, its inadequate understanding of 'culture' and ethnicity, its ethnocentric/middle class bias, its blindness to structural forces, and its blame-the-victim implications (cf. Leacock ed. 1971, Valentine 1968, Waxman 1977, Stack 1974). Despite the negative scholarly consensus on Lewis's theory, the alternative discussions either tend towards economic reductionism (Ryan 1971, Steinberg 1981, Wilson 1978)

or else ultimately minimize the reality of profound marginalization and destruction—some of it internalized—that envelop a disproportionate share of the inner city poor (cf. Stack 1974, Valentine 1978; see critiques by Maxwell 1988, Wilson 1988). More importantly, the media, public policy-makers and a large proportion of inner city residents themselves continue to subscribe to a popularized blame-the-victim/culture of poverty concept that has not been adequately rebutted by scholars.

The inner city residents described in the ethnographic vignette above are the pariahs of urban industrial US society. They seek their income and subsequently their identity and the meaning in their life through what they perceive to be high-powered careers 'on the street.' They partake of ideologies and values and share symbols which form the basis of an 'inner city street culture' completely excluded from the mainstream economy and society but ultimately derived from it. Most of them have a few direct contacts with non–inner city residents, and when they do it is usually with people who are in a position of domination: teachers in school, bosses, police officers, and later parole or probation officers.

How can one understand the complicated ideological dynamic accompanying inner city poverty without falling into a hopelessly idealistic culture of poverty and blame-the-victim interpretation? Structural, political economy reinterpretations of the inner city dynamic emphasize historical processes of labour migration in the context of institutionalized ethnic discrimination. They dissect the structural transformations in the international economy which are destroying the manufacturing sector in the United States and are swelling the low wage, low prestige service sector (cf. Davis 1987; Sassen-Koob 1986; Steinberg 1981; Tabb and Sawers, eds., 1984; Wilson 1978, 1987). These analyses address the structural confines of the inner city dynamic but fall prey to a passive interpretation of human action and subscribe to a weakly dialectic interpretation of the relationship between ideological processes and material reality, or between culture and class.

Although ultimately traceable directly to being products of international labour migrations in a transnational world economy, street-level inner city residents are more than merely passive victims of historical economic transformations or of the institutionalized discrimination of a perverse political and economic system. They do not passively accept their fourth-class citizen fate. They are struggling determinedly—just as ruthlessly as the railroad and oil robber-barons of the previous century and the investment-banker 'yuppies' of today—to earn money, demand dignity and lead meaningful lives. Tragically, it is that very process of struggle against—yet within—the system which exacerbates the trauma of their community and which destroys hundreds of thousands of lives on the individual level.

In the day-to-day experience of the street-bound inner city resident, unemployment and personal anxiety over the inability to provide one's family with a minimal standard of living translates itself into intra-community crime, intra-community drug abuse, intra-community violence. The objective, structural desperation of a population without a viable economy, and facing systematic barriers of ethnic discrimination and ideological marginalization, becomes charged at the community level into self-destructive channels.

Most importantly, the 'personal failure' of those who survive on the street is articulated in the idiom of race. The racism imposed by the larger society becomes internalized on a personal level. Once again, although the individuals in the ethnographic fragment at the beginning of this paper are the victims of long-term historical and structural transformations, they do not analyse their difficult situation from a political economy perspective. In their struggle to survive and even to be successful, they enforce on a day-to-day level the details of the trauma and cruelty of their lives on the excluded margins of US urban society.

CULTURAL REPRODUCTION THEORY

Theorists of education have developed a literature on processes of social and cultural reproduction which focus on the ideological domination of the poor and the working class in the school setting (cf. Giroux 1983). Although some of the social reproduction approaches tend towards an economic reductionism or a simple, mechanical functionalism (cf. Bowles and Gintis 1977), the more recent variants emphasize the complexity and contradictory nature of the dynamic of ideological domination (Willis 1983). There are several ethnographies which document how the very process whereby students resist school, channels them into marginal roles in the economy for the rest of their lives (cf. Willis 1977; Macleod 1987). Other ethnographically-based interpretations emphasize how success for inner city African-American students requires a rejection of their ethnic identity and cultural dignity (Fordham 1988).

There is no reason why these theories of cultural resistance and ideological domination have to be limited to the institutional school setting. Cultural reproduction theory has great potential for shedding light on the interaction between structurally induced cultural resistance and self-reinforced marginalization at the street-level in the inner city experience. The violence, crime and substance abuse plaguing the inner city can be understood as the manifestations of a 'culture of resistance' to mainstream, white racist, and economically exclusive society. This 'culture of resistance,' however, results in greater oppression and self-destruction. More concretely, refusing to accept the outside society's racist role playing and refusing to accept low wage, entry-level jobs, translates into high crime rates, high addiction rates and high intra-community violence.

Most of the individuals in the above ethnographic description are proud that they are not being exploited by 'the White Man,' but they feel 'like fucking assholes' for being poor. All of them have previously held numerous jobs in the legal economy in their lives. Most of them hit the street in their early teens working odd jobs as delivery boys and baggers in supermarkets and *bodegas*. Most of them have held the jobs that are recognized as among the least desirable in US society. Virtually all of these street participants have had deeply negative personal experiences in the minimum-wage labour market, owing to abusive, exploitative and often racist bosses or supervisors. They see the illegal, underground economy as not only offering superior wages, but also a more dignified work place. For example, Gato had formerly worked for the ASPCA, cleaning out the gas chambers where stray dogs and cats are killed. Bennie had been fired six months earlier from a night shift job as security guard on the violent ward for the criminally insane on Wards Island; Chino had been fired a year ago from a job installing high altitude storm windows on skyscrapers following an accident which temporarily blinded him in the right eye. Upon being disabled he discovered that his contractor had hired him illegally through an arrangement with a corrupt union official who had paid him half the union wage, pocketing the rest, and who had not taken health insurance for him. Chino also claimed that his foreman from Pennsylvania was a 'Ku Klux Klanner' and had been especially abusive to him as he was a black Puerto Rican. In the process of recovering from the accident, Chino had become addicted to crack and ended up in the hospital as a gunshot victim before landing a job at Papito's crack house. Julio's last legal job before selling crack was as an off-the-books messenger for a magazine catering to New York yuppies. He had become addicted to crack, began selling possessions from out of his home and finally was thrown out by his wife who had just given birth to his son, who carried his name as Julio the IIIrd, on public assistance. Julio had quit his messenger job in favour of stealing car radios for a couple of hours at night in the very same neighbourhood where he had been delivering messages for ten hour days at just above minimum wage. Nevertheless, after a close encounter with the police Julio begged his cousin for a job selling in his crack house. Significantly, the sense of responsibility, success and prestige that selling crack gave him enabled him to kick his crack habit and replace it by a less expensive and destructive powder cocaine and alcohol habit.

The underground economy, consequently, is the ultimate 'equal opportunity employer' for inner city youth (cf. Kornblum and Williams 1985). As Davis (1987: 75) has noted for Los Angeles, the structural economic incentive to participate in the drug economy is overwhelming:

> With 78,000 unemployed youth in the Watts-Willowbrook area, it is not surprising that there are now 145 branches of the rival Crips and Bloods gangs in South L.A., or that the jobless resort to the opportunities of the burgeoning 'Crack' economy.

The individuals 'successfully' pursuing careers in the 'crack economy' or any other facet of the underground economy are no longer 'exploitable' by legal society. They speak with anger at their former low wages and bad treatment. They make fun of friends and acquaintances—many of whom come to buy drugs from them—who are still employed in factories, in service jobs, or in what they (and most other people) would call 'shitwork.' Of course, many others are less self-conscious about the reasons for their rejection of entry-level, mainstream employment. Instead, they think of themselves as lazy and irresponsible. They claim they quit their jobs in order to have a good time on the street. Many still pay lip service to the value of a steady, legal job. Still others cycle in and out of legal employment supplementing their bouts at entry-level jobs through part-time crack sales in an almost perverse parody of the economic subsidy of the wage labour sector by semi-subsistence peasants who cyclically engage in migratory wage labour in third world economies (cf. Meillassoux 1981; Wallerstein 1977).

THE CULTURE OF TERROR IN THE UNDERGROUND ECONOMY

The culture of resistance that has emerged in the underground street-level economy in opposition to demeaning, underpaid employment in the mainstream economy engenders violence. In the South American context of extreme political repression and racism against Amerindians and Jews, anthropologist Michael Taussig has argued that 'cultures of terror' emerge to become ' . . . a high-powered tool for domination and a principal medium for political practice' (1984: 492). Unlike Taussig's examples of the 1910s

Putumayo massacres and the 1970s Argentine torture chambers, domination in the case of the inner city's culture of terror is self-administered even if the root cause is generated or even imposed externally. With the exception of occasional brutality by policemen or the bureaucratized repression of the social welfare and criminal justice institutions (cf. Davis 1988), the physical violence and terror of the inner city are largely carried out by inner city residents themselves.

Regular displays of violence are necessary for success in the underground economy—especially at the street-level drug dealing world. Violence is essential for maintaining credibility and for preventing rip-off by colleagues, customers and hold-up artists. Indeed, upward mobility in the underground economy requires a systematic and effective use of violence against one's colleagues, one's neighbours and, to a certain extent, against oneself. Behaviour that appears irrationally violent and self-destructive to the middle class (or the working class) outside observer, can be reinterpreted according to the logic of the underground economy, as a judicious case of public relations, advertising, rapport building and long-term investment in one's 'human capital development.'

The importance of one's reputation is well illustrated in the fieldwork fragment at the beginning of this paper. Gato and I were mugged because Gato had a reputation for being 'soft' or 'pussy' and because I was publicly unmasked as *not being* an undercover cop: hence safe to attack. Gato tried to minimize the damage to his future ability to sell on that corner by not turning and running. He had pranced sideways down the street, though being beaten with a baseball bat and kicked to the ground twice. Significantly, I found out later that it was the second time this had happened to Gato this year. Gato was not going to be upwardly mobile in the underground economy because of his 'pussy' reputation and he was further cementing his fate with an increasingly out of control addiction to crack.

Employers or new entrepreneurs in the underground economy are looking for people who can demonstrate their capacity for effective violence and terror. For example, in the eyes of Papito, the owner of the string of crack franchises I am currently researching, the ability of his employees to hold up under gunpoint is crucial as stick-ups of dealing dens are not infrequent. In fact, since my fieldwork began in 1986, the *botanica* has been held up twice. Julio happened to be on duty both times. He admitted to me that he had been very nervous when they held the gun to his temple and had asked for money and crack. Nevertheless, not only did he withhold some of the money and crack that was hidden behind the bogus *botanica* merchandise, but he also later exaggerated to Papito the amount that had been stolen in order to pocket the difference.

On several occasions in the midst of long conversations with active criminals (i.e. once with a dealing-den stick-up artist, several times with crack dealers, and once with a former bank robber) I asked them to explain how they were able to trust their partners in crime sufficiently to ensure the longevity and effectiveness of their enterprise. To my surprise I was not given any righteous diatribes about blood-brotherhood trustworthiness or any adulations of boy-hood loyalty. Instead, in each case, in slightly different language I was told somewhat aggressively: 'What do you mean how do I trust him? You should ask "How does he trust me?"' Their ruthlessness is their security: 'My support network is me, myself and I.' They made these assertions with such vehemence as to appear threatened by the concept that their security and success might depend upon the trustworthiness of their partner or their employer. They were claiming—in one case angrily—that they were not dependent upon trust: because they were tough enough to command respect and enforce all contracts they entered into. The 'How can they trust me?' was said with smug pride, perhaps not unlike the way a stockbroker might brag about his access to inside information on an upcoming hostile takeover deal.

At the end of the summer Chino demonstrated clearly the how-can-I-be-trusted dynamic. His cocaine snorting habit had been degenerating into a crack addiction by the end of the summer, and finally one night he was forced to flee out of state to a cousin's when he was unable to turn in the night's receipts to his boss Papito following a binge. Chino also owed Papito close to a thousand dollars for bail that Papito had posted when he was arrested for selling crack at the *botanica* a few months ago. Almost a year later when Papito heard that Chino had been arrested for jumping bail he arranged through another associate incarcerated in the same prison (Rikers Island) to have Chino beaten up before his trial date.

My failure to display a propensity for violence in several instances cost me the respect of the members of the crack scene that I frequented. This was very evident when I turned down Julio and Chino's offer to search for Bennie after he mugged Gato and me. Julio had despairingly exclaimed that I 'still [thought] like a *blanquito*,' genuinely disappointed that I was not someone with common sense and self-respect.

These concrete examples of the cultivation of violent public behaviour are the extreme cases of individuals relying on the underground economy for their income and dependent upon cultivating terror in order to survive. Individuals involved in street activity cultivate the culture of terror in order to intimidate competitors, maintain credibility, develop new contacts, cement partnerships, and ultimately to have a good time. For the most part they are not conscious of this process. The culture of terror becomes a myth and a role model with rules and satisfactions all its own which ultimately has a traumatic impact on the majority of Spanish Harlem residents—who are drug free and who work honestly at poorly remunerated legal jobs, 9 to 5 plus overtime.

PURSUING THE AMERICAN DREAM

It is important to understand that the underground economy and the violence emerging out of it are not propelled by an irrational cultural logic distinct from that of mainstream USA. On the contrary, street participants are frantically pursuing the 'American dream.' The assertions of the culture of poverty theorists that the poor have been badly socialized and do not share mainstream values is wrong. On the contrary, ambitious, energetic, inner city youths are attracted into the underground economy in order to try frantically to get their piece of the pie as fast as possible. They often even follow the traditional US model for upward mobility to the letter by becoming aggressive private entrepreneurs. They are the ultimate rugged individualists braving an unpredictable frontier where fortune, fame and destruction are all just around the corner. Hence Indio, a particularly enterprising and ambitious young crack dealer who was aggressively carving out a new sales point, shot his brother in the spine and paralysed him for life while he was high on angel dust in a battle over sales rights. His brother now works for him selling on crutches. Meanwhile, the shooting has cemented Indio's reputation and his workers are awesomely disciplined: 'If he shot his brother he'll shoot anyone.' Indio reaffirms this symbolically by periodically walking his turf with an oversized gold chain and name plate worth several thousand dollars hanging around his neck.

The underground economy and the culture of terror are experienced as the most realistic routes to upward mobility. Entry-level jobs are not seen as viable channels to upward mobility by high school dropouts. Drug selling or other illegal activity appear as the most effective and realistic options for getting rich within one's lifetime. Many of the street dealers claim to be strictly utilitarian in their involvement with crack and they snob their clients despite the fact that they usually have considerable alcohol and powder cocaine habits themselves. Chino used to chant at his regular customers 'Come on, keep on killing yourself; bring me that money; smoke yourself to death; make me rich.'

Even though street sellers are employed by the

owner of a sales point for whom they have to maintain regular hours, meet sales quotas and be subject to being fired, they have a great deal of autonomy and power in their daily (or nightly) routine. The boss only comes once or twice a shift to drop off drugs and pick up money. Frequently, it is a young messenger who is sent instead. Sellers are often surrounded by a bevy of 'thirsty' friends and hanger-oners—frequently young teenage women in the case of male sellers—willing to run errands, pay attention to conversations, lend support in arguments and fights and provide sexual favours for them on demand because of the relatively large amounts of money and drugs passing through their hands. In fact, even youths who do not use drugs will hang out and attempt to befriend respectfully the dealer just to be privy to the excitement of people coming and going, copping and hanging; money flowing, arguments, detectives, and stick-up artists—all around danger and excitement. Other non-users will hang out to be treated to an occasional round of beer, Bacardi or, on an off night, Thunderbird.

The channel into the underground economy is by no means strictly economic. Besides wanting to earn 'crazy money,' people choose 'hoodlum' status in order to assert their dignity at refusing to 'sling a mop for the white man' (cf. Anderson 1976: 68). Employment or better yet self-employment—in the underground economy—accords a sense of autonomy, self-dignity and an opportunity for extraordinary rapid short-term upward mobility that is only too obviously unavailable in entry-level jobs. Opulent survival without a 'visible means of support' is the ultimate expression of success and it is a viable option. There is plenty of visible proof of this to everyone on the street as they watch teenage crack dealers drive by in convertible Suzuki Samurai jeeps with the stereo blaring, 'beem' by in impeccable BMWs, or—in the case of the middle-aged dealers—speed around in well waxed Lincoln Continentals. Anyone can aspire to be promoted to the level of a seller perched on a 20-speed mountain bike with a beeper by their side. In fact, many youths not particularly active in the drug trade run around with beepers on their belts just pretending to be big-time. The impact of the sense of dignity and worth that can accompany selling crack is illustrated by Julio's ability to overcome his destructive addiction to crack only after getting a job selling it: 'I couldn't be messin' up the money. I couldn't be fucking up no more! Besides, I had to get respect.'

In New York City the insult of working for entry-level wages amidst extraordinary opulence is especially painfully perceived by Spanish Harlem youths who have grown in abject poverty only a few blocks from all-white neighbourhoods commanding some of the highest real estate values in the world. As messengers, security guards or xerox machine operators in the corporate headquarters of the Fortune 500 companies, they are brusquely ordered about by young white executives who sometimes make monthly salaries superior to their yearly wages and who do not even have the time to notice that they are being rude.

It could be argued that Manhattan sports a *de facto* apartheid labour hierarchy whereby differences in job category and prestige correlate with ethnicity and are often justified—consciously or unconsciously—through a racist logic. This humiliating confrontation with New York's ethnic/occupational hierarchy drives the street-bound cohort of inner city youths deeper into the confines of their segregated neighbourhood and the underground economy. They prefer to seek out meaning and upward mobility in a context that does not constantly oblige them to come into contact with people of a different, hostile ethnicity wielding arbitrary power over them. In the underground economy, especially in the world of substance abuse, they never have to experience the silent subtle humiliations that the entry-level labour market—or even merely a daily subway ride downtown—invariably subjects them to.

In this context the crack high and the rituals and struggles around purchasing and using the drug are comparable to the millenarian religions that sweep colonized peoples attempting to resist oppression in the context of accelerated social trauma—whether it be the Ghost dance of the Great Plains Amerindians, the 'cargo cults' of Melanesia, the Mamachi movement of the Guaymi Amerindians in Panama, or even religions such as Farrakhan's Nation of Islam and the Jehovah's Witnesses in the heart of the inner city (cf. Bourgois 1986, 1989). Substance abuse in general, and crack in particular, offer the equivalent of a millenarian metamorphosis. Instantaneously users are transformed from being unemployed, depressed high school dropouts, despised by the world—and secretly convinced that their failure is due to their own inherent stupidity, 'racial laziness' and disorganization—into being a mass of heart-palpitating pleasure, followed only minutes later by a jaw-gnashing crash and wideawake alertness that provides their life with concrete purpose: get more crack—fast!

One of the most dramatic illustrations within the dynamic of the crack economy of how a cultural dynamic of resistance to exploitation can lead contradictorily to greater oppression and ideological domination is the conspicuous presence of women in the growing cohort of crack addicts. In a series of ten random surveys undertaken at Papito's crack franchises, women and girls represented just under 50% of the customers. This contrasts dramatically to the estimates of female participation in heroin addiction in the late 1970s.

The painful spectacle of young, emaciated women milling in agitated angst around crack copping corners and selling their bodies for five dollars, or even merely for a puff on a crack stem, reflects the growing emancipation of women in all aspects of inner city life, culture and economy. Women—especially the emerging generation which is most at risk for crack addiction—are no longer as obliged to stay at home and maintain the family. They no longer so readily sacrifice public life or forgo independent opportunities to generate personally disposable income. This is documented by the frequent visits to the crack houses by pregnant women and by mothers accompanied by toddlers.

A more neutral illustration of the changed position of women in street culture outside the arena of substance abuse is the growing presence of young women on inner city basketball courts. Similarly, on the national level, there are conclusive statistics documenting increased female participation in the legal labour market—especially in the working class Puerto Rican community. By the same token, more women are also resisting exploitation in the entry-level job market and are pursuing careers in the underground economy and seeking self-definition and meaning through intensive participation in street culture.

Although women are using the drug and participating intensively in street culture, traditional gender relations still largely govern income-generating strategies in the underground economy. Most notably, women are forced disproportionately to rely on prostitution to finance their habits. The relegation of women to the traditional street role of prostitution has led to a flooding of the market for sex, leading to a drop in the price of women's bodies and to an epidemic rise in venereal disease among women and newborn babies.

Contradictorily, therefore, the underlying process of emancipation which has enabled women to demand equal participation in street culture and to carve out an expanded niche for themselves in the underground economy has led to a greater depreciation of women as ridiculed sex objects. Addicted women will tolerate a tremendous amount of verbal and physical abuse in their pursuit of a vial of crack, allowing lecherous men to humiliate and ridicule them in public. Chino, who is married and is the father of nine children, refers to the women who regularly service him with oral sex as 'my moufs' [mouths]. He enjoys calling out to these addicted women from across the street, 'Yo, there goes my mouf! Come on over here.' Such a public degradation of a cohort of women who are conspicuously present on the street cannot be neutral. It ultimately reinforces the ideological domination of women in general.

DE-LEGITIMIZING DOMINATION

How can one discuss and analyse the phenomenon of street-level inner city culture and violence without reproducing and confirming the very ideological relationships that are its basis? In his discussion of the culture of terror, Taussig notes that it is precisely the narratives about the torture and violence of the repressive societies which ' . . . are in themselves evidence of the process whereby a culture of terror was created and sustained' (1984: 279). The superhuman power that the media has accorded to crack serves a similar mythical function. The *New York Times* has run articles and interviews with scientists that portray crack as if it were a miraculous substance beyond the power of human beings to control (cf. 25 June, 1988: 1). They 'prove' this by documenting how quickly rats will ecstatically kill themselves when provided with cocaine upon demand. Catheterized rats push the cocaine lever to the exclusion of the nutrient lever until they collapse exhausted to die of thirst.

The alleged omnipotence of crack coupled with even the driest recounting of the overpowering statistics on violence ultimately allows US society to absolve itself of any real responsibility for the inner city phenomena. The mythical dimensions of the culture of terror push economics and politics out of the picture and enable the US to maintain in some of its larger cities a level of ethnic segregation and economic marginalization that are unacceptable to any of the other wealthy, industrialized nations of the world, with the obvious exception of South Africa. Worse yet, on the level of theory, because of the continued domination—even in their negation—of the North America-centred culture of poverty theories, this discussion of the ideological implications of the underground economy may take readers full circle back to a blame-the-victim interpretation of inner city oppression.

NOTES

1. A *botanica* is a herbal pharmacy and *santeria* utility store.
2. This research was funded by the United States Bureau of the Census, the Wenner-Gren Foundation for Anthropological Research, two Washington University Junior Faculty Summer Research grants, and Lottery Funds and an Affirmative Action Grant from San Francisco State University. An expanded version of this article will be appearing in a special issue of *Contemporary Drug Problems* devoted to crack in the United States.

   Pseudonyms have been used in order to disguise identities of persons referred to.

REFERENCES

Anderson, Elijah. 1976. *A Place on the Corner*. Chicago: U. of Chicago.

Bourgois, Philippe. 1986. The Miskitu of Nicaragua: Politicized Ethnicity. *A.T.* 2:2: 4–9.

———. 1989. *Ethnicity at Work: Divided Labour on a Central American Banana Plantation*. Baltimore: Johns Hopkins U.P.

Bowles, Samuel and Herbert Gintis. 1977. *Schooling in Capitalist America*. New York: Basic Books.

Davis, Mike. 1987. *Chinatown*, Part Two? The 'Internationalization' of Downtown Los Angeles. *New Left Review* 164: 65–86.

Davis, Mike, with Sue Ruddick. 1988. Los Angeles: Civil Liberties Between the Hammer and the Rock. *New Left Review* 1970: 37–60.

Fordham, Signithia. 1988. Racelessness as a Factor in Black Students' School Success: Pragmatic Strategy or Pyrrhic Victory? *Harvard Educational Review* 58:1: 54–84.

Giroux, Henry. 1983. Theories of Reproduction and Resistance in the New Sociology of Education: A Critical Analysis. *Harvard Educational Review* 53:3: 257–293.

Kornblum, William and Terry Williams. 1985. *Growing Up Poor*. Lexington, MA.: Lexington Books.

Leacock, Eleanor Burke. ed. 1971. *The Culture of Poverty: A Critique*. New York: Simon and Schuster.

Lewis, Oscar. 1966. The Culture of Poverty. In *Anthropological Essays* pp. 67–80. New York: Random House.

Macleod, Jay. 1987. *Ain't No Makin' It*. Boulder, Colorado: Westview P.

Maxwell, Andrew. 1988. The Anthropology of Poverty in Black Communities: A Critique and Systems Alternative. *Urban Anthropology* 17:2&3: 171–191.

Meillassoux, Claude. 1981. *Maidens, Meal and Money*. Cambridge: Cambridge U.P.

Ryan, William. 1986[1971]. Blaming the Victim. In *Taking Sides: Clashing Views on Controversial Social Issues* pp. 45–52. ed. Kurt Finsterbusch and George McKenna. Guilford, CT: Dushkin Publishing Group.

Sassen-Koob, Saskia. 1986. New York City: Economic Restructuring and Immigration. *Development and Change* 17:1: 87–119.

Stack, Carol. 1974. *All Our Kin: Strategies for Survival in a Black Community*. New York: Harper & Row.

Steinberg, Stephen. 1981. *The Ethnic Myth: Race, Ethnicity and Class in America*. New York: Atheneum.

Tabb, William and Larry Sawers, eds. 1984. *Marxism and the Metropolis: New Perspectives in Urban Political Economy*. New York: Oxford U.P.

Taussig, Michael. 1984. Culture of Terror—Space of Death, Roger Casement's Putumayo Report and the Explanation of Torture. *Comparative Studies in Society and History* 26:3: 467–497.

Valentine, Charles. 1968. *Culture and Poverty*. Chicago: U. of Chicago P.

Valentine, Bettylou. 1978. *Hustling and Other Hard Work*. NY: Free P.

Wallerstein, Emanuel. 1977. Rural Economy in Modern World Society. *Studies in Comparative International Development* 12:1: 29–40.

Waxman, Chaim. 1977. *The Stigma of Poverty: A Critique of Poverty Theories and Policies*. NY: Pergamon.

Willis, Paul. 1983. Cultural Production and Theories of Reproduction. In *Race, Class and Education*, pp. 107–138. eds. Len Barton and Stephen Walker. London: Croom-Helm.

———. 1977. *Learning to Labor: How Working Class Kids Get Working Class Jobs*. Aldershot, England: Gower.

Wilson, William Julius. 1978. *The Declining Significance of Race: Blacks and Changing American Institutions*. Chicago: U. of Chicago P.

———. 1987. *The Truly Disadvantaged: The Inner City, the Underclass and Public Policy*. Chicago: U. of Chicago.

6

PROFILE OF ANTHROPOLOGISTS
Corporate Anthropologists

Jennifer J. Laabs

Most anthropological work is still done in other cultures. Today, however, an increasing number of anthropologists are bringing their expertise to the corporate world. The concept of culture and the ethnographic methods of anthropology that originally developed on the African savannahs, the Australian outback, the Arctic tundra, and the bush country of the New Guinea Highlands are now being applied to understand and advance corporate cultures as well as to enhance the social organization of shops and offices. From Xerox to General Motors to Nissan, corporate executives find that anthropologists can help them to see through different eyes.

Recent business anthropology aims to improve working conditions within offices, develop understandings of the importance of corporate culture, provide market research insights through participant observation rather than survey research, develop products through observation of people in natural settings, and provide insights into other cultures to facilitate a corporation's expansion into the global economy.

While anthropologists have been working with businesses since the 1930s, the 1980s witnessed exceptional growth in this field due to the globalization of business activity and the increased awareness of the importance of culture for business.

As you read this selection, ask yourself the following questions:

☐ *What are the four fields of anthropology, and what are some of the areas of applied anthropological work?*

☐ *What are the similarities and differences between business anthropology and other forms of cultural anthropology?*

☐ *What is meant by the "culture" of a business?*

☐ *How can anthropologists help corporations perform better in a global environment?*

☐ *How can a corporate "origin myth" stimulate creative thinking?*

The following terms discussed in this selection are included in the Glossary at the back of the book:

archaeology
biological anthropology
corporate culture
cultural anthropology
linguistic anthropology
origin myth

Chances are, an anthropologist wouldn't be the first business expert you'd call if you wanted to build a better mousetrap—or a better HR program. Anthropologists aren't exactly listed as consultants in the phone book between *accountant* and *attorney*. But maybe they should be.

Although calling an anthropologist might seem like an unusual answer to a business dilemma, many companies have found that anthropologists' expertise as cultural scientists is quite useful in gaining insight about human behavior within their corporate digs.

Anthropology, by definition, is "the science of human beings," and studies people in relation to their "distribution, origin, classification, relationship of races, physical character, environmental and social relations and culture" (according to *Webster's Ninth New Collegiate Dictionary*).

Although there are many types of anthropologists (see "They Dig up Rocks, Don't They?"), most people have only heard of the archaeology (stones and bones) variety. But there's much more to them than that.

Anthropologists study many different areas of business, but essentially they're all people-watchers of one sort or another. Business anthropologists have been studying the corporate world for years (since the early 1900s), on such varied topics as how to encourage more creativity or how best to integrate multicultural learning techniques into an organization's training program.

There are only a dozen business anthropologists who actually use the title of *anthropologist*, but there are about 200 currently working in and for corporate America.

Lorna M. McDougall, a staff anthropologist at Arthur Andersen's Center for Professional Education in St. Charles, Illinois, for example, currently is studying why people from some cultures learn best from lectures, although others learn best through interactive learning.

Her background includes linguistics study at Trinity College in Dublin, Ireland, and social anthropological study at Oxford. She also has a specialty in medical anthropology, and has worked in a variety of organizations and universities.

McDougall has been a key player in shaping the firm's Business English Language Immersion Training (ELIT) program, directed by the company's management development group, to which McDougall reports.

The ELIT program builds both a common language skill for communication between people who speak English as a second language (there are approximately 800 million in the world), and an awareness of each culture's unique approach to business encounters. The results of her work have helped instructors, who train Andersen consultants working in 66 countries, be better teachers. They've also helped students become better learners.

The center is almost a mini-United Nations, and has many of the same kinds of intercultural opportunities and challenges, but also is a melting pot of sorts in which she studies many types of cultural issues. "We're in a unique position to be able to use people's information and exchange it," says McDougall.

Arthur Andersen's product essentially is its people, and keeping them trained and in top shape to consult alongside other Andersen employees in many different countries is a cultural and business challenge that many global firms are facing these days. Although the company has been global for many years, delivering clear, effective training for consultants continues to be an issue.

McDougall is part of Andersen's corporate strategy, says Pete Pesce, managing director for Arthur Andersen's human resources worldwide. "An anthropologist brings a lot of value to an organization," says Pesce. Although McDougall is the company's first onsite anthropologist and has been with Arthur Andersen only one year, she's going to be even more valuable in the future because of the increasing worldwide scope of the company's operations, says Pesce.

Because the organization has more than 56,000 employees and has spent, for example, 7.4% of its annual revenue in 1990 ($309 million) on training and education, the company is committed to enhancing its education programs using expertise that such disciplines as anthropology can offer.

What is that expertise? "Business anthropology, like all anthropology, is based on observing and analyzing group values and behavior in a cultural context. We focus on *what* people in a cultural group do, *how many* of them do it and *how what they do* affects the individuals in the group," she says.

"Business anthropologists seek to identify the connections between national culture and organizational culture," explains McDougall. Just as other cultural scientists, she helps identify some of the major cultural variables within and between organizations and the various ways that these differences impact:

- Structure

- Strategy

- Operations

- Communications

- Behavior.

From a cross-cultural standpoint, McDougall's job was to analyze what Arthur Andersen instructors

THEY DIG UP ROCKS, DON'T THEY?

When most people think of anthropologists, they think of the most popular kind—those who dig up ancient artifacts and try to make sense of past life forms and cultures. These "stones and bones" scientists are only a fraction of the forms that anthropology takes: *Academic anthropology* dates back to the late 19th century. It was formalized by the establishment of the American Anthropological Association (AAA) in 1902, which currently has 11,000 members. In contrast with anthropology in Europe and Latin America, American academic anthropology is distinguished by its "four-field approach" including:

- Cultural anthropology
- Archaeology
- Biological anthropology
- Linguistic anthropology.

There are many other subgroups within these four areas.

Applied anthropology dates back to World War II when anthropologists worked for the federal government. The Society for Applied Anthropology (SFAA), founded in 1941, has 3,000 members. The National Association for the Practice of Anthropology (NAPA), was formed in 1983 and overlaps membership of the SFAA. Many of these *applied* and *practicing* anthropologists work for government agencies and non-profit groups. Their work includes:

- Agricultural development
- Education
- Family planning
- Legal system development
- Natural resources management
- Public health and nutrition
- Social impact assessment.

Business anthropology traces its origins to the 1930s, but only since the early 1980s have anthropologists been working for such major corporations as General Motors, Xerox, Nissan and McDonnell Douglas.   — *JL*

(usually partners) and students do in the classroom and how they interpret those events.

"When I came in to study this program, I used an anthropological methodology to take a look at what was happening," she says. She listened in on classroom sessions and conducted many face-to-face interviews. "I then analyzed that data from an anthropological perspective," says McDougall. She noticed, for example, that people from certain cultures are used to two-way communication in the classroom, although others just sit quietly while the "professor lectures." To do otherwise, in their minds, would be disrespectful.

"It isn't necessarily an inherent feature of the human mind that people learn in one way or another," says McDougall. It's more a question of how people have *learned to learn*, and how the company's training can incorporate all types of learning styles for the best possible retention of the material by everyone. "What we're really doing is facilitating," she says.

Changes were made in the objectives of the training program. For example, another component was added—a cultural orientation module, which helps the company's staff and managers become more aware of multicultural diversity issues and how those behaviors are affecting their business interactions.

As a result of the changes, the "students" have been more cooperative and better learners inside the classroom, explains McDougall. Noticeably more intercultural socializing has taken place outside the classroom as well—something management hadn't anticipated. "It's important to realize that when you're looking at the effectiveness of cross-cultural training, you want to look at the outcome in improved relations between the people involved," she explains.

Pesce, from a human resources perspective, has found that the organizational values are the same throughout the firm's many offices globally because of the company's emphasis on homogeneous training and orientation. "I've travelled around the world and talked to employees," he says. "What I see clearly is that the values of the firm are very, very consistent. When our people talk about our organization, they talk about it in the same light in terms of quality, values, delivering client service and developing our people."

McDougall also teaches some of the management development classes, and is involved in the company's "train the trainers" program. In addition, she presents special classes to the company's human resources managers on cultural sensitivity issues.

"Recently, I was in London meeting with our

AN ANTHROPOLOGIST'S TOOL KIT

By Lorna M. McDougall

Anthropologists rely on a large historical and current geographical data bank for new ideas and new applications of old ideas. For example, when we look at the history of work, we can trace it from the survival activities common to higher primates—getting food and shelter—through the stages of human evolution and history.

What we see is that, as work becomes further removed from the direct provision of needs, the issue of motivation arises. We know that many of the great states: Greek, Roman, Mayan, Egyptian, African, Indian, Chinese, to mention only a few, approached work and productivity using a variety of rewards, incentives and disciplinary measures. They also had to deal with what we would recognize as business issues: strategic planning, accounting, finance and inventory management.

A wide-ranging cultural approach shows us that the issues any society faces today aren't necessarily new—nor are the issues new for management. On the contrary, approaching things from a comparative perspective, we can see that in our time we have made progress in finding creative alternatives for productivity in the context of today's values and culturally diverse work force.

The value of this knowledge is that it can readily stimulate creative thinking. It helps us to realize that nothing is written in stone, and that we are dealing with situations that always have been challenging. We aren't deficient just because these situations continue.

On the contrary, we need to realize that our current proactive approach to such situations, which involves actually studying how to improve them, rather than just wrestling with them, is a significant advancement. Management problems have been around a long time, but management development is our creative response to dealing with them.

directors of human resources for our Europe, the Middle East, India and Africa divisions," says Pesce. "Their interest in dealing with working standards is very keen. The challenge is to understand the differences in cultures, and in work and family values—the differences between Spain and Germany, for example. Lorna will be very helpful to us in that whole process."

Other areas she is studying involve such topics as:

- Leadership
- Creativity
- Productivity
- Delegation.

Areas for McDougall's anthropological study have been identified in a variety of ways. Sometimes members of the management development team propose ideas; other times, McDougall identifies them. Some recent topics have included teaching associates the cultural meaning of gestures and selecting colors for computer screens used in training.

"Colors have symbolic connections that are culture-specific," explains McDougall. "For example, in some cultures, white is associated with marriage, but in others it's associated with death. Others associate blue with death. In some cultures pink is considered feminine and in others yellow is."

Another project that McDougall is helping develop is an Experienced Hire Orientation program to help new hires assimilate more rapidly into the company's corporate culture. "We would apply what anthropologists call *oral transmission* of beliefs, practices and values by having established personnel pass on the firm's history and traditions by word of mouth, rather than in writing," explains McDougall.

For now, her work has been centered at the St. Charles facility, but in the future she might travel to the company's other worldwide locations for other research projects.

ANTHROPOLOGY BOOSTS CREATIVITY

"What good are zero defects, if you aren't even making the right product?" asks Roger P. McConochie, a St. Charles, Illinois-based anthropologist who consults with businesses on a variety of topics.

McConochie asks a thought-provoking question. Some companies are looking to people like him to help answer it, because it opens up the corporate agenda to the bigger picture: What really is a company's business all about?

One business person, who has benefited from the anthropological approach, came to this conclusion: "What is our product? It isn't hardware, and it isn't even customer satisfaction, excellence, quality, TQM, or those other buzzwords from the '80s," says Mark T. Grace, operations development manager for Houston-based Generon Systems (a division of Dow Chemical and British Oxygen Corp.). Although the company manufactures nitrogen-separation equipment, Grace says: "We have only one product: innovation."

"Today we're the best in the world at what we do," says Grace, "but if we keep doing things the same way for another two or three years, we'll be out of business. That's how quickly this industry is changing and that's how tough our competition is. Our challenge on a daily basis is to redesign our equipment so that it's more efficient: space-efficient, weight-efficient, cost-efficient."

In his business, creativity is everything, he continues. "The problem is putting people into a group and having them freely share their ideas. Each person wants individual credit for his or her ideas, yet the best ideas emerge from interaction." Although the company even has "idea rooms" in which people can draw their ideas and put them up on the wall, Grace explains, "We were stuck. So at one meeting, I said, 'We've tried everything else, why not bring in an anthropologist?'"

He called McConochie, president of Corporate Research International, for suggestions on how to incorporate culturally correct ways of getting staff to contribute. Since then, McConochie, and his associate, Harvard-educated Anthony Giannini, president of The Corporate DaVinci, Ltd., have been an anthropological sounding board for Grace.

Generon's problem is fairly typical in business. But it isn't the company's fault, say these anthropologists, because today's business people are products of the competitive jungle in which they live and work. Although competition may be good among rivals, it often doesn't work within a single organizational culture, as evidenced by the fact that creativity gets stifled. People have a hard time leaving their cultural imprints at the front door.

To understand present society, anthropologists look to the past. From their perspective, McConochie and Giannini liken successful business strategy to the Renaissance period in Europe (between the 14th and 16th centuries), when such individuals as Leonardo da Vinci were guided by many values, including the aesthetics of beauty and the spiritual and emotional sides of humanity.

"During the Renaissance, new institutions were being formed and reformed and the individual was rediscovered," says Giannini. Da Vinci's *The Last Supper*, for example, was the first painting that got away from depicting human figures in a flat and mono-chromatic way. "You had, for the very first time, real people," he notes.

At that time, there was a blending of many human interests and cultures into almost every facet of life, including work. But that approach, for the most part, was abandoned somewhere along the way.

What was lost? "A concern with the human side of things, a concern with the non-quantifiable," says Mc-Conochie. He and Giannini say they think business would benefit from getting back to that holistic approach to thinking. "We believe in numbers; and we believe in measurements, but we also believe that there are elements to life and elements to corporate practice that can't be put into numbers."

Today, compartmentalization of human thinking is rampant, but the challenge of globalization requires businesses to rethink that strategy. Such techniques as "bridging" or "scaffolding" allow workers to use the many facets of their collective conscious to come up with solutions to current problems. It also can help them better understand colleagues from other cultures. Anything less, they say, falls short.

Giannini and McConochie created *The Corporate DaVinci*—a program for corporate Renaissance, in which they help organizations rethink their corporate history and recreate their corporate myths. "In anthropological terms, we would call it an *origin myth*. Every tribe in the jungle has a story of how it came to be," says McConochie. And so do companies. They don't usually think about it, but if often helps people remember how they came to be, and how they fit into history.

For example, when Giannini took the program to Ford Motor Co., he began the first session with a brief history of the wheel: From its invention to modern-day transportation. "In just 15 minutes, they had a fresh way of looking at the work they were doing day by day," says McConochie. "It was no longer just going out and pushing cars off the assembly line and selling them to get their sales figures up for the year. They were participating in the human drama."

Why is this so important? Because companies need a clear "ego sense": a continual sense of organizational self over time, says McConochie. Most anthropologists talk in terms of thousands, or even millions, of years. People begin to see that their lives, in the grander scheme of things, last only an instant. They also see, however, that what they do has an impact on the historical continuum and gives workers a feeling of oneness.

TEN DIMENSIONS OF CORPORATE BEAUTY

1. Purpose. Is there a clear and unifying purpose to the product or service you're auditing?
2. Integrity. Does the product or service do what it was originally designed to do?
3. Simplicity. Is the product or service as simple as possible in structure, content, operation, and so on? Do corporate standards exist for simplicity in design?
4. Symmetry/Asymmetry. Is it physically symmetrical? *Pleasing to the eye?* Is it logically symmetrical? *Pleasing to the mind?* Is there operational harmony between the various parts? *Pleasing to the ear?* Does it feel symmetrical? *Pleasing to the touch? Smell? Taste?* Is it pleasing to your sense of proportional order in all respects? *Pleasing to the emotions?*
5. Balance. Does the product or service justify its existence? Are its gains worth its costs? Does it fit in with the rest of your product or service family?
6. Brilliancy. Compared to other competitive products and services, does this product or service sparkle on its own? Where does it lack sparkle?
7. Suggestiveness. Does the use of this product or service strongly evoke images of client or customer success in multiple domains, such as how designer clothes may suggest a boost in social status?
8. Clarity. Is the product or service easily understood? Is it easily used?
9. Adaptability. How adaptable to sudden change in the marketplace is the product or service? Are there any breakthroughs looming on the technology horizon that will change the picture?
10. Perenniality. Is the product or service an annual or perennial entity? Will it last at least two years? More than five, 10 or 15 years?

"What defines us as human beings is that, despite the differences across cultures, we're all trying to create meaning in our lives," says McConochie. "From my experience in corporations, the people on the shop floor have as much need for meaning in their lives as the people in the boardroom," he explains. "Everybody wants fewer defects at a lower cost. That's fine," says McConochie. "I'm not sure that's enough."

Corporations have been trapped by the concept that all that people on the shop floor need is to sleep, eat and get paid at the end of the week—and if you give them those basics, it's enough to motivate them. This isn't so, explains McConochie, who has consulted with many types of businesses, including aviation companies. Even chief executive officers won't work any harder if you double their salaries. "What you need to do is give them an opportunity to be creative, and an opportunity for challenge and growth," he explains. Creativity also must be supported in corporate culture—in word and deed.

"Right at the top of their corporate mission statement, organizations ought to have a special credo that reads 'Beauty in our products and services, and in the creative means of their production, is a corporate goal of the highest order,'" says Giannini.

Everyone can be creative—they just need some tools to help broaden their thinking. Giannini and McConochie's Corporate DaVinci program includes a segment called *The Aesthetic Audit* (see "Ten Dimensions of Corporate Beauty"), which gives people a guide to use as a springboard into the creative process.

For example, if you went to the hardware store, and picked up a simple screw or nut, you could examine it and ask, "Does it suit its purpose?" Then you'd move on to the other points. Does it demonstrate integrity? If it's corroded, has sharp edges that might cut the person using it, or lacks brilliancy and symmetry, for example, you might round the edges and paint it.

"Typically, I find that executives give low ratings to 60 to 70% of their products and services in at least half of these dimensions," says Giannini. Looking at their own products with *focused eyes*, companies then go on to make better products, and also create new ones. It gives colleagues a set of questions from which to start, so they can work together creatively.

Employees also can benefit from cognitive and cultural training, so they understand where ideas come from and how those ideas vary across societal boundaries. For example, these anthropologists include such topics in their program as:

- Organization of Thought Across Cultures

- The Multicultural Technician

- Cognitive Emotions Across Cultures

- Multicultural Business Thinking in Action.

Can corporations actually blend science with poetry? Production with art? Business with aesthetics? Anthropologists who reach from one culture to another—bringing the best cognitive and cultural artifacts from the past into the present—say it *is* possible, and may be just the bridge that sparks innovation of the future.

7

Shakespeare in the Bush

Laura Bohannan

Communication is an essential characteristic of human social life. Through language we socialize our children and pass down cultural values from generation to generation. Communication forms and defines relations among individuals as well as among groups. Because communication is so natural, we seldom ask a critical question: When we speak, does the listener understand?

At a minimum, communication involves a sender, a receiver, and a shared "code" for exchanging information. When an individual or group sends a message, the sender anticipates that those who receive the message will interpret and understand the message in the way the sender intended. Miscommunication is, of course, an unfortunately common phenomenon that can lead to fist fights, divorces, and wars.

What most of us do not appreciate is the degree to which culture affects our interpretations of messages. As Laura Bohannan tells the tale of Hamlet, we gradually discover how particular behaviors or events can have very different meanings in different places. What is interesting is that the miscommunication of interpretational differences is not a result of poor language or translation abilities. Miscommunication is not a result of speaking too quickly or not loudly enough—it reflects cultural differences.

As you read this selection, ask yourself the following questions:

☐ What were the author's original beliefs about the universality of the classics—such as Hamlet?

☐ How did the Tiv elders react to the marriage of Hamlet's mother to his uncle? How was this different from Hamlet's own emotional reaction?

☐ Why do the Tiv believe a chief should have more than one wife?

☐ As the author tells the story, consider how the elders interpret various actions so as to fit Tiv culture and in so doing redefine the central meaning of the play.

The following terms discussed in this selection are included in the Glossary at the back of the book:

age grade
agnatic
cultural relativism
levirate
polygyny
socialization

Just before I left Oxford for the Tiv in West Africa, conversation turned to the season at Stratford. "You Americans," said a friend, "often have difficulty with Shakespeare. He was, after all, a very English poet, and one can easily misinterpret the universal by misunderstanding the particular."

From *Natural History*, 1966. Reprinted by permission of the author.

I protested that human nature is pretty much the same the whole world over; at least the general plot and motivation of the greater tragedies would always be clear—everywhere—although some details of custom might have to be explained and difficulties of translation might produce other slight changes. To end an argument we could not conclude, my friend gave me a copy of *Hamlet* to study in the African bush: it would, he hoped, lift my mind above its primitive surroundings, and possibly I might, by prolonged meditation, achieve the grace of correct interpretation.

It was my second field trip to that African tribe, and I thought myself ready to live in one of its remote sections—an area difficult to cross even on foot. I eventually settled on the hillock of a very knowledgeable old man, the head of a homestead of some hundred and forty people, all of whom were either his close relatives or their wives and children. Like the other elders of the vicinity, the old man spent most of his time performing ceremonies seldom seen these days in the more accessible parts of the tribe. I was delighted. Soon there would be three months of enforced isolation and leisure, between the harvest that takes place just before the rising of the swamps and the clearing of new farms when the water goes down. Then, I thought, they would have even more time to perform ceremonies and explain them to me.

I was quite mistaken. Most of the ceremonies demanded the presence of elders from several homesteads. As the swamps rose, the old men found it too difficult to walk from one homestead to the next, and the ceremonies gradually ceased. As the swamps rose even higher, all activities but one came to an end. The women brewed beer from maize and millet. Men, women, and children sat on their hillocks and drank it.

People began to drink at dawn. By midmorning the whole homestead was singing, dancing, and drumming. When it rained, people had to sit inside their huts: there they drank and sang or they drank and told stories. In any case, by noon or before, I either had to join the party or retire to my own hut and my books. "One does not discuss serious matters when there is beer. Come, drink with us." Since I lacked their capacity for the thick native beer, I spent more and more time with *Hamlet*. Before the end of the second month, grace descended on me. I was quite sure that *Hamlet* had only one possible interpretation, and that one universally obvious.

Early every morning in the hope of having some serious talk before the beer party, I used to call on the old man at his reception hut—a circle of posts supporting a thatched roof above a low mud wall to keep out wind and rain. One day I crawled through the low doorway and found most of the men of the homestead sitting huddled in their ragged clothes on stools, low plank beds, and reclining chairs, warming themselves against the chill of the rain around a smoky fire. In the center were three pots of beer. The party had started.

The old man greeted me cordially. "Sit down and drink." I accepted a large calabash full of beer, poured some into a small drinking gourd, and tossed it down. Then I poured some more into the same gourd for the man second in seniority to my host before I handed my calabash over to a young man for further distribution. Important people shouldn't ladle beer themselves.

"It is better like this," the old man said, looking at me approvingly and plucking at the thatch that had caught in my hair. "You should sit and drink with us more often. Your servants tell me that when you are not with us, you sit inside your hut looking at a paper."

The old man was acquainted with four kinds of "papers": tax receipts, bride price receipts, court fee receipts, and letters. The messenger who brought him letters from the chief used them mainly as a badge of office, for he always knew what was in them and told the old man. Personal letters for the few who had relatives in the government or mission stations were kept until someone went to a large market where there was a letter writer and reader. Since my arrival, letters were brought to me to be read. A few men also brought me bride price receipts, privately, with requests to change the figures to a higher sum. I found moral arguments were of no avail, since in-laws are fair game, and the technical hazards of forgery difficult to explain to an illiterate people. I did not wish them to think me silly enough to look at any such papers for days on end, and I hastily explained that my "paper" was one of the "things of long ago" of my country.

"Ah," said the old man. "Tell us."

I protested that I was not a storyteller. Storytelling is a skilled art among them; their standards are high and the audiences critical—and vocal in their criticism. I protested in vain. This morning they wanted to hear a story while they drank. They threatened to tell me no more stories until I told them one of mine. Finally, the old man promised that no one would criticize my style "for we know you are struggling with our language." "But," put in one of the elders, "you must explain what we do not understand, as we do when we tell you our stories." Realizing that here was my chance to prove *Hamlet* universally intelligible, I agreed.

The old man handed me some more beer to help me on with my storytelling. Men filled their long wooden pipes and knocked coals from the fire to place in the pipe bowls; then, puffing contentedly, they sat back to listen. I began in the proper style, "Not yesterday, not yesterday, but long ago, a thing occurred. One night three men were keeping watch outside the homestead of the great chief, when suddenly they saw the former chief approach them."

"Why was he no longer their chief?"

"He was dead," I explained. "That is why they were troubled and afraid when they saw him."

"Impossible," began one of the elders, handing his pipe on to his neighbor, who interrupted, "Of course it wasn't the dead chief. It was an omen sent by a witch. Go on."

Slightly shaken, I continued. "One of these three was a man who knew things"—the closest translation for scholar, but unfortunately it also meant witch. The second elder looked triumphantly at the first. "So he spoke to the dead chief saying, 'Tell us what we must do so you may rest in your grave,' but the dead chief did not answer. He vanished, and they could see him no more. Then the man who knew things—his name was Horatio—said this event was the affair of the dead chief's son, Hamlet."

There was a general shaking of heads round the circle. "Had the dead chief no living brothers? Or was this son the chief?"

"No," I replied. "That is, he had one living brother who became the chief when the elder brother died."

The old men muttered: such omens were matters for chiefs and elders, not for youngsters; no good could come of going behind a chief's back; clearly Horatio was not a man who knew things.

"Yes, he was," I insisted, shooing a chicken away from my beer. "In our country the son is next to the father. The dead chief's younger brother had become the great chief. He had also married his elder brother's widow only about a month after the funeral."

"He did well," the old man beamed and announced to the others, "I told you that if we knew more about Europeans, we would find they really were very like us. In our country also," he added to me, "the younger brother marries the elder brother's widow and becomes the father of his children. Now, if your uncle, who married your widowed mother, is your father's full brother, then he will be a real father to you. Did Hamlet's father and uncle have one mother?"

His question barely penetrated my mind; I was too upset and thrown off balance by having one of the most important elements of *Hamlet* knocked straight out of the picture. Rather uncertainly I said that I thought they had the same mother, but I wasn't sure—the story didn't say. The old man told me severely that these genealogical details made all the difference and that when I got home I must ask the elders about it. He shouted out the door to one of his younger wives to bring his goatskin bag.

Determined to save what I could of the mother motif, I took a deep breath and began again. "The son Hamlet was very sad because his mother had married again so quickly. There was no need for her to do so, and it is our custom for a widow not to go to her next husband until she has mourned for two years."

"Two years is too long," objected the wife, who had appeared with the old man's battered goatskin bag. "Who will hoe your farms for you while you have no husband?"

"Hamlet," I retorted without thinking, "was old enough to hoe his mother's farms himself. There was no need for her to remarry." No one looked convinced. I gave up. "His mother and the great chief told Hamlet not to be sad, for the great chief himself would be a father to Hamlet. Furthermore, Hamlet would be the next chief: therefore he must stay to learn the things of a chief. Hamlet agreed to remain, and all the rest went off to drink beer."

While I paused, perplexed at how to render Hamlet's disgusted soliloquy to an audience convinced that Claudius and Gertrude had behaved in the best possible manner, one of the younger men asked me who had married the other wives of the dead chief.

"He had no other wives," I told him.

"But a chief must have many wives! How else can he brew beer and prepare food for all his guests?"

I said firmly that in our country even chiefs had only one wife, that they had servants to do their work, and that they paid them from tax money.

It was better, they returned, for a chief to have many wives and sons who would help him hoe his farms and feed his people; then everyone loved the chief who gave much and took nothing—taxes were a bad thing.

I agreed with the last comment, but for the rest fell back on their favorite way of fobbing off my questions: "That is the way it is done, so that is how we do it."

I decided to skip the soliloquy. Even if Claudius was here thought quite right to marry his brother's widow, there remained the poison motif, and I knew they would disapprove of fratricide. More hopefully I resumed, "That night Hamlet kept watch with the three who had seen his dead father. The dead chief again appeared, and although the others were afraid, Hamlet followed his dead father off to one side. When they were alone, Hamlet's dead father spoke."

"Omens can't talk!" The old man was emphatic.

"Hamlet's dead father wasn't an omen. Seeing him might have been an omen, but he was not." My audience looked as confused as I sounded. "It *was* Hamlet's dead father. It was a thing we call a 'ghost.'" I had to use the English word, for unlike many of the neighboring tribes, these people didn't believe in the survival after death of any individuating part of the personality.

"What is a 'ghost'? An omen?"

"No, a 'ghost' is someone who is dead but who walks around and can talk, and people can hear him and see him but not touch him."

They objected. "One can touch zombis."

"No, no! It was not a dead body the witches had animated to sacrifice and eat. No one else made Hamlet's dead father walk. He did it himself."

"Dead men can't walk," protested my audience as one man.

I was quite willing to compromise. "A 'ghost' is the dead man's shadow."

But again they objected. "Dead men cast no shadows."

"They do in my country," I snapped.

The old man quelled the babble of disbelief that arose immediately and told me with that insincere, but courteous, agreement one extends to the fancies of the young, ignorant, and superstitious, "No doubt in your country the dead can also walk without being zombis." From the depths of his bag he produced a withered fragment of kola nut, bit off one end to show it wasn't poisoned, and handed me the rest as a peace offering.

"Anyhow," I resumed, "Hamlet's dead father said that his own brother, the one who became chief, had poisoned him. He wanted Hamlet to avenge him. Hamlet believed this in his heart, for he did not like his father's brother." I took another swallow of beer. "In the country of the great chief, living in the same homestead, for it was a very large one, was an important elder who was often with the chief to advise and help him. His name was Polonius. Hamlet was courting his daughter, but her father and her brother . . . (I cast hastily about for some tribal analogy) warned her not to let Hamlet visit her when she was alone on her farm, for he would be a great chief and so could not marry her."

"Why not?" asked the wife, who had settled down on the edge of the old man's chair. He frowned at her for asking stupid questions and growled, "They lived in the same homestead."

"That was not the reason," I informed them. "Polonius was a stranger who lived in the homestead because he helped the chief, not because he was a relative."

"Then why couldn't Hamlet marry her?"

"He could have," I explained, "but Polonius didn't think he would. After all, Hamlet was a man of great importance who ought to marry a chief's daughter, for in his country a man could have only one wife. Polonius was afraid that if Hamlet made love to his daughter, then no one else would give a high price for her."

"That might be true," remarked one of the shrewder elders, "but a chief's son would give his mistress's father enough presents and patronage to more than make up the difference. Polonius sounds like a fool to me."

"Many people think he was," I agreed. "Meanwhile Polonius sent his son Laertes off to Paris to learn the things of that country, for it was the homestead of a very great chief indeed. Because he was afraid that Laertes might waste a lot of money on beer and women and gambling, or get into trouble by fighting, he sent one of his servants to Paris secretly, to spy out what

Laertes was doing. One day Hamlet came upon Polonius's daughter Ophelia. He behaved so oddly he frightened her. Indeed"—I was fumbling for words to express the dubious quality of Hamlet's madness— "the chief and many others had also noticed that when Hamlet talked one could understand the words but not what they meant. Many people thought that he had become mad." My audience suddenly became more attentive. "The great chief wanted to know what was wrong with Hamlet, so he sent for two of Hamlet's age mates (school friends would have taken long explanation) to talk to Hamlet and find out what troubled his heart. Hamlet, seeing that they had been bribed by the chief to betray him, told them nothing. Polonius, however, insisted that Hamlet was mad because he had been forbidden to see Ophelia, whom he loved."

"Why," inquired a bewildered voice, "should anyone bewitch Hamlet on that account?"

"Bewitch him?"

"Yes, only witchcraft can make anyone mad, unless, of course, one sees the beings that lurk in the forest."

I stopped being a storyteller, took out my notebook and demanded to be told more about these two causes of madness. Even while they spoke and I jotted notes, I tried to calculate the effect of this new factor on the plot. Hamlet had not been exposed to the beings that lurk in the forest. Only his relatives in the male line could bewitch him. Barring relatives not mentioned by Shakespeare, it had to be Claudius who was attempting to harm him. And, of course, it was.

For the moment I staved off questions by saying that the great chief also refused to believe that Hamlet was mad for the love of Ophelia and nothing else. "He was sure that something much more important was troubling Hamlet's heart."

"Now Hamlet's age mates," I continued, "had brought with them a famous storyteller. Hamlet decided to have this man tell the chief and all his homestead a story about a man who had poisoned his brother because he desired his brother's wife and wished to be chief himself. Hamlet was sure the great chief could not hear the story without making a sign if he was indeed guilty, and then he would discover whether his dead father had told him the truth."

The old man interrupted, with deep cunning, "Why should a father lie to his son?" he asked.

I hedged: "Hamlet wasn't sure that it really was his dead father." It was impossible to say anything, in that language, about devil-inspired visions.

"You mean," he said, "it actually was an omen, and he knew witches sometimes send false ones. Hamlet was a fool not to go to one skilled in reading omens and divining the truth in the first place. A man-who-sees-the-truth could have told him how his father died, if he really had been poisoned, and if there was witchcraft in it; then Hamlet could have called the elders to settle the matter."

The shrewd elder ventured to disagree. "Because his father's brother was a great chief, one-who-sees-the-truth might therefore have been afraid to tell it. I think it was for that reason that a friend of Hamlet's father—a witch and an elder—sent an omen so his friend's son would know. Was the omen true?"

"Yes," I said, abandoning ghosts and the devil; a witch-sent omen it would have to be. "It was true, for when the storyteller was telling his tale before all the homestead, the great chief rose in fear. Afraid that Hamlet knew his secret, he planned to have him killed."

The stage set of the next bit presented some difficulties of translation. I began cautiously. "The great chief told Hamlet's mother to find out from her son what he knew. But because a woman's children are always first in her heart, he had the important elder Polonius hide behind a cloth that hung against the wall of Hamlet's mother's sleeping hut. Hamlet started to scold his mother for what she had done."

There was a shocked murmur from everyone. A man should never scold his mother.

"She called out in fear, and Polonius moved behind the cloth. Shouting, 'A rat!' Hamlet took his machete and slashed through the cloth." I paused for dramatic effect. "He had killed Polonius!"

The old men looked at each other in supreme disgust. "That Polonius truly was a fool and a man who knew nothing! What child would not know enough to shout, 'It's me!'" With a pang, I remembered that these people are ardent hunters, always armed with bow, arrow, and machete; at the first rustle in the grass an arrow is aimed and ready, and the hunter shouts "Game!" If no human voice answers immediately, the arrow speeds on its way. Like a good hunter Hamlet had shouted, "A rat!"

I rushed in to save Polonius's reputation. "Polonius did speak. Hamlet heard him. But he thought it was the chief and wished to kill him to avenge his father. He had meant to kill him earlier that evening. . . ." I broke down, unable to describe to these pagans, who had no belief in individual afterlife, the difference between dying at one's prayers and dying "unhousell'd, disappointed, unaneled."

This time I had shocked my audience seriously. "For a man to raise his hand against his father's brother and the one who has become his father—that is a terrible thing. The elders ought to let such a man be bewitched."

I nibbled at my kola nut in some perplexity, then pointed out that after all the man had killed Hamlet's father.

"No," pronounced the old man, speaking less to me than to the young men sitting behind the elders. "If your father's brother has killed your father, you must appeal to your father's age mates; *they* may avenge him. No man may use violence against his senior relatives." Another thought struck him. "But if his father's brother had indeed been wicked enough to bewitch Hamlet and make him mad that would be a good story indeed, for it would be his fault that Hamlet, being mad, no longer had any sense and thus was ready to kill his father's brother."

There was a murmur of applause. *Hamlet* was again a good story to them, but it no longer seemed quite the same story to me. As I thought over the coming complications of plot and motive, I lost courage and decided to skim over dangerous ground quickly.

"The great chief," I went on, "was not sorry that Hamlet had killed Polonius. It gave him a reason to send Hamlet away, with his two treacherous age mates, with letters to a chief of a far country, saying that Hamlet should be killed. But Hamlet changed the writing on their papers, so that the chief killed his age mates instead." I encountered a reproachful glare from one of the men whom I had told undetectable forgery was not merely immoral but beyond human skill. I looked the other way.

"Before Hamlet could return, Laertes came back for his father's funeral. The great chief told him Hamlet had killed Polonius. Laertes swore to kill Hamlet because of this, and because his sister Ophelia, hearing her father had been killed by the man she loved, went mad and drowned in the river."

"Have you already forgotten what we told you?" The old man was reproachful. "One cannot take vengeance on a madman; Hamlet killed Polonius in his madness. As for the girl, she not only went mad, she was drowned. Only witches can make people drown. Water itself can't hurt anything. It is merely something one drinks and bathes in."

I began to get cross. "If you don't like the story, I'll stop."

The old man made soothing noises and himself poured me some more beer. "You tell the story well, and we are listening. But it is clear the elders of your country have never told you what the story really means. No, don't interrupt! We believe you when you say your marriage customs are different, or your clothes and weapons. But people are the same everywhere; therefore, there are always witches and it is we, the elders, who know how witches work. We told you it was the great chief who wished to kill Hamlet, and now your own words have proved us right. Who were Ophelia's male relatives?"

"There were only her father and her brother." Hamlet was clearly out of my hands.

"There must have been many more; this also you must ask of your elders when you get back to your country. From what you tell us, since Polonius was dead, it must have been Laertes who killed Ophelia, although I do not see the reason for it."

We had emptied one pot of beer, and the old men argued the point with slightly tipsy interest. Finally one of them demanded of me, "What did the servant of Polonius say on his return?"

With difficulty I recollected Reynaldo and his mission. "I don't think he did return before Polonius was killed."

"Listen," said the elder, "and I will tell you how it was and how your story will go, then you may tell me if I am right. Polonius knew his son would get into trouble, and so he did. He had many fines to pay for fighting, and debts from gambling. But he had only two ways of getting money quickly. One was to marry off his sister at once, but it is difficult to find a man who will marry a woman desired by the son of a chief. For if the chief's heir commits adultery with your wife, what can you do? Only a fool calls a case against a man who will someday be his judge. Therefore Laertes had to take the second way: he killed his sister by witchcraft, drowning her so he could secretly sell her body to the witches."

I raised an objection. "They found her body and buried it. Indeed Laertes jumped into the grave to see his sister once more—so, you see, the body was truly there. Hamlet, who had just come back, jumped in after him."

"What did I tell you?" The elder appealed to the others. "Laertes was up to no good with his sister's body. Hamlet prevented him, because the chief's heir, like a chief, does not wish any other man to grow rich and powerful. Laertes would be angry, because he would have killed his sister without benefit to himself. In our country he would try to kill Hamlet for that reason. Is this not what happened?"

"More or less," I admitted. "When the great chief found Hamlet was still alive, he encouraged Laertes to try to kill Hamlet and arranged a fight with machetes between them. In the fight both the young men were wounded to death. Hamlet's mother drank the poisoned beer that the chief meant for Hamlet in case he won the fight. When he saw his mother die of poison, Hamlet, dying, managed to kill his father's brother with his machete."

"You see, I was right!" exclaimed the elder.

"That was a very good story," added the old man, "and you told it with very few mistakes. There was just one more error, at the very end. The poison Hamlet's mother drank was obviously meant for the survivor of the fight, whichever it was. If Laertes had won, the great chief would have poisoned him, for no one would know that he arranged Hamlet's death. Then, too, he need not fear Laertes' witchcraft; it takes a strong heart to kill one's only sister by witchcraft.

"Sometime," concluded the old man, gathering his ragged toga about him, "you must tell us some more stories of your country. We, who are elders, will instruct you in their true meaning, so that when you return to your own land your elders will see that you have not been sitting in the bush, but among those who know things and who have taught you wisdom."

8

Preserving Language Diversity

H. Russell Bernard

In recent history, languages have been disappearing at an alarming rate. The modern world's 6,000 languages may diminish to but a few hundred over the next century, thereby decreasing the diversity of thought processes and expression. When Christopher Columbus landed in the New World 500 years ago, there were 1,000 languages. Of the 187 North American Indian languages, only about 35 remain. Genocide eliminated the people and the languages of Tasmania in the brief period between 1803 and 1835. Around the globe today further linguistic decline follows the expansion of dominant cultures and the devaluation of ethnic traditions. Parents sometimes feel their children will profit if they learn the dominant culture and language, often to the exclusion of their traditional culture and language. Sometimes these acculturation processes are further assisted by government agencies or public policies that encourage or require proficiency in nontraditional languages. In some cases, policies aimed at eradicating diversity have given way, in recent years, to enlightened policies that embrace it. However, it is one thing to become aware of a problem and another to develop a solution.

Shakespeare's Hamlet, discussed in the previous selection, is an oral performance (a play) also passed on and preserved through literature. The vast majority of languages spoken today also have rich oral traditions, but few possess any literature. H. Russell Bernard believes that we may be able to preserve language diversity by using computer technology that provides an opportunity for native peoples to produce literature in their own language—and he is doing something about it.

As you read this selection, ask yourself the following questions:

☐ Why is it important to preserve linguistic diversity?

☐ While most languages today have writing systems, they lack a written literary tradition. Why is this the case?

☐ How did the development of new technologies of the early 1980s dramatically change the ability to write native texts?

☐ In what ways—political, economic, and social—can preserving native languages benefit ethnic groups?

The following terms discussed in this selection are included in the Glossary at the back of the book:

ethnic group
lexicon
literacy
orthography

Reproduced by permission of the Society for Applied Anthropology from *Human Organization*, Vol. 51, No. 1, Spring 1992, pp. 82–89.

In 1987, Jesús Salinas and I conceived a plan for the development of a center in Mexico where Indian people could learn to read and write their own languages using microcomputers. More importantly, they would be able to print and publish their own works, in their own languages, on topics of their own choice. The idea was to make it possible for Indian people to save their languages from extinction.

This paper is about how that center came about, and about how we hope to extend the work to help preserve thousands of native languages throughout the world. First, though, I address the issue of why I believe anthropologists must work to preserve linguistic diversity.

THE PROBLEM

Depending on how you count them, there are between 3000 and 6000 languages spoken in the world today. Only 276 languages, however, are spoken by a million people or more.[1] About 80–90% of all languages are spoken by indigenous peoples like the Zuni, the Samoans, and the Jívaro. Taken together, all these peoples comprise less than 10% of the world's population.

In other words, about 80–90% of all linguistic diversity is today vested in 10% of the world's population. A few native language communities, like the Aymara and the Tswana, are large and robust. Most are small and fragile. Languages are vanishing quickly.

Languages have always come and gone. Neither the language of Jesus nor that of Caesar are spoken today. But languages seem to be disappearing faster than ever before. My guess is that there are about 15% fewer languages today than there were in 1500 AD.

As an anthropologist, I'm alarmed at this prospect. It's not that I worship language diversity for its own sake. Nor do I want to preserve a lot of cultural-linguistic groups for my own (or my colleagues') pleasure of studying them. I'm concerned instead that humanity itself, the species *H. sapiens*, may be at evolutionary risk. The wholesale disappearance of languages, and what I will argue is the consequent reduction of cultural diversity, may threaten our survival.

I say "may threaten" because I have no way to test my hunch. But consider: 40,000 years ago, there were no more than 15 million humans in the world (Cohen 1977:54). Today, there are over 5 billion of us. We have occupied the Americas, the string of smaller Pacific Islands, Australia, New Zealand, and Greenland. We've adapted to jungles, deserts, and the arctic. By any reasonable measure, H. sapiens sapiens is an evolutionary success story.

It is practically an article of faith in anthropology that the adaptive success of our species was due to

"culture." Culture implies ideas and the communication of ideas through language. Linguistic diversity, then, is at least the correlate of (though not the cause of) diversity of adaptational ideas—ideas about transferring property (or even the idea of property itself), curing illness, acquiring food, raising children, distributing power, or settling disputes.[2]

By this reasoning, any reduction of language diversity diminishes the adaptational strength of our species because it lowers the pool of knowledge from which we can draw. We know that the reduction of biodiversity today threatens all of us. I think we are conducting an experiment to see what will happen to humanity if we eliminate "cultural species" in the world. This is a reckless experiment. If we don't like the way it turns out, there's no going back.

TRIBAL LANGUAGES REMAIN UNWRITTEN

Before 1500 AD, reading was an extremely rare skill. Since Johannes Gutenberg's improvements in the printing press, however, literacy and printing have been spreading around the world. (See Eisenstein 1979 for a review of the effects of printing on the West.) Still, more than 500 years after Gutenberg, most languages of the world remain unwritten—without any literary tradition, without books.

It's not for lack of writing systems. Virtually all indigenous languages have writing systems, usually alphabets. Some alphabets are more and some are less standardized, but missionaries and linguists over the past 500 years have seen to it that every extant language can be written. A few indigenous literary traditions have flourished in the past or are flourishing now (Zulu, Xhosa, and Luo in Africa; Cherokee and Navajo in North America; Quechua and Aymara in South America, to name a few), and a great many peoples have two or three books in their native language: a formal grammar, a dictionary, and a translation of the Bible.

Still, what most native languages lack is native authors who write books in their own native languages. They lack *popular* literacy, where people read newspapers and books regularly and write letters to one another as a matter of course. I argue that without popular literacy, all but a few native languages will soon disappear. And when nonwritten languages disappear, they disappear forever.[3]

BILINGUAL EDUCATION AND WRITING

There are, to be sure, many bilingual education programs in the world. In those programs, native children learn to read and write in both their first language and in the major national language of their country. In Africa, Latin America, North America, Asia, and the Pacific Islands, governments spend millions of dollars every year on such programs. In Mexico alone, there are 56 Indian languages, spoken by 8–10 million people, and there are bilingual (Indian/Spanish) school programs in half of those languages.

In Canada, there are 70 Indian and Eskimo languages, with active literacy training programs in Cree, Ojibwa, Montagnais, and Inuit (Eskimo), among others. (Burnaby 1985 offers an excellent overview of how native writing is taught in Canada.) There are nearly 38 American Indian languages still spoken by more than 1000 people each in the US. There are bilingual education programs in schools on most major Indian reservations.

These programs do not produce popular literacy, however—at least not in the native language. Children typically learn to read primers and, in church-related programs, the Bible in their native language. They learn special alphabets and spend hundreds of hours of their childhood composing simple sentences, but they don't grow up to write books in that language. The tribal languages of the world therefore remain largely unwritten. Bilingual education programs do not produce true native literacy, because they are not, in general, meant to produce true native literature.[4]

WHY TRIBAL LANGUAGES REMAIN UNWRITTEN

There are several reasons why bilingual education programs have failed to produce either popular literacy or sustained traditions of native literature:

1. Many people who speak nonwritten languages believe that by giving up their language—by not speaking it at home—they will impart some economic advantage to their children. They reason that the minority language creates an indelible mark that prevents people from getting jobs in the economic mainstream.[5]

   There is some truth to this reasoning. Native peoples are almost everywhere discriminated against when it comes to competing for jobs in national economies. Giving up one's language and culture, however, does not automatically bring economic benefits. I'll have more to say about this later.

2. In some cases there are competing alphabets. People argue about which alphabet to use and don't get down to the serious business of writing. Different alphabets are often the result of missionaries from different faiths or denominations competing for the allegiance of native people. I have seen competing interest groups (both native and foreign) battle for decades over how best to represent a particular sound in a particular language.

3. Even when there is just one accepted alphabet, it may be too complex. I have seen alphabets so unwieldy they cripple the efforts of native people who want to write native language books.

   This problem is particularly common in alphabets devised to write tone languages. Euroamerican missionaries and linguists find it next to impossible to read tone languages correctly unless tones are marked. They make up cumbersome writing systems, and insist that tone be marked. Then they convince native people that the language cannot be written "correctly" unless tones are marked.

   Native speakers of tone languages usually don't need to see tones marked in writing.[6] They discern the correct tones from the context. Consider the sentence: "The man /bit/ /sit/ /kit/ /lit/ his lip" and suppose you had to choose one of the words in brackets. No native speaker of English would fail this test. Similarly, native speakers of a tone language can usually choose the right meaning of a word in context.

   We could, of course, devise more ambiguous examples, such as "The child was quite /mad/ /bad/." This is the sort of example used, in bilingual teaching materials around the world, to convince native people that they have to mark tones. But people rarely have to make choices among such ambiguities in isolated sentences. Instead, sentences and thoughts occur in the context of paragraphs and whole texts.

   Even if ambiguous sentences do create problems once in a while, that's a small price to pay for the ability to write. In my experience, it comes down to this: if native people have to write tone languages by marking all the tones, they simply don't write at all. I'll return to this later, too.

4. It costs too much to print books. Despite these problems, there are native speakers of tribal languages who want to write books. There are even some who have written lengthy texts. Those books remain unpublished because the costs of modern printing technology are too high.

   If a speaker of, say, Mixtec, in Mexico, wrote a 200-page manuscript in that language, no commercial printer could afford to produce the book. It would require a complete new family of type. Even if individual characters could be manufactured (an expensive item), no typesetter could understand the text and the proofs would be riddled with errors. Correcting those errors would take a lot of time and expense.

A realistic print run for a book in Mixtec might come to 300 or 400 copies. The cost per book, assuming 150 pages of text, would be around $8, just for photoreproduction and the least expensive binding. That figure leaps to about $15 when the costs of typesetting and editing are included. That's about 45,000 Mexican pesos, or two days' wages for a laborer in rural areas of the country.

MICROCOMPUTERS AND NATIVE LITERACY

Beginning in 1971, I taught Jesús Salinas Pedraza, a Ñähñu Indian from the state of Hidalgo in Mexico, to read and write his own language.[7] We used a modified version of an alphabet that had been developed by missionary linguists (from the Summer Institute of Linguistics) some years before.

During the 1970s, under support from the National Science Foundation and the National Endowment for the Humanities, Salinas wrote a description of his own, Ñähñu, culture. I translated and annotated his ethnography and entered the text into a mainframe word processor. Two bilingual (Ñähñu-English) books resulted from that effort. One was a volume of folk tales (Bernard and Salinas 1976), and the other was a volume on the ethnography of the Ñähñu people (Salinas and Bernard 1978).

In order to use the mainframe word processor, I had to make some adjustments. The existing alphabet contained several symbols that did not appear on a standard terminal keyboard. So, for example, the letter ä in Ñähñu sounds something like the "aw" in the word "paw." That sound is written with a character that looks like a backwards c in the International Phonetic Alphabet. Since the letter c is not needed in Ñähñu, I used it to represent the "aw" sound.

The problem was that Salinas and other Ñähñu bilingual educators didn't like the compromised writing system that I'd concocted. I thought it would be easy for people to use whatever letters were available on the IBM keyboard to represent the sounds of their particular language. I was annoyed when Salinas and other Ñähñu educators balked at using the standard IBM keyboard to write their language. I insisted that they adjust their needs to the available technology. They insisted that the technology should serve their needs, not the other way around.

They were absolutely right, but it was only 1981. The then-current wisdom in linguistics was that writing systems for previously nonwritten languages should be constructed from characters available on standard keyboards. The idea, of course, was to make writing systems accessible (Fishman 1977:xiii). Word processors were still pretty clumsy. Hardly anyone thought about using them to write Spanish or French, much less the exotic, nonwritten languages of the world.

A couple of early word processors for the Apple II series allowed the user to build new characters that would appear on the screen, and print them exactly as they appeared on the screen. One of those word processors, appropriately called *Gutenberg*, also had its own programming language that gave the user control over page layout, and it took advantage of the downloading capacity of the early Apple dot matrix printers to permit the use of multiple type fonts. The Apple II/Gutenberg system of the early 1980s made it possible (with a lot of effort) to do basic desktop publishing.

I used that system to design a Ñähñu word processor and taught Salinas to use it. The system contained all the characters that Salinas and his colleagues had asked for, and Salinas wrote an ethnography of more than 250,000 words on the Ñähñu word processor. The annotated translation of that ethnography appeared in Bernard and Salinas (1989).

I cannot emphasize enough the importance of our being able to produce the Ñähñu alphabet on the screen. Suppose you want to produce the character u. It's not in ASCII, but you can still program any reasonably sophisticated word processor to construct that character. First, create a macro so that striking ^u (Control-u) produces the string u$@ on the screen. Second, define the dollar sign ($) as the ASCII character for the backspace, and define the ampersand (@) as the ASCII character for underline. The macro would be interpreted during printing to produce the underlined u.

This works, of course, but it is aesthetically unpleasing. It is so unpleasing, in fact, that people won't use it unless they have to. (For a long time in the evolution of word processing, American programs required the use of this clumsy, ugly procedure even for writing Spanish and French.) Using Gutenberg, Salinas could write the special characters of Ñähñu directly to the screen in 1981. By 1984, he was so comfortable writing Ñähñu on the Apple II that I began to consider how we could extend the technology to others.

EXTENDING THE TECHNOLOGY TO OTHER LANGUAGES IN MEXICO

That's how we came, in 1987, to develop a plan for a center where Indian people could learn to read and write and publish books in their own languages using microcomputers. The center is sponsored by four organizations: The National Directorate for Indian Education (the part of Mexico's Ministry of Education in charge of bilingual, Indian-Spanish education programs); the Interamerican Indian Institute; the Center for Advanced Studies in Social Anthropology (CIESAS); and the Department of Anthropology at the University of Florida.

The native literacy center began operations in August 1988 at the Oaxaca, Mexico headquarters of CIESAS. The head of CIESAS in Oaxaca is Salomon Nahmad. The literacy center has received funding from the Jessie Ball du Pont Foundation and a grant of equipment from Apple Computer, Inc. Salinas runs the center, together with Josefa González, a Mixtec Indian from the state of Oaxaca. (Seven language families are represented in the state of Oaxaca, with 16 major Indian languages spoken by more than a million people.)

In the first phase of the project (which ended in May 1991), Indians applied to spend up to three months at the literacy center. The trainees were mostly bilingual school teachers. They were already literate in Spanish, so they needed only to transfer the technology of literacy to the creation of documents in their previously nonwritten languages. They found it very easy to do, once they learned to use a word processor that produced the characters they needed.

In other words, Mixtecs learned to use a Mixtec-Spanish word processor; Chinantecs learned to use a Chinantec-Spanish word processor; and so on. While at the center, the Indian teachers produced a chunk of original writing (prose or poetry) on a topic of their own choosing (ethnography, biography, etc.). In the second phase of the project, now underway, those literary works are being edited, published, and distributed to the people of the various language communities. There are plans to select a few of the works for expansion, translation into Spanish, and publication in bilingual editions for wider distribution.

Even now, the Oaxaca native literacy project relies on the old Gutenberg software and the Apple II series hardware, but change is coming. In the current, second phase of the project, we are setting up a complete desktop publishing center, based on IBM-compatible hardware (and Windows), capable of handling all the various characters needed.[8]

So far, 60 people, representing ten different Mexican languages, have trained at the Oaxaca native literacy center. They have produced works in Ñähñu, Mixtec, Zapotec, Chatino, Amuzgo, Chinantec, and Mazatec. In every case, the trainees wrote directly in their own languages. In the next stage of the project, the authors-teachers will use their books to teach adults and children of their home regions to read.

The microcomputer has *not* made it possible for most Indians in Mexico to afford books. It has made it clear, however, that many native people want to write books. People everywhere want to read. Since there is no more potent force for literacy than an author (who quite naturally wants others to read his or her work), it follows that if we want to help people become literate we should help as many of them as possible to become authors.

EXTENDING THE TECHNOLOGY TO SOUTH AMERICA

In April 1989, Salinas and I presented a demonstration of our work at the meeting of the Society for Applied Anthropology in Santa Fe, New Mexico. Norman Whitten, Professor of Anthropology at the University of Illinois, offered to help bring this new technology to Ecuador. During the summer and fall of 1989, E. Chango, a trilingual (Shwara-Quichua-Spanish) school teacher from Ecuador spent three months at the center in Oaxaca. Salinas and González taught Chango using the common medium of Spanish, just as they have taught Mexican speakers of Chinantec to write Chinantec.

Chango was supported by the Sacha Runa Foundation. During his stay, he produced a 50-page text, in Ecuadorean Quichua, about Shwara culture. (Quichua is spoken by about 5 million people in Ecuador. It is different from Quechua, which is spoken by about 6 million people in Peru and Bolivia.) In 1990, according to Whitten, Chango acquired a computer system of his own in Ecuador and began teaching others to read and write Quichua and Shwara.

EXTENDING THE TECHNOLOGY TO AFRICA

In July 1988, Salinas and I presented a demonstration of our work at the XIIth International Congress of Anthropological and Ethnological Sciences held in Zagreb, Yugoslavia. Paul Nchoji Nkwi, head of anthropology at the University of Yaoundé, Cameroon, suggested that the technology might be used to help the Kom people of Cameroon to write books in their language, too.

The Kom kingdom is part of the North West

Province of Cameroon, an area formerly controlled by the British. Kom is spoken by about 127,000 people, and Nkwi is himself a Kom. Almost all Kom people are bilingual in English and Kom, and all educated Kom people are fully literate in English. According to Nkwi, many Kom people would read Kom books—if any were available.

Nkwi and I applied to the Wenner-Gren Foundation for Anthropological Research for funds, and in August 1989, I spent two weeks training five speakers of Kom to use a microcomputer and to produce text in their native language. The five participants in the two-week course included two bilingual (Kom-English) school teachers, a recently graduated lawyer from the University of Yaoundé, a graduate student of anthropology, and a Catholic priest.

THE TONE PROBLEM

Like most nonwritten languages, Kom has an alphabet, but it has little else in the way of an orthography. An orthography is a set of rules for writing a language. English orthography, for example, consists of an alphabet plus a massive set of conventions for spelling words in the language, another set of conventions for syllabification of words, another for punctuation, and so on. All those orthographic rules have developed out of a large body of literature in English. To get an idea of how large the set of orthographic conventions is for, say, American English, think of Webster's International Dictionary, where the conventions are listed.

Furthermore, there are different conventions for different dialects of English. For example, "labor" is spelled "labour" in Britain; "night" is spelled "nite" in tabloid newspapers in the US. Rules for placement of commas and quotation marks vary from one English-speaking country to another.

Indeed, conventions for spelling and punctuation change within one country over any reasonably long time, as authors of various literatures take liberties with this and that rule and as the public accepts or disposes of the changes. Until recently, Americans used a circumflex o in the word "rôle"; it's gone now, although some British publishers still use it. The ç in "façade" is almost gone, too, and other changes are going on all the time.

Still, the most basic part of any orthography is the set of characters that are used conventionally to write a particular language—its alphabet. The first alphabet for Kom was developed by German missionaries in the 1880s. Various other religious and secular groups contributed over the years to the evolution of the currently favored Kom alphabet.

The five participants in the Kom language writing project were all familiar with the current alphabet (though none of them had ever written a substantial text in Kom). The task was to transfer their skill in writing English to writing Kom, using the alphabet they knew.

There was an immediate problem, however. Kom is a language with three tones. As I noted earlier, native speakers of most tone languages do not need to see tones in order to read a text correctly. Non-native speakers of English complain bitterly about how hard it is to pronounce words that are written in English. "How does one know where to put the stress on a word?" they ask. Native speakers have some difficulty as children, but adults do not need to see stress marked in writing in order to read English fluently.[9]

Spanish is often mentioned as an example of a "rational" writing system. For the most part, the five vowel letters /a e i o u/ represent five distinct sounds, and the accents in Spanish tell the reader where to put the stress on words that do not have predictable stress. Words in Spanish that end in r, for example, are normally stressed on the final syllable; there is no need to mark stress with an accent unless that rule is violated.

Today, many Spanish writers are leaving out the accent marks. Will the convenience that this represents to writers and to publishers overcome the force of tradition? Maybe not, but native speakers of Spanish clearly do not need to see accents in order to read their language fluently. Spanish-speaking scholars around the world who communicate by electronic mail are writing messages without accents, since electronic mail systems (like IBM's Bitnet, used by many academics around the world) simply do not permit accents.[10]

The Kom speakers in the Cameroon project learned in school that they had to mark the tones in their writing of Kom if they wanted others to be able to read their work. I programmed a character set that included all the vowels with the tones, and taught the participants how to access these characters. The problem was, of course, that the system was cumbersome. Each sound required its own character.

For example, if the sound /a/ can be pronounced in high, or low, or rising tone, then you need three different characters on a keyboard to represent that fact: á, à, and â, for example. Multiply that by all the vowels that can take different tones (including the vowel ü in Kom, pronounced much as the ü in German), and you can see the problem: to type Kom on a computer keyboard, you would have to learn the placement of dozens of extra keys. And most of those extra keys are going to be hard to access (Control-i, for example, or even Control-Shift-i).

By the third day of the two-week session, all five of

the participants had abandoned the tones. One of the school teachers insisted to the end that the tones should be marked; that is, he felt it was somehow more correct to do so. There is no argument against this position, any more than there is an argument against those Spanish speakers who reject the idea of giving up accent marks. Tradition is its own explanation and it must be respected. But the simple fact is that two weeks after we had begun, those five Kom speakers had produced a corpus of 25,000 words of *casual, adult, literate* Kom.

It was *casual* literature: by the end of the two weeks, the participants would turn on the computer in the morning and just start typing Kom without hesitation. Anything they could say they could write. It was *adult* literature: it was not the sort of thing one sees in school primers ("Paul's father is going to the field to plant corn"), but was instead composed of complex sentences. It was *literate* literature: it was not a bunch of disconnected sentences of the sort one finds in reading tutorials. It was flowing Kom text that ran on for pages and pages, was organized around some theme (the lawyer, for example, had recently married and wrote about customary Kom marriage contracts), and had something to say.

All five participants in the group read one another's texts. At the end of the two weeks, the group held a special ceremony to which two dozen other Kom people were invited. The priest wrote a speech, in Kom, without any marked tones, describing the group's experiences over the preceding two weeks. One of the school teachers delivered that speech, in unhesitating locution, after one preliminary reading.

The evidence so far, then, is that Kom people do not need to mark tones in their writing any more than we need to mark stress or "rationalize" English spelling. We can, in other words, tolerate a lot of ambiguity in our writing systems. Word processing made it possible to test this assertion about the marking of tones in Kom as it had, in fact, in Mexico earlier. (There are many examples of how much ambiguity human beings can tolerate in their writing systems. Modern Hebrew is written entirely without marking vowels.)

WORD PROCESSING AND OTHER ORTHOGRAPHIC CONVENTIONS

Word processing also made it possible for the Kom people to shortcut the process of convention-building in the rest of their orthography. At one point in the two-week training session, I right justified one of the Kom texts, just to see what it looked like, and the participants asked to learn how to do it. This innovation led to their developing various rules of punctuation. Right-hand justification looks attractive, but if a language uses long words, then there are inevitably big, ugly spaces in right-justified text.

The cure for those spaces is the clever use of hyphens. The user right justifies the text and looks at the spaces in each line. He or she then decides a) whether a line has too many spaces, and, if it does, b) exactly how to hyphenate the first word of the following line. When the word is hyphenated and the paragraph is re-justified, the spaces on the offending line are filled in. The next line may now have offending spaces, and so the process is repeated, all the way through the text.

The Kom participants in the course worked together on putting the hyphens into one text. At each line they discussed how to hyphenate certain words, and whether some words should be hyphenated at all. In some cases, they decided that long words were really composed of two stand-alone words. They separated these words rather than hyphenating them. Taking the development of English orthography as a historical benchmark, decades of convention-building were squeezed into those discussions about how to hyphenate Kom words in order to achieve the prettiest right-justified output possible.

MAKING DICTIONARIES

There is a final point regarding the use of computers in the preservation of previously nonwritten languages. As any language acquires a corpus of literature, it acquires the basis for a growing, context-sensitive dictionary. The first edition of Webster's dictionary of American English was a fraction of the size of the latest edition. That dictionary grew to its enormous present size because the printing presses of the US have churned out so much literature in the last two hundred years. Generations of dictionary builders have combed that literature, searching for newly coined words, new uses for old words, and word obsolescences as well.

By contrast, it is common for a fieldworking linguist to produce a dictionary of perhaps 5000 words after a decade of studying a nonwritten language.[11] Many tribal languages are still without good dictionaries. At a minimum, the 25,000-word corpus of literature that the Kom group produced in two weeks contains 2000 unique words. We can now use a program that collects the unique words in a text, alphabetizes those words, and presents them on a screen for input of the information needed in a dictionary database (part of speech, plural form, conjugations, etc.).

DISCUSSION

My experience with these projects leads me to two conclusions.

1. Teaching people to read primers and Bibles does not produce authors; it produces readers. Printing presses and publishing houses produce authors. This rule is no different today for nonliterate languages than it was in late medieval times in Europe (Davis 1981, Eisenstein 1979).

2. Teaching a few highly motivated people to *write and print* their own books can help many people become literate. Authors want others to read what they have written and are anxious to help people learn to do so.

Between 1940–1958, Navajo literature and newspapers began to appear, but Navajos themselves were not authors of books and articles in Navajo (Young 1977:469). Programs to promote Navajo were implemented at several universities (Northwestern and MIT, for example). These programs, along with the demonstration school at Rough Rock and Tribal Youth Conferences fostered pride in Navajo culture (Young 1977). Navajo authors began to write books in Navajo. More and more Navajos speak Navajo these days, rather than fewer and fewer. I think this trend is related to the increasing presence of Navajo written literature.

WHAT CAN WE DO?

The technology of printing is too expensive to make publication of books in most native languages commercially attractive. Microcomputers and desktop publishing reduce the cost of publication, but this technology is still more than most native language communities can afford.

On the other hand, this technology is not too expensive for government agencies, private development agencies, foundations that support literacy training, missionary groups, and local community self-help groups. The technology can even be supplied by individuals: anthropologists or linguists, for example, or native people of means who may want to help local schools.

There are some objections. Clearly, when the choice is between food and computers, the computers must wait. But anthropologists (and missionaries) are not usually faced with such choices.

Some may also argue that insisting on the importance of written literature may make native people "disdain their own discourse" (Verne 1981:302). One response to this objection is that, while both the written and the oral word offer exciting possibilities, in order to gain the power of literacy we must give up the beauty and power of the oral word. "We have to die to continue living" (Ong 1982:15).

Both arguments are wrong. While literacy is today a correlate of more technologically developed peoples, it is debatable whether literacy causes some kind of "great divide" among cultures of the world. Goody (1977:18, 1986) takes the strong position that acquisition of literacy transforms the nature of cognitive processes, as does Ong (1982:15), but other researchers question this conclusion (Cole and Scribner 1981, Finnegan 1988).

Moreover, oral traditions remain strong in the most literate societies. People pay a lot of money to see a Broadway play, and while the script may exist somewhere as a written document, it has no relevance to most theater-goers whose appreciation of the performance comes from exposure to an oral and visual experience. The same can be said for movies, television shows, and country music. There are differences in spontaneously generated works of music and theater and works that are rehearsed from scripts. But oral/visual performance traditions remain strong even in the most technologically advanced societies.

Even if literacy does cause some kind of fundamental change in the human condition, it is extreme hubris to conclude that, while this transformation has happened to us, it should not happen to still-preliterate peoples.

The critical argument, however, is this: even if literacy causes some irreversible change in thought and culture, it is better to preserve language diversity than to preserve orality.

In the end, it comes to that. There were 260 Aboriginal languages in Australia, but only 40 or 50 were in daily use in the 1970s by just 40,000 speakers (Wurm 1981:23).[12] In the Americas, hundreds of languages have become extinct since contact with Europeans, and many more have only a few elderly speakers left. Our humanistic interest demands that we respond to these facts. Nothing less than the richness of human knowledge is at stake.

If the humanistic perspective is too impractical, and if the species-survival argument too hypothetical, then consider the material implications of language-and-politics events in India, Belgium, Canada, Lithuania, and Estonia. People everywhere apparently understand that cultural uniqueness—ethnicity—reinforces their claim to a share of political power, land, jobs, and other resources in ethnically heterogeneous states. A unique language is a powerful force in legitimating those claims.

Neither literacy nor a unique language is always a key to development, of course. Eastman (1983:86) shows how promoting native languages may be used to deny people access to resources. She points out that in South Africa, many people are given primary instruction in their native languages (Xhosa, Zulu), and then denied further education. Without mastery of English and Afrikaans, native people have no access to those in power, nor even to one another.

More typical, however, is the case of some islands off the west coast of Ireland. According to O'Brien (1979:88), the people there complained in 1977 that they were receiving less state funds because they were English speakers. People of Gaelic-speaking islands, they said, who were in similar social and economic circumstances, were receiving more. This case is particularly interesting because it involves a state that had taken an official stand in favor of developing an ancestral tongue. The efforts to push for the use of Gaelic in Ireland have been less successful than hoped for by language planners, hence the use of the promise of general state revenues to promote the language.

Finally, consider the recent case of a group of Mexican Indians who sued a power company. The company had received funding from an international development agency to build a hydroelectric generator, which required building a dam. The resulting lake in back of the dam was due to flood out thousands of acres of the Indians' ancestral lands. The power company offered to pay for the land, of course, and the government appealed to the Indians to accept the offer.

The government argued it was the Indians' patriotic duty, as Mexicans, to accept the offer and help provide needed electricity for development of the nation. The Indians argued that the offer was inadequate, but they also said that they wanted their land so that they could retain their identity. The lawyers for the power company noted that only a few elderly people in the Indian community spoke the Indian language anymore and that none of the younger generation was learning the language. How, the lawyers asked, did the Indians expect to convince anyone of their claim to special ethnic status if they didn't speak their own language? How, indeed?

NOTES

1. My thanks to Joseph Grimes for the data on which this count was based.
2. There is an old debate, of course, about whether people think different thoughts *because* they speak different languages. My own position on this debate is that people who speak one language can grasp new thoughts that happen to originate with speakers of another language, no matter what the two languages happen to be. Whatever one's position in this debate, though, it is a matter of fact that language diversity is a correlate of cultural diversity.
3. A very interesting case of casual, popular literacy without printing of books is found among the Vai people of Liberia. The Vai use a locally invented syllabary for keeping ledgers and for writing letters. They do not, apparently, produce literature with the script (Cole and Scribner 1981).
4. In the rest of this paper I use the term "literature" to mean only *written* documents. *Oral literature* is neither less valuable nor less interesting than written literature. But it is not a substitute for written literature in my argument regarding language preservation, so I exclude it from further discussion.
5. Many Americans will recognize this pattern from their own youth, when their parents forbade the use of anything but English in their homes. Price (1979:41) cites a modern example: the women of Bagnols-sur-Cèze in France deny they ever heard of Provençal and forbid men from introducing it into family conversations. The women are concerned that their children won't learn proper French if Provençal is encouraged.
6. Venezky (1977:39) notes that in 1930, the International African Institute concluded that tones could be omitted from African languages when the context made it clear what the writer wanted to convey. De Francis (1950) concluded that the ambiguity that would result from not marking tones in Chinese would be small enough to leave them out of any alphabetic writing system. In 1958, however, the Pinyin romanization of Chinese was adopted by the People's Republic of China. That system did include four tones. Non-native speakers of Chinese, of course, welcomed the marking of tones. I know of no tests, however, to see whether native speakers of any Chinese language would require tone marking in an alphabetic system.
7. The Ñähñu are generally known in the literature as the Otomí. The name "Otomí" has negative connotations in Mexican Spanish. Many Ñähñu people today prefer to be known by the name they call themselves.
8. 286-level technology is now inexpensive, and the latest version of WordPerfect allows users to define any character they need for their text (although one can only see the characters on the screen in "view document" mode). Special characters can be programmed for on-screen display with the Duke Language Toolkit and an EGA monitor. (The Toolkit, from Duke University, works with PC-Write, a popular, full-featured word processor that produces plain ASCII text.) Other software is also becoming available for handling special screen and print fonts.
9. This does not mean that English spelling is the best it could possibly be, only that it is not as bad as myths would make it.
10. Lack of the enye /ñ/ is another matter. Spanish speakers with whom I have electronic mail communication use either /ny/ or /^n/. Doing so avoids embarrassing situations like having to write /ano/, "ass," for /año/, "year."
11. The corpus of text that a linguist collects is oral. In any language, most people get along with 5000 words or less (Ong 1982:107). So a linguist who transcribes everyday speech, or perhaps a few folk tales, is not likely to run into more than about 5000 words. A large body of folk tales is likely to contain many more words.

12. There are quite a few Aboriginal authors in Australia, and they feel the loss of their ancestral languages deeply (Davis and Hodge 1985:11, 25). They make their living writing in English. Unless they write books in their ancestral languages, those languages are doomed to quick extinction. Should Aboriginal authors, therefore, feel obliged to write in Aboriginal languages? Absolutely not. The Oaxaca project demonstrates that there are many, many potential authors among people who speak languages that have no literary tradition. Providing many people with the tools to write and print books will not guarantee language survival, but it will make language survival possible.

REFERENCES CITED

Bernard, H. R. and J. Salinas Pedraza. 1976. Otomí Folk Tales, Parables and Jokes. Chicago: University of Chicago Press.

———. 1989. Native Ethnography: A Mexican Indian Describes His Culture. Newbury Park, CA: Sage.

Burnaby, B. 1985. Promoting Native Writing Systems in Canada. Toronto: Ontario Institute for Studies in Education.

Cohen, M. 1977. The Food Crisis in Prehistory. New Haven, CT: Yale University Press.

Cole, M. and S. Scribner. 1981. The Psychology of Literacy. Cambridge: Harvard University Press.

Davis, N. Z. 1981. Printing and the People. In Literacy and Social Development in the West. H. J. Graff, ed. Pp. 69–95. Cambridge: Cambridge University Press.

Davis, J. and B. Hodge, eds. 1985. Aboriginal Writing Today. Canberra: Australian Institute of Aboriginal Studies.

De Francis, J. 1950. Nationalism and Language Reform in China. Princeton: Princeton University Press.

Eastman, C. 1983. Language Planning. San Francisco. Chandler and Sharp.

Eisenstein, E. 1979. The Printing Press as an Agent of Change: Communications and Cultural Transformations in Early Modern Europe. 2 vols. Cambridge: Cambridge University Press.

Finnegan, R. 1988. Literacy and Orality. Oxford: Basil Blackwell.

Fishman, J., ed. 1977. Advances in the Creation of Writing Systems. The Hague: Mouton.

Goody, J. 1977. The Domestication of the Savage Mind. Cambridge: Cambridge University Press.

———. 1986. The Logic of Writing and the Organization of Society. Cambridge: Cambridge University Press.

O'Brien, T. 1979. Economic Support for Minority Languages. In The Future of Cultural Minorities. A. E. Alcock, B. K. Taylor, and J. M. Welton, eds. Pp. 82–101. London: Macmillan.

Ong, W. J. 1982. Orality and Literacy. New York: Methuen.

Price, G. 1979. The Present Position and Viability of Minority Languages. In The Future of Cultural Minorities. A. E. Alcock, B. K. Taylor, and J. M. Welton, eds. Pp. 30–43. London: Macmillan.

Salinas Pedraza, J. and H. R. Bernard. 1978. The Otomí. Albuquerque: University of New Mexico Press.

Venezky, R. L. 1977. Principles of the Design of Practical Writing Systems. In Advances in the Creation of Writing Systems. J. Fishman, ed. Pp. 37–54. The Hague: Mouton.

Verne, E. 1981. Literacy and Industrialization. In Literacy and Social Development in the West. H. J. Graff, ed. Pp. 286–303. Cambridge: Cambridge University Press.

Wurm, S. A. 1981. Papua New Guinea, Australia, French Polynesia, Solomon Islands, the New Hebrides, New Caledonia. In Linguistic Composition of the Nations of the World. H. Kloss and G. McConnell, eds. Vol. 4 [all]. Quebec: Laval University Press.

Young, R. 1977. Written Navajo: A Brief History. In Advances in the Creation of Writing Systems. J. Fishman, ed. Pp. 459–470. The Hague: Mouton.

9

"To Give Up On Words":
Silence in Western Apache Culture[1]

Keith H. Basso

Can you imagine working on a four-person cattle crew for several days without being introduced to or speaking with one of the other members, whom you did not know? For the Apache, this is a normal occurrence; they do not feel obligated to introduce strangers to one another. Instead, the Apache believe that when the time is right, the strangers will begin speaking to each other.

Would you find it uncomfortable to go on a date and sit in silence for an hour because you had only recently met your companion? What would you think if after returning home from several months' absence your parents and relatives didn't speak to you for several days? While these situations seem unusual to us, they are considered appropriate among the Apache. While it seems "natural" to us that when people first meet introductions are in order and that when friends and relatives reunite greetings and "catching up" will immediately follow, this is not the case for all cultures.

Those familiar with the television show "Northern Exposure" may consider how the reticence of Native American character Marilyn Whirlwind contrasts with the behavior of the other characters. This example demonstrates how communicating across cultural boundaries can be fraught with uncertainty and misunderstanding. In this selection Keith Basso shows how, among the Apache, certain situations call for silence rather than communication, and how silence makes sense within its cultural context.

As you read this selection, ask yourself the following questions:

☐ *What are some of the ways silence is used in American communication, and how are they different from those in Apache culture?*

☐ *How are the meaning and function of silence affected by the social and cultural context?*

☐ *What is the critical factor in an Apache's decision to speak or keep silent?*

☐ *How do Apache interact upon meeting a stranger, courting, welcoming children home, getting cussed out, and being with people who are sad?*

☐ *Despite the variety of situations in which Apache are silent, what is the underlying determinant?*

The following terms discussed in this selection are included in the Glossary at the back of the book:

hypothesis
informant
kinship
socialization
sociolinguistics
status

From *Southwestern Journal of Anthropology*, Vol. 26, No. 3, Autumn 1970, pp. 213–230.

It is not the case that a man who is silent says nothing.

—Anonymous

I

Anyone who has read about American Indians has probably encountered statements which impute to them a strong predilection for keeping silent or, as one writer has put it, "a fierce reluctance to speak except when absolutely necessary." In the popular literature, where this characterization is particularly widespread, it is commonly portrayed as the outgrowth of such dubious causes as "instinctive dignity," "an impoverished language," or, perhaps worst of all, the Indians' "lack of personal warmth." Although statements of this sort are plainly erroneous and dangerously misleading, it is noteworthy that professional anthropologists have made few attempts to correct them. Traditionally, ethnographers and linguists have paid little attention to cultural interpretations given to silence or, equally important, to the types of social contexts in which it regularly occurs.

This study investigates certain aspects of silence in the culture of the Western Apache of east-central Arizona. After considering some of the theoretical issues involved, I will briefly describe a number of situations—recurrent in Western Apache society—in which one or more of the participants typically refrain from speech for lengthy periods of time.[2] This is accompanied by a discussion of how such acts of silence are interpreted and why they are encouraged and deemed appropriate. I conclude by advancing an hypothesis that accounts for the reasons that the Western Apache refrain from speaking when they do, and I suggest that, with proper testing, this hypothesis may be shown to have relevance to silence behavior in other cultures.

II

A basic finding of sociolinguistics is that, although both language and language usage are structured, it is the latter which responds most sensitively to extra-linguistic influences (Hymes 1962, 1964; Ervin-Tripp 1964, 1967; Gumperz 1964; Slobin 1967). Accordingly, a number of recent studies have addressed themselves to the problem of how factors in the social environment of speech events delimit the range and condition the selection of message forms (cf. Brown and Gilman 1960; Conklin 1959; Ervin-Tripp 1964, 1967; Frake 1964; Friedrich 1966; Gumperz 1961, 1964; Martin 1964). These studies may be viewed as taking the now famil-

iar position that verbal communication is fundamentally a decision-making process in which, initially, a speaker, having elected to speak, selects from among a repertoire of available codes that which is most appropriately suited to the situation at hand. Once a code has been selected, the speaker picks a suitable channel of transmission and then, finally, makes a choice from a set of referentially equivalent expressions within the code. The intelligibility of the expression he chooses will, of course, be subject to grammatical constraints. But its acceptability will not. Rules for the selection of linguistic alternates operate on features of the social environment and are commensurate with rules governing the conduct of face-to-face interaction. As such, they are properly conceptualized as lying outside the structure of language itself.

It follows from this that for a stranger to communicate appropriately with the members of an unfamiliar society it is not enough that he learn to formulate messages intelligibly. Something else is needed: a knowledge of what kinds of codes, channels, and expressions to use in what kinds of situations and to what kinds of people—as Hymes (1964) has termed it, an "ethnography of communication."

There is considerable evidence to suggest that extra-linguistic factors influence not only the use of speech but its actual occurrence as well. In our own culture, for example, remarks such as "Don't you know when to keep quiet?" "Don't talk until you're introduced," and "Remember now, no talking in church" all point to the fact that an individual's decision to speak may be directly contingent upon the character of his surroundings. Few of us would maintain that "silence is golden" for all people at all times. But we feel that silence is a virtue for some people some of the time, and we encourage children on the road to cultural competence to act accordingly.

Although the form of silence is always the same, the function of a specific act of silence—that is, its interpretation by and effect upon other people—will vary according to the social context in which it occurs. For example, if I choose to keep silent in the chambers of a Justice of the Supreme Court, my action is likely to be interpreted as a sign of politeness or respect. On the other hand, if I refrain from speaking to an established friend or colleague, I am apt to be accused of rudeness or harboring a grudge. In one instance, my behavior is judged by others to be "correct" or "fitting"; in the other, it is criticized as being "out of line."

The point, I think, is fairly obvious. For a stranger entering an alien society, a knowledge of when *not* to speak may be as basic to the production of culturally acceptable behavior as a knowledge of what to say. It stands to reason, then, that an adequate ethnography of communication should not confine itself exclusively to the analysis of choice within verbal repertoires. It should also, as Hymes (1962, 1964) has suggested, specify those conditions under which the members of the society regularly decide to refrain from verbal behavior altogether.

III

The research on which this paper is based was conducted over a period of sixteen months (1964–1969) in the Western Apache settlement of Cibecue, which is located near the center of the Fort Apache Indian Reservation in east-central Arizona. Cibecue's 800 residents participate in an unstable economy that combines subsistence agriculture, cattle-raising, sporadic wage-earning, and Government subsidies in the form of welfare checks and social security benefits. Unemployment is a serious problem, and substandard living conditions are widespread.

Although Reservation life has precipitated far-reaching changes in the composition and geographical distribution of Western Apache social groups, consanguineal kinship—real and imputed—remains the single most powerful force in the establishment and regulation of interpersonal relationships (Kaut 1957; Basso 1970). The focus of domestic activity is the individual "camp," or *gową́ą́*. This term labels both the occupants and the location of a single dwelling or, as is more apt to be the case, several dwellings built within a few feet of each other. The majority of *gową́ą́* in Cibecue are occupied by nuclear families. The next largest residential unit is the *gotáá* (camp cluster), which is a group of spatially localized *gową́ą́*, each having at least one adult member who is related by ties of matrilineal kinship to persons living in all the others. An intricate system of exogamous clans serves to extend kinship relationships beyond the *gową́ą́* and *gotáá* and facilitates concerted action in projects, most notably the presentation of ceremonials, requiring large amounts of manpower. Despite the presence in Cibecue of a variety of Anglo missionaries and a dwindling number of medicine men, diagnostic and curing rituals, as well as the girls' puberty ceremonial, continue to be performed with regularity (Basso 1966, 1970). Witchcraft persists in undiluted form (Basso 1969).

IV

Of the many broad categories of events, or scenes, that comprise the daily round of Western Apache life, I shall deal here only with those that are coterminous with what Goffman (1961, 1964) has termed "focused gatherings" or "encounters." The concept *situation*, in keeping with established usage, will refer inclusively to the location of such a gathering, its physical setting, its point in time, the standing behavior patterns that accompany it, and the social attributes of the persons involved (Hymes 1962, 1964; Ervin-Tripp 1964, 1967).

In what follows, however, I will be mainly concerned with the roles and statuses of participants. The reason for this is that the critical factor in the Apache's decision to speak or keep silent seems always to be the nature of his relationships to other people. To be sure, other features of the situation are significant, but apparently only to the extent that they influence the perception of status and role.[3] What this implies, of course, is that roles and statuses are not fixed attributes. Although they may be depicted as such in a static model (and often with good reason), they are appraised and acted upon in particular social contexts and, as a result, subject to redefinition and variation.[4] With this in mind, let us now turn our attention to the Western Apache and the types of situations in which, as one of my informants put it, "it is right to give up on words."

V

1. "Meeting strangers" (*nda dòhwáá'iłtsééda*). The term, *nda*, labels categories at two levels of contrast. At the most general level, it designates any person—Apache or non-Apache—who, prior to an initial meeting, has never been seen and therefore cannot be identified. In addition, the term is used to refer to Apaches who, though previously seen and known by some external criteria such as clan affiliation or personal name, have never been engaged in face-to-face interaction. The latter category, which is more restricted than the first, typically includes individuals who live on the adjacent San Carlos Reservation, in Fort Apache settlements geographically removed from Cibecue, and those who fall into the category *kii dòhandáágo* (non-kinsmen). In all cases, "strangers" are separated by social distance. And in all cases it is considered appropriate, when encountering them for the first time, to refrain from speaking.

The type of situation described as "meeting strangers" (*nda dòhwáá'iłtsééda*) can take place in any number of different physical settings. However, it occurs most frequently in the context of events such as fairs and rodeos, which, owing to the large number of people in attendance, offer unusual opportunities for chance encounters. In large gatherings, the lack of verbal communication between strangers is apt to go unnoticed, but in smaller groups it becomes quite conspicuous. The following incident, involving two strangers who found themselves part of a four-man round-up crew, serves as a good example. My informant, who was also a member of the crew, recalled the following episode:

> One time, I was with A, B, and X down at Gleason Flat, working cattle. That man, X, was from East Fork [a community nearly 40 miles from Cibecue] where B's wife was from. But he didn't know A, never knew him before, I guess. First day, I worked with X. At night, when we camped, we talked with B, but X and A didn't say anything to each other. Same way, second day. Same way, third. Then, at night on fourth day, we were sitting by the fire. Still, X and A didn't talk. Then A said, "Well, I know there is a stranger to me here, but I've been watching him and I know he is all right." After that, X and A talked a lot. . . . Those two men didn't know each other, so they took it easy at first.

As this incident suggests, the Western Apache do not feel compelled to "introduce" persons who are unknown to each other. Eventually, it is assumed, strangers will begin to speak. However, this is a decision that is properly left to the individuals involved, and no attempt is made to hasten it. Outside help in the form of introductions or other verbal routines is viewed as presumptuous and unnecessary.

Strangers who are quick to launch into conversation are frequently eyed with undisguised suspicion. A typical reaction to such individuals is that they "want something," that is, their willingness to violate convention is attributed to some urgent need which is likely to result in requests for money, labor, or transportation. Another common reaction to talkative strangers is that they are drunk.

If the stranger is an Anglo, it is usually assumed that he "wants to teach us something" (i.e., give orders or instructions) or that he "wants to make friends in a hurry." The latter response is especially revealing, since Western Apaches are extremely reluctant to be hurried into friendships—with Anglos or each other. Their verbal reticence with strangers is directly related to the conviction that the establishment of social relationships is a serious matter that calls for caution, careful judgment, and plenty of time.

2. "Courting" (*líígoláá*). During the initial stages of courtship, young men and women go without speaking for conspicuous lengths of time. Courting may occur in a wide variety of settings—practically anywhere, in fact—and at virtually any time of the day or night, but it is most readily observable at large public gatherings such as ceremonials, wakes, and rodeos. At these events, "sweethearts" (*zééde*) may stand or sit (sometimes holding hands) for as long as an hour without exchanging a word. I am told by adult informants that the young people's reluctance to speak may be-

come even more pronounced in situations where they find themselves alone.

Apaches who have just begun to court attribute their silence to "intense shyness" (*'isté'*) and a feeling of acute "self-consciousness" (*dàyéézi*) which, they claim, stems from their lack of familiarity with one another. More specifically, they complain of "not knowing what to do" in each other's presence and of the fear that whatever they say, no matter how well thought out in advance, will sound "dumb" or "stupid."[5]

One informant, a youth 17 years old, commented as follows:

> It's hard to talk with your sweetheart at first. She doesn't know you and won't know what to say. It's the same way towards her. You don't know how to talk yet . . . so you get very bashful. That makes it sometimes so you don't say anything. So you just go around together and don't talk. At first, it's better that way. Then, after a while, when you know each other, you aren't shy anymore and can talk good.

The Western Apache draw an equation between the ease and frequency with which a young couple talks and how well they know each other. Thus, it is expected that after several months of steady companionship sweethearts will start to have lengthy conversations. Earlier in their relationship, however, protracted discussions may be openly discouraged. This is especially true for girls, who are informed by their mothers and older sisters that silence in courtship is a sign of modesty and that an eagerness to speak betrays previous experience with men. In extreme cases, they add, it may be interpreted as a willingness to engage in sexual relations. Said one woman, aged 32:

> This way I have talked to my daughter. "Take it easy when boys come around this camp and want you to go somewhere with them. When they talk to you, just listen at first. Maybe you won't know what to say. So don't talk about just anything. If you talk with those boys right away, then they will know you know all about them. They will think you've been with many boys before, and they will start talking about that."

3. "Children, coming home" (*čogoše nakáii*). The Western Apache lexeme *iltá'ìnatsáá* (reunion) is used to describe encounters between an individual who has returned home after a long absence and his relatives and friends. The most common type of reunion, *čogoše nakáii* (children, coming home), involves boarding school students and their parents. It occurs in late May or early in June, and its setting is usually a trading post or school, where parents congregate to await the arrival of buses bringing the children home. As the latter disembark and locate their parents in the crowd, one anticipates a flurry of verbal greetings. Typically, how-

ever, there are few or none at all. Indeed, it is not un-usual for parents and child to go without speaking for as long as 15 minutes.

When the silence is broken, it is almost always the child who breaks it. His parents listen attentively to everything he says but speak hardly at all themselves. This pattern persists even after the family has reached the privacy of its camp, and two or three days may pass before the child's parents seek to engage him in sustained conversation.

According to my informants, the silence of West-ern Apache parents at (and after) reunions with their children is ultimately predicated on the possibility that the latter have been adversely affected by their experi-ences away from home. Uppermost is the fear that, as a result of protracted exposure to Anglo attitudes and values, the children have come to view their parents as ignorant, old-fashioned, and no longer deserving of respect. One of my most thoughtful and articulate in-formants commented on the problem as follows:

> You just can't tell about those children after they've been with White men for a long time. They get their minds turned around sometimes . . . they forget where they come from and get ashamed when they come home be-cause their parents and relatives are poor. They forget how to act with these Apaches and get mad easy. They walk around all night and get into fights. They don't stay at home.
>
> At school, some of them learn to want to be White men, so they come back and try to act that way. But we are still Apaches! So we don't know them anymore, and it is like we never knew them. It is hard to talk to them when they are like that.

Apache parents openly admit that, initially, chil-dren who have been away to school seem distant and unfamiliar. They have grown older, of course, and their physical appearance may have changed. But more fun-damental is the concern that they have acquired new ideas and expectations which will alter their behavior in unpredictable ways. No matter how pressing this concern may be, however, it is considered inappropri-ate to directly interrogate a child after his arrival home. Instead, parents anticipate that within a short time he will begin to divulge information about himself that will enable them to determine in what ways, if any, his views and attitudes have changed. This, the Apache say, is why children do practically all the talking in the hours following a reunion, and their parents remain unusually silent.

Said one man, the father of two children who had recently returned from boarding school in Utah:

> Yes, it's right that we didn't talk much to them when they came back, my wife and me. They were away for a long time, and we didn't know how they would like it,

being home. So we waited. Right away, they started to tell stories about what they did. Pretty soon we could tell they liked it, being back. That made us feel good. So it was easy to talk to them again. It was like they were before they went away.

4. "Getting cussed out" (*šiłditéé*). This lexeme is used to describe any situation in which one individual, angered and enraged, shouts insults and criticisms at another. Although the object of such invective is in most cases the person or persons who provoked it, this is not always the case, because an Apache who is truly beside himself with rage is likely to vent his feelings on anyone whom he sees or who happens to be within range of his voice. Consequently, "getting cussed out" may involve large numbers of people who are totally innocent of the charges being hurled against them. But whether they are innocent or not, their response to the situation is the same. They refrain from speech.

Like the types of situations we have discussed thus far, "getting cussed out" can occur in a wide variety of physical settings: at ceremonial dancegrounds and trading posts, inside and outside wickiups and houses, on food-gathering expeditions and shopping trips—in short, wherever and whenever individuals lose control of their tempers and lash out verbally at persons nearby.

Although "getting cussed out" is basically free of setting-imposed restrictions, the Western Apache fear it most at gatherings where alcohol is being consumed. My informants observed that especially at "drinking parties" (*dá'idlą́ą́*), where there is much rough joking and ostensibly mock criticism, it is easy for well-intentioned remarks to be misconstrued as insults. Provoked in this way, persons who are intoxicated may become hostile and launch into explosive tirades, often with no warning at all.

The silence of Apaches who are "getting cussed out" is consistently explained in reference to the belief that individuals who are "enraged" (*haškéé*) are also ir-rational or "crazy" (*bìné'idįį*). In this condition, it is said, they "forget who they are" and become oblivious to what they say or do. Concomitantly, they lose all concern for the consequences of their actions on other people. In a word, they are dangerous. Said one informant:

> When people get mad they get crazy. Then they start yelling and saying bad things. Some say they are going to kill somebody for what he has done. Some keep it up that way for a long time, maybe walk from camp to camp, real angry, yelling, crazy like that. They keep it up for a long time, some do.
>
> People like that don't know what they are saying, so you can't tell about them. When you see someone like that, just walk away. If he yells at you, let him say what-

ever he wants to. Let him say anything. Maybe he doesn't mean it. But he doesn't know that. He will be crazy, and he could try to kill you.

Another Apache said:

When someone gets mad at you and starts yelling, then just don't do anything to make him get worse. Don't try to quiet him down because he won't know why you're doing it. If you try to do that, he may just get worse and try to hurt you.

As the last of these statements implies, the Western Apache operate on the assumption that enraged persons—because they are temporarily "crazy"—are difficult to reason with. Indeed, there is a widely held belief that attempts at mollification will serve to intensify anger, thus increasing the chances of physical violence. The appropriate strategy when "getting cussed out" is to do nothing, to avoid any action that will attract attention to oneself. Since speaking accomplishes just the opposite, the use of silence is strongly advised.

5. "Being with people who are sad" (nde dò-biłgòzóóda bigáá). Although the Western Apache phrase that labels this situation has no precise equivalent in English, it refers quite specifically to gatherings in which an individual finds himself in the company of someone whose spouse or kinsman has recently died. Distinct from wakes and burials, which follow immediately after a death, "being with people who are sad" is most likely to occur several weeks later. At this time, close relatives of the deceased emerge from a period of intense mourning (during which they rarely venture beyond the limits of their camps) and start to resume their normal activities within the community. To persons anxious to convey their sympathies, this is interpreted as a sign that visitors will be welcomed and, if possible, provided with food and drink. To those less solicitous, it means that unplanned encounters with the bereaved must be anticipated and prepared for.

"Being with people who are sad" can occur on a foot-path, in a camp, at church, or in a trading post; but whatever the setting—and regardless of whether it is the result of a planned visit or an accidental meeting—the situation is marked by a minimum of speech. Queried about this, my informants volunteered three types of explanations. The first is that persons "who are sad" are so burdened with "intense grief" (dółgozóóda) that speaking requires of them an unusual amount of physical effort. It is courteous and considerate, therefore, not to attempt to engage them in conversation.

A second native explanation is that in situations of this sort verbal communication is basically unneces-

sary. Everyone is familiar with what has happened, and talking about it, even for the purpose of conveying solace and sympathy, would only reinforce and augment the sadness felt by those who were close to the deceased. Again, for reasons of courtesy, this is something to be avoided.

The third explanation is rooted in the belief that "intense grief," like intense rage, produces changes in the personality of the individual who experiences it. As evidence for this, the Western Apache cite numerous instances in which the emotional strain of dealing with death, coupled with an overwhelming sense of irrevocable personal loss, has caused persons who were formerly mild and even-tempered to become abusive, hostile, and physically violent.

That old woman, X, who lives across Cibecue Creek, one time her first husband died. After that she cried all the time, for a long time. Then, I guess she got mean because everyone said she drank a lot and got into fights. Even with her close relatives, she did like that for a long time. She was too sad for her husband. That's what made her like that; it made her lose her mind.

My father was like that when his wife died. He just stayed home all the time and wouldn't go anywhere. He didn't talk to any of his relatives or children. He just said, "I'm hungry. Cook for me." That's all. He stayed that way for a long time. His mind was not with us. He was still with his wife.

My uncle died in 1911. His wife sure went crazy right away after that. Two days after they buried the body, we went over there and stayed with those people who had been left alone. My aunt got mad at us. She said, "Why do you come over here? You can't bring my husband back. I can take care of myself and those others in my camp, so why don't you go home." She sure was mad that time, too sad for someone who died. She didn't know what she was saying because in about one week she came to our camp and said, "My relatives, I'm all right now. When you came to help me, I had too much sadness and my mind was no good. I said bad words to you. But now I am all right and I know what I am doing."

As these statements indicate, the Western Apache assume that a person suffering from "intense grief" is likely to be disturbed and unstable. Even though he may appear outwardly composed, they say, there is always the possibility that he is emotionally upset and therefore unusually prone to volatile outbursts. Apaches acknowledge that such an individual might welcome conversation in the context of "being with people who are sad," but, on the other hand, they fear it might prove incendiary. Under these conditions, which resemble those in Situation No. 4, it is considered both expedient and appropriate to keep silent.

6. "Being with someone for whom they sing" (*nde bìdádìstááha bigą́ą́*). The last type of situation to be described is restricted to a small number of physical locations and is more directly influenced by temporal factors than any of the situations we have discussed so far. "Being with someone for whom they sing" takes place only in the context of "curing ceremonials" (*gòjìtáł; èdotáł*). These events begin early at night and

come to a close shortly before dawn the following day. In the late fall and throughout the winter, curing ceremonials are held inside the patient's wickiup or house. In the spring and summer, they are located outside, at some open place near the patient's camp or at specially designated dance grounds where group rituals of all kinds are regularly performed.

Prior to the start of a curing ceremonial, all persons in attendance may feel free to talk with the patient; indeed, because he is so much a focus of concern, it is expected that friends and relatives will seek him out to offer encouragement and support. Conversation breaks off, however, when the patient is informed that the ceremonial is about to begin, and it ceases entirely when the presiding medicine man commences to chant. From this point on, until the completion of the final chant next morning, it is inappropriate for anyone except the medicine man (and, if he has them, his aides) to speak to the patient.[6]

In order to appreciate the explanation Apaches give for this prescription, we must briefly discuss the concept of "supernatural power" (*diyi'*) and describe some of the effects it is believed to have on persons at whom it is directed. Elsewhere (Basso 1969:30) I have defined "power" as follows:

> The term *diyi'* refers to one or all of a set of abstract and invisible forces which are said to derive from certain classes of animals, plants, minerals, meteorological phenomena, and mythological figures within the Western Apache universe. Any of the various powers may be acquired by man and, if properly handled, used for a variety of purposes.

A power that has been antagonized by disrespectful behavior towards its source may retaliate by causing the offender to become sick. "Power-caused illnesses" (*kásitį́ diyi' bił*) are properly treated with curing ceremonials in which one or more medicine men, using chants and various items of ritual paraphernalia, attempt to neutralize the sickness-causing power with powers of their own.

Roughly two-thirds of my informants assert that a medicine man's power actually enters the body of the patient; others maintain that it simply closes in and envelops him. In any case, all agree that the patient is brought into intimate contact with a potent supernat-

ural force which elevates him to a condition labeled *gòdiyó'* (sacred, holy).

The term *gòdiyó'* may also be translated as "potentially harmful" and, in this sense, is regularly used to describe classes of objects (including all sources of power) that are surrounded with taboos. In keeping with the semantics of *gòdiyó'*, the Western Apache explain that, besides making patients holy, power makes them potentially harmful. And it is this transformation, they explain, that is basically responsible for the cessation of verbal communication during curing ceremonials.

Said one informant:

> When they start singing for someone like that, he sort of goes away with what the medicine man is working with (i.e., power). Sometimes people they sing for don't know you, even after it (the curing ceremonial) is over. They get holy, and you shouldn't try to talk to them when they are like that . . . it's best to leave them alone.

Another informant made similar comments:

> When they sing for someone, what happens is like this: that man they sing for doesn't know why he is sick or which way to go. So the medicine man has to show him and work on him. That is when he gets holy, and that makes him go off somewhere in his mind, so you should stay away from him.

Because Apaches undergoing ceremonial treatment are perceived as having been changed by power into something different from their normal selves, they are regarded with caution and apprehension. Their newly acquired status places them in close proximity to the supernatural and, as such, carries with it a very real element of danger and uncertainty. These conditions combine to make "being with someone for whom they sing" a situation in which speech is considered disrespectful and, if not exactly harmful, at least potentially hazardous.

VI

Although the types of situations described above differ from one another in obvious ways, I will argue in what follows that the underlying determinants of silence are in each case basically the same. Specifically, I will attempt to defend the hypothesis that keeping silent in Western Apache culture is associated with social situations in which participants perceive their relationships *vis-à-vis* one another to be ambiguous and/or unpredictable.

Let us begin with the observation that, in all the situations we have described, *silence is defined as appro-*

priate with respect to a specific individual or individuals. In other words, the use of speech is not directly curtailed by the setting of a situation nor by the physical activities that accompany it but, rather, by the perceived social and psychological attributes of at least one focal participant.

It may also be observed that, in each type of situation, *the status of the focal participant is marked by ambiguity*—either because he is unfamiliar to other participants in the situation or because, owing to some recent event, a status he formerly held has been changed or is in a process of transition.

Thus, in Situation No. 1, persons who earlier considered themselves "strangers" move towards some other relationship, perhaps "friend" (šìdikéé), perhaps "enemy" (šìkédndíí). In Situation No. 2, young people who have had relatively limited exposure to one another attempt to adjust to the new and intimate status of "sweetheart." These two situations are similar in that the focal participants have little or no prior knowledge of each other. Their social identities are not as yet clearly defined, and their expectations, lacking the foundation of previous experience, are poorly developed.

Situation No. 3 is somewhat different. Although the participants—parents and their children—are well known to each other, their relationship has been seriously interrupted by the latter's prolonged absence from home. This, combined with the possibility that recent experiences at school have altered the children's attitudes, introduces a definite element of unfamiliarity and doubt. Situation No. 3 is not characterized by the absence of role expectations but by the participants' perception that those already in existence may be outmoded and in need of revision.

Status ambiguity is present in Situation No. 4 because a focal participant is enraged and, as a result, considered "crazy." Until he returns to a more rational condition, others in the situation have no way of predicting how he will behave. Situation No. 5 is similar in that the personality of a focal participant is seen to have undergone a marked shift which makes his actions more difficult to anticipate. In both situations, the status of focal participants is uncertain because of real or imagined changes in their psychological makeup.

In Situation No. 6, a focal participant is ritually transformed from an essentially neutral state to one which is contextually defined as "potentially harmful." Ambiguity and apprehension accompany this transition, and, as in Situations No. 4 and 5, established patterns of interaction must be waived until the focal participant reverts to a less threatening condition.

This discussion points up a third feature characteristic of all situations: *the ambiguous status of focal participants is accompanied either by the absence or suspension*

of established role expectations. In every instance, nonfocal participants (i.e., those who refrain from speech) are either uncertain of how the focal participant will behave towards them or, conversely, how they should behave towards him. Stated in the simplest way possible, their roles become blurred with the result that established expectations—if they exist—lose their relevance as guidelines for social action and must be temporarily discarded or abruptly modified.

We are now in a position to expand upon our initial hypothesis and make it more explicit.

1. In Western Apache culture, the absence of verbal communication is associated with social situations in which the status of local participants is ambiguous.

2. Under these conditions, fixed role expectations lose their applicability and the illusion of predictability in social interaction is lost.

3. To sum up and reiterate: keeping silent among the Western Apache is a response to uncertainty and unpredictability in social relations.

VII

The question remains to what extent the foregoing hypothesis helps to account for silence behavior in other cultures. Unfortunately, it is impossible at the present time to provide anything approaching a conclusive answer. Standard ethnographies contain very little information about the circumstances under which verbal communication is discouraged, and it is only within the past few years that problems of this sort have engaged the attention of sociolinguists. The result is that adequate cross-cultural data are almost completely lacking.

As a first step towards the elimination of this deficiency, an attempt is now being made to investigate the occurrence and interpretation of silence in other Indian societies of the American Southwest. Our findings at this early stage, though neither fully representative nor sufficiently comprehensive, are extremely suggestive. By way of illustration, I quote below from portions of a preliminary report prepared by Priscilla Mowrer (1970), herself a Navajo, who inquired into the situational features of Navajo silence behavior in the vicinity of Tuba City on the Navajo Reservation in east-central Arizona.

I. *Silence and Courting:* Navajo youngsters of opposite sexes just getting to know one another say nothing, except to sit close together and maybe hold hands. . . . In public, they may try not to let on that they are interested in each other, but in private it is another matter. If the girl is at a gathering where the boy is also present, she may go off by herself. Falling in step, the boy will generally follow. They may just walk around or find some place to sit down. But, at first, they will not say anything to each other.

II. *Silence and Long Absent Relatives:* When a male or female relative returns home after being gone for six months or more, he (or she) is first greeted with a handshake. If the returnee is male, the female greeter may embrace him and cry—the male, meanwhile, will remain dry-eyed and silent.

III. *Silence and Anger:* The Navajo tend to remain silent when being shouted at by a drunk or angered individual because that particular individual is considered temporarily insane. To speak to such an individual, the Navajo believe, just tends to make the situation worse. . . . People remain silent because they believe that the individual is not himself, that he may have been witched, and is not responsible for the change in his behavior.

IV. *Silent Mourning:* Navajos speak very little when mourning the death of a relative. . . . The Navajo mourn and cry together in pairs. Men will embrace one another and cry together. Women, however, will hold one another's hands and cry together.

V. *Silence and the Ceremonial Patient:* The Navajo consider it wrong to talk to a person being sung over. The only people who talk to the patient are the medicine man and a female relative (or male relative if the patient is male) who is in charge of food preparation. The only time the patient speaks openly is when the medicine man asks her (or him) to pray along with him.

These observations suggest that striking similarities may exist between the types of social contexts in which Navajos and Western Apaches refrain from speech. If this impression is confirmed by further research, it will lend obvious cross-cultural support to the hypothesis advanced above. But regardless of the final outcome, the situational determinants of silence seem eminently deserving of further study. For as we become better informed about the types of contextual variables that mitigate against the use of verbal codes, we should also learn more about those variables that encourage and promote them.

BIBLIOGRAPHY

Basso, Keith H. 1966. *The Gift of Changing Woman.* Bureau of American Ethnology, bulletin 196.

———. 1969. *Western Apache Witchcraft.* Anthropological Papers of the University of Arizona, no. 15.

———. 1970. *The Cibecue Apache.* New York: Holt, Rinehart and Winston, Inc.

Brown, R. W., and Albert Gilman. 1960. "The Pronouns of Power and Solidarity," in *Style in Language* (ed. by T. Sebeok), pp. 253–276. Cambridge: The Technology Press of Massachusetts Institute of Technology.

Conklin, Harold C. 1959. Linguistic Play in Its Cultural Context. *Language* 35:631–636.

Ervin-Tripp, Susan. 1964. "An Analysis of the Interaction of Language, Topic and Listener," in *The Ethnography of Communication* (ed. by J. J. Gumperz and D. Hymes), pp. 86–102. *American Anthropologist,* Special Publication, vol. 66, no. 6, part 2.

———. 1967. *Sociolinguistics.* Language-Behavior Research Laboratory, Working Paper no. 3. Berkeley: University of California.

Frake, Charles O. 1964. "How to Ask for a Drink in Subanun," in *The Ethnography of Communication* (ed. by J. J. Gumperz and D. Hymes), pp. 127–132. *American Anthropologist,* Special Publication, vol. 66, no. 6, part 2.

Friedrich, P. 1966. "Structural Implications of Russian Pronomial Usage," in *Sociolinguistics,* (ed. by W. Bright), pp. 214–253. The Hague: Mouton.

Garfinkel, H. 1967. *Studies in Ethnomethodology.* Englewood Cliffs, N. J.: Prentice-Hall, Inc.

Goffman, E. 1961. *Encounters: Two Studies in the Sociology of Interaction.* Indianapolis: The Bobbs-Merrill Co., Inc.

———. 1963. *Behavior in Public Places.* Glencoe, Ill.: Free Press.

———. 1964. "The Neglected Situation," in *The Ethnography of Communication* (ed. by J. J. Gumperz and D. Hymes), pp. 133–136. *American Anthropologist,* Special Publication, vol. 66, no. 6, part 2.

Gumperz, John J. 1961. Speech Variation and the Study of Indian Civilization. *American Anthropologist* 63: 976–988.

———. 1964. "Linguistic and Social Interaction in Two Communities," in *The Ethnography of Communication* (ed. by J. J. Gumperz and D. Hymes), pp. 137–153. *American Anthropologist,* Special Publication, vol. 66, no. 6, part 2.

———. 1967. "The Social Setting of Linguistic Behavior," in *A Field Manual for Cross-Cultural Study of the Acquisition of Communicative Competence (Second Draft)* (ed. by D. I. Slobin), pp. 129–134. Berkeley: University of California.

Hymes, Dell. 1962. "The Ethnography of Speaking," in *Anthropology and Human Behavior* (ed. by T. Gladwin and W. C. Sturtevant), pp. 13–53. Washington, D. C.: The Anthropological Society of Washington.

———. 1964. "Introduction: Toward Ethnographies of Communication," in *The Ethnography of Communication* (ed. by J. J. Gumperz and D. Hymes), pp. 1–34. *American Anthropologist,* Special Publication, vol. 66, no. 6, part 2.

Kaut, Charles R. 1957. *The Western Apache Clan System: Its Origins and Development.* University of New Mexico Publications in Anthropology, no. 9.

Martin, Samuel. 1964. "Speech Levels in Japan and Korea," in *Language in Culture and Society* (ed. by D. Hymes), pp. 407–415. New York: Harper and Row.

Mowrer, Priscilla. 1970. Notes on Navajo Silence Behavior. MS, University of Arizona.

Slobin, Dan I. (ed.). 1967. *A Field Manual for Cross-Cultural Study of the Acquisition of Communicative Competence (Second Draft).* Berkeley: University of California.

NOTES

1. At different times during the period extending from 1964–1969 the research on which this paper is based was

supported by U. S. P. H. S. Grant MH-12691-01, a grant from the American Philosophical Society, and funds from the Doris Duke Oral History Project at the Arizona State Museum. I am pleased to acknowledge this support. I would also like to express my gratitude to the following scholars for commenting upon an earlier draft: Y. R. Chao, Harold C. Conklin, Roy G. D'Andrade, Charles O. Frake, Paul Friedrich, John Gumperz, Kenneth Hale, Harry Hoijer, Dell Hymes, Stanley Newman, David M. Schneider, Joel Sherzer, and Paul Turner. Although the final version gained much from their criticisms and suggestions, responsibility for its present form and content rests solely with the author. A preliminary version of this paper was presented to the Annual Meeting of the American Anthropological Association in New Orleans, Louisiana, November 1969. A modified version of this paper is scheduled to appear in *Studies in Apachean Culture and Ethnology* (ed. by Keith H. Basso and Morris Opler), Tucson: University of Arizona Press, 1970.

2. The situations described in this paper are not the only ones in which the Western Apache refrain from speech. There is a second set—not considered here because my data are incomplete—in which silence appears to occur as a gesture of respect, usually to persons in positions of authority. A third set, very poorly understood, involves ritual specialists who claim they must keep silent at certain points during the preparation of ceremonial paraphernalia.

3. Recent work in the sociology of interaction, most notably by Goffman (1963) and Garfinkel (1967), has led to the suggestion that social relationships are everywhere the major determinants of verbal behavior. In this case, as Gumperz (1967) makes clear, it becomes methodologically unsound to treat the various components of communicative events as independent variables. Gumperz (1967) has presented a hierarchical model, sensitive to dependency, in which components are seen as stages in the communication process. Each stage serves as the input for the next. The basic stage, i.e., the initial input, is "social identities or statuses." For further details see Slobin 1967:131–134.

4. I would like to stress that the emphasis placed on social relations is fully in keeping with the Western Apache interpretation of their own behavior. When my informants were asked to explain why they or someone else was silent on a particular occasion, they invariably did so in terms of *who* was present at the time.

5. Among the Western Apache, rules of exogamy discourage courtships between members of the same clan (*kii àłhánigo*) and so-called "related" clans (*kii*), with the result that sweethearts are almost always "non-matrilineal kinsmen" (*dòhwàkíída*). Compared to "matrilineal kinsmen" (*kii*), such individuals have fewer opportunities during childhood to establish close personal relationships and thus, when courtship begins, have relatively little knowledge of each other. It is not surprising, therefore, that their behavior is similar to that accorded strangers.

6. I have witnessed over 75 curing ceremonials since 1961 and have seen this rule violated only 6 times. On 4 occasions, drunks were at fault. In the other 2 cases, the patient fell asleep and had to be awakened.

10

Problems in Pocatello:

A Study in Linguistic Misunderstanding

Barbara Joans

In an earlier selection, Laura Bohannan showed us how the story of Hamlet was reinterpreted by the Tiv and understood by them in a way far different than Shakespeare intended. In this selection, Barbara Joans describes a similar case of cross-cultural misunderstanding. This situation did not occur in faraway Africa, but right in our backyard. The case involved communication between agency officials and a group of Native American women in Idaho. Two differences between this misunderstanding and the interpretation of Hamlet in the earlier selection are: first, the misunderstanding that developed in this situation has concrete consequences; second, neither of the parties realized until after the fact that they were miscommunicating. Paradoxically, serious miscommunication problems are most likely when both parties believe they are communicating well. People who recognize that their messages are not being understood have the opportunity to clarify their meaning. In this case, the Native American women understood English and erroneously thought they understood the language of bureaucratic regulations as well.

Other examples of cultural miscommunication show a lack of agreement of meaning or semantic domain of a word when it gets translated from one language to another. In the context of health care, for example, miscommunication between physician and patient can have profound consequences. Cross-cultural interactions, whether social, business, or political, are fraught with pitfalls and require sensitivity to these various issues in culture and communication.

As you read this selection, ask yourself the following questions:

☐ Do you think the crux of the problem was words (that is, vocabulary) or meanings?

☐ How do you think the power differential between the government agency and the Native American women might have affected the behavior during the meetings in which the rules were explained?

☐ In a variety of arenas, people who are not completely conversant with the dominant culture come into contact with powerful social institutions and organizations such as schools, factories, and social service agencies. In such situations miscommunication, conflict, and personal frustration are likely consequences. What sort of system might reduce the likelihood of cross-cultural misunderstandings?

☐ How did the anthropologist's attention to culture and communication lead her to participate in this case?

The following terms discussed in this selection are included in the Glossary at the back of the book:

culture brokers
linguistics
mediator

Reproduced by permission of Society for Applied Anthropology from *Practicing Anthropology*, 6(3/4):6, 8, 1984.

In November, 1978, the Pocatello Social Service Agency accused six older Bannock-Shoshoni women from the Fort Hall reservation of withholding financial information while receiving supplemental security income (SSI). The women were charged with fraud and ordered to repay the SSI payments. With the help of an Idaho legal aid office, the women contested the agency ruling on repayment. Legal Aid contended that the women were misinformed of SSI rules and of their individual responsibilities. The social service agency claimed the women knew the rules and chose to ignore them. When the disagreement ended up in court, I was asked to help out. The issue seemed clear. *Did the Indian women understand what was expected of them?*

BACKGROUND

In December, 1978, a lawyer from the Idaho Legal Aid Services requested my aid on behalf of the Bannock-Shoshoni women. As a cultural anthropologist and Director of Women's Re-Entry at Idaho State University, I was the logical person to contact. This was a fortunate meeting all around, as I had been trying, unsuccessfully, to make contact with Fort Hall Indians all year. Fort Hall and Pocatello are two ends of a wide spectrum.

Pocatello is a poor railroad town situated in the southeast portion of Idaho. Major employment comes from the fertilizer plant and other heavy industry and marginal ranch and farm lands. In spite of the poverty and general hardness of people's lives, there are prevailing attitudes of rugged individualism and pride in the pioneering spirit of town ancestors. There is also a small state university of surprising vitality. Pocatello is a town of extremes.

Situated about ten miles out of town is the Fort Hall Indian reservation. Over 1,000 Bannock-Shoshoni live, farm, and work at Fort Hall. While the reservation is large, most of it is desert. Few Indians do more than scrape a meager living from the soil. For supplemental income they make pottery and jewelry which they sell to the local townspeople. Some of the Indians rent part of their lands to local Anglos for a small yearly income. Fort Hall is an Indian cultural center hosting intertribal feasts, dances, sweat lodges, pow-wows, initiations, and meetings all summer long. The Bannock-Shoshoni maintain a vital political/cultural role in the western Indian community. They provide meeting places for many tribes.

The close proximity of Fort Hall and Pocatello assures continuous contact between the two populations. Unfortunately, frequent meetings are not often beneficial to either group. Typical culture contact takes place in such non-neutral spaces as local bars, unemploy-ment and welfare lines, and hospital clinics. Old antagonisms fanned by years of mutual prejudice reinforce debilitating stereotypes. The two communities may live side-by-side, but there is little positive cultural exchange and even less mutual understanding.

THE PROBLEM

The lack of understanding between the two communities crystallized around the issue of SSI payments. Six older (all past sixty) Bannock-Shoshoni women were having trouble with the Pocatello social service agency that handled their SSI account. The women were accused of withholding information from the agency and receiving unreported monies. Several of the women had small parcels of land at Fort Hall which they were able to rent to neighboring Anglos. They received between one and two thousand dollars in rental income. They rented the land in January, but did not receive payment on the land until the following December.

Under SSI regulations, the women were required to report all income. The Pocatello SSI explained, in English, at reservation community lunches that all monies had to be accounted for. The women did not report the rental of their lands in December when they received payment. SSI claimed that the income should have been reported as soon as the land was rented. Because it was not immediately reported, the SSI people stopped all checks and demanded that the women pay back the monies they had received during the year. To compound the problem, several women were sent extra checks which they assumed they could keep. They reasoned that if the government sent them money, the government knew what it was doing. SSI wanted all the monies returned. The payments in question amounted to around $2,000, and the women had no way of repaying it. They went to see the legal aid lawyer and he came to see me.

PROBLEM SOLVING: THE METHODOLOGY

The SSI workers claimed that the rules and regulations had been fully explained. The legal aid lawyer wanted to know if, in my estimation, this was so. *Did the Indian women understand what was expected of them?*

I used language as the criterion for cultural understanding. Since all the verbal exchanges between SSI staff and Bannock-Shoshoni were in English, I decided to use the women's comprehension of English as the index for general cultural understanding. If the women sufficiently understood English, then the SSI staff would have justification in their claims. If, on the other hand, the women's comprehension of English was minimal, a case for misunderstanding SSI rules could be made. Drawing from my general knowledge of language (anthropological training but not specific training in linguistics), I created a three-part system to test the English language sophistication of the Indian women. Levels 1, 2, and 3 were the categories.

Level 1

This consisted of everyday common speech. For example:—How are you?—I am fine—Are you cold?—Do you need a coat?—Are you hungry?—Each of the women understood and was able to communicate on Level 1 English.

Level 2

This consisted of language joking behavior. Could the women understand non-literal sentences? Could they share in joke-making behavior about local Pocatello officials? We had spoken often about their contempt for Pocatello officials and I knew they disapproved of town politics. But could they understand the double-entendres, the mixed meanings, the puns, and the jokes? At this level, only one woman was able to follow my conversation and understand the linguistic ambiguities and joking statements. The one Indian woman who understood English Level 2 participated in joking behavior and made outrageous comments about the nature of the Pocatello political system. With her alone, I tested for Level 3.

Level 3

This consisted of understanding the rules and regulations governing Indian lives and the ability to articulate these rules. I tested for Level 3 by first enquiring about Indian laws. Did the woman understand how the Indian police operated on the reservation? She did. Could she articulate an understanding of tribal policies, laws and rules? She could. Did she understand how Pocatello police operated? She did not. Could she understand Indian councils? Yes. Did she understand Pocatello town councils? No. I saw that she was not able to translate rules from Indian society to Pocatello society on Level 3 using English as the language of communication. I concluded from her lack of Level 3 understanding that there were severe cultural misunderstandings between her and the Pocatello SSI people. The SSI people thought that the Bannock-Shoshoni women knew what they were talking about when they described procedures in English. I was in a position to demonstrate that they did not.

Since it was my job to determine how much En-glish the Bannock-Shoshoni women actually understood, I devised methods to keep me in frequent communication. I visited the women at their homes, at the lawyer's office, at my office, and at the reservation trading post. Using the traditional methodologies of participant observation, I stayed with the Indian women about three months. At the end of that time I was able to conclude that while they were all talking English, the Indian women and the agency people used English with very different meanings. The Indian women did not understand what was expected of them.

PROBLEM SOLVING: THE PROCESS

The next problem was how to make my knowledge acceptable to the judge. I had to prove culture conflict and cultural misunderstanding. These women looked like they talked English, but, in reality, they didn't have a clear idea of what the SSI people were telling them. The women were all in their late 60s and early 70s, and had lived most of their lives on the Indian reservation where they had very little voluntary contact with English. Their normal, everyday language was either Bannock or Shoshoni.

THE RESULTS

For my court appearance it was necessary to prepare an anthropological brief documenting the linguistic and cultural misunderstanding. I had to supply a bibliography dealing with other cases of cultural misunderstanding. I also had to submit my much shortened vitae as evidence of credentials enabling me to research contact situations. Then I was permitted to testify. The legal aid lawyer and I chose to use the evidence from the Bannock-Shoshoni woman who was most proficient in English (Level 2) for our first test case. We stated:

- That the SSI people always came to the reservation on busy days when many things were happening.

- That the SSI people always spoke to a large number of people during a community lunch and never gave individuals specific attention.

- That the SSI people always spoke English and the Indian women did not understand English sufficiently to comply with their demands. The Indian women never understood Level 3, the level of laws and rules.

- Therefore, the Bannock-Shoshoni women should not lose their SSI benefits, nor should they have to pay any monies back.

After considering our evidence, the judge ruled that the women did not have to return any money. He decided that there was too great a possibility that the women did not understand the SSI instructions and, therefore, could not be held responsible for either failing to report rent monies before they received them or failing to return checks that should not have been sent. The judge added that in the future the SSI would have to use a Bannock-Shoshoni interpreter when they went to the reservation to describe program requirements.

By using linguistic patterns as criteria for cultural understanding, I was able to initiate a program of action anthropology in Idaho. Interpreters are now used in all contact situations between town agencies and reservation peoples. For the first time in Idaho, variant cultural patterns were accepted in court as determinants of behavior. Through these actions the Bannock-Shoshoni women have gained some control over their economic resources.

11

A Cultural Approach to Male–Female Miscommunication

Daniel N. Maltz and Ruth A. Borker

Of the 60,000 or so words in the English language, the typical, educated adult uses about 2,000. Five hundred of these words alone can convey over 14,000 meanings. But even with all these alternatives, this is not the central problem of miscommunication in America. Rather, interethnic and cross-sex conversations are the central problem—because the participants possess different subcultural rules for speaking.

Conversation is a negotiated activity. Within a given culture, conversations rely upon unspoken understandings about tone of voice, visual cues, silence, minimal responses (such as "mm hmm"), and a variety of other subtle conventions. A cultural approach to male–female conversation highlights unconscious meanings that can lead members of one group to misinterpret the intent of others. Evidence suggests, for example, that women use the response "mm hmm" to indicate they are listening while men use the same response to indicate they are agreeing. Thus, a man who does not provide such cues may indicate to a female conversation partner that he is not listening whereas a woman may appear to keep changing her mind when giving the same cue. This and similar insights are found throughout this selection and indicate the need for attention to be paid to communication across cultural and subcultural boundaries.

As you read this selection, ask yourself the following questions:

☐ *What are some of the differences in the ways men and women talk to each other that have been noted in earlier research?*

☐ *How do differences between men and women in conversational style reflect differences in power in the larger society?*

☐ *If men and women exist in different linguistic subcultures, how and when were these subcultures learned? How does the world of girls differ from the world of boys?*

☐ *What kinds of miscommunications occur in cross-sex conversation?*

☐ *Can you think of situations that have occurred in your own life that can be better understood after reading this cultural analysis of cross-sex conversation?*

The following terms discussed in this selection are included in the Glossary at the back of the book:

gender
metalinguistics
sex roles
social networks
sociolinguistics
subculture

Reprinted with permission from John L. Gumperz (ed.), *Language and Social Identity*, 1982. Cambridge University Press.

INTRODUCTION

This chapter presents what we believe to be a useful new framework for examining differences in the speaking patterns of American men and women. It is based not on new data, but on a reexamination of a wide variety of material already available in the scholarly literature. Our starting problem is the nature of the different roles of male and female speakers in informal cross-sex conversations in American English. Our attempts to think about this problem have taken us to preliminary examination of a wide variety of fields often on or beyond the margins of our present competencies: children's speech, children's play, styles and patterns of friendship, conversational turn-taking, discourse analysis, and interethnic communication. The research which most influenced the development of our present model includes John Gumperz's work on problems in interethnic communication (1982) and Marjorie Goodwin's study of the linguistic aspects of play among black children in Philadelphia (1978, 1980a, 1980b).

Our major argument is that the general approach recently developed for the study of difficulties in cross-ethnic communication can be applied to cross-sex communication as well. We prefer to think of the difficulties in both cross-sex and cross-ethnic communication as two examples of the same larger phenomenon: cultural difference and miscommunication.

THE PROBLEM OF CROSS-SEX CONVERSATION

Study after study has shown that when men and women attempt to interact as equals in friendly cross-sex conversations they do not play the same role in interaction, even when there is no apparent element of flirting. We hope to explore some of these differences, examine the explanations that have been offered, and provide an alternative explanation for them.

The primary data on cross-sex conversations come from two general sources: social psychology studies from the 1950s such as Soskin and John's (1963) research on two young married couples and Strodbeck and Mann's (1956) research on jury deliberations, and more recent sociolinguistic studies from the University of California at Santa Barbara and the University of Pennsylvania by Candace West (Zimmerman and West 1975; West and Zimmerman 1977; West 1979), Pamela Fishman (1978), and Lynette Hirschman (1973).

WOMEN'S FEATURES

Several striking differences in male and female contributions to cross-sex conversation have been noticed in these studies.

First, women display a greater tendency to ask questions. Fishman (1978:400) comments that "at times I felt that all women did was ask questions," and Hirschman (1973:10) notes that "several of the female–male conversations fell into a question–answer pattern with the females asking the males questions."

Fishman (1978:408) sees this question-asking tendency as an example of a second, more general characteristic of women's speech, doing more of the routine "shitwork" involved in maintaining routine social interaction, doing more to facilitate the flow of conversation (Hirschman 1973:3). Women are more likely than men to make utterances that demand or encourage responses from their fellow speakers and are therefore, in Fishman's words, "more actively engaged in insuring interaction than the men" (1978:404). In the earlier social psychology studies, these features have been coded under the general category of "positive reactions" including solidarity, tension release, and agreeing (Strodbeck and Mann 1956).

Third, women show a greater tendency to make use of positive minimal responses, especially "mm hmm" (Hirschman 1973:8), and are more likely to insert "such comments throughout streams of talk rather than [simply] at the end" (Fishman 1978:402).

Fourth, women are more likely to adopt a strategy of "silent protest" after they have been interrupted or have received a delayed minimal response (Zimmerman and West 1975; West and Zimmerman 1977:524).

Fifth, women show a greater tendency to use the pronouns "you" and "we," which explicitly acknowledge the existence of the other speaker (Hirschman 1973:6).

MEN'S FEATURES

Contrasting contributions to cross-sex conversations have been observed and described for men.

First, men are more likely to interrupt the speech of their conversational partners, that is, to interrupt the speech of women (Zimmerman and West 1975; West and Zimmerman 1977; West 1979).

Second, they are more likely to challenge or dispute their partners' utterances (Hirschman 1973:11).

Third, they are more likely to ignore the comments of the other speaker, that is, to offer no response or acknowledgment at all (Hirschman 1973:11), to respond slowly in what has been described as a "delayed minimal response" (Zimmerman and West 1975:118), or to respond unenthusiastically (Fishman 1978).

Fourth, men use more mechanisms for controlling the topic of conversation, including both topic development and the introduction of new topics, than do women (Zimmerman and West 1975).

Finally, men make more direct declarations of fact or opinion than do women (Fishman 1978:402), including suggestions, opinions, and "statements of orientation" as Strodbeck and Mann (1956) describe them, or "statements of focus and directives" as they are described by Soskin and John (1963).

EXPLANATIONS OFFERED

Most explanations for these features have focused on differences in the social power or in the personalities of men and women. One variant of the social power argument, presented by West (Zimmerman and West 1975; West and Zimmerman 1977), is that men's dominance in conversation parallels their dominance in society. Men enjoy power in society and also in conversation. The two levels are seen as part of a single social-political system. West sees interruptions and topic control as male displays of power—a power based in the larger social order but reinforced and expressed in face-to-face interaction with women. A second variant of this argument, stated by Fishman (1978), is that while the differential power of men and women is crucial, the specific mechanism through which it enters conversation is sex-role definition. Sex roles serve to obscure the issue of power for participants, but the fact is, Fishman argues, that norms of appropriate behavior for women and men serve to give power and interactional control to men while keeping it from women. To be socially acceptable as women, women cannot exert control and must actually support men in their control. In this casting of the social power argument, men are not necessarily seen to be consciously flaunting power, but simply reaping the rewards given them by the social system. In both variants, the link between macro and micro levels of social life is seen as direct and unproblematic, and the focus of explanation is the general social order.

Sex roles have also been central in psychological explanations. The primary advocate of the psychological position has been Robin Lakoff (1975). Basically, Lakoff asserts that, having been taught to speak and act like 'ladies,' women become as unassertive and insecure as they have been made to sound. The impossible task of trying to be both women and adults, which Lakoff sees as culturally incompatible, saps women of confidence and strength. As a result, they come to pro-

duce the speech they do, not just because it is how women are supposed to speak, but because it fits with the personalities they develop as a consequence of sex-role requirements.

The problem with these explanations is that they do not provide a means of explaining why these specific features appear as opposed to any number of others, nor do they allow us to differentiate between various types of male–female interaction. They do not really tell us why and how these specific interactional phenomena are linked to the general fact that men dominate within our social system.

AN ALTERNATIVE EXPLANATION: SOCIOLINGUISTIC SUBCULTURES

Our approach to cross-sex communication patterns is somewhat different from those that have been previously proposed. We place the stress not on psychological differences or power differentials, although these may make some contribution, but rather on a notion of cultural differences between men and women in their conceptions of friendly conversation, their rules for engaging in it, and, probably most important, their rules for interpreting it. We argue that American men and women come from different sociolinguistic subcultures, having learned to do different things with words in a conversation, so that when they attempt to carry on conversations with one another, even if both parties are attempting to treat one another as equals, cultural miscommunication results.

The idea of distinct male and female subcultures is not a new one for anthropology. It has been persuasively argued again and again for those parts of the world such as the Middle East and southern Europe in which men and women spend most of their lives spatially and interactionally segregated. The strongest case for sociolinguistic subcultures has been made by Susan Harding from her research in rural Spain (1975).

The major premise on which Harding builds her argument is that speech is a means for dealing with social and psychological situations. When men and women have different experiences and operate in different social contexts, they tend to develop different genres of speech and different skills for doing things with words. In the Spanish village in which she worked, the sexual division of labor was strong, with men involved in agricultural tasks and public politics while women were involved in a series of networks of personal relations with their children, their husbands, and their female neighbors. While men developed their verbal skills in economic negotiations and public political argument, women became more verbally adept at a quite different mode of interactional manipulation with words: gossip, social analysis, subtle information gathering through a carefully developed technique of verbal prying, and a kind of second-guessing the thoughts of others (commonly known as 'women's intuition') through a skillful monitoring of the speech of others. The different social needs of men and women, she argues, have led them to sexually differentiated communicative cultures, with each sex learning a different set of skills for manipulating words effectively.

The question that Harding does not ask, however, is, if men and women possess different subcultural rules for speaking, what happens if and when they try to interact with each other? It is here that we turn to the research on interethnic miscommunication.

INTERETHNIC COMMUNICATION

Recent research (Gumperz 1977, 1978a, 1978b, 1979; Gumperz and Tannen 1978) has shown that systematic problems develop in communication when speakers of different speech cultures interact and that these problems are the result of differences in systems of conversational inference and the cues for signalling speech acts and speaker's intent. Conversation is a negotiated activity. It progresses in large part because of shared assumptions about what is going on.

Examining interactions between English-English and Indian-English speakers in Britain (Gumperz 1977, 1978a, 1979; Gumperz et al. 1977), Gumperz found that differences in cues resulted in systematic miscommunication over whether a question was being asked, whether an argument was being made, whether a person was being rude or polite, whether a speaker was relinquishing the floor or interrupting, whether and what a speaker was emphasizing, whether interactants were angry, concerned, or indifferent. Rather than being seen as problems in communication, the frustrating encounters that resulted were usually chalked up as personality clashes or interpreted in the light of racial stereotypes which tended to exacerbate already bad relations.

To take a simple case, Gumperz (1977) reports than Indian women working at a cafeteria, when offering food, used a falling intonation, e.g., "gravy," which to them indicated a question, something like "do you want gravy?" Both Indian and English workers saw a question as an appropriate polite form, but to English-English speakers a falling intonation signalled not a question, which for them is signalled by a rising intonation such as "gravy," but a declarative statement, which was both inappropriate and extremely rude.

A major advantage of Gumperz's framework is that it does not assume that problems are the result of bad faith, but rather sees them as the result of individuals wrongly interpreting cues according to their own rules.

THE INTERPRETATION OF MINIMAL RESPONSES

How might Gumperz's approach to the study of conflicting rules for interpreting conversation be applied to the communication between men and women? A simple example will illustrate our basic approach: the case of positive minimal responses. Minimal responses such as nods and comments like "yes" and "mm hmm" are common features of conversational interaction. Our claim, based on our attempts to understand personal experience, is that these minimal responses have significantly different meanings for men and women, leading to occasionally serious miscommunication.

We hypothesize that for women a minimal response of this type means simply something like "I'm listening to you; please continue," and that for men it has a somewhat stronger meaning such as "I agree with you" or at least "I follow your argument so far." The fact that women use these responses more often than men is in part simply that women are listening more often than men are agreeing.

But our hypothesis explains more than simple differential frequency of usage. Different rules can lead to repeated misunderstandings. Imagine a male speaker who is receiving repeated nods or "mm hmm"s from the woman he is speaking to. She is merely indicating that she is listening, but he thinks she is agreeing with everything he says. Now imagine a female speaker who is receiving only occasional nods and "mm hmm"s from the man she is speaking to. He is indicating that he doesn't always agree; she thinks he isn't always listening.

What is appealing about this short example is that it seems to explain two of the most common complaints in male–female interaction: (1) men who think that women are always agreeing with them and then conclude that it's impossible to tell what a woman really thinks, and (2) women who get upset with men who never seem to be listening. What we think we have here are two separate rules for conversational maintenance which come into conflict and cause massive miscommunication.

SOURCES OF DIFFERENT CULTURES

A probable objection that many people will have to our discussion so far is that American men and women interact with one another far too often to possess different subcultures. What we need to explain is how it is that men and women can come to possess different cultural assumptions about friendly conversation.

Our explanation is really quite simple. It is based on the idea that by the time we have become adults we possess a wide variety of rules for interacting in different situations. Different sets of these rules were learned at different times and in different contexts. We have rules for dealing with people in dominant or subordinate social positions, rules which we first learned as young children interacting with our parents and teachers. We have rules for flirting and other sexual encounters which we probably started learning at or near adolescence. We have rules for dealing with service personnel and bureaucrats, rules we began learning when we first ventured into the public domain. Finally, we have rules for friendly interaction, for carrying on friendly conversation. What is striking about these last rules is that they were learned not from adults but from peers, and that they were learned during precisely that time period, approximately age 5 to 15, when boys and girls interact socially primarily with members of their own sex.

The idea that girls and boys in contemporary America learn different ways of speaking by the age of five or earlier has been postulated by Robin Lakoff (1975), demonstrated by Andrea Meditch (1975), and more fully explored by Adelaide Haas (1979). Haas's research on school-age children shows the early appearance of important male–female differences in patterns of language use, including a male tendency toward direct requests and information giving and a female tendency toward compliance (1979:107).

But the process of acquiring gender-specific speech and behavior patterns by school-age children is more complex than the simple copying of adult "genderlects" by preschoolers. Psychologists Brooks-Gunn and Matthews (1979) have labelled this process the "consolidation of sex roles"; we call it learning of gender-specific 'cultures.'

Among school-age children, patterns of friendly social interaction are learned not so much from adults as from members of one's peer group, and a major feature of most middle-childhood peer groups is homogeneity; "they are either all-boy or all-girl" (Brooks-Gunn and Matthews 1979). Members of each sex are learning self-consciously to differentiate their behavior from that of the other sex and to exaggerate these differences. The process can be profitably compared to accent divergence in which members of two groups that wish to become clearly distinguished from one another socially acquire increasingly divergent ways of speaking.[1]

Because they learn these gender-specific cultures

from their age-mates, children tend to develop stereotypes and extreme versions of adult behavior patterns. For a boy learning to behave in a masculine way, for example, Ruth Hartley (1959, quoted in Brooks-Gunn and Matthews 1979:203) argues that:

> both the information and the practice he gets are distorted. Since his peers have no better sources of information than he has, all they can do is pool the impressions and anxieties they derived from their early training. Thus, the picture they draw is oversimplified and overemphasized. It is a picture drawn in black and white, with little or no modulation and it is incomplete, including a few of the many elements that go to make up the role of the mature male.

What we hope to argue is that boys and girls learn to use language in different ways because of the very different social contexts in which they learn how to carry on friendly conversation. Almost anyone who remembers being a child, has worked with school-age children, or has had an opportunity to observe school-age children can vouch for the fact that groups of girls and groups of boys interact and play in different ways. Systematic observations of children's play have tended to confirm these well-known differences in the ways girls and boys learn to interact with their friends.

In a major study of sex differences in the play of school-age children, for example, sociologist Janet Lever (1976) observed the following six differences between the play of boys and that of girls: (1) girls more often play indoors; (2) boys tend to play in larger groups; (3) boys' play groups tend to include a wider age range of participants; (4) girls play in predominantly male games more often than vice versa; (5) boys more often play competitive games, and (6) girls' games tend to last a shorter period of time than boys' games.

It is by examining these differences in the social organization of play and the accompanying differences in the patterns of social interaction they entail, we argue, that we can learn about the sources of male–female differences in patterns of language use. And it is these same patterns, learned in childhood and carried over into adulthood as the bases for patterns of single-sex friendship relations, we contend, that are potential sources of miscommunication in cross-sex interaction.

THE WORLD OF GIRLS

Our own experience and studies such as Goodwin's (1980b) of black children and Lever's (1976, 1978) of white children suggest a complex of features of girls' play and the speech within it. Girls play in small groups, most often in pairs (Lever 1976; Eder and Hallinan 1978; Brooks-Gunn and Matthews 1979), and their play groups tend to be remarkably homogeneous in terms of age. Their play is often in private or semi-private settings that require participants be invited in. Play is cooperative and activities are usually organized in noncompetitive ways (Lever 1976; Goodwin 1980b). Differentiation between girls is not made in terms of power, but relative closeness. Friendship is seen by girls as involving intimacy, equality, mutual commitment, and loyalty. The idea of 'best friend' is central for girls. Relationships between girls are to some extent in opposition to one another, and new relationships are often formed at the expense of old ones. As Brooks-Gunn and Matthews (1979:280) observe, "friendships tend to be exclusive, with a few girls being exceptionally close to one another. Because of this breakups tend to be highly emotional," and Goodwin (1980a:172) notes that "the non-hierarchical framework of the girls provides a fertile ground for rather intricate processes of alliance formation between equals against some other party."

There is a basic contradiction in the structure of girls' social relationships. Friends are supposed to be equal and everyone is supposed to get along, but in fact they don't always. Conflict must be resolved, but a girl cannot assert social power or superiority as an individual to resolve it. Lever (1976), studying fifth-graders, found that girls simply could not deal with quarrels and that when conflict arose they made no attempt to settle it; the group just broke up. What girls learn to do with speech is cope with the contradiction created by an ideology of equality and cooperation and a social reality that includes differences and conflict. As they grow up they learn increasingly subtle ways of balancing the conflicting pressures created by a female social world and a female friendship ideology.

Basically girls learn to do three things with words: (1) to create and maintain relationships of closeness and equality, (2) to criticize others in acceptable ways, and (3) to interpret accurately the speech of other girls.

To a large extent friendships among girls are formed through talk. Girls need to learn to give support, to recognize the speech rights of others, to let others speak, and to acknowledge what they say in order to establish and maintain relationships of equality and closeness. In activities they need to learn to create cooperation through speech. Goodwin (1980a) found that inclusive forms such as "let's," "we gonna," "we could," and "we gotta" predominated in task-oriented activities. Furthermore, she found that most girls in the

group she studied made suggestions and that the other girls usually agreed to them. But girls also learn to exchange information and confidences to create and maintain relationships of closeness. The exchange of personal thoughts not only expresses closeness but mutual commitment as well. Brooks-Gunn and Matthews (1979:280) note of adolescent girls:

> much time is spent talking, reflecting, and sharing intimate thought. Loyalty is of central concern to the 12- to 14-year old girl, presumably because, if innermost secrets are shared, the friend may have 'dangerous knowledge' at her disposal.

Friendships are not only formed through particular types of talk, but are ended through talk as well. As Lever (1976:4) says of 'best friends,' "sharing secrets binds the union together, and 'telling' the secrets to outsiders is symbolic of the 'break-up.'"

Secondly, girls learn to criticize and argue with other girls without seeming overly aggressive, without being perceived as either 'bossy' or 'mean,' terms girls use to evaluate one another's speech and actions. Bossiness, ordering others around, is not legitimate because it denies equality. Goodwin (1980a) points out that girls talked very negatively about the use of commands to equals, seeing it as appropriate only in role play or in unequal relationships such as those with younger siblings. Girls learn to direct things without seeming bossy, or they learn not to direct. While disputes are common, girls learn to phrase their arguments in terms of group needs and situational requirements rather than personal power or desire (Goodwin 1980a). Meanness is used by girls to describe nonlegitimate acts of exclusion, turning on someone, or withholding friendship. Excluding is a frequent occurrence (Eder and Hallinan 1978), but girls learn over time to discourage or even drive away other girls in ways that don't seem to be just personal whim. Cutting someone is justified in terms of the target's failure to meet group norms and a girl often rejects another using speech that is seemingly supportive on the surface. Conflict and criticism are risky in the world of girls because they can both rebound against the critic and can threaten social relationships. Girls learn to hide the source of criticism; they present it as coming from someone else or make it indirectly through a third party (Goodwin 1980a, 1980b).

Finally, girls must learn to decipher the degree of closeness being offered by other girls, to recognize what is being withheld, and to recognize criticism. Girls who don't actually read these cues run the risk of public censure or ridicule (Goodwin 1980). Since the currency of closeness is the exchange of secrets which can be used against a girl, she must learn to read the intent and loyalty of others and to do so continuously, given the system of shifting alliances and indirect expressions of conflict. Girls must become increasingly sophisticated in reading the motives of others, in determining when closeness is real, when conventional, and when false, and to respond appropriately. They must learn who to confide in, what to confide, and who not to approach. Given the indirect expression of conflict, girls must learn to read relationships and situations sensitively. Learning to get things right is a fundamental skill for social success, if not just social survival.

THE WORLD OF BOYS

Boys play in larger, more hierarchically organized groups than do girls. Relative status in this ever-fluctuating hierarchy is the main thing that boys learn to manipulate in their interactions with their peers. Nondominant boys are rarely excluded from play but are made to feel the inferiority of their status positions in no uncertain terms. And since hierarchies fluctuate over time and over situation, every boy gets his chance to be victimized and must learn to take it. The social world of boys is one of posturing and counterposturing. In this world, speech is used in three major ways: (1) to assert one's position of dominance, (2) to attract and maintain an audience, and (3) to assert oneself when other speakers have the floor.

The use of speech for the expression of dominance is the most straightforward and probably the best-documented sociolinguistic pattern in boys' peer groups. Even ethological studies of human dominance patterns have made extensive use of various speech behaviors as indices of dominance. Richard Savin-Williams (1976), for example, in his study of dominance patterns among boys in a summer camp uses the following speech interactions as measures of dominance: (1) giving of verbal commands or orders, such as "Get up," "Give it to me," or "You go over there"; (2) name calling and other forms of verbal ridicule, such as "You're a dolt"; (3) verbal threats or boasts of authority, such as "If you don't shut up, I'm gonna come over and bust your teeth in"; (4) refusals to obey orders; and (5) winning a verbal argument as in the sequence: "I was here first" / "Tough," or in more elaborate forms of verbal duelling such as the 'dozens.'[2]

The same patterns of verbally asserting one's dominance and challenging the dominance claims of others form the central element in Goodwin's (1980a) observations of boys' play in Philadelphia. What is easy to

forget in thinking about this use of words as weapons, however, is that the most successful boy in such interaction is not the one who is most aggressive and uses the most power-wielding forms of speech, but the boy who uses these forms most successfully. The simple use of assertiveness and aggression in boys' play is the sign not of a leader but of a bully. The skillful speaker in a boys' group is considerably more likeable and better liked by his peers than is a simple bully. Social success among boys is based on knowing both how and when to use words to express power as well as knowing when not to use them. A successful leader will use speech to put challengers in their place and to remind followers periodically of their nondominant position, but will not browbeat unnecessarily and will therefore gain the respect rather than the fear of less dominant boys.

A second sociolinguistic aspect of friendly interaction between boys is using words to gain and maintain an audience. Storytelling, joke telling, and other narrative performance events are common features of the social interaction of boys. But actual transcripts of such storytelling events collected by Harvey Sacks (Sacks 1974; Jefferson 1978) and Goodwin (1980a), as opposed to stories told directly to interviewers, reveal a suggestive feature of storytelling activities among boys: audience behavior is not overtly supportive. The storyteller is frequently faced with mockery, challenges and side comments on his story. A major sociolinguistic skill which a boy must apparently learn in interacting with his peers is to ride out this series of challenges, maintain his audience, and successfully get to the end of his story. In Sacks's account (1974) of some teenage boys involved in the telling of a dirty joke, for example, the narrator is challenged for his taste in jokes (an implication that he doesn't know a dirty joke from a non-dirty one) and for the potential ambiguity of his opening line "Three brothers married three sisters," not, as Sacks seems to imply, because audience members are really confused, but just to hassle the speaker. Through catches,[3] put-downs, the building of suspense, or other interest-grabbing devices, the speaker learns to control his audience. He also learns to continue when he gets no encouragement whatever, pausing slightly at various points for possible audience response but going on if there is nothing but silence.

A final sociolinguistic skill which boys must learn from interacting with other boys is how to act as audience members in the types of storytelling situations just discussed. As audience member as well as storyteller, a boy must learn to assert himself and his opinions. Boys seem to respond to the storytelling of other boys not so much with questions on deeper implications or with minimal-response encouragement as with side comments and challenges. These are not meant primarily to interrupt, to change topic, or to change the direction of the narrative itself, but to assert the identity of the individual audience member.

WOMEN'S SPEECH

The structures and strategies in women's conversation show a marked continuity with the talk of girls. The key logic suggested by Kalčik's (1975) study of women's rap groups, Hirschman's (1973) study of students and Abrahams's (1975) work on black women is that women's conversation is interactional. In friendly talk, women are negotiating and expressing a relationship, one that should be in the form of support and closeness, but which may also involve criticism and distance. Women orient themselves to the person they are talking to and expect such orientation in return. As interaction, conversation requires participation from those involved and back-and-forth movement between participants. Getting the floor is not seen as particularly problematic; that should come about automatically. What is problematic is getting people engaged and keeping them engaged—maintaining the conversation and the interaction.

This conception of conversation leads to a number of characteristic speech strategies and gives a particular dynamic to women's talk. First, women tend to use personal and inclusive pronouns, such as 'you' and 'we' (Hirschman 1973). Second, women give off and look for signs of engagement such as nods and minimal response (Kalčik 1975; Hirschman 1973). Third, women give more extended signs of interest and attention, such as interjecting comments or questions during a speaker's discourse. These sometimes take the form of interruptions. In fact, both Hirschman (1973) and Kalčik (1975) found that interruptions were extremely common, despite women's concern with politeness and decorum (Kalčik 1975). Kalčik (1975) comments that women often asked permission to speak but were concerned that each speaker be allowed to finish and that all present got a chance to speak. These interruptions were clearly not seen as attempts to grab the floor but as calls for elaboration and development, and were taken as signs of support and interest. Fourth, women at the beginning of their utterances explicitly acknowledge and respond to what has been said by others. Fifth, women attempt to link their utterance to the one preceding it by building on the previous utterance or talking about something parallel or related to it. Kalčik (1975) talks about strategies of tying together, filling in, and serializing as signs of

women's desire to create continuity in conversation, and Hirschman (1973) describes elaboration as a key dynamic of women's talk.

While the idiom of much of women's friendly talk is that of support, the elements of criticism, competition, and conflict do occur in it. But as with girls, these tend to take forms that fit the friendship idiom. Abrahams (1975) points out that while 'talking smart' is clearly one way women talk to women as well as to men, between women it tends to take a more playful form, to be more indirect and metaphoric in its phrasing and less prolonged than similar talk between men. Smartness, as he points out, puts distance in a relationship (Abrahams 1975). The target of criticism, whether present or not, is made out to be the one violating group norms and values (Abrahams 1975). Overt competitiveness is also disguised. As Kalčik (1975) points out, some stories that build on preceding ones are attempts to cap the original speaker, but they tend to have a form similar to supportive ones. It is the intent more than the form that differs. Intent is a central element in the concept of 'bitchiness,' one of women's terms for evaluating their talk, and it relates to this contradiction between form and intent, whether putting negative messages in overtly positive forms or acting supportive face to face while not being so elsewhere.

These strategies and the interactional orientation of women's talk give their conversation a particular dynamic. While there is often an unfinished quality to particular utterances (Kalčik 1975), there is a progressive development to the overall conversation. The conversation grows out of the interaction of its participants, rather than being directed by a single individual or series of individuals. In her very stimulating discussion, Kalčik (1975) argues that this is true as well for many of the narratives women tell in conversation. She shows how narrative "kernels" serve as conversational resources for individual women and the group as a whole. How and if a "kernel story" is developed by the narrator and/or audience on a particular occasion is a function of the conversational context from which it emerges (Kalčik 1975:8), and it takes very different forms at different tellings. Not only is the dynamic of women's conversation one of elaboration and continuity, but the idiom of support can give it a distinctive tone as well. Hannerz (1969:96), for example, contrasts the "tone of relaxed sweetness, sometimes bordering on the saccharine," that characterizes approving talk between women, to the heated argument found among men. Kalčik (1975:6) even goes so far as to suggest that there is an "underlying esthetic or organizing principle" of "harmony" being expressed in women's friendly talk.

MEN'S SPEECH

The speaking patterns of men, and of women for that matter, vary greatly from one North American subculture to another. As Gerry Philipsen (1975:13) summarizes it, "talk is not everywhere valued equally; nor is it anywhere valued equally in all social contexts." There are striking cultural variations between subcultures in whether men consider certain modes of speech appropriate for dealing with women, children, authority figures, or strangers; there are differences in performance rules for storytelling and joke telling; there are differences in the context of men's speech; and there are differences in the rules for distinguishing aggressive joking from true aggression.

But more surprising than these differences are the apparent similarities across subcultures in the patterns of friendly interaction between men and the resemblances between these patterns and those observed for boys. Research reports on the speaking patterns of men among urban blacks (Abrahams 1976; Hannerz 1969), rural Newfoundlanders (Faris 1966; Bauman 1972), and urban blue-collar whites (Philipsen 1975; LeMasters 1975) point again and again to the same three features: storytelling, arguing and verbal posturing.

Narratives such as jokes and stories are highly valued, especially when they are well performed for an audience. In Newfoundland, for example, Faris (1966:242) comments that "the reason 'news' is rarely passed between two men meeting in the road—it is simply not to one's advantage to relay information to such a small audience." Loud and aggressive argument is a second common feature of male–male speech. Such arguments, which may include shouting, wagering, name-calling, and verbal threats (Faris 1966:245), are often, as Hannerz (1969:86) describes them, "debates over minor questions of little direct import to anyone," enjoyed for their own sake and not taken as signs of real conflict. Practical jokes, challenges, put-downs, insults, and other forms of verbal aggression are a third feature of men's speech, accepted as normal among friends. LeMasters (1975:140), for example, describes life in a working-class tavern in the Midwest as follows:

> It seems clear that status at the Oasis is related to the ability to "dish it out" in the rapid-fire exchange called "joshing": you have to have a quick retort, and preferably one that puts you "one up" on your opponent. People who can't compete in the game lose status.

Thus challenges rather than statements of support are a typical way for men to respond to the speech of other men.

WHAT IS HAPPENING IN CROSS-SEX CONVERSATION

What we are suggesting is that women and men have different cultural rules for friendly conversation and that these rules come into conflict when women and men attempt to talk to each other as friends and equals in casual conversation. We can think of at least five areas, in addition to that of minimal responses already discussed, in which men and women probably possess different conversational rules, so that miscommunication is likely to occur in cross-sex interaction.

1. There are two interpretations of the meaning of questions. Women seem to see questions as a part of conversational maintenance, while men seem to view them primarily as requests for information.

2. There are two conventions for beginning an utterance and linking it to the preceding utterance. Women's rules seem to call for an explicit acknowledgment of what has been said and making a connection to it. Men seem to have no such rule and in fact some male strategies call for ignoring the preceding comments.

3. There are different interpretations of displays of verbal aggressiveness. Women seem to interpret overt aggressiveness as personally directed, negative, and disruptive. Men seem to view it as one conventional organizing structure for conversational flow.

4. There are two understandings of topic flow and topic shift. The literature on storytelling in particular seems to indicate that men operate with a system in which topic is fairly narrowly defined and adhered to until finished and in which shifts between topics are abrupt, while women have a system in which topic is developed progressively and shifts gradually. These two systems imply very different rules for and interpretations of side comments, with major potential for miscommunication.

5. There appear to be two different attitudes towards problem sharing and advice giving. Women tend to discuss problems with one another, sharing experiences and offering reassurances. Men, in contrast, tend to hear women, and other men, who present them with problems as making explicit requests for solutions. They respond by giving advice, by acting as experts, lecturing to their audiences.[4]

CONCLUSIONS

Our purpose in this paper has been to present a framework for thinking about and tying together a number of strands in the analysis of differences between male and female conversational styles. We hope to prove the intellectual value of this framework by demonstrating its ability to do two things: to serve as a model both of and for sociolinguistic research.

As a model *of* past research findings, the power of our approach lies in its ability to suggest new explanations of previous findings on cross-sex communication while linking these findings to a wide range of other fields, including the study of language acquisition, of play, of friendship, of storytelling, of cross-cultural miscommunication, and of discourse analysis. Differences in the social interaction patterns of boys and girls appear to be widely known but rarely utilized in examinations of sociolinguistic acquisition or in explanations of observed gender differences in patterns of adult speech. Our proposed framework should serve to link together these and other known facts in new ways.

As a model *for* future research, we hope our framework will be even more promising. It suggests to us a number of potential research problems which remain to be investigated. Sociolinguistic studies of school-age children, especially studies of the use of speech in informal peer interaction, appear to be much rarer than studies of young children, although such studies may be of greater relevance for the understanding of adult patterns, particularly those related to gender. Our framework also suggests the need for many more studies of single-sex conversations among adults, trying to make more explicit some of the differences in conversational rules suggested by present research. Finally, the argument we have been making suggests a number of specific problems that appear to be highly promising lines for future research:

1. A study of the sociolinguistic socialization of 'tomboys' to see how they combine male and female patterns of speech and interaction;

2. An examination of the conversational patterns of lesbians and gay men to see how these relate to the sex-related patterns of the dominant culture;

3. An examination of the conversational patterns of the elderly to see to what extent speech differences persist after power differences have become insignificant;

4. A study of children's cultural concepts for talking about speech and the ways these shape the acquisition of speech styles (for example, how does the concept of 'bossiness' define a form of behavior which little girls must learn to recognize, then censure, and finally avoid?);

5. An examination of 'assertiveness training' programs for women to see whether they are really teaching women the speaking skills that politically skillful men learn in boyhood or are merely teaching women how to act like bossy little girls or bullying little boys and not feel guilty about it.

We conclude this paper by reemphasizing three of the major ways in which we feel that an anthropological perspective on culture and social organization can prove useful for further research on differences between men's and women's speech.

First, an anthropological approach to culture and cultural rules forces us to reexamine the way we interpret what is going on in conversations. The rules for interpreting conversations are, after all, culturally determined. There may be more than one way of understanding what is happening in a particular conversation and we must be careful about the rules we use for interpreting cross-sex conversations, in which the two participants may not fully share their rules of conversational inference.

Second, a concern with the relation between cultural rules and their social contexts leads us to think seriously about differences in different kinds of talk, ways of categorizing interactional situations, and ways in which conversational patterns may function as strategies for dealing with specific aspects of one's social world. Different types of interaction lead to different ways of speaking. The rules for friendly conversation between equals are different from those for service encounters, for flirting, for teaching, or for polite formal interaction. And even within the apparently uniform domain of friendly interaction, we argue that there are systematic differences between men and women in the way friendship is defined and thus in the conversational strategies that result.

Third and finally, our analysis suggests a different way of thinking about the connection between the gender-related behavior of children and that of adults. Most discussions of sex-role socialization have been based on the premise that gender differences are greatest for adults and that these adult differences are learned gradually throughout childhood. Our analysis, on the other hand, would suggest that at least some aspects of behavior are most strongly gender-differentiated during childhood and that adult patterns of friendly interaction, for example, involve learning to overcome at least partially some of the gender-specific cultural patterns typical of childhood.

NOTES

1. The analogy between the sociolinguistic processes of dialect divergence and genderlect divergence was pointed out to us by Ron Macaulay.

2. In the strict sense the term, 'dozens' refers to a culturally specific form of stylized argument through the exchange of insults that has been extensively documented by a variety of students of American black culture and is most frequently practiced by boys in their teens and pre-teens. Recently folklorist Simon Bronner (1978) has made a convincing case for the existence of a highly similar but independently derived form of insult exchange known as 'ranking,' 'mocks,' or 'cutting' among white American adolescents. What we find striking and worthy of note is the tendency for both black and white versions of the dozens to be practiced primarily by boys.

3. 'Catches' are a form of verbal play in which the main speaker ends up tricking a member of his or her audience into a vulnerable or ridiculous position. In an article on the folklore of black children in South Philadelphia, Roger Abrahams (1963) distinguishes between catches which are purely verbal and tricks in which the second player is forced into a position of being not only verbally but also physically abused as in the following example of a catch which is also a trick:

   A: Adam and Eve and Pinch-Me-Tight
      Went up the hill to spend the night.
      Adam and Eve came down the hill.
      Who was left?
   B: Pinch-Me-Tight
   [A pinches B]

   What is significant about both catches and tricks is that they allow for the expression of playful aggression and that they produce a temporary hierarchical relation between a winner and loser, but invite the loser to attempt to get revenge by responding with a counter-trick.

4. We thank Kitty Julien for first pointing out to us the tendency of male friends to give advice to women who are not necessarily seeking it and Niyi Akinnaso for pointing out that the sex difference among Yoruba speakers in Nigeria in the way people respond verbally to the problems of others is similar to that among English speakers in the U.S.

12

PROFILE OF AN ANTHROPOLOGIST

Living Abroad:
Cross-Cultural Training for Families

Lillian Trager

Travelers sometimes feel disoriented. People in another country eat different food, they speak different languages, and they do not have the same manners. On the one hand this makes international travel exciting; on the other hand it can make living abroad extraordinarily stressful. That stress, sometimes called culture shock, is regularly experienced by anthropological fieldworkers. Just as learning another language takes work and training, learning to live in another culture is a problem we should not take lightly.

It is a cliché to say that the world is shrinking, especially in the fields of business and commerce. In the future, many more families will experience living in another culture. Cross-cultural training for employees and their families, like the training described in this selection, can help in building bridges of communication that are in fact necessary for adapting to the small world (a global village) that we will inhabit in the next century.

As you read this selection, ask yourself the following questions:

☐ *How do linguistic and cultural isolation add to the difficulties of adapting to a new culture for the families of businesspeople?*

☐ *Why is it generally easier for an employee to move abroad than for his or her spouse?*

☐ *Is it easier for an American to move overseas than it is for a foreigner to move here?*

☐ *Do you think it makes good economic sense for companies to provide cross-cultural training for employees? How about for spouses and children?*

☐ *How would an anthropological approach to cross-cultural training differ from more common programs? What are differences between short-term and long-term problems of adaptation to another culture?*

The following terms discussed in this selection are included in the Glossary at the back of the book:

culture shock
ethnocentrism
sex roles

Reproduced by permission of Society for Applied Anthropology from *Practicing Anthropology*, 9(3):5, 11, 1987.

A young Latin American woman accompanied her husband to an industrial community in Southern Wisconsin, where he was to work for a large multinational company for some months. The company helped them find a furnished apartment in a semi-suburban area of the city. Every day the husband left for work and his wife sat in the nearly bare apartment. She had not met other employees or their spouses, nor had she been able to meet others in the neighborhood. She spoke little English, and despite a sizeable Spanish-speaking population in the city, she had no basis for interaction with people in it. Not surprisingly, she was very unhappy and most anxious for her husband's assignment to end so that they could return home.

An Australian woman who had travelled widely and lived in a number of countries moved to Nigeria when her Scottish husband, an engineer, was sent there to supervise a road construction project. They settled in a sizeable provincial city, where they had a large house and several servants. As in the case of the Latin American woman, the husband went to work each day, leaving his wife in the house with essentially nothing to do except care for her two-year-old child. Despite the size of the city, there were few other European expatriates living there, and although much of the local population spoke at least some English, she had no basis for meeting people in the community. With servants, she was not even forced out to go shopping. When I met her, some two months after she had come to live in the city, she had interacted with no one except her husband, two-year-old child, and servants.

Despite the obvious differences in the situation of these two women, their cases are not unusual. When Americans go overseas to live, they often find themselves in situations where they feel isolated and alienated from the people around them. Non-Americans have similar experiences when they come to live in the United States; an English woman living in the same Wisconsin community as the Latin American complained bitterly about the difficulty of getting to know people in the city.

In the literature on intercultural interaction and cross-cultural training, it is the generally received wisdom that it is far easier for someone who is *working* in a new cultural setting than it is for family members who accompany him or her. The employee has a specific institutional context to deal with, and in many cases, especially in international business, that institutional context may not differ greatly from the one at home. Spouse and children, on the other hand, confront a range of new institutions, and do not always have ready-made settings in which to meet others. While most cases described, like those above, focus on the problems of women, and to some extent children, in fact the same types of difficulties are encountered by

the much smaller number of men who accompany their wives overseas.

Despite the recognition of the difficulties of living abroad, as opposed to working abroad, cross-cultural training programs place relatively little emphasis on this. As one consultant to international business explained to me, companies are concerned with the effective work performance of their employees and may be willing to train them to perform better, but they are not particularly anxious to spend money to prepare other family members. What can be done to assist people going abroad to live, and what role exists for anthropologists?

In the remainder of this article, I discuss several types of training activities that may be useful and briefly describe one program and the type of audience that seems to exist for such a program. Anthropologists may contribute significantly both through their knowledge of culture in general and through their in-depth knowledge of specific societies and cultures. However, there must be a willingness to translate that knowledge into terms and perspectives that will be valuable for non-anthropologists who wish to interact and communicate in new cultural contexts.

LEVELS OF TRAINING AND THE ROLES OF ANTHROPOLOGISTS

Programs to introduce people to issues in cross-cultural interaction and communication may operate at several levels. The most basic consists of assistance in coping with the practicalities of everyday living in a new environment—how to shop, how to find housing, how to deal with servants, types of schools, etc. This is the most commonly offered type of training. Many large multinational firms, for example, send employees and their spouses to short intensive courses which usually focus on the basics. Similarly, some consulting firms in American cities have set up programs for new arrivals, mainly the spouses of foreign executives. For example, several firms in the New York City area assist with the day-to-day problems of settling in the U.S. With the exception of Overseas Briefing Associates, run by Alison Lanier, all focus on the immediate problems of arrival. While anthropologists could no doubt provide or participate in such training, there is nothing which would make this type of introductory material the special province of anthropologists.

On the other hand, the more successful, and I would argue more useful, type of cross-cultural training does very much depend on anthropological understanding. Beyond the most immediate basic needs, cross-cultural training programs at the next level include an introduction to the basic concepts necessary for understanding differences in communication and interaction patterns. These may be introduced as general issues that will be confronted by anyone going to live in a new cultural context, regardless of the specific society. The overall goal is to help make people aware of cultural differences and of how such differences affect communication and interaction patterns.

Topics considered in such training include ethnocentrism, culture shock, nonverbal communication patterns, and value differences in such basic areas as friendship and sex roles. Implicit in this is increased understanding of one's own culture. In other words, cross-cultural training of this type tries to make explicit the things one does "naturally" and to provide a basis for understanding that such patterns are not necessarily natural for people elsewhere. The result is that people are led to expect that there will be differences and are given pointers for helping to understand and interpret those different behaviors when they are confronted.

What I have just described may sound much like the first part of a standard cultural anthropology course, and to some extent it is, but most such courses do not focus on understanding cultural differences as a basis for interaction between individuals from different cultural backgrounds. Anthropologists have specific expertise that provides the basis for anthropological concepts which are used, and often taken out of context, by those who organize such programs. Thus, "culture shock" is dealt with as an essentially psychological process with a predictable time-span and set of reactions: during the first few weeks you will feel elated; by the second month you will be depressed; and then you will settle down and adjust. The more important issue that culture shock is a result of being without cultural cues, and that over time one may learn new cues, is much less emphasized in much of the cross-cultural training currently taking place.

The third level for cross-cultural training provides detail on a specific culture and society and focuses especially on the issues of long-term adjustment and integration. It is usually after the initial settling-in takes place that family members have the greatest difficulties. The problem, as expressed both by Americans who have lived overseas in a variety of circumstances and by those who have come to the U.S. to live for several years, seems to be one of "meeting people" outside of very narrow confines. For example, wives of business executives overseas note the difficulty of meeting people outside of their husband's company and of learning about society beyond the "golden ghetto."

Anthropologists with knowledge of a specific society can help prepare people for interacting with people there, not only by providing information on cultural practices but also by helping point out ways in which they can learn further about the society and culture on their own. The most successful long-term adjustment seems to be that of individuals who develop a specific interest in some aspect of the culture and use that as a basis for both learning about the society and for meeting people. For example, the wife of an American academic on sabbatical in Sweden decided she wanted to learn Swedish folk fiddling, while the wife of a U.N. employee in Thailand became an expert on Thai temples. An anthropologist doing such training cannot tell people what to explore, but can help them to know of the possibilities in a particular cultural context. In doing such in-depth training, anthropologists need to be willing to translate their own knowledge into new terms and perspectives and particularly to examine issues of interaction, rather than simply provide information on the culture. Often, the best resources to aid in this area are not standard ethnographies. For example, in Nigeria a useful introduction for non-Nigerians is a humorous book written some years ago by Nigerian journalist Peter Enahoro, *How to Be a Nigerian*.

LIVING ABROAD: A WORKSHOP AND A COURSE

My first foray into cross-cultural training for families going overseas resulted from discussions and interviews with wives of foreign executives in Racine, Wisconsin. In 1978 I organized a three-session workshop through the university and focused it specifically on the problems faced by families. I drew on resource people in the area, including people who had themselves lived overseas, and began to develop my own materials as well as to explore those materials that were commercially available (e.g. from the Experiment in International Living and SIETAR). The resulting workshop convinced me that there was a need and an audience, but some time elapsed before I was able to pursue the idea further. In subsequent workshops some years later, jointly organized with Dick Ammann and Wendy Leeds-Hurwitz, we did not focus specifically on families overseas, but rather concentrated on general cross-cultural training first for a broad audience, and secondly for educators and businesspeople.

In the meantime, I designed and introduced a for-credit evening course, entitled "Living Abroad." This, like the first workshop, was primarily concerned with issues confronting families, as well as individuals, who for whatever reason are planning to live in a cultural environment different from their own. The clientele for this course has included businesspeople and their wives as well as others with interest in travel and living overseas. About half of the students have been full-time undergraduates while others have been community residents.

Whereas the workshops have concentrated on general issues, using role playing, simulations, and other exercises, in the course it has been possible to examine specific cultures. Students have been asked to focus on a specific society and to try to explore cultural patterns that an American living in that society would have to deal with. The results have been mixed, as it is frequently difficult for students to find appropriate materials. However, students get an opportunity to explore some of the ways in which cultural differences may affect interaction patterns. In some cases, they have also been able to meet with and interview foreign students from the societies they are studying, and to discuss with them problems they have had learning about American society and culture.

In summary, cross-cultural training for people planning to live in a society different from their own can be valuable, especially if it moves beyond the basics of the initial settling-in problems to consider issues in cross-cultural communication and interaction and, beyond that, to a consideration of specific cultural patterns. Although there is a considerable amount of cross-cultural training now taking place, especially for business executives, there is room for anthropologists to play a more prominent role in designing and conducting such training.

13

Ancient Genes and Modern Health

S. Boyd Eaton and Melvin Konner

The best available evidence about prehistory is that early humans were scavengers and gatherers of wild plants, not mighty hunters. This idea might at first seem far removed from the daily worries of people in complex societies like the United States. What do the food-getting methods of prehistoric people have to do with us and our world?

Two points are relevant here. First, anthropologists believe that food-getting and food-producing systems have been important factors in historical change (see Selection 16, "The Worst Mistake in the History of the Human Race"). Second, a major problem confronting Western society has been the rise in particular chronic illnesses—sometimes called the diseases of civilization—that ultimately kill most Americans. In this article, Boyd Eaton and Melvin Konner demonstrate how information from paleoanthropology and the study of contemporary hunters and gatherers can shed new light on the origins of some present-day health problems.

As you read this selection, ask yourself the following questions:

☐ What is the difference between biological and cultural evolution?

☐ Do biological and cultural evolution advance at the same rate? If not, what sorts of things might happen as cultural changes occur faster than biological changes?

☐ What was the diet of our Paleolithic ancestors?

☐ What sort of nutritional changes accompanied the development of agriculture?

☐ What sort of illnesses are found in the West but not among hunters and gatherers?

☐ In addition to diet, what other lifestyle differences are related to chronic illness in the Western world?

The following terms discussed in this selection are included in the Glossary at the back of the book:

Cro-magnon
cultural evolution
epidemiology
foraging
hunter-gatherers
Paleolithic
Paleontology

For the past ten years we have been investigating the proposition that the major chronic illnesses which afflict humans living in affluent industrialized Western nations are promoted by a mismatch between our ge-

"Diet: Paleolithic Genes and Twentieth Century Health." S. Boyd Eaton and Melvin Konner, *Anthroquest*, 1985. Reprinted by permission of the L.S.B. Leakey Foundation.

netic constitution and a variety of lifestyle factors which have bioenvironmental relevance. The diseases include atherosclerosis with its sequels of heart attacks, strokes and peripheral vascular disease; adult-onset diabetes; many important forms of cancer; hypertension (high blood pressure); emphysema; and obesity. The main lifestyle variables are diet, exercise patterns and exposure to abusive substances—chiefly alcohol and tobacco. We have taken the basic position that the genetic constitution of humanity, which controls our physiology, biochemistry and metabolism, has not been altered in any fundamental way since *Homo sapiens sapiens* first became widespread. In contrast, cultural evolution during the relatively brief period since the appearance of agriculture has been breathtakingly rapid, so that genes selected over the preceding geologic eras must now function in a foreign and, in many ways, hostile Atomic Age milieu.

In order to better understand our current lifestyle/genetic discord and to appreciate what steps might be taken to eliminate its harmful etiologic consequences, we needed to determine, as best we could, the actual constituents of our ancestral lifestyle. For most people speculation about our Stone Age ancestors exerts a strong fascination: How did they live, what did they look like, how did they differ from us and how were they similar? For us, the effort to characterize their nutritional practices and the exercise patterns necessitated by their daily activities has been exciting as well as scientifically rewarding. The bulk of our understanding has come from the fields of paleontology, anthropology, epidemiology and nutritional science.

Paleontology is the study of fossil remains. For example, the stature of Paleolithic humans can be estimated from the length of femora (thigh bones) according to a formula which relates total height to femoral length; it is not necessary to have all the bony components of a skeleton to make this determination. Such studies have shown that humans living in the eastern Mediterranean area 30,000 years ago were probably tall; males averaged 177.1 cm (5′9¾″) and females 166.5 cm (5′5½″), whereas in 1960 Americans averaged 174.2 cm (5′8½″) and 163.4 cm (5′4½″) respectively.

Skeletal height and pelvic depth both probably reflect nutritional factors, especially protein intake. With the advent of agriculture, animal protein intake decreased markedly so that average stature for both men and women ultimately declined by over 10 centimeters. The same phenomenon, a decrease in the animal protein content of the diet around the time that agriculture first appeared, is also documented by analysis of strontium/calcium ratios in bony remains. Strontium reaches the skeletons of living animals mainly through ingestion of plant foods so that herbivores have higher strontium levels in their bones than do carnivores. Studies of strontium/calcium ratios in the bones of humans who lived just before and during the changeover to agriculture confirm that the consumption of meat declined relative to that of vegetable foods around this period.

Skeletons also indicate muscularity; the prominence of muscular insertion sites and the area of articular surfaces both vary directly with the forces exerted by the muscles acting on them. Analyses of these features show that average preagricultural humans were apparently generally stronger than those who lived thereafter, including us today. Because of their hardness, teeth are very well represented in paleontological material. It is a telling comment about our current consumption of sugar (which approaches 125 lbs per person per year in the United States) that only about two percent of teeth from the Late Paleolithic period exhibit dental caries whereas some recent European populations have had more than 70 percent of their teeth so affected.

Anthropology is a broad discipline which includes the study of recent hunter-gatherers whose lives can be considered to mirror those of our remote ancestors in many ways. Of course, there are important differences: Such people have been increasingly forced from the most environmentally desirable areas into desert, arctic or jungle habitats where the food quest must be far more difficult than it was for Paleolithic hunter-gatherers who exploited the most abundant and fruitful regions then available without competition from encroaching civilization. On the other hand, the technology of recent foragers is more advanced than that available to those living 25,000 years ago; an excellent example is the bow and arrow, perhaps developed no earlier than 10 to 15 thousand years ago. Nevertheless, study of recent hunter-gatherers does provide a kind of window into the Stone Age world; the nutrition, physical attributes and health of individuals who have such parallel lives must be reasonably similar despite the millennia which separate them in time.

Anthropologists have studied over 50 hunter-gatherer societies sufficiently well to justify nutritional generalizations about them. When data from these groups are analyzed statistically, the average values all center around a subsistence pattern of 35 percent meat and 65 percent vegetable foods (by weight). There is, of course, considerable variation; arctic peoples may eat up to 90 percent animal products, whereas arid desert dwellers may obtain only 15 percent of their diet from such sources. Nevertheless, these data allow us to reasonably conclude that Paleolithic humans had a roughly similar range of subsistence patterns.

Epidemiology is the study of disease patterns. When a pathologic condition, such as lung cancer, is common in a specified population, for example, cigarette smokers, and uncommon in another specified group, such as nonsmokers, differences between the two groups may bear on the etiology of the disease condition under scrutiny. Information derived from various epidemiologic investigations can be used to help estimate what sorts of diseases might have afflicted Paleolithic humans and which ones must have been uncommon. For example, in today's world, people who consume a minimal amount of saturated fat tend to have little coronary heart disease and a relatively low incidence of cancer involving the breast, uterus, prostate and colon. If we could be confident that the Stone Age diet contained little saturated fat we could rationally assume that individuals living then had a lower incidence of heart disease and cancers related to fat intake than do persons living in affluent, industrialized Western nations today. Similar arguments might be made concerning hypertension (as related to dietary sodium, potassium and calcium) and, of course, lung cancer and emphysema (cigarettes). A tempting assumption is that, since illnesses of this sort tend to become manifest in older persons, Paleolithic humans (whose life expectancy was less than ours) would not have had the opportunity to develop them, no matter what their lifestyle. However, epidemiologists and pathologists have shown that young people in the Western world commonly have developing, asymptomatic forms of these illnesses, but hunter-gatherer youths do not. Furthermore, those members of technologically primitive cultures who survive to the age of 60 or more remain relatively free from these disorders, unlike their "civilized" counterparts.

Nutritional science furthers evaluation of Paleolithic life by providing analyses of the foods such people were likely to have eaten. An understanding of their overall nutrition is impossible without knowing that, although they ate more red meat than we do now, they nevertheless consumed much less saturated fat since wild game has less than a fifth the fat found in the domesticated animals currently bred and raised for meat production. Similarly, nutrition analyses of the wild, uncultivated fruits, vegetables and nuts eaten by recent hunter-gatherers allow us to estimate the average nutritional values of the plant foods our ancestors ate. To this end we have been able to accumulate nutritional data characterizing 43 different wild animals ranging from kangaroos to wart hogs and 153 different wild vegetable foods—mainly roots, beans, nuts, tubers and fruit but including items as diverse as truffles and seed pods. The search for this information has been challenging but entertaining; how else would one learn that bison meat contains only 40 mg of cholesterol per 100 grams of tissue or that the Australian green plum has the world's highest known vitamin C content (3150 mg per 100 grams)!

When information from these disparate scientific disciplines is correlated and coordinated, what is the picture that emerges? What was the diet of our ancestors; what are other important ways in which their lifestyle differs from ours; and do these differences have any relationship to the chronic illnesses from which we suffer, but from which recent hunter-gatherers seem immune?

To address the most straightforward, but certainly not unimportant, issues first, it is clear that our Stone Age ancestors were rarely if ever exposed to tobacco and alcohol. The manufacture of barley beer can be dated as early as 7000 years ago, but there is no convincing evidence for consumption of alcohol before this time and recent technologically primitive groups have not been found to manufacture alcoholic beverages. Similarly, there is no indication that tobacco was available in Eurasia prior to the voyages of discovery only 500 years ago. But Late Paleolithic peoples were probably not altogether free from abusive substances; several recent hunter-gatherer groups have used some form of consciousness-altering drugs for ceremonial purposes and it seems likely that similar agents may have been available in the Late Stone Age although their use could hardly have been as prevalent as is currently the case.

The physical demands of life in the Late Paleolithic period insured that our ancestors, both men and women, were strong, fit, lean, and muscular. Their bones prove that they were robust—they resemble those of today's superior athletes. Furthermore, hunter-gatherers studied in the last 150 years have been trim and athletic in their appearance.

Modern nutritionists generally feel that items from four basic food groups—meat and fish, vegetables, nuts and fruits, milk and milk products, and breads and cereals—are necessary for a balanced diet. But during the Paleolithic period older children and adults derived all their nutrients from the first two groups: wild game and vegetables, fruits and nuts. Except for very young children, who were weaned much later than they are today, no one had any dairy foods at all and they apparently made comparatively little use of grain. Their only "refined" carbohydrate was honey, available only seasonally and obtained painfully. They seem to have eaten little seafood until fairly late in prehistory, though this assumption is questionable since the ancient sea level was much lower (because of water locked up in the extensive glaciers of that period) and the sites of Paleolithic seacoast dwellers are now under water.

After weaning, Paleolithic humans drank water, but the beverages we now consume generally deliver an appreciable caloric load as they quench our thirst. Mundane as it is, this example illustrates a pervasive pattern—caloric concentration. Since our meat is fattier, it contains more calories per unit weight (typically two to three times as many) than does wild game. Furthermore, the plant foods we eat are commonly refined and adulterated so that their basic caloric load is multiplied: french fries have more than twice and potato chips over five times the calories present in an equal weight of baked potato. Pumpkin pie has ten times the calories found in the same weight of pumpkin served alone.

The salt added to our foods as a seasoning and as a preservative insures that we now consume an average of six times the daily sodium intake of Paleolithic humans. In a similar vein, the process of refining carbohydrate foods provides us with quantities of sugar and white flour far in excess of what was available to our ancestors while reducing our complex carbohydrate (starch) and dietary fiber intake much below the levels they consumed. Not only do we eat twice the fat eaten by Stone Agers, its nature is different. Structural fat is a necessary constituent of cellular membranous structures; this type of fat is predominantly polyunsaturated in nature and was the major fat consumed by our remote ancestors. Conversely, depot or storage fat is the main type found in the adipose tissue stores of domesticated animals; this variety of fat is largely saturated and is very prominent in today's diets. Like game available now, the wild animals eaten 25,000 years ago had minimal depot fat; accordingly humans then ate considerably more polyunsaturated than saturated fat—but the reverse obtains in 20th century affluent Western nations.

To summarize, these observations indicate that the Cro-Magnons and similar Late Paleolithic peoples consumed nearly three times the amount of protein we do, about a sixth of the sodium, more potassium, more calcium (which is very interesting in view of the prevalence of osteoporosis in today's society), and considerably more vitamin C (though not the amounts megavitamin enthusiasts would recommend). They ate about the same amount of carbohydrate that we do; however, it was predominantly in the form of starch and other complex carbohydrates, providing a good deal more dietary fiber than we have in our diet. For them refined carbohydrate and simple sugar, from honey and fruit, were available only seasonally and in limited amounts. They ate only half the fat we consume in 20th century America and their fat was more polyunsaturated than saturated in nature.

Certain aspects of our ancestors' physical fitness bear further emphasis: Their "exercise program" was lifelong, it developed both endurance and strength, it applied to men and women alike, and the activities which comprised their "workouts" varied predictably with seasonal changes. Today's fitness enthusiasts might well ponder these Paleolithic training guidelines. Preagricultural humans were more like decathlon athletes than either marathoners or power lifters; our genes appear to have been programmed for

the synergism which results when endurance and strength occur together. A lifelong program was unavoidable for them; for us it requires strategic planning. Really long-term training in just one exercise mode is almost impossible to maintain; overtraining, boredom and burn-out tend to overcome even the most intense dedication. Paleolithic men and women were spared these phenomena because the activities of each season differed from those of the next. The Russians have perhaps unconsciously recreated these circumstances in a training approach they call "periodization." This system employs planned daily, weekly and quarterly variation in the mode, volume and intensity of exercise so that training remains fresh and invigorating, not dull and endlessly repetitive. Perhaps this recapitulation of our ancestral pattern partially explains the success their athletes have experienced in international competition.

What about the proposition we advanced at the beginning of this article: Do the diseases of civilization result from the mismatch between our genes and our current lifestyle? The evidence is strong that such a connection exists. In important respects the lifestyle of Paleolithic humans, that for which our genes have been selected, parallels recommendations made by the American Cancer Society, the American Heart Association, the American Diabetes Association and the Senate Select Committee on Nutrition. Furthermore, recent hunter-gatherers have been essentially free from the chronic illnesses which kill most Americans.

Anthropology, paleontology, medicine, epidemiology and nutrition can be likened to the facets of a prism, each providing a different view of the same subject. Our subject is the health and disease of persons living in affluent, industrialized Western society and when views provided by diverse scientific disciplines converge, the resulting implications acquire profound significance. There is nothing especially distinctive about human hunter-gatherers in biochemical and physiological terms. What they ate and how they lived fall well within the broad mammalian spectrum. During the past 10,000 years, however, humans have exceeded the bounds. Many of the lifestyle factors we now take for granted (particularly sedentary living, alcohol, tobacco and our high salt, high saturated fat, high refined carbohydrate diet) are unique in free-living vertebrate experience. They constitute a deviation so extreme that our bodies have responded by developing forms of illness not otherwise seen in nature. These are the diseases of civilization.

14

You Are What You Eat:
Religious Aspects of the Health Food Movement

Jill Dubisch

Food is a basic biological need, a fundamental ingredient for the survival of a group. The environment often determines what sorts of foods are available and also influences which foods are culturally preferred and which are prohibited. Culture, however, is the final arbiter of what is acceptable to eat. We eat cows but not horses. We eat pheasant but not the bald eagle, since the latter is a sacred symbol. We eat lettuce but avoid dandelion in our salads. We may find eating raw fish disgusting but don't mind cooking the unborn young of a dumb and helpless bird that doesn't know enough to hide its eggs.

Culture defines what is appropriate to eat, and, at the same time, what you eat may define your membership in a culture or subculture. What a family eats for breakfast or lunch often reflects its ethnic background or geographic location—bagels and lox, grits, or refried beans. Some people are conspicuous in their pronouncements of what they do or do not eat because this projects their self-image. In that very real sense, you are what you eat.

As you read this selection, ask yourself the following questions:

☐ *The author indicates that she is looking at food as a system of symbols expressing a world view. What does that mean?*

☐ *In what ways does the health food movement seem to you like a religion?*

☐ *The author notes a number of symbolic oppositions, like nature/culture and pure/impure. What are some of the other oppositions she mentions and what is their significance?*

☐ *How does what you eat (for example, wheat germ and honey) communicate membership in the movement?*

☐ *How might understanding the dynamics of health food beliefs be helpful in improving public health by reducing tobacco, alcohol, or crack consumption?*

The following terms discussed in this selection are included in the Glossary at the back of the book:

mana
taboo
world view

Dr. Robbins was thinking how it might be interesting to make a film from Adelle Davis' perennial best seller, *Let's Eat Right to Keep Fit*. Representing a classic confrontation between good and evil—in this case nutrition versus unhealthy diet—the story had definite box office appeal. The role of the hero, Protein, probably should be filled by Jim Brown, although Burt Reynolds undoubtedly would pull strings to get the part. Sunny Doris Day would be a clear choice to play the heroine, Vitamin C, and Orson Welles, oozing saturated fatty acids from the pits of his flesh, could win an Oscar for his interpretation of the villainous Cholesterol. The film might begin on a stormy night in the central nervous system. . . .

—Tom Robbins, *Even Cowgirls Get the Blues*

Reprinted by permission of the author.

I intend to examine a certain way of eating; that which is characteristic of the health food movement, and try to determine what people are communicating when they choose to eat in ways which run counter to the dominant patterns of food consumption in our society. This requires looking at health foods as a system of symbols and the adherence to a health food way of life as being, in part, the expression of belief in a particular world view. Analysis of these symbols and the under-laying world view reveals that, as a system of beliefs and practices, the health food movement has some of the characteristics of a religion.

Such an interpretation might at first seem strange since we usually think of religion in terms of a belief in a deity or other supernatural beings. These notions, for the most part, are lacking in the health food move-ment. However, anthropologists do not always con-sider such beliefs to be a necessary part of a religion. Clifford Geertz, for example, suggests the following broad definition:

> A religion is (1) a system of symbols which acts to (2) es-tablish powerful, pervasive, and long-lasting moods and motivations in men by (3) formulating conceptions of a general-order of existence and (4) clothing these con-ceptions with such an aura of factuality that (5) the moods and motivations seem uniquely realistic. (Geertz 1965:4)

Let us examine the health food movement in the light of Geertz's definition.

HISTORY OF THE HEALTH FOOD MOVEMENT

The concept of "health foods" can be traced back to the 1830s and the Popular Health movement, which com-bined a reaction against professional medicine and an emphasis on lay knowledge and health care with broader social concerns such as feminism and the class struggle (see Ehrenreich and English 1979). The Popu-lar Health movement emphasized self-healing and the dissemination of knowledge about the body and health to laymen. One of the early founders of the movement, Sylvester Graham (who gave us the graham cracker), preached that good health was to be found in temper-ate living. This included abstinence from alcohol, a vegetarian diet, consumption of whole wheat prod-ucts, and regular exercise. The writings and preachings of these early "hygienists" (as they called themselves) often had moral overtones, depicting physiological and spiritual reform as going hand in hand (Shryock 1966).

The idea that proper diet can contribute to good health has continued into the twentieth century. The discovery of vitamins provided for many health food people a further "natural" means of healing which could be utilized instead of drugs. Vitamins were pro-moted as health-giving substances by various writers, including nutritionist Adelle Davis, who has been per-haps the most important "guru" of health foods in this century. Davis preached good diet as well as the use of vitamins to restore and maintain health, and her books have become the best sellers of the movement. (The ti-tles of her books, *Let's Cook It Right*, *Let's Get Well*, *Let's Have Healthy Children*, give some sense of her ap-proach.) The health food movement took on its present form, however, during the late 1960s, when it became part of the "counterculture."

Health foods were "in," and their consumption be-came part of the general protest against the "establish-ment" and the "straight" life-style. They were associ-ated with other movements centering around social concerns, such as ecology and consumerism (Kandel and Pelto 1980:328). In contrast to the Popular Health movement, health food advocates of the sixties saw the establishment as not only the medical profession but also the food industry and the society it represented. Food had become highly processed and laden with col-orings, preservatives, and other additives so that pu-rity of food became a new issue. Chemicals had also be-come part of the food-growing process, and in reaction terms such as "organic" and "natural" became watch-words of the movement. Health food consumption re-ceived a further impetus from revelations about the high sugar content of many popular breakfast cereals which Americans had been taught since childhood to think of as a nutritious way to start the day. (Kellogg, an early advocate of the Popular Health movement, would have been mortified, since his cereals were orig-inally designed to be part of a hygienic regimen.)

Although some health food users are members of formal groups (such as the Natural Hygiene Society, which claims direct descent from Sylvester Graham), the movement exists primarily as a set of principles and practices rather than as an organization. For those not part of organized groups, these principles and practices are disseminated, and contact is made with other members of the movement, through several means. The most important of these are health food stores, restaurants, and publications. The two most prominent journals in the movement are *Prevention* and *Let's Live*, begun in 1920 and 1932 respectively (Hongladarom 1976).

These journals tell people what foods to eat and how to prepare them. They offer advice about the use of vitamins, the importance of exercise, and the danger of pollutants. They also present testimonials from faithful practitioners. Such testimonials take the form of articles that recount how the author overcame a physical problem through a health food approach, or letters from readers who tell how they have cured their ailments by following methods advocated by the journal or suggested by friends in the movement. In this manner, such magazines not only educate, they also articulate a world view and provide evidence and support for it. They have become the "sacred writings" of the movement. They are a way of "reciting the code"—the cosmology and moral injunctions—which anthropologist Anthony F. C. Wallace describes as one of the important categories of religious behavior (1966:57).

IDEOLOGICAL CONTENT OF THE HEALTH FOOD MOVEMENT

What exactly is the health food system? First, and most obviously, it centers around certain beliefs regarding the relationship of diet to health. Health foods are seen as an "alternative" healing system, one which people turn to out of their dissatisfaction with conventional medicine (see, for example, Hongladarom 1976). The emphasis is on "wellness" and prevention rather than on illness and curing. Judging from letters and articles found in health food publications, many individuals' initial adherence to the movement is a type of conversion. A specific medical problem, or a general dissatisfaction with the state of their health, leads these converts to an eventual realization of the "truth" as represented by the health food approach, and to a subsequent change in life-style to reflect the principles of that approach. "Why This Psychiatrist 'Switched,'" published in *Prevention* (September 1976), carries the following heading: "Dr. H. L. Newbold is a great advocate of better nutrition and a livelier life style. But it took a personal illness to make him see the light." For those who have experienced such conversion, and for others who become convinced by reading about such experiences, health food publications serve an important function by reinforcing the conversion and encouraging a change of life-style. For example, an article entitled "How to Convert Your Kitchen for the New Age of Nutrition" (*Prevention*, February 1975) tells the housewife how to make her kitchen a source of health for her family. The article suggests ways of reorganizing kitchen supplies and reforming cooking by substituting health foods for substances detrimental to health, and also offers ideas on the preparation of nutritious and delicious meals which will convert the family to this new way of eating without "alienating" them. The pamphlet *The Junk Food Withdrawal Manual* (Kline 1978), details how an individual can, step by step, quit eating junk foods and adopt more healthful eating habits. Publications also urge the readers to convert others by letting them know how much better health foods are than junk foods. Proselytizing may

take the form of giving a "natural" birthday party for one's children and their friends, encouraging schools to substitute fruit and nuts for junk food snacks, and even selling one's own baking.

Undergoing the conversion process means learning and accepting the general features of the health food world view. To begin with, there is great concern, as there is in many religions, with purity, in this case, the purity of food, of water, of air. In fact, there are some striking similarities between keeping a "health food kitchen" and the Jewish practice of keeping kosher. Both make distinctions between proper and improper foods, and both involve excluding certain impure foods (whether unhealthful or non-kosher) from the kitchen and table. In addition, a person concerned with maintaining a high degree of purity in food may engage in similar behavior in either case—reading labels carefully to check for impermissible ingredients and even purchasing food from special establishments to guarantee ritual purity.

In the health food movement, the basis of purity is healthfulness and "naturalness." Some foods are considered to be natural and therefore healthier; this concept applies not only to foods but to other aspects of life as well. It is part of the large idea that people should work in harmony with nature and not against it. In this respect, the health food cosmology sets up an opposition of nature (beneficial) versus culture (destructive), or, in particular, the health food movement against our highly technological society. As products of our industrialized way of life, certain foods are unnatural; they produce illness by working against the body. Consistent with this view is the idea that healing, like eating, should proceed in harmony with nature. The assumption is that the body, if allowed to function naturally, will tend to heal itself. Orthodox medicine, on the other hand, with its drugs and surgery and its non-holistic approach to health, works against the body. Physicians are frequently criticized in the literature of the movement for their narrow approach to medical problems, reliance on drugs and surgery, lack of knowledge of nutrition, and unwillingness to accept the validity of the patient's own experience in healing himself. It is believed that doctors may actually cause further health problems rather than effecting a cure. A short item in *Prevention*, "The Delivery Is Normal—But the Baby Isn't," recounts an incident in which drug-induced labor in childbirth resulted in a mentally retarded baby. The conclusion is "nature does a good job—and we should not, without compelling reasons, try to take over" (*Prevention*, May 1979:38).

The healing process is hastened by natural substances, such as healthful food, and by other "natural" therapeutic measures such as exercise. Vitamins are also very important to many health food people, both for maintaining health and for healing. They are seen as components of food which work with the body and are believed to offer a more natural mode of healing than drugs. Vitamins, often one of the most prominent products offered in many health food stores, provide the greatest source of profit (Hongladarom 1976).

A basic assumption of the movement is that certain foods are good for you while others are not. The practitioner of a health food way of life must learn to distinguish between two kinds of food: those which promote well-being ("health foods") and those which are believed to be detrimental to health ("junk foods"). The former are the only kind of food a person should consume, while the latter are the antithesis of all that food should be and must be avoided. The qualities of these foods may be described by two anthropological concepts, *mana* and *taboo*. Mana is a type of beneficial or valuable power which can pass to individuals from sacred objects through touch (or, in the case of health foods, by ingestion). Taboo, on the other hand, refers to power that is dangerous; objects which are taboo can injure those who touch them (Wallace 1966: 60–61). Not all foods fall clearly into one category or the other. However, those foods which are seen as having health-giving qualities, which contain *mana*, symbolize life, while *taboo* foods symbolize death. ("Junk food is . . . dead. . . . Dead food produces death," proclaims one health food manual [Kline 1978:2–4].) Much of the space in health food publications is devoted to telling the reader why to consume certain foods and avoid others ("Frozen, Creamed Spinach: Nutritional Disaster," *Prevention*, May 1979; "Let's Sprout Some Seeds," *Better Nutrition*, September 1979).

Those foods in the health food category which are deemed to possess an especially high level of *mana* have come to symbolize the movement as a whole. Foods such as honey, wheat germ, yogurt, and sprouts are seen as representative of the general way of life which health food adherents advocate, and Kandel and Pelto found that certain health food followers attribute mystical powers to the foods they consume. Raw food eaters speak of the "life energy" in uncooked foods. Sprout eaters speak of their food's "growth force" (1980:336).

Qualities such as color and texture are also important in determining health foods and may acquire symbolic value. "Wholeness" and "whole grain" have come to stand for healthfulness and have entered the jargon of the advertising industry. Raw, coarse, dark, crunchy, and cloudy foods are preferred over those which are cooked, refined, white, soft, and clear. (See chart.)

Thus dark bread is preferred over white, raw milk over pasteurized, brown rice over white. The convert must learn to eat foods which at first seem strange and even exotic and to reject many foods which are components of the Standard American diet. A McDonald's hamburger, for example, which is an important symbol of America itself (Kottack 1978), falls into the category of "junk food" and must be rejected.

Just as the magazines and books which articulate the principles of the health food movement and serve as a guide to the convert can be said to comprise the sacred writings of the movement, so the health food store or health food restaurant is the temple where the purity of the movement is guarded and maintained. There individuals find for sale the types of food and other substances advocated by the movement. One does not expect to find items of questionable purity, that is, substances which are not natural or which may be detrimental to health. Within the precincts of the temple adherents can feel safe from the contaminating forces of the larger society, can meet fellow devotees, and can be instructed by the guardians of the sacred area (see, for example, Hongladarom 1976). Health food stores may vary in their degree of purity. Some sell items such as coffee, raw sugar, or "natural" ice cream which are considered questionable by others of the faith. (One health food store I visited had a sign explaining that it did not sell vitamin supplements, which it considered to be "unnatural," i.e., impure.)

People in other places are often viewed as living more "naturally" and healthfully than contemporary Americans. Observation of such peoples may be used to confirm practices of the movement and to acquire ideas about food. Healthy and long-lived people like the Hunza of the Himalayas are studied to determine the secrets of their strength and longevity. Cultures as yet untainted by the food systems of industrialized nations are seen as examples of what better diet can do. In addition, certain foods from other cultures—foods such as humus, falafel, and tofu—have been adopted into the health food repertoire because of their presumed healthful qualities.

Peoples of other times can also serve as models for a more healthful way of life. There is in the health food movement a concept of a "golden age," a past which provides an authority for a better way of living. This past may be scrutinized for clues about how to improve contemporary American society. An archaeologist, writing for *Prevention* magazine, recounts how "I Put Myself on a Caveman Diet—Permanently" (*Prevention*, September 1979). His article explains how he improved his health by utilizing the regular exercise and simpler foods which he had concluded from his research were probably characteristic of our prehistoric ancestors. A general nostalgia about the past seems to exist in the health food movement, along with the feeling that we have departed from a more natural pattern of eating practiced by earlier generations of

Health Food World View

	Health Foods	Junk Foods	
cosmic *oppositions*	LIFE, NATURE	DEATH, CULTURE	
basic values and desirable attributes	holistic, organic harmony with body and nature natural and real harmony, self- sufficiency, independence homemade, small scale layman competence and understanding	fragmented, mechanistic working against body and nature manufactured and artificial disharmony, dependence mass-produced professional esoteric knowledge and jargon	undesirable attributes
beneficial qualities of food	whole coarse dark crunchy raw cloudy	processed refined white soft cooked clear	harmful qualities
specific foods with mana	yogurt* honey* carob soybeans* sprouts* fruit juices herb teas foods from other cultures: humus, falafel, kefir, tofu, stir-fried vegetables, pita bread	ice cream, candy sugar* chocolate beef overcooked vegetables soft drinks* coffee*, tea "all-American" foods: hot dogs, McDonald's hamburgers*, potato chips, Coke	specific taboo foods
	return to early American values, "real" American way of life	corruption of this original and better way of life and values	

*Denotes foods with especially potent mana or taboo.

Americans (see, for example, Hongladarom 1976). (Sylvester Graham, however, presumably did not find the eating habits of his contemporaries to be very admirable.)

The health food movement is concerned with more than the achievement of bodily health. Nutritional problems are often seen as being at the root of emotional, spiritual, and even social problems. An article entitled "Sugar Neurosis" states "Hypoglycemia (low blood sugar) is a medical reality that can trigger wife-beating, divorce, even suicide" (*Prevention*, April 1979: 110). Articles and books claim to show the reader how to overcome depression through vitamins and nutrition and the movement promises happiness and psychological well-being as well as physical health. Social problems, too, may respond to the health food approach. For example, a probation officer recounts how she tried changing offenders' diets in order to change their behavior. Testimonials from two of the individuals helped tell "what it was like to find that good nutrition was their bridge from the wrong side of the law and a frustrated, unhappy life to a vibrant and use-

ful one" (*Prevention*, May 1978:56). Thus, through more healthful eating and a more natural life-style, the health food movement offers its followers what many religions offer: salvation—in this case salvation for the body, for the psyche, and for society.

Individual effort is the keystone of the health food movement. An individual can take responsibility for his or her own health and does not need to rely on professional medical practitioners. The corollary of this is that it is a person's own behavior which may be the cause of ill health. By sinning, by not listening to our bodies, and by not following a natural way of life, we bring our ailments upon ourselves.

The health food movement also affirms the validity of each individual's experience. No two individuals are alike: needs for different vitamins vary widely; some people are more sensitive to food additives than others; each person has his or her best method of achieving happiness. Therefore, the generalized expertise of professionals and the scientifically verifiable findings of the experts may not be adequate guides for you, the individual, in the search of health. Each person's experience has meaning; if something works for you, then it works. If it works for others also, so much the better, but if it does not, that does not invalidate your own experience. While the movement does not by any means disdain all scientific findings (and indeed they are used extensively when they bolster health food positions), such findings are not seen as the only source of confirmation for the way of life which the health food movement advocates, and the scientific establishment itself tends to be suspect.

In line with its emphasis on individual responsibility for health, the movement seeks to deprofessionalize knowledge and place in every individual's hands the information and means to heal. Drugs used by doctors are usually available only through prescription, but foods and vitamins can be obtained by anyone. Books, magazines, and health food store personnel seek to educate their clientele in ways of healing themselves and maintaining their own health. Articles explain bodily processes, the effects of various substances on health, and the properties of foods and vitamins.

The focus on individual responsibility is frequently tied to a wider concern for self-sufficiency and self-reliance. Growing your own organic garden, grinding your own flour, or even, as one pamphlet suggests, raising your own cow are not simply ways that one can be assured of obtaining healthful food; they are also expressions of independence and self-reliance. Furthermore, such practices are seen as characteristic of an earlier "golden age" when people lived natural lives. For example, an advertisement for vitamins appearing in a digest distributed in health food stores shows a mother and daughter kneading bread together. The heading reads "America's discovering basics." The copy goes on, "Baking bread at home has been a basic family practice throughout history. The past several decades, however, have seen a shift in the American diet to factory-produced breads. . . . Fortunately, today there are signs that more and more Americans are discovering the advantage of baking bread themselves." Homemade bread, home-canned produce, sprouts growing on the window sill symbolize what are felt to be basic American values, values supposedly predominant in earlier times when people not only lived on self-sufficient farms and produced their own fresh and more natural food, but also stood firmly on their own two feet and took charge of their own lives. A reader writing to *Prevention* praises an article about a man who found "new life at ninety without lawyers or doctors," saying "If that isn't the optimum in the American way of living, I can't imagine what is!" (*Prevention*, May 1978:16). Thus although it criticizes the contemporary American way of life (and although some vegetarians turn to Eastern religions for guid-

ance—see Kandel and Pelto 1980), the health food movement in general claims to be the true faith, the proponent of basic American-ness, a faith from which the society as a whole has strayed.

SOCIAL SIGNIFICANCE OF THE HEALTH FOOD MOVEMENT FOR AMERICAN ACTORS

Being a "health food person" involves more than simply changing one's diet or utilizing an alternative medical system. Kandel and Pelto suggest that the health food movement derives much of its popularity from the fact that "food may be used simultaneously to cure or prevent illness, as a religious symbol and to forge social bonds. Frequently health food users are trying to improve their health, their lives, and sometimes the world as well" (1980:332). Use of health foods becomes an affirmation of certain values and a commitment to a certain world view. A person who becomes involved in the health food movement might be said to experience what anthropologist Anthony F. C. Wallace has called "mazeway resynthesis." The "mazeway" is the mental "map" or image of the world which each individual holds. It includes values, the environment and the objects in it, the image of the self and of others, the techniques one uses to manipulate the environment to achieve desired end states (Wallace 1966:237). Resynthesis of this mazeway—that is, the creation of new "maps," values, and techniques—commonly occurs in times of religious revitalization, when new religious movements are begun and converts to them are made. As individuals, these converts learn to view the world in a new manner and to act accordingly. In the case of the health food movement, those involved learn to see their health problems and other dissatisfactions with their lives as stemming from improper diet and living in disharmony with nature. They are provided with new values, new ways of viewing their environment, and new techniques for achieving their goals. For such individuals, health food use can come to imply "a major redefinition of self-image, role, and one's relationship to others" (Kandel and Pelto 1980:359). The world comes to "make sense" in the light of this new world view. Achievement of the desired end states of better health and an improved outlook on life through following the precepts of the movement gives further validation.

It is this process which gives the health food movement some of the overtones of a religion. As does any new faith, the movement criticizes the prevailing social values and institutions, in this case the health-threatening features of modern industrial society. While an individual's initial dissatisfaction with prevailing beliefs and practices may stem from experiences with the conventional medical system (for example, failure to find a solution to a health problem through visits to a physician), this dissatisfaction often comes to encompass other facets of the American way of life. This further differentiates the "health food person" from mainstream American society (even when the difference is justified as a return to "real" American values).

In everyday life the consumption of such substances as honey, yogurt, and wheat germ, which have come to symbolize the health food movement, does more than contribute to health. It also serves to represent commitment to the health food world view. Likewise, avoiding those substances, such as sugar and white bread, which are considered "evil" is also a mark of a health food person. Ridding the kitchen of such items—a move often advocated by articles advising readers on how to "convert" successfully to health foods—is an act of ritual as well as practical significance. The symbolic nature of such foods is confirmed by the reactions of outsiders to those who are perceived as being inside the movement. An individual who is perceived as being a health food person is often automatically assumed to use honey instead of sugar, for example. Conversely, if one is noticed using or not using certain foods (e.g., adding wheat germ to food, not eating white sugar), this can lead to questions from the observer as to whether or not that individual is a health food person (or a health food "nut," depending upon the questioner's own orientation).

The symbolic nature of such foods is especially important for the health food neophyte. The adoption of a certain way of eating and the renunciation of mainstream cultural food habits can constitute "bridge-burning acts of commitment" (Kandel and Pelto 1980:395), which function to cut the individual off from previous patterns of behavior. However, the symbolic activity which indicates this cutting off need not be as radical as a total change of eating habits. In an interview in *Prevention*, a man who runs a health-oriented television program recounted an incident in which a viewer called up after a show and announced excitedly that he had changed his whole life-style—he had started using honey in his coffee! (*Prevention*, February 1979:89). While recognizing the absurdity of the action on a practical level, the program's host acknowledged the symbolic importance of this action to the person involved. He also saw it as a step in the right direction since one change can lead to another. Those who sprinkle wheat germ on cereal, toss alfalfa sprouts with a salad, or pass up an ice cream cone for yogurt are not only demonstrating a concern for health but also affirming their commitment to a particular life-style and symbolizing adherence to a set of values and a world view.

CONCLUSION

As this analysis has shown, health foods are more than simply a way of eating and more than an alternative healing system. If we return to Clifford Geertz's definition of religion as a "system of symbols" which produces "powerful, pervasive, and long-lasting moods and motivations" by "formulating conceptions of a general-order of existence" and making them appear "uniquely realistic," we see that the health food movement definitely has a religious dimension. There is, first, a system of symbols, in this case based on certain kinds and qualities of food. While the foods are believed to have health-giving properties in themselves, they also symbolize a world view which is concerned with the right way to live one's life and the right way to construct a society. This "right way" is based on an approach to life which stresses harmony with nature and the holistic nature of the body. Consumption of those substances designated as "health foods," as well as participation in other activities associated with the movement which also symbolize its world view (such as exercising or growing an organic garden) can serve to establish the "moods and motivations" of which Geertz speaks. The committed health food follower may come to experience a sense of spiritual as well as physical well-being when he or she adheres to the health food way of life. Followers are thus motivated to persist in this way of life, and they come to see the world view of this movement as correct and "realistic."

In addition to its possession of sacred symbols and its "convincing" world view, the health food movement also has other elements which we usually associate with a religion. Concepts of mana and taboo guide the choice of foods. There is a distinction between the pure and impure and a concern for the maintenance of purity. There are "temples" (health food stores and other such establishments) which are expected to maintain purity within their confines. There are "rabbis," or experts in the "theology" of the movement and its application to everyday life. There are sacred and instructional writings which set out the principles of the movement and teach followers how to utilize them. In addition, like many religious movements, the health food movement harkens back to a "golden age" which it seeks to recreate and assumes that many of the ills of the contemporary world are caused by society's departure from this ideal state.

Individuals entering the movement, like individuals entering any religious movement, may undergo a process of conversion. This can be dramatic, resulting from the cure of an illness or the reversal of a previous state of poor health, or it can be gradual, a step-by-step changing of eating and other habits through exposure to health food doctrine. Individuals who have undergone conversion and mazeway resynthesis, as well as those who have tested and confirmed various aspects of the movement's prescriptions for better health and a better life, may give testimonials to the faith. For those who have adopted, in full or in part, the health food world view, it provides, as do all religions, explanations for existing conditions, answers to specific problems, and a means of gaining control over one's existence. Followers of the movement are also promised "salvation," not in the form of afterlife, but in terms of enhanced physical well being, greater energy, longer life-span, freedom from illness, and increased peace of mind. However, although the focus is this-worldly, there is a spiritual dimension to the health food movement. And although it does not center its world view around belief in supernatural beings, it does posit a higher authority—the wisdom of nature—as the source of ultimate legitimacy for its views.

Health food people are often dismissed as "nuts" or "food faddists" by those outside the movement. Such a designation fails to recognize the systematic nature of the health food world view, the symbolic significance of health foods, and the important functions which the movement performs for its followers. Health foods offer an alternative or supplement to conventional medical treatment, and a meaningful and effective way for individuals to bring about changes in lives which are perceived as unsatisfactory because of poor physical and emotional health. It can also provide for its followers a framework of meaning which transcends individual problems. In opposing itself to the predominant American life-style, the health food movement sets up a symbolic system which opposes harmony to disharmony, purity to pollution, nature to culture, and ultimately, as in many religions, life to death. Thus while foods are the beginning point and the most important symbols of the health food movement, food is not the ultimate focus but rather a means to an end: the organization of a meaningful world view and the construction of a satisfying life.

REFERENCES

Ehrenreich, Barbara, and Deidre English. 1979. *For Her Own Good: 150 Years of the Experts' Advice to Women*. Garden City, N.Y.: Anchor Press/Doubleday.

Geertz, Clifford. 1965. "Religion as a Cultural System." In Michael Banton, ed., *Anthropological Approaches to the Study of Religion*. A.S.A. Monograph No. 3. London: Tavistock Publications Ltd.

Hongladarom, Gail Chapman. 1976. "Health Seeking Within the Health Food Movement." Ph.D. Dissertation: University of Washington.

Kandel, Randy F., and Gretel H. Pelto. 1980. "The Health Food Movement: Social Revitalization or Alternative Health Maintenance System." In Norge W. Jerome, Randy F. Kandel, and Gretel H. Pelto, eds., *Nutritional Anthropology*. Pleasantville, N.Y.: Redgrave Publishing Co.

Kline, Monte. 1978. *The Junk Food Withdrawal Manual*. Total Life, Inc.

Kottak, Conrad. 1978. "McDonald's as Myth, Symbol, and Ritual." In *Anthropology: The Study of Human Diversity*. New York: Random House.

Shryock, Richard Harrison. 1966. *Medicine in America: Historical Essays*. Baltimore: Johns Hopkins University Press.

Wallace, Anthony F. C. 1966. *Religion: An Anthropological View*. New York: Random House.

15

Chinese Table Manners:
You Are *How* You Eat

Eugene Cooper

I had been looking forward to this dinner with an important client for over a week. We were going to close the biggest deal of my career. He arrived on time, and I ordered a bit of wine. It was a fancy restaurant and I was trying to behave appropriately; I tucked my napkin neatly on my lap and lifted my wine glass carefully with my little finger extended in the way I had always seen it done. But what began well, began to go awry. I looked on in horror as my client ladled a number of different dishes together into a soup bowl, lifted it to his mouth and began to shovel it in. I was so embarrassed by this display of bad manners that I hoped no one I knew would happen by. My face must have betrayed my thoughts, but my client did not let on. He simply asked if I was not enjoying my food since I had left the dishes flat on the table. This took me by surprise, because I realized for the first time that he was looking at me and finding my behavior odd. Our smiles became realizations and turned to laughter. Luckily, we had a good sense of humor about our ethnocentrism. Somebody should have warned us; this could have been a real disaster.

Consider yourself warned. Table manners, like a great many everyday events, are heavily laden with cultural meaning. Understanding culturally prescribed behaviors is of practical importance, not merely interesting. More anthropologists need to be involved in cross-cultural training for situations where there is likely to be interaction between people from different cultures or ethnic groups.

As you read this selection, ask yourself the following questions:

☐ How does one determine which culture's table manners are better? Why do we judge people by their manners?

☐ What are the important distinctions in Chinese food?

☐ Which food is the most basic and a necessary part of every Chinese meal? What about your own culture?

☐ What does it mean in China if you leave your rice bowl on the table while eating from it?

☐ What is the overriding rule of Chinese table customs?

☐ How do the Chinese feel about eating alone? Why?

The following terms discussed in this selection are included in the Glossary at the back of the book:
cultural values
ethnology
symbol

Reproduced by permission of Society for Applied Anthropology from *Human Organization*, 45(2):179–184, 1986.

"Etiquette of this kind (not putting half eaten meat back in the bowl, [not] wiping one's nose on one's sleeve) is not superficial, a matter for the surface rather than the depths; refined ways of acting are so internalized as to make alternative behavior truly 'disgusting,' 'revolting,' 'nauseous,' turning them into some of the most highly charged and deeply felt of intra-social differences, so that 'rustic' behavior is not merely quaint but barbarous" (Goody 1982:140).

"Probably no common practice is more diversified than the familiar one of eating in company, for what Europeans consider as correct and decent may by other races be looked upon as wrong or indelicate. Similarly, few social observances provide more opportunities for offending the stranger than the etiquette of the table" (Hammerton 1936:23).

Our shrinking world makes encounters with people of other cultures increasingly common in our life experiences. Whether in the conduct of business, in interactions with our "ethnic" neighbors, or as visitors to other countries, we are frequently called on to communicate with others whose assumptions about what constitutes appropriate behavior are widely different from our own.

In such contexts, it is often difficult to know whether habits and customs one takes for granted in one's own home may be creating unfavorable impressions in one's host's home. No less an authority than Confucius, writing more than two thousand years ago, was aware of the potential difficulties involved in intercultural communication, and provided the following advice: "When entering a country inquire of its customs. When crossing a border, inquire of the prohibitions" (Li Chi 1971:17).

Among such customs and prohibitions, those associated with behavior at the table can make an enormous difference in the way one is perceived by a foreign host.

As regards the Chinese in particular, the way one handles oneself at the table gives off signals of the clearest type as to what kind of a person one is, and it is all too easy to offend, as I hope to show. At the same time, however, it is easy enough to equip oneself with a few simple points to bear in mind that will not only pleasantly surprise one's Chinese host, but also convince him or her that one is a sensitive, cultivated, courteous, respectful, and considerate individual.

Surprisingly, for a civilization which has generated so many handbooks of its various cuisines, China has not produced any popular guidebooks for table manners of the Emily Post variety. The field, of course, has for the most part been preempted by the *Li Chi*—records of etiquette and ceremonial—most of which is said to date from the early Han. Indeed, many of the themes which characterize contemporary Chinese table manners are present in the minute descriptions of behaviors appropriate to people of various stations in all the gradations of Han social structure, such as the prescription to yield or defer. However, one is hard pressed to find a general rough and ready guide to contemporary Chinese table manners of anything more than the most superficial kind, usually present in popular Chinese cookbooks for Western audiences.

The absence of attention to table manners may be the result of the fact that table manners are among those habits most taken for granted—rules no grownup needs instruction in. A Chinese culinary enthusiast of my acquaintance assures me that table manners are not important in Chinese history, being far outweighed by the scarcity of food generally as the major issue. Nevertheless, an examination of Chinese table manners provides sufficient contrast with Western table habits in terms of structure and performance, as to make significant features of Chinese etiquette emerge in comparison—features taken for granted by the native.

Those few who have written on the subject (Chang 1977; Hsü and Hsü 1977) generally qualify as bicultural individuals with sufficient experience of both Chinese and Western rules to tease out the areas of contrastive significance. My five years of field research (and eating) in Hong Kong, and eight years of marriage to a Chinese woman who taught me Chinese table manners as to a child, also qualify me for the assignment, although my former European colleagues at the University of Hong Kong might question my credentials as an expert on Western etiquette, to be sure.

BASIC STRUCTURES AND PARAPHERNALIA

To begin with, it is useful to consider K. C. Chang's (1977) broad outline of the important distinctions in Chinese food between food (*shih*) and drink (*yin*), and then within the category food, between *fan* (grain/rice) and *ts'ai* (dishes). Chang establishes a hierarchy with grain as the base, vegetables and fruit as next least expendable, and meat as most expendable in the preparation of a meal. Fish would probably fall between vegetables and meat at least as far as contemporary Hong Kong is concerned, particularly if one includes the enormous variety of preserved fish available.

In any event, it is fair to say that a Chinese meal is not a meal without *fan*. The morning food event, at which rice is not normally taken, or if so is taken as gruel, is not thought of as a meal. When Chinese speak of a full day's eating fare, it is two square meals per day rather than three. Thus rice (or grain) defines a meal, and its treatment and consumption are circumscribed in a number of ways.

It will be helpful, however, to lay out the general paraphernalia with which the diner is equipped, and the structure in which it is deployed before returning to the rules governing rice. On this subject, Hsü and Hsü (1977:304) have written:

> The typical Chinese dining table is round or square, the *ts'ai* dishes are laid in the center, and each participant in the meal is equipped with a bowl for *fan*, a pair of chopsticks, a saucer, and a spoon. All at the table take from the *ts'ai* dishes as they proceed with the meal.

The *ts'ai* dishes are typically shared by all, and must be treated much as common property, whereas one's bowl is a private place which comes directly in touch with the mouth. The chopsticks are of both the mouth and the table, and mediate between. They are thin, and when employed appropriately only touch the one piece or small quantity a person touches first. Many Westerners find the habit of sharing from a common plate potentially unhygienic, and one might be tempted to dismiss this as a bit of ethnocentricity. However, the point has recently been made by no less an authority than Communist party secretary Hu Yaobang, who called attention to the unsanitary character of traditional Chinese eating habits and urged change.

One employs the chopsticks to take from the common plate and place food in one's bowl, then one raises the bowl to the mouth and pushes food into the mouth with the chopsticks. Hsü and Hsü state, "The diner who lets his *fan* bowl stay on the table and eats by picking up lumps of *fan* from the bowl is expressing disinterest in or dissatisfaction with the food. If he or she is a guest in someone's house, that is seen as an open insult to the host" (1977:304). Since one's bowl is a private place, "good manners do not preclude resting a piece of meat (or other items) in one's bowl between bites" (1977:304). However, one never puts a partially chewed piece of anything back into one of the common plates (I would not have thought this necessary to mention; however, an otherwise culturally sensitive person I know had the audacity to do so recently so it may bear mentioning.) Also, it is extremely poor manners to suck or bite your chopsticks.

In some cases the bowl may be substituted for by a spoon, as, for example, when one goes out to lunch with one's workmates, and each diner is supplied with a flat plate piled high with rice topped with roast pork, chicken, duck and/or *lap cheong* (Chinese sausage), or with a helping of a single *ts'ai* dish (the latter known as *hui fan*).

Eating rice off a flat plate with chopsticks alone is not an easy task. Westerners exasperated with the use of chopsticks often feel their most intense frustration when trying to accomplish this task, and are often re-

duced to picking up small bits of rice with the ends of their chopsticks and placing them in the mouth. Seeming to pick at one's food in this way is not good manners and marks one as an incompetent foreign devil, confirming in most Chinese minds all of their previous prejudices about *guailos*.

No self-respecting Chinese would attempt to eat rice directly from a flat plate without first piling the rice onto, or scooping the rice into, a spoon. One eats the *ts'ai* or meat with one's chopsticks, but rice is most often carried to the mouth in a spoon. The spoon stands in for the bowl in the mini-context of an individual serving, and one can also think of the bowl itself as serving in the capacity of an enlarged spoon in the context of regular dining as well.

Rice is usually doled out from a common pot by the host or hostess. When someone has filled your rice bowl for you, it is accepted with two hands. To accept rice with one hand suggests disinterest, disrespect, and carelessness. One places the full bowl in front of oneself and waits until everyone has been served. It is very impolite to begin eating before everyone at the table has had his bowl filled with rice. When one has finished the rice in one's bowl, one does not continue to eat of the common *ts'ai* dishes. To eat *ts'ai* without rice in one's bowl is to appear a glutton interested only in *ts'ai*, of which one must consume a great deal to get full without rice. Depending on the degree of intimacy of a relationship, one may, when eating at the home of a friend or acquaintance, rise from the table to refill one's bowl with rice from the rice pot in the kitchen. However, at formal occasions one's host will usually be alert enough to notice when one's rice bowl is empty and move to fill it before one might be forced to request more rice. When one rises to get more rice, the host will usually insist on taking one's bowl and filling it. One may decline such assistance if the host is a close friend by simply saying "I'll serve myself."

At banquets one is expected to fill up on *ts'ai*, and consumption of too much rice may be a sign of disrespect to the quality of the *ts'ai* dishes. No rice should ever be left over in one's bowl at the end of the meal.

> As children we were always taught to leave not a single grain of *fan* in our bowl when we finished. Our elders strongly impressed on us that each single grain of rice or corn was obtained through the drops of sweat of the tillers of the soil (Hsü and Hsü 1977:308).

A corollary of this rule is never to take so much rice, or anything else for that matter, in your bowl as to be unable to finish it. It is also extremely disrespectful of the meal and of one's host to leave bits of rice on the table around one's bowl, and Chinese children are often told that each of these grains will materialize as a pockmark on the face of their future spouse.

As regards the *ts'ai*, it is important to note again that it is arrayed for all to share. Generally speaking, especially on formal occasions, one does not serve oneself without first offering to others, at least those seated immediately to either side. This applies also to the taking of tea, and one generally fills a neighbor's cup before taking tea for oneself. When tea is poured for you, it is customary to tap the table with your fingers to convey your thanks.

The overriding rule of Chinese table customs is deference. Defer to others in everything. Be conscious of the need to share what is placed in common. This means don't eat only from those dishes that you like.

> One very common point of instruction from parents to children is that the best mannered person does not allow co-diners to be aware of what his or her favorite dishes are by his or her eating pattern (Hsü and Hsü 1977:304).

When taking from the common dishes one should also only take in such proportions that everyone else will be left with a roughly equivalent amount. It is polite to take the remains of a common *ts'ai* dish after a new dish has been brought out. The desirability of the remains is diminished by the introduction of a new dish, and the remains of the old become fair game. However, it is rather poor manners to incline a common plate toward oneself and scrape the remains into one's bowl. This "looking in the mirror" evokes the idea of narcissistic concern with oneself.

In general, young should defer to old in order of eating, and on formal occasions when guests are present children may even be excluded from the dining table until the adults are finished, or seated at a table separate from the adults. In the household of the boss of the factory where I did my fieldwork, apprentices commonly sat with the boss at the family table, but were relegated to the children's table at the New Year's feast.

A host will usually signal that it is appropriate to begin eating, after each person at the table has taken rice, by picking up his chopsticks and saying "*sik fan.*" When a guest has eaten his fill, he indicates that he is finished by putting down his chopsticks and encouraging others still eating to take their time. They in turn will inquire if the guest is full, and if he is he should say so. Upon finishing one may either remain at the table or leave. A guest of honor is expected to remain until all are finished.

In addition, one should be careful not to take large mouthfuls, to refrain from making noise while chewing, and to try to maintain the same pace of eating as others at the table. In contrast to Western etiquette in which "toothpicks are never used outside the privacy of one's room" (McLean 1941:63), toothpicks are provided at most Chinese tables and it is not impolite to give one's teeth a thorough picking at the table, provided one covers one's mouth with the opposite hand.

Spitting is not good manners at a Chinese table, although this is a rule often honored more in the breach. Spittoons are often provided in Chinese restaurants, both as a repository for waste water and tea used to sterilize one's utensils, and for expectorations of various sorts. Often the contents of the spittoons threaten to get up and walk away, so vile are the contents. The floor is fair game in many restaurants for just about anything remaining in one's mouth not swallowable, such as small bits of bone or gristle. Hong Kong has improved considerably in this regard in the recent years, but in working-class restaurants and *daipaidongs*, spitting is still quite common.

INFLECTIONS OF GENERAL PRINCIPLES

Having laid out these basic ground rules, it remains to explore how these rules are inflected in the various contexts in which food events occur in contemporary Hong Kong. These contexts are many and varied, ranging from informal and intimate occasions when the family is together at home for a meal, to the more formal occasions involving elaborate feasts usually held in restaurants. Somewhat intermediate between these are the meals eaten out, but in somewhat less formal contexts—from breakfast taken at *dim saam* houses, lunches taken at foodstalls with workmates, to evening meals prepared in restaurants for individual diners (*hak fan*), and midnight snacks. Expectations as to appropriate comportment at the table will also vary with region of origin, age, and class position.

For example, for Cantonese a full meal usually includes soup, and many Cantonese feel uncomfortable leaving the table without having partaken of soup. The minimal structure of the Cantonese meal includes not just *fan* (grain) and *ts'ai* (dishes), but also soup. This minimal structure is served up in what is known as *hak fan*, a specialty of some restaurants (usually Shanghainese) in which one may choose from a daily set menu of *hak* dishes, served with an extra large bowl of rice and the soup of the day. *Hak fan* is designed for people who must eat alone for some reason, not considered the most desirable circumstances. Two Chinese who knew each other would not sit down at the same table and order two individual dishes of *hak fan*. They would surely grasp the opportunity of sharing the greater variety available to each through social eating.

Jack Goody has likened eating alone to defecating in public (1982:306) because of the absence of the social in meeting essentially biological needs. *Hak fan* assures that even taken alone, the minimum structural entity of a Cantonese meal is available to be consumed. This basic structure is also revealed in a variety of thermos containers used for carrying lunch to work which are equipped with compartments for rice, *ts'ai* and soup. Since the contexts in which food events occur in Hong Kong are so varied, soup is not always the focus of attention. Proceeding through the ordinary day's food events from morning to evening will give us occasion to note context-linked inflections of our general principles.

As mentioned previously, the morning food event does not pass muster as a meal, largely due to the absence of rice. Still, there are a variety of contexts in which this event may take place. At home, the morning food event usually involves rice from the evening before boiled down to congee with a variety of pickles and condiments tossed in or served on the side. This is usually grabbed quickly in the kitchen on the way out to work, if it is eaten at all, and seldom involves the entire family seated at a single table.

Eaten out, the morning food event may take several forms. Consistent with the quick and superficial character of the event at home is the food event taken at a food stall of *daipaidong*, of which several different types serve suitable breakfast fare—congee (most commonly with preserved egg and pork), *yautiu* (unsweetened fried dough strips), hot *dao-jeung* (soy bean milk), *jucheung fen* (rolled rice noodles), all served with tea, usually in a glass.

Eating at a *daipaidong*, and even in some restaurants, one assumes the probability that the chopsticks, stuffed together in a can and set at the center of the table for individual diners to take, as well as one's cup, bowl, and spoon, will not have been properly washed. A brief ritualized washing usually precedes the meal in which one pours a glass of boiling hot tea into one's glass, stirring the ends of the chopsticks in the water to sterilize them, pouring the still hot water into one's bowl where one's cup and spoon are immersed and sterilized. The wash water is then thrown out, usually on the street in the case of a *daipaidong*, or in a spittoon at a restaurant, and one is prepared to commence eating. Occasionally, one is even provided with a separate bowl for washing one's eating implements, filled by one's waiter with boiling water from a huge kettle.

At a *daipaidong* for breakfast, one usually shares a table with a stranger, or perhaps a neighbor or workmate, depending on whether one eats near home or near work. In any case, one's portion is usually one's own, and the rules of formal dining apply only in the most general terms. Food is usually taken with dispatch, as one is usually rushing to work or to school, and the idea is just to put something in one's stomach to suppress hunger till the first meal of the day—*ng fan* (lunch).

The slightly more formal morning food event is *dim saam*, referred to most often as *yam ch'a* (drink tea). "Drinking tea" again refers to something less than a "meal," although on weekends, taken with one's family at a large table, *dim saam* often involves the consumption of large quantities of buns, dumplings, rice noodles in various shapes, a variety of innards, and the like. One sits down, is approached by one's waiter, or in fancier restaurants by a host or hostess, who will inquire what kind of tea one will be drinking—*sao mei, bo lei, soy sin*, and that old perceived favorite of *guailos*—*heung pien* (jasmine). When the tea arrives the host will fill everyone's cup and the meal may begin.

One acquires food from carts pushed around by young children and/or aged women, and less frequently by older men. One may find oneself sharing a table with strangers, or with regular customers who eat at the same restaurant at the same time every morning. Going to *yam ch'a* on a regular schedule assures one of continuous contact with the usual crowd, and it is common to find oneself seated at the same table with many of the same people each morning. While polite conversation is the general rule, more juicy gossip is not inappropriate as the relationship between morning diners becomes more familiar.

Generally, each diner is aware of what he has consumed, and the position of the plates may be adjusted where they have been ambiguously placed so the waiter can figure the tab. One eats from one's own plates under such circumstances, and pays for one's own plates; however, it is polite to fill the tea cup of one's neighbor from one's own pot if one is acquainted with him or her. There are still some restaurants in Hong Kong which serve tea in a covered bowl, quite literally stuffed with tea, and poured into a cup to be drunk, extremely dark, but the standard tea pot has replaced the bowl as a tea vessel in most restaurants.

A table shared with strangers or neighbors is usually an informal arrangement in which one eats one's own food. However, taking *dim saam* may also be a more formal occasion, especially on weekends, or when one has been *cheng*-ed (asked out). In such circumstances many of the rules of formal dining apply, i.e., the food on the table is common and should only be taken in such proportions that enough is left for others. One may order dishes one likes from the passing wagons, but one should always offer to others before taking from the dish for oneself. The dishes accumulate somewhat at random due to the vagaries of the itinerary of the carts, so there is no formal order to the dishes' arrival, although sweeter dishes are usually taken last.

Dim saam often trails off into lunch on formal or informal occasions, and by noon after the diners have warmed up with a few *dim saam* dishes, it is polite to inquire of one's fellow diners whether a plate of noodles or rice (a real meal) is in order, and if so, to order such dishes from the kitchen from one's waiter. Varieties of *dim saam* are also available from *daipaidong* as well, sometimes served up in individual portions to go.

The midday food event in Hong Kong includes rice or a reasonable substitute (rice noodles, bean noodles, wheat noodles), and is most often taken during a lunch hour break from factory or office labor. A variety of choices confront the Hong Kong worker eating out for lunch. Food stalls serve a variety of dishes, usually in individual portions on flat plates heaped high with rice, and covered with a single *ts'ai* dish. A glass of tea is usually served, and doubles again as a vessel for sterilizing one's chopsticks and spoon. Blue collar workers I knew in Hong Kong would often consume a full-to-the-brim tea tumbler of high octane spirits with such meals, and trundle back to work with the warm glow and slightly glazed look of a two-martini-lunch executive.

A plate of noodles may also be ordered from stalls specializing in such things. These may be served in individual portions, but given the easy divisibility of noodle dishes it is common for workmates to order a variety of noodle dishes and share them in common. A portion is lifted from the plate to one's bowl; with chopsticks initially, when the noodles are easily grasped in quantity; with help from the spoon as the plate gets progressively emptied. The setting of shared common dishes makes the general rules of the table outlined above once again applicable.

Co-workers will often go out to lunch at large *dim saam* restaurants, catch the tail end of the morning *dim saam* and order a variety of more substantial noodle or rice dishes. Where eating has taken place in common, and occasionally even where individual portions have been served, it is unusual for the check to be divided. Someone usually pays the whole tab. Among workmates, or those who often eat together, there is an implicit assumption that in the long run reciprocity will be achieved. It is not impolite among status equals to grab the check and pay for one's fellow diner, but this is not polite if the status difference is too great. Fights over the check occasionally occur in a way which evokes the potlatches of Northwest Coast Indians in which a status hierarchy is confirmed. Paying the check validates one's status superiority over one's fellow diners. Of course, the wider social setting must also be taken into account. One may be desirous of seeking a favor of an important person, in which case paying the check may serve as a mild form of pressure in which the obligation of reciprocity is finessed, enjoining one's fellow diner to comply with one's request. Food events are first and foremost social events.

The evening meal taken at home usually includes some warmed over *ts'ai* from the previous day's meal plus an increment of newly prepared dishes. It is not good manners to ignore the leftovers, despite the fact that they may not be quite as attractive as when served the day before. The general rules of the table apply, although the intimate setting of the family at home makes their application somewhat less formal. Still and all, parents will most commonly instruct children as to the appropriate forms of behavior at the table in this setting, and the children must show that they understand and are learning. In many working-class homes in Hong Kong it is still common for the men to eat first, with the women joining later and/or hovering over the meal without ever formally sitting down.

At more formal dinners or at banquets or feasts associated with weddings, New Year's, funerals or festivals, the primacy of the *fan* and the secondary character of the *ts'ai* dishes is reversed, with attention devoted to the quality of the *ts'ai* dishes (Hsü and Hsü 1977:307), and rice not served till last. Thus at a banquet one may eat *ts'ai* without rice in one's bowl, and one is expected to fill up on *ts'ai* such that when the rice is finally served, one can only take a token portion, which is to say, this has been a real feast.

> During festivals and especially when acting as hosts all Chinese seem to ignore their sense of frugality and indulge in extravagance. *Ts'ai* dishes are served in abundance. The host or hostess will heap the guests' saucers with piece after piece of meat, fish, chicken and so on, in spite of repeated excuses or even protests on the guests' part. When *fan* is finally served, most around the table are full and can at best nibble a few grains (Hsü and Hsü 1977:307).

By the time the rice has been served at a banquet the diner has already had a share of cold appetizer, several stir fry dishes, or whole chickens, ducks, fish, soup, and a sweet/salty dessert. The emphasis on whole items (with head and tail attached) symbolizes completeness and fullness, and evokes these meanings at the table. One tries to serve fish, *yü*, a homophone for surplus, *yü*, to sympathetically bring about that condition in one's guests.

It is not polite to turn over a fish at the table. Rather, when the side facing up has been finished, the skeleton is lifted off to leave the meat underneath exposed. Apparently, turning over the fish is taboo among boat people, since the fish symbolizes the boat which will capsize sympathetically if a fish is turned over. Waiters in Hong Kong are never sure which of their customers are boat folk and might take offense, so they generally refrain from turning over any fish and apparently the practice has now become general.

A variety of prestige foods, such as shark's fin

soup and the various eight precious dishes, are served at banquets more for the social recognition they confer than for the pleasure derived from their consumption (see de Garine 1976:150).

Conceptually, whiskey belongs with grain from which it is distilled and may be taken with food as a rice substitute. On formal occasions in Hong Kong scotch or VSOP Cognac is the rule, served straight in water tumblers, and often diluted with Seven-Up.

Another food event of note in Hong Kong is *siu yeh*—loosely translated as snacks. Usually taken late in the evening, they may include anything from congee, noodles and won ton, to roast pork, duck or chicken, to *hung dao sa* (sweet red bean soup—hot or iced) and *dao-fufa* (sweet bean curd usually flavored with almond). *Siu yeh* is usually served in individual portions. If you go out for won ton mein, everyone gets his own bowl. If you order duck's neck soup with rice, you are served an individual helping of soup, and an individual bowl of rice. Depending on the class of restaurant you take your *siu yeh* in, you may or may not find it advisable to wash your utensils with tea.

Itinerant street vendors with wheeled carts dispense a variety of prepared *siu yeh* in some residential neighborhoods, calling housewives and amahs to the street clutching their large porcelain bowls, or doling out cuttlefish parts to schoolchildren on street corners.

In all these contexts the general pattern that emerges is one that centers on deference, in thinking first of the other, in suppressing one's inclination to satiate oneself before the other has had a chance to begin, in humility. One yields to the other before satisfying one's own urges. At the macro level of China's great tradition, one finds such behavior characteristic of the *chün-tzu*, the individual skilled in the *li* (etiquette, rites, and ceremonies). He is one also skilled in the art of *jang*—of yielding, of accomplishing without activity, of boundless generosity, of cleaving to the *li*. There is even something of a Taoist resonance in all this, getting at things indirectly, without obvious instrumental effort.

Generally, it can be stated that the degree to which a Chinese practices the rules of etiquette marks his class position with respect to his fellow Chinese; although the degree to which the behavior of lower-class

people at the table is informed by these rules should not be underestimated. Disregard of the rules on the part of a Chinese is regarded with as much distaste by their fellows as the faux pas normally committed by Westerners, except that the latter can be excused by their hopeless, if expected, ignorance.

It does not take much study for a Westerner to perform well enough at the table to impress most Chinese, since their expectations are exceedingly low. Keeping in mind a few simple things without slavishly parading one's knowledge, one can usually avoid provoking disgust and revulsion, and convince one's fellow diners that one is sensitive to others on their own terms, as well as to the world at large. Among the most basic of cultural patterns, learned early in life, the degree to which one observes these patterns has a lot to do with the way one is perceived as a person in Chinese terms.

Simple knowledge of the structural contexts, behavioral expectations, and symbolic associations of food events can provide access across social boundaries that would otherwise be less easily breached, and make it possible to more easily achieve one's goals. Table manners are part of an inventory of symbolic behaviors that may be manipulated, finessed, and encoded to communicate messages about oneself. For the Chinese, as for almost everyone else, you are *how* you eat.

REFERENCES

Chang, K. C. (ed.), 1977, Introduction. In *Food in Chinese Culture*. New Haven: Yale University Press.

de Garine, I., 1976, Food, Tradition and Prestige. In *Food, Man and Society*. D. Walcher, N. Kretchmer, and H. L. Barnett, eds. New York: Plenum Press.

Goody, J., 1982, *Cooking, Cuisine and Class*. Cambridge: Cambridge University Press.

Hammerton, J. A., 1936, *Manners and Customs of Mankind*, Vol. I. New York: W. M. A. Wise.

Hsü, F. L. K., and V. Y. N. Hsü, 1977, Modern China: North. In *Food in Chinese Culture*. K. C. Chang, ed. New Haven: Yale University Press.

Li Chi, 1971, *Chü Li, Part I*. Taipei: World Publishing.

McLean, N. B., 1941, *The Table Graces: Setting, Service and Manners for the American House without Servants*. Peoria, IL: Manual Arts Press.

16

The Worst Mistake in the History of the Human Race

Jared Diamond

What we eat and how we eat, as we have seen in previous selections, are important both nutritionally and culturally. This selection takes us a step further, suggesting that how we get what we eat—through gathering and hunting versus agriculture, for example—has dramatic consequences. This seems pretty obvious. We all imagine what a struggle it must have been before the development of agriculture. We think of our ancestors spending their days searching for roots and berries to eat, or out at the crack of dawn, hunting wild animals. We now know, as discussed by Boyd Eaton and Melvin Konner in Selection 13, that this was not quite the case. Nevertheless, isn't it really better to simply go to the refrigerator, open the door, and reach for a container of milk to pour into a bowl of flaked grain for your regular morning meal? What could be simpler and more nutritious?

There are many things that we seldom question; the truth seems so evident and the answers obvious. One such sacred cow is the tremendous prosperity brought about by the agricultural revolution. This selection is a thought-provoking introduction to the connection between culture and agriculture. The transition from food foraging to farming (what archaeologists call the neolithic revolution) may have been the worst mistake in human history or its most important event. You be the judge. But for better or worse,

this cultural evolution has occurred and the world will never be the same again.

As you read this selection, ask yourself the following questions:

☐ *What is the fundamental difference between the progressivist view and the revisionist interpretation?*

☐ *How did the development of agriculture affect people's health?*

☐ *What three reasons explain the changes brought about by the development of agriculture?*

☐ *How did the development of agriculture affect social equality, including gender equality?*

The following terms discussed in this selection are included in the Glossary at the back of the book:

agricultural development
domestication of plants and animals
evolutionary anthropology
hunter-gatherers
neolithic
social stratification

To science we owe dramatic changes in our smug self image. Astronomy taught us that our earth isn't the center of the universe but merely one of billions of heavenly bodies. From biology we learned that we weren't specially created by God but evolved along with millions of other species. Now archaeology is demolishing another sacred belief: that human history over the past million years has been a long tale of progress. In particular, recent discoveries suggest that the adoption of agriculture, supposedly our most decisive step toward a better life, was in many ways a cat-

Jared Diamond / ©1987 Discover Magazine.

astrophe from which we have never recovered. With agriculture came the gross social and sexual inequality, the disease and despotism, that curse our existence.

At first, the evidence against this revisionist interpretation will strike twentieth century Americans as irrefutable. We're better off in almost every respect than the people of the Middle Ages, who in turn had it easier than cavemen, who in turn were better off than apes. Just count our advantages. We enjoy the most abundant and varied foods, the best tools and material goods, some of the longest and healthiest lives, in history. Most of us are safe from starvation and predators. We get our energy from oil and machines, not from our sweat. What neo-Luddite among us would trade his life for that of a medieval peasant, a caveman, or an ape?

For most of our history we supported ourselves by hunting and gathering: we hunted wild animals and foraged for wild plants. It's a life that philosophers have traditionally regarded as nasty, brutish, and short. Since no food is grown and little is stored, there is (in this view) no respite from the struggle that starts anew each day to find wild foods and avoid starving. Our escape from this misery was facilitated only 10,000 years ago, when in different parts of the world people began to domesticate plants and animals. The agricultural revolution gradually spread until today it's nearly universal and few tribes of hunter-gatherers survive.

From the progressivist perspective on which I was brought up, to ask "Why did almost all our hunter-gatherer ancestors adopt agriculture?" is silly. Of course they adopted it because agriculture is an efficient way to get more food for less work. Planted crops yield far more tons per acre than roots and berries. Just imagine a band of savages, exhausted from searching for nuts or chasing wild animals, suddenly gazing for the first time at a fruit-laden orchard or a pasture full of sheep. How many milliseconds do you think it would take them to appreciate the advantages of agriculture?

The progressivist party line sometimes even goes so far as to credit agriculture with the remarkable flowering of art that has taken place over the past few thousand years. Since crops can be stored, and since it takes less time to pick food from a garden than to find it in the wild, agriculture gave us free time that hunter-gatherers never had. Thus it was agriculture that enabled us to build the Parthenon and compose the B-minor Mass.

While the case for the progressivist view seems overwhelming, it's hard to prove. How do you show that the lives of people 10,000 years ago got better when they abandoned hunting and gathering for farming? Until recently, archaeologists had to resort to indirect tests, whose results (surprisingly) failed to support the progressivist view. Here's one example of an indirect test: Are twentieth century hunter-gatherers really worse off than farmers? Scattered throughout the world, several dozen groups of so-called primitive people, like the Kalahari Bushmen, continue to support themselves that way. It turns out that these people have plenty of leisure time, sleep a good deal, and work less hard than their farming neighbors. For instance, the average time devoted each week to obtaining food is only 12 to 19 hours for one group of Bushmen, 14 hours or less for the Hadza nomads of Tanzania. One Bushman, when asked why he hadn't emulated neighboring tribes by adopting agriculture, replied, "Why should we, when there are so many mongongo nuts in the world?"

While farmers concentrate on high-carbohydrate crops like rice and potatoes, the mix of wild plants and animals in the diets of surviving hunter-gatherers provides more protein and a better balance of other nutrients. In one study, the Bushmen's average daily food intake (during a month when food was plentiful) was 2,140 calories and 93 grams of protein, considerably greater than the recommended daily allowance for people of their size. It's almost inconceivable that Bushmen, who eat 75 or so wild plants, could die of starvation the way hundreds of thousands of Irish farmers and their families did during the potato famine of the 1840s.

So the lives of at least the surviving hunter-gatherers aren't nasty and brutish, even though farmers have pushed them into some of the world's worst real estate. But modern hunter-gatherer societies that have rubbed shoulders with farming societies for thousands of years don't tell us about conditions before the agricultural revolution. The progressivist view is really making a claim about the distant past: that the lives of primitive people improved when they switched from gathering to farming. Archaeologists can date that switch by distinguishing remains of wild plants and animals from those of domesticated ones in prehistoric garbage dumps.

How can one deduce the health of the prehistoric garbage makers, and thereby directly test the progressivist view? That question has become answerable only in recent years, in part through the newly emerging techniques of paleopathology, the study of signs of disease in the remains of ancient peoples.

In some lucky situations, the paleopathologist has almost as much material to study as a pathologist today. For example, archaeologists in the Chilean deserts found well preserved mummies whose medical conditions at time of death could be determined by autopsy. And feces of long-dead Indians who lived in dry caves in Nevada remain sufficiently well preserved to be examined for hookworm and other parasites.

Usually the only human remains available for study are skeletons, but they permit a surprising number of deductions. To begin with, a skeleton reveals its owner's sex, weight, and approximate age. In the few cases where there are many skeletons, one can construct mortality tables like the ones life insurance companies use to calculate expected life span and risk of death at any given age. Paleopathologists can also calculate growth rates by measuring bones of people of different ages, examine teeth for enamel defects (signs of childhood malnutrition), and recognize scars left on bones by anemia, tuberculosis, leprosy, and other diseases.

One straightforward example of what paleopathologists have learned from skeletons concerns historical changes in height. Skeletons from Greece and Turkey show that the average height of hunter-gatherers toward the end of the ice ages was a generous 5'9" for men, 5'5" for women. With the adoption of agriculture, height crashed, and by 3000 B.C. had reached a low of only 5'3" for men, 5' for women. By classical times heights were very slowly on the rise again, but modern Greeks and Turks have still not regained the average height of their distant ancestors.

Another example of paleopathology at work is the study of Indian skeletons from burial mounds in the Illinois and Ohio river valleys. At Dickson Mounds, located near the confluence of the Spoon and Illinois rivers, archaeologists have excavated some 800 skeletons that paint a picture of the health changes that occurred when a hunter-gatherer culture gave way to intensive maize farming around A.D. 1150. Studies by George Armelagos and his colleagues then at the University of Massachusetts show these early farmers paid a price for their new-found livelihood. Compared to the hunter-gatherers who preceded them, the farmers had a nearly 50 per cent increase in enamel defects indicative of malnutrition, a fourfold increase in iron-deficiency anemia (evidenced by a bone condition called porotic hyperostosis), a threefold rise in bone lesions reflecting infectious disease in general, and an increase in degenerative conditions of the spine, probably reflecting a lot of hard physical labor. "Life expectancy at birth in the pre-agricultural community was about twenty-six years," says Armelagos, "but in the post-agricultural community it was nineteen years. So these episodes of nutritional stress and infectious disease were seriously affecting their ability to survive."

The evidence suggests that the Indians at Dickson Mounds, like many other primitive peoples, took up farming not by choice but from necessity in order to feed their constantly growing numbers. "I don't think

most hunter-gatherers farmed until they had to, and when they switched to farming they traded quality for quantity," says Mark Cohen of the State University of New York at Plattsburgh, co-editor, with Armelagos, of one of the seminal books in the field, *Paleopathology at the Origins of Agriculture.* "When I first started making that argument ten years ago, not many people agreed with me. Now it's become a respectable, albeit controversial, side of the debate."

There are at least three sets of reasons to explain the findings that agriculture was bad for health. First, hunter-gatherers enjoyed a varied diet, while early farmers obtained most of their food from one or a few starchy crops. The farmers gained cheap calories at the cost of poor nutrition. (Today just three high-carbohydrate plants—wheat, rice, and corn—provide the bulk of the calories consumed by the human species, yet each one is deficient in certain vitamins or amino acids essential to life.) Second, because of dependence on a limited number of crops, farmers ran the risk of starvation if one crop failed. Finally, the mere fact that agriculture encouraged people to clump together in crowded societies, many of which then carried on trade with other crowded societies, led to the spread of parasites and infectious disease. (Some archaeologists think it was crowding, rather than agriculture, that promoted disease, but this is a chicken-and-egg argument, because crowding encourages agriculture and vice versa.) Epidemics couldn't take hold when populations were scattered in small bands that constantly shifted camp. Tuberculosis and diarrheal disease had to await the rise of farming, measles and bubonic plague the appearance of large cities.

Besides malnutrition, starvation, and epidemic diseases, farming helped bring another curse upon humanity: deep class divisions. Hunter-gatherers have little or no stored food, and no concentrated food sources, like an orchard or a heard of cows: they live off the wild plants and animals they obtain each day. Therefore, there can be no kings, no class of social parasites who grow fat on food seized from others. Only in farming population could a healthy, non-producing elite set itself above the disease-ridden masses. Skeletons from Greek tombs at Mycenae *c.* 1500 B.C. suggest that royals enjoyed a better diet than commoners, since the royal skeletons were two or three inches taller and had better teeth (on the average, one instead of six cavities or missing teeth). Among Chilean mummies from *c.* A.D. 1000, the élite were distinguished not only by ornaments and gold hair clips but also by a fourfold lower rate of bone lesions caused by disease.

Similar contrasts in nutrition and health persist on a global scale today. To people in rich countries like the U.S., it sounds ridiculous to extol the virtues of hunting and gathering. But Americans are an élite, dependent on oil and minerals that must often be imported from countries with poorer health and nutrition. If one could choose between being a peasant farmer in Ethiopia or a Bushman gatherer in the Kalahari, which do you think would be the better choice?

Farming may have encouraged inequality between the sexes, as well. Freed from the need to transport their babies during a nomadic existence, and under pressure to produce more hands to till the fields, farming women tended to have more frequent pregnancies than their hunter-gatherer counterparts—with consequent drains on their health. Among the Chilean mummies, for example, more women than men had bone lesions from infectious disease.

Women in agricultural societies were sometimes made beasts of burden. In New Guinea farming communities today I often see women staggering under loads of vegetables and firewood while the men walk empty-handed. Once while on a field trip there studying birds, I offered to pay some villagers to carry supplies from an airstrip to my mountain camp. The heaviest item was a 110-pound bag of rice, which I lashed to a pole and assigned to a team of four men to shoulder together. When I eventually caught up with the villagers, the men were carrying light loads, while one small woman weighing less than the bag of rice was bent under it, supporting its weight by a cord across her temples.

As for the claim that agriculture encouraged the flowering of art by providing us with leisure time, modern hunter-gatherers have at least as much free time as do farmers. The whole emphasis on leisure time as a critical factor seems to me misguided. Gorillas have had ample free time to build their own Parthenon, had they wanted to. While post-agricultural technological advances did make new art forms possible and preservation of art easier, great paintings and sculptures were already being produced by hunter-gatherers 15,000 years ago, and were still being produced as recently as the last century by such hunter-gatherers as some Eskimos and the Indians of the Pacific Northwest.

Thus with the advent of agriculture an élite became better off, but most people became worse off. Instead of swallowing the progressivist party line that we chose agriculture because it was good for us, we must ask how we got trapped by it despite its pitfalls.

One answer boils down to the adage "Might makes right." Farming could support many more people than hunting, albeit with a poorer quality of life. (Population densities of hunter-gatherers are rarely over one person per ten square miles, while farmers

average 100 times that.) Partly, this is because a field planted entirely in edible crops lets one feed far more mouths than a forest with scattered edible plants. Partly, too, it's because nomadic hunter-gatherers have to keep their children spaced at four-year intervals by infanticide and other means, since a mother must carry her toddler until it's old enough to keep up with the adults. Because farm women don't have that burden, they can and often do bear a child every two years.

As population densities of hunter-gatherers slowly rose at the end of the ice ages, bands had to choose between feeding more mouths by taking the first steps toward agriculture, or else finding ways to limit growth. Some bands chose the former solution, unable to anticipate the evils of farming, and seduced by the transient abundance they enjoyed until population growth caught up with increased food production. Such bands outbred and then drove off or killed the bands that chose to remain hunter-gatherers, because a hundred malnourished farmers can still outfight one healthy hunter. It's not that hunter-gatherers abandoned their life style, but that those sensible enough not to abandon it were forced out of all areas except the ones farmers didn't want.

At this point it's instructive to recall the common complaint that archaeology is a luxury, concerned with the remote past, and offering no lessons for the present. Archaeologists studying the rise of farming have reconstructed a crucial stage at which we made the worst mistake in human history. Forced to choose between limiting population or trying to increase food production, we chose the latter and ended up with starvation, warfare, and tyranny.

Hunter-gatherers practiced the most successful and longest-lasting life style in human history. In contrast, we're still struggling with the mess into which agriculture has tumbled us, and it's unclear whether we can solve it. Suppose that an archaeologist who had visited us from outer space were trying to explain human history to his fellow spacelings. He might illustrate the results of his digs by a 24-hour clock on which one hour represents 100,000 years of real past time. If the history of the human race began at midnight, then we would now be almost at the end of our first day. We lived as hunter-gatherers for nearly the whole of that day, from midnight through dawn, noon, and sunset. Finally, at 11:54 p.m., we adopted agriculture. As our second midnight approaches, will the plight of famine-stricken peasants gradually spread to engulf us all? Or will we somehow achieve those seductive blessings that we imagine behind agriculture's glittering façade, and that have so far eluded us?

17

Agricultural Development and the Quality of Life

Peggy F. Barlett and Peter J. Brown

American culture values progress. We seem to believe that new is better, and, as a nation, we seem to think that "progress is our most important product." We expect most change to be improvement, which means, most of the time, increased production, profits, and material possessions. As a society we are rich, but in what ways are we better off? This question has been raised by anthropologists studying diet (Selection 13), leisure time (Selection 20), and gender equality (Selection 23). These anthropological questions lead many people to wonder about their own values and expectations for life: Are these determined by you or by your culture?

In this article, Peggy Barlett and Peter Brown discuss the ambiguous but important concept of "quality of life." In rural areas throughout the world, increased agricultural production spurred on by the expansion of a world market has significantly changed people's lives. For most farmers, this progress has been possible only with some real costs— trade-offs—in traditional values and life satisfaction. From an anthropological view, economic development can bring increases in perceived needs that can never be satisfied. As cultures change through increased agricultural production, people may have more material possessions but be less satisfied.

As you read this selection, ask yourself the following questions:

☐ *What is meant by trade-offs in the process of agricultural development?*

☐ *What are some of the difficulties in defining the quality of life in a cross-culturally valid way?*

☐ *Why has the U.S. economy followed the capital-intensive pathway of agricultural development?*

☐ *What causes people to change their perceptions about the "necessities" of life? What is the role of culture contact in this process?*

The following terms discussed in this selection are included in the Glossary at the back of the book:

agricultural development
cultural evolution
fallow
population pressure
slash-and-burn techniques

One of the paradoxes of modern life is the persistence of suffering and deep dissatisfaction among people who enjoy an unparalleled abundance of material goods. The paradox is at least as old as our modern age. Ever since the benefits and costs of industrial technology became apparent, opinion has been divided over whether we are progressing or declining (Johnson 1982:200 [Selection 20]).

Agricultural development is usually considered synonymous with "progress" in the Western world, but does agricultural development always improve the "quality of life" for farmers and their communi-

From *Agriculture and Human Values*, 1985. Reprinted by permission.

ties? What are the human dimensions of the transformation of agriculture? Anthropological research shows that the relationship between agricultural development and the quality of life is much more complex than simple "progress." As Johnson indicates above, there are both costs and benefits associated with major economic changes, and these costs and benefits are difficult to interpret because they vary from culture to culture. We feel that agricultural development both harms and enhances life quality. We reject the simplistic notion that "new is better" and that increased agricultural production will automatically improve peoples' lives. However, it is wrong to ignore this important question simply because it is value laden or hard to measure.

In this paper we explore the relationship between agricultural development and the quality of life using concepts and examples from cultural anthropology. We explore the question by emphasizing the systematic patterns of trade-offs inherent in economic and social transformations. The concept "quality of life" must be seen as involving both an objective, measurable reality and a subjective, unquantifiable reality, which includes a person's ability to achieve culturally prescribed goals. Agricultural development can change the objective conditions of life, but it can also alter perceptions and goals, and these changes can sometimes move in opposite directions, both to increase and decrease "quality of life."

THE ANTHROPOLOGICAL PERSPECTIVE: CULTURAL EVOLUTION AND LIFE QUALITY

Respect for the values and lifeways of other societies is essential for an accurate understanding of changing quality of life. The knowledge, technology, values and beliefs of a society form a complex interconnected whole which is passed down from generation to generation; this is the central anthropological concept of culture. Cultural systems are highly adaptable, and as such form the core of human survival, allowing our species to inhabit and prosper in all environments of the world. The interconnected aspect of culture means that if one part changes, others will be affected; if, for instance, an economy changes, then we can and should expect that people's family life, politics, and religion will also be affected. In the past anthropology was limited to the study of primitive peoples, but today it includes the study of contemporary cultures in developing as well as developed nations. In this way, anthropologists bring a cross-cultural perspective to understandings about patterns of socio-economic change.

Quality of life is seen by anthropologists not only in terms of contemporary cultural diversity but also in the dimension of time. Using a long-term evolutionary view, there are basic stages in cultural evolution from "hunting and gathering" societies, through tribal and chiefdom phases, to agricultural and industrial states. In the historical evolution of complex societies like the one in which we live, there are some clear, unmistakable trends: population sizes get larger; economic systems become more complex and specialized; more energy is harnessed and consumed; social systems become unequal; and belief systems generally become more elaborate, reinforcing the economic and political trends.

From this perspective, the domestication of plants and animals emerges as one of the most important events in human history. Current archeological evidence indicates that the emergence of farming was not a sudden revolutionary event, but a slow, gradual process which occurred independently in Mesopotamia, the Indus valley, southern China, ancient Mexico and ancient Peru (Service 1975). The economic shift towards agriculture provided the foundation of ancient civilizations that followed the economic transformation in those five locations. The production of surplus food through farming allowed the economic specialization of the first cities and the elaboration of knowledge and art which are sometimes synonymous with civilization. It is logical that Western historians have interpreted this general cultural change as "progress."

The cultural changes following the domestication of plants and animals also involved some rather hefty costs. With the first agriculturally based state societies there also appeared the first kings, armies, jails, taxes, and war. For the bulk of the population, agriculture and civilization meant more work and a less nutritious diet than had been the case with more "primitive" cultures based on hunting and gathering. When we consider early slave-based states, for example, it is obvious that civilization improved life quality only for certain social segments. Because of these types of trade-offs involved in historical processes, the anthropological perspective does not allow a simple label like "progress" to be applied to complex cultural evolution. As cultures change, things get different, not necessarily better.

An important finding of recent anthropology was that the life among hunting and gathering societies like that of the !Kung San of Botswana is not "nasty, brutish, and short," as Westerners have traditionally believed. On the contrary, the San have more leisure time than most other societies, and adults average two to three days of subsistence work per week with six to eight hours of work in each of those days (Lee 1979:256–278). The San also enjoy an abundant and nutritious diet, compared to most agricultural societies, and have a flexible and intimate social system characterized by sharing, independence, cooperation and humor. Recent research on other band societies seems to support these findings that hunting and gathering peoples live lives with few material possessions, but what might be considered a high quality of life. The !Kung themselves describe a decline in their life quality brought by government control as well as the loss of territory to herding and agricultural people.

> Before the white people came, we did what our hearts wanted. We lived in different places, far apart, and when our hearts wanted to travel, we traveled. *We were not poor.* We had everything we could carry. No one told us what to do. Now the white people tell us to stay in this place. There are too many people. There's no food to gather. Game is far away and people are dying of tuberculosis. But when I was a little girl, we left sickness behind us when we moved (Volkman 1982:20; emphasis added).

DEFINING THE QUALITY OF LIFE

In general, there are two social scientific strategies for attempting to measure the quality of life. Most common is the definition of social indicators, that is, objective material measures such as per capita income, life expectancy, employment figures, morbidity/mortality rates, and the availability of certain consumer goods. Social indicators attempt to measure objectively peoples' life conditions, both wealth and health. A second, and less widespread strategy is subjective, attempting to measure life quality in terms of individuals' assessments of their life circumstances and life satisfaction. This subjective approach emphasizes the role of perception both in terms of life expectations and current life circumstances.

The methodological rigor associated with social indicators is impressive, but there is clearly no consensus on which statistical measures best comprise a standard quality of life scale. There is always the nagging question of the cross-cultural validity of "objective" social indicators since they ignore variations in beliefs and value concerning what is important in life. Because values, life expectations, and perceptions of the "good life" vary between cultural groups, it may be as difficult to define a universal scale of life quality as it would be to define a universal scale of beauty. This is not to imply, however, that minimal requirements in terms of basic human needs for food, shelter, and clothing cannot be identified. Such material conditions for the continuation of life may be considered *necessary but not sufficient* conditions for a high quality of life.

While objective quality of life indicators may be useful scientific tools for legislators and policy makers who wish to measure the efficacy of social and economic development programs, they often obscure important variations in the quality of life. For instance, infant mortality statistics are nearly identical for two cantons in Costa Rica that have sharply distinct situations (OFIPLAN 1979). One canton includes a large urban population, some light industry, and good medical facilities. Its high infant mortality rate can be attributed to the density of population, lack of adequate urban employment for many families, very concentrated landholdings in its rural areas, and lack of alternate income sources for these landless rural families. Infant mortality would seem to be strongly correlated with social class and inadequate nourishment. The contrasting canton is a sparsely populated frontier area with less concentrated landholdings and little unemployment. Its high infant mortality rate can be attributed more to difficult transportation and poor medical facilities rather than to malnourishment and underemployment of the population. Quality of life indicators obscure the great variation of wealth in the first canton, and the much lower and less skewed income levels in the second canton.

In addition to these problems in reducing complex issues to quantitative measures, quality of life measures can in some cases be inherently ethnocentric. For example, in using a measure of formal education, access to Western medicine, or income, the researcher assumes a more Western culture is better, and movement toward Western standards of living implies "progress." People judge their life circumstances through comparisons with others; this is the basis of the social scientific concept, "relative deprivation." There may be changing standards of comparison because of new perceptions of the necessities of life, or because of new comparison groups. As the case of the !Kung San shows, lack of material possessions does not always imply poverty. A subjective perspective of quality of life, based on the people's own perceptions, needs to be added to social indicators, to achieve a less biased view.

In applying the quality of life concept, a neglected question has been the extent to which the needs, values, aspirations, and life expectations as defined by a particular group of people can be met in their current life circumstances. These needs, values, and aspirations are by necessity defined differently by diverse ethnic or class groups, and also at various points in a process of historical cultural change. Material possessions, for instance, will be important to some groups as in modern Western culture, but irrelevant in others. The ability to maintain close ties with large family groups is essential for some cultures, while such contact would be burdensome to others. This diversity is important when analyzing how the "trade-offs" of agricultural development influence the quality of life. A culturally relativistic approach would therefore first examine a people's perceived needs and desires and then compare it to the objective reality of life circumstances. Quality of life might be conceived of as a ratio of objective social indicators to culturally defined perceptions of needs and life expectations. As we show below, both parts of this equation can change simultaneously in a process of agricultural development.

This approach allows for different strategies for achieving a high quality of life: to increase the capability to meet needs, or to reduce perceived needs and life expectations. Schumacher (1973) has argued that the former is an approach to life satisfaction typical of industrial capitalism while the latter represents a "Buddhist" approach. This second strategy is not generally recognized in discussions of quality of life among developmental practitioners or government agencies, but is revealed by a less ethnocentric approach to the issue.

WHAT IS AGRICULTURAL DEVELOPMENT?

Agricultural development is one label that can be given to a complex process of change in food production systems. As human populations have grown over the centuries, early methods of shifting agriculture have been replaced by permanent plow agriculture, characterized by draft animals and a short fallow period. Research on the evolution of cultural methods shows a transition from long fallow systems in which crop land is used only one year out of 25, to medium and short fallow systems where the land is cultivated every year (Netting 1977; Boserup 1965; Brookfield and Hart 1971). Slash-and-burn techniques that are necessary to remove a forest cover are replaced by plowing techniques to remove weeds and cultivate the soil. In this process, human labor in agriculture is supplemented by draft animals or by machines. When compared with the earliest agricultural technology, plow agriculture requires not only more intensive use of land but also more human labor per unit of output (Boserup 1965).

The causes of agricultural intensification are complex, but the single most important determinant in most of the world areas is population pressure (Gleave and White 1969; Boserup 1965; Spooner 1972; Brown and Podolefsky 1976). As the numbers of people increase for a given area of territory, agricultural methods become more sophisticated. In some cases contact with other groups creates the desire for consumer goods, especially through trade, and this culture contact can also result in agricultural intensification

(Rawski 1972; Barlett 1982). Increased taxation or colonial expropriation of resources can have the same effect (Geertz 1963; White 1973).

With the advent of the industrial revolution, the process of agricultural evolution split into two distinct paths. Western European nations have generally followed one path in which industrial goods are emphasized in the production process and farm labor is generally replaced with capital. The other path is best exemplified by wet rice cultivation in Asia: it involves extraordinarily high investments of human labor in very small plots. This labor-intensive path usually includes sophisticated irrigation systems and public investments in canals and terraces. A result of this type of agriculture intensification is often a complete restructuring of the ecosystem to maximize food production. Although the productivity of agricultural labor declines on this path, the productive output per acre increases.

In the capital-intensive path of agricultural development, the production process becomes increasingly more diversified. Some parts of the production process, although not commonly conceived of as agriculture, are turned over to industries separate from the farm (such as the substitution of commercial fertilizer for farm manure). These industries produce chemicals, tractors, and silos for the use of farmers, thereby adding much more capital and labor investment to the overall process of food production. Importantly, such increased specialization also removes the farmer from direct control over important aspects of agricultural production, although he or she may orchestrate the process. Industrial agriculture also modifies the ecosystem more than traditional plow methods, not only through massive clearings of plots but also with the introduction of herbicides and pesticides into the environment.

Considering either the labor-intensive path or the capital-intensive path of agricultural development, there are major changes in four areas: the amount of work required to grow food increases; the amount of energy invested in food production increases; the sophistication of necessary tools increases; and the ecosystem is dramatically altered. These are all aspects of a general process of cultural change which can be called agricultural *intensification*.

AGRICULTURAL "PROGRESS" AND THE QUALITY OF LIFE

Although agricultural development actually has two alternative paths, only the capital intensive path is considered "development" or "progress" by Western experts and policy makers. Most agricultural development programs, modeled after the Western capital-intensive path, seek to replace on-farm labor with machinery and chemicals as well as to increase the productivity of the land with commercial fertilizers and improved crop varieties. The success of increasing productivity by U.S. and Western European farmers is clear. However, important trade-offs are often not recognized in agricultural development planning. For example, we noted above the farmer's loss of control over critical aspects of the production system. Another trade-off in capital-intensive agriculture is that it sometimes results in a lower quality food product. The quality of hybrid tomatoes sold in most grocery stores is one example; the lower protein content of hybrid corn is another. The introduction of these hybrid corn varieties into the U.S. increases profits for corn producers, but forces livestock producers to find a new protein source to replace the lost food value in corn. Peruvian fishmeal was once imported for this purpose, but today soybeans are commonly used. The cost of these substitutes is often not included in the estimates of the success of hybrid corn varieties.

Has the development of agriculture in the U.S. led to an improvement in the quality of life? Most policy makers have equated "improved quality of life" with "increased consumption of purchased goods" and farmers are certainly consuming more goods now than in previous generations. But as farmers in the U.S. have become more and more linked to a complex industrial and market system, their self-sufficiency has declined. Farmers' purchases of food at the grocery store are now similar to non-farmers, and consumer goods that were once rare are now purchased regularly. There is little doubt that capital-intensive farming provides more cash with which to buy more goods now, as the result of the development process.

Farmers' increased consumption of purchased goods is achieved at the cost of certain other aspects of the quality of life. The quality of work time, for example, has clearly diminished for those people who used to be independent farmers but who today are workers in fertilizer or machine factories. These workers may not do the arduous tasks that face farmers at certain points of the year, but they lose the variety of farm work and also lose control over their daily schedule of activities. Farmers consistently place a high value on "being one's own boss" and making one's own independent decisions. Trade-offs such as this are hard to include when trying to create a total judgment of a change in the quality of life.

Quality of life, the ability to meet perceived needs, is not automatically improved by agricultural development. Despite the ability of U.S. farmers to purchase more goods, like everyone else in capitalist society, they are likely to be caught in the consumer trap. The "consumer trap" means that the more one is able to consume, the more one desires to consume. Because "needs" escalate, development does not necessarily increase the ability to meet those needs. As U.S. farmers have become more a part of the wider consumer society, they experience constant pressure for more consumer goods, for the farm as well as for the family. This increasing desire to consume leads to pressures for greater intensification in farm production, which can push the farm into yet another spiral of more work, more energy, and more capital. Just as industry finds itself on a growth treadmill, so is agriculture told: "Grow or die."

A CROSS-CULTURAL MODEL

The relationship of agricultural development to the issue of quality of life may be seen as a circular process of intensification of production and consumption. Figure 1 diagrams some aspects of that process. Agricultural intensification leads in most situations to an increase in the labor expended in food production. This labor intensification may involve a lower quality of work experience for many workers and sometimes even a lower quality product. Environmental and technological changes usually accompany the process, which results in more sales of products and more money for the consumption of goods. An increase in perceived needs accompanies this process, however, and thus increased consumption does not automatically lead to an improved subjective assessment of life quality.

The desire for further consumption may stimulate another cycle of increased intensification in order to increase production. As explained above, this spiral begins as the result of a long evolutionary history of population pressure, conquest, and trade. In contemporary developing societies, however, it is maintained by the market pressures on consumers. From this perspective, then, as long as the developmental process pushes farmers to be more and more involved in the market, the market will exert pressure to expand their perceived "needs." Since the perceived ability to meet those needs is an essential component of the quality of life, agricultural development is inherently incapable of increasing the level of satisfaction and the quality of life among farmers.

COSTA RICA

These same issues of intensification, trade-offs, and the consumer trap can be seen in a mountainous area of rural Costa Rica, where the process of agricultural in-

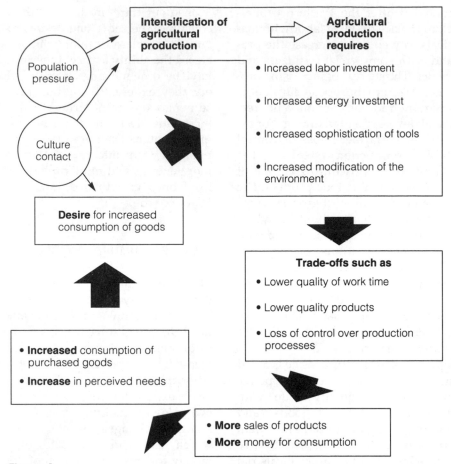

Figure 1
A model of the vicious cycle of agricultural intensification and increases in
perceived needs.

tensification has occurred rapidly in one generation (Barlett 1982). Having abandoned their traditional fallow system, the majority of farmers are now using each plot of land to produce several crops each year. The adoption of tobacco as a cash crop allows many households to harvest corn, beans, and tobacco in one annual sequence on each plot. To achieve this level of production, farmers must now work much harder, both in terms of longer hours of work and in terms of harder work digging tobacco terraces by hand each year. Farmers in this area of Costa Rica invest over four times the work for this triple cropping sequence than for the traditional corn and beans sequence. Tobacco also requires considerably more capital (for fertilizer, chemicals, and equipment), increasing per acre costs over 700% for these "more modern" farmers.

Ecological adaptations and the security of rural life are also affected. The intensity of cultivation without the traditional fallow periods, together with the heavy use of chemicals, has increased problems with plant diseases and insect infestations in the area. Some farmers report feeling nauseated or having headaches

after using the chemicals required by their tobacco contract. Another trade-off is the necessity to finance tobacco on credit, jeopardizing future income should one year's harvest be damaged. Many farmers see farming as much more stressful and risky now than it used to be.

Tobacco is, however, a profitable crop and gives farmers three times more cash per acre than any other land use option. With more money to consume, tobacco producers are proud of their increased consumption. They are able to build nicer houses, buy televisions and refrigerators, invest in more land and livestock, and eat a more varied diet. On the other hand, development has also brought changes in cultural perceptions of the necessities of life in rural Costa Rica. Television exposes them to an urban middle-class lifestyle, and peasant farmers who were barefoot a generation ago now want stereos and cars as well as shoes and new fashions. Even for those without television, the increased contact with the city, government officials, tobacco company personnel, and bank officials all affect their perceived needs. It would be impossible for the scientific observer to say that agricultural development has clearly led to an improved ability to meet their perceived needs.

SARDINIA

Another case of trade-offs associated with agricultural intensification is the history of industrial cheese production in Sardinia, Italy (Brown 1979; Berger 1981). Traditionally, shepherds from all zones of the island maintained flocks of sheep on non-arable land and produced *pecorino* cheese out in the countryside at the sheepfold enclosures. While most of this production was for local consumption, some cheese was sold to itinerant merchants who imported it to mainland Italy. In the local economy, cheese, meat, and lambs were bartered by shepherd families for food, services, rent payments, and necessities; the remainder of cheese sold to merchants was a source of cash for what little there was to purchase.

Around 1910, cheese production became industrialized with the advent of centralized cheese factories (*casefici*) financed by investors from Romagna in mainland Italy. Gradually, most herders in coastal and foothill zones, with the notable exception of the Barbagia highlands, were transformed into simple milk producers, selling milk daily to the factories. This economic transformation was possible not simply because local brokers for the factories offered cash for milk and hence reduced some economic risk. Industrial cheese production occurred simultaneously with an increased demand for cash and the availability of consumer goods.

The intensified production system has had a number of important consequences. On the negative side, shepherds' work lives are more monotonous, their profit margins much narrower, and their hours longer because flocks have been expanded up to four times the traditional size (Sabattini and Moro 1973). Similarly, the cheese produced by the industrial process is considered to be of inferior quality (Counihan 1981). On the positive side, the shift has allowed shepherds to live permanently in town and to purchase consumer goods like Fiats and motor scooters which make commutes to flocks easier. Most shepherds, however, must use donkeys for some part of their commute and now face the additional burden of transporting milk to roads for transfer to the cheese factory trucks. From the shepherds' view, the greatest advantage of the *caseficio* system is their ability to live a more "civilized" life in town, but the demands for cash in this modern consumer-oriented society are boundless.

Interestingly, *caseficio*-contracted shepherds envy their counterparts, primarily from the Barbagia high-

lands, who produce their own cheese and have remained independent of the factories. These traditional shepherds have also increased production, and they achieve much higher incomes by selling their own cheese. The original produce is considered tastier and brings a higher price in the market. Traditional producers tend to be more self-sufficient in food production, but their families still participate fully in the cash-based consumer society. In terms of material indicators, industrial and traditional shepherds may not be very different, but in terms of the strong cultural value placed on independence, the cost of industrialization has been heavy.

RURAL UNITED STATES

Agricultural development in the U.S. shows several of the trade-offs noted above. The "cost-price squeeze" currently facing U.S. farmers is a natural result of the increased diversification of capital-intensive agriculture (Schertz 1979). Today, U.S. farmers sell their products for low prices in a world market glutted with food. They operate an intensified farming system that requires capital that must be borrowed at high interest rates, fertilizers and chemicals whose prices rise sharply each year, and machinery whose costs also reflect the rising costs of living in the U.S. (Tweeten 1981). Rising energy prices provide an additional burden to the farmer (Buttel et al., 1980). The "squeeze" on farmers' profits is severe and is forcing many families out of farming. The number of farmers is declining rapidly all over the country, and farms are becoming bigger as the result. On those farms that are left, the capital and energy invested per unit of output has increased, showing the familiar intensification and the use of resources to produce food (Pimentel 1973; U.S.D.A. 1979, 1981).

Families forced off the farm usually end up in factory work or similar wage labor. Most see these jobs as much less desirable than farming and lament the monotony of the work, the loss of control over their lives, and the necessity to be "indoors" and away from growing things. For these people, agricultural development is usually a decline in the quality of work life.

In Georgia, farmers have suffered an unusually severe period of drought, together with the national cost-price squeeze (Barlett 1984). Facing profits that have fallen to zero year after year, one older farmer was asked if he thought we could go back to an era of lower consumption standards. He replied, "Most of those younger farmers would rather jump in the river." The perceived needs for cars, new homes, luxury vacations, or even an air-conditioned tractor make this period of financial hardship doubly difficult. The increased sophistication of farming has led again to an increase in perceived needs and no perceived improvement in the quality of life.

CONCLUSION

The three ethnographic examples above help illustrate the complex interaction of agricultural development and the quality of life. In this paper we have examined both the concepts of agricultural development and quality of life in the framework of cultural relativism and cultural evolution. It is important to recognize that in the process of intensified or industrialized production, both the material measures of life quality and a people's value and attitudes about "necessities" can change. In capital-intensive economic systems, perceptions of need can fuel the market demand for increased production. When this is the case, it will be impossible to assume that increased agricultural production will necessarily improve a society's quality of life.

REFERENCES

Barlett, Peggy F. 1982. *Agricultural Choice and Change: Decision Making in a Costa Rican Community*. New Brunswick, N.J.: Rutgers Press.

———. 1984. "Microdynamics of Debt, Drought & Default in South Georgia." *American Journal of Agricultural Economics* 66(5): 836–843.

Berger, Allen. 1981. "The Effects of Capitalism on the Social Structure of Pastoral Villages in Highland Sardinia." *Michigan Discussions in Anthropology*, Vol. 3.

Boserup, Ester. 1965. *The Conditions of Agricultural Growth*. Chicago: Aldine.

Brookfield, H. C. and D. Hart. 1971. *Melanesia: A Geographical Interpretation of an Island World*. London: Methuen.

Brown, Paula and Aaron Podolefsky. 1976. "Population Density, Agricultural Intensity, Land Tenure, and Group Size in the New Guinea Highlands." *Ethnology* 15:211–238.

Brown, Peter J. 1979. *Cultural Adaptations to Endemic Malaria and the Socioeconomic Effects of Malaria Eradication in Sardinia*. Ph.D. Dissertation, Department of Anthropology, S.U.N.Y. Stony Brook.

Buttel, Frederick H. et al. 1980. "Energy and Small Farms: A Review of Existing Research." Paper II of the National Rural Center, Small Farms Project. Washington, D.C.

Counihan, Carole M. 1981. *Food, Culture, and Political Economy: An Investigation of Changing Lifestyles in the Sardinian Town of Bosa*. Ph.D. Dissertation, Department of Anthropology, University of Massachusetts.

Geertz, Clifford. 1963. *Agricultural Involution*. Berkeley: University of California Press.

Gleave, M. B. and H. P. White. 1969. "Population Density and Agricultural Systems in West Africa." In *Environment and Land Use in Africa*. M. F. Thomas and G. W. Whittington, eds. (pps. 273–300). London: Methuen.

Johnson, Allen. 1982. "In Search of the Affluent Society." In *Anthropology: Contemporary Perspectives* (3d ed.). D. Hunter and P. Whitten, eds. (pps. 200–225). Boston: Little, Brown.

Lee, Richard Borshay. 1979. *The !Kung San: Men, Women and Work in a Foraging Society*. NY: Cambridge University Press.

Netting, Robert McC. 1977. *Cultural Ecology*. Menlo Park: Cummings.

OFIPLAN. 1979. *Mapa de Pobreza de Costa Rica*. San Jose: Oficina de Planificacion Nacional y Politica Economica.

Pimental, David, et al. 1973. "Food Production and the Energy Crisis." *Science* 182:443–449.

Rawsky, Evelyn Sakakida. 1972. *Agricultural Change and the Peasant Economy of South China*. Cambridge, Mass.: Harvard University Press.

Sabattini, Gianfranco and Beniamino Moro. 1973. *Il Sistema Economica della Sardegna*. Cagliari: Editrice Sarda.

Schertz, Lyle P. et al. 1979. *Another Revolution in U.S. Farming?* USDA Agricultural Economic Report #441. Washington: U.S. Government Printing Office.

Schumacher, E. F. 1973. *Small Is Beautiful*. NY: Harper and Row.

Service, Elman R. 1975. *Origins of the State and Civilization*. NY: Norton.

Spooner, Brian. 1972. *Population Growth*. Cambridge, Mass.: MIT Press.

Tweeten, Luther. 1981. "Agriculture at a Crucial Evolutionary Crossroads." *Research in Domestic and International Agribusiness Management* 2:1–15.

U.S.D.A. 1979. *Structure Issues of American Agriculture*. Economics, Statistics and Cooperatives Service: Agricultural Economic Report 438. Washington, D.C.: U.S. Government Printing Office.

———. 1981. *A Time to Choose: Summary Report on the Structure of Agriculture*. Washington, D.C.: U.S. Government Printing Office.

Volkman, Toby Alice. 1982. *The San in Transition*. Cultural Survival and D.E.R. Occasional Paper 9. Cambridge, Mass.: Cultural Survival.

White, Benjamin. 1973. "Demand for Labor and Population Growth in Colonial Java." *Human Ecology* 1(3): 217–244.

18

The Agrarian Basis of Conflict in Central America

Billie R. DeWalt

Central American foreign policy has plagued United States leaders for decades. Our southern neighbors have been beset by armed revolutions and political upheavals that have been impossible to quell. What have been the sources of these conflicts? While some may blame ideologies introduced by outside influences, it is clear that there must be a foundation of disenchantment with existing conditions before revolutionary ideologies can gain a foothold.

The previous selection described the complex interaction between agricultural development and the quality of life. In this selection, Billie DeWalt describes economic principles and government policies that have effected changes in the patterns of landholding in Central America. These changes, he argues, have created crisis and conflict. Peasant agriculturalists have become an underemployed urban poor struggling to survive as shoeshine boys, servants, and street vendors. Does Central America need more arms to battle rebels in the streets, or more fundamental social and economic reforms to provide a permanent solution?

As you read this selection, ask yourself the following questions:

☐ How have the price-structuring policies of Central American countries affected small farmers?

☐ What is the concept of "comparative advantage"? Does it appear to make sense? And how have policies derived from this principle affected Central America?

☐ What effect does increased emphasis on pasture land and beef cattle have on agricultural labor, small farmers, employment, nutrition, and the environment?

☐ Why is land reform so crucial in Central America? What happens to those pushed out of the countryside into the urban centers?

The following terms discussed in this selection are included in the Glossary at the back of the book:

agrarian
land concentration
social stratification

The current headlines on Central America have provoked many questions concerning the causes of political upheaval in the region. A revolution has succeeded in Nicaragua, revolutions continue in El Salvador and Guatemala, and Honduras is being turned into an armed camp. Even Costa Rica, the only one of the five Central American republics with a significant democratic tradition, has become embroiled in conflict with its neighbors and has experienced internal unrest.

Presented in this essay are some comparative data on the agrarian systems of Central America. The principal objective is to demonstrate that recent agricultural trends, especially the concentration of land ownership resulting from the growth of the cattle industry, have contributed to the conflicts occurring in Central America. Four major points will be emphasized:

1. that the agricultural sector is extraordinarily important in the economies and to the people of Central America;

2. that the agrarian sector of these societies has historically been marked by an emphasis on export commodities;

3. that the export orientation and associated processes have helped to cause an extremely unequal distribution of land and a lack of employment opportunities in Central America; and

4. that these in turn have had a significant role in creating the social, economic, and political instability in the region.

It is difficult to obtain accurate current information on the agricultural sector; therefore, the author has relied largely on data before 1979, a time that predates the Nicaraguan Revolution and the latest outbreak of civil war in El Salvador. As we will see, the agrarian processes described here have developed over a long period of time and are still continuing in several of the republics. In other countries the changes that are now occurring are direct consequences of the current revolutionary ferment in the region.

The percentage of the population directly involved in agriculture is still an important segment in all of the countries. In 1980 it ranged from a low of 29 percent in Costa Rica to a high of 63 percent in Honduras, and was over 50 percent in El Salvador and Guatemala. The percentage contribution of the gross domestic product made by agriculture was also substantial, ranging from a low of 18.5 percent in Costa Rica to a high of 33.5 percent in Nicaragua.[1]

While all of the Central American countries have been devoting substantial effort to industrialization, agriculture has been an important part of their attempts to finance this industrialization. Throughout Latin America, countries count on the agricultural sector to produce staples to feed their rapidly growing and urbanizing populations. Price policies have generally been structured to keep the costs of basic foodstuffs to a minimum. These policies are presumed to serve the needs of urban dwellers and factory workers. However, these "cheap food" strategies have often served as disincentives for production because it is simply not profitable enough for farmers to cultivate basic staples. As Alain de Janvry has shown, the effect of cheap food policies has been increasingly to reduce small farmers to the margin of existence as they are generally the producers of basic commodities. They continue to try to produce enough for their own sub-

sistence but do not find it worthwhile to try to produce a surplus for the market.[2]

Another way in which agriculture is used to finance industrialization is that a substantial part of the Central American countries' foreign exchange is earned from agricultural exports. In 1978 agricultural products comprised well over 50 percent of the total exports in all of the countries, and almost 70 percent in Guatemala and Honduras. This percentage had increased since 1971 in all of the countries except for El Salvador and Honduras where it had declined slightly.[3] At the same time that the governments of Central America have been implementing cheap food policies, they have generally provided subsidies and credit for the capitalist sector of agriculture to try to stimulate the production of export commodities such as bananas, coffee, sugar cane, beef, and cotton. The goal of such policies is to earn scarce foreign exchange.

Cheap food policies and an emphasis on export agriculture are both based on a belief in comparative advantage, the idea that a country should produce those products for which it is most favorably endowed in terms of natural resources, labor skills, cost advantages, or other factors. The concept of comparative advantage is an essential element of the free trade policies advocated by liberal economists since Adam Smith.[4] As will be seen, these policies have not been kind to Central America.

Export agriculture has been a significant part of Central America's linkage with the world market since it was colonized by the Spanish. In many areas of Central America, cacao was a vital export crop as far back as 1540. Indigo was another early export commodity until it was replaced by synthetic dyes in the middle of the nineteenth century.[5] This was around the time that coffee became important. Bananas and other tropical fruits were added around the turn of the century and have been supplemented in more recent times by cotton, sugar cane, and beef cattle.[6] The region has followed policies designed to make use of its comparative advantage—its tropical location—to export products to the rest of the world.

One major problem for Central America has been that these agricultural exports are extremely vulnerable to "boom and bust cycles"; that is, depending on world demand, prices fluctuate wildly. When demand rises the prices for agricultural products also rise, giving more individuals in more countries an incentive to plant them. This often results in overproduction that will sometimes cause prices to drop precipitously. Because demand for these products is relatively inelastic (as prices drop, consumption does not rise significantly), low prices continue for several years until supply decreases. Further contributing to the instability of demand is that many of these crops are subject to substitution effects. Just as indigo was replaced by synthetic substitutes, the demand for cotton declined as synthetic fabrics were increasingly used in clothing (a process that began to reverse after the steep rises in oil prices after 1973). High sugar prices several years ago led to the increasing use of corn sweeteners, and the world sugar market has been slack ever since.

These bust cycles reduce the profits of the landowners, leading to three economically rational responses on their part. First, those who can afford to do so attempt to expand their holdings still further so that they maintain their profits by earning smaller margins on greater production. Second, they diversify to spread their risks over a larger number of crops. The expansion into cotton, sugar cane, African palm, melons, beef cattle, and other crops may be seen as part of this strategy.[7] Finally, they seek to reduce their costs of production, most typically by attempting to reduce labor costs through the use of increased technology, such as machinery or herbicides, or by shifting to less labor-intensive crops.

A good example of such processes comes from southern Honduras, the region in which I have been working periodically since June 1981. This area is inhospitable. The coastal plain around the Gulf of Fonseca is not extensive. There is a dry season from December until May, and there is usually another extended dry period during the rainy season that makes agriculture risky. During the colonial period, indigo and sugar cane were cultivated in this region and some scrub cattle were raised, but the area was a backwater compared with other regions of Central America. Although some coffee was grown in the south, agrarian capitalism and an emphasis on export agriculture did not penetrate this region until after 1950. After this date, sugar cane, cotton, and especially cattle production for the international trade began to change the region's agrarian systems.[8]

Sugar cane and cotton are both crops that, while cultivated by large landowners, provide significant labor opportunities for the small farmers and landless people. The cane is cut by workers using machetes, while the cotton is picked by hand. During the past several years, however, the world market for both of these commodities has been in a bust cycle. The two large sugar cane mills are in danger of closing because of heavy debts, and cotton cultivation has become more and more unprofitable because production requires increasing amounts of pesticides to control insects. This has caused many farmers to continue a trend—the conversion of their lands to pasture for cattle production—which was begun in the late 1950s and early 1960s. Under current conditions, the main requirement for cattle production is having large extensions of pasture land. The expansion of production thus requires clearing all available land for pasture, and, when possible, purchasing and/or renting more land.

The change in land use patterns is dramatic. Between the 1952 and 1974 agricultural censuses in southern Honduras, the amount of land in pasture increased by 50 percent, reaching over 60 percent of the total land area in 1974. This has occurred in both lowlands and highlands. One of the ways in which the process is facilitated is that many landholders rent forest land to the poor who clear it to produce subsistence crops. Pasture is interplanted with these crops so that after a year or two of cultivation the landholder is left with a permanent pasture. The poor have only the option of attempting to rent the increasingly scarce areas of forest land.[9]

Why are landowners so interested in cattle and pasture? One landowner in southern Honduras explained her reasons. She reported that in the past she had grown cotton on her lands. In recent years, with the unpredictability of prices on the world market, the high costs of chemicals, fuel, machinery, and the problems associated with hiring workers, she has decided that the crop is too risky and unprofitable. With just three or four hired hands, she can effectively manage a herd of several hundred cattle. Input costs are lower, and, while prices are still unpredictable, it is common practice to hold on to the animals when prices are too low.[10]

The conversion of land to pasture is going on all over Central America. Land utilization patterns for Honduras and Costa Rica show that only a little over 6 percent of the land in both countries is used for export crops like bananas, coffee, cotton, and sugar cane. While some may criticize the multinational corporations that control the production and/or marketing of these commodities, at least their production employs a substantial amount of labor. However, at present, over 50 percent of the land in both countries is devoted to pasture for cattle, an export commodity that employs relatively little labor.[11]

The growth of cattle production in the five Central American countries has been phenomenal. Between 1959 and 1979 the number of cattle increased by 80 percent, from 6.9 million to 12.4 million head. While meat production in these countries increased by over 185 percent, consumption has barely increased, and per capita consumption actually declined in Honduras and Costa Rica. The reason is that exports of beef have risen even faster (about 500 percent in the last twenty years) than production.[12] The United States is the biggest consumer of exported beef, using it for hamburger, pet foods, and other processed meats.

The effects of turning Central America into a large cattle ranch are profound. Many people have noted the ecological costs, especially the destruction of forests as more and more land is cleared for pasture. In addition, as small farmers and agricultural laborers are displaced from good lands, they are forced into using marginal, often steep-sloped lands in order to produce their subsistence crops. Increased soil erosion is the result. There are no nutritional benefits for the majority of local people; in fact, cattle are competing with poor people for scarce land and food. The pastures to feed cattle replace land that people could use to feed themselves. There are no employment benefits; the main reason for the expansion of cattle production is precisely because so little labor is required. Finally, because cattle production requires extensive amounts of land, larger landholders continue to try to expand their holdings, thus exacerbating inequalities in access to land.[13]

The result of the concentration on export agriculture, especially beef, is that these Central American agrarian systems are now plagued by the dual problems of extreme inequities of land distribution and decreasing employment opportunities.

Table 1 indicates the concentration of landholdings that existed in Central America before the Nicaraguan Revolution. Although in several cases agricultural censuses have not been carried out for many years and the data are now quite old, in most countries land concentration is growing rather than declining.[14] A small percentage of the landholders has had control over a large part of the land, while the majority of landholders has had access only to small plots of land. For example, at the time of the last census in El Salvador only .7 percent of the population controlled almost 39 percent of the land. Meanwhile, almost 87 percent of the landholders were owners of plots of less than five hectares that comprised only 19.6 percent of the cultivated land. In addition, almost 41 percent of the population was completely landless.[15]

A similar pattern prevailed in Nicaragua until the Sandinista Revolution. Anastasio Somoza's family owned one-half of all the farms over five hundred hectares and controlled about one-quarter of all industry. This concentration of land and wealth, and the corruption and abuse of power that went along with it, was one of the principal reasons why so many segments of the populace united to overthrow his regime.[16] The data for the other Central American countries are similar. Guatemala, Honduras, and Costa Rica also have been characterized by an extremely skewed distribution of landholdings.

The revolution that took place in Nicaragua and those in process in El Salvador and Guatemala have roots that go beyond the agrarian issue. Yet the inequalities in the agrarian system are among the most critical stimuli to revolution. One of the rallying cries

Table 1   CONCENTRATION OF AGRICULTURAL LANDHOLDINGS IN CENTRAL AMERICA

Country	Percentage of Landholders	Percentage of Land Controlled
NICARAGUA (1963)[a]		
< 5 hectares	50.8%	3.5%
>100 hectares	5.0	58.8
EL SALVADOR (1971)[a]		
< 5 hectares	86.9	19.6
>100 hectares	.7	38.9
GUATEMALA (1970)[b] (estimates)		
< 4 hectares	83.3	12.3
>350 hectares	.5	42.4
HONDURAS (1974)[c]		
< 5 hectares	63.8	1.8
>100 hectares	9.1	44.1
COSTA RICA (1973)[d]		
< 4.76 hectares	35.0	1.5
>100 hectares	8.4	67.0

[a] J. W. Wilkie and S. Haber, eds., *Statistical Abstract of Latin America*, vol. 22 (Los Angeles, 1983).

[b] World Bank, *Guatemala: Economic and Social Position and Prospects* (Washington, DC, 1978). While these are estimated figures, they generally agree with the data from the 1964 agricultural census, presented in Wilkie and Haber, *Statistical Abstract of Latin America*.

[c] *Censo Nacional Agropecuario 1974, Tomo II, Tenencia de la Tierra* (Tegucigalpa, 1978).

[d] These data were computed from Table 11 of Mitchell A. Seligson, *Peasants of Costa Rica and the Development of Agrarian Capitalism* (Madison, WI, 1980). The data in Seligson's table were originally expressed in terms of *manzanas*, a unit of land that is equivalent to .69 hectare. For this reason I have used lands that are under 4.76 hectares for my comparison.

of the Sandinista Revolution was "land for whoever works it!" and agrarian reform is still a major issue there.

Although a proposal of agrarian reform set in motion the CIA-directed coup that toppled the democratically elected government of Jacobo Arbenz in Guatemala in 1954, the U.S. government apparently perceives the necessity of agrarian reform.[17] To try to correct some of the gross inequalities in Central America and to take some of the pressure off friendly regimes, the United States has been providing funds for agrarian reform efforts. This is being attempted in El Salvador despite right-wing opposition which has extended to the murder of two U.S. government advisers and the head of the Salvadoran Institute of Agrarian Transformation in January 1981. Even in Costa Rica, which thus far has remained an island of democracy in a sea of military dictatorships, agrarian reform has been promoted with the assistance of the U.S. government. As Mitchell A. Seligson has said, "land reform is seen as an imperative for the future stability of the Costa Rican countryside."[18]

The reason why land reform is so crucial is that jobs are not being created in the industrial sector fast enough to absorb either the increasing population or the people who are being pushed out of the rural areas. This is because the process of industrialization in Central America has followed a path similar to that of agriculture, emphasizing capital-intensive rather than labor-intensive development. As Harley Browning and Bryan Roberts have shown for Latin America as a whole, the percentage of the population employed in industry barely increased, from 18.6 percent in 1950 to only 21.2 percent in 1979.[19] Table 2 demonstrates the same trend for the Central American countries. The percentage of the population engaged in agriculture is declining, and the industrial sector has not expanded at nearly the same rate. In the past twenty years, the percentage of the population in agriculture has dropped as little as 7 percent in Honduras and as much as 22 percent in Costa Rica. The percentage employed in industry in the five countries has increased only between 4 and 7 percent. As a result, the rural landless and the small farmer are caught in a squeeze. They are increasingly pushed out of the countryside into the urban areas in which few decent jobs await them. There they either join the ranks of unemployed or, more typically, become engaged in the informal service sector of the economy as shoeshine boys, servants, or street vendors. This has been the true sector of growth in Central American economies, especially in Nicaragua and Costa Rica.

The agrarian processes described above have created greater numbers of underemployed urban poor and continue to exacerbate the already glaring inequalities existing in these countries. The agrarian problems of Central America suggest that hundreds of millions of dollars of military assistance, the training of thousands of troops, and the presence and even participation of U.S. troops are not likely to quell for long the revolutionary fires burning in the region.

Much more fundamental social and economic reforms are needed to provide a permanent solution. These include meaningful agrarian reform; price policies that are not antithetical to the production of basic grains; improved distribution of services such as health, education, and water and sanitation; more widespread participation in government and planning; and elimination of corruption and abuse of power. Without such reforms first, the $8 billion in economic assistance recommended by the Kissinger Commission is only likely to worsen the problem. Walter LaFeber recently has argued that one of the effects of the immensely popular Alliance for Progress during the Kennedy administration was to make revolutions inevitable. The alliance did result in unprecedented economic growth rates in Latin America, but the growth occurred along the lines of capital-intensive strategies, thus creating fewer jobs for the poor who were and still are the most needy beneficiaries. In addition, the economic benefits were largely usurped by the oligarchs who controlled banks and mercantile businesses. Consequently, economic growth created greater inequality and fed revolutionary sentiment.[20]

Given the prevailing conditions in the four Central American republics to which the $8 billion in economic assistance would flow, there is a strong likelihood that, even if the money were to be used for its intended purposes, it would not help. These funds would most likely go into developing capital-intensive industries and into expanding export agriculture. For the agricultural sector, this is likely to continue to engender the concentration of landholdings and the investment in commodities and technologies that minimize labor costs. These developments have a greater likelihood of further lining the pockets of the rich and ignoring the fundamental needs of the poor for land and/or jobs with which to earn a decent living.

Table 2 PERCENTAGE CHANGE IN THE DISTRIBUTION OF THE LABOR FORCE IN CENTRAL AMERICA[a]

	Agriculture		Industry		Services	
	1960	1980	1960	1980	1960	1980
Honduras	70%	63%	11%	15%	19%	23%
El Salvador	62	50	17	22	21	27
Nicaragua	62	43	16	20	22	37
Guatemala	67	55	14	21	19	25
Costa Rica	51	29	19	23	30	48

[a] World Bank, World Development Report, 1983 (New York, 1983), pp. 188–89.

NOTES

1. The percentages of the population involved in agriculture in 1980 may be found in Table 2. Percentages for the contribution of agriculture to the gross domestic product were 18.5 in Costa Rica, 27.5 in El Salvador, 28.3 in Honduras, 28.4 in Guatemala, and 33.5 in Nicaragua. These data may be found in J. W. Wilkie and S. Haber, eds., Statistical Abstract of Latin America, vol. 22 (Los Angeles, 1983), pp. 291, 293–95.
2. Alain de Janvry, The Agrarian Question and Reformism in Latin America (Baltimore, 1981), pp. 157–73.
3. The actual percentages of exports contributed by agriculture for 1978 were 53.4 for El Salvador, 58.1 for Costa Rica, 58.9 for Nicaragua, 68.2 for Honduras, and 68.9 for Guatemala. See Wilkie and Haber, Statistical Abstract of Latin America, pp. 402, 406–07, 409, 411.
4. See Joan Robinson, Aspects of Development and Underde-

velopment (Cambridge, MA, 1979), pp. 102–03. In her critique of free trade and comparative advantage, Robinson notes that this idea is dependent upon two assumptions, neither of which holds in the modern world. First, the argument is made in terms of comparisons of static equilibrium conditions in which each trading nation is characterized by full employment of resources and balanced payments. Second, because all countries are treated as having the same level of development, unequal exchange is not part of the model.

5. Murdo MacLeod, *Spanish Central America: A Socio-economic History, 1520–1720* (Berkeley, 1973). This is an excellent source for the early history of agricultural exports in Central America.

6. A very good general reference, particularly on the importance of coffee and bananas in Central American history, is Ralph Woodward, *Central America: A Nation Divided* (New York, 1976), esp. pp. 149–202. More in-depth accounts of the significance of agricultural export commodities may be found in Tommie Sue Montgomery, *Revolution in El Salvador: Origins and Evolution* (Boulder, CO, 1982), esp. pp. 34–46; John A. Booth, *The End and the Beginning: The Nicaraguan Revolution* (Boulder, CO, 1982), esp. pp. 20–26; Mitchell A. Seligson, *Peasants of Costa Rica and the Development of Agrarian Capitalism* (Madison, WI, 1980), esp. pp. 14–72; Jefferson C. Boyer, *Agrarian Capitalism and Peasant Praxis in Southern Honduras* (Ann Arbor, MI, 1983), esp. pp. 62–95; and Richard N. Adams, *Crucifixion by Power: Essays on Guatemalan Social Structure, 1944–1966* (Austin, TX, 1970), esp. pp. 353–79.

7. See Montgomery, *Origins and Evolution*, p. 45 for an account of this in El Salvador in the 1920s.

8. See Boyer, *Agrarian Capitalism*, pp. 59–61; Billie R. DeWalt and Kathleen M. DeWalt, *Farming Systems Research in Southern Honduras*, Report No. 1, Department of Sociology, University of Kentucky, Lexington; Billie R. DeWalt, "The Cattle Are Eating the Forest," *Bulletin of the Atomic Scientists* 39 (1983): 18–23.

9. See DeWalt, "The Cattle Are Eating the Forest," pp. 20–21.

10. Although this landowner did not mention it, another advantage of cattle is that they are quite maneuverable. Estimates are that 200,000 of Nicaragua's cattle were smuggled out of the country into Honduras between the beginning of the revolution and mid-1981 (see Joseph Collins, *What Difference Could a Revolution Make?* [San Francisco, 1982], p. 45). It is also common for Hondurans to smuggle their cattle into El Salvador or Guatemala where prices are higher.

11. These data were obtained by the author from the following sources: for Costa Rica, unpublished accounts from Proyecto de Información Agropecuario del Istmo Centroamericano, Instituto Interamericano de Coop-

eración para la Agricultura, San Jose, Costa Rica; for Honduras, compiled from various volumes of the Censo Nacional Agropecuario, Dirección General de Estadistica y Censos, Republica de Honduras, Tegucigalpa, 1977 and 1978.

12. Between 1959 and 1979 the number of cattle increased by 44.4 percent in El Salvador, 60 percent in Nicaragua, 69.2 percent in Honduras, 100 percent in Costa Rica, and 125 percent in Guatemala. These data are reported in Billie R. DeWalt, "Microcosmic and Macrocosmic Processes of Agrarian Change in Southern Honduras," in Billie R. DeWalt and Pertti J. Pelto, eds., *Microlevel/Macrolevel Linkages in Anthropological Theory and Research* (Boulder, CO, n.d.). These percentages are derived from data presented in several U.S. Department of Agriculture foreign circulars entitled "Livestock and Meat" and published between 1959 and 1983.

13. Other discussions of these processes may be found in Douglas Shane, *Hoofprints of the Forest: An Inquiry into the Beef Cattle Industry in the Tropical Forest Areas of Latin America* (Washington, DC, 1980); James Nations and Daniel Komer, "Indians, Immigrants and Beef Exports: Deforestation in Central America," *Cultural Survival Quarterly* 6 (1982): 8–12; Seligson, *Peasants of Costa Rica*, p. 164; and DeWalt, "The Cattle Are Eating the Forest."

14. For Costa Rica see Seligson, *Peasants of Costa Rica*, p. 148; for Honduras see Boyer, *Agrarian Capitalism*, pp. 85–96; and for El Salvador see Martin Diskin, "Land Reform in El Salvador: An Evaluation," *Culture and Agriculture* 13 (1981): 1–7.

15. Diskin, "Land Reform in El Salvador," p. 1.

16. It is interesting to note that in the United States there is a similar pattern of landownership, with about 1 percent of the owners controlling 40 percent of the land. Over 78 percent of the landholders have access to only about 3 percent of the land. The major difference is that in this country there are many more alternative employment possibilities for those who do not have access to land. See Ann Mariano, "A Homesite Is a Lot," *Washington Post National Weekly Edition*, February 13, 1984, p. 21.

17. On Mexico's continuing agrarian problems see Gustavo Esteva, *The Struggle for Rural Mexico* (South Hadley, MA, 1983); on Nicaragua see Collins, *What Difference Could a Revolution Make?* p. 79; and on Guatemala see Stephen Schlesinger and Stephen Kinzer, *Bitter Fruit: The Untold Story of the American Coup in Guatemala* (Garden City, NY, 1982), pp. 75–77.

18. Seligson, *Peasants of Costa Rica*, p. 123.

19. Harley Browning and Bryan Roberts, "Urbanization, Sectoral Transformation, and the Utilization of Labor in Latin America," *Comparative Urban Research* 8 (1980): 86–103.

20. Walter LaFeber, *Inevitable Revolutions: The United States in Central America* (New York, 1983), pp. 148–55.

19

The Domestication of Wood in Haiti:

A Case Study in Applied Evolution

Gerald F. Murray

In its annual report on the state of the planet, the World-watch Institute describes the growing shortage of wood for fuel and construction throughout the Third World. The problem is most acute in densely populated areas with a long history of agriculture. In these areas, peasant farmers or members of their families may spend several hours each day finding firewood. Because forests take such a long time to grow and such a short time to cut down, reforestation is a worldwide ecological challenge.

As described in this selection, Haiti has a severe deforestation problem that is closely related to wider issues of poverty and overpopulation. In this context, traditional reforestation projects, with ponderous education components on the value of trees, had failed miserably. Anthropologist Gerald Murray, who had done research on land tenure among rural Haitian peasants, had the rare opportunity to design and implement an alternative project in forestry and agricultural development. His anthropological understanding of the economic system and culture of the Haitian people clearly paid off. The project represents applying cultural anthropology at its best.

As you read this selection, ask yourself the following questions:

- ☐ *Why does Haiti have a deforestation problem?*

- ☐ *How was Gerald Murray's anthropological alternative project different from traditional reforestation programs?*

- ☐ *Why was using particular kinds of trees important for the project?*

- ☐ *What accounted for the Haitian peasants' enthusiasm for the idea of trees as a cash crop?*

- ☐ *What is meant by the title of this piece?*

The following terms discussed in this selection are included in the Glossary at the back of the book:

arable land
domestication of plants and animals
horticulture
population pressure
reforestation
swidden
usufruct rights

Reprinted from *Anthropological Praxis*, edited by Robert M. Wulff and Shirley J. Fiske, 1987, by permission of Westview Press, Boulder, Colorado.

PROBLEM AND CLIENT

Expatriate tree lovers, whether tourists or developmental planners, often leave Haiti with an upset stomach. Though during precolonial times the island Arawaks had reached a compromise with the forest, their market-oriented colonial successors saw trees as something to be removed. The Spaniards specialized in exporting wood from the eastern side of the island, whereas the French on the western third found it more profitable to clear the wood and produce sugar cane, coffee, and indigo for European markets. During the nineteenth century, long after Haiti had become an independent republic, foreign lumber companies cut and exported most of the nation's precious hardwoods, leaving little for today's peasants.

The geometric increase in population since colonial times—from an earlier population of fewer than half a million former slaves to a contemporary population of more than six million—and the resulting shrinkage of average family holding size have led to the evolution of a land use system devoid of systematic fallow periods. A vicious cycle has set in—one that seems to have targeted the tree for ultimate destruction. Not only has land pressure eliminated a regenerative fallow phase in the local agricultural cycle; in addition the catastrophic declines in per hectare food yields have forced peasants into alternative income-generating strategies. Increasing numbers crowd into the capital city, Port-au-Prince, creating a market for construction wood and charcoal. Poorer sectors of the peasantry in the rural areas respond to this market by racing each other with axes and machetes to cut down the few natural tree stands remaining in remoter regions of the republic. The proverbial snowball in Hades is at less risk than a tree in Haiti.

Unable to halt the flows either of wood into the cities or of soil into the oceans, international development organizations finance studies to measure the volume of these flows (50 million trees cut per year is one of the round figures being bandied about) and to predict when the last tree will be cut from Haiti. Reforestation projects have generally been entrusted by their well-meaning but short-sighted funders to Duvalier's Ministry of Agriculture, a kiss-of-death resource channeling strategy by which the Port-au-Prince jobs created frequently outnumber the seedlings produced. And even the few seedlings produced often died in the nurseries because the peasants were understandably reluctant to cover their scarce holdings with state-owned trees. Project managers had been forced to resort to "food for work" strategies to move seedlings out of nurseries onto hillsides. And peasants have endeavored where possible to plant the trees on somebody else's hillsides and to enlist their livestock as allies in the subsequent removal of this dangerous vegetation.

This generalized hostility to tree projects placed the U.S. Agency for International Development (AID)/Haiti mission in a bind. After several years of absence from Haiti in the wake of expulsion by Francois Duvalier, AID had reestablished its presence under the government of his son Jean Claude. But an ambitious Integrated Agricultural Development Project funded through the Ministry of Agriculture had already given clear signs of being a multimillion-dollar farce. And an influential congressman chairing the U.S. House Ways and Means Committee—consequently exercising strong control over AID funds worldwide—had taken a passionate interest in Haiti. In his worldwide travels this individual had become adept at detecting and exposing developmental charades. And he had been blunt in communicating his conviction that much of what he had seen in AID/Haiti's program was precisely that. He had been touched by the plight of Haiti and communicated to the highest AID authorities his conviction about the salvific power of contraceptives and trees and his determination to have AID grace Haiti with an abundant flow of both. And he would personally visit Haiti (a convenient plane ride from Washington, D.C.) to inspect for himself, threatening a worldwide funding freeze if no results were forthcoming. A chain reaction of nervous "yes sirs" speedily worked its way down from AID headquarters in Washington to a beleaguered Port-au-Prince mission.

The pills and condoms were less of a problem. Even the most cantankerous congressman was unlikely to insist on observing them in use and would probably settle for household distribution figures. Not so with the trees. He could (and did) pooh-pooh nursery production figures and asked to be taken to see the new AID forests, a most embarrassing request in a country where peasants creatively converted daytime reforestation projects into nocturnal goat forage projects. AID's reaction was twofold—first, to commission an immediate study to explain to the congressman and others why peasants refused to plant trees (for this they called down an AID economist); and second, to devise some program strategy that would achieve the apparently unachievable: to instill in cash-needy, defiant, pleasant charcoalmakers a love, honor, and respect for newly planted trees. For this attitudinal transformation, a task usually entrusted to the local armed forces, AID/Haiti invited an anthropologist to propose an alternative approach.

PROCESS AND PLAYERS

During these dynamics, I completed a doctoral dissertation on the manner in which Haitian peasant land tenure had evolved in response to internal population growth. The AID economist referred to above exhaustively reviewed the available literature, also focusing on the issue of Haitian peasant land tenure, and produced for the mission a well-argued monograph (Zuvekas 1978) documenting a lower rate of landlessness in Haiti than in many other Latin American settings but documenting as well the informal, extralegal character of the relationship between many peasant families and their landholdings. This latter observation was interpreted by some in the mission to mean that the principal determinant of the failure of tree planting projects was the absence among peasants of legally secure deeds over their plots. Peasants could not be expected to invest money on land improvements when at mildest the benefits could accrue to another and at worst the very improvements themselves could lead to expropriation from their land. In short, no massive tree planting could be expected, according to this model, until a nationwide cadastral reform granted plot-by-plot deeds to peasant families.

This hypothesis was reputable but programmatically paralyzing because nobody dreamed that the Duvalier regime was about to undertake a major cadastral reform for the benefit of peasants. Several AID officers in Haiti had read my dissertation on land tenure (Murray 1977), and I received an invitation to advise the mission. Was Haitian peasant land tenure compatible with tree planting? Zuvekas' study had captured the internally complex nature of Haitian peasant land tenure. But the subsequent extrapolations as to paralyzing insecurity simply did not seem to fit with ethnographic evidence. In two reports (Murray 1978a, 1978b) I indicated that peasants in general feel secure about their ownership rights over their land. Failure to secure plot-by-plot surveyed deeds is generally a cost-saving measure. Interclass evictions did occur, but they were statistically rare; instead most land disputes were intrafamilial. A series of extralegal tenure practices had evolved—preinheritance land grants to young adult dependents, informal inheritance subdivisions witnessed by community members, fictitious sales to favored children, complex community-internal share-cropping arrangements. And though these practices produced an internally heterogeneous system with its complexities, there was strong internal order. Any chaos and insecurity tended to be more in the mind of observers external to the system than in the behavior of the peasants themselves. There was a danger that the complexities of Haitian peasant land

tenure would generate an unintended smokescreen obscuring the genuine causes of failure in tree planting projects.

What then were these genuine causes? The mission, intent on devising programming strategies in this domain, invited me to explore further, under a contract aimed at identifying the "determinants of success and failure" in reforestation and soil conservation projects. My major conclusion was that the preexisting land tenure, cropping, and livestock systems in peasant Haiti were perfectly adequate for the undertaking of significant tree planting activities. Most projects had failed not because of land tenure or attitudinal barriers among peasants but because of fatal flaws in one or more key project components. Though my contract called principally for analysis of previous or existing projects, I used the recommendation section of the report to speculate on how a Haiti-wise anthropologist would program and manage reforestation activities if he or she had the authority. In verbal debriefings I jokingly challenged certain young program officers in the mission to give me a jeep and carte blanche access to a $50,000 checking account, and I would prove my anthropological assertions about peasant economic behavior and produce more trees in the ground than their current multimillion-dollar Ministry of Agriculture charade. We had a good laugh and shook hands, and I departed confident that the report would be as dutifully perused and as honorably filed and forgotten as similar reports I had done elsewhere.

To my great disbelief, as I was correcting Anthro 101 exams some two years later, one of the program officers still in Haiti called to say that an Agroforestry Outreach Project (AOP) had been approved chapter and verse as I had recommended it; and that if I was interested in placing my life where my mouth had been and would leave the ivory tower to direct the project, my project bank account would have not $50,000, but $4 million. After several weeks of hemming and hawing and vigorous negotiating for leave from my department, I accepted the offer and entered a new (to me) role of project director in a strange upside-down world in which the project anthropologist was not a powerless cranky voice from the bleachers but the chief of party with substantial authority over general project policy and the allocation of project resources. My elation at commanding resources to implement anthropological ideas was dampened by the nervousness of knowing exactly who would be targeted for flak and ridicule if these ideas bombed out, as most tended to do in the Haiti of Duvalier.

The basic structural design of AOP followed a tripartite conceptual framework that I proposed for analyzing projects. Within this framework a project is composed of three essential systemic elements: a technical base, a benefit flow strategy, and an institutional delivery strategy. Planning had to focus equally on all three; I argued that defects in one would sabotage the entire project.

Technical Strategy

The basic technical strategy was to make available to peasants fast-growing wood trees (*Leucaena leucocephala, Cassia siamea, Azadirachta indica, Casuarina equisetifolia, Eucalyptus camaldulensis*) that were not only drought resistant but also rapid growing, producing possible four-year harvest rotations in humid lowland areas (and slower rotations and lower survival rates in arid areas) and that were good for charcoal and basic construction needs. Most of the species mentioned also restore nutrients to the soil, and some of them coppice from a carefully harvested stump, producing several rotations before the need for replanting.

Of equally critical technical importance was the use of a nursery system that produced light-weight microseedlings. A project pickup truck could transport over 15,000 of these microseedlings (as opposed to 250 traditional bag seedlings), and the average peasant could easily carry over 500 transportable seedlings at one time, planting them with a fraction of the ground preparation time and labor required for bulkier bagged seedlings. The anthropological implications of this nursery system were critical. It constituted a technical breakthrough that reduced to a fraction the fossil-fuel and human energy expenditure required to transport and plant trees.

But the technical component of the project incorporated yet another element: the physical juxtaposition of trees and crops. In traditional reforestation models, the trees are planted in large unbroken monocropped stands. Such forests or woodlots presuppose local land tenure and economic arrangements not found in Haiti. For the tree to make its way as a cultivate into the economy of Haitian peasants and most other tropical cultivators, reforestation models would have to be replaced by agroforestry models that entail spatial or temporal juxtaposition of crops and trees. Guided by prior ethnographic knowledge of Haitian cropping patterns, AOP worked out with peasants various border planting and intercropping strategies to make tree planting feasible even for small holding cultivators.

Benefit Flow Strategies

With respect to the second systemic component, the programming of benefit flows to participants, earlier projects had often committed the fatal flaw of defining project trees planted as *pyebwa leta* (the state's trees). Authoritarian assertions by project staff concerning sanctions for cutting newly planted trees created fears among peasants that even trees planted on their own land would be government property. And several peasants were frank in reporting fears that the trees might eventually be used as a pretext by the government or the "Company" (the most common local lexeme used to refer to projects) for eventually expropriating the land on which peasants had planted project trees.

Such ambiguities and fears surrounding benefit flows paralyze even the technically soundest project. A major anthropological feature of AOP was a radical frontal attack on the issue of property and usufruct rights over project trees. Whereas other projects had criticized tree cutting, AOP promulgated the heretical message that trees were meant to be cut, processed, and sold. The only problem with the present system, according to project messages, was that peasants were cutting nature's trees. But once the landowner "mete fos li deyo" (expends his resources) and plants and cares for his or her own wood trees on his or her own land, the landowner has the same right to harvest and sell wood as corn or beans.

I was inevitably impressed at the impact that this blunt message had when I delivered it to groups of prospective peasant tree planters. Haitian peasants are inveterate and aggressive cash-croppers; many of the crops and livestock that they produce are destined for immediate consignment to local markets. For the first time in their lives, they were hearing a concrete proposal to make the wood tree itself one more marketable crop in their inventory.

But the message would ring true only if three barriers were smashed.

1. The first concerned the feared delay in benefits. Most wood trees with which the peasants were familiar took an impractically long time to mature. There fortunately existed in Haiti four-year-old stands of leucaena, cassia, eucalyptus, and other project trees to which we could take peasant groups to demonstrate the growth speed of these trees.

2. But could they be planted on their scanty holdings without interfering with crops? Border and row planting techniques were demonstrated, as well as intercropping. The average peasant holding was about a hectare and a half. If a cultivator planted a field in the usual crops and then planted 500 seedlings in the same field at 2 meters by 2 meters, the seedlings would occupy

only a fifth of a hectare. And they would be far enough apart to permit continued cropping for two or three cycles before shade competition became too fierce. That is, trees would be planted on only a fraction of the peasant's holdings and planted in such a way that they would be compatible with continued food growing even on the plots where they stood. We would then calculate with peasants the potential income to be derived from these 500 trees through sale as charcoal, polewood, or boards. In a best-case scenario, the gross take from the charcoal of these trees (the least lucrative use of the wood) might equal the current annual income of an average rural family. The income potential of these wood trees clearly would far offset any potential loss from decreased food production. Though it had taken AID two years to decide on the project, it took about twenty minutes with any group of skeptical but economically rational peasants to generate a list of enthusiastic potential tree planters.

3. But there was yet a third barrier. All this speculation about income generation presupposed that the peasants themselves, and not the government or the project, would be the sole owners of the trees and that the peasants would have unlimited rights to the harvest of the wood whenever they wished. To deal with this issue, I presented the matter as an agreement between cultivator and the project: We would furnish the free seedlings and technical assistance; the cultivators would agree to plant 500 of these seedlings on their own land and permit project personnel to carry out periodic survival counts. We would, of course, pay no wages or "Food for Work" for this planting. But we would guarantee to the planters complete and exclusive ownership of the trees. They did not need to ask for permission from the project to harvest the trees whenever their needs might dictate, nor would there be any penalties associated with early cutting or low survival. If peasants changed their minds, they could rip out their seedlings six months after planting. They would never get any more free seedlings from us, but they would not be subject to any penalties. There are preexisting local forestry laws, rarely enforced, concerning permissions and minor taxes for tree cutting. Peasants would have to deal with these as they had skillfully done in the past. But from our project's point of view, we relinquish all tree ownership rights to the peasants who accept and plant the trees on their property.

Cash-flow dialogues and ownership assurances such as these were a far cry from the finger-wagging ecological sermons to which many peasant groups had been subjected on the topic of trees. Our project technicians developed their own messages; but central to all was the principle of peasant ownership and usufruct of AOP trees. The goal was to capitalize on the preexisting fuel and lumber markets, to make the wood tree one more crop in the income-generating repertoire of the Haitian peasant.

Institutional Strategy

The major potential fly in the ointment was the third component, the institutional component. To whom would AID entrust its funds to carry out this project? My own research had indicated clearly that Haitian governmental involvement condemned a project to certain paralysis and possible death, and my report phrased that conclusion as diplomatically as possible. The diplomacy was required to head off possible rage, less from Haitian officials than from certain senior officers in the AID mission who were politically and philosophically wedded to an institution-building strategy. Having equated the term "institution" with "government bureaucracy," and having defined their own career success in terms, not of village-level resource flows, but of voluminous and timely bureaucracy-to-bureaucracy cash transfers, such officials were in effect marshaling U.S. resources into the service of extractive ministries with unparalleled track records of squandering and/or pilfering expatriate donor funds.

To the regime's paradoxical credit, however, the blatant openness and arrogance of Duvalierist predation had engendered an angry willingness in much of Haiti's development community to explore other resource flow channels. Though the nongovernmental character of the proposal provoked violent reaction, the reactionaries in the Haiti mission were overridden by their superiors in Washington, and a completely nongovernmental implementing mode was adopted for this project.

The system, based on private voluntary organizations (PVOs), worked as follows.

1. AID made a macrogrant to a Washington-based PVO (the Pan American Development Foundation, PADF) to run a tree-planting project based on the principles that had emerged in my research. At the Haiti mission's urging, PADF invited me to be chief of party for the project and located an experienced accountant in Haiti to be financial administrator. PADF in addition recruited three American agroforesters who, in

addition to MA-level professional training, had several years of overseas village field experience under their belts. Early in the project they were supplemented by two other expatriates, a Belgian and a French Canadian. We opened a central office in Port-au-Prince and assigned a major region of Haiti to each of the agroforesters, who lived in their field regions.

2. These agroforesters were responsible for contacting the many village-based PVOs working in their regions to explain the project, to emphasize its microeconomic focus and its difference from traditional reforestation models, to discuss the conditions of entry therein, and to make technical suggestions as to the trees that would be appropriate for the region.

3. If the PVO was interested, we drafted an agreement in which our mutual contributions and spheres of responsibility were specified. The agreements were not drafted in French (Haiti's official language) but in Creole, the only language spoken by most peasants.

4. The local PVO selected *animateurs* (village organizers) who themselves were peasants who lived and worked in the village where trees would be planted. After receiving training from us, they contacted their neighbors and kin, generated lists of peasants interested in planting a specified number of trees, and informed us when the local rains began to fall. At the proper moment we packed the seedlings in boxes customized to the particular region and shipped them on our trucks to the farmers, who would be waiting at specified drop-off points at a specified time. The trees were to be planted within twenty-four hours of delivery.

5. The animateurs were provided with Creole language data forms by which to gather ecological, land use, and land tenure data on each plot where trees would be planted and certain bits of information on each peasant participant. These forms were used to follow up, at periodic intervals, the survival of trees, the incidence of any problems (such as livestock depredation, burning, disease), and—above all—the manner in which the farmer integrated the trees into cropping and livestock patterns, to detect and head off any unintended substitution of food for wood.

RESULTS AND EVALUATION

The project was funded for four years from October 1981 through November 1985. During the writing of the project paper we were asked by an AID economist to estimate how many trees would be planted. Not knowing if the peasants would in fact plant any trees, we nervously proposed to reach two thousand peasant families with a million trees as a project goal. Fiddling with his programmed calculator, the economist informed us that that output would produce a negative internal rate of return. We would need at least two million trees to make the project worth AID's institutional while. We shrugged and told him cavalierly to up the figure and to promise three million trees on the land of six thousand peasants. (At that time I thought someone else would be directing the project.)

Numbers of Trees and Beneficiaries

Though I doubted that we could reach this higher goal, the response of the Haitian peasants to this new approach to tree planting left everyone, including myself, open mouthed. Within the first year of the project, one million trees had been planted by some 2,500 peasant households all over Haiti. My fears of peasant indifference were now transformed into nervousness that we could not supply seedlings fast enough to meet the demand triggered by our wood-as-a-cash-crop strategy. Apologetic village animateurs informed us that some cultivators who had not signed up on the first lists were actually stealing newly planted seedlings from their neighbors' fields at night. They promised to catch the scoundrels. If they did, I told them, give the scoundrels a hug. Their pilfering was dramatic proof of the bull's-eye nature of the anthropological predictions that underlie the project.

By the end of the second year (when I left the project), we had reached the four-year goal of three million seedlings and the project had geared up and decentralized its nursery capacity to produce several million seedlings per season (each year having two planting seasons). Under the new director, a fellow anthropologist, the geometric increase continued. By the end of the fourth year, the project had planted, not its originally agreed-upon three million trees, but twenty million trees. Stated more accurately, some 75,000 Haitian peasants had enthusiastically planted trees on their own land. In terms of its quantitative outreach, AOP had more than quintupled its original goals.

Wood Harvesting and Wood Banking

By the end of its fourth year the project had already received an unusual amount of professional research attention by anthropologists, economists, and foresters. In addition to AID evaluations, six studies had been released on one or another aspect of the project (Ashley

1986; Balzano 1986; Buffum and King 1985; Conway 1986; Grosenick 1985; McGowan 1986). As predicted, many peasants were harvesting trees by the end of the fourth year. The most lucrative sale of the wood was as polewood in local markets, though much charcoal was also being made from project trees.

Interestingly, however, the harvesting was proceeding much more slowly than I had predicted. Peasants were "clinging" to their trees and not engaging in the clear cutting that I hoped would occur, as a prelude to the emergence of a rotational system in which peasants would alternate crops with tree cover that they themselves had planted. This technique would have been a revival, under a "domesticated" mode, of the ancient swidden sequence that had long since disappeared from Haiti. Though such a revival would have warmed anthropological hearts, the peasants had a different agenda. Though they had long ago removed nature's tree cover, they were extremely cautious about removing the tree cover that they had planted. Their economic logic was unassailable. Crop failure is so frequent throughout most of Haiti, and the market for wood and charcoal so secure, that peasants prefer to leave the tree as a "bank" against future emergencies. This arboreal bank makes particular sense in the context of the recent disappearance from Haiti of the peasant's traditional bank, the pig. A governmentally mandated (and U.S. financed) slaughter of all pigs because of fears of African swine fever created a peasant banking gap that AOP trees have now started to fill.

THE ANTHROPOLOGICAL DIFFERENCE

Anthropological findings, methods, and theories clearly have heavily influenced this project at all stages. We are dealing, not with an ongoing project affected by anthropological input, but with a project whose very existence was rooted in anthropological research and whose very character was determined by ongoing anthropological direction and anthropologically informed managerial prodding.

My own involvement with the project spanned several phases and tasks:

1. Proposal of a theoretical and conceptual base of AOP, and concept of "wood as a cash crop."

2. Preliminary contacting of local PVOs to assess preproject interest.

3. Identification of specific program measures during project design.

4 Preparation of social soundness analysis for the AID project paper.

5. Participation as an outside expert at the meetings in AID Washington at which the fate of the project was decided.

6. Participation in the selection and in-country linguistic and cultural training of the agroforesters who worked for the project.

7. Direction and supervision of field operations.

8. Formative evaluation of preliminary results and the identification of needed midcourse corrections.

9. Generation of several hundred thousand dollars of supplemental funding from Canadian and Swiss sources and internationalization of the project team.

10. Preparation of publications about the project (Murray 1984, 1986).

In addition to my own participation in the AOP, four other anthropologists have been involved in long-term commitments to the project. Fred Conway did a preliminary study of firewood use in Haiti (Conway 1979). He subsequently served for two years as overall project coordinator within AID/Haiti. More recently he has carried out revealing case study research on the harvesting of project trees (Conway 1986). Glenn Smucker likewise did an early feasibility study in the northwest (Smucker 1981) and eventually joined the project as my successor in the directorship. Under his leadership, many of the crucial midcourse corrections were introduced. Ira Lowenthall took over the AID coordination of the project at a critical transitional period and has been instrumental in forging plans for its institutional future. And Anthony Balzano has carried out several years of case study fieldwork on the possible impact of the tree-planting activities on the land tenure in participating villages. All these individuals have PhDs, or are PhD candidates, in anthropology. And another anthropologist in the Haiti mission, John Lewis, succeeded in adapting the privatized umbrella agency outreach model for use in a swine repopulation project. With the possible exception of Vicos, it would be hard to imagine a project that has been as heavily influenced by anthropologists.

But how specifically has anthropology influenced the content of the project? There are at least three major levels at which anthropology has impinged on the content of AOP.

1. *The Application of Substantive Findings.* The very choice of "wood as a marketable crop" as the fundamental theme of the project stemmed from ethnographic knowledge of the cash-oriented foundations of Haitian peasant horti-

culture and knowledge of current conditions in the internal marketing system. Because of ethnographic knowledge I was able to avoid succumbing to the common-sense inclination to emphasize fruit trees (whose perishability and tendency to glut markets make them commercially vulnerable) and to choose instead a fast-growing wood tree. There is a feverishly escalating market for charcoal and construction wood that cannot be dampened even by the most successful project. And there are no spoilage problems with wood. The peasants can harvest it when they want. Furthermore, ethnographic knowledge of Haitian peasant land tenure—which is highly individualistic—guided me away from the community forest schemes that so many development philosophers seem to delight in but that are completely inappropriate to the social reality of Caribbean peasantries.

2. *Anthropological Methods.* The basic research that led up to the project employed participant observation along with intensive interviewing with small groups of informants to compare current cost/benefit ratios of traditional farming with projected cash yields from plots in which trees are intercropped with food on four-year rotation cycles. A critical part of the project design stage was to establish the likelihood of increased revenues from altered land use behaviors. During project design I also applied ethnographic techniques to the behavior of institutional personnel. The application of anthropological notetaking on 3-by-5 slips, not only with peasants but also with technicians, managers, and officials, exposed the institutional roots of earlier project failures and stimulated the proposal of alternative institutional routes. Furthermore, ethno-scientific elicitation of folk taxonomies led to the realization that whereas fruit trees are classified as a crop by Haitian peasants, wood trees are not so classified. This discovery exposed the need for the creation of explicit messages saying that wood can be a crop, just as coffee, manioc, and corn can. Finally, prior experience in Creole-language instrument design and computer analysis permitted me to design a baseline data gathering system.

3. *Anthropological Theory.* My own thinking about tree planting was heavily guided by cultural-evolutionary insights into the origins of agriculture. The global tree problem is often erroneously conceptualized in a conservationist or ecological framework. Such a perspective is very short-sighted for anthropologists. We are aware of an ancient food crisis, when humans still hunted and gathered, that was solved, not by the adoption of conservationist practices, but rather by the shift into a domesticated mode of production. From hunting and gathering we turned to cropping and harvesting. I found the analogy with the present tree crisis conceptually overpowering. Trees will reemerge when and only when human beings start planting them aggressively as a harvestable crop, not when human consciousness is raised regarding their ecological importance. This anthropological insight (or bias), nourished by the aggressive creativity of the Haitian peasants among whom I had lived, swayed me toward the adoption of a dynamic "domestication" paradigm in proposing a solution to the tree problem in Haiti. This evolutionary perspective also permitted me to see that the cash-cropping of wood was in reality a small evolutionary step, not a quantum leap. The Haitian peasants already cut and sell natural stands of wood. They already plant and sell traditional food crops. It is but a small evolutionary step to join these two unconnected streams of Haitian peasant behavior, and this linkage is the core purpose of the Agroforestry Outreach Project.

Broader anthropological theory also motivated and justified a nongovernmental implementing mode for AOP. Not only AID but also most international development agencies tend to operate on a service model of the state. This idealized model views the basic character of the state as that of a provider of services to its population. Adherence to this theoretically naive service model has led to the squandering of untold millions of dollars in the support of extractive public bureaucracies. This waste is justified under the rubric of institution building—assisting public entities to provide the services that they are supposed to be providing.

But my anthropological insights into the origins of the state as a mechanism of extraction and control led me to pose the somewhat heretical position that the predatory behavior of Duvalier's regime was in fact not misbehavior. Duvalier was merely doing openly and blatantly what other state leaders camouflage under rhetoric. AID's search of nongovernmental implementing channels for AOP, then, was not seen as a simple emergency measure to be employed under a misbehaving regime but rather as an avenue of activity that might be valid as an option under many or most regimes. There is little justification in either ethnology or anthropological theory for viewing the state as the proper recipient of developmental funds. This theoretical insight permitted us to argue for a radically nongovernmental mode of tree-planting support in AOP. In short, sensitivity to issues in anthropological theory played a profound role in the shaping of the project.

Would AOP have taken the form it did without these varied types of anthropological input? Almost certainly not. Had there been no anthropological input, a radically different scenario would almost certainly have unfolded with the following elements.

1. AID would probably have undertaken a reforestation project—congressional pressure alone would have ensured that. But the project would have been based, not on the theme of "wood as a peasant cash-crop," but on the more traditional approach to trees as a vehicle of soil conservation. Ponderous educational programs would have been launched to teach the peasants about the value of trees. Emphasis would have been placed on educating the ignorant and on trying to induce peasants to plant commercially marginal (and nutritionally tangential) fruit trees instead of cash-generating wood trees.

2. The project would have been managed by technicians. The emphasis would probably have been on carrying out lengthy technical research concerning optimal planting strategies and the combination of trees with optimally effective bench terraces and other soil conservation devices. The outreach problem would have been given second priority. Throughout Haiti hundreds of thousands of dollars have been spent on numerous demonstration projects to create terraced, forested hillsides, but only a handful of cooperative local peasants have been induced to undertake the same activities on their own land.

3. The project would almost certainly have been run through the Haitian government. When after several hundred thousand dollars of expenditures few trees were visible, frustrated young AID program officers would have gotten finger-wagging lectures about the sovereign right of local officials to use donor money as they see fit. And the few trees planted would have been defined as *pyebwa leta* (the government's trees), and peasants would have been sternly warned against ever cutting these trees, even the ones planted on their own land. And the peasants would soon turn the problem over to their most effective ally in such matters, the

free-ranging omnivorous goat, who would soon remove this alien vegetation from the peasant's land.

Because of anthropology, the Agroforestry Outreach Project has unfolded to a different scenario. It was a moving experience for me to return to the village where I had done my original fieldwork (and which I of course tried to involve in the tree-planting activities) to find several houses built using the wood from leucaena trees planted during the project's earliest phases. Poles were beginning to be sold, although the prices had not yet stabilized for these still unknown wood types. Charcoal made from project trees was being sold in local markets. For the first time in the history of this village, people were "growing" part of their house structures and their cooking fuel. I felt as though I were observing (and had been a participant in) a replay of an ancient anthropological drama, the shift from an extractive to a domesticated mode of resource procurement. Though their sources of food energy had been domesticated millennia ago, my former village neighbors had now begun replicating this transition in the domain of wood and wood-based energy. I felt a satisfaction at having chosen a discipline that could give me the privilege of participating, even marginally, in this very ancient cultural-evolutionary transition.

REFERENCES

Ashley, Marshall D. 1986. *A Study of Traditional Agroforestry Systems in Haiti and Implications for the USAID/Haiti Agroforestry Outreach Project.* Port-au-Prince: University of Maine Agroforestry Outreach Research Project.

Balzano, Anthony. 1986. *Socioeconomic Aspects of Agroforestry in Rural Haiti.* Port-au-Prince: University of Maine Agroforestry Outreach Research Project.

Buffum, William, and Wendy King. 1985. *Small Farmer Decision Making and Tree Planting: Agroforestry Extension Recommendations.* Port-au-Prince: Haiti Agroforestry Outreach Project.

Conway, Frederick. 1979. *A Study of the Fuelwood Situation in Haiti.* Port-au-Prince: USAID.

———. 1986. *The Decision Making Framework for Tree Planting Within the Agroforestry Outreach Project.* Port-au-Prince: University of Maine Agroforestry Outreach Research Project.

Grosenick, Gerald. 1985. *Economic Evaluation of the Agroforestry Outreach Project.* Port-au-Prince: University of Maine Agroforestry Outreach Research Project.

McGowan, Lisa A. 1986. *Potential Marketability of Charcoal, Poles, and Planks Produced by Participants in the Agroforestry Outreach Project.* Port-au-Prince: University of Maine Agroforestry Outreach Research Project.

Murray, Gerald F. 1977. *The Evolution of Haitian Peasant Land Tenure: A Case Study in Agrarian Adaptation to Population Growth.* Ph.D. dissertation, Columbia University, New York.

———. 1978a. *Hillside Units, Wage Labor, and Haitian Peasant Land Tenure: A Strategy for the Organization of Erosion Control.* Port-au-Prince: USAID.

———. 1978b. *Informal Subdivisions and Land Insecurity: An Analysis of Haitian Peasant Land Tenure.* Port-au-Prince: USAID.

———. 1979. *Terraces, Trees, and the Haitian Peasant: An Assessment of 25 Years of Erosion Control in Rural Haiti.* Port-au-Prince: USAID.

———. 1984. "The Wood Tree as a Peasant Cash-Crop: An Anthropological Strategy for the Domestication of Energy." In A. Valdman and R. Foster, eds., *Haiti—Today and Tomorrow: An Interdisciplinary Study.* New York: University Press of America.

———. 1986. "Seeing the Forest While Planting the Trees: An Anthropological Approach to Agroforestry in Rural Haiti." In D. W. Brinkerhoff and J. C. Garcia-Zamor, eds., *Politics, Projects, and Peasants: Institutional Development in Haiti.* New York: Praeger, pp. 193–226.

Smucker, Glenn R. 1981. *Trees and Charcoal in Haitian Peasant Economy: A Feasibility Study.* Port-au-Prince: USAID.

Zuvekas, Clarence. 1978. *Agricultural Development in Haiti: An Assessment of Sector Problems, Policies, and Prospects under Conditions of Severe Soil Erosion.* Washington, D.C.: USAID.

20

In Search of the Affluent Society

Allen Johnson

The world is sometimes divided into the haves and have-nots. We who live in the technologically complex, rich societies have little doubt that our place is assured among the haves. Those who live in the technologically simple, poor societies, we believe, are certainly among the have-nots. We ethnocentrically presume, without a doubt, that we are better off. "Primitive" society is seen in polar contrast to our own. If we are high-tech, they are technologically simple. If we live long, they die young. If we are free, they are slaves to tradition. If we are a society blessed by an abundance of leisure, then they must be constantly pressed by the neverending struggle for survival. These contrasts seem so obvious that they are seldom questioned. Our beliefs legitimate our quest for progress and our desire to transfer our technological skill to a variety of technologically simple societies.

Should we be so smug? Here is another case where we can put our undocumented assumptions to the test. Remember that American society is ignorant about the lifeways of other peoples and the satisfactions and frustrations they feel in their daily lives. In this article, Allen Johnson questions the basic assumption that technology and a host of labor-saving devices have given rise to a new leisure society. Anthropologists do not advocate the return to a "primitive" lifestyle and would not choose to do so themselves, but we challenge you to question your assumptions about other peoples and other lifeways. These questions have forced some anthropologists to rethink what is meant by the "economic development" of poorer countries.

As you read this selection, ask yourself the following questions:

☐ *What do the terms "affluence" and "quality of life" mean to you?*

☐ *Into what three categories does the author divide time?*

☐ *Who spends more time working (production time)— the technologically simple Machiguenga or the technologically complex French?*

☐ *Do you believe that economic growth has given us more leisure time?*

☐ *What might be other uses of Allen Johnson's method for studying time allocation?*

The following terms discussed in this selection are included in the Glossary at the back of the book:

ethnocentrism
horticulture
time-allocation study

One of the paradoxes of modern life is the persistence of suffering and deep dissatisfaction among people who enjoy an unparalleled abundance of material goods. The paradox is at least as old as our modern age. Ever since the benefits and costs of industrial technology became apparent, opinion has been divided over whether we are progressing or declining.

The debate grows particularly heated when we compare our civilization with the cultures of "primitive" or "simpler" peoples. At the optimistic extreme, we are seen as the beneficiaries of an upward development that has brought us from an era in which life was said to be "nasty, brutish, and short," into one of ease, affluence, and marvelous prospects for the future. At the other extreme, primitives are seen as enjoying idyllic lives of simplicity and serenity, from which we have descended dangerously through an excess of greed. The truth is a complex mix of these two positions, but it is striking how difficult it is to take a balanced view. We are attracted irresistibly to either the optimistic or the pessimistic position.

The issue is of more than academic interest. The modern world is trying to come to grips with the idea of "limits to growth" and the need to redistribute wealth. Pressures are mounting from the environment on which we depend and from the people with whom we share it. Scientists, planners, and policy makers are now talking about "alternative futures," trying to marshal limited resources for the greater good of humanity. In this context it is useful to know whether people living in much simpler economies than our own really do enjoy advantages we have lost.

In his book *The Affluent Society*, economist John Kenneth Galbraith accepts the optimistic view, with some reservations. According to him, the modern trend has been toward an increase in the efficiency of production; working time has decreased while the standard of living has risen through a growth in purchasing power. One of Galbraith's reservations is that he does not see this growth as an unmitigated good. He sees our emphasis on acquiring goods as left over from times when the experience of poverty was still real and thinks we are ready to acknowledge our wealth and reduce our rates of consumption. The trend over the last 100 years toward a shorter work week, he argues, demonstrates that we are relinquishing some of our purchasing power in exchange for greater leisure.

Galbraith's view that modern affluence both brings us greater leisure and fills our basic needs better than any previous economic system is widespread. Yet the first part of this view is almost certainly wrong, and the second is debatable. Anthropologist Marshall Sahlins has shown that hunting-and-gathering economies, such as those found among the Australian aborigines and the San of southern Africa, require little work (three to four hours per adult each day) to provide ample and varied diets. Although they lack our abundance of goods, material needs are satisfied in a leisurely way, and in their own view, people are quite well off.

Sahlins points out that there are two roads to affluence: our own, which is to produce more, and what he calls the Buddhist path, which is to be satisfied with

less. Posing the problem of affluence in this way makes it clear that affluence depends not only on material wealth but also on subjective satisfaction. There is apparently plenty of room for choice in designing a life of affluence.

Recent studies of how people in different societies spend their time allow us to make a fairly objective comparison of primitive and modern societies. In one analysis, Alexander Szalai studied middle-class French couples residing in six cities in France—Arras, Besançon, Chalon-sur-Saône, Dunkerque, Épinal, and Metz. Orna Johnson and I, both of us anthropologists, collected similar data when we lived among the Machiguenga Indians of Peru for some 18 months, which were spread over one long and two shorter visits.

The Machiguenga live in extended family groups scattered throughout the Amazon rain forest. They spend approximately equal amounts of time growing food in gardens carved out of the surrounding forest and in hunting, fishing, and collecting wild foods. They are self-sufficient; almost everything they consume is produced by their own labors using materials that are found close at hand. Despite some similarities in how the French and the Machiguenga spend their time (for instance, in the way work is apportioned between the sexes), the differences between the societies are applicable to our purposes.

For reasons that will become clear, we divide ways of spending time into three categories: production time, consumption time, and free time. Production time refers to what we normally think of as work, in which goods and services are produced either for further production (capital goods) or for direct consumption (consumption goods). Consumption time refers to time spent using consumption goods. Eating, and what we think of as leisure time—watching television, visiting amusement parks, playing tennis—is spent this way. Free time is spent in neither production nor consumption; it includes sheer idleness, rest, sleep, and chatting.

Of course, these three categories of time are arbitrary. We could eliminate the difference between consumption time and free time, for example by pointing out that the French consume beds and the Machiguenga consume mats during sleep. But we want to distinguish time spent at movies or driving a car from time spent doing nothing—sitting idly by the door or casually visiting neighbors. This supports a main contention of our research: that little agreement now exists on exactly how to measure the differences between dissimilar societies.

For comparative purposes, we broke down our data into five categories of people, two for the Machiguenga and three for the French. For the relatively sim-

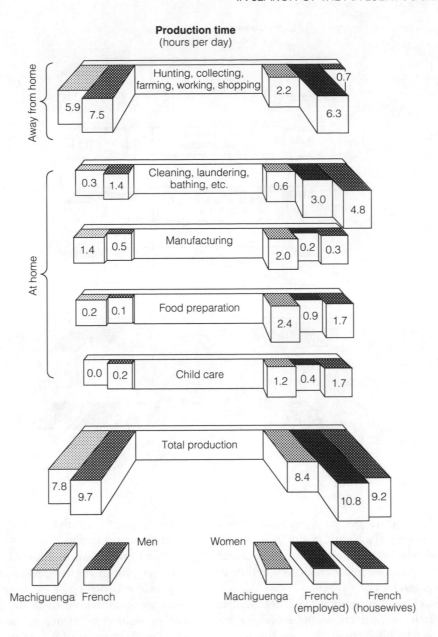

Production time
(hours per day)

Away from home — Hunting, collecting, farming, working, shopping — 5.9 7.5 / 2.2 0.7 6.3

At home:
Cleaning, laundering, bathing, etc. — 0.3 1.4 / 0.6 3.0 4.8
Manufacturing — 1.4 0.5 / 2.0 0.2 0.3
Food preparation — 0.2 0.1 / 2.4 0.9 1.7
Child care — 0.0 0.2 / 1.2 0.4 1.7

Total production — 7.8 9.7 / 8.4 10.8 9.2

Men — Machiguenga French

Women — Machiguenga French (employed) French (housewives)

ple Machiguenga society, a division by gender was sufficient for studying patterns in time use. But for the more complex French society, a male-female breakdown was insufficient because such a division does not allow for working women. We divided the French data into three categories: men, working women, and housewives.

In production time French workers, both men and women, spend more time working outside the home than the Machiguenga do. French men work one and a half hours more per day away from home than do Machiguenga men; employed French women work four hours more per day than do Machiguenga women. French housewives work less outside the home than Machiguenga women do, but they make up for this difference by exceeding their Machiguenga counterparts in work inside the home. French men spend more time working inside the home than do Machiguenga men. All told, French men spend more time engaged in production than do Machiguenga men, and French women (both working and housewives) spend more time in production activities than do Machiguenga women.

The French score equal to or higher than the Machiguenga on all measures of consumption. French men spend more than three times as many hours in consumption as do Machiguenga men; French women consume goods at four or five times the rate of Machiguenga women, depending on whether they are employed or are housewives.

It is in the category of free time that the Machiguenga clearly surpass the French. Machiguenga men

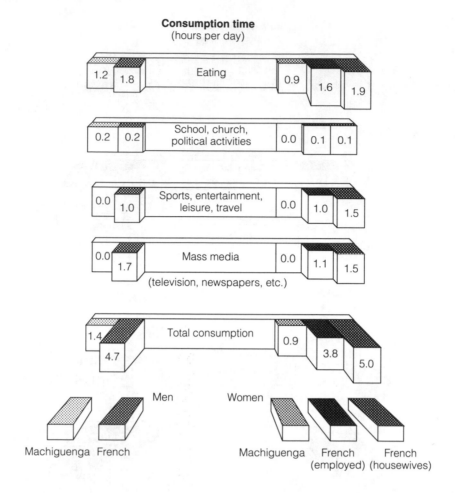

Consumption time
(hours per day)

Eating
1.2 | 1.8 | 0.9 | 1.6 | 1.9

School, church, political activities
0.2 | 0.2 | 0.0 | 0.1 | 0.1

Sports, entertainment, leisure, travel
0.0 | 1.0 | 0.0 | 1.0 | 1.5

Mass media
0.0 | 1.7 | 0.0 | 1.1 | 1.5
(television, newspapers, etc.)

Total consumption
1.4 | 4.7 | 0.9 | 3.8 | 5.0

Men   Women

Machiguenga French   Machiguenga French   French
                                        (employed) (housewives)

spend more than 14 hours per day engaged in free time, compared with nearly 10 hours for their French counterparts, and Machiguenga women have much more free time than French women do—whether or not the French women work.

The immediate question concerns differences in the overall pattern. It seems undeniable, as Sahlins has argued, that modern technological progress has not resulted in more free time for most people. The shrinking of the work week in the last century is probably nothing more than a short-term wrinkle in the historical trend toward longer work weeks. If our modern economy provides us with more goods, it is not simply because technical efficiency has increased. Indeed, the trend toward a shorter work week ended with World War II; since then, the length of the work week has remained about the same.

The increase of consumption time at the expense of free time is both a loss and a gain. Here we encounter a subtle, complex problem. Increased consumption may add excitement and pleasure to what would otherwise be considered boring time. On the other hand, this increase has the effect of crowding time with consumption activities so that people begin to feel that

"time is short"—which may detract from the enjoyment of consumption.

Economist Staffan Burenstam Linder has looked at the effects of higher production and consumption of goods on our sense of time. To follow his argument we must move from the level of clock time to that of subjective time, as measured by our inner sense of the tempo of our lives. According to Linder, as a result of producing and consuming more, we are experiencing an increasing scarcity of time. This works in the following way. Increasing efficiency in production means that each individual must produce more goods per hour; increased productivity means, though it is not often mentioned in this context, that to keep the system going we must consume more goods. Free time gets converted into consumption time because time spent neither producing nor consuming comes increasingly to be viewed as wasted. Linder's theory may account for the differences between the ways the Machiguenga and the French use their time.

The increase in the value of time (its increasing scarcity) is felt subjectively as an increase in tempo or pace. We are always in danger of being slow on the

Free time
(hours per day)

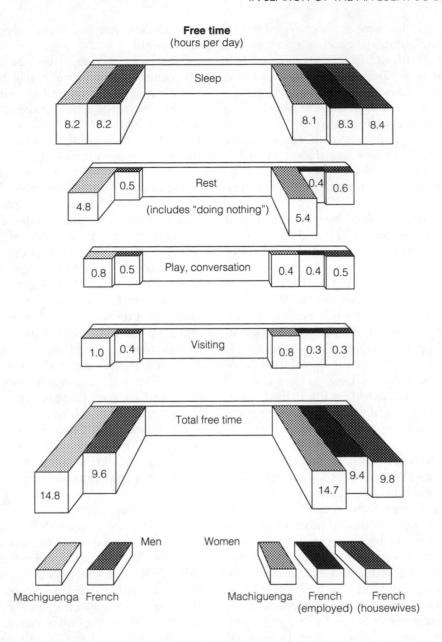

Sleep

8.2 8.2   8.1 8.3 8.4

Rest

0.5   0.4 0.6

4.8   5.4

(includes "doing nothing")

Play, conversation

0.8 0.5   0.4 0.4 0.5

Visiting

1.0 0.4   0.8 0.3 0.3

Total free time

9.6   9.4 9.8

14.8   14.7

Men   Women

Machiguenga French   Machiguenga French   French
                                          (employed) (housewives)

production line or late to work; and in our leisure we are always in danger of wasting time. I have been forcefully impressed with this aspect of time during several field visits to the Machiguenga. It happens each time I return to their communities that, after a period of two or three days, I sense a definite decrease in time pressure; this is a physiological as well as a psychological sensation.

This feeling of a leisurely pace of life reflects the fact that among the Machiguenga daily activities are never hurried or desperate. Each task is allotted its full measure of time, and free time is not felt to be boring or lost but is accepted as entirely natural. These feelings last throughout the field visit, but when I return home I am conscious of the pressure and sense of hurry building up to its former level. Something similar,

though fleeting, happens on vacation trips—but here the pressure to consume, to see more sights while traveling, or to get one's money's worth in entertainment constantly asserts itself, and the tempo is usually kept up.

Linder sees a kind of evolutionary progression from "time surplus" societies through "time affluence" societies, ending with the "time famine" society of developed countries. The famine is expressed not only in a hectic pace, but also in a decline of activities in which goods are not consumed rapidly enough, such as spending time with the elderly and providing other social services. As Galbraith has pointed out, we neglect basic social needs because they are seen as economically unproductive.

Not only do we use our time for almost frantic consumption, but more of our time is also devoted to caring for the increasing number of goods we possess. The Machiguenga devote three to four times more of their production time at home to manufacturing (cloth and baskets, for example) than they do to maintenance activities, such as cleaning and doing the laundry; the French pattern is the reverse. This may help account for the failure of modern housewives to acquire more leisure time from their appliances, a situation that has prompted anthropologist Marvin Harris to refer to appliances as "labor-saving devices that don't save work."

On both objective and subjective grounds, then, it appears that economic growth has not given us more leisure time. If anything, the increasingly hectic pace of leisure activities detracts from our enjoyment of play, even when the increased stimulation they bring is taken into account. When we consider the abundance of goods, however, the situation is obviously different. The superiority of modern industrial technology in producing material goods is clear. The Machiguenga, and other people at a similar technological level, have no doubts on this score either. Despite their caution, which outsiders are apt to label "traditionalism," they really do undertake far-reaching changes in their ways of life in order to obtain even small quantities of industrial output.

One area in which the Machiguenga clearly need (and warmly welcome) Western goods is medicine. Despite hopeful speculations in popular writings that Amazon Indians have secret herbal remedies that are effective against infections, cancer, and other conditions, the curative powers of Machiguenga medicine are circumscribed. Antibiotics, even the lowly sulfa pill, are highly effective and much in demand for skin sores, eye infections, and other painful endemic health problems. Medicines to control such parasites as amoebae and intestinal worms bring immediate relief to a community, although people are eventually reinfected. In terms of human well-being, then, even the most romantic defender of the simple life must grant that modern medicines improve the lives of primitive people.

I am much less certain about what other Western goods to offer as evidence of the comparative lack of affluence among the Machiguenga. They have a great abundance of food, for example; they produce at least twice as many calories of food energy as they consume. (The excess production is not surplus so much as a security margin in case someone should fall ill or relatives unexpectedly come to stay for a time.) The Machiguenga diet is highly varied and at times very tasty. The people are attractive and healthy, with no apparent signs of malnutrition. Although they are somewhat underweight by modern standards, these standards may reflect average weights of modern populations that the Machiguenga would regard as overweight.

The highly productive food economy of the Machiguenga depends on metal tools obtained from Peruvian traders. Without an outside source of axes, the Machiguenga would have to give up their semi-sedentary existence and roam the forest as nomads. Should this happen, they could support fewer people in the same territory—but, if other hunter-collector groups can be used as evidence, nomadic life would result in even shorter workdays. Once again, in quantities of food as well as in quantities of time, the Machiguenga fit Sahlin's model of primitive affluence.

Our affluence exceeds Machiguenga affluence, but as in the case of time, there is the quality of life to take into account. My personal experiences in the field illustrate this aspect of the contrast. In preparing to leave for our first year-long visit to the Machiguenga, Orna and I decided to limit ourselves to the clothing and supplies that would fit into two trunks. This decision led to much agonizing over what to take and what to leave behind. Although we had both been in the field before, we had never gone anywhere quite so remote and we could not imagine how we would get along with so few goods.

The truth, however, was that we were absurdly oversupplied. As our field work progressed we used less and less of our store of goods. It even became a burden to us, since our possessions had to be dried in the sun periodically to prevent rot. As we grew close to the people we were living among, we began to be embarrassed by having so many things we did not really need.

Once, after a long rainy period, I laid my various footgear side by side in the sun to dry. There were a pair of hiking boots, a pair of canvas-topped jungle boots, and two pairs of sneakers. Some men came to visit and began inspecting the shoes, fingering the materials, commenting on the cleats, and trying them on for size. Then the discussion turned to how numerous my shoes were, and one man remarked that I had still another pair. There were protests of disbelief and I was asked if that was true. I said, "No, that's all I have." The man then said, "Wait," and went inside the house, returning with an "extra pair" of sneakers that I had left forgotten and unused in a corner of the room for months. This was not the only occasion on which I could not keep track of my possessions, a deficiency unknown to the Machiguenga.

My feelings about this incident were compounded when I discovered that, no matter which pair of shoes I wore, I could never keep up with these men, whose bare feet seemed magically to grip the slipperiest rocks or to find toe holds in the muddy trails. At about this time I was reading Alfred Russel Wallace's narrative of his years in the Amazon, in which he relates that his boots soon wore out and he spent his remaining time there barefoot—an achievement that continues to fill me with awe. My original pride in being well shod was diminished to something closely resembling embarrassment.

This experience brings up the question of whether goods are needed in themselves or because demand for them had been created by the producers. Galbraith stresses that we cannot simply assume that goods are produced to meet people's real needs. The billions of dollars spent each year on advertising indicate that not all consumer wants arise from basic needs of the individual, but that some are created in consumers by the producers themselves. This turns things around. Instead of arguing, as economists usually do, that our economic system serves us well, we are forced to consider that it may be we who serve the system by somehow agreeing to want the things it seems bent on producing, like dozens of kinds of shoes.

To most economists there is no justification for criticizing the purchasing habits of modern consumers. Purchases simply reflect personal preference, and it smacks of arrogance and authoritarianism to judge the individual decisions of free men and women. Economist Kenneth Boulding has referred sarcastically to such attempts as "theonomics." Economists assume that if there were more satisfying pathways of consumption, people would choose them. But the role of advertising in creating wants leaves open the question of the relationship between the consumption of goods and the fulfillment of needs.

When the task is to consume more, there are three ways of complying. One is to increase the amount of time spent consuming; this is one way the French differ from the Machiguenga. Another way is to increase the total number of goods we possess and to devote less time to each one individually. In a sense, this is what I was doing with five pairs of shoes. The third way is to increase the elaborateness (and hence the cost of production) of the items we consume. The following instance, which took place at a Machiguenga beer feast, demonstrates that even those manufactured items we consider most practical are both elaborate and costly.

At Machiguenga beer feasts, which last for two or three days until the beer is gone, men often make recreational items like drums and toys. At one beer feast that had been going on for a day and a half, I watched a drum being made. The monkey-skin drumheads were being readied, and I noticed that the man next to me was about to make holes in the edge of the skin for the gut that would be used to tighten the drumhead. I had in my pocket an elaborate knife of fine steel, which had among its dozen separate functions (scissors, file, tweezers, etc.) a leather punch. By the time I had pulled the knife out and opened the punch, my neighbor had already made a perfect hole with a scrap of broken kitchen knife he had kept close at hand.

Then he noticed my knife and wanted to see it. He noted its fine workmanship and passed it around to others, who tested its sharpness and opened all its parts, asking me to explain each one. They wanted to know how much it cost and how they could obtain one.

I interpret this experience in two ways. First, the knife was overelaborate. The Machiguenga met all their own needs for clothing, shelter, and containers with much simpler tools. Second, the elaborateness of the knife was itself an attraction, and its remarkable design and quality of materials could not help but draw the men's attention. They wanted the knife—not craving it, but willing to make serious efforts to get it or something similar if the opportunity arose. It is characteristic of a developed culture's contact with small, isolated societies that the developed culture is not met as a whole, but rather in highly selective ways that emphasize manufactured goods and the aura of the great, mysterious power that made them.

Our examples do not prove that the Machiguenga enjoy a higher quality of life than people who live in an industrial society, but they are not intended to. They do show that the quantitative abundance of consumption goods does not automatically guarantee an advantage to the consumer. And although our experiences among the Machiguenga make it easy to argue for the high quality of their lives—as reflected in their warm family ties, peaceable manners, good humor, intimacy with nature, and impressive integrity—it is also true that we would have regarded a permanent life there as a great personal sacrifice. Orna and I came home partly because it is home, where our lives have meaning, and partly because we did not want to go without some creature comforts that we, for better or worse, regard as highly desirable.

It seems likely, however, that an increasing supply of creature comforts and stimulation will bring us into a dangerous relationship with our environment. Such a confrontation might lead us to think about the costs involved in producing and consuming less. In traditional terms this is almost unthinkable, because the relative affluence of communities has been restricted to quantitative measures such as per capita income or gross national product, which can only increase (good), stay the same (bad), or decline (worse). But these numerical measures, which always discover the highest standard of living in the developed nations of the West, do not necessarily touch on all the factors that contribute to a good quality of life. The concept of quality of life suggests something more complex: a balancing out of diverse satisfactions and dissatisfactions, not all of which are bought and sold in the marketplace.

Social scientists are trying to develop a broad range of indexes, such as those called "social indicators," that attempt to measure the quality of individual well-being. It has not been the theoreticians but the planners directly involved in applying economic thought to directed social changes, like urban renewal and rural development, who have insisted on such measures. Instead of relying on a single measure, like per capita income, they have added unemployment rates, housing, mental health, cultural and educational resources, air quality, government efficiency, and social participation. Communities, or nations, may rank low on one measure but high on another, and this makes comparisons both fairer and more realistic.

Even here problems remain. For one thing, the social indicators themselves sometimes sacrifice understanding of quality for measures of quantity. For example, the measure of "mental health" has been the suicide rate per 100,000 population—surely a restricted interpretation of the concept. Despite its obvious shortcomings, the measure has the advantage of specifying exactly what we mean by the term "mental health." In comparing communities or cultures we need standard measures, even though quality and quantity are ultimately incompatible.

When we discuss non-Western societies, the existing social indicators do not work very well. Unem-ployment, housing, and mental health all become hard to define. Economists, for example, often label free time in other cultures as "hidden unemployment"; by clever use of this negative term, they have transformed what might be a good thing into something that sounds definitely bad. In our case, Machiguenga housing, made of palm fronds, palm wood, and various tropical hardwoods, would never qualify as good housing in terms of a housing code, but it is cool, well ventilated, comfortable, and secure. Thus we are still far from developing criteria that allow us to compare the quality of life, or affluence, in diverse societies.

The economy of the United States is changing rapidly. Yet when we try to construct models of the alternative futures open to us, we falter because we lack the means to evaluate them. To turn this process over to the marketplace is not the same as turning it over to the "people" in some absolute democratic sense. People's behavior in the marketplace is strongly influenced, often by subterfuge, by producers who try to convince them that their interests coincide.

To accept the influence of the producers of goods without criticism, while labeling all other efforts to influence consumer patterns as "interference" or "theonomics," amounts to simple bias. Certainly a degree of open-mindedness about what a good quality of life is, and more efforts at learning about the quality of life in other communities, are invaluable as we chart our uncertain future.

21

Eating Christmas in the Kalahari

Richard Borshay Lee

An economy is a social system for the production, exchange, and consumption of goods and services. Using this definition, anthropologists believe that all human societies have economies and that economic systems can work without money and markets. In the previous selection we saw that people in different societies spend different amounts of time in working and relaxing.

People in food-foraging societies, like the !Kung San described in this selection, have received much attention by anthropologists. To a large degree, this is because they represent (at least by analogy) the original lifestyle of our ancestors. A major discovery of research on food foragers is that their life is not "nasty, brutish, and short." In fact, in Selection 13 Eaton and Konner argued that food foragers' diet might be an ideal one for people living in industrialized societies.

In the hunter-gatherer economy, anthropologists have discovered, the exchange of goods is based on rules of gift giving or reciprocity. In this selection, Richard Lee tells of his surprise at the !Kung San's lack of appreciation of a Christmas gift. As we have already seen, a group's customs and rules about appropriate social behavior can reflect important cultural values. When people act in unexpected ways, anthropologists see this as an opportunity to better understand their culture and world view. That is the case in this selection.

All people give gifts to each other, but there are rules and obligations about those gifts. In our own society there are rules about the polite way to receive a present. We are supposed to act appreciative (even if we hate the gift) because the gift is less important than the social relationship at stake. The !Kung break those rules, but in the process, Richard Lee discovers that there are important cultural messages behind their "impoliteness."

As you read this selection, ask yourself the following questions:

☐ Why did Richard Lee feel obligated to give a valuable gift to the !Kung at Christmas? Why did they think he was a miser?

☐ Why did the !Kung people's insults about the impending gift bother the anthropologist so much? Were the people treating him in a special way?

☐ What does Lee mean by saying, "There are no totally generous acts?" Do you agree?

☐ What are some cultural rules about gift giving in our own society?

The following terms discussed in this selection are included in the Glossary at the back of the book:

cultural values
economy
egalitarian society
hunter-gatherers
reciprocal gift

The !Kung Bushmen's knowledge of Christmas is thirdhand. The London Missionary Society brought the holiday to the southern Tswana tribes in the early nineteenth century. Later, native catechists spread the idea far and wide among the Bantu-speaking pastoralists, even in the remotest corners of the Kalahari Desert. The Bushmen's idea of the Christmas story, stripped to its essentials, is "praise the birth of white man's god-chief": what keeps their interest in the holiday high is the Tswana-Herero custom of slaughtering an ox for his Bushmen neighbors as an annual goodwill gesture. Since the 1930s, part of the Bushmen's annual round of activities has included a December congregation at the cattle posts for trading, marriage brokering, and several days of trance dance feasting at which the local Tswana headman is host.

As a social anthropologist working with !Kung Bushmen, I found that the Christmas ox custom suited my purposes. I had come to the Kalahari to study the hunting and gathering subsistence economy of the !Kung, and to accomplish this it was essential not to provide them with food, share my own food, or interfere in any way with their food-gathering activities. While liberal handouts of tobacco and medical supplies were appreciated, they were scarcely adequate to erase the glaring disparity in wealth between the anthropologist, who maintained a two-month inventory of canned goods, and the Bushmen, who rarely had a day's supply of food on hand. My approach, while paying off in terms of data, left me open to frequent accusations of stinginess and hardheartedness. By their lights, I was a miser.

The Christmas ox was to be my way of saying thank you for the cooperation of the past year; and since it was to be our last Christmas in the field, I determined to slaughter the largest, meatiest ox that money could buy, insuring that the feast and trance dance would be a success.

Through December I kept my eyes open at the wells as the cattle were brought down for watering. Several animals were offered, but none had quite the grossness that I had in mind. Then, ten days before the holiday, a Herero friend led an ox of astonishing size and mass up to our camp. It was solid black, stood five feet high at the shoulder, had a five-foot span of horns, and must have weighed 1,200 pounds on the hoof. Food consumption calculations are my specialty, and I quickly figured that bones and viscera aside, there was enough meat—at least four pounds—for every man, woman, and child of the 150 Bushmen in the vicinity of /ai/ai who were expected at the feast.

Having found the right animal at last, I paid the Herero £20 ($56) and asked him to keep the beast with his herd until Christmas day. The next morning word spread among the people that the big solid black one

was the ox chosen by /ontah (my Bushman name; it means, roughly, "whitey") for the Christmas feast. That afternoon I received the first delegation. Ben!a, an outspoken sixty-year-old mother of five, came to the point slowly.

"Where were you planning to eat Christmas?"

"Right here at /ai/ai," I replied.

"Alone or with others?"

"I expect to invite all the people to eat Christmas with me."

"Eat what?"

"I have purchased Yehave's black ox, and I am going to slaughter and cook it."

"That's what we were told at the well but refused to believe it until we heard it from yourself."

"Well, it's the black one," I replied expansively, although wondering what she was driving at.

"Oh, no!" Ben!a groaned, turning to her group. "They were right." Turning back to me she asked, "Do you expect us to eat that bag of bones?"

"Bag of bones! It's the biggest ox at /ai/ai."

"Big, yes, but old. And thin. Everybody knows there's no meat on that old ox. What did you expect to eat off of it, the horns?"

Everybody chuckled at Ben!a's one-liner as they walked away, but all I could manage was a weak grin.

That evening it was the turn of the young men. They came to sit at our evening fire. /gaugo, about my age, spoke to me man-to-man.

"/ontah, you have always been square with us," he lied. "What has happened to change your heart? That sack of guts and bones of Yehave's will hardly feed one camp, let alone all the Bushmen around /ai/ai." And he proceeded to enumerate the seven camps in the /ai/ai vicinity, family by family. "Perhaps you have forgotten that we are not few, but many. Or are you too blind to tell the difference between a proper cow and an old wreck? That ox is thin to the point of death."

"Look, you guys," I retorted, "that is a beautiful animal, and I'm sure you will eat it with pleasure at Christmas."

"Of course we will eat it: it's food. But it won't fill us up to the point where we will have enough strength to dance. We will eat and go home to bed with stomachs rumbling."

That night as we turned in, I asked my wife, Nancy, "What did you think of the black ox?"

"It looked enormous to me. Why?"

"Well, about eight different people have told me I got gypped; that the ox is nothing but bones."

"What's the angle?" Nancy asked. "Did they have a better one to sell?"

"No, they just said that it was going to be a grim Christmas because there won't be enough meat to go around. Maybe I'll get an independent judge to look at the beast in the morning."

Bright and early, Halingisi, a Tswana cattle owner, appeared at our camp. But before I could ask him to give me his opinion on Yehave's black ox, he gave me the eye signal that indicated a confidential chat. We left the camp and sat down.

"/ontah, I'm surprised at you; you've lived here for three years and still haven't learned anything about cattle."

"But what else can a person do but choose the biggest, strongest animal one can find?" I retorted.

"Look, just because an animal is big doesn't mean that it has plenty of meat on it. The black one was a beauty when it was younger, but now it is thin to the point of death."

"Well I've already bought it. What can I do at this stage?"

"Bought it already? I thought you were just considering it. Well, you'll have to kill it and serve it, I suppose. But don't expect much of a dance to follow."

My spirits dropped rapidly. I could believe that Ben!a and /gaugo just might be putting me on about the black ox, but Halingisi seemed to be an impartial critic. I went around that day feeling as though I had bought a lemon of a used car.

In the afternoon it was Tomazo's turn. Tomazo is a fine hunter, a top trance performer . . . and one of my most reliable informants. He approached the subject of the Christmas cow as part of my continuing Bushman education.

"My friend, the way it is with us Bushmen," he began, "is that we love meat. And even more than that, we love fat. When we hunt we always search for the fat ones, the ones dripping with layers of white fat: fat that turns into a clear, thick oil in the cooking pot, fat that slides down your gullet, fills your stomach and gives you a roaring diarrhea," he rhapsodized.

"So, feeling as we do," he continued, "it gives us pain to be served such a scrawny thing as Yehave's black ox. It is big, yes, and no doubt its giant bones are good for soup, but fat is what we really crave and so we will eat Christmas this year with a heavy heart."

The prospect of a gloomy Christmas now had me worried, so I asked Tomazo what I could do about it.

"Look for a fat one, a young one . . . smaller, but fat. Fat enough to make us //gom (evacuate the bowels), then we will be happy."

My suspicions were aroused when Tomazo said that he happened to know a young, fat, barren cow that the owner was willing to part with. Was Tomazo working on commission, I wondered? But I dispelled this unworthy thought when we approached the Herero owner of the cow in question and found that he had decided not to sell.

The scrawny wreck of a Christmas ox now became the talk of the /ai/ai water hole and was the first news told to the outlying groups as they began to come in from the bush for the feast. What finally convinced me that real trouble might be brewing was the visit from u!au, an old conservative with a reputation for fierceness. His nickname meant spear and referred to an incident thirty years ago in which he had speared a man to death. He had an intense manner; fixing me with his eyes, he said in clipped tones:

"I have only just heard about the black ox today, or else I would have come earlier. /ontah, do you honestly think you can serve meat like that to people and avoid a fight?" He paused, letting the implications sink in. "I don't mean fight you, /ontah; you are a white man. I mean a fight between Bushmen. There are many fierce ones here, and with such a small quantity of meat to distribute, how can you give everybody a fair share? Someone is sure to accuse another of taking too much or hogging all the choice pieces. Then you will see what happens when some go hungry while others eat."

The possibility of at least a serious argument struck me as all too real. I had witnessed the tension that surrounds the distribution of meat from a kudu or gemsbok kill, and had documented many arguments that sprang up from a real or imagined slight in meat distribution. The owners of a kill may spend up to two hours arranging and rearranging the piles of meat under the gaze of a circle of recipients before handing them out. And I knew that the Christmas feast at /ai/ai would be bringing together groups that had feuded in the past.

Convinced now of the gravity of the situation, I went in earnest to search for a second cow; but all my inquiries failed to turn one up.

The Christmas feast was evidently going to be a disaster, and the incessant complaints about the meagerness of the ox had already taken the fun out of it for me. Moreover, I was getting bored with the wisecracks, and after losing my temper a few times, I resolved to serve the beast anyway. If the meat fell short, the hell with it. In the Bushmen idiom, I announced to all who would listen:

"I am a poor man and blind. If I have chosen one that is too old and too thin, we will eat it anyway and see if there is enough meat there to quiet the rumbling of our stomachs."

On hearing this speech, Ben!a offered me a rare word of comfort. "It's thin," she said philosophically, "but the bones will make a good soup."

At dawn Christmas morning, instinct told me to turn over the butchering and cooking to a friend and take off with Nancy to spend Christmas alone in the bush. But curiosity kept me from retreating. I wanted to see what such a scrawny ox looked like on butchering, and if there *was* going to be a fight, I wanted to catch every word of it. Anthropologists are incurable that way.

The great beast was driven up to our dancing ground, and a shot in the forehead dropped it in its tracks. Then, freshly cut branches were heaped around the fallen carcass to receive the meat. Ten men volunteered to help with the cutting. I asked /gaugo to make the breast bone cut. This cut, which begins the butchering process for most large game, offers easy access for removal of the viscera. But it allows the hunter to spot-check the amount of fat on an animal. A fat game animal carries a white layer up to an inch thick on the chest, while in a thin one, the knife will quickly cut to the bone. All eyes fixed on his hand as /gaugo, dwarfed by the great carcass, knelt to the breast. The first cut opened a pool of solid white in the black skin. The second and third cut widened and deepened the creamy white. Still no bone. It was pure fat; it must have been two inches thick.

"Hey /gau," I burst out, "that ox is loaded with fat. What's this about the ox being too thin to bother eating? Are you out of your mind?"

"Fat?" /gau shot back. "You call that fat? This wreck is thin, sick, dead!" And he broke out laughing. So did everyone else. They rolled on the ground, paralyzed with laughter. Everybody laughed except me; I was thinking.

I ran back to the tent and burst in just as Nancy was getting up. "Hey, the black ox. It's fat as hell! They were kidding about it being too thin to eat. It was a joke or something. A put-on. Everyone is really delighted with it."

"Some joke," my wife replied. "It was so funny that you were ready to pack up and leave /ai/ai."

If it had indeed been a joke, it had been an extraordinarily convincing one, and tinged, I thought, with more than a touch of malice as many jokes are. Nevertheless, that it was a joke lifted my spirits considerably, and I returned to the butchering site where the shape of the ox was rapidly disappearing under the axes and knives of the butchers. The atmosphere had become festive. Grinning broadly, their arms covered with blood well past the elbow, men packed chunks of meat into the big cast-iron cooking pots, fifty pounds to the load, and muttered and chuckled all the while about the thinness and worthlessness of the animal and /ontah's poor judgment.

We danced and ate that ox two days and two nights; we cooked and distributed fourteen potfuls of meat and no one went home hungry and no fights broke out.

But the "joke" stayed in my mind. I had a growing feeling that something important had happened in my relationship with the Bushmen and that the clue lay in the meaning of the joke. Several days later, when most of the people had dispersed back to the bush camps, I raised the question with Hakekgose, a Tswana man who had grown up among the !Kung, married a !Kung girl, and who probably knows the culture better than any other non-Bushman.

"With us whites," I began, "Christmas is supposed to be the day of friendship and brotherly love. What I can't figure out is why the Bushmen went to such lengths to criticize and belittle the ox I had bought for the feast. The animal was perfectly good and their jokes and wisecracks practically ruined the holiday for me."

"So it really did bother you," said Hakekgose. "Well, that's the way they always talk. When I take my rifle and go hunting with them, if I miss, they laugh at me for the rest of the day. But even if I hit and bring one down, it's no better. To them, the kill is always too small or too old or too thin; and as we sit down on the kill site to cook and eat the liver, they keep grumbling, even with their mouths full of meat. They say things like, 'Oh, this is awful! What a worthless animal! Whatever made me think that this Tswana rascal could hunt!'"

"Is this the way outsiders are treated?" I asked.

"No, it is their custom; they talk that way to each other too. Go and ask them."

/gaugo had been one of the most enthusiastic in making me feel bad about the merit of the Christmas ox. I sought him out first.

"Why did you tell me the black ox was worthless, when you could see that it was loaded with fat and meat?"

"It is our way," he said smiling. "We always like to fool people about that. Say there is a Bushman who has been hunting. He must not come home and announce like a braggart, 'I have killed a big one in the bush!' He must first sit down in silence until I or someone else comes up to his fire and asks, 'What did you see today?' He replies quietly, 'Ah, I'm no good for hunting. I saw nothing at all (pause) just a little tiny one.' Then I smile to myself," /gaugo continued, "because I know he has killed something big.

"In the morning we make up a party of four or five people to cut up and carry the meat back to the camp. When we arrive at the kill we examine it and cry out, 'You mean to say you have dragged us all the way out here in order to make us cart home your pile of bones? Oh, if I had known it was this thin I wouldn't have come.' Another one pipes up, 'People, to think I gave up a nice day in the shade for this. At home we may be hungry but at least we have nice cool water to drink.' If the horns are big, someone says, 'Did you think that somehow you were going to boil down the horns for soup?'

"To all this you must respond in kind. 'I agree,' you say, 'this one is not worth the effort; let's just cook the liver for strength and leave the rest for the hyenas. It is not too late to hunt today and even a duiker or steenbok would be better than this mess.'

"Then you set to work nevertheless; butcher the animal, carry the meat back to the camp and everyone eats," /gaugo concluded.

Things were beginning to make sense. Next, I went to Tomazo. He corroborated /gaugo's story of the obligatory insults over a kill and added a few details of his own.

"But," I asked, "why insult a man after he has gone to all that trouble to track and kill an animal and when he is going to share the meat with you so that your children will have something to eat?"

"Arrogance," was his cryptic answer.

"Arrogance?"

"Yes, when a young man kills much meat he comes to think of himself as a chief or a big man, and he thinks of the rest of us as his servants or inferiors. We can't accept this. We refuse one who boasts, for someday his pride will make him kill somebody. So we always speak of his meat as worthless. This way we cool his heart and make him gentle."

"But why didn't you tell me this before?" I asked Tomazo with some heat.

"Because you never asked me," said Tomazo, echoing the refrain that has come to haunt every field ethnographer.

The pieces now fell into place. I had known for a long time that in situations of social conflict with Bushmen I held all the cards. I was the only source of tobacco in a thousand square miles, and I was not incapable of cutting an individual off for noncooperation. Though my boycott never lasted longer than a few days, it was an indication of my strength. People resented my presence at the water hole, yet simultaneously dreaded my leaving. In short I was a perfect target for the charge of arrogance and for the Bushmen tactic of enforcing humility.

I had been taught an object lesson by the Bushmen; it had come from an unexpected corner and had hurt me in a vulnerable area. For the big black ox was to be the one totally generous, unstinting act of my year at /ai/ai and I was quite unprepared for the reaction I received.

As I read it, their message was this: There are no totally generous acts. All "acts" have an element of calculation. One black ox slaughtered at Christmas does not wipe out a year of careful manipulation of gifts given to serve your own ends. After all, to kill an animal and share the meat with people is really no more than the Bushmen do for each other every day and with far less fanfare.

In the end, I had to admire how the Bushmen had played out the farce—collectively straight-faced to the end. Curiously, the episode reminded me of the *Good Soldier Schweik* and his marvelous encounters with authority. Like Schweik, the Bushmen had retained a thoroughgoing skepticism of good intentions. Was it this independence of spirit, I wondered, that had kept them culturally viable in the face of generations of contact with more powerful societies, both black and white? The thought that the Bushmen were alive and well in the Kalahari was strangely comforting. Perhaps, armed with that independence and with their superb knowledge of their environment, they might yet survive the future.

22

If Only They Would Listen:

The Anthropology of Business and the Business of Anthropology

S. Brian Burkhalter

On a symbolic level, the style of this article beautifully illustrates the duality of cultural anthropology on the contemporary scene. On the one hand, anthropologists have applied their knowledge to organizations—such as businesses—in industrial society. At the same time, however, anthropology as a discipline has remained true to its roots of traditional fieldwork in other cultures. You can take the anthropologist out of the other culture, but you can't take the other culture out of the anthropologist. This duality helps create the anthropological imagination. *It provides anthropologists with a way of seeing that is distinct from the viewpoints of other academic disciplines. Anthropologists are broadly exposed to a wide variety of lifeways, forms of social organization, and belief systems.*

Anthropology, as you have seen, is a discipline with much to offer in terms of understanding culture and behavior of human groups. Because of this, anthropology has much to offer to the fields of business and marketing, as was described in Selection 6 ("Corporate Anthropologists"). Indeed, the history of anthropological work in the area of industrial organization is long. Recently, popular books like In Search of Excellence *have demonstrated that successful corporations are becoming aware of their own cultures and how their corporate culture is related to creativity and productivity. In business, culture can also be a matter of dollars and "sense."*

As you read this selection, ask yourself the following questions:

- ☐ *What does the author mean by the anthropology of business?*

- ☐ *Given your understanding of the concept of culture, what do you think is meant by the term "corporate culture"?*

- ☐ *Why might anthropology be particularly valuable in international business and international marketing?*

The following terms discussed in this selection are included in the Glossary at the back of the book:

corporate culture   ethnography
ethnic groups

The air of the small town was laden with red dust that felt gritty against the eyes. But what I felt most were the heat of the early afternoon and the relentless glare of the tropical sun. Outside there was no shade, for the citizens of Itaituba, perhaps to prove their mastery over the nearby jungle, had hewn down almost every tree, and buildings baked beside the broad, glittering Tapajos River, a tributary of the Amazon. I had come to town to buy supplies before returning upstream to the villages of the Mundurucu Indians and on this, the 24th of May, 1980, stood by a cash register and counted my change.

"That's the thief!" shouted a stout, young man in a red tee-shirt as he pointed at me. He spoke quickly, and I could not understand his excited Portuguese. But I

Reproduced by permission of Society for Applied Anthropology from *Practicing Anthropology*, 7(4): 18–20.

could not miss the fifteen or so armed soldiers who surrounded me or the polite, cautious man in plain clothes who identified himself as the Capitão of the police.

It is at times like these that one hopes one can answer the most important questions or, at the very least, understand what they are. And it is the search to determine these questions that directs sensitive ethnography. You may wonder, for example, just what my fieldwork among the Mundurucu Indians of Central Brazil has to do with business and commerce, and thereby to the anthropology of business and the business of anthropology.

MUNDURUCU COMMERCE

Consider the wristwatches, the portable shortwave radios, the battery-powered record players, the new clothes. Mundurucu no longer make pottery; they use aluminum pots and pans. Only old women occasionally weave hammocks; others always buy theirs from riverboat traders, missionaries, government Indian agents, or merchants in town. Small boys stalk lizards with bows and arrows, but their fathers hunt with shotguns and rifles. Face and body tattoos of elders are not seen on men and women middle-aged and younger, who also forgo perforating their earlobes in traditional fashion. To anyone sporting novelties, they ask a question not heard a few decades ago: "How much does it cost?" Mundurucu know money and love it.

But it was not the love of money so much as the desire for goods that induced village after village to move to distant river banks where riverboat merchants plied their trade. Diets changed as people relied more on fish and less on game. Tools, dress, and housing types became indistinguishable from those of Brazilian peasant neighbors. And there were cheap perfumes, plastic icons, and peroxide to bleach their children's hair. Travel to regional towns became easier, and there men could buy cigarettes, liquor, and the embraces of local prostitutes.

Mundurucu history reflects their growing reliance on trade. Dense jungle and row after row of rapids on the Tapajos River made reaching the territory difficult for outsiders, but Mundurucu attacks on the Portuguese prompted a punitive expedition against them in 1795, and they were soundly defeated. The Portuguese victors, however, offered them machetes, axes, cloth, and other goods to act as mercenaries against other tribes of the region, and this the Mundurucu did, taking heads as trophies and spreading terror among their enemies.

Their Indian neighbors subdued, they sought other ways to gain access to these goods, bartering manioc flour to Brazilian rubber tappers, then learning to tap rubber themselves. Merchants advanced credit and kept their books, so that these Indians, like many of their Brazilian peasant neighbors, were kept in perpetual debt. Their land was demarcated as a reservation, and missionaries, government Indian agents, and itinerant merchants all became active in trading with the Mundurucu. In the mid 1950s gold was discovered to the north of their reservation, and from Brazilian miners Mundurucu learned to dig alluvial deposits, run the dirt through sluices, and pan the sediment for gold dust. These techniques were applied to streams within their reservation, and output was rewarding enough to make it worthwhile, but not so great as to attract miners from more productive sites downstream to the north.

Just thirty years ago, Robert and Yolanda Murphy studied these same people to find them ignorant of banknotes and eager to catch a glimpse of the tiny people hiding within the Murphys' radio (Robert Murphy, personal communication). But now radios are common, and cruzeiros quickly spent. Gone are the days of relying on credit and barter alone; now Mundurucu deal in cash.

Their transformation is far from unique; it mimics the experience of tribe after tribe in Amazonia and throughout the world. To lose sight of the impact of money, of trade with the outside world, or of the wealth of introduced goods would seriously distort our understanding of them as a people and a culture undergoing change.

This leads us to business and commerce, but I should add one note before exploring our roles as anthropologists in these enterprises. Business is inevitable; our food, clothing, and shelter depend upon transactions carried out within a capitalist system. To observe that this is so is neither to condemn nor to condone this economic arrangement. Business is not so much immoral as it is amoral, and it appears to me that we would do well to study it as we would any other social phenomenon. In applying our skills to the business world, we must take care to exercise due concern for those affected by our actions, but this should not inhibit our interest.

THE ANTHROPOLOGY OF BUSINESS

Beads of perspiration ran down my forehead, stinging my eyes, and the air seemed thick and heavy as I faced the local militia and tried to make sense out of what my accuser was saying. How I loved Brazil, truly—the lively strains of the *samba*, friendships warmed by *cachaca*, children laughing on the wharves, stoic peasants fishing from canoes. Fieldwork had demanded patience above all things, patience with malaria, patience with inevitable delay, patience with bureaucracy. And so, resolved to be patient and calm, to maintain my poise, I began to understand the charges against me. I was being accused of having helped sell my red-shirted antagonist a stolen car some four months earlier, when, in fact, I had been deep within the jungle. If only they would listen. . . .

My role of late has been a double one, encouraging my friends in anthropology to consider options in business, where I feel they have much to contribute, and encouraging business scholars to concern themselves with what anthropology has to offer to them. If only they would listen to each other, there could be a fruitful meshing of interests.

Anthropologists have contributed little to the growing volume of scholarly work on the conduct and scope of business, although, clearly, we should have much to say about it. Consider, for example, corporate culture, a notion in vogue among business scholars. Surely this is a subject which we should feel comfortable exploring. Furthermore, closer links to business offer the very real prospect of employment for trained anthropologists able and willing to help solve particular problems. Corporate managers beset with hosts of opportunities, costs, and questions need to know such things as how their corporations actually function and how this differs from its organizational chart and as how its operations could be streamlined, made more effective, broadened or narrowed in scope, or otherwise "improved." Participant-observers may offer insights that others may neither be in a position nor have the training to offer. How are business decisions made? Who influences these decisions, how do they do so, and why? Some answers may be obvious—and thus less interesting—but some may not be immediately evident at all. How does such decision-making behavior affect a corporation's response to its outside environment: How does it enhance or reduce the firm's ability to compete?

Personnel and labor problems also invite anthropological contributions. If management is considered aloof and uncaring by its employees, what can be done to improve labor relations and to offer a higher quality work-life? Here, the anthropologist as a consultant working with unions and management could play the role of a disinterested third party, providing an understanding of the social context in which such problems arise. Teams of anthropologists could achieve an even more holistic view in such situations.

Consulting anthropologists could also offer services to small businesses, especially those that are "starting up." What sort of store is or is not appropriate for a particular neighborhood? What appeal will a shop have and to which ethnic group or social class? These may seem obvious questions—and clients may be reluctant to consult us on them—but they should not be underestimated. A pizza shop may not prosper in a Chinese neighborhood, and a Greek community may or may not frequent a boutique selling imported French fashions. Such preferences, however, can, to a certain degree, be assessed in advance using ethnographic methods, and results could be valuable not only to small businesses, but also to the communities involved, which might need goods or services that a small business would be glad to provide.

Our contributions need not be limited to these considerations. The interactions between government and business in the guise of federal, state, or even municipal efforts to encourage business growth, to foster the establishment of minority-owned businesses, or to stimulate business activity in economically depressed areas are further examples of projects in which anthropological consultants could be of tremendous service. What steps a local government should follow to encourage the development of business in decaying urban neighborhoods and how residents would be likely to respond to various measures are matters that anthropologists are well-equipped to research and for which they could provide feasible policy guidelines.

In brief, in any business or public situation requiring extensive knowledge about how a local community, ethnic group, or group of businessmen think, feel, believe, and act, there is an opportunity for applied anthropologists to make policy suggestions based on ethnographic research.

Problems, of course, abound. To research a question, we need to know what the question is, and clients may not be quite sure what they need or desire from us. It is not enough to agree that "things aren't working here." Problems should be stated in such a way that they are manageable. Often the formulation of questions and the search for solutions will be a team effort, so applied anthropologists should get used to working with engineers, city planners, government officials, and businessmen.

Again, there are ethical problems. Anthropologists conducting research for businesses or for public agencies must be sensitive to any restrictions imposed on subsequent scholarly publications based on this research. Even more importantly, we must try to ensure that our findings are not used to harm the interests of the communities we study. These and like concerns will appear and reappear in consulting work in business, and we must anticipate areas of conflict in advance and become skillful in using contracts to protect our interests and those of the people studied.

THE ANTHROPOLOGY OF MARKETING

All eyes in the store turned toward me, and passers-by stopped to gawk and listen. I was bigger than any one of the soldiers, and that, I was sure, did not make them happy. One had his hand on his hip, and, as I watched him out of the corner of my eye, I wondered if it rested on his pistol. My shirt was tucked in, and I was glad of it, for this proved that I did not carry a gun. The Capitão asked for my identity card, and, calmly and deliberately, I fished my passport from my right front trouser pocket. The passport was wrapped in plastic, and as I unwrapped it I joked about it, saying that this protected it from water, for I had already been clumsy enough to fall in the river once. No one laughed, and I felt very nervous.

I said that I had other documents in a bag that I had checked when entering the store and offered to get them. The Capitão showed no interest. The face of one soldier seemed restless, bored, eager for action, and I did not want to provoke him.

Thought after thought vied for my attention during the first brief moments of this confrontation, and I contemplated spending weeks or months in the town jail, which I imagined was filthy, ill-equipped, and dangerous. I realized, with a shudder, that I did not know what my rights were or whether or not they would be respected. Curiously, I did not feel fear. But, as voices rose in argument, I considered the prospect of jail, incarceration in the Amazon, being trapped behind iron bars in the tropics. . . .

We can imprison ourselves in paradigms that are too restrictive, definitions of what anthropology is that are too inflexible to allow us to explore promising avenues of research. In a moment, I will sketch some work I believe anthropologists can do in marketing and international business, two of my particular interests.

Let us begin by noticing that studying exchange has long interested anthropologists. Boas's work among the Indians of the North Pacific Coast, Malinowski's study of the kula ring of the Trobriand Islands, and Marcel Mauss's "Essai sur le don" are early examples. The anthropological literature is replete with discussions of exchange as can be seen in the work of Claude Lévi-Strauss, Melville Herskovits, Edward Spicer, Robert F. Murphy, Marvin Harris, Clifford Geertz, Manning Nash, and Marshall Sahlins, to name but a few.

With this in mind, consider the definition of marketing proposed by Philip Kotler in his classic text *Principles of Marketing*: "Marketing is human activity directed at satisfying needs and wants through exchange processes." Were we to adopt a normative view of definitions, we could claim that this encompasses much of anthropology and might well be surprised to learn we had been studying marketing all along.

In its focus on consumers and on marketing behavior, however, the marketing literature has largely taken either a data-analytical, modelling approach or a psychological approach. Scant recognition has been accorded to cultural influences. But, although psychological aspects are important, exchange is primarily a social and cultural phenomenon intended to satisfy economic ends. Anthropologists have much to say concerning the cultural dimensions of marketing, and we have scarcely been heard.

This is not to say that anthropologists have ignored marketing altogether; it is instructive to consider some titles that bridge the gap between the two fields. Examples are George M. Foster's "The Folk Economy of Rural Mexico with Special Reference to Marketing," Charles Winick's "Anthropology's Contributions to Marketing," David E. Allen's "Anthropological Insights into Customer Behaviour," Alan S. Marcus's "How Agencies Can Use Anthropology in Advertising," John F. Sherry, Jr.'s "Gift Giving in Anthropological Perspective," and Norbert Dannhaeuser's *Contemporary Trade Strategies in the Philippines: A Study in Marketing Anthropology*. My own *Amazon Gold Rush: Markets and the Mundurucu Indians* explored how an Indian group behaved as consumers. Since 1978, the American Anthropological Association has co-sponsored one of the major marketing journals, *The Journal of Consumer Research*. Other cultural anthropologists, like Walter J. Dickie of Creative Research, Inc. (*Anthropology Newsletter*, December 1982, p. 7), and Steve Barnett of Planmetrics, Inc. (*The Wall Street Journal*, 7 July 1983, p. 25), both University of Chicago Ph.D.s, have put their ethnographic skills to use doing marketing research for consulting firms.

Conducting international business in general and international marketing in particular demands sensitivity to cultural differences in behavior and expectations, and the scope for practical advice from applied anthropologists is tremendous. Vast differences in cultural norms determine what is considered proper and tasteful advertising, what are appropriate colors for packaging, what are the most appealing sizes of units offered for sale, and what are the most effective means of promoting a product. Practices vary greatly. What is a token of regard in one country may be deemed a bribe in another. Customs regulations may be designed to encourage exports and to discourage imports, while appealing to concerns like consumer safety or fairness in advertising. This contrast between latent and manifest intentions should be familiar to consulting anthropologists.

Knowing the importance of credit and how credit is managed could be of help to marketers wanting to increase sales. Such information could influence, for instance, the type of outlet chosen or the advertising media used. My observations of purchasing in an Amazonian peasant village provide a pertinent example. Here, the shopkeeper is seen as a patron, and goods are often bought on credit. This is sometimes advantageous to the buyer, as when medicines or food are needed and money is unavailable. More often, it is to his disadvantage, for the shopkeeper minds the books, not always fairly, and does not fear losing customers if prices are high because they cannot afford to risk losing his patronage by buying elsewhere. The norms governing his patron-client relation relate to the customer's need for security in times of want and to the shopkeeper's willingness to profit from this.

The social context of purchasing should not be ignored. Thus, besides noting that a farmer buys an item in a country general store situated at the intersection of two state roads, we should seek to learn what social relations permeate the interactions between the farmer and the merchant. Are they relatives or old friends? How long have they known each other? What activities do they pursue in common, such as hunting and fishing, attending church picnics, promoting the county fair? Are purchases made on credit or with cash? Are acts of purchasing often just an excuse for the buyer to socialize by joining the men hanging about the general store?

What could such information on the social context mean to management? In some cases, marketing strategies could be affected considerably. If the relations between buyer and seller exclusive of the act of purchasing are more important than product attributes, then it might be wise to retail one's product in a greater number of smaller stores than in fewer larger ones, where prices may be lower but customer-merchant relations more attenuated. Such decisions would depend upon the market segment targeted and upon the product's appeal to those of various social classes, ethnic groups, age categories, and regions.

Anthropological guidance may also help avoid tragic mistakes. Recall the marketing of Nestle's powdered infant formula to areas where water sources were contaminated. Nestle's later efforts to defend itself from international reproach are reprehensible, but the initial decision to launch the product in such areas was at base an error that anthropologists could have

prevented. Anyone with extensive knowledge of these regions would have been familiar with the threat diarrhea poses to infants and known that it was induced by contaminated water. Had this advice been sought and heeded, possibly millions of infant lives could have been spared.

THE MARKETING OF ANTHROPOLOGY

The voices that rose in argument were voices in my defense. Two friends from the government Indian agency, FUNAI, had accompanied me to the store, and one, Francisco, argued furiously. He showed his identity card to prove that he worked with FUNAI and claimed that I had been with him in the jungle four months earlier. When my accuser declared that the thief had been from São Paulo, Francisco retorted that my accent and passport clearly showed that I was an American and that the only reason I was suspected was because I had blonde hair like the thief.

The debate was so quickly paced that I could not get a word in; this, I suspect, was an advantage. But, as Francisco confided to me, the two of them had beards, and, in rural Brazil, bearded ones were often considered sympathizers with Fidel Castro and, hence, not to be trusted. Perhaps they were not the best people to press my case.

When we reflect upon how we, as anthropologists, can best press our case to market our skills, it is evident that we should strive to enhance our credibility with the clients we seek to serve. Physicians in white lab coats, jealous of their title "doctor," do so; investment bankers on Wall Street do so when they dress up in their dark blue, pin-striped suits and carry attache cases. When I began my fieldwork among the Mundurucu, I confess that the style of dress adopted by the men—pastel-colored slacks (often patched or dirty) and tight-fitting short-sleeve shirts worn unbuttoned in front—seemed a bit uncouth. It is droll to think that, at the end of my fieldwork two years later, I dressed that way and thought nothing of it. Further, I became accustomed to walking somewhat as they did, to holding my shoulders as they did, and to having conversations without looking at the person with whom I was speaking just as they did. We must adapt ourselves to our social environment.

This is but an illustration of a frame of mind. To succeed as applied anthropologists in commerce, we need to be mindful of what we can do to attract customers. It is this sort of talk, I know, that sends shudders down the spines of anthropologists, for we value intensely our status as "marginals" and our critical, "gadfly" tradition. It is far more comfortable to ponder aloud the ethical dilemmas we may face as consultants than to reorient ourselves toward seeking to satisfy clients. But both, alas, are important.

Consider what we have to overcome. One has only to recall the opening paragraph of Franz Boas's *Anthropology and Modern Life*, first published in 1928, to realize how relevant his words are today: *Anthropology is often considered a collection of curious facts, telling about the peculiar appearance of exotic people and describing their strange customs and beliefs. It is looked upon as an entertaining diversion, apparently without any bearing upon the conduct of life of civilized communities.* Boas sought to challenge this conception, as did other anthropologists during and since World War II, especially during the last decade, but, nonetheless, it remains.

An internship program is a clever way to market our services. From the viewpoint of the candidate for the master's or Ph.D. degree, the internship establishes his or her credentials as an applied anthropologist while he or she gathers data for the thesis. But it is the appreciation that the host agency or business has for what the intern has accomplished once the internship has been completed that makes for good marketing. It creates a demand for these services, just as manufacturers try to do when they give out samples of their products.

The internship offers a further advantage in that it encourages the student to adapt to meet the demands of the host agency or business. If you will excuse my behaviorism, applied anthropology is what applied anthropologists do when they apply their skills. If there is no call for these skills, they will not be applied. The successful practitioner, then, must be market-oriented. This should remind us to ask: "what is our product?" and "what is our business?" Too narrow or inflexible a response to these questions may eventually mean, as the makers of horse-drawn carriages, wooden barrels, and oil-burning lamps at length discovered about themselves, that we have no product and no business at all.

PROSPECTS FOR THE FUTURE

Perhaps it was my passport, perhaps my accent, perhaps the spirited defense by my friend Francisco. My accuser began to stammer and blush, having discovered his mistake. He first asked my pardon and that of Francisco and shook my hand. He apologized to the Capitão, to all of us again, and appeared embarrassed and defeated. In his haste to get even with those who had cheated him, he had pointed his finger at the wrong man. The Capitão indicated that I could go. The soldiers seemed disappointed, but, what could they do? It was clear that I was innocent.

Just then a small white car screeched to a halt outside the store and raised a thick cloud of red dust. Out jumped a thin man in shorts and a striped shirt—the *chefe* of FUNAI headquarters. Word spreads quickly in small towns, and an unknown passer-by had warned him of my plight. He ran up to us, declaring that it was absolutely ridiculous to have accused me of selling the stolen car. The Capitão must have felt a bit sheepish, for they were good friends. The case against me was closed.

As the crowd dispersed and the soldiers wandered reluctantly away, Francisco, my other friend, and I gathered our purchases and caught a ride back to FUNAI headquarters with the *chefe*. Francisco urged me to get a lawyer and prosecute for false arrest. The *chefe* laughed and declared that he would chide the Capitão with "what kind of monkey was this?" the next time they sat down to play cards. I felt that tempered uncertainty one experiences after a narrow escape. Strangely enough, I was neither angry nor offended, just greatly relieved. I mused about how I loved doing anthropology and delighted in the thought of what a novel entry this incident would make in my fieldnotes. Working as an ethnographer in Brazil seemed, in some indescribable sense, a charmed existence. I welcomed the next challenge and wondered: "what is in store for me next?"

The answer now seems clear: another anthropological adventure in fields no less exotic.

23

Society and Sex Roles

Ernestine Friedl

Americans pride themselves on their concern about social justice. We believe, or at least say we believe, in equal rights and equal access to education, jobs, and other opportunities. As such, understanding the social and historical origins of inequality should be important to us for both intellectual and policy reasons. One of the many inequalities that remain in our society and in societies throughout the world is the asymmetrical relations between men and women. Indeed, the dominant position of men is so pervasive that people often assume that this is the "natural" (read biological) relationship between the sexes. Anthropology, as we have seen, is a discipline that challenges us to question such fundamental assumptions.

In this selection, Ernestine Friedl examines contemporary hunter-gatherer societies and in so doing suggests that male dominance stems from economic control over resources. Differences in cultural perception about gender are closely related not only to economic patterns but also to the organization of families and the institution of marriage.

As you read this selection, ask yourself the following questions:

- [ ] Looking at the historical and anthropological records, how frequently do we find gender equality?

- [ ] What is the source of male power in hunter-gatherer societies?

- [ ] Why don't women hunt?

- [ ] Based on this reading, how will the changing position of women in the American labor force affect gender roles?

- [ ] What is the value of cross-cultural studies for understanding problems such as sexism in our own society?

The following terms discussed in this selection are included in the Glossary at the back of the book:

egalitarian society
gender
human universal
hunter-gatherers
nomadic band
reciprocal gift
sex roles
shaman

"Women must respond quickly to the demands of their husbands," says anthropologist Napoleon Chagnon describing the horticultural Yanomamo Indians of Venezuela. When a man returns from a hunting trip, "the woman, no matter what she is doing, hurries home and quietly but rapidly prepares a meal for her husband. Should the wife be slow in doing this, the husband is within his rights to beat her. Most reprimands . . . take the form of blows with the hand or with a piece of firewood. . . . Some of them chop their wives with the sharp edge of a machete or axe, or shoot them with a barbed arrow in some nonvital area, such as the buttocks or leg."

Among the Semai agriculturalists of central Malaya, when one person refuses the request of another, the offended party suffers *punan*, a mixture of

From "Society and Sex Roles" by Ernestine Friedl from *Human Nature* magazine, April 1978. Copyright © 1978 by Human Nature, Inc. Reprinted by permission of the publisher.

emotional pain and frustration. "Enduring *punan* is commonest when a girl has refused the victim her sexual favors," reports Robert Dentan. "The jilted man's 'heart becomes sad.' He loses his energy and his appetite. Much of the time he sleeps, dreaming of this lost love. In this state he is in fact very likely to injure himself 'accidentally.'" The Semai are afraid of violence; a man would never strike a woman.

The social relationship between men and women has emerged as one of the principal disputes occupying the attention of scholars and the public in recent years. Although the discord is sharpest in the United States, the controversy has spread throughout the world. Numerous national and international conferences, including one in Mexico sponsored by the United Nations, have drawn together delegates from all walks of life to discuss such questions as the social and political rights of each sex, and even the basic nature of males and females.

Whatever their position, partisans often invoke examples from other cultures to support their ideas about the proper role of each sex. Because women are clearly subservient to men in many societies, like the Yanomamo, some experts conclude that the natural pattern is for men to dominate. But among the Semai no one has the right to command others, and in West Africa women are often chiefs. The place of women in these societies supports the argument of those who believe that sex roles are not fixed, that if there is a natural order, it allows for many different arrangements.

The argument will never be settled as long as the opposing sides toss examples from the world's cultures at each other like intellectual stones. But the effect of biological differences on male and female behavior can be clarified by looking at known examples of the earliest forms of human society and examining the relationship between the technology, social organization, environment, and sex roles. The problem is to determine the conditions in which different degrees of male dominance are found, to try to discover the social and cultural arrangements that give rise to equality or inequality between the sexes, and to attempt to apply this knowledge to our understanding of the changes taking place in modern industrial society.

As Western history and the anthropological record have told us, equality between the sexes is rare; in most known societies females are subordinate. Male dominance is so widespread that it is virtually a human universal; societies in which women are consistently dominant do not exist and have never existed.

Evidence of a society in which women control all strategic resources like food and water, and in which women's activities are the most prestigious has never been found. The Iroquois of North America and the Lovedu of Africa came closest. Among the Iroquois, women raised food, controlled its distribution, and helped to choose male political leaders. Lovedu women ruled as queens, exchanged valuable cattle, led ceremonies, and controlled their own sex lives. But among both the Iroquois and the Lovedu, men owned the land and held other positions of power and prestige. Women were equal to men; they did not have ultimate authority over them. Neither culture was a true matriarchy.

Patriarchies are prevalent, and they appear to be strongest in societies in which men control significant goods that are exchanged with people outside the family. Regardless of who produces food, the person who gives it to others creates the obligations and alliances that are at the center of all political relations. The greater the male monopoly on the distribution of scarce items, the stronger their control of women seems to be. This is most obvious in relatively simple hunter-gatherer societies.

Hunter-gatherers, or foragers, subsist on wild plants, small land animals, and small river or sea creatures gathered by hand; large land animals and sea mammals hunted with spears, bows and arrows, and blow guns; and fish caught with hooks and nets. The 300,000 hunter-gatherers alive in the world today include the Eskimos, the Australian aborigines, and the Pygmies of Central Africa.

Foraging has endured for two million years and was replaced by farming and animal husbandry only 10,000 years ago; it covers more than 99 percent of human history. Our foraging ancestry is not far behind us and provides a clue to our understanding of the human condition.

Hunter-gatherers are people whose ways of life are technologically simple and socially and politically egalitarian. They live in small groups of 50 to 200 and have neither kings, nor priests, nor social classes. These conditions permit anthropologists to observe the essential bases for inequalities between the sexes without the distortions induced by the complexities of contemporary industrial society.

The source of male power among hunter-gatherers lies in their control of a scarce, hard to acquire, but necessary nutrient—animal protein. When men in a hunter-gatherer society return to camp with game, they divide the meat in some customary way. Among the !Kung San of South Africa, certain parts of the animal are given to the owner of the arrow that killed the beast, to the first hunter to sight the game, to the one who threw the first spear, and to all men in the hunting party. After the meat has been divided, each hunter distributes his share to his blood relatives and his in-laws, who in turn share it with others. If an animal is large enough, every member of the band will receive some meat.

Vegetable foods, in contrast, are not distributed beyond the immediate household. Women give food to their children, to their husbands, to other members of the household, and rarely, to the occasional visitor. No one outside the family regularly eats any of the wild fruits and vegetables that are gathered by the women.

The meat distributed by the men is a public gift. Its source is widely known, and the donor expects a reciprocal gift when other men return from a successful hunt. He gains honor as a supplier of a scarce item and simultaneously obligates others to him.

These obligations constitute a form of power or control over others, both men and women. The opinions of hunters play an important part in decisions to move the village; good hunters attract the most desirable women; people in other groups join camps with good hunters; and hunters, because they already participate in an internal system of exchange, control exchange with other groups for flint, salt, and steel axes. The male monopoly on hunting unites men in a system of exchange and gives them power; gathering vegetable food does not give women equal power even among foragers who live in the tropics, where the food collected by women provides more than half the hunter-gatherer diet.

If dominance arises from a monopoly on big-game hunting, why has the male monopoly remained unchallenged? Some women are strong enough to participate in the hunt and their endurance is certainly equal to that of men. Dobe San women of the Kalahari Desert in Africa walk an average of 10 miles a day carrying from 15 to 33 pounds of food plus a baby.

Women do not hunt, I believe, because of four interrelated factors: variability in the supply of game; the different skills required for hunting and gathering; the incompatibility between carrying burdens and hunting; and the small size of seminomadic foraging populations.

Because the meat supply is unstable, foragers must make frequent expeditions to provide the band with gathered food. Environmental factors such as seasonal and annual variation in rainfall often affect the size of the wildlife population. Hunters cannot always find game, and when they do encounter animals, they are not always successful in killing their prey. In northern latitudes, where meat is the primary food, periods of starvation are known in every generation. The irregularity of the game supply leads hunter-gatherers in areas where plant foods are available to depend on these predictable foods a good part of the time. Someone must gather the fruits, nuts, and roots and carry them back to camp to feed unsuccessful hunters, children, the elderly, and anyone who might not have gone foraging that day.

Foraging falls to the women because hunting and gathering cannot be combined on the same expedition. Although gatherers sometimes notice signs of game as they work, the skills required to track game are not the same as those required to find edible roots or plants. Hunters scan the horizon and the land for traces of large game; gatherers keep their eyes to the ground, studying the distribution of plants and the texture of the soil for hidden roots and animal holes. Even if a woman who was collecting plants came across the track of an antelope, she could not follow it; it is impossible to carry a load and hunt at the same time. Running with a heavy load is difficult, and should the animal be sighted, the hunter would be off balance and could neither shoot an arrow nor throw a spear accurately.

Pregnancy and child care would also present difficulties for a hunter. An unborn child affects a woman's body balance, as does a child in her arms, on her back, or slung at her side. Until they are two years old, many hunter-gatherer children are carried at all times, and until they are four, they are carried some of the time.

An observer might wonder why young women do not hunt until they become pregnant, or why mature women and men do not hunt and gather on alternate days, with some women staying in camp to act as wet nurse for the young. Apart from the effects hunting might have on a mother's milk production, there are two reasons. First, young girls begin to bear children as soon as they are physically mature and strong enough to hunt, and second, hunter-gatherer bands are so small that there are unlikely to be enough lactating women to serve as wet nurses. No hunter-gatherer group could afford to maintain a specialized female hunting force.

Because game is not always available, because hunting and gathering are specialized skills, because women carrying heavy loads cannot hunt, and because women in hunter-gatherer societies are usually either pregnant or caring for young children, for most of the last two million years of human history men have hunted and women have gathered.

If male dominance depends on controlling the supply of meat, then the degree of male dominance in a society should vary with the amount of meat available and the amount supplied by the men. Some regions, like the East African grasslands and the North American woodlands, abounded with species of large mammals; other zones, like tropical forests and semideserts, are thinly populated with prey. Many elements affect the supply of game, but theoretically, the less meat provided exclusively by the men, the more egalitarian the society.

All known hunter-gatherer societies fit into four basic types: those in which men and women work together in communal hunts and as teams gathering edible plants, as did the Washo Indians of North America; those in which men and women each collect their own plant foods although the men supply some meat to the group, as do the Hadza of Tanzania; those in which male hunters and female gatherers work apart but return to camp each evening to share their acquisitions, as do the Tiwi of North Australia; and those in which the men provide all the food by hunting large game, as do the Eskimo. In each case the extent of male dominance increases directly with the proportion of meat supplied by individual men and small hunting parties.

Among the most egalitarian of hunter-gatherer societies are the Washo Indians, who inhabited the valleys of the Sierra Nevada in what is now southern California and Nevada. In the spring they moved north to Lake Tahoe for the large fish runs of sucker and native trout. Everyone—men, women, and children—participated in the fishing. Women spent the summer gathering edible berries and seeds while the men continued to fish. In the fall some men hunted deer but the most important source of animal protein was the jack rabbit, which was captured in communal hunts. Men and women together drove the rabbits into nets tied end to end. To provide food for the winter, husbands and wives worked as teams in the late fall to collect pine nuts.

Since everyone participated in most food-gathering activities, there were no individual distributors of food and relatively little difference in male and female rights. Men and women were not segregated from each other in daily activities; both were free to take lovers after marriage; both had the right to separate whenever they chose; menstruating women were not isolated from the rest of the group; and one of the two major Washo rituals celebrated hunting while the other celebrated gathering. Men were accorded more prestige if they had killed a deer, and men directed decisions about the seasonal movement of the group. But if no male leader stepped forward, women were permitted to lead. The distinctive feature of groups such as the Washo is the relative equality of the sexes.

The sexes are also relatively equal among the Hadza of Tanzania but this near-equality arises because men and women tend to work alone to feed themselves. They exchange little food. The Hadza lead a leisurely life in the seemingly barren environment of the East African Rift Gorge that is, in fact, rich in edible berries, roots, and small game. As a result of this abundance, from the time they are 10 years old, Hadza men and women gather much of their own food. Women take their young children with them into the bush, eating as they forage, and collect only enough food for a light family meal in the evening. The men eat berries and roots as they hunt for small game, and

should they bring down a rabbit or a hyrax, they eat the meat on the spot. Meat is carried back to the camp and shared with the rest of the group only on those rare occasions when a poisoned arrow brings down a large animal—an impala, a zebra, an eland, or a giraffe.

Because Hadza men distribute little meat, their status is only slightly higher than that of the women. People flock to the camp of a good hunter and the camp might take on his name because of his popularity, but he is in no sense a leader of the group. A Hadza man and a woman have an equal right to divorce and each can repudiate a marriage simply by living apart for a few weeks. Couples tend to live in the same camp as the wife's mother but they sometimes make long visits to the camp of the husband's mother. Although a man may take more than one wife, most Hadza males cannot afford to indulge in this luxury. In order to maintain a marriage, a man must support both his wife and his mother-in-law with some meat and trade goods, such as beads and cloth, and the Hadza economy gives few men the wealth to provide for more than one wife and mother-in-law. Washo equality is based on cooperation; Hadza equality is based on independence.

In contrast to both these groups, among the Tiwi of Melville and Bathurst Islands off the northern coast of Australia, male hunters dominate female gatherers. The Tiwi are representative of the most common form of foraging society, in which the men supply large quantities of meat, although less than half the food consumed by the group. Each morning Tiwi women, most with babies on their backs, scatter in different directions in search of vegetables, grubs, worms, and small game such as bandicoots, lizards, and opossums. To track the game, they use hunting dogs. On most days women return to camp with some meat and with baskets full of *korka*, the nut of the native palm, which is soaked and mashed to make a porridge-like dish. The Tiwi men do not hunt small game and do not hunt every day, but when they do they often return with kangaroo, large lizards, fish, and game birds.

The porridge is cooked separately by each household and rarely shared outside the family, but the meat is prepared by a volunteer cook, who can be male or female. After the cook takes one of the parts of the animal traditionally reserved for him or her, the animal's "boss," the one who caught it, distributes the rest to all near kin and then to all others residing with the band. Although the small game supplied by the women is distributed in the same way as the big game supplied by the men, Tiwi men are dominant because the game they kill provides most of the meat.

The power of Tiwi men is clearest in their betrothal practices. Among the Tiwi, a woman must always be married. To ensure this, female infants are betrothed at birth and widows are remarried at the gravesides of their late husbands. Men form alliances by exchanging daughters, sisters, and mothers in marriage and some collect as many as 25 wives. Tiwi men value the quantity and quality of food many wives can collect and the many children they can produce.

The dominance of the men is offset somewhat by the influence of adult women in selecting their next husbands. Many women are active strategists in the political careers of their male relatives, but to the exasperation of some sons attempting to promote their own futures, widowed mothers sometimes insist on selecting their own partners. Women also influence the marriages of their daughters and granddaughters, especially when the selected husband dies before the bestowed child moves to his camp.

Among the Eskimo, representative of the rarest type of forager society, inequality between the sexes is matched by inequality in supplying the group with food. Inland Eskimo men hunt caribou throughout the year to provision the entire society, and maritime Eskimo men depend on whaling, fishing, and some hunting to feed their extended families. The women process the carcasses, cut and sew skins to make clothing, cook, and care for the young; but they collect no food of their own and depend on the men to supply all the raw material for their work. Since men provide all the meat, they also control the trade in hides, whale oil, seal oil, and other items that move between the maritime and inland Eskimos.

Eskimo women are treated almost exclusively as objects to be used, abused, and traded by men. After puberty all Eskimo girls are fair game for any interested male. A man shows his intentions by grabbing the belt of a woman and if she protests, he cuts off her trousers and forces himself upon her. These encounters are considered unimportant by the rest of the group. Men offer their wives' sexual services to establish alliances with trading partners and members of hunting and whaling parties.

Despite the consistent pattern of some degree of male dominance among foragers, most of these societies are egalitarian compared with agricultural and industrial societies. No forager has any significant opportunity for political leadership. Foragers, as a rule, do not like to give or take orders, and assume leadership only with reluctance. Shamans (those who are thought to be possessed by spirits) may be either male or female. Public rituals conducted by women in order to celebrate the first menstruation of girls are common, and the symbolism in these rituals is similar to that in the ceremonies that follow a boy's first kill.

In any society, status goes to those who control the distribution of valued goods and services outside the family. Equality arises when both sexes work side by side in food production, as do the Washo, and the products are simply distributed among the workers. In such circumstances, no person or sex has greater access to valued items than do others. But when women make no contribution to the food supply, as in the case of the Eskimo, they are completely subordinate.

When we attempt to apply these generalizations to contemporary industrial society, we can predict that as long as women spend their discretionary income from jobs on domestic needs, they will gain little social recognition and power. To be an effective source of power, money must be exchanged in ways that require returns and create obligations. In other words, it must be invested.

Jobs that do not give women control over valued resources will do little to advance their general status. Only as managers, executives, and professionals are women in a position to trade goods and services, to do others favors, and therefore to obligate others to them. Only as controllers of valued resources can women achieve prestige, power, and equality.

Within the household, women who bring in income from jobs are able to function on a more nearly equal basis with their husbands. Women who contribute services to their husbands and children without pay, as do some middle-class Western housewives, are especially vulnerable to dominance. Like Eskimo women, as long as their services are limited to domestic distribution they have little power relative to their husbands and none with respect to the outside world.

As for the limits imposed on women by their procreative functions in hunter-gatherer societies, childbearing and child care is organized around work as much as work is organized around reproduction. Some foraging groups space their children three to four years apart and have an average of only four to six children, far fewer than many women in other cultures. Hunter-gatherers nurse their infants for extended periods, sometimes for as long as four years. This custom suppresses ovulation and limits the size of their families. Sometimes, although rarely, they practice infanticide. By limiting reproduction, a woman who is gathering food has only one child to carry.

Different societies can and do adjust the frequency of birth and the care of children to accommodate whatever productive activities women customarily engage in. In horticultural societies, where women work long hours in gardens that may be far from home, infants get food to supplement their mothers' milk, older children take care of younger children, and pregnancies are widely spaced. Throughout the world, if a society requires a woman's labor, it finds ways to care for her children.

In the United States, as in some other industrial societies, the accelerated entry of women with preschool children into the labor force has resulted in the development of a variety of child-care arrangements. Individual women have called on friends, relatives, and neighbors. Public and private child-care centers are growing. We should realize that the declining birth rate, the increasing acceptance of childless or single-child families, and a de-emphasis on motherhood are adaptations to a sexual division of labor reminiscent of the system of production found in hunter-gatherer societies.

In many countries where women no longer devote most of their productive years to childbearing, they are beginning to demand a change in the social relationship of the sexes. As women gain access to positions that control the exchange of resources, male dominance may be archaic, and industrial societies may one day become as egalitarian as the Washo.

24

Child Care in China

Bruce Dollar

In the previous selection, we saw that gender roles are related to conditions of economic control and the exchange of resources. Such comparisons lead anthropologists to study the causes and effects of increasing numbers of women entering business, industry, and the service economy. This social and economic change affects the family and children, primarily those of preschool age.

Postrevolutionary China is a country where a large proportion of women work outside the home. China, then, provides an example of a society in which public, preschool child-care facilities are used on a large scale. Indeed, the widespread availability of child care for working parents provides a stark contrast to our own society. A second difference between China and our own culture is the values adults attempt to instill in their children.

The schoolroom is a place where children learn models of social interaction. Much of what is learned in school is not part of the curriculum but rather has to do with cultural values and explanations of how our social systems work. Most American parents would feel comfortable with the values learned in the Chinese kindergarten. Yet these fundamental orientations and values are quite different from those actually taught in our schools. In their early encounters with public education, as we shall see in the next selection, American children learn the importance of competition and the desire to outperform their classmates.

Studies in postrevolutionary China provide a vivid cross-cultural contrast with our own society.

As you read this selection, ask yourself the following questions:

- ☐ *What major values do caregivers attempt to instill in Chinese children?*

- ☐ *What form of child care is provided for the infants of working mothers?*

- ☐ *What sorts of punishment are used in kindergarten?*

- ☐ *Why did Mao consider women working outside the home so important?*

- ☐ *Has the large population of women in the labor force in China contributed to the decline of the family or to social or psychological problems for youth?*

The following terms discussed in this selection are included in the Glossary at the back of the book:
cultural values
egalitarian society
institutions
sex roles

The old art of China watching is giving way to China witnessing, and one quality of the new China that seems inevitably to impress all recent visitors is the extraordinary vibrancy of Chinese children, from the very youngest to the adolescents, who already tower so noticeably over their grandparents. During my own recent trip within China, my companions and I saw for ourselves the exuberant self-confidence that seems to infuse all Chinese kids, whether they are performing for strangers, participating in a classroom exercise, or playing by themselves.

"Ours is a socialist society; everything is done according to plan." This pronouncement, with which our

With permission from *Saturday Review of Education*, May 1973.

various Chinese hosts so frequently prefaced their answers to our questions, provides a starting point for understanding how this spirit of exuberance has been achieved. Although Chinese society is largely decentralized to encourage local self-sufficiency and diversification, the whole is knit together by an administrative structure that is more or less uniform from city to city and, somewhat less, from commune (or network of villages) to commune. It is a framework that provides an efficient system of communication and has helped produce a remarkable social cohesion based on commonly held goals and values—which themselves are informed by the teachings of Mao Tse-tung.

The consensus is particularly apparent with respect to the care and training of the young. This is hardly surprising when one considers the enormous stock the Chinese place in producing what they call "revolutionary successors," an apt phrase in a country where revolutionary consciousness has been maintained largely through vivid comparisons with the "bitter past," and where the problem of continuing the revolution into succeeding generations is paramount.

Thus, throughout our visit we constantly encountered—with amazing consistency at various points along a 2,500-mile itinerary—several major ideas about child rearing in the numerous conversations we had with people in child-related institutions: families, nurseries, kindergartens, and schools. These themes—especially the subordination of personal to social needs, respect for productive labor, altruism, cooperation, and the integration of physical with intellectual labor—together describe the kind of citizen China hopes to produce. The techniques employed to achieve these values are in practice virtually from infancy.

During the years before primary schools, which begin at the age of seven, a series of public child care facilities is available to parents who wish to use them. In the cities, where patterns are more uniform, a mother's maternity leave (paid) usually terminates 56 days after birth. Since breast-feeding is the rule in China, the mother may then place her child in the nursing room at her place of work. Most work institutions—factories, hospitals, and government offices, for example—provide this facility for their employees. In a typical arrangement the mother has two half-hour breaks, plus lunch, to visit and nurse her baby during the work day. After work the baby returns home with the mother.

Nursing rooms provide care for infants up to one and a half years old; then they may be sent to one of the various kinds of nurseries. Some of these are attached to the work place or located in the home neighborhood; they may be open only during the work day, or they may be "live-in" nurseries, where children stay overnight and go home on weekends. Kindergartens,

usually located in the residential areas, generally care for children from three and a half to seven years old and may also be either part-time or full-time.

In a country in which over 90 percent of all women of working age do work, it might be expected that a similar percentage of children would therefore receive some kind of institutional care. But there are options. The most common is to leave the child in the care of grandparents, who frequently live with the family. Another alternative is to make arrangements with a friend or neighbor. Estimates vary from place to place, but in most cities no more than half the children of nursery school age are in attendance. For kindergarten the figures are higher, especially in the cities, where attendance is over 80 percent.

Since child care is decentralized, different localities often make their own arrangements, which may not conform to the usual patterns. This is particularly true of rural areas, where a lack of resources and the persistence of custom probably account for a lower incidence of public child care facilities. One small village we visited, the Sha Shih Yu Brigade in northeast China, had no permanent facility; only during harvest time, when all hands were needed in the fields, was there organized care for small children. A child care center located in a coal mining area near Tangshan, on the other hand, served 314 children divided into at least five separate age groups, from 56 days to six years old.

How do these institutions work to socialize the children under their care? And what are they like for the kids? In spite of the diversity in organizational structure, the remarkable similarity from place to place, both in the values espoused and the methods used to inculcate them, seems to support a number of generalizations.

One quality that is sure to strike an American observer is the preponderance and the style of group activities. A common example is the "cultural performance," usually presented for visitors. Whether they are songs from a revolutionary opera, dances to celebrate a harvest, or a program of folk melodies played on traditional Chinese instruments, these performances are always presented by groups, and it is impossible to pick out a "star."

Although there were exceptions, many early child care facilities we visited seemed rather poorly supplied with the variety of toys and materials that the conventional wisdom in the United States says should be on hand to enrich and enliven a child's environment. Although this may have been due to a simple inability to pay for more equipment, the teachers we spoke to did not seem to consider it a shortcoming. Perhaps this is because Chinese children are generally expected to rely on each other for stimulation—at any rate, this seems to be the effect. The situation provides an interesting contrast to that in the United States, where the highly desired "rich environment" often means that kids interact with inanimate materials more than they do with other people.

The small children we saw were not without playthings, however. There was always at least one toy for each child—typically a rubber or plastic doll of a worker, a peasant, or a soldier. Rocking horses were also common, as were military toys and playground equipment that could accommodate many children. But in general the emphasis was on group play. One recent American visitor to a Chinese nursery school reports noticing that the blocks seemed awfully heavy for small children. "Exactly!" beamed the teachers. "That fosters mutual help."

Chinese teachers actively encourage such group behavior as cooperation, sharing, and altruism. "We praise a child when he shows concern for others' interests," said one kindergarten teacher. "For example, at meal time teachers give out bowls and chop sticks. If a youngster gets a nicer bowl and gives it to someone else, we praise him for it. Or when the children are asked to select a toy and a child gives the best one to a classmate, we praise that, too."

Even in a competitive situation, this teacher said, helping another is more important than winning. "When the children run in a relay race, sometimes one will fall down, especially if he's small. If another child stops to help him get up or to see if he's all right, even though his own team might fall behind, we encourage this." The approach contrasts markedly with methods used in the Soviet Union, another country that stresses the collective in its child-rearing practices. There, competition is discouraged between individuals but promoted between groups. Each child is made aware of his importance within his group—say, a row in his classroom—and then competes fiercely for the rewards of a group victory. The Chinese seem genuinely to eschew even this form of competition in favor of straightforward mutual help and cooperation.

But how do teachers deal with improper behavior and matters of discipline? Here is how the question was answered in a conversation with three staff members of a full-time kindergarten in Peking:

Q: What kinds of behavior do you discourage in the children?

A: We criticize those who take toys or other things from others. Or if children beat each other—we criticize that.

Q: Exactly how do you handle such a situation—say, two kids fighting?

A: First, the teacher must understand the reason for the fight. For instance, one might have taken a toy from the other, and the second child hit him. In that case, the teacher will criticize both. This criticism is carried out alone, unless it took place in the class; in that case it will be done in front of the class so that all the children will understand what was wrong. Criticism is to make children understand what was wrong and why.

Q: What kind of punishment do you use?

A: There is no punishment.

Q: Well, what if a child were really intractable? Would you use some mild sanction, such as depriving him of some free play time on the playground?

A: (At this point all three women broke into smiles at our incredulity. Waving their hands back and forth to underscore their words, they said): No, no, nothing like that. We believe in persuasion.

Q: Do other children ever participate in criticism?

A: Generally, no. Unless a third child saw what happened—then he'll be asked to tell.

Q: Let's say the incident was unobserved by any third party and the two kids involved give conflicting versions of what happened. Then how does the teacher act?

A: If the teacher finds a contradiction when both tell what happened, she will try to educate the children. She will note that everyone can make a mistake, including the teachers. The mistake that led to the fight is not important, she will say, but telling the truth is very important. At this point the children will probably tell the truth.

This sounded like fine theory, but it provoked some skepticism among those of us who had been teachers. What about teachers who do not have the patience to use such positive techniques? we asked. How do you deal with teachers who don't observe the school's policy? The reply: "We all—teachers and leadership—have the same goal: to cultivate revolutionary successors. So we all work together and help each other. We study our profession together. We have regular criticism and self-criticism sessions, and sometimes we help each other on specific problems."

If we had not already seen many teachers in action here and elsewhere on our trip, we might have been dissatisfied with this answer. But we were constantly struck by the teachers' apparent love for their work in all the early child care institutions we visited. These women, we learned (there were no men), were chosen for their jobs after having shown a particular interest in children, and "sensitivity and love for children" were the criteria most often cited for their recruitment. Credentials were secondary. Since the Cultural Revolution, the amount of training teachers receive has ranged all the way from university graduation to short-term training classes and "learning through practice."

Three of us in the group who were especially interested in child rearing and education often asked to see child care centers and schools under normal operating conditions. Our guides accommodated these requests by arranging for us to stay behind after the formal tour to make a low-key visit to a kindergarten, say, without the rest of the group. Some of our most revealing insights occurred during our observation of everyday free playground activities.

One afternoon, for example, at the child care center serving workers of the Fan Ga Chong coal mine area near Tangshan, I spent nearly an hour outside among the four-and-a-half to six-year-olds and their teachers, or "nurses." Here was the one place where I saw what might be called a disruptive child—a little boy who, in the United States, would probably have been labeled hyperkinetic and put on Ritalin. While the other 50 or so children busied themselves with various games—rope jumping, drop the handkerchief, tricycle riding, playing with toys and each other—this boy ran constantly from place to place, trying to be in on everything at once and occasionally interfering with someone else's fun. The nurses, who themselves were taking part in the games, were obviously aware of the boy's actions, but they made no fuss over him. Instead, each time he ran by a nurse, she would reach out, place her hand on the back of his head, and gently guide him away from trouble or toward an activity he might like—usually with a few soothing words. Soon he was off again, and once or twice it was necessary to intervene when he began picking on another child. But always the adults acted cheerfully and patiently, and the boy never became a center of attention. His actions were the closest thing to aggressive or disruptive behavior among children that I saw on the entire trip.

After visiting several classrooms at the Pei Hai Kindergarten, a full-time kindergarten located in a park in Peking, I spent an even longer time on the playground watching free play. Once again I was struck by the way teachers enthusiastically joined in. The children, well over a hundred of them, had formed into a variety of play groups. Some played on slides, a merry-go-round, monkey bars, and swings. Some were organized into class-sized groups for games. Others were in smaller groups, jumping rope or kicking a ball around. There were kids in pairs and kids alone. One

gleeful little boy, holding aloft a leafy twig, ran, danced, and twirled with it till he fell down from dizziness. And ranging over the whole playground, sweeping past and through everyone else's games, was a whooping pack of boys chasing a soccer ball, a laughing teacher in the lead.

In one group that especially caught my eye, seven or eight girls were jumping rope, taking turns at the ends of a pink plastic rope and lining up to jump one by one. No teacher was with them. They were very absorbed and used chants and songs to accompany each jumper. Several times while I watched, a minor controversy of some kind would erupt and everything would come to a halt. Maybe it concerned whose turn was next on the rope or how many times one had jumped before missing. Whatever it was, the whole group would come together and heatedly debate their points. With no single girl taking charge, they would quickly work out a settlement that seemed to satisfy everyone and then resume their jumping with all the gusto of before. These little girls were good jumpers, incidentally. So good that after a while they attracted an audience: six little boys found chairs, lined them up to form a small gallery, and proceeded to join in the jumping chants, applauding for each jumper. Great fun for all, highly organized, and by all indications spontaneous and undirected by adults.

In the United States the growing demand for facilities for the care of infants and preschool children has provoked a chorus of urgent questions: Doesn't a baby need a single individual to relate to and identify with as mother? How can a mother be sure that those to whom she entrusts her child will teach the same values she holds? Isn't it the mother's natural role to care for her own children? What is the effect of institutionalized child care on the family?

Obviously, the answers the Chinese have found to these questions are not directly applicable to this country. Yet the insights they provide can be instructive as we seek our own solutions.

There is a strong likelihood that the average child in China will undergo "multiple mothering" of some kind. Even if the mother does not choose to leave her infant in the nursing room where she works, chances are the child will wind up in the care of a neighbor or the grandmother. Offsetting this diversity of "mothers," however, is the near-uniform consensus of values and methods of child rearing I have described. This consistency seems to go a long way toward providing young children with the kind of security we in the United States might normally associate only with single mothering.

Another aspect of multiple or "shared" mothering, as Ruth Sidel, author of the excellent recent book *Women & Child Care in China*, points out, "is that infants can thrive physically and emotionally if the mother-surrogates are constant, warm, and giving. Babies in China are not subjected to serial mothering; we were repeatedly told that aunties (i.e., nurses) and teachers rarely leave their jobs. And they are warm and loving with the children. The children show none of the lethargy or other intellectual, emotional, or physical problems of institutionalized children. Quite the opposite!"

"Everything is planned," and the position of mothers in China is the consequence of a society-wide effort to provide for the economic liberation of women. In keeping with Mao Tse-tung's edict calling for "genuine equality between the sexes," a broad series of programs, including birth control information and prenatal care with maternity leave, in addition to the system of child care facilities, is underway to assume the full participation of women in "building socialism." The objects of unspeakable oppression in prerevolutionary society, Chinese women today have been thoroughly integrated into the labor force, both in factory and commune. And a growing number of them are entering professions—for example, 50 percent of the medical students are now women.

Despite the enormous progress, even the Chinese will concede that full parity with men is not yet a reality. Top government, military, and management posts continue to be mostly male preserves. However, women do wield considerable political and administrative power at the local level, where they often run the smallest governmental units, the neighborhood revolutionary committees.

But the key to liberation is still economic independence, which depends on the availability of work. Since 1971 a new source of work for women has appeared: the so-called housewives' factories. These have been organized locally by women who live in housing areas like the Kung Kiang Workers' Residential Area in Shanghai, and whose husbands work in the various nearby factories. As they describe it to us, the housewives were looking for ways in which they could contribute productively to the revolution without hav-

ing to leave the residential area. So they set up their own light industries in workshops near their homes, and by working full- or part-time were able to produce needed commodities, such as flashlight bulbs or men's trousers, while earning extra money for themselves. The entire operation in each case was staffed and run by women.

Since nearly all working-age women in China today work and are no longer economically dependent on their husbands or families, one might well wonder about the effects of these conditions on the family.

By all available evidence the family is thriving in China, and the individual household continues to be the basic social unit. A featured item in every home we visited, as ubiquitous as a portrait of Chairman Mao, was a display of a great many photographs of family members, usually pressed under a piece of glass on top of a bureau or framed on the wall. Our host or hostess would invariably point this out with pride. Signs of active and full participation in family life were everywhere, and all generations were included. A man out with his children is a common sight, as is a child with a grandmother or grandfather.

Parents are obviously revered by children, and so are grandparents. In fact, the complete absence of a "generation gap" is a striking phenomenon to an American. Not only are grandparents well integrated into family life, but old people who have no family or who are disabled live in well-tended "respect for aged" homes and are given important functions that serve the neighborhood.

Far from undermining the family structure, we were repeatedly told, jobs for women and day care for children have made home life easier, having eliminated many former sources of friction and frustration. A major factor here is undoubtedly the mass commitment to working for the betterment of China. Personal gratification seems to derive from each individual's knowledge that he or she makes an important contribution, no matter how small, to the national effort and that the benefits of this contribution, and others like it, will be distributed to all.

25

American Schoolrooms:
Learning the Nightmare

Jules Henry

Cultural values are reflected in social institutions. In institutions of socialization like schools, culture is re-created for a new generation—an important theme in the previous selection, on postrevolutionary China. There is a critical linkage between a society's economic system, the organization of institutions, and the cultural values that are taught young children. Consider this provocative view of the unconscious cultural learning that goes on in American elementary schools.

When studying other societies, anthropologists often conclude that there are important differences between what the natives say they are doing and what they actually are doing. We are somewhat less comfortable when such an observation is made about our own society. In ideal terms, we believe that our educational institutions encourage cooperation, creativity, and free expression, allowing individual students to fulfill their own potential. But in this selection, Jules Henry argues that the function of education is to bind the mind and spirit, to make children fit the culture as it already exists. An institution like the school, therefore, functions as a mechanism of social control. Some of this control comes from people in positions of authority, but much of it is located in peer pressure to conform to the culture of the group.

Teachers (like parents) are probably doing this unconsciously, even when they are trying to make learning fun. In the process of education, children learn to sing off key— along with the rest of the group—and also learn not to question certain things. The author believes that American children also learn to become destructively competitive and that this produces deep-seated fear of failure in their per-

sonalities. Paradoxically, while learning these parts of our culture might ultimately drive some students to succeed, others learn to fail.

American cultural values, including competition and individual achievement, fit our capitalist economy and social meritocracy. The structure of the institutions of socialization, including tests and grades, probably influenced you to read this.

As you read this selection, ask yourself the following questions:

☐ This selection is about 30 years old. How have American schoolrooms changed or stayed the same over that time period? Does the author's description fit your experience?

☐ What does the author mean that students "learn to be absurd?"

☐ Identify several cultural values that are expressed in schools.

☐ What do you think "education" should be? Are there any positive functions of the "noise" in classrooms?

The following terms discussed in this selection are included in the Glossary at the back of the book:

cultural values
sanctions
social control
socialization

School is an institution for drilling children in cultural orientations. Educators have attempted to free the school from drill, but have failed because they have always chosen the most obvious "enemy" to attack. Furthermore, with every enemy destroyed, new ones are installed among the old fortifications that are the enduring contradictory maze of the culture. Educators think that when they have made arithmetic or spelling into a game; made it unnecessary for children to "sit up straight"; defined the relation between teacher and children as democratic; and introduced plants, fish, and hamsters into schoolrooms, they have settled the problem of drill. They are mistaken.

The paradox of the human condition is expressed more in education than elsewhere in human culture, because learning to learn has been and continues to be *Homo sapiens'* most formidable evolutionary task. Although it is true that mammals, as compared to birds and fishes, have to learn so much that it is difficult to say by the time we get to chimpanzees which behavior is inborn and which is learned, the learning task has become so enormous for man that today, education, along with survival, constitutes a major preoccupation. In all the fighting over education we are simply saying that after a million years of struggling to become human, we are not yet satisfied that we have mastered the fundamental human task, learning.

Another learning problem inherent in the human condition is this: We must conserve culture while changing it, we must always be *more* sure of surviving than of adapting. When a new idea appears, our first concern *as animals* must be that it does not kill us; then, and only then, can we look at it from other points of view. In general, primitive people solved this problem simply by walling their children off from new possibilities by educational methods that, largely through fear, so narrowed the perceptual sphere that nontraditional ways of viewing the world became unthinkable.

The function of education has never been to free the mind and the spirit of man, but to bind them. To the end that the mind and spirit of his children should never escape, *Homo sapiens* has wanted acquiescence, not originality, from his offspring. It is natural that this should be so, for where every man is unique there is no society, and where there is no society there can be no man. Contemporary American educators think they want creative children, yet it is an open question as to what they expect these children to create. If all through school the young were provoked to question the Ten Commandments, the sanctity of revealed religion, the foundations of patriotism, the profit motive, the two-party system, monogamy, the laws of incest, and so on, we would have more creativity than we could handle. In teaching our children to accept fundamentals of social relationships and religious beliefs without question we follow the ancient highways of the human race.

American classrooms, like educational institutions anywhere, express the values, preoccupations, and fears found in the culture as a whole. School has no choice; it must train the children to fit the culture as it is. School can give training in skills; it cannot teach creativity. Since the creativity that *is* encouraged—as in science and mathematics, for example—will always be that which satisfies the cultural drives at the time, all the American school can do is nurture that creativity when it appears.

Creative intellect is mysterious, devious, and irritating. An intellectually creative child may fail in social studies, for example, simply because he cannot understand the stupidities he is taught to believe as "fact." He may even end up agreeing with his teachers that he is "stupid" in social studies. He will not be encouraged to play among new social systems, values, and relationships, if for no other reason than that the social studies teachers will perceive such a child as a poor student. Furthermore, such a child will simply be unable to fathom the absurdities that seem transparent *truth* to the teacher. What idiot believes in the "law of supply and demand," for example? But the children who do, tend to *become* idiots; and learning to be an idiot is part of growing up! Or, as Camus put it, learning to be *absurd*. Thus the intellectually creative child who finds it impossible to learn to think the absurd the truth, who finds it difficult to accept absurdity as a way of life, usually comes to think himself stupid.

Schools have therefore never been places for the stimulation of young minds; they are the central conserving force of the culture, and if we observe them closely they will tell us much about the cultural pattern that binds us.

Much of what I am now going to say pivots on the inordinate capacity of a human being to learn more than one thing at a time. A child writing the word "August" on the board, for example, is not only learning the word "August," but also how to hold the chalk without making it squeak, how to write clearly, how to keep going even though the class is tittering at his slowness, how to appraise the glances of the children

The author of this article used the term *man* to refer to humanity in general. The term is not used by modern anthropologists because, to many people, it reflects an unconscious sexist bias in language and rhetoric. At the time that this article was written, however, the generalized *man* was a common convention in writing. In the interest of historical accuracy we have not changed the wording in this article, but students should be aware that nonsexist terms (*humans, people, Homo sapiens,* and so on) are preferred. —The Editors.

From *Columbia University Forum*, Spring 1963, pp. 24–30 by permission of Columbia University Press.

in order to know whether he is doing it right or wrong. If a classroom can be compared to a communications system—a flow of messages between teacher (transmitter) and pupils (receivers)—it is instructive to recall another characteristic of communications systems applicable to classrooms: their inherent tendency to generate *noise*. *Noise*, in communications theory, applies to all those random fluctuations of the system that cannot be controlled, the sounds that are not part of the message. The striking thing about the child is that along with his "messages about spelling" he learns all the noise in the system also. But—and mark this well—it is *not* primarily the message (the spelling) that constitutes the most important subject matter to be learned, but the noise! The most significant cultural learning—primarily the cultural drives—are communicated as *noise*. Let us see the system operate in some of the contemporary suburban classrooms my students and I studied over a period of six years.

> It is March 17 and the children are singing songs from Ireland and her neighbors. The teacher plays on the piano, while the children sing. While some children sing, a number of them hunt in the index, find a song belonging to one of Ireland's neighbors, and raise their hands in order that they may be called on to name the next song. The singing is of that pitchless quality always heard in elementary school classrooms. The teacher sometimes sings through a song first, in her off-key, weakishly husky voice.

The usual reason for this kind of song period is that the children are "broadened" while they learn something about music and singing. But what the children in fact learn about singing is to sing like everybody else. (This phenomenon—the standard, elementary school pitchlessness of the English-speaking world—was impressive enough for D. H. Lawrence to mention it in *Lady Chatterley's Lover*. The difficulty in achieving true pitch is so pervasive among us that missionaries carry it with them to distant jungles, teaching the natives to sing hymns off key. Hence on Sundays we would hear our Pilagá Indian friends, all of them excellent musicians in the Pilagá scale, carefully copy the missionaries by singing Anglican hymns, translated into Pilagá, off key exactly as sharp or as flat as the missionaries sang.) Thus one of the first things a child with a good ear learns in elementary school is to be musically stupid; he learns to doubt or to scorn his innate musical capacities.

But possibly more important than this is the use to which teacher and pupils put the lesson in ways not related at all to singing or to Ireland and her neighbors. To the teacher this was an opportunity to let the children somehow share the social aspects of the lesson with her. The consequence was distraction from

singing as the children hunted in the index, and the net result was to activate the children's drives toward competition, achievement, and dominance. In this way the song period was scarcely a lesson in singing, but rather one in extorting the maximal benefit for the Self from *any* situation.

The first lesson a child has to learn when he comes to school is that lessons are not what they seem. He must then forget this and act as if they were. This is the first step toward "school mental health"; it is also the first step in becoming absurd. The second lesson is to put the teachers' and students' criteria in place of his own. The child must learn that the proper way to sing is tunelessly and not the way he hears the music; that the proper way to paint is the way the teacher says, not the way he sees it; that the proper attitude is not pleasure, but competitive horror at the success of his classmates, and so on. And these lessons must be so internalized that he will fight his parents if they object. The early schooling process is not successful unless it has produced in the child an acquiescence in its criteria, unless the child *wants* to think the way school has taught him to think. What we see in kindergarten and the early years of school is the pathetic surrender of babies. How could it be otherwise?

Now nothing so saps self-confidence as alienation from the Self. It would follow that school, the chief agent in the process, must try to provide the children with "ego support," for culture tries to remedy the ills it creates. Hence the effort to give children recognition in our schools. Hence the conversion of the songfest into an exercise in Self-realization. That anything essential was nurtured in this way, is an open question, for the kind of individuality that was recognized as the children picked titles out of the index was mechanical, without a creative dimension, and under the strict control of the teacher. In short, the school metamorphoses the child, giving it the kind of Self the school can manage, and then proceeds to minister to the Self it has made.

We can see this at work in another example:

> The observer is just entering her fifth-grade classroom for the observation period. The teacher says, "Which one of you nice, polite boys would like to take (the observer's) coat and hang it up?" From the waving hands, it would seem that all would like to claim the honor. The teacher chooses one child, who takes the observer's coat. . . . The teacher conducted the arithmetic lessons mostly by asking, "Who would like to tell the answer to the next problem?" This question was followed by the usual large and agitated forest of hands, with apparently much competition to answer.

What strike us here are the precision with which the teacher was able to mobilize the potentialities in the boys for the proper social behavior, and the speed with which they responded. The large number of waving hands proves that most of the boys have already become absurd; but they have no choice. Suppose they sat there frozen?

A skilled teacher sets up many situations in such a way that *a negative attitude can be construed only as treason.* The function of questions like, "Which one of you nice, polite boys would like to take (the observer's) coat and hang it up?" is to bind the children into absurdity—to compel them to acknowledge that absurdity is existence, to acknowledge that it is better to exist absurd than not to exist at all. The reader will have observed that the question is not put, "Who *has* the answer to the next problem?" but, "Who *would like to tell*" it? What at one time in our culture was phrased as a challenge to skill in arithmetic, becomes here an invitation to group participation. The essential issue is that *nothing is but what it is made to be by the alchemy of the system.*

In a society where competition for the basic cultural goods is a pivot of action, people cannot be taught to love one another. It thus becomes necessary for the school to teach children how to hate, and without appearing to do so, for our culture cannot tolerate the idea that babes should hate each other. How does the school accomplish this ambiguity? Obviously through fostering competition itself, as we can see in an incident from a fifth-grade arithmetic lesson.

> Boris had trouble reducing 12/16 to the lowest terms, and could only get as far as 6/8. The teacher asked him quietly if that was as far as he could reduce it. She suggested he "think." Much heaving up and down and waving of hands by the other children, all frantic to correct him. Boris pretty unhappy, probably mentally paralyzed. The teacher, quiet, patient, ignores the others and concentrates with look and voice on Boris. After a minute or two, she turns to the class and says, "Well, who can tell Boris what the number is?" A forest of hands appears, and the teacher calls Peggy. Peggy says that four may be divided into the numerator and the denominator.

Boris's failure has made it possible for Peggy to succeed; his misery is the occasion for her rejoicing. This is the standard condition of the contemporary American elementary school. To a Zuñi, Hopi, or Dakota Indian, Peggy's performance would seem cruel beyond belief, for competition, the wringing of success from somebody's failure, is a form of torture foreign to those noncompetitive cultures. Yet Peggy's action seems natural to us; and so it is. How else would you run our world?

Looked at from Boris's point of view, the nightmare at the blackboard was, perhaps, a lesson in controlling himself so that he would not fly shrieking from the room under enormous public pressure. Such experiences force every man reared in our culture, over and over again, night in, night out, even at the pinnacle of success, to dream not of success, but of failure. In school the external nightmare is internalized for life. Boris was not learning arithmetic only; he was learning the *essential nightmare also. To be successful in our culture one must learn to dream of failure.*

When we say that "culture teaches drives and values" we do not state the case quite precisely. We should say, rather, that culture (and especially the school) provides the occasions in which drives and values are *experienced in events* that strike us with *overwhelming and constant force.* To say that culture "teaches" puts the matter too mildly. Actually culture invades and infests the mind as an obsession. If it does not, it will be powerless to withstand the impact of critical differences, to fly in the face of contradiction, to so engulf the mind that the world is seen only as the culture decrees it shall be seen, to compel a person to be absurd. The central emotion in obsession is fear, and the central obsession in education is fear of failure. In school, one becomes absurd through being afraid; but paradoxically, *only by remaining absurd can one feel free from fear.*

Let us see how absurdity is reinforced: consider this spelling lesson in a fourth-grade class.

> The children are to play "spelling baseball," and they have lined up to be chosen for the two teams. There is much noise, but the teacher quiets it. She has selected a boy and a girl and sent them to the front of the room as team captains to choose their teams. As the boy and girl pick the children to form their teams, each child takes a seat in orderly succession around the room. Apparently they know the game well. Now Tom, who has not yet been chosen, tries to call attention to himself in order to be chosen. Dick shifts his position to be more in the direct line of vision of the choosers, so that he may not be overlooked. He seems quite anxious. Jane, Tom, Dick, and one girl whose name the observer does not know are the last to be chosen. The teacher even has to remind the choosers that Dick and Jane have not been chosen. . . .
>
> The teacher now gives out words for the children to spell, and they write them on the board. (Each word is a pitched ball, and each correctly spelled word is a base hit. The children move around the room from base to base as their teammates spell the words correctly.) The outs seem to increase in frequency as each side gets near the children chosen last. The children have great difficulty spelling "August." As they make mistakes, those in the seats say, "No!" The teacher says, "Man on third." As a child at the board stops and thinks, the teacher says, "There's a time limit; you can't take too long, honey." At last, after many children fail on "August" one child gets it right and returns, grinning with pleasure, to her seat. . . . The motivation level in this game seems terrific. All

the children seem to watch the board, to know what's right and wrong, and seem quite keyed up. There is no lagging in moving from base to base. The child who is now writing "Thursday" stops to think after the first letter, and the children snicker. He stops after another letter. More snickers. He gets the word wrong. There are frequent signs of joy from the children when their side is right.

"Spelling baseball" is an effort to take the "weariness, the fever, and the fret" out of spelling by absurdly transforming it into a competitive game. Children are usually good competitors, though they may never become good spellers; and although they may never learn to *spell* success, they know what it *is*, how to go after it, and how it feels not to have it. A competitive game is indicated when children are failing, because the drive to succeed in the *game* may carry them to victory over the subject matter. But once a spelling lesson is cast in the form of a game of baseball a great variety of *noise* enters the system; because the sound of *baseball* (the baseball "messages") cannot but be *noise* in a system intended to communicate *spelling*. If we reflect that one could not settle a baseball game by converting it into a spelling lesson, we see that baseball is bizarrely irrelevant to spelling. If we reflect further that a child who is a poor speller might yet be a magnificent ballplayer, we are even further impressed that learning spelling through baseball is learning by absurd association.

In making spelling into a baseball game one drags into the classroom whatever associations a child may have to the impersonal sorting process of kid baseball, but there are differences between the baseball world and the "spelling baseball" world also. One's failure is paraded before the class minute upon minute, until, when the worst spellers are the only ones left, the conspicuousness of the failures has been enormously increased. Thus the *noise* from baseball is amplified by a *noise* factor specific to the classroom.

It should not be imagined that I "object" to all of this, for in the first place I am aware of the indispensable social functions of the spelling game, and in the second place, I can see that the rendering of failure conspicuous cannot but intensify the quality of the essential nightmare, and thus render an important service to the culture. Without nightmares human culture has never been possible. Without hatred competition cannot take place except in games.

The unremitting effort by the system to bring the cultural drives to a fierce pitch must ultimately turn the children against one another; and though they cannot punch one another in the nose or pull one another's hair in class, they can vent some of their hostility in carping criticism of one another's work. Carping criticism, painfully evident in almost any American classroom, is viciously destructive of the early tillage of those creative impulses we say we cherish.

Listen to a fifth-grade class: The children are taking turns reading stories they have made up. Charlie's is called *The Unknown Guest*.

> "One dark, dreary night, on a hill a house stood. This house was forbidden territory for Bill and Joe, but they were going in anyway. The door creaked, squealed, slammed. A voice warned them to go home. They went upstairs. A stair cracked. They entered a room. A voice said they might as well stay and find out now; and their father came out. He laughed and they laughed, but they never forgot their adventure together."
>
> Teacher: Are there any words that give you the mood of the story?
> Lucy: He could have made the sentences a little better . . . .
> Teacher: Let's come back to Lucy's comment. What about his sentences?
> Gert: They were too short. (Charlie and Jeanne have a discussion about the position of the word "stood" in the first sentence.)
> Teacher: Wait a minute; some people are forgetting their manners. . . .
> Jeff: About the room: the boys went up the stairs and one "cracked," then they were in the room. Did they fall through the stairs, or what?
> The teacher suggests Charlie make that a little clearer. . . .
> Teacher: We still haven't decided about the short sentences. Perhaps they make the story more spooky and mysterious.
> Gwynne: I wish he had read with more expression instead of all at one time.
> Rachel: Not enough expression.
> Teacher: Charlie, they want a little more expression from you. I guess we've given you enough suggestions for one time. (Charlie does not raise his head, which is bent over his desk as if studying a paper.) Charlie! I guess we've given you enough suggestions for one time, Charlie, haven't we?

If American children fail while one of their number succeeds, they carp. And why not? We must not let our own "inner Borises" befog our thinking. A competitive culture endures by tearing people down. Why blame the children for doing it?

The contemporary school is not all horrors; it has its gentler aspects as well. Nearing a conclusion, let us examine impulse release and affection as they appear in the suburban classrooms.

Impulse is the root of life, and its release in the right amount, time, and place is a primary concern of culture. Nowadays the problem of impulse release takes on a special character because of the epoch's commitment to "letting down the bars." This being the case, teachers have a task unique in the history of education: the fostering of impulse release rather than the installation of controls. Everywhere controls are breaking down, and firmness with impulse is no part of contemporary pedagogy of "the normal child." Rather, impulse release, phrased as "spontaneity," "life adjustment," "democracy," "permissiveness," and "mothering," has become a central doctrine of education. It persists despite tough-minded critics from the Eastern Seaboard who concentrate on curriculum. The teachers know better; the real, persisting, subject matter is *noise*.

How can the teacher release children's emotions without unchaining chaos? How can she permit so much *noise* and not lose the message? Were they alive, the teachers I had in P.S. 10 and P.S. 186 in New York City, who insisted on absolute silence, would say that chaos does prevail in many modern classrooms and that the message *is* lost. But lest old-fashioned readers argue that the social structure has fallen apart, I will point out what does *not* happen: The children do not fight or wrestle, run around the room, throw things, sing loudly, or whistle. The boys do not attack the girls or vice versa. Children do not run in and out of the room. They do not make the teacher's life miserable. All this occurs when the social structure *is* torn down, but in the average suburban classrooms we studied, it never quite happens. Why not? Here are some excerpts from an interview with a second-grade teacher I'll call Mrs. Olan:

> In the one-room schoolhouse in which I first taught, the children came from calm homes. There was no worry about war, and there was no TV or radio. Children of today know more about what is going on; they are better informed. So you can't hold a strict rein on them.
>
> Children need to enjoy school and like it. They also need their work to be done; it's not all play. You must get them to accept responsibility and to do work on their own.

To the question, "What would you say is your own particular way of keeping order in the classroom?" Mrs. Olan says:

> Well, I would say I try to get that at the beginning of the year by getting this bond of affection and relationship between the children and me. And we do that with stories; and I play games *with* them—don't just teach them how to play. It's what you get from living together comfortably. We have "share" times. . . . These are the things that contribute toward discipline. Another thing in discipline—it took me a long time to learn it, too: I thought I was the boss, but I learned that even with a child, if you speak to him as you would to a neighbor or a friend you get a better response than if you say, "Johnny, do this or that."

Mrs. Olan has a creed: Love is the path to discipline through permissiveness; and school is a continu-

ation of family life, in which the values of sharing and democracy lead to comfortable living and ultimately to discipline. She continues:

> With primary children the teacher is a mother during the day; they have to be able to bring their problems to you. They get love and affection at home, and I see no reason not to give it in school.

To Mrs. Olan, mother of a 21-year-old son, second-grade children are pussy-cats. When asked, "Do you think the children tend to be quieter if the teacher is affectionate?" she says:

> If a teacher has a well-modulated voice and a pleasing disposition, her children are more relaxed and quiet. Children are like kittens: If kittens have a full stomach and lie in the sun they purr. If the atmosphere is such that the children are more comfortable, they are quiet. It is comfortable living that makes the quiet child. When you are shouting at them and they're shouting back at you, it isn't comfortable living.

It is clear to the observer that Mrs. Olan is no "boss," but lodges responsibility in the children. She clarifies the matter further:

> It means a great deal to them to give their own direction. When problems do come up in the room we talk them over and discuss what is the right thing to do when this or that happens. Usually you get pretty good answers. They are a lot harder on themselves than I would be; so if any punishment comes along like not going to an assembly you have group pressure.

As the interviewer was leaving, Mrs. Olan remarked, "My children don't rate as high (on achievement tests) as other children. I don't push, and that's because I believe in comfortable living." *Noise* has indeed become subject matter.

In such classrooms the contemporary training for impulse release and fun is clear. There the children are not in uniform, but in the jerkins and gossamer of *A Midsummer Night's Dream*; it is a sweet drilling without pain. Since impulse and release and fun are a major requirement of the classroom, and since they must be contained within the four walls, the instrument of containment can only be affection. The teacher must therefore become a parent, for it is a parent above all who deals with the impulses of the child.

It is hard for us to see, since we consider most people inherently replaceable, that there is anything remarkable in a parent-figure like a teacher showering the symbols of affection on a child for a year and then letting him walk out of her life. However, this is almost unheard of outside the stream of Western civilization; and even in the West it is not common. As a matter of fact, the existence of *children* willing to accept such demonstrations is in itself an interesting phenomenon, based probably on the obsolescence of the two-parent family. (Today our children *do not have enough parents*, because parents are unable to do all that has to be done *by* parents nowadays.) The fact that a teacher can be demonstrative without inflicting deep wounds on *herself* implies a character structure having strong brakes on involvement. Her expressions of tenderness, then, must imply "so far and no farther"; and over the years, children must come to recognize this. If this were not so, children would have to be dragged shrieking from grade to grade and teachers would flee teaching, for the mutual attachment would be so deep that its annual severing would be too much for either to bear. And so this noise, too, teaches two lessons important to today's culture. From regular replacement-in-affection children learn that the affection-giving figure, the teacher, is replaceable also, and so they are drilled in uninvolvement. Meanwhile, they learn that the symbols of affectivity can be used ambiguously, and that they are not binding—that they can be scattered upon the world without commitment.

Again, the reader should not imagine that I am "against" affectionate classrooms. They are a necessary adjunct to contemporary childhood and to the socialization of parenthood (the "three-parent family")

at this stage of our culture. Meanwhile, the dialectic of culture suggests that there is some probability that when love like this enters by the door, learning leaves by the transom.

What, then, is the central issue? The central issue is *love of knowledge* for its own sake, not as the creature of drive, exploited largely for survival and for prestige. Creative cultures have loved the "beautiful person"— meditative, intellectual, and exalted. As for the individual, the history of great civilizations reveals little except that creativity has had an obstinate way of emerging only in a few, and that it has never appeared in the mass of the people. Loving the beautiful person more, we may alter this.

The contemporary school is a place where children are drilled in very general cultural orientations, and where subject matter becomes to a very considerable extent the instrument for instilling them. Because school deals with masses of children, it can manage only by reducing children all to a common definition. Naturally that definition is determined by the cultural preoccupations and so school creates the *essential nightmare* that drives people away from something (in our case, failure) and toward something (success). Today our children, instead of loving knowledge, become embroiled in the nightmare.

26

Family Planning, Amazon Style

Warren M. Hern

Family planning, excessive population growth, contraception, and abortion are some of the most incendiary issues in contemporary America. But America is not alone. These issues can strike in the heart of the Amazon as readily as in a technological society, and often with devastating results.

We often find that development and change for some comes at the expense of others. Increasing opportunities for wage labor may result in increased poverty and ill health. "Progress" may strip the land of its trees and the rivers of their fish, thus ending ways of life that have existed for a thousand years. While change may be unavoidable, and in some cases beneficial, it can be more thoughtful.

Thoughtless attempts to impose external morals have often led to social and cultural transformations that were clearly unanticipated. The decline of polygyny—the practice of several wives marrying a single husband—may be an example. Apparently, the practice of polygyny has some functionality in the culture and economy of the Shipibo people of the Amazon. In the selection following this one we find that polyandry—the practice of several husbands marrying one wife—has functionality in Tibet. While cultural values and behaviors must change, it is important to understand that these values exist in a larger social and cultural system, and that it will be affected also.

As you read this selection, ask yourself the following questions:

☐ *How has the Shipibo environment changed over the past thirty years?*

☐ *Have the Shipibo benefitted from the introduction of logging, cattle ranching, commercial fishing, and banana and rice farming and the resulting opportunities for wage labor?*

☐ *Why would the author refer to high fertility as a new health problem?*

☐ *How does polygyny affect birth rates?*

☐ *How do you feel about polygyny as a traditional cultural value, as a possible means of devaluing women, and as a method of controlling population growth?*

The following terms discussed in this selection are included in the Glossary at the back of the book:

epidemic
infanticide
polygyny
population pressure

"When you come back, don't forget to bring *toötimarau*," Chomoshico called to me. I was leaving the Shipibo Indian village of Manco Capac, on the banks of the Pisqui River in the Peruvian Amazon, where I had

been doing medical research. Chomoshico was nearing the end of her eleventh pregnancy. She already had seven living children. Neither she nor her husband wants more. "Enough. Clothes cost," they told me. "I'm tired of having children," she said. "I almost died with the last one." Her husband has tuberculosis.

Toötimarau means "medicine to keep from being pregnant"—birth control. I knew I could promise

Chomoshico worm medicine for her children's parasites, and I might be able to bring her vitamins and iron for her pregnancy, even medicine for tuberculosis. But while I could informally provide other kinds of medical care, I could not arrange to bring her birth control without risking reprisals from politicians who are against it. The Shipibo have been asking me for *toöti-marau* for more than twenty-five years, but I haven't been able to arrange any yet. I can only refer them to a Peruvian doctor in Pucallpa, many days away by canoe. Most can never get there. The men even pull me aside to ask if I know about an operation to "fix" men—vasectomy—and, again, I tell them the name of my medical colleague in Pucallpa.

In the same village, a few weeks before, a young girl had died on her thirteenth birthday trying to give birth to twins. And in that girl's natal village, just up the river, I had just seen my first case of frank starvation among the Shipibo Indians, with whom I had worked as a physician and scientist since 1964. The starving man had tuberculosis. His family, which would normally have taken care of someone so ill, was away working for a logging company.

Chomoshico's desperate request for birth control, the death of the thirteen-year-old girl, and the plight of the starving man are all related. The Shipibo's own high fertility, uncontrolled by any effective means, is compounding the problem of the population pressure created by an influx of outsiders, who are moving into Shipibo territory and destroying the natural resources.

The Shipibo Indians who live along the Ucayali River and its tributaries, such as the Pisqui, notice that the fish are getting smaller and harder to find, and that the game animals they rely on during the rainy season—when fish are almost impossible to catch—are more elusive than in the past. Palm leaves for thatching roofs seem scarcer, and people have to trek long distances, sometimes a mile or more, to gather firewood, once available a few steps away. People are aware that their own village is growing, that they do not know all its inhabitants, that the village school is crowded. Sometimes they have to go all day without eating fish. The Shipibo word for fish, *piti*, is also their word for food: a Shipibo without fish is truly poor.

In this crisis, the Shipibo are not alone. The Peruvian government has urged desperate people from the crowded coastal cities and Andean communities to settle and live in the jungle "paradise." They have. Pucallpa, the major port on the Ucayali, the "highway" river that becomes the Amazon, was probably an aboriginal Shipibo settlement (its Shipibo name means "red earth"). In the 1940s, just before the trans-Andes highway was put through to Pucallpa from Lima, the settlement's population was about 2,500. When I first visited Pucallpa in 1964, the population had grown to about 25,000. It was a raw, dusty, frontier town with dirt streets and Saturday night gunfights. More than 250,000 people live there now—a hundredfold increase in fifty years.

With the local waters already depleted, fishing boats from Pucallpa speed downstream more than 150 miles, where they take all fish more than two inches long with drift nets, pack the fish in ice, and start back up the river. The smaller fish are discarded to rot. There is not much left for the Shipibo, for the mestizo colonists from elsewhere in Peru, for the large fish, for the alligators, or for the wading birds that used to line the shores of the Ucayali. Areas around Pucallpa that were covered by canopy rain forest in 1964 now look like Oklahoma. The hundreds of bird species that enlivened the forest have been replaced by emaciated cows. Swamps filled with fish are replaced by causeways carrying buses and motorcycles. Twenty years ago, a traveler camped on the beach of the Ucayali River could not sleep for the sounds of fish splashing and alligators hunting them. There aren't enough fish to keep one awake now; the traveler is kept awake by the whine of fishermen's outboard motors.

Instead of living by subsistence fishing and horticulture, as the Shipibo principally do, their new neighbors exploit the environment to make money. First come the timber cutters, followed by cattle ranchers, commercial fishermen, and the farmers of bananas, rice, and other cash crops. The resultant deforestation and flooding have eliminated some crops and game animals that were sources of food for the Shipibo in the rainy season. The Shipibo themselves are drawn into the money economy and sometimes sell products from scarce animals (such as water turtle eggs) in order to get cash.

The Shipibo painfully admit that, although they work much harder than before, they don't have enough money for clothes (which they used to make by hand from woven cloth) and schoolbooks for their children (not a factor thirty years ago). They now have to buy food at times, even though it was previously plentiful.

The Shipibo (and the closely related Conibo) are the dominant indigenous people of the upper Peruvian Amazon. They have survived there for about a thousand years, but only by battling fiercely with other tribes and exhibiting a pragmatic tenacity in the face of colonization. Before the European conquest, they may have numbered more than 50,000. By the early twentieth century, fewer than 3,000 remained. Somehow they escaped the further decimation or complete extinction that befell many other Amazon tribes exposed to European diseases, enslavement, intertribal warfare sponsored by rubber tappers, and other openly genocidal attempts to rid the Amazon of its native inhabitants. Their population is now about 30,000 and growing.

The last smallpox epidemic was in 1964. But now, in addition to the modern plagues of tuberculosis and cholera, the Shipibo have a new health problem: high fertility, which places pressure on resources and takes a heavy toll among Shipibo women.

In the past the Shipibo controlled their birth rate and population growth in a variety of ways: by sexual abstinence, by abortion (using pressure on the uterus), by infanticide, and by the use of herbal contraceptives. Knowledge of these contraceptives was passed down through the generations from mother to daughter, from grandmother to granddaughter. But several things happened to interrupt this tradition. The horrifying epidemics that wiped out whole villages following European contact prompted shamans in related tribes to forbid the practices of infanticide and abortion. The Shipibo shamans may also have taken this step, but more likely, Christian missionaries played a role in disrupting the cultural traditions that controlled fertility. In 1697, the Shipibo massacred a group of Franciscans who were insisting that the Shipibo give up polygyny (multiple wives). Today, the custom remains strong in some parts of the Shipibo culture area but is declining in villages close to centers of Western influence.

Even though polygyny allows some men to have more offspring than others, it permits women to have fewer children with longer intervals between births. This arrangement has several important effects: it allows women to recover from each pregnancy; it allows children to gain maturity before being weaned and placed on a diet of all solid foods; and it reduces the total number of children borne by individual women. The result for the group is that women have a better chance of recovering from pregnancy and therefore of living longer, and child survival is better.

These advantages of polygyny are often cited by members of traditional societies, whose strategy is, not to have as many children as possible, but to have as many as possible that survive to adulthood. A final result of polygyny, paradoxically, is that community fertility could be restrained.

My acquaintance with Shipibo methods of controlling fertility began in 1964, when I was a third-year medical student from the University of Colorado. I had just finished working intensively for several months at the Hospital Amazonico "Albert Schweitzer" near Pucallpa, and had traveled to the Shipibo village of Paococha to learn about native ideas concerning the nature, treatment, and control of disease. A Shipibo friend who was helping me, Ambrosio, came to me one

day to tell me that his wife was bleeding to death: she had just had a baby. Ambrosio asked me to see her, and I treated his wife for retained membranes and postpartum uterine atony (relaxation of the uterus). She recovered, and he asked me what I could do for me. I told him I would like to learn about medicines that women use to control pregnancy. His aunt Julia was the local expert.

From Julia I learned that Shipibo women have several such herbal preparations. One of the most common is called *toötimahuaste* (*toöti* means "pregnancy," *ma* means "not," and *huaste* means "herb"). Taken as a tea during three successive menstrual periods, it is supposed to cause sterility.

In 1969, for my master of public health thesis, I returned to the village to conduct a more formal census and collect the inhabitants' reproductive histories. I asked the Shipibo women in my survey if they knew about these medicines and if they used them. They roared with laughter at the idea of a male gringo asking these intimate questions in their language. Then they usually told me that they knew about them; many had used them. Some of the women had seriously harmed themselves by using highly toxic natural substances in a desperate attempt to control fertility.

At first I was puzzled to find that women who had used the herbal contraceptives had more children, on the average, than those who hadn't. This turned out to be because older women, who had already had many children, were more likely to have used the herbal contraceptives. But my doubts about the effectiveness of the traditional contraceptives were renewed when I analyzed the results of my two population studies in 1964 and 1969. The Shipibo in Paococha turned out to have the highest fertility ever recorded for a human group, with a woman having an average of ten births during her reproductive life.

Moreover, their rate of population growth was nearly 4.9 percent per year, with the population doubling every 14.5 years. Such a population explosion had to be fairly recent, for if such a rate had been in effect for very long the population would have been huge. The phenomenon could not be completely explained by better medical care (some of which I had provided) and a declining death rate. Either the herbal contraceptives didn't work, or I wasn't getting all the information.

There were two other factors. By 1969, a large extended family from down the Ucayali river, at the periphery of the Shipibo territory, moved into Paococha. Several of the men had multiple wives. (The local, "downtown" Shipibo assured me that, unlike themselves, the new family was composed of *salvajes*—savages—and that they practiced the old ways, including polygyny.) Because missionaries and schoolteachers discouraged it, this family structure was becoming rare.

The second factor was suggested to me when I remembered that the Shipibo always observed certain taboos, including "dieting," when taking medications of any kind. I asked the women what they did when they took *toötimahuaste*. They replied that one cannot eat salt, honey from the forest or other sweets, ripe bananas, and certain kinds of fish. And a woman taking *toötimahuaste* may not have sex. This would mean an abstinence of three months or more. Right away, I suspected what epidemiologists call a "secondary non-causal association" between the use of herbal contraceptives and fewer pregnancies.

Postpartum sexual abstinence is often linked with polygyny in tribal societies. The woman who has just given birth may not sleep with her husband for a period of time, which may be from three months to three years. During that time her husband sleeps with one of the other wives. In Shipibo tradition, it is not uncommon for a man to have two or three wives. Because women in polygynous marriages might be better able to observe the sexual abstinence associated with herbal contraceptives, and because this might help these women have longer birth intervals, I speculated that a decline in the practice of polygyny could be contributing to the community's high fertility.

To be sure of this, I had to determine that, on average, the birth intervals were indeed longer for women in polygynous marriages than for women in monogamous marriages and that fertility was actually lower for the former than for the latter. Further, I wanted to determine if the rates of polygyny differed among the villages, and if so, whether less polygyny is associated with lower or higher community fertility. By studying Shipibo villages that were separated by long distances and had different levels of cultural contact with Western society, I could compare the relationship between polygyny and fertility.

Up on the Pisqui River, Shipibo lives are more traditional than in the Shipibo villages lining the Ucayali. The Pisqui is much smaller and fluctuates more quickly than the Ucayali. It contains fewer fish and other edible wildlife. The Pisqui Shipibo live more by hunting and gathering than their Ucayali brethren. They are more isolated from outside influences, and have been since at least early colonial times.

In 1983 and 1984, I studied eight Shipibo villages in different states of cultural transition. Six of the villages were as much as sixty miles up the Pisqui. The results of the study showed that polygyny is generally more common on the Pisqui, and that longer birth intervals occur in the polygynous unions there. In some Pisqui villages, 45 percent of the women were in polygynous marriages, whereas in Paoyhän, a new Shipibo village on the Ucayali, only about 5 percent of the women were in this kind of union.

Comparing the birth interval lengths and fertility of all women, regardless of their villages, I found that, on average, the birth intervals for women in polygynous marriages were thirty-four months—four months longer than those of women in monogamous marriages. And most significant, women in monogamous marriages had 1.3 more children during their reproductive lives than women in polygynous marriages. Accordingly, in villages where polygyny was more common, the average intervals between births were longer and community fertility rates were lower.

The most acute health problem for the Shipibo, as both they and I see it, is epidemic disease—tuberculosis, cholera, and influenza, to mention a few. These diseases carry off the older people who know the cultural traditions, and they carry off many children. But the long-term problem is high fertility, which is placing pressure on the diminishing resources. Weakened by increasingly poor nutrition, the Shipibo are more vulnerable to epidemics. In their case, population growth means poverty and disease.

For Shipibo women, high fertility means sickness and death. They have an extremely high rate of cervical cancer, which is probably related, among other things, to early childbearing and many pregnancies. I estimate that the maternal mortality ratio—the proportion of women who die from pregnancy and childbirth—is roughly one for every hundred live births, one hundred times higher than in the United States.

A larger question raised by studies such as mine is whether we really understand how fast the world's population is growing and will grow in the future. The Shipibo are essentially not counted in the Peruvian census, and neither are their mestizo and other Shipibo neighbors. Numbers sent to the government offices are highly inaccurate (but then I, for one, never received a U.S. census form in 1990).

From my experiences in Latin America, I would speculate that official census counts are missing at least one in ten people and perhaps every fourth person. Some of those groups excluded appear to have population growth rates of more than 3.5 percent. If this is true—and if it is similarly true in other parts of the developing world—world population growth rates may not only be higher than official estimates but may also grow higher as traditional societies like the Shipibo experience rapid cultural change.

Human population growth is not new. But there was a time, long past, when it took 100,000 years for world population to double. Soon after agriculture was invented, the doubling time dropped to 700 years. Now our population is doubling every 35 to 40 years. What happened?

While there are many answers, one emerges from this study and others like it: many human societies that controlled their fertility in the past have lost the tradition of doing so in the frenzy of modern cultural change. The old methods that reduced births have not yet been replaced by the new technologies of fertility control. The result is chaos, suffering, more cultural change, and in some cases, even more rapid population growth. Where will it stop?

For the Shipibo it stops when the beloved *yoshan-shico* (grandmother) dies of tuberculosis and takes with her the ancient Amazon traditions of pottery making and weaving and knowledge of the plants and seasons. It stops with the loss of half the village's children to a measles epidemic. It stops with the death of a beautiful thirteen-year-old girl in childbirth. It stops when the village chief, a vigorous and intelligent young man, dies of cholera. It stops when the legendary hunter of *piache*, a giant fish once commonly found in Amazon lakes, returns after three days in the bush with his canoe empty and his harpoon unused. His family gets by on another meal of banana porridge.

It stops when the bright but superfluous young men and women of the village leave for the city, where they can get low-level jobs and survive. Their village education, which kept them from the forest and from learning their environment and own culture, has given them only minimal skills for life in town, where they sometimes conceal their cultural identity to get jobs.

It stopped for Ambrosio's wife when she died, exhausted, trying to give birth the next time, at the end of her twelfth pregnancy. The previous child proved to be mentally retarded, probably the result of a two-day labor and difficult delivery. For Ambrosio, a friendly man with a mischievous smile and quick wit, it stopped when he died from tetanus two years later. For Julia, who became one of my dearest friends in life, a woman who had outlived two husbands and thrown out several others, who was fiercely independent and could hunt and fish with the men, who was a skilled artist and walking library of Shipibo culture, it stopped when she started coughing blood and bled to death in a few minutes in front of her horrified family. The Shipibo are being forced to choose between buying tuberculosis medicine for people like Julia and building schools for their children.

For me, there are few things as delightful as the sound of Shipibo children laughing. The Shipibo love their children, and it shows. But what is ahead for people like Chomoshico and her husband and children? The inexorable arithmetic of population growth is upon them, and the consequences for their environment and families are plain to see. As a public health physician, I cannot help noticing that the Shipibo's fertility problems are inseparable from their other health problems and the changes going on around them. I also cannot help noticing that each family, with few exceptions, wants to limit its fertility but has no safe, effective means of doing so. That is not a scientific issue, but a political problem that neither I nor the Shipibo can solve.

27

When Brothers Share a Wife

Melvyn C. Goldstein

Marriage is a social institution that formalizes certain aspects of the relationship between males and females. It is an institution that evokes in us deep-seated emotions about questions of right and wrong, good and evil, and traditional versus modern. Within families, arguments may occur about what is appropriate premarital behavior, what is a proper marriage ceremony, and how long a marriage should last. Although these arguments may be traumatic for parents and their offspring, from a cross-cultural perspective, they generally involve minor deviations from the cultural norms. In contrast, anthropology textbooks describe an amazing variety of marriage systems that fulfill both biological and social functions. This selection will show just how different things could be.

Social institutions are geared to operate within and adapt to the larger social and ecological environment. This was the case in the earlier selections on gender roles (23) and family planning (26); the organization of the family must also be adapted to the ecology. For example, the nuclear family is more adapted to a highly mobile society than is an extended family unit that includes grandparents and others. As society increasingly focuses on technical education, career specialization, and therefore geographic mobility for employment purposes, a system has evolved that emphasizes the nuclear family over the extended family. In a similar way, fraternal polyandry in Tibet, as described in this selection, can meet the social, demographic, and ecological needs of its region.

As you read this selection, ask yourself the following questions:

☐ What is meant by the term "fraternal polyandry"?

☐ Is this the only form of marriage allowed in Tibet?

☐ How do husbands and wives feel about the sexual aspects of sharing a spouse?

☐ Why would Tibetans choose fraternal polyandry?

☐ How is the function of fraternal polyandry like that of nineteenth-century primogeniture in England?

The following terms discussed in this selection are included in the Glossary at the back of the book:

arable land
corvée
fraternal polyandry
monogamy
nuclear family
population pressure
primogeniture

Eager to reach home, Dorje drives his yaks hard over the 17,000-foot mountain pass, stopping only once to rest. He and his two older brothers, Pema and Sonam, are jointly marrying a woman from the next village in a few weeks, and he has to help with the preparations.

With permission from *Natural History*, Vol. 96, No. 3; Copyright the American Museum of Natural History, 1987.

Dorje, Pema, and Sonam are Tibetans living in Limi, a 200-square-mile area in the northwest corner of Nepal, across the border from Tibet. The form of marriage they are about to enter—fraternal polyandry in anthropological parlance—is one of the world's rarest forms of marriage but is not uncommon in Tibetan society, where it has been practiced from time immemorial. For many Tibetan social strata, it traditionally represented the ideal form of marriage and family.

The mechanics of fraternal polyandry are simple. Two, three, four, or more brothers jointly take a wife, who leaves her home to come and live with them. Traditionally, marriage was arranged by parents, with children, particularly females, having little or no say. This is changing somewhat nowadays, but it is still unusual for children to marry without their parents' consent. Marriage ceremonies vary by income and region and range from all the brothers sitting together as grooms to only the eldest one formally doing so. The age of the brothers plays an important role in determining this: very young brothers almost never participate in actual marriage ceremonies, although they typically join the marriage when they reach their midteens.

The eldest brother is normally dominant in terms of authority, that is, in managing the household, but all the brothers share the work and participate as sexual partners. Tibetan males and females do not find the sexual aspect of sharing a spouse the least bit unusual, repulsive, or scandalous, and the norm is for the wife to treat all the brothers the same.

Offspring are treated similarly. There is no attempt to link children biologically to particular brothers, and a brother shows no favoritism toward his child even if he knows he is the real father because, for example, his older brothers were away at the time the wife became pregnant. The children, in turn, consider all of the brothers as their fathers and treat them equally, even if they also know who is their real father. In some regions children use the term "father" for the eldest brother and "father's brother" for the others, while in other areas they call all the brothers by one term, modifying this by the use of "elder" and "younger."

Unlike our own society, where monogamy is the only form of marriage permitted, Tibetan society allows a variety of marriage types, including monogamy, fraternal polyandry, and polygyny. Fraternal polyandry and monogamy are the most common forms of marriage, while polygyny typically occurs in cases where the first wife is barren. The widespread practice of fraternal polyandry, therefore, is not the outcome of a law requiring brothers to marry jointly. There is choice, and in fact, divorce traditionally was relatively simple in Tibetan society. If a brother in a polyandrous marriage became dissatisfied and wanted to separate, he simply left the main house and set up his own household. In such cases, all the children stayed in the main household with the remaining brother(s), even if the departing brother was known to be the real father of one or more of the children.

The Tibetans' own explanation for choosing fraternal polyandry is materialistic. For example, when I asked Dorje why he decided to marry with his two brothers rather than take his own wife, he thought for a moment, then said it prevented the division of his family's farm (and animals) and thus facilitated all of them achieving a higher standard of living. And when I later asked Dorje's bride whether it wasn't difficult for her to cope with three brothers as husbands, she laughed and echoed that rationale of avoiding fragmentation of the family land, adding that she expected to be better off economically, since she would have three husbands working for her and her children.

Exotic as it may seem to Westerners, Tibetan fraternal polyandry is thus in many ways analogous to the way primogeniture functioned in nineteenth-century England. Primogeniture dictated that the eldest son inherited the family estate, while younger sons had to leave home and seek their own employment—for example, in the military or the clergy. Primogeniture maintained family estates intact over generations by permitting only one heir per generation. Fraternal polyandry also accomplishes this but does so by keeping all the brothers together with just one wife so that there is only one set of heirs per generation.

While Tibetans believe that in this way fraternal polyandry reduces the risk of family fission, monogamous marriages among brothers need not necessarily precipitate the division of the family estate: brothers could continue to live together, and the family land could continue to be worked jointly. When I asked Tibetans about this, however, they invariably responded that such joint families are unstable because each wife is primarily oriented to her own children and interested in their success and well-being over that of the children of other wives. For example, if the youngest brother's wife had three sons while the eldest brother's wife had only one daughter, the wife of the youngest brother might begin to demand more resources for her children since, as males, they represent the future of the family. Thus, the children from different wives in the same generation are competing sets of heirs, and this makes such families inherently unstable. Tibetans perceive that conflict will spread from the wives to their husbands and consider this likely to cause family fission. Consequently, it is almost never done.

Although Tibetans see an economic advantage to fraternal polyandry, they do not value the sharing of a wife as an end in itself. On the contrary, they articulate a number of problems inherent in the practice. For example, because authority is customarily exercised by the eldest brother, his younger male siblings have to subordinate themselves with little hope of changing their status within the family. When these younger brothers are aggressive and individualistic, tensions and difficulties often occur despite there being only one set of heirs.

In addition, tension and conflict may arise in

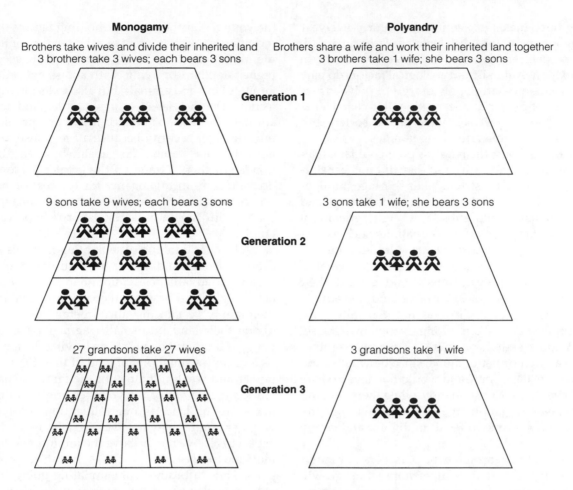

Monogamy

Brothers take wives and divide their inherited land
3 brothers take 3 wives; each bears 3 sons

Generation 1

Polyandry

Brothers share a wife and work their inherited land together
3 brothers take 1 wife; she bears 3 sons

9 sons take 9 wives; each bears 3 sons

Generation 2

3 sons take 1 wife; she bears 3 sons

27 grandsons take 27 wives

Generation 3

3 grandsons take 1 wife

polyandrous families because of sexual favoritism. The bride normally sleeps with the eldest brother, and the two have the responsibility to see to it that the other males have opportunities for sexual access. Since the Tibetan subsistence economy requires males to travel a lot, the temporary absence of one or more brothers facilitates this, but there are also other rotation practices. The cultural ideal unambiguously calls for the wife to show equal affection and sexuality to each of the brothers (and vice versa), but deviations from this ideal occur, especially when there is a sizable difference in age between partners in the marriage.

Dorje's family represents just such a potential situation. He is fifteen years old and his two older brothers are twenty-five and twenty-two years old. The new bride is twenty-three years old, eight years Dorje's senior. Sometimes such a bride finds the youngest husband immature and adolescent and does not treat him with equal affection; alternatively, she may find his youth attractive and lavish special attention on him. Apart from this consideration, when a younger male like Dorje grows up, he may consider his wife "ancient" and prefer the company of a woman his own age or younger. Consequently, although men and women do not find the idea of sharing a bride or a bridegroom

repulsive, individual likes and dislikes can cause familial discord.

Two reasons have commonly been offered for the perpetuation of fraternal polyandry in Tibet: that Tibetans practice female infanticide and therefore have to marry polyandrously, owing to a shortage of females; and that Tibet, lying at extremely high altitudes, is so barren and bleak that Tibetans would starve without resort to this mechanism. A Jesuit who lived in Tibet in the eighteenth century articulated this second view: "One reason for this most odious custom is the sterility of the soil, and the small amount of land that can be cultivated owing to the lack of water. The crops may suffice if the brothers all live together, but if they form separate families they would be reduced to beggary."

Both explanations are wrong, however. Not only has there never been institutionalized female infanticide in Tibet, but Tibetan society gives females considerable rights, including inheriting the family estate in the absence of brothers. In such cases, the woman takes a bridegroom who comes to live in her family and adopts her family's name and identity. Moreover, there is no demographic evidence of a shortage of females. In Limi, for example, there were (in 1974) sixty females and fifty-three males in the fifteen- to thirty-five-year age category, and many adult females were unmarried.

The second reason is also incorrect. The climate in Tibet is extremely harsh, and ecological factors do play a major role perpetuating polyandry, but polyandry is not a means of preventing starvation. It is characteristic, not of the poorest segments of the society, but rather of the peasant landowning families.

In the old society, the landless poor could not realistically aspire to prosperity, but they did not fear starvation. There was a persistent labor shortage throughout Tibet, and very poor families with little or no land and few animals could subsist through agricultural labor, tenant farming, craft occupations such as carpentry, or by working as servants. Although the per person family income could increase somewhat if brothers married polyandrously and pooled their wages, in the absence of inheritable land, the advantage of fraternal polyandry was not generally sufficient to prevent them from setting up their own households. A more skilled or energetic younger brother could do as well or better alone, since he would completely control his income and would not have to share it with his siblings. Consequently, while there was and is some polyandry among the poor, it is much less frequent and more prone to result in divorce and family fission.

An alternative reason for the persistence of fraternal polyandry is that it reduces population growth (and thereby reduces the pressure on resources) by relegating some females to lifetime spinsterhood. Fraternal polyandrous marriages in Limi (in 1974) averaged 2.35 men per woman, and not surprisingly, 31 percent of the females of child-bearing age (twenty to forty-nine) were unmarried. These spinsters either continued to live at home, set up their own households, or worked as servants for other families. They could also become Buddhist nuns. Being unmarried is not synonymous with exclusion from the reproductive pool. Discreet extramarital relationships are tolerated, and actually half of the adult unmarried women in Limi had one or more children. They raised these children as single mothers, working for wages or weaving cloth and blankets for sale. As a group, however, the unmarried women had far fewer offspring than the married women, averaging only 0.7 children per woman, compared with 3.3 for married women, whether polyandrous, monogamous, or polygynous. While polyandry helps regulate population, this function of polyandry is not consciously perceived by Tibetans and is not the reason they consistently choose it.

If neither a shortage of females nor the fear of starvation perpetuates fraternal polyandry, what motivates brothers, particularly younger brothers, to opt for this system of marriage? From the perspective of the younger brother in a landholding family, the main incentive is the attainment or maintenance of the good life. With polyandry, he can expect a more secure and higher standard of living, with access not only to his family's land and animals, but also to its inherited collection of clothes, jewelry, rugs, saddles, and horses. In addition, he will experience less work pressure and much greater security because all responsibility does not fall on one "father." For Tibetan brothers, the question is whether to trade off the greater personal freedom inherent in monogamy for the real or potential economic security, affluence, and social prestige associated with life in a larger, labor-rich polyandrous family.

A brother thinking of separating from his polyandrous marriage and taking his own wife would face various disadvantages. Although in the majority of Tibetan regions all brothers theoretically have rights to their family's estate, in reality Tibetans are reluctant to divide their land into small fragments. Generally, a younger brother who insists on leaving the family will receive only a small plot of land, if that. Because of its power and wealth, the rest of the family usually can block any attempt of the younger brother to increase his share of land through litigation. Moreover, a younger brother may not even get a house and cannot expect to receive much above the minimum in terms of movable possessions, such as furniture, pots, and pans. Thus, a brother contemplating going it on his own must plan on achieving economic security and the good life not through inheritance but through his own work.

The obvious solution for younger brothers—creating new fields from virgin land—is generally not a feasible option. Most Tibetan populations live at high altitudes (above 12,000 feet), where arable land is extremely scarce. For example, in Dorje's village, agriculture ranges only from about 12,900 feet, the lowest point in the area, to 13,300 feet. Above that altitude, early frost and snow destroy the staple barley crop. Furthermore, because of the low rainfall caused by the Himalayan rain shadow, many areas in Tibet and northern Nepal that are within appropriate altitude range for agriculture have no reliable sources of irrigation. In the end, although there is plenty of unused land in such areas, most of it is either too high or too arid.

Even where unused land capable of being farmed exists, clearing the land and building the substantial terraces necessary for irrigation constitute a great undertaking. Each plot has to be completely dug out to a depth of two to two and a half feet so that the large rocks and boulders can be removed. At best, a man might be able to bring a few new fields under cultivation in the first years after separating from his brothers, but he could not expect to acquire substantial amounts of arable land this way.

In addition, because of the limited farmland, the Tibetan subsistence economy characteristically includes a strong emphasis on animal husbandry. Tibetan farmers regularly maintain cattle, yaks, goats, and sheep, grazing them in the areas too high for agriculture. These herds produce wool, milk, cheese, butter, meat, and skins. To obtain these resources, however, shepherds must accompany the animals on a daily basis. When first setting up a monogamous household, a younger brother like Dorje would find it difficult to both farm and manage animals.

In traditional Tibetan society, there was an even more critical factor that operated to perpetuate fraternal polyandry—a form of hereditary servitude somewhat analogous to serfdom in Europe. Peasants were tied to large estates held by aristocrats, monasteries, and the Lhasa government. They were allowed the use of some farmland to produce their own subsistence but were required to provide taxes in kind and corvée (free labor) to their lords. The corvée was a substantial hardship, since a peasant household was in many cases required to furnish the lord with one laborer daily for most of the year and more on specific occasions such as the harvest. This enforced labor, along with the lack of new land and the ecological pressure to pursue both agriculture and animal husbandry, made polyandrous families particularly beneficial. The polyandrous family allowed an internal division of adult labor, maximizing economic advantage. For example, while the wife worked the family fields, one brother could perform the lord's corvée, another could look after the animals, and a third could engage in trade.

Although social scientists often discount other people's explanations of why they do things, in the case of Tibetan fraternal polyandry, such explanations are very close to the truth. The custom, however, is very sensitive to changes in its political and economic milieu and, not surprisingly, is in decline in most Tibetan areas. Made less important by the elimination of the traditional serf-based economy, it is disparaged by the dominant non-Tibetan leaders of India, China, and Nepal. New opportunities for economic and social mobility in these countries, such as the tourist trade and government employment, are also eroding the rationale for polyandry, and so it may vanish within the next generation.

28

Law, Custom, and Crimes Against Women:

The Problem of Dowry Death in India

John van Willigen and V. C. Channa

Anthropologists find many societies with unusual customs, beliefs, and behaviors. Usually they discover, after careful study and reflection, that these perform some useful function within the society, as in the case of polygyny and polyandry discussed in the previous two selections. But is this always the case? Must we assume that simply because a custom exists it is healthy for the members of society? We think not, and the Christians who were fed to lions and the Aztec slaves who were sacrificed to a bloodthirsty god would most likely agree.

Times change; hunters and gatherers plant crops, tribal people rush headlong into peasantry, and small-scale farmers become urban wage earners. Traditions that helped maintain a healthy society in one context may become dysfunctional in another. For better or worse, traditions and beliefs run deep and are almost impossible to unlearn. It is the nature of culture to resist change.

As you will read, the practice of dousing a bride with kerosene and creating a human torch certainly indicates that the payment of dowry is a traditional practice gone awry. This said, what can be done? Laws, even those that carry serious penalties, are light ammunition against the armor of strongly held cultural beliefs. Governments will solve such problems only through public policy based on in-depth cultural understanding.

As you read this selection, ask yourself the following questions:

☐ What do you think the authors mean when they suggest that dowry death presents a problem for ethnologists because of ethnological theory's functional cast?

☐ Why does the institution of dowry make college education problematic for some young women?

☐ What are the present-day approaches to solving the dowry death problem?

☐ How can women's access to production roles and property, delocalization of social control, and economic transformation affect the problem of dowry death?

☐ Dowry-related violence in India is related to the economic value of women. What might be said about the relationship between the economic position and the social status of women in America?

The following terms discussed in this selection are included in the Glossary at the back of the book:

caste
cultural materialism
demography
dowry
ethnology
peasants
sex roles

A 25-year-old woman was allegedly burnt to death by her husband and mother-in-law at their East Delhi home yesterday. The housewife, Mrs. Sunita, stated before her death at the Jaya Prakash Narayana Hospital that members of her husband's family had been harassing her for bringing inadequate dowry.

The woman told the Shahdara subdivisional magistrate that during a quarrel over dowry at their Pratap Park house yesterday, her husband gripped her from behind while the mother-in-law poured kerosene over her clothes.

Her clothes were then set ablaze. The police have registered a case against the victim's husband, Suraj Prakash, and his mother.

—Times of India, February 19, 1988

This routinely reported news story describes what in India is termed a "bride-burning" or "dowry death." Such incidents are frequently reported in the newspapers of Delhi and other Indian cities. In addition, there are cases in which the evidence may be ambiguous, so that deaths of women by fire may be recorded as kitchen accidents, suicides, or murders. Dowry violence takes a characteristic form. Following marriage and the requisite giving of dowry, the family of the groom makes additional demands for the payment of more cash or the provision of more goods. These demands are expressed in unremitting harassment of the bride, who is living in the household of her husband's parents, culminating in the murder of the woman by members of her husband's family or by her suicide. The woman is typically burned to death with kerosene, a fuel used in pressurized cook stoves, hence the use of the term "bride-burning" in public discourse.

Dowry death statistics appear frequently in the press and parliamentary debates. Parliamentary sources report the following figures for married women 16 to 30 years of age in Delhi: 452 deaths by burning for 1985; 478 for 1986 and 300 for the first six months of 1987 (Bhatia 1988). There were 1,319 cases reported nationally in 1986 (Times of India, January 10, 1988). Police records do not match hospital records for third degree burn cases among younger married women; far more violence occurs than the crime reports indicate (Kumari 1988).

There is other violence against women related both directly and indirectly to the institution of dowry. For example, there are unmarried women who commit suicide so as to relieve their families of the burden of providing a dowry. A recent case that received national attention in the Indian press involved the triple suicide of three sisters in the industrial city of Kanpur. A pho-

Reproduced by permission of the Society for Applied Anthropology from *Human Organization*, Vol. 50, No. 4, 1991, pp. 369–377.

tograph was widely published showing the three young women hanging from ceiling fans by their scarves. Their father, who earned about 4000 Rs. [rupees] per month, was not able to negotiate marriage for his oldest daughter. The grooms were requesting approximately 100,000 Rs. Also linked to the dowry problem is selective female abortion made possible by amniocentesis. This issue was brought to national attention with a startling statistic reported out of a seminar held in Delhi in 1985. Of 3000 abortions carried out after sex determination through amniocentesis, only one involved a male fetus. As a result of these developments, the government of the state of Maharashtra banned sex determination tests except those carried out in government hospitals.

The phenomenon of dowry-death presents a difficult problem for the ethnologist. Ethnological theory, with its residual functionalist cast, still does not deal effectively with the social costs of institutions of what might be arguably referred to as custom gone bad, resulting in a culturally constituted violence syndrome.

This essay examines dowry and its violent aspects, and some of the public solutions developed to deal with it in India. Our work consists of a meta-analysis of some available literature. We critique the legal mechanisms established to regulate the cultural institution of dowry and the resultant social evils engendered by the institution, and argue that policies directed against these social evils need to be constructed in terms of an underlying cause rather than of the problem itself. We consider cause, an aspect of the problem infrequently discussed in public debate. As Saini asserts, "legal academicians have shown absolutely no interest in the causal roots of dowry as practiced in contemporary India" (1983:143).

THE INSTITUTION

Since ancient times, the marriage of Hindus has required the transfer of property from the family of the bride to the family of the groom. Dowry or *daan dehej* is thought by some to be sanctioned by such religious texts as the *Manusmriti*. Seen in this way, dowry is a religious obligation of the father of a woman and a matter of *dharma* (religious duty) whereby authority over a woman is transferred from her father to her husband. This transfer takes different forms in different communities in modern India (Tambiah 1973). In public discussion, the term "dowry" covers a wide range of traditional payments and expenses, some presented to the groom's family and others to be retained by the bride. Customs have changed through time. The financial burdens of gifts and the dowry payments per se are exacerbated by the many expenses associated with the marriage celebration itself, but dowry payment is especially problematic because of its open-ended nature. As Tambiah notes, "marriage payments in India usually comprise an elaborate series of payments back and forth between the marrying families" and "this series extends over a long period of time and persists after marriage" (1973:92). Contemporary cases such as the death of Mrs. Sunita, often revolve around such continued demands.

A daughter's marriage takes a long time to prepare and involves the development of an adaptive strategy on the part of her family. An important part of the strategy is the preparation for making dowry payments; family consumption may be curtailed so as to allow accumulation of money for dowry. Seeing to marriage arrangements may be an important aspect of retirement planning. The dowries that the family receives on behalf of their sons may be "rolled over" to deal with the daughter's requirements. Families attempt to cultivate in both their sons and daughters attributes that will make them more attractive in marriage negotiations. Many things besides dowry are considered in negotiations: "non-economic" factors have demonstrable effect on the expectations for dowry and the family's strategy concerning the dowry process.

Education is a variable to be considered in the negotiation process. Education of young women is somewhat problematic because suitable husbands for such women must also be college educated. The parents of such young men demand more dowry for their sons. A consideration in sending a young woman to college will therefore be her parents' capacity to dower her adequately so as to obtain an appropriate groom. In any case, education is secondary to a man's earning power and the reputation of a woman's family. Education is, however, important in the early stages of negotiation because of the need to coordinate the level of the education of the men and women. Education qualifications are also less ambiguously defined than other dimensions of family reputation. Physical attractiveness is a consideration, but it is thought somewhat unseemly to emphasize this aspect of the decision.

Advertisements in newspapers are used for establishing marriage proposals (Aluwalia 1969, Niehoff 1959, Weibe and Ramu 1971), but contacts are more typically established through kin and other networks. Some marriages may be best termed "self-arranged," and are usually called "love marriages." In these cases, young men and women may develop a relationship independent of their families and then ask that negotiations be carried out on their behalf by family representatives.

Analysis of matrimonial advertisements shows some of the attributes considered to be important.

Listed in such advertisements are education, age, income and occupation, physical attributes, *gotra* (a kind of unilineal descent group) membership, family background, place of residence, personality features, consideration of dowry, time and type of marriage, and language.

Consideration of dowry and other expenditures are brought out early in the negotiations and can serve as a stumbling block. Dowry negotiations can go on for some time. The last stage is the actual "seeing of the groom" and the "seeing of the bride," both rather fleeting encounters whose position at the end of the process indicates their relative lack of importance.

Marriage is a process by which two families mutually evaluate each other. The outcome of the negotiations is an expression of the relative worth of the two persons, a man and a woman, and, by extension, the worth of their respective families. This estimation of worth is expressed in marriage expenditures, of which dowry is but a part. There are three possible types of expenditures: cash gifts, gifts of household goods, and expenditures on the wedding celebration itself. The cash gift component of the dowry goes to the groom's father and comes to be part of his common household fund. The household goods are for use by the groom's household, although they may be used to establish a separate household for the newlyweds. When separate accommodations are not set up, the groom's family may insist that the goods do not duplicate things they already have.

Dates for marriages are set through consideration of horoscopes; horoscopy is done by professional astrologers (*pandits*). This practice leads to a concentration of marriage dates and consequent high demand for marriage goods and services at certain times of the year. During marriage seasons, the cost of jewelry, furniture, clothes, musicians' services and other marriage related expenditures goes up, presumably because of the concentration of the demand caused by the astrologers.

The expenditures required of the woman's family for the wedding in general and the dowry in particular are frequently massive. Paul reports, for a middle-class Delhi neighborhood, that most dowries were over 50,000 Rs. (1986). Srinivas comments that dowries over 200,000 Rs. are not uncommon (1984).[1]

ETHNOLOGICAL THEORIES ABOUT DOWRY

Dowry had traditionally been discussed by ethnologists in the context of the functionalist paradigm, and much theorizing about dowry appears to be concerned with explaining the "contribution" that the institution makes to social adaptation. The early theoretician

Westermarck interpreted dowry as a social marker of the legitimacy of spouse and offspring, and as a mechanism for defining women's social roles and property rights in the new household (Westermarck 1921:428). Murdock suggests that dowry may confirm the contract of marriage (1949). Dowry is interpreted by Friedl as a means to adjust a woman to her affinal home as it rearranges social relationships including the social separation of the man from his parents (1967). Dowry payments are public expressions of the new relationship between the two families, and of the social status of the bride and groom.

Dowry is seen in the social science literature as a kind of antemortem or anticipated inheritance by which a widow is assured of support, and provision for her offspring (Friedl 1967; Goody 1973, 1976). It transfers money to where the women will be and where they will reproduce; as a result, resources are also placed where the children will benefit, given the practice of patrilineal inheritance of immovable, economically valuable property like farm land.

In India, dowry is also seen as an expression of the symbolic order of society. According to Dumont, dowry expresses the hierarchal relations of marriage in India and lower status of the bride (Dumont 1957). The amount of dowry given is an expression of prestige. The capacity to buy prestige through dowry increases the potential for social mobility (Goody 1973). Dowry is a kind of delayed consumption used to demonstrate or improve social rank (Epstein 1960).

There is a significant discontinuity between discussions of dowry in the ethnological theory and in public discourse. Certainly the dowry problem does appear in the writing of contemporary ethnologists, but it is simply lamented and left largely uninterpreted and unexplained.

THE EXTANT SOLUTIONS TO THE PROBLEM

The Dowry Prohibition Act of 1961, as amended in 1984 and 1986, is the primary legal means for regulating the dowry process and controlling its excesses. The laws against dowry are tough. Dowry demand offenses are "cognizable" (require no warrant) and non-bailable, and the burden of proof is on the accused. There are, in fact, convictions under the law.

The act defines dowry as "any property of valuable security given or agreed to be given either directly or indirectly—(a) by one party to a marriage to the other party to a marriage; or (b) by parents of either party to a marriage or by any other person, to either party to the marriage or to any other person" (Government of India 1986:1). The act makes it illegal to give or take dowry, "If any person after the com-

mencement of this act, gives or takes or abets the giving or taking of dowry, he shall be punishable with imprisonment for a term which shall not be less than five years; and with fine which shall not be less than fifteen thousand rupees or the amount of the value of such dowry which ever is more" (Government of India 1986:1). While this section unambiguously prohibits dowry, the third section allows wedding presents to be freely given. Thus the law does not apply to "presents which are given at the time of marriage to the bride (without demand having been made in that behalf)" (Government of India 1986:1). Identical provisions apply to the groom. Furthermore, all such presents must be listed on a document before the consummation of the marriage. The list is to contain a brief description and estimation of the value of the gifts, name of presenting person, and the relationship that person has with the bride and groom. This regulation also provides "that where such presents are made by or on the behalf of the bride or any other person related to the bride, such presents are of a customary nature and the value thereof is not excessive having regard to the financial status of the person by whom, or on whose behalf, such presents are given" (Government of India 1986:2). Amendments made in 1984 make it illegal for a person to demand dowry with the same penalty as under the earlier "giving and taking" provision. It was also declared illegal to advertise for dowry, such an offense being defined as not bailable, with the burden of proof on the accused person.

This legislation was coupled with some changes in the Indian Penal Code that legally established the concept of "dowry death." That is, "where the death of a woman is caused by any burns or bodily injury or occurs otherwise than under normal circumstances within seven years of her marriage and it is shown that soon before her death she was subjected to cruelty or harassment by her husband or any relative of her husband for, or in connection with, any demand for dowry, such death shall be called 'dowry death,' and such husband or relative shall be deemed to have caused her death" (Government of India 1987:4). The Indian Evidence Act of 1871 was changed so as to allow for the presumption of guilt under the circumstances outlined above. Changes in the code allowed for special investigation and reporting procedures of deaths by apparent suicide of women within seven years of marriage if requested by a relative. There were also newly defined special provisions for autopsies.

To this point, however, these legal mechanisms have proved ineffective. According to Sivaramayya, the "act has signally failed in its operation" (1984:66). Menon refers to the "near total failure" of the law (1988:12). A similar viewpoint is expressed by Srinivas, who wrote, "The Dowry Prohibition Act of 1961 has been unanimously declared to be an utterly ineffective law" (1984:29).

In addition to the legal attack on dowry abuses, numerous public groups engage in public education campaigns. In urban settings, the most noteworthy of these groups are specialized research units such as the Special Cell for Women of the Tata Institute of Social Sciences (Bombay), and the Center for Social Research (New Delhi). Also involved in the effort are private voluntary organizations such as the Crimes Against Women Cell, Karmika, and Sukh Shanti.

These groups issue public education advertising on various feminist issues. The anti-dowry advertisement of the Federation of Indian Chambers of Commerce and Industry Ladies Organization exemplifies the thrust of these campaigns. In the following advertisement, which was frequently run in the winter of 1988 in newspapers such as the Times of India, a photograph of a doll dressed in traditional Indian bridal attire was shown in flames.

> Every time a young bride dies because of dowry demands, we are all responsible for her death. Because we allow it to happen. Each year in Delhi hospitals alone, over 300 brides die of third degree burns. And many more deaths go unreported. Most of the guilty get away. And we just shrug helplessly and say, "what can we do?" We can do a lot.
>
> Help create social condemnation of dowry. Refuse to take or give dowry. Protest when you meet people who condone the practice. Reach out and help the girl being harassed for it. Act now.
>
> Let's fight it together.
>
> As parents, bring up educated, self-reliant daughters. Make sure they marry only after 18. Oppose dowry; refuse to even discuss it. If your daughter is harassed after marriage stand by her.
>
> As young men and women, refuse marriage proposals where dowry is being considered. As friends and neighbors, ostracize families who give or take dowry. Reach out to help victims of dowry harassment.
>
> As legislators and jurists, frame stronger laws. Ensure speedy hearings, impose severe punishments. As associations, give help and advice. Take up the challenge of changing laws and attitudes of society. Let us all resolve to fight the evil. If we fight together we can win.
>
> SAY NO TO DOWRY.

Also engaged in anti-dowry work are peasant political action groups such as Bharatiya Kisan Union (BKU). BKU consists of farmers from western Uttar Pradesh whose political program is focused more generally on agricultural issues. The group sponsored a massive 25-day demonstration at Meerut, Uttar Pradesh, in 1988. The leadership used the demonstration to announce a social reform program, most of it dealing with marriage issues. According to news ser-

vice reports, "The code of social reforms includes fixing the maximum number of persons in a marriage party at 11, no feasts relating to marriage, and no dowry except 10 grams of gold and 30 grams of silver" (Times of India, February 11, 1988). Buses plying rural roads in western Uttar Pradesh are reported to have been painted with the slogan "The bride is the dowry." Private campaigns against dowry occur in the countryside as well as among the urban elites, although it is likely that the underlying motivations are quite different.

POLICY ANALYSIS

Our argument is based on the assumption that social problems are best dealt with by policies directed at the correction of causative factors, rather than at the amelioration of symptoms. While current legal remedies directly confront dowry violence, the linkage between cause and the problematic behavior is not made. Here we develop an argument consisting of three components: women's access to production roles and property; delocalization of social control; and economic transformation of society. The pattern of distribution of aspects of the institution of dowry and its attendant problems is important to this analysis. Although dowry practices and the related crimes against women are distributed throughout Indian society, the distribution is patterned in terms of geography, caste rank, socioeconomic rank, urban/rural residence, and employment status of the women. In some places and among some people there is demonstrably more violence, more intensity of dowry practices, and more commitment to dowry itself. Much of the distributional data are problematic in one way or another. The most frequent problem is that the studies are not based on national samples. Furthermore, the interpretation of results is often colored by reformist agendas. There is a tendency to deemphasize differences in frequency from one segment of the population to another so as to build support of dowry death as a general social reform issue. Nevertheless, while the data available for these distributions are of inconsistent quality, they are interpretable in terms of our problem.

Women's Access to Production Roles and Property

Dowry violence is most frequent in north India. Some say that it is an especially severe problem in the Hindi Belt (i.e., Uttar Pradesh, Haryana, Punjab, Delhi, Bihar) (Government of India 1974:75). It is a lesser, albeit increasing problem in the south. There is also a north/

south difference in the marriage institution itself. To simplify somewhat, in the north hypergamy is sought after in marriage alliances, in which case brides seek grooms from higher rank descent groups within their caste group (Srinivas 1984). In the south, marriages are more typically isogamous.

The literature comparing north and south India indicates important contrasts at both the ecological and the institutional levels. Based on conceptions developed by Boserup (1970) in a cross-cultural comparative framework on the relationship between the farming system and occupational role of women, Miller (1981) composed a model for explaining the significant north-south differences in the juvenile sex ratio [the ratio of males to females ten years of age and below]. The farming systems of the north are based on "dry-field plow cultivation," whereas in the south the farming systems are dominated by "swidden and wet-rice cultivation" (Miller 1981:28). These two systems make different labor demands. In the wet rice or swidden systems of the south, women are very important sources of labor. In the north, women's involvement in agricultural production is limited. According to Miller, women in the north are excluded from property holding and receive instead a "dowry of movables." In the south, where women are included in the production activities, they may receive "rights to land" (Miller 1981:28). In the north, women are high-cost items of social overhead, while in the south, women contribute labor and are more highly valued. In the north there is a "high cost of raising several daughters" while in the south there is "little liability in raising several daughters." There is thus "discrimination against daughters" and an "intense preference for sons" in the north, and "appreciation for daughters" and "moderate preference for sons" in the south. Miller thus explains the unbalanced-toward-males juvenile sex ratios of the north and the balanced sex ratios of the south (Miller 1981:27–28). The lower economic value of women in the north is expressed in differential treatment of children by sex. Females get less food, less care, and less attention, and therefore they have a higher death rate. In general the Boserup and Miller economic argument is consistent with Engels's thesis about the relationship between the subordination of women and property (Engels 1884, Hirschon 1984:1).

Miller extended her analysis of juvenile sex ratios to include marriage costs (including dowry), female labor participation, and property owning, and found that property owning was associated with high marriage costs and low female labor force participation, both of which were associated with high juvenile sex ratios. That is, the death rate of females is higher when marriage costs are high and women are kept from remunerative employment. Both of these patterns are as-

sociated with the "propertied" segment of the population (Miller 1981:156–159). Her data are derived from the secondary analysis of ethnographic accounts. The literature concerning the distribution of dowry practices and dowry death is consistent with these results.

Miller's analysis shows a general pattern of treatment of females in India. Their access to support in various forms is related to their contribution to production (Miller 1981). This analysis does not explain the problem of dowry violence, but it does demonstrate a fundamental pattern within which dowry violence can be interpreted.

The distribution of dowry varies by caste. In her study of dowry violence victims in Delhi, Kumari found that members of the lower ranking castes report less "dowry harassment" than do those in higher ranking castes (Kumari 1988:31). These results are consistent with Miller's argument since the pattern of exclusion of women from economic production roles varies by caste. Women of lower castes are less subject to restrictions concerning employment outside the realm of reproduction within the household. These women are often poor and uneducated, and are subject to other types of restrictions.

In the framework of caste, dowry practices of higher caste groups are emulated by lower caste groups. This process is known as "Sanskritization" and it may relate to the widely held view that dowry harassment is increasing in lower ranking castes. Sanskritization is the process by which lower ranked caste groups attempt to raise their rank through the emulation of higher rank castes. The emulation involves discarding certain behaviors (such as eating meat or paying bride price) and adopting alternatives (Srinivas 1969). Attitudinal research shows that people of the lower socio-economic strata have a greater commitment to dowry than do those of higher strata (Hooja 1969, Khanna and Verghese 1978, Paul 1986). Although the lower and middle classes are committed to dowry, the associated violence, including higher death rates, is more typically a middle class problem (Kumari 1988).

Employment status of women has an effect on dowry. In her survey of dowry problems in a south Delhi neighborhood, Paul (1986) found that the amount of dowry was less for employed middle class women than it was for the unemployed. This pattern is also suggested by Verghese (1980) and van der Veen (1972:40), but disputed by others (Murickan 1975). This link is also manifested among tribal people undergoing urbanization. Tribal people, ranked more toward the low end of the social hierarchy, typically make use of bride price (i.e., a payment to the bride's family) rather than dowry (Karve 1953). As these groups become more integrated into national life, they will shift to dowry practices to emulate high castes while their women participate less in gainful employment (Luthra 1983). Croll finds a similar relationship in her analysis of post-revolutionary China. She says, "it is the increased value attributed to women's labor which is largely responsible for the decline in the dowry" (1984:58).

Both Kumari (1988) and Srinivas (1984) developed arguments based on non-economic factors. Kumari in effect indicated that if dowry could be explained in economic terms, marriage would be simply a calculation of the value of a woman: if the value were high, bride price would be paid, and if the value were low, dowry transactions would occur. This formulation was presented as a refutation of Madan's dowry-as-compensation argument (Kumari 1988). We agree that reducing this practice to purely economic terms is an absurdity. The argument is not purely economic, but it is certainly consistent with a cultural materialist perspective (Harris 1979) in which symbolic values are shaped by an underlying material relationship that is the basis for the construction of cultural reality.

Delocalization of Social Control

Dowry violence is more frequent in cities (Saini 1983). Delhi has the reputation of having a high frequency of problems of dowry (Srinivas 1984:7). The urban-rural distribution pattern may be a manifestation of the effects of the delocalization of dowry. Dowry, when operative in the relationships among local caste groups in related villages, was to an extent self-regulating through caste *panchayats* (councils) and by the joint families themselves. These groups easily reach into peoples' lives. By contrast, the national level laws have inadequate reach and cannot achieve regulation. While in some areas caste groups continue to function to limit abuses, these groups are less effective in urban settings. Population movements and competition with state level social control mechanisms limit the effectiveness of self-regulation. A government commission study of women's status argues "that because of changed circumstances in which a son generally has a separate establishment and has a job somewhere away from home, the parents cannot expect much help from him, and so they consider his marriage as the major occasion on which their investment in his education can be recovered" (Government of India 1974:74). These views are consistent with the research results reported by Paul, who demonstrates that dowry amounts are higher among people who have migrated to Delhi and those who live in nuclear families, because the families in general and the women in particular are less subject to social constraints (Paul 1986). New brides do not seem to have adequate support networks in urban settings.

Economic Transformation of Society

The custom of dowry has been thrown into disarray by inflationary pressures. The consumer price index for urban non-manual workers has increased from its reference year of 1960 value of 100 to 532 for 1984–85 (Government of India 1987). The media of dowry exchange have changed dramatically because of the increasing availability of consumer goods. It has become increasingly difficult to prepare for giving dowry for a daughter or sister. Sharma argues that, in part, dowry problems are caused by rapid change in the nature of consumer goods which made it no longer possible to accumulate gift goods over a long period as the latest styles in material goods could not be presented (1984:70–71).

The current regime of individual dowry seeking and giving is constituted as a kind of rational behavior. That is, it is achieved through choice, is consistent with certain values, and serves to increase someone's utility. There are a number of things sought by the groom's family in these transactions. Wealth and family prestige are especially important. The family prestige "bought" with marriage expenditures, which is relevant to both the bride and groom's side in the transaction, is no doubt very much worth maximizing in the Indian context. From the perspective of the bride's family, dowry payments involve trading present consumption for future earning power for their daughter through acquiring a groom with better qualities and connections. In a two-tier, gender segregated, high unemployment, inflationary economy such as that of India, one can grasp the advantage of investing in husbands with high future earning potential. It is also possible to argue that in societies with symbolic mechanisms of stratification, it is expected that persons will attempt to make public displays of consumption in order to improve their overall performance and so to take advantage of the ambiguities of the status hierarchy system. The demand for both symbolic goods and future earnings is highly elastic. Family connections, education, and wealth seem especially important in India, and they all serve as hedges against inflation and poverty. With women having limited access to jobs and earning lower pay, it is rational to invest in a share of the groom's prospects. If you ask people why they give dowry when their daughters are being married they say, "because we love them." On the other hand, grooms' families will find the decision to forgo dowry very difficult.

SUMMARY

The distributional data indicate that the relationship between the way females are treated in marriage and their participation in economic production is consistent with Miller's development of the Boserup hypothesis. It is assumed that the pattern of maltreatment of females has been subject to various controls operating at the levels of family, caste, and community. Urbanization reduces the effectiveness of these mechanisms, thus increasing the intensity of the problem. This trend is exacerbated by the economic transformations within contemporary Indian society. It is our viewpoint that policies developed to reduce dowry-related violence will fail if they do not increase the economic value of women.

The criminalization of dowry may have been a politically useful symbol, but it has not curtailed the practice. As dowry is attacked, the state has not adequately dealt with the ante-mortem inheritance aspect of the custom. If dowry continues to provide a share of the family wealth to daughters before the death of the parents, then legally curtailing the practice is likely to damage the economic interests of women in the name of protecting them. One might argue that the primary legal remedy for the dowry problem actually makes it worse because it limits the transfer of assets to women. Perhaps this is why research on attitudes toward dowry indicates a continued positive commitment to the institution (Mathew 1987). India is a society in which most people (most particularly the elite) have given and received dowry; most people are even today giving and taking dowries. Declaring dowry a crime creates a condition in which the mass of society are technically criminals. The moral-legal basis of society suffers, and communal, parochial, and other fissiparous forces are encouraged.

To be effective, anti-dowry legislation must make sure that the social utility provided by dowry practices be displaced to practices that are less problematic, and that the apparent causes of the practice be attacked. To do so would mean that attempts to eradicate the social evils produced by the dowry institution need to be based on an examination of women's property rights so as to increase their economic access. Traditional Hindu customs associated with inheritance give sons the right from birth to claim the so-called ancestral properties. This principle is part of the Mitakshara tradition of Hindu law, which prevails throughout India except in Bengal, Kerala, Assam, and northern parts of Orissa. These properties are obtained from father, paternal grandfather, or paternal great-grandfather. According to Sivaramayya (1984:71), "The Hindu Succession Act (the law which controls inheritance) did not abrogate this right by birth which exists in favor of a son, paternal grandson and paternal great grandson. The availability of the right in favor of these male descendants only is a discrimination against daughters." The right is derived from ancient texts. According to Tambiah (1973:95), the Dharmasastras provide that it is "essentially males who inherit the patrimony while women are entitled to maintenance, marriage expenses and gifts." While the Hindu Succession Act abrogates much traditional law, it specifically accepts the principle of male birth right to the property of the joint family. That is, "When a male Hindu dies after the commencement of the Act, having at the time of death an interest in a Mitakshara coparcenary property, his interest in the property shall devolve by survivorship upon the surviving members of the coparcenary and not in accordance with this Act" (Government of India 1985:3). The Hindu Succession Act in its most recent form provides for the intestate or testamentary inheritance of a female of a share of the family property. Yet the prior right of males at birth is not abrogated. Hindu males own a share of the family rights at birth; females can inherit it. Testamentary succession overrides the principle of intestate succession, and therefore the interests of females can be usurped simply by writing a will. The other procedures for a female to renounce an interest in family property are very simple. Moreover, according to Sivaramayya (1984:58), "no specific formality is required for the relinquishment of the interest beyond the expression of a clear intention to that effect." Instruments of relinquishment can be and are forged.

The ante-mortem inheritance function of dowry has been eroded or perhaps supplanted by transfer of goods to the groom's family for their consumption and the expression of the so-called prestige of the family. Indeed social science commentary on dowry in India suggests that this aspect of dowry is relatively unimportant in any case because only a small portion of the total marriage expenditure is under the bride's control. There is evidence that even the clothing and ornaments and other personal property of the bride are being usurped (Verghese 1980). Implementation of a gender-neutral inheritance law as advocated by the Government of India Committee on the Status of Women may serve to increase the economic value of women in general, while it serves as an alternative to the ante-mortem inheritance aspect of dowry. Since dowry constitutes a kind of ante-mortem inheritance, it is logical to change the inheritance laws in conjunction with the restrictions on dowry behavior. Sisters as well as brothers need to have a share in the family wealth from birth, and that right should be associated with legal procedures that increase the difficulty of alienation of property rights. There is no question that such a procedure would serve to erode the stability of the patrilineal family by diluting its economic base.

The Government of India has passed legislation such as the Hindu Succession Act (1955) and the Hindu Adoption and Maintenance Act (1956), both of which inter-alia provide for a woman's right of inheritance from her father. For example, under the Adoption and Maintenance Act, a woman has a claim of rights of maintenance from her husband's father in case she is widowed. Moreover, she has the right to claim inheritance from her deceased husband's estate. In spite of these changes, inheritance provisions are quite different for males and females. The Chief Justice of the Supreme Court of India, Honorable Mr. Justice Y. V. Chandrachud wrote that in spite of changes, "some inequalities like the right of birth in favor of a son, paternal grandson and paternal great grandson still persist" (1984:vii). Provision of females with equal rights to inherit ancestral property from birth, or from a bequest, or at the death may reduce dowry problems. Furthermore, property that is allowed to remain in the name of the deceased for any length of time, as is frequently the case in India, should revert to the state. As it stands, property may remain in the name of a deceased ancestor, while his descendants divide it informally among themselves.

The establishment of a gender-neutral inheritance law represents a significant shift in public policy. We argue that there is a link between pro-male property laws and violence toward women. While we assert this position, we also need to recognize that the proerty laws give coherence and stability to an essential Indian institution, the joint family. The Mitakshara principle of male inheritance rights is both a reflection and a cause of family solidarity. Modifying this principle in an attempt to reduce violence toward women could have a deleterious effect on family coherence. In addition, the fundamental nature of these institutions makes it inconceivable that there would be substantial resistance to these changes. Yet if one considers this issue in historic terms, it is apparent that during the 20th century, legal change is in the direction of gender neutrality, a process that started with the Hindu Law of Inheritance (Amendment) Act (1929) and the Hindu Succession Act (1956), and continues through judicial decisions to the present (Diwan 1988:384). As Diwan notes in reference to the changes brought by the Hindu Succession Act of 1956, "the Mitakshara bias towards preference of males over females and of agnates over cognates has been considerably whittled down" (1988:358). Such change is not easy. The changes brought with the Hindu Succession Act in 1956 were achieved only after overcoming "stiff resistance from the tradition-

alists" (Government of India 1974:135). The same report states, "The hold of tradition, however, was so strong that even while introducing sweeping changes, the legislators compromised and retained in some respects the inferior position of women" (Government of India 1974:135). It must be remembered that the texts that are the foundations of contemporary law include legislation (such as the Hindu Succession Act itself), case law, and religious texts, so that the constitutional question is also a question for religious interpretation, despite the constitutional commitment to secularism.

We are advocating further steps toward gender neutrality of the inheritance laws so that women and men will receive an equal share under intestate succession, and have an equal chance to be testamentary heirs. The law should thus be gender-neutral while still permitting a range of decisions allowing property to stay in a male line if the holder of the property so chooses. The required social adjustment could be largely achieved through the decisions of a family, backed by the power of the state. Families could express their preferences, but the state would not serve to protect the economic interests of males. The process could involve the concept of birthright as well as succession at death. We do not choose to engage those arguments, but do point out that the rapid aging of the Indian population may suggest that a full abrogation of the Mitakshara principle of birthright would be the best social policy because doing so would give older people somewhat greater control over their property in an economy virtually devoid of public investment in social services for older people (Bose and Gangrade 1988, Sharma and Dak 1987).

There are precedents for such policy at the state level. In Andhra Pradesh, the Hindu Succession Act was amended to provide for a female's birthright interest in the Mitakshara property. In Kerala, the Mitakshara property concept was legally abrogated altogether. Other gender asymmetries in the laws of India need to be attacked. The overall goal of policy should be to increase the economic value of women.

Ethnological theory directs our attention to social recognition of marriage and property transfer as functionally important features of the institution. The state can provide a means of socially recognizing marriage through registration and licensure. The law expresses no explicit preference for traditional marriage ritual, and it is possible to have a civil marriage under the provisions of the Special Marriage Act (1954) through registration with a magistrate. Nevertheless, this system co-exists parallel with the traditional system of marriage, which is beyond the reach of state control. Other marriages may be registered under this act if the persons involved so choose, and if a ceremony has been carried out. These special marriages are an alternative to an unregistered marriage.

We conclude that a useful mechanism for state control of dowry problems is the establishment of universal marriage registration, which does not exist at the present time. Marriage registration is also called for by the first Round Table on Social Audit of Implementation of Dowry Legislation (Bhatia 1988), which may serve to provide some monitoring of dowry abuses and perhaps to manifest the state's interest in an effective marriage institution. It would be naive to assume that such a policy would be widely honored, but as it is, low-income persons do not get married because they do not have the resources for marriage under the traditional non-state controlled regime. There are numerous reform groups that organize mass marriage ceremonies of village people so as to help them escape the burden of marriage expenditures. The point is that compliance is a large problem even under current circumstances.

In conclusion, we feel that the causes of the dowry problems are a product of the low economic value of women, loss of effective social control of abuse through delocalization, and pressures caused by economic transformation. The traditional family, caste group, and community controls which have been reduced in effectiveness should be replaced by state functions. The foundation of state control is universal marriage registration and licensure. The impact of the economic value of women on the problem is indicated by the transition from bride price to dowry among tribal people. It is also associated with a reduction in the extent of gainful employment and lower dowry amounts demonstrated for employed women. A broad program to increase the economic value of women would be the most useful means of dealing with the problem of dowry. Further restrictions on dowry without providing for a radically different property right for females is probably not in the interests of Indian women, since dowry represents ante-mortem inheritance. This underlying paradox may explain the commitment to dowry revealed in attitudinal research with Indian women, even though it is also an important feminist issue. The alternatives include the abolishment of the legal basis for the joint family as a corporate unit as has been done in Kerala, or the legal redefinition of the joint family as economically duolineal, as has occurred in Andhra Pradesh.

NOTE

1. For purposes of comparison, a mid-career Indian academic might be paid 60,000 Rs. per year.

REFERENCES CITED

Aluwalia, H. 1969. Matrimonial Advertisements in Panjab. *Indian Journal of Social Work* 30:55–65.
Bhatia, S. C. 1988. Social Audit of Dowry Legislation. Delhi: Legal Literacy Project.
Bose, A. B., and K. D. Gangrade. 1988. *The Aging in India, Problems and Potentialities.* New Delhi: Abhinav.
Boserup, Ester. 1970. *Women's Role in Economic Development.* New York: St. Martin's Press.
Chandrachud, Y. V. 1984. Foreword. In *Inequalities and the Law.* B. Sivaramayya, ed. Pp. iv–vi. Lucknow: Eastern Book Company.
Croll, Elisabeth. 1984. The Exchange of Women and Property: Marriage in Post-revolutionary China. In *Women and Property—Women as Property.* Renee Hirschon, ed. Pp. 44–61. London/New York: Croom Helm/St. Martin's Press.
Diwan, Paras. 1988. *Modern Hindu Law, Codified and Uncodified.* Allahabad: Allahabad Law Agency.
Dumont, Louis. 1957. *Hierarchy and Marriage Alliance in South Indian Kinship.* London: Royal Anthropological Institute.
Engels, Fredrich. 1884. *The Origin of Family, Private Property and the State.* New York: International.
Epstein, T. Scarlett. 1960. Peasant Marriage in South India. *Man in India* 40:192–232.
Friedl, Ernestine. 1967. *Vasilika, A Village in Modern Greece.* New York: Holt, Rinehart and Winston.
Goody, Jack. 1973. Bridewealth and Dowry in Africa and Eurasia. In *Bridewealth and Dowry.* Jack Goody and S. J. Tambiah, eds. Pp. 1–58. Cambridge: Cambridge University Press.
———. 1976. *Production and Reproduction, A Comparative Study of the Domestic Domain.* Cambridge: Cambridge University Press.
Government of India. 1974. *Towards Equality: Report of the Committee on the Status of Women.* New Delhi: Government of India, Ministry of Education and Social Welfare.
———. 1985. The Hindu Succession Act. New Delhi: Government of India.
———. 1986. The Dowry Prohibition Act, 1961 (Act No. 28 of 1961) and Connected Legislation (as on 15th January, 1986). New Delhi: Government of India.
———. 1987. *India 1986, A Reference Manual.* Delhi: Ministry of Information and Broadcasting.
Harris, Marvin. 1979. *Cultural Materialism: The Struggle for a Science of Culture.* New York: Random House.
Hirschon, Renee. 1984. Introduction: Property, Power and Gender Relations. In *Women and Property—Women as Property.* Renee Hirschon, ed. Pp. 1–22. London/New York: Croom Helm/St. Martin's Press.
Hooja, S. L. 1969. *Dowry System in India.* New Delhi: Asia Press.
Karve, Irawati. 1953. *Kinship Organization in India.* Bombay: Asia Publishing.
Khanna, G. and M. Verghese. 1978. *Indian Women Today.* New Delhi: Vikas Publishing House.
Kumari, Ranjana. 1988. Practice and Problems of Dowry: A Study of Dowry Victims in Delhi. In *Social Audit of Dowry Legislation.* S. C. Bhatia, ed. Pp. 27–37. Delhi: Legal Literacy Project.
Luthra, A. 1983. Dowry Among the Urban Poor, Perception and Practice. *Social Action* 33:207.

Mathew, Anna. 1987. Attitudes Toward Dowry. *Indian Journal of Social Work* 48:95–102.

Menon, N. R. Madhava. 1988. The Dowry Prohibition Act: Does the Law Provide the Solution or Itself Constitute the Problem? In *Social Audit of Dowry Legislation.* S. C. Bhatia, ed. Pp. 11–26. Delhi: Legal Literacy Project.

Miller, Barbara D. 1981. *The Endangered Sex, Neglect of Female Children in Rural North India.* Ithaca, NY: Cornell University Press.

Murdock, George P. 1949. *Social Structure.* New York: Macmillan.

Murickan, J. 1975. Women in Kerala: Changing Socioeconomic Status and Self Image. In *Women in Contemporary India.* A. de Souza, ed. Pp. 73–95. Delhi: Manohar.

Niehoff, Arthur H. 1959. A Study of Matrimonial Advertisements in North India. *Eastern Anthropologist* 12:37–50.

Paul, Madan C. 1986. *Dowry and the Position of Women in India. A Study of Delhi Metropolis.* New Delhi: Inter India Publishers.

Saini, Debi. 1983. Dowry Prohibition Law, Social Change and Challenges in India. *Indian Journal of Social Work* 44(2):143–147.

Sharma, M. L. and T. Dak. 1987. *Aging in India, Challenge for the Society.* Delhi: Ajanta Publications.

Sharma, Ursula. 1984. Dowry in North India: Its Consequences for Women. In *Women and Property—Women as Property.* Renee Hirschon, ed. Pp. 62–74. London/ New York: Croom Helm/St. Martin's Press.

Sivaramayya, B. 1984. *Inequalities and the Law.* Lucknow: Eastern Book Company.

Srinivas, M. N. 1969. *Social Change in Modern India.* Berkeley, CA: University of California Press.

———. 1984. *Some Reflections on Dowry.* Delhi: Oxford University Press.

Tambiah, S. J. 1973. Dowry and Bridewealth and the Property Rights of Women in South Asia. In *Bridewealth and Dowry.* Jack Goody and S. J. Tambiah, eds. Pp. 59–169. Cambridge: Cambridge University Press.

van der Veen, Klaus W. 1972. *I Give Thee My Daughter—A Study of Marriage and Hierarchy Among the Anavil Brahmins of South Gujarat.* Assen: Van Gorcum.

Verghese, Jamila. 1980. *Her Gold and Her Body.* New Delhi: Vikas Publishing House.

Weibe, P. O. and G. N. Ramu. 1971. A Content Analysis of Matrimonial Advertisements. *Man in India* 51:119–120.

Westermarck, Edward. 1921. *The History of Human Marriage.* London: MacMillan and Co.

29

The Kpelle Moot

James L. Gibbs, Jr.

Some scholars argue that law, like marriage, is a major institution found in all societies, although in widely divergent forms. Others argue that law exists only where some individual or group possesses the authority to impose punishments. Debates about what is and what isn't law aside, conflict exists in all societies. Further, all societies have culturally defined mechanisms by which people attempt to settle their differences.

Conflict-management procedures must be geared to meet the needs of particular social systems. In the urban centers of Western society, people live in faceless anonymity. Relations between people can be characterized as single interest. For example, generally a person's landlord is neither kin nor neighbor. The landlord-tenant relationship is not complicated by any other social bonds. A person who has a car accident is unlikely to have run into a friend or a relative. Our legal system, with its narrow focus on the grievance itself, fits our social system of one-dimensional relationships.

In small-scale social systems, people are often involved with one another on multiple levels. A landlord may also be a neighbor and a relative. In such settings, people are born, grow up, grow old, and die in the same community. Because their social relationships are long-term and highly valued, people in such communities need to resolve disputes in a way that maintains good relations.

Today in the United States, government agencies and grassroots organizations are establishing programs—Neighborhood Justice Centers or Dispute Resolution Centers—based on models of consensus and conciliation. According to the Citizen's Dispute Resolution Handbook, the potential of local-level conflict resolution was originally recognized in the work of an anthropologist who had described these processes in Africa.

As you read this selection, ask yourself the following questions:

☐ How are formal courtroom hearings different from moots?

☐ In what kinds of cases is the formal court effective and in what kinds is it ineffective?

☐ How is a mediator different from a judge?

☐ What is the function of the blessing at the beginning of the moot?

☐ In contrast to the official court, how does the procedure used during the moot facilitate harmony and reconciliation?

☐ Why does the author consider the moot therapeutic?

The following terms discussed in this selection are included in the Glossary at the back of the book:

clan
culture area
extended family
mediator
moot
multiple relationship
palaver
patrilineal
single-interest relationship
social control

Reprinted from James L. Gibbs, "The Kpelle Moot," *Africa*, Vol. 33, No. 1, 1963.

Africa as a major culture area has been characterized by many writers as being marked by a high development of law and legal procedures.[1] In the past few years research on African law has produced a series of highly competent monographs such as those on law among the Tiv, the Barotse, and the Nuer.[2] These and related shorter studies have focused primarily on formal processes for the settlement of disputes, such as those which take place in a courtroom, or those which are, in some other way, set apart from simpler measures of social control. However, many African societies have informal, quasi-legal, dispute-settlement procedures, supplemental to formal ones, which have not been as well studied, or—in most cases—adequately analysed.

In this paper I present a description and analysis of one such institution for the informal settlement of disputes, as it is found among the Kpelle of Liberia; it is the moot, the *bɛrɛi mu meni saa* or 'house palaver.' Hearings in the Kpelle moot contrast with those in a court in that they differ in tone and effectiveness. The genius of the moot lies in the fact that it is based on a covert application of the principles of psychoanalytic theory which underlie psychotherapy.

The Kpelle are a Mande-speaking, patrilineal group of some 175,000 rice cultivators who live in Central Liberia and the adjoining regions of Guinea. This paper is based on data gathered in a field study which I carried out in 1957 and 1958 among the Liberian Kpelle of Panta Chiefdom in north-east Central Province.

Strong corporate patrilineages are absent among the Kpelle. The most important kinship group is the virilocal polygynous family which sometimes becomes an extended family, almost always of the patrilineal variety. Several of these families form the core of a residential group, known as a village quarter, more technically, a clan-barrio.[3] This is headed by a quarter elder who is related to most of the household heads by real or putative patrilineal ties.

Kpelle political organization is centralized although there is no single king or paramount chief, but a series of chiefs of the same level of authority, each of whom is superordinate over district chiefs and town chiefs. Some political functions are also vested in the tribal fraternity, the Poro, which still functions vigorously. The form of political organization found in the area can thus best be termed the polycephalous associational state.

The structure of the Kpelle court system parallels that of the political organization. In Liberia the highest court of a tribal authority and the highest tribal court chartered by the Government is that of a paramount chief. A district chief's court is also an official court. Disputes may be settled in these official courts or in un-

official courts, such as those of town chiefs or quarter elders. In addition to this, grievances are settled informally in moots, and sometimes by associational groupings such as church councils or cooperative work groups.

In my field research I studied both the formal and informal methods of dispute settlement. The method used was to collect case material in as complete a form as possible. Accordingly, immediately after a hearing, my interpreter and I would prepare verbatim transcripts of each case that we heard. These transcripts were supplemented with accounts—obtained from respondents—of past cases or cases which I did not hear litigated. Transcripts from each type of hearing were analysed phrase by phrase in terms of a frame of reference derived from jurisprudence and ethno-law. The results of the analysis indicate two things: first, that courtroom hearings and moots are quite different in their procedures and tone, and secondly, why they show this contrast.

Kpelle courtroom hearings are basically coercive and arbitrary in tone. In another paper[4] I have shown that this is partly the result of the intrusion of the authoritarian values of the Poro into the courtroom. As a result, the court is limited in the manner in which it can handle some types of disputes. The court is particularly effective in settling cases such as assault, possession of illegal charms, or theft where the litigants are not linked in a relationship which must continue after the trial. However, most of the cases brought before a Kpelle court are cases involving disputed rights over women, including matrimonial matters which are usually cast in the form of suits for divorce. The court is particularly inept at settling these numerous matrimonial disputes because its harsh tone tends to drive spouses farther apart rather than to reconcile them. The moot, in contrast, is more effective in handling such cases. The following analysis indicates the reasons for this.[5]

The Kpelle *bɛrɛi mu meni saa*, or 'house palaver,' is an informal airing of a dispute which takes place before an assembled group which includes kinsmen of the litigants and neighbors from the quarter where the case is being heard. It is a completely *ad hoc* group, varying greatly in composition from case to case. The matter to be settled is usually a domestic problem: alleged mistreatment or neglect by a spouse, an attempt to collect money paid to a kinsman for a job which was not completed, or a quarrel among brothers over the inheritance of their father's wives.

In the procedural description which follows I shall use illustrative data from the Case of the Ousted Wife:

Wama Nya, the complainant, had one wife, Yua. His older brother died and he inherited the widow, Yokpo, who moved into his house. The two women were classificatory sisters. After Yokpo moved in, there was strife in the household. The husband accused her of staying out late at night, of harvesting rice without his knowledge, and of denying him food. He also accused Yokpo of having lovers and admitted having had a physical struggle with her, after which he took a basin of water and 'washed his hands of her.'

Yokpo countered by denying the allegations about having lovers, saying that she was accused falsely, although she had in the past confessed the name of one lover. She further complained that Wama Nya had assaulted her and, in the act, had committed the indignity of removing her headtie, and had expelled her from the house after the ritual hand-washing. Finally, she alleged that she had been thus cast out of the house at the instigation of the other wife who, she asserted, had great influence over their husband.

Kɔlɔ Waa, the Town Chief and quarter elder, and the brother of Yokpo, was the mediator of the moot, which decided that the husband was mainly at fault, although Yua and Yokpo's children were also in the wrong. Those at fault had to apologize to Yokpo and bring gifts of apology as well as local rum[6] for the disputants and participants in the moot.

The moot is most often held on a Sunday—a day of rest for Christians and non-Christians alike—at the home of the complainant, the person who calls the moot. The mediator will have been selected by the complainant. He is a kinsman who also holds an office such as town chief or quarter elder, and therefore has some skill in dispute settlement. It is said that he is chosen to preside by virtue of his kin tie, rather than because of his office.

The proceedings begin with the pronouncing of blessings by one of the oldest men of the group. In the Case of the Ousted Wife, Gbenai Zua, the elder who pronounced the blessings, took a rice-stirrer in his hand and, striding back and forth, said:

This man has called us to fix the matter between him and his wife. May ɣala (the supreme, creator deity) change his heart and let his household be in good condition. May ɣala bless the family and make them fruitful. May He bless them so they can have food this year. May He bless the children and the rest of the family so they may always be healthy. May He bless them to have good luck. When Wama Nya takes a gun and goes in the bush, may he kill big animals. May ɣala bless us to enjoy the meat. May He bless us to enjoy life and always have luck. May ɣala bless all those who come to discuss this matter.

The man who pronounces the blessings always carries a stick or a whisk (kpung) which he waves for effect as he paces up and down chanting his injunctions. Participation of spectators is demanded, for the blessings are chanted by the elder (kpung namu or 'kpung owner') as a series of imperatives, some of which he repeats. Each phrase is responded to by the spectators who answer in unison with a formal response, either e ka ti (so be it), or a low, drawn-out eeee. The kpung namu delivers his blessings faster and faster, building up a rhythmic interaction pattern with the other participants. The effect is to unite those attending in common action before the hearing begins. The blessing focuses attention on the concern with maintaining harmony and the well-being of the group as a whole.

Everyone attending the moot wears their next-to-best clothes or, if it is not Sunday, everyday clothes. Elders, litigants, and spectators sit in mixed fashion, pressed closely upon each other, often overflowing onto a veranda. This is in contrast to the vertical spatial separation between litigants and adjudicators in the courtroom. The mediator, even though he is a chief, does not wear his robes. He and the oldest men will be given chairs as they would on any other occasion.

The complainant speaks first and may be interrupted by the mediator or anyone else present. After he has been thoroughly quizzed, the accused will answer and will also be questioned by those present. The two parties will question each other directly and question others in the room also. Both the testimony and the questioning are lively and uninhibited. Where there are witnesses to some of the actions described by the parties, they may also speak and be questioned. Although the proceedings are spirited, they remain orderly. The mediator may fine anyone who speaks out of turn by requiring them to bring some rum for the group to drink.

The mediator and others present will point out the various faults committed by both the parties. After everyone has been heard, the mediator expresses the consensus of the group. For example, in the Case of the Ousted Wife, he said to Yua: 'The words you used towards your sister were not good, so come and beg her pardon.'

The person held to be mainly at fault will then formally apologize to the other person. This apology takes the form of the giving of token gifts to the wronged person by the guilty party. These may be an item of clothing, a few coins, clean hulled rice, or a combination of all three. It is also customary for the winning party in accepting the gifts of apology to give, in return, a smaller token such as a twenty-five cent piece[7] to show his 'white heart' or good will. The losing party is also lightly 'fined'; he must present rum or beer to the mediator and the others who heard the case. This is consumed by all in attendance. The old man then pronounces blessings again and offers thanks for the restoration of harmony within the group, and asks that all continue to act with good grace and unity.

An initial analysis of the procedural steps of the moot isolates the descriptive attributes of the moot and shows that they contrast with those of the courtroom hearing. While the airing of grievances is incomplete in courtroom hearings, it is more complete in the moot. This fuller airing of the issues results, in many marital cases, in a more harmonious solution. Several specific features of the house palaver facilitate this wider airing of grievances. First, the hearing takes place soon after a breach has occurred, before the grievances have hardened. There is no delay until the complainant has time to go to the paramount chief's or district chief's headquarters to institute suit. Secondly, the hearing takes place in the familiar surroundings of a home. The robes, writs, messengers, and other symbols of power which subtly intimidate and inhibit the parties in the courtroom, by reminding them of the physical force which underlies the procedures, are absent. Thirdly, in the courtroom the conduct of the hearing is firmly in the hands of the judge but in the moot the investigatory initiative rests much more with the parties themselves. Jurisprudence suggests that, in such a case, more of the grievances lodged between the parties are likely to be aired and adjusted. Finally, the range of relevance applied to matters which are brought out is extremely broad. Hardly anything mentioned is held to be irrelevant. This too leads to a more thorough ventilation of the issues.

There is a second surface difference between court and moot. In a courtroom hearing, the solution is, by and large, one which is imposed by the adjudicator. In the moot the solution is more consensual. It is, therefore, more likely to be accepted by both parties and hence more durable. Several features of the moot contribute to the consensual solution: first, there is no unilateral ascription of blame, but an attribution of fault to both parties. Secondly, the mediator, unlike the chief in the courtroom, is not backed by political authority and the physical force which underlies it. He cannot jail parties, nor can he levy a heavy fine. Thirdly, the sanctions which are imposed are not so burdensome as to cause hardship to the losing party or to give him or her grounds for a new grudge against the other party. The gifts for the winning party and the potables for the spectators are not as expensive as the fines and the court costs in a paramount chief's court. Lastly, the ritualized apology of the moot symbolizes very concretely the consensual nature of the solution.[8] The public offering and acceptance of the tokens of apology indicate that each party has no further grievances and that the settlement is satisfactory and mutually acceptable. The parties and spectators drink together to symbolize the restored solidarity of the group and the rehabilitation of the offending party.

This type of analysis describes the courtroom hearing and the moot, using a frame of reference derived from jurisprudence and ethno-law which is explicitly comparative and evaluative. Only by using this type of comparative approach can the researcher select features of the hearings which are not only unique to each of them, but theoretically significant in that their contribution to the social-control functions of the proceedings can be hypothesized. At the same time, it enables the researcher to pin-point in procedures the cause for what he feels intuitively: that the two hearings contrast in tone, even though they are similar in some ways.

However, one can approach the transcripts of the trouble cases with a second analytical framework and emerge with a deeper understanding of the implications of the contrasting descriptive attributes of the court and the house palaver. Remember that the coercive tone of the courtroom hearing limits the court's effectiveness in dealing with matrimonial disputes, especially in effecting reconciliations. The moot, on the other hand, is particularly effective in bringing about reconciliations between spouses. This is because the moot is not only conciliatory, but *therapeutic*. Moot procedures are therapeutic in that, like psychotherapy, they re-educate the parties through a type of social learning brought about in a specially structured interpersonal setting.

Talcott Parsons[9] has written that therapy involves four elements: support, permissiveness, denial of reciprocity, and manipulation of rewards. Writers such as Frank,[10] Klapman,[11] and Opler[12] have pointed out that the same elements characterize not only individual psychotherapy, but group psychotherapy as well. All four elements are writ large in the Kpelle moot.

The patient in therapy will not continue treatment very long if he does not feel support from the therapist or from the group. In the moot the parties are encouraged in the expression of their complaints and feelings because they sense group support. The very presence of one's kinsmen and neighbors demonstrates their concern. It indicates to the parties that they have a real problem and that the others are willing to help them to help themselves in solving it. In a parallel vein, Frank, speaking of group psychotherapy, notes that: 'Even anger may be supportive if it implies to a patient that others take him seriously enough to get angry at him, especially if the object of the anger feels it to be directed toward his neurotic behavior rather than himself as a person.'[13] In the moot the feeling of support also grows out of the pronouncement of the blessings which stress the unity of the group and its harmonious goal, and it is also undoubtedly increased by the absence of the publicity and expressive symbols of political power which are found in the courtroom.

Permissiveness is the second element in therapy. It indicates to the patient that everyday restrictions on making anti-social statements or acting out anti-social impulses are lessened. Thus, in the Case of the Ousted Wife, Yua felt free enough to turn to her ousted co-wife (who had been married leviratically) and say:

> You don't respect me. You don't rely on me any more. When your husband was living, and I was with my husband, we slept on the farm. Did I ever refuse to send you what you asked me for when you sent a message? Didn't I always send you some of the meat my husband killed? Did I refuse to send you anything you wanted? When your husband died and we became co-wives, did I disrespect you? Why do you always make me ashamed? The things you have done to me make me sad.

Permissiveness in the therapeutic setting (and in the moot) results in catharsis, in a high degree of stimulation of feelings in the participants and an equally high tendency to verbalize these feelings.[14] Frank notes that: 'Neurotic responses must be expressed in the therapeutic situation if they are to be changed by it.'[15] In the same way, if the solution to a dispute reached in a house palaver is to be stable, it is important that there should be nothing left to embitter and undermine the decision. In a familiar setting, with familiar people, the parties to the moot feel at ease and free to say *all* that is on their minds. Yokpo, judged to be the wronged party in the Case of the Ousted Wife, in accepting an apology, gave expression to this when she said:

> I agree to everything that my people said, and I accept the things they have given me—I don't have *anything else* about them on my mind. (*My italics.*)

As we shall note below, this thorough airing of complaints also facilitates the gaining of insight into and the unlearning of idiosyncratic behaviour which is socially disruptive. Permissiveness is rooted in the lack of publicity and the lack of symbols of power. But it stems, too, from the immediacy of the hearing, the locus of investigatory initiative with the parties, and the wide range of relevance.

Permissiveness in therapy is impossible without the denial of reciprocity. This refers to the fact that the therapist will not respond in kind when the patient acts in a hostile manner or with inappropriate affection. It is a type of privileged indulgence which comes with being a patient. In the moot, the parties are treated in the same way and are allowed to hurl recriminations that, in the courtroom, might bring a few hours in jail as punishment for the equivalent of contempt of court. Even though inappropriate views are not responded to in kind, neither are they simply ignored. There is denial of *congruent* response, not denial of *any* response whatsoever. In the *bɛrɛi mu meni saa*, as in group psychotherapy, 'private ideation and conceptualization are brought out into the open and all their

facets or many of their facets exposed. The individual gets a "reading" from different bearings on the compass, so to speak,[16] and perceptual patterns . . . are joggled out of their fixed positions. . . .'[17]

Thus, Yua's outburst against Yokpo quoted above was not responded to with matching hostility, but its inappropriateness was clearly pointed out to her by the group. Some of them called her aside in a huddle and said to her:

> You are not right. If you don't like the woman, or she doesn't like you, don't be the first to say anything. Let her start and then say what you have to say. By speaking, if she heeds some of your words, the wives will scatter, and the blame will be on you. Then your husband will cry for your name that you have scattered his property.

In effect, Yua was being told that, in view of the previous testimony, her jealousy of her co-wife was not justified. In reality testing, she discovered that her view of the situation was not shared by the others and, hence was inappropriate. Noting how the others responded, she could see why her treatment of her co-wife had caused so much dissension. Her interpretation of her new co-wife's actions and resulting premises were not shared by the co-wife, nor by the others hearing a description of what had happened. Like psychotherapy, the moot is gently corrective of behavior rooted in such misunderstandings.

Similarly, Wama Nya, the husband, learned that others did not view as reasonable his accusing his wife of having a lover and urging her to go off and drink with the suspected paramour when he passed their house and wished them all a good evening. Reality testing for him taught him that the group did not view this type of mildly paranoid sarcasm as conducive to stable marital relationships.

The reaction of the moot to Yua's outburst indicates that permissiveness in this case was certainly not complete, but only relative, being much greater than in the courtroom. But without this moderated immunity the airing of grievances would be limited, and the chance for social relearning lessened. Permissiveness in the moot is incomplete because, even there, prudence is not thrown to the winds. Note that Yua was not told not to express her feelings at all, but to express them only after the co-wife had spoken so that, if the moot failed, she would not be in an untenable position. In court there would be objection to her blunt speaking out. In the moot the objection was, in effect, to her speaking *out of turn*. In other cases the moot sometimes fails, foundering on this very point, because the parties are *too* prudent, all waiting for the others to make the first move in admitting fault.

The manipulation of rewards is the last dimension

of therapy treated by Parsons. In this final phase of therapy[18] the patient is coaxed to conformity by the granting of rewards. In the moot one of the most important rewards is the group approval which goes to the wronged person who accepts an apology and to the person who is magnanimous enough to make one.

In the Case of the Ousted Wife, Kɔlɔ Waa, the mediator, and the others attending decided that the husband and the co-wife, Yua, had wronged Yokpo. Kɔlɔ Waa said to the husband:

> From now on, we don't want to hear of your fighting. You should live in peace with these women. If your wife accepts the things which the people have brought you should pay four chickens and ten bottles of rum as your contribution.

The husband's brother and sister also brought gifts of apology, although the moot did not explicitly hold them at fault.

By giving these prestations, the wrong-doer is restored to good grace and is once again acting like an 'upright Kpelle' (although, if he wishes, he may refuse to accept the decision of the moot). He is eased into this position by being grouped with others to whom blame is also allocated, for, typically, he is not singled out and isolated in being labelled deviant. Thus, in the Case of the Ousted Wife, the children of Yokpo were held to be at fault in 'being mean' to their step-father, so that blame was not only shared by one 'side,' but ascribed to the other also.

Moreover, the prestations which the losing party is asked to hand over are not expensive. They are significant enough to touch the pocketbook a little; for the Kpelle say that if an apology does not cost something other than words, the wrong-doer is more likely to repeat the offending action. At the same time, as we noted above, the tokens are not so costly as to give the loser additional reason for anger directed at the other party which can undermine the decision.

All in all, the rewards for conformity to group expectations and for following out a new behaviour pattern are kept within the deviant's sight. These rewards are positive, in contrast to the negative sanctions of the courtroom. Besides the institutionalized apology, praise and acts of concern and affection replace fines and jail sentences. The mediator, speaking to Yokpo as the wronged party, said:

> You have found the best of the dispute. Your husband has wronged you. All the people have wronged you. You are the only one who can take care of them because you are the oldest. Accept the things they have given to you.

The moot in its procedural features and procedural sequences is, then, strongly analogous to psychotherapy. It is analogous to therapy in the structuring of the role of the mediator also. Parsons has indicated that, to do his job well, the therapist must be a member of two social systems: one containing himself and his patient; and the other, society at large.[19] He must not be seduced into thinking that he belongs only to the therapeutic dyad, but must gradually pull the deviant back into a relationship with the wider group. It is significant, then, that the mediator of a moot is a kinsman who is also a chief of some sort. He thus represents both the group involved in the dispute and the wider community. His task is to utilize his position as kinsman as a lever to manipulate the parties into living up to the normative requirements of the wider society, which, as chief, he upholds. His major orientation must be to the wider collectivity, not to the particular goals of his kinsmen.

When successful, the moot stops the process of alienation which drives two spouses so far apart that they are immune to ordinary social-control measures such as a smile, a frown, or a pointed aside.[20] A moot is not always successful, however. Both parties must have a genuine willingness to cooperate and a real concern about their discord. Each party must be willing to list his grievances, to admit his guilt, and make an open apology. The moot, like psychotherapy, is impotent without well-motivated clients.

The therapeutic elements found in the Kpelle moot are undoubtedly found in informal procedures for settling disputes in other African societies also; some of these are reported in literature and others are not. One such procedure which seems strikingly parallel to the Kpelle *bɛrɛi mu meni saa* has been described by J. H. M. Beattie.[21] This is the court of neighbors or *rukurato rw'enzarwa* found in the Banyoro kingdom of Uganda. The group also meets as an *ad hoc* assembly of neighbors to hear disputes involving kinsmen or neighbors.[22]

The intention of the Nyoro moot is to 'reintegrate the delinquent into the community and, if possible, to achieve reconciliation without causing bitterness and resentment; in the words of an informant, the institution exists "to finish off people's quarrels and to abolish bad feeling."'[23] This therapeutic goal is manifested in the manner in which the dispute is resolved. After a decision is reached the penalty imposed is always the same. The party held to be in the wrong is asked to bring beer (four pots, modified downwards according to the circumstances) and meat, which is shared with the other party and all those attending the *rukurato*. The losing party is also expected to 'humble himself, not only to the man he has injured but to the whole assembly.'[24]

Beattie correctly points out that, because the council of neighbors has no power to enforce its decision, the shared feast is *not* to be viewed primarily as a penalty, for the wrong-doer acts as a host and also shares in the food and drink. 'And it is a praiseworthy thing; from a dishonourable status he is promoted to an honourable one . . . '[25] and reintegrated into the community.[26]

Although Beattie does not use a psychoanalytic frame of reference in approaching his material, it is clear that the communal feast involves the manipulation of rewards as the last step in a social-control measure which breaks the progressive alienation of the deviance cycle. The description of procedures in the *rukurato* indicates that it is highly informal in nature, convening in a room in a house with everyone 'sitting around.' However, Beattie does not provide enough detail to enable one to determine whether or not the beginning and intermediate steps in the Nyoro moot show the permissiveness, support, and denial of reciprocity which characterize the Kpelle moot. Given the structure and outcome of most Nyoro councils, one would surmise that a close examination of their proceedings[27] would reveal the implicit operation of therapeutic principles.

The fact that the Kpelle court is basically coercive and the moot therapeutic does not imply that one is dysfunctional while the other is eufunctional. Like Beattie, I conclude that the court and informal dispute-settlement procedures have separate but complementary functions. In marital disputes the moot is oriented to a couple as a dyadic social system and serves to reconcile them wherever possible. This is eufunctional from the point of view of the couple, to whom divorce would be dysfunctional. Kpelle courts customarily treat matrimonial matters by granting a divorce. While this may be dysfunctional from the point of view of the couple, because it ends their marriage, it may be eufunctional from the point of view of society. Some marriages, if forced to continue, would result in adultery or physical violence at best, and improper socialization of children at worst. It is clear that the Kpelle moot is to the Kpelle court as the domestic and family relations courts (or commercial and labour arbitration boards) are to ordinary courts in our own society. The essential point is that both formal and informal dispute-settlement procedures serve significant functions in Kpelle society and neither can be fully understood if studied alone.[28]

NOTES

1. The field work on which this paper is based was carried out in Liberia in 1957 and 1958 and was supported by a grant from the Ford Foundation, which is, of course, not responsible for any of the views presented here. The data were analyzed while the writer was the holder of a pre-doctoral National Science Foundation Fellowship. The writer wishes to acknowledge, with gratitude, the support of both foundations. This paper was read at the Annual Meeting of the American Anthropological Association in Philadelphia, Pennsylvania, in November 1961. The dissertation, in which this material first appeared, was directed by Philip H. Gulliver, to whom I am indebted for much stimulating and provocative discussion of many of the ideas here. Helpful comments and suggestions have also been made by Robert T. Holt and Robert S. Merrill.

   Portions of the material included here were presented in a seminar on African Law conducted in the Department of Anthropology at the University of Minnesota by E. Adamson Hoebel and the writer. Members of the seminar were generous in their criticisms and comments.

2. Paul J. Bohannan, *Justice and Judgment among the Tiv*, Oxford University Press, London, 1957; Max Gluckman, *The Judicial Process among the Barotse of Northern Rhodesia*, Manchester University Press, 1954; P. P. Howell, *A Handbook of Nuer Law*, Oxford University Press, London, 1954.

3. Cf. George P. Murdock, *Social Structure*, Macmillan, New York, 1949, p. 74.

4. James L. Gibbs, Jr., 'Poro Values and Courtroom Procedures in a Kpelle Chiefdom,' *Southwestern Journal of Anthropology* (in press). A detailed analysis of Kpelle courtroom procedures and of procedures in the moot together with transcripts appears in: James L. Gibbs, Jr., *Some Judicial Implications of Marital Instability among the Kpelle* (unpublished Ph.D. Dissertation, Harvard University, Cambridge, Mass., 1960).

5. What follows is based on a detailed case study of moots in Panta Chiefdom and their contrast with courtroom hearings before the paramount chief of that chiefdom. Moots, being private, are less susceptible to the surveillance of the anthropologist than courtroom hearings, thus I have fewer transcripts of moots than of court cases. The analysis presented here is valid for Panta Chiefdom and also valid, I feel, for most of the Liberian Kpelle area, particularly the north-east where people are, by and large, traditional.

6. This simple distilled rum, bottled in Monrovia and retailing for twenty-five cents a bottle in 1958, is known in the Liberian Hinterland as 'cane juice' and should not be confused with imported varieties.

7. American currency is the official currency of Liberia and is used throughout the country.

8. Cf. J. F. Holleman, 'An Anthropological Approach to Bantu Law (with special reference to Shona law)' in the *Journal of the Rhodes-Livingstone Institute*, vol. x, 1950, pp. 27–41. Holleman feels that the use of tokens for effecting apologies—or marriages—shows the proclivity for reducing events of importance to something tangible.

9. Talcott, Parsons, *The Social System*, The Free Press, Glencoe, Ill., 1951, pp. 314–19.

10. Jerome D. Frank, 'Group Methods in Psychotherapy,' in *Mental Health and Mental Disorder: A Sociological Approach*, edited by Arnold Rose, W. W. Norton Co., New York, pp. 524–35.

11. J. W. Klapman, *Group Psychotherapy: Theory and Practice*, Grune & Stratton, New York, 1959.

12. Marvin K. Opler, 'Values in Group Psychotherapy,' *International Journal of Social Psychiatry*, vol. iv, 1959, pp. 296–98.

13. Frank, op. cit., p. 531.

14. Ibid.

15. Ibid.

16. Klapman, op. cit., p. 39.

17. Ibid., p. 15.

18. For expository purposes the four elements of therapy are described as if they always occur serially. They may, and do, occur simultaneously also. Thus, all four of the factors may be implicit in a single short behavioural sequence. Parsons (op. cit.) holds that these four elements are common not only to psychotherapy but to all measures of social control.

19. Parsons, op. cit., p. 314. Cf. loc. cit., chap. 10.

20. Cf. Parsons, op. cit., chap. 7. Parsons notes that in any social-control action the aim is to avoid the process of alienation, that 'vicious-cycle' phenomenon whereby each step taken to curb the non-conforming activity of the deviant has the effect of driving him further into his pattern of deviance. Rather, the need is to 'reach' the deviant and bring him back to the point where he is susceptible to the usual everyday informal sanctions.

21. J. H. M. Beattie, 'Informal Judicial Activity in Bunyoro,' *Journal of African Administration*, vol. ix, 1957, pp. 188–95.

22. Disputes include matters such as a son seducing his father's wives, a grown son disobeying his father, or a husband or wife failing in his or her duties to a spouse. Disputes between unrelated persons involve matters like quarrelling, abuse, assault, false accusations, petty theft, adultery, and failure to settle debts. (Ibid., p. 190.)

23. Ibid., p. 194.

24. Beattie, op. cit., p. 194.

25. Ibid., p. 193.

26. Ibid., p. 195. Moreover, Beattie also recognizes the functional significance of the Nyoro moots, for he notes that: 'It would be a serious error to represent them simply as clumsy, "amateur" expedients for punishing wrong-doers or settling civil disputes at an informal, sub-official level.' (Ibid.)

27. The type of examination of case materials that is required demands that field workers should not simply record cases that meet the 'trouble case' criterion (cf. K. N. Llewellyn and E. A. Hoebel, *The Cheyenne Way*, Norman, Okla., University of Oklahoma Press, 1941; and E. A. Hoebel, *The Law of Primitive Man*, Cambridge, Mass., Harvard University Press, 1954), but that cases should be recorded in some transcript-like form.

28. The present study has attempted to add to our understanding of informal dispute-settlement procedures in one African society by using an eclectic but organized collection of concepts from jurisprudence, ethno-law, and psychology. It is based on the detailed and systematic analysis of a few selected cases, rather than a mass of quantitative data. In further research a greater variety of cases handled by Kpelle moots should be subjected to the same analysis to test its merit more fully.

30

Legal Planning in Papua New Guinea

Richard Scaglion

When small-scale societies come under the control of larger governments, as in colonial situations, those governments impose some form of "civilized" law. Unfortunately, these imposed legal systems often do not fit the indigenous social system. Western legal systems seem to focus on narrowing issues and applying standardized rules and procedures. Legal systems in small-scale societies, as you've seen in the previous selection, tend to be flexible and to focus on people and social relationships.

New Guinea, the second largest island on the globe, is located north of Australia. Isolated by sparsely populated malarial zones separating the coast from the interior, over a million people lived in high mountains unknown to the outside world until the lust for gold drove Australian prospectors into the interior during the early 1930s. With the exception of some early patrols and missionary activity, very little was known about the highlands until the 1950s. With over seven hundred languages and thousands of tribal groups on the island, the creation of culturally appropriate government policy was an issue of great concern for the new nation of Papua New Guinea.

Anthropologists have played important roles as researchers and consultants in planning for this new nation. Richard Scaglion's research, described in this article, was done at the request of the Papua New Guinea Law Reform Commission. He was asked to help the Commission better understand the character of customary law. Such research and anthropological input is important in culturally heterogeneous nations like Papua New Guinea, or, for that matter, the United States.

A postscript to this selection describes the changes that have come about in Papua New Guinea since this original study.

As you read this selection, ask yourself the following questions:

☐ Why did the constitution of Papua New Guinea mandate the development of a national legal system based on customary law?

☐ How are yams and sex related to conflict among the Abelam people?

☐ What are the two different uses of yams in Abelam conflict management?

☐ How does the Abelam view of the formal legal system differ from their view of their traditional system?

☐ What are some of the characteristics of Abelam conflict management that should be considered in developing a legal system based on customary law?

The following terms discussed in this selection are included in the Glossary at the back of the book:

affinal
age grade
big man
cross-cutting ties
exogamous
lineage

moiety system
moot
patrilineal
patrilocal
totem

From *Oceania*, 1981. Reprinted by permission of *Oceania*.

Acknowledging 'the worthy customs and traditional wisdoms of our people,' the Constitution of Papua New Guinea recognizes customary law as a basis for the development of a self-reliant national legal system. The constitution also calls for a fundamental re-orientation 'toward Papua New Guinean forms of participation, consultation and consensus.' Implied is the presumption of unity in Melanesian perceptions of basic customary law, and an expectation that common attitudes and principles can provide an appropriate foundation for a national legal system.

While there is a large corpus of information about traditional law in specific Papua New Guinea societies (see Potter 1973 for an annotated bibliography), very little cross-cultural research on Papua New Guinea customary law has been done.

It is by no means certain that such common underlying principles of customary law in Papua New Guinea as may exist could in fact be integrated into a national legal system. The purpose of this paper is to examine traditional patterns and perceptions of law and conflict management of one society, the Samukundi Abelam, and to consider some of the implications of these patterns for the development of a national legal system in Papua New Guinea.

ETHNOGRAPHIC BACKGROUND

The Abelam people, known particularly for their art work, cult houses (the famous *haus tamberan*) and the growing of ceremonial long yams, inhabit the area of land between the middle Sepik river and the Prince Alexander coastal ranges of the East Sepik Province of Papua New Guinea. Customary law among the Abelam was first examined by Kaberry (1941–42) for the Mamukundi Abelam, although, like many of the early ethnographers of law in Papua New Guinea, Kaberry was not primarily concerned with the implications of her findings for national legal development.

The focus of this study is the Samukundi or Western Abelam (Scaglion 1976:40–53), a subgroup having a particularly elaborate form of the yam complex found elsewhere in the Sepik area (Forge 1966, Lea 1969, Tuzin 1972). Primary data were collected in Neligum, one of the northernmost Abelam villages, between November 1974 and January 1976, and during a number of subsequent field trips. Neligum, with a population of approximately 550, is located virtually on the slopes of the Prince Alexander Mountains.

The Samukundi Abelam year is divided into two major segments linked to the horticultural cycle. From August through January, most Abelam men are involved in growing certain varieties of long yams (*Dioscorea alata*) in special yam gardens. Since these

ceremonial yams are important indicators of social status and prestige, great effort is invested in their cultivation. A series of taboos is observed to ensure successful yam growth, including curtailment of sexual activity and general avoidance of conflict both inside and outside the village. The belief that social discord and sexual intercourse have a negative effect on the growth of ceremonial yams produces a social environment in which adultery and other conflict-producing sexual behavior rarely occurs, and in which other forms of conflict are often suppressed or moderated in the interests of the yams. Following the yam harvest, a period of ceremonial activity begins. This portion of the year, between February and July, is devoted largely to yam festivals and male initiation activities. During this period, sexual activities resume and repressed hostilities re-emerge, resulting in an increase in conflict. Thus Samukundi Abelam culture is characterized by marked seasonality in conflict management practices (Scaglion 1976) as well as in demographic patterns (Scaglion 1978) and other forms of social behavior (Scaglion and Condon 1979).

TRADITIONAL CONFLICT MANAGEMENT

Traditionally, the Abelam do not categorize types of disputes except perhaps to distinguish between mild and severe 'trouble.' All disputes are referred to merely as *paaw* or 'trouble,' and many arise over almost any issue. A few types of disputes arise fairly frequently and, when pressed, many informants will describe in general terms the situations which gave rise to them. Frequently mentioned are: (a) problems involving women, either sexual rivalries or fights between in-laws over mistreatment of women; (b) disagreements over yams and the equality of yam exchanges; (c) disputes over land ownership; (d) thefts of garden produce and other products, particularly the cutting of someone else's sago or coconuts; and (e) the killing of another person's dog or pig. This last situation arises fairly frequently when garden fences are inadequate and dogs or pigs enter and ruin crops. The garden owner blames the animal owner for not watching over his animal and demands compensation for the ruined crops. The animal owner blames the garden owner for not securing his fence and demands compensation for the slaughtered animal. Also mentioned as types of conflict situations are (f) problems involving sorcery; and (g) domestic problems. These categories are actually frequently occurring trouble situations rather than formal legal 'categories' analogous to those found in Western jurisprudence.

Abelam do distinguish various strategies for the management of conflict, although they rarely make generalizations about *paaw* or 'trouble' and its relationship with these conflict management strategies. Informants are quite willing to explain the details of any particular case, however, indicating the motivations for each actor's actions. As a consequence, the general principles described herein have been abstracted from case studies. During the period of research investigation, all conflict cases were documented using a case study approach (Black and Metzger, 1963; Epstein 1967; Frake 1969; Gulliver 1969). Sixty-five extended cases were collected, together with forty-six detailed memory (historical) cases. General principles were checked through the use of hypothetical cases wherever possible, although this methodology was not entirely successful. Most informants not only showed a distinct lack of interest in my attempts to formulate any general statements about traditional conflicts, but also displayed a frustrating refusal to make any definite statements about cases in the abstract. 'Someone might do it that way,' 'someone would do that if he felt like it,' were common responses to abstract hypothetical cases. Thus even hypothetical cases had to be described using specific individuals and situations: 'What if X's pig ruined six yams from Y's garden?'

Despite these difficulties, certain general patterns or trends emerge from the case material. Perhaps the most significant pattern involved procedural differences in conflict management depending upon the social relationship between disputants.

SOCIAL ORGANIZATION

The Abelam are nominally patrilineal and patrilocal with members of patrilineal lineages (subclans) usually living in close proximity, often within a single hamlet. Abelam clans are named, totemic kin groups, with each clan having a bird totem (*njambu*) for which it is named. Lineages are nominally patrilineal kin groups but are unnamed and strictly exogamous. Clans are ideally exogamous, but some flexibility was observed. There is a dual moiety system with villages divided into geographical halves by one moiety system (*kumandji/kwiendji*) and into ceremonial halves by another (*ara* moiety structure). These two moiety systems cross-cut one another.

Politically, the basic autonomous unit is the village group, comprised of approximately 200–700 individuals. The larger village groups consist of two or more village segments (generally noted as villages in the Village Directory 1968). Thus Neligum is actually a village group comprised of two village segments, usually called Neligum 1 (Upper Neligum) and Neligum 2 (Lower Neligum).

Each village segment is spatially divided into hamlets, each of which consists of one or more lineages, and ritually separated into ceremonial groups. Each ceremonial group has its own cult house or ceremonial house around which ritual life centres. Ceremonial groups are comprised of the residents of several hamlets, who are generally closely related both geographically and genealogically. They usually have an agnatic clan core with a number of affinal and other accretions. Traditionally there were no formally designated political leaders, only big men (*nemandu*), subclan elders who exerted (and still exert) their influence through respect gained by virtue of their success in growing long yams and also through oratory, political experience, wealth and (formerly) warfare.

Hence there are two basic idioms for the consideration of social organization: one which might be termed geographical/political, consisting of hamlets, ceremonial groups and village segments, all of which can (for all practical purposes) be plotted spatially on a map; and another which is a social construct, primarily kinship based, consisting of lineages, clans, and *ara* moieties. To this latter system may be added age-grade initiation groups.

A present-day Western Abelam's loyalties are primarily to his lineage and to his ceremonial group. Clan membership is of lesser importance; and younger men will even be unsure of who is and is not in their own clan. One often hears the names of ceremonial groups (these are geographical names of the *amés* of ceremonial grounds) discussed as a political unit, while clan names are virtually never used in this way.

PROCEDURE

It is these geographical/political units, then, which form the basis for procedural differences in conflict management: differences are seen in conflict cases which arise between members of the same ceremonial groups, between members of different ceremonial groups within the same village, and between residents of different villages. This categorization of types of conflict according to the affiliation of the disputants correlates with the three major mechanisms for the traditional management of conflict. These mechanisms are: (a) moots, literally 'talk' (*kundi*); (b) yam exchanges; and (c) fighting. The first two of these mechanisms are still important means for managing conflicts.

Moots (Kundi)

When trouble (*paaw*) breaks out in the village, big men call together informal meetings of concerned parties for 'talk,' or simply show up at the scene of the dispute. Trouble between members of the same ceremonial group usually involves the big men of that group attempting mediation by stressing the importance of ceremonial group solidarity and seeking to convince either or both parties of their fault. Frequently the litigants will be members of the same lineage or the same clan, or will have the same clan totem. In such cases, the big men may stress the importance of solidarity in these social groupings. Intra-ceremonial group disputes are often resolved by this type of mediation. Compensation payments are sometimes negotiated, in which shell rings (*yuwa*) are used to validate payment. Even when restitution is in kind (e.g., a pig returned for a speared pig) a shell ring is usually included in the payment.

When the parties have reached agreement, the big man who has acted as the main mediator often performs a therapeutic ceremony. He first receives a shell ring from each disputant. Holding these rings, he chants a special conciliatory song known as *ngwayé kundi*, afterwards giving each disputant the other's shell ring. Each disputant holds a small quantity of lime on the leaves of the *narandu* plant, a symbol of peace. Holding the other's shell ring, each disputant then smears the lime on his counterpart's chest, after which the disputants clasp hands. This ring exchange is said to 'kill' the trouble.

The *ngwayé kundi* song is a frequently used conciliatory technique, and variations are used at all levels of conflict resolution. It may be used to effectively stop fighting, or to signal the end of a conflict situation. Disputes within the ceremonial group rarely involve violence and, even when they do, other members of the ceremonial group rarely become involved because of conflicting loyalties arising from their close and constant interaction with all of the disputants. Consequently the *ngwayé kundi* technique is often used in conjunction with a ring exchange to formalize the end of intra-ceremonial group conflict. The following summary of a case which occurred a few months before my initial arrival in Neligum illustrates this use of the *ngwayé kundi* technique.

Case Summary 1

Kaprélép* and Paal, living in the same ceremonial group, were having affairs with each other's wives. Each knew, but for a time neither said anything. Finally, Kaprélép confronted Paal and began to heap

abuse on him after which he (Kaprélép) picked up a stone and hit Paal over the head, knocking him semi-conscious. Paal's patri-parallel cousin who was in the same clan but had moved into a different ceremonial group from the disputants, happened to be nearby. He grabbed Kaprélép by the throat and began strangling him. Others pulled them apart.

Nyamio, a big man from the ceremonial group of the disputants, heard the noise, and, when he arrived, calmed down all the disputants including Paal, who had revived. They all had an informal meeting at which both principals agreed to leave the other's wife alone and forget the trouble. In order to formalize the agreement, Nyamio suggested that they exchange shell rings.

Later that day each gave one of his shell rings to Nyamio, who held one in each hand. After the disputants had rubbed lime on one another's chests as previously described, Nyamio sang the *ngwayé kundi* after which he gave each man the other's shell ring, thus 'killing' the trouble.

The above case also illustrates the fact that, even when intra-ceremonial group disputes involve violence, the violence rarely escalates into spearfighting. *Kundi* mediation techniques are usually sufficient to settle the dispute and where the trouble is serious, ring exchange and *ngwayé kundi* techniques may be used as a formal end to the dispute.

Yam Exchanges

Yam exchanges have a dual function in Abelam conflict management; they serve to both terminate disputes and to prolong them non-violently. Disputes between members of different ceremonial groups which are not settled through mediation often result in yam exchanges.

The dispute termination function of the yam exchange involves an equal and simultaneous exchange of ceremonial long yams, pigs, and shell rings. Again, the exchange validates the settlement and 'kills' the trouble.

The same sort of an exchange, undertaken in a different spirit, actually continues the dispute but channels aggressions into a patterned, socially acceptable and non-violent form. One disputant gives a number of especially large yams, together with a pig, to his adversary, and challenges him to match them. These exchanges may take place repeatedly, and over a period of several years, with the man who cannot match the other's yams losing prestige. A challenge to a yam exchange may prevent a fight. One case was recorded in which, in a potentially explosive situation where one

---

*This name is a pseudonym, as are all names used in the cases. The names used are actually types of birds in the Abelam language.

man was threatening to spear another, the threatened man kept face and prevented the fight by the challenge: 'You talk about fighting but your yams are inferior.' This statement shamed his opponent into an exchange.

Fighting. Traditionally, disputes between members of different villages often resulted in spear fights, with large pitched battles occasionally occurring. Raiding between enemy villages was frequent and casualties were not uncommon.

Disputes within the village but involving members of different ceremonial groups sometimes also resulted in spear fights. However, since the hostile groups ultimately had to unite against enemy villages for purposes of defence, casualties were few and mechanisms were available to stop the fighting. The leaves of the aforementioned *narandu* plant, tied together with yellow flowers (again symbolizing peace) could be hoisted on a pole during a fight. This constituted a powerful taboo against further fighting, and anyone who broke it would sicken and die, be killed by sorcery or be speared. The *narandu* was only hoisted, however, either before casualties occurred, or when they were equal.

The *ngwayé kundi* was often used in conjunction with the *narandu* to stop fights. In such cases, the *ngwayé kundi* was used as a ritualized style of argument and verbal conciliation. Unlike ordinary verbal statements, however, the *ngwayé kundi* could not be interrupted for any reason, and tempers usually cooled during its delivery. The *ngwayé kundi* which was sung as an interruption during a fight often was repeated later at the ritual exchange of rings, where other *ngwayé kundi* songs could be sung, as previously described for intra-ceremonial group disputes.

The use of the *ngwayé kundi* as an interruptive device during fighting is illustrated by the following summary of a case that occurred in the mid-1940s. The case involved members of two ceremonial groups and, as frequently happened in such cases, resulted in a spear fight.

Case Summary 2

A man from Lower Neligum induced the wife of an important man from Upper Neligum to leave her husband and live with him. The cuckolded husband got his brother and classificatory son (BroSo) together, and the three, armed with spears, set out for Lower Neligum. Upon arrival they called out for the wife's lover, who arrived after a brief period of time together with several heavily armed men from his own hamlet. A fight began, and quite a few spears were thrown although no one was injured. Finally a big man from Lower Neligum, a member of the same ceremonial group as the fighting group from Lower Neligum, who had not been involved in the fighting, stepped in with the *narandu* peace symbol hoisted on a pole to prevent further fighting. He proceeded to sing an *ngwayé kundi*. This ended the fight; the wife later returned to her husband in Upper Neligum.

While there is no clear one-to-one relationship between affiliation of parties and type of conflict management technique, disputes within the ceremonial group are usually settled through *kundi* techniques. Within the village, disputes are usually managed through the two yam exchange techniques, although big man intervention may be successful. At times fighting resulted. Disputes involving persons from different villages almost inevitably resulted in fighting, although at times yam exchange techniques were used.

The three traditional conflict management techniques described above, *kundi*, yam exchange and fighting, and the affiliation of disputants can be briefly diagrammed as follows [see chart below].

It should be noted that the above discussion stresses procedural rather than substantive law. This is in keeping with the Abelam process of conflict management, in which 'rules' are abstractions by the ethnographer. For the Abelam, *paaw* or 'trouble' needs to be resolved, and the ways in which it is resolved constitute the realm of customary law.

Kundi	Yam Exchanges	Fighting
Disputants in same ceremonial group		
	Disputants in different ceremonial groups in the same village	
		Disputants in different villages

TRADITIONAL PERCEPTIONS OF LAW AND CONFLICT

The Abelam concept of conflict is based upon patterns of duality and balanced opposition. Individuals and groups involved in conflict are hypothetically equal, and stories of families or clans allying themselves with a particular litigant because his side 'was weak' are common. This principle is illustrated in many stories and legends: adversaries are typically brothers in conflict. Despite the importance of elder brother-younger brother distinctions among the Abelam, conflict stories often stress balance in dispute situations by not making such distinctions. These principles of duality and balanced opposition are illustrated in the following story which explains the origins of fighting:

> Two men got some breadfruit sap from the forest. They wanted to mix it with water and use the mixture to catch birds of paradise. They brought the sap down to the water and began to mix it.
>
> Meanwhile, many birds were hiding under roots in the forest. A black cockatoo was the first to come out. He moved the roots aside and looked around. Then the other birds came out.
>
> As the men were watching this, two female birds of paradise came out, saw the men, and hurried away. The men immediately fell in love with the birds of paradise, threw the breadfruit sap away into the forest, and followed the two birds.
>
> When the men finally caught up with the birds, they asked them, 'Where did you come from? We were preparing breadfruit sap, we saw you, you ran away, and we have followed you.' 'We are only women,' replied the birds. 'We came down to the stream to wash and we saw you putting the sap in the water, so we turned back.'
>
> 'We like you two and want to marry you,' said the men. 'No, we can't marry you because you have bodies. If you get rid of your bodies, then we can get married,' replied the birds.
>
> The two brothers, Ganjambwi and Maurongi, went back to their village at Imbia. They fashioned spear tips from bamboo, and hardened the tips in a fire. Then they shaved spear shafts from the black palm. They wove cord for binding the spears; after which they bound, strengthened and decorated the weapons.
>
> The brothers then got a taro leaf (*Colocasia indica* or Elephant's ear) which they put on the ground. Into it they scraped coconuts and poured the water from them. Then they ate and drank until they were stuffed. One brother said, 'You can't leave me like this, you must kill me.' The other brother said, 'You can't leave me like this, you must kill me.' So the two got their spears and each went around one side of the house. Each then ran around to the front and they began to fight.
>
> Their sons came out and saw them fighting and said, 'Stop, you can't do that!' The fathers went back around to the sides of the house and came running to the front again, this time 'sumsuming' (a ritualized and standardized display of spear fighting intent). Then they really began to fight. They simultaneously threw their spears into one another's stomachs and killed each other.
>
> After they died, they were transformed into forms similar to the birds of paradise women, after which they went to their area and married them.
>
> Men came from all around to hear the story of what had happened, and to learn about how to fight.

As is common with Abelam stories, a song accompanies the tale. The song associated with this particular tale is a mourning song sung by the mother of the two dead brothers, lamenting what had happened.

PERCEPTIONS OF THE INTRODUCED LEGAL SYSTEM

The government and by extension the court system is viewed quite differently from the traditional system. The perception is one of unilateral power which is not consistent with traditional balance. Most Abelam do not view the formal legal system as able to be manipulated by them, and do not view judges as mediators. For this reason, Abelam are often hesitant to bring cases to court, do not often appeal unfavourable decisions, and often are affected by bluffs by legally sophisticated individuals who threaten to take them to court.

This view of the court system has developed mainly because of historical events beginning with the first European contact and continuing until the recent past. German labour recruiters, English and Australian gold prospectors, and government officers were viewed as powerful outsiders who were clearly able to impose their will on the Abelam. Consequently, Abelam view court proceedings in much the same spirit. A magistrate makes a decision with power to compel compliance. Abelam rarely understand the mediation and arbitration functions of magistrates in civil cases.

As a result, conflicts which are 'settled' in court are not really thought to be over unless the parties have reached a mutually acceptable traditional agreement. The following case summary illustrated one such incident in which a conflict case was 'settled' in court and independently 'settled' outside of court by an extension of traditional procedures:

Case Summary 3

Gwatnjé was employed as a medical assistant at the hospital. He was married to a woman from a nearby village where he had taken up residence. One evening he saw another woman from this village, a patient, whom he liked. He asked her to have sexual relations with him and, when she refused, threatened her with sorcery, explaining that he could give her an injection that would kill her. She was afraid and acceded to Gwatnjé's wishes.

Later she told her husband Siwi, who went out looking for Gwatnjé. Siwi did not carry spears, and intended to fight only with his hands (indicating a dispute of only a minor nature). Siwi found Gwatnjé and began to fight with him when he was hit from behind by Gwatnjé's brother-in-law, Kugulé.

After *kundi* mediation failed to satisfy Siwi's demands for compensation, he took the matter to court. The magistrate ordered that Gwatnjé be removed from his position at the hospital for taking advantage of the patient, and also committed him to three months in hard labour.

Siwi, feeling that he had not paid back Kugulé for his part in the dispute, went out looking for him. Unable to find him, he saw instead Kugulé's brother whom he assaulted with a stone and injured seriously.

After Gwatnjé returned from his sentence, it was decided in *kundi* mediation that things were fairly well balanced, and that the matter should be laid to rest. A ring exchange was agreed upon.

The exchange was held in Kugulé's hamlet area. Gwatnjé's lineage, led by his father, came to the hamlet carrying spears and peace signs: the *narandu* together with two orange-like fruits called *mban*, skewered on a palm leaf spine and resting side by side, representing the unification of the antagonistic groups. The shell ring was carried prominently and decorated with the *narandu*. Also, a medium sized yam and a sprouted coconut were carried in, laid down, and later matched by Siwi.

After the two rings and yams were duly displayed and compared, *ngwayé kundi* songs were sung by the big men in the three disputants' lineages. The rings were then exchanged by Gwatnjé and Siwi as previously described with lime being rubbed on each other's chest. Following this, there was a series of ritual songs, the theme being unification between Gwatnjé's and his wife's villages, during which food was eaten.

There was some discussion about Kugulé's participation. He brought out a ring, but Siwi did not have another, so it was agreed that they would exchange K10* in cash, which they did.

Later the exchanged yams would be planted ra-

ther than eaten and the spouted coconuts would be planted as a permanent reminder of the settlement.

DISCUSSION

The overall pattern which has emerged from the above description of Abelam conflict management is one of procedural flexibility with a stress on dispute settlement rather than 'administration of justice.' Rarely are abstract rules or precedents discussed, other than to say that a particular action 'was not the proper way to behave.' Decisions are generally reached on a case-by-case basis through consensus. Consequently, cases which are structurally similar by the standards of Western jurisprudence may be handled quite differently depending upon the relationship among parties to the dispute, the relative status of participants, and the history of conflict among these persons. This model of conflict management is relatively common in small scale societies where disputants are in multiplex relationships.

What then are the implications for the development of the national legal system in Papua New Guinea? Flexibility in dispute management practices in a single society would suggest that formal restatements of customary law beyond a general level would have limited value. Customary law is less a system of application of formal legal rules or norms to a given fact situation than a system for ensuring a just solution through compromise. Furthermore, customary law has always been flexible and responsive to changing social situations. This feature of customary law is particularly important in contemporary Papua New Guinea where social change continues to be rapid. Formal and detailed restatements of customary law could destroy flexibility and freeze customary law at a single and quickly out-dated point in time.

A legal system which is adaptable to a variety of social conditions would seem to be both necessary and desirable in Papua New Guinea. Flexible rules of evidence and procedure could be instituted. Magistrates should use mediative or arbitrative techniques in preference to adjudicative procedures. Reconciliation in the first instance is an approach already taken in the Village Courts Act. This system, based upon knowledgeable local magistrates applying customary law to disputes under their own jurisdiction, would seem to be a desirable form of legal adaptability (Scaglion 1979).

Yet, given the rapidly changing patterns of migration and urbanization in Papua New Guinea, some form of national unification and integration would seem to be a desirable aim. General restatements of customary legal principles may underline broad com-

---

*Ten Papua New Guinea Kina. At the time of this case, the kina was at parity with the Australian dollar.

mon principles of customary law which could provide a basis for a uniquely Melanesian national legal system. Samukundi Abelam conflict management is strikingly dissimilar to Western law in the areas of family law and succession and in matters relating to communal ownership of land and property. Detailed research on the other ethnic groups is needed to provide comparable material to identify the extent to which unification might be possible in these areas. It is important, however, not to lose sight of the importance of flexibility in the law. If we are to extrapolate from the Samukundi Abelam case, 'the worthy customs and traditional wisdoms of our people' would caution against unnecessary legal formalism in Papua New Guinea.

POSTSCRIPT

A few years after the basic research described above was completed, the Law Reform Commission of Papua New Guinea established a Customary Law Project. Its purpose was to conduct research on the nature of customary law throughout the country and to investigate the extent to which these customs could form the basis for a unique national legal system. Yet, as previously stated, Papua New Guinea is an extraordinarily diverse country. Its roughly 4 million people represent almost a thousand different cultural traditions. Would so many different people and cultures share any basic legal principles at all? Even if they did, would these principles—which operate smoothly in small-scale, relatively homogeneous tribal societies—still work in a large, pluralistic nation-state?

In 1979 I was hired to direct this project. My previous research had made it clear to me that we shouldn't attempt to 'write lawbooks' for hundreds of different tribes. A more profitable approach would be to investigate the *process* of conflict management. How were conflict cases actually handled in various cultures? The Customary Law Project employed students from the University of Papua New Guinea to collect such cases, usually by working in their home areas. Eventually some 600 detailed cases from all parts of the country were gathered. Through a computer retrieval system, these customary law cases were made available to legal practitioners for use in actual national court cases to help develop a Papua New Guinea common law.

The customary case materials were also used to find underlying principles of Melanesian customary law and to identify social problems caused by rapid cultural and economic change. For example, the Law Reform Commission staff prepared a draft bill that would recognize customary compensation payments, which Melanesians commonly use for settling disputes, while at the same time setting some limits on the amounts demanded and paid. A Family Law Bill was drafted that would formally recognize certain customary marriage arrangements, such as polygyny, that were prohibited under Australian law. The project also supported the development of a system of Village Courts (mentioned above). These courts give the power of law to traditional leaders but still allow them to arbitrate according to their own local customs. Village Courts thus integrate customary law with the national legal system and yet permit individual courts to exercise the procedural flexibility found by previous research to be so important in Melanesian customary law.

My own active involvement with the project (described in Scaglion 1987) ended in 1981. However, the Law Reform Commission is continuing its research into Papua New Guinea customary law. From the standpoint of applied anthropology, I believe that one of the most important accomplishments of the project was to focus attention on the procedures and underlying principles of customary law rather than on the formal 'rules' with which lawyers are often concerned. Melanesians themselves are more concerned with restoring disrupted social relationships than with upholding such 'rules.' Thus the application of anthropological theory and methods has hopefully had an impact in developing a national legal system for Papua New Guinea.

REFERENCES

Black, M. and Metzger, D. 1965. Ethnographic Description and the Study of Law. *American Anthropologist* 67:141.

Epstein, A. L. 1967. The Case Method in the Field of Law, *In* A. L. Epstein (ed.), *The Craft of Social Anthropology*. London: Tavistock, 153–180.

Forge, J. A. W. 1966. Art and Environment in the Sepik. *Proceedings of the Royal Anthropological Institute* 1965:23–31.

Frake, C. O. 1969. Struck by Speech: The Yakan Concept of Litigation. *In* L. Nader (ed.), *Law in Culture and Society*, Chicago: Aldine, 147.

Gulliver, P. H. 1969. Introduction to Case Studies of Law in Non-Western Societies. *In* L. Nader (ed.), *Law in Culture and Society*. Chicago: Aldine, 11–23.

Kaberry, P. 1941–42. Law and Political Organization in the Abelam Tribe, New Guinea. *Oceania* 11:233–258, 345–367.

Lea, D. A. M. 1969. Access to Land among Swidden Cultivators: An Example from New Guinea. *Australian Geographical Studies* 7:137–152.

Potter, M. 1973. *Traditional Law in Papua New Guinea: An Annotated and Selected Bibliography*. Canberra: Australian National University Press.

Scaglion, R. 1976. *Seasonal Patterns in Western Abelam Conflict*

Management Practices. Ph.D. Thesis, University of Pittsburgh.

———. 1978. Seasonal Births in a Western Abelam Village, Papua New Guinea. *Human Biology* 50:313–323.

———. 1979. Formal and Informal Operations of a Village Court in Maprik. *Melanesian Law Journal* 7:116–129.

———. 1987. Customary Law Development in Papua New Guinea. *In* R. M. Wulff and S. J. Fiske (eds.), *Anthropo-*

logical Praxis: Translating Knowledge into Action, Boulder: Westview, 98–108.

Scaglion, R. and Condon, R. G. 1979. Abelam Yam Beliefs and Sociorhythmicity: A study in chronoanthropology. *Journal of Biosocial Science* 11:17–25.

Tuzin, D. 1972. Yam Symbolism in the Sepik: An interpretative account. *Southwestern Journal of Anthropology* 28:230–254.

31

Contemporary Warfare in the New Guinea Highlands

Aaron Podolefsky

Within political units—whether tribes or nations—there are well-established mechanisms for handling conflict non-violently. James Gibbs's ethnographic description of the Kpelle moot (Selection 29) illustrated some traditional means of conflict resolution within society. Between politically autonomous groups, however, few mechanisms exist. Consequently, uncontained conflict may expand into armed aggression—warfare. In both primitive and modern forms, warfare always causes death, destruction, and human suffering. It is certainly one of the major problems confronting humankind.

New Guinea highlanders can tell you why they go to war—to avenge ghosts or to exact revenge for the killing of one of their own. As we have seen in previous selections, people do not seem to comprehend the complex interrelationship among the various parts of their own social system. Throughout the world, anthropologists find that people do not fathom the causes of their own social behavior. If they did, finding solutions would certainly be a far simpler matter.

The leaders of Papua New Guinea see intertribal fighting as a major social problem with severe economic consequences. Although fighting itself may be age-old, the reemergence of warfare in this area in the 1970s appears to have a new set of causes. In this selection, Aaron Podolefsky shows how the introduction of Western goods may have inadvertently resulted in changes in economic arrangements, marriage patterns, and, ultimately, warfare.

As you read this selection, ask yourself the following questions:

☐ What is the theoretical orientation (research strategy) of this paper?

☐ When did tribal fighting reemerge as a national problem in New Guinea?

☐ How did intertribal marriage constrain the expansion of minor conflict into warfare?

☐ How has the rate of intertribal marriage changed? Why did it change?

☐ How are the introduction of Western goods, trade, marriage, and warfare interrelated?

The following terms discussed in this selection are included in the Glossary at the back of the book:

affinal kin
aggression
agnatic
blood relatives
cross-cutting ties
cultural materialism
lineage
multiplex relationships
pacification
tribe

From *Ethnology*, 1984. Reprinted by permission of *Ethnology*.

After decades of pacification and relative peace, intergroup warfare reemerged in the Papua New Guinea highlands during the late 1960s and early 1970s, only a few years before national independence in 1975. Death and destruction, martial law, and delay in highlands development schemes have been the outcome.

Most explanations of the resurgence either posit new causes (such as psychological insecurity surrounding political independence from Australian rule or disappointment at the slow speed of development) or attribute the increased fighting to relaxation of government controls which suppressed fighting since the pacification process began. None of the explanations thus far advanced has looked at changes in the structure or infrastructure of highlands societies themselves which could account for behavioral changes in the management of conflict.

This paper employs a cultural materialist strategy in which the efficacy of explanatory models are ranked: infrastructure, structure, and superstructure.[1] From a macrosociological perspective, infrastructural changes unintentionally induced during the colonial era resulted in changes in the structural relations between groups. These changes reduced existing (albeit weak) indigenous mechanisms constraining conflict. Traditionally, groups maintained differential access to resources such as stone used for axes and salt. Axe heads and salt were produced in local areas and traded for valuables available elsewhere. I argue that the introduction and distribution of items such as salt and steel axes reduced the necessity for trade, thereby altering the need for intertribal marriage as well as reducing extratribal contacts of a type which facilitated marriage between persons of different tribes. The reduction of intertribal marriage, over time, resulted in a decay of the web of affinal and nonagnatic kin ties which had provided linkages between otherwise autonomous tribal political units. Thus, the resurgence of tribal fighting is, in part, a result of the reduction of constraints which might otherwise have facilitated the containment of conflict rather than its expansion into warfare. This view sees warfare as one possible end result of a process of conflict management.

An advantage of this strategy is that it suggests a testable hypothesis which runs counter to conventional wisdom and informed opinion that the rate of intertribal marriage would increase after pacification. Some researchers believed that once tribal fighting ended men would be able to wander farther afield and develop relationships with single teenage girls over a wide area. Pacification, then, might reasonably be expected to result in an increase in intertribal marriage. An increase or lack of change in the rate of intergroup marriage since contact would invalidate the explanation. The hypothesis will be tested on data collected in the Gumine District, Simbu (formerly Chimbu) Province, Papua New Guinea.

BACKGROUND

Warfare in traditional highlands societies has been regarded as chronic, incessant, or endemic, and is said to have been accepted as a part of social living in most areas. Indeed, the pattern of warfare was one of the most continuous and violent on record.

However, hostilities were neither random nor did highlanders live in a perpetual state of conflict with all surrounding groups. Some neighboring groups maintained relations of permanent hostility and had little to do with one another. In contrast, most neighboring tribes intermarried and attended one another's ceremonies.

Pacification was an early goal of the colonial administration. By the end of the 1930s fighting was rare in the vicinity of Simbu province government stations. By 1940 Australian authority was accepted and attacks on strangers and tribal fighting had nearly ended, although the entire highlands was not pacified until the 1960s. This period also witnessed the introduction of Western goods such as salt and the steel axe.

Change came quickly to New Guinea. Sterling writes in 1943: "Headhunters and cannibals a generation ago, most of the natives of British New Guinea have now become so accustomed to the ways of the whites that they have been trained as workers and even to assist in administering the white man's law."

From the end of World War II through the 1970s, educational and business opportunities expanded, local government and village courts were introduced, and national self-government was attained in 1975. Highlanders came to expect that development would lead to material gains.[2]

Tribal warfare began to reemerge as a significant national problem in about 1970, five years before independence. By 1973 the government had become concerned that the situation might deteriorate to a point that they could no longer effectively administer parts of the highlands. In 1972, according to government report, 28 incidents involving 50 or more persons were reported in the Western Highlands District. A decade later, Bill Wormsley (1982) reports 60 fights per year in the Enga Province (the figures are of course not directly comparable). Although the level of fighting declined in Enga during 1980 due to the declaration of a state of emergency, it increased again in 1981 and 1982. Martial law has also been declared in the Simbu Province. Deaths lead to payback killing and to demands for compensation payments. Inflated demands for "excess" compensation further compound the problem.

Of the five major theories of warfare outlined by Koch in 1974 (biological evolution, psychological theories, cultural evolution, ecological adaptation, and social-structure analysis), scholars have used only psychological theories and social-structural analysis to explain the recent emergence of tribal warfare.

Some researchers favor explanations which combine the traditional cultural heritage of violence with issues in development. Others seem to argue that the problem lies in the Enga's perception that the government, especially the courts, has become weaker and that this had led to the breakdown in law and order. Rob Gordon notes, however, that the police force in Enga has increased from 72 in 1970 to 300 in 1981, and that the average sentence for riotous behavior has grown from 3 months in 1970 to 9.6 months in 1978–9 with no apparent deterrent effect. Kiaps (field officers), Gordon suggests, have in fact lost power for several reasons. Most interesting from the perspective of the present analysis involves the kiaps' loss of control over access to goods. He (1983:209) states that "The importance that the Enga attach to trade-goods should not be underestimated." An old Engan is quoted as saying "The first Kiaps gave beads, salt, steel axes—everyone wanted it so they all followed the Kiap and stopped fighting. We stopped fighting because we did not want to lose the source of these things." I would add that once they "followed the kiaps" for these goods, previous important trade relations no longer needed to be kept up. In a 1980 study, Gordon also acknowledges problems created by intergroup suspicion, generational conflict exacerbated by education, and decline in men's houses and clan meetings. Similarly, Paula Brown (1982a) believes that pacification was a temporary effect in which fighting was suppressed. The Simbu do not see the government as holding power.

Explanations also combine development problems with psychologically oriented theories. Contemporary violence is sometimes thought to be a protest rising out of psychological strain created by the drastic social change of an imposed economic and political system. In a 1973 paper Bill Standish describes the period leading up to independence as one of stress, tension, and insecurity. He argues that the fighting is an expression of primordial attachments in the face of political insecurity surrounding national independence from Australian colonial rule. Paula Brown (1982a, 1982b) suggests that during the colonial period expectations for the future included security, wealth, and the improvement of life. "Disappointment that these goals have not been realized is expressed in disorder." She suggests that what is needed is a political movement rather than the imposition of Western institutions and suppression of fighting.

The present paper cannot and does not formally refute any of these explanations. Indeed, some make a great deal of sense and fill in part of a very complex picture. However, it is difficult to evaluate the validity of these explanations since very little data are presented. For example, Standish (1973) presents no evidence to assess whether, in fact, the level of stress has changed over time (precontact, postcontact, or independence era), or whether stress is associated with fighting or even with differential levels of awareness about independence, the latter likely expressing itself geographically around centers of population and development.

ETHNOGRAPHIC BACKGROUND— THE MUL COMMUNITY

Mul lies approximately 3 miles east of the Gumine District Headquarters and 32 miles south of Kundiawa, the capital of the Simbu province. The Gumine patrol post was established in 1954. During the early 1960s a dirt road was constructed linking Gumine to the capital and within a few years the road was extended through Mul. Lying at an elevation of about 5,500 feet, Mul is the central portion of a larger tribal territory which extends steeply from the southern edge of the Marigl Gorge to elevations of 8 to 9,000 feet.

The area is densely populated. Land is either cultivated or fallow in grass or scrub regrowth. Individually owned trees are scattered and there are a yearly increasing number of coffee trees. With 295 persons per square mile on cultivatable land, this density is high compared with other highland groups (see Brown and Podolefsky 1976).

The people of Mul are Simbus. Social relations and cultural patterns follow in most important respects those extensively documented by Paula Brown in numerous publications. I will describe here only those dimensions of organization most directly relevant to the resurgence of tribal fighting.

Mul residents trace kinship though males, and their social groupings are patrilineal. Hierarchical segments link themselves as father/son, while parallel segments are seen as brothers. Individuals, however, are less concerned with this overall construct and tend to interact in terms of group composition and alignments. The likelihood of an individual conflict escalating into warfare is directly related to the structural distance between conflicting parties.

The largest political group to unite in warfare is the tribe, a group of several thousand individuals. Tribes are segmented into clans whose members see themselves as a unified group. Generally, individually owned plots of land tend to cluster and people can point out rough boundaries between adjacent clans. Plots of land belonging to members of a particular subclan tend to cluster within the clan area. The subclan section (or one-blood group) is the first to mobilize for warfare. The potential for expansion of such conflicts depends to a large degree on whether the relative position of the groups in the segmentary system lends itself to opposing alignments at the higher levels of segmentation and upon the past relations between the groups.

Unlike subclan sections in most highlands societies there is no restriction upon fighting between sections of the subclan. Within the subclan section, however, there are moral restrictions on internal fighting. If comembers become extremely angry they may attack with fists, clubs, or staffs, but not with axes, arrows, or spears. These restrictions are related to the notion that members of the subclan have "one-blood," and that this common blood should not be shed.

Segmentary principles operate in situations of cooperation as well as conflict. Members of a subclan section may enclose garden plots within a single fence and cooperate in the construction of men's houses. Brown (1970:99–103) similarly notes that in the central Simbu transactions between clans and tribes are competitive while those within the clan are reciprocal. Generally speaking, in terms of proximity of land holdings and residence, cooperation in gardening and house construction and the willingness to unite in common defense and ceremonial exchange, the solidarity of a social group is inversely related to the position in the segmentary hierarchy.

Cross-cutting these segmentary principles are a variety of interpersonal ties (e.g., affinal and other nonagnatic relations, exchange ties and personal friendships) which affect behavior in conflict situations. It is these ephemeral or transitory linkages which provide the avenues through which structurally autonomous tribal groups interact.

MARRIAGE AND WARFARE

Marriage and warfare are linked in the minds of New Guinea highlanders. Early writers report indigenous notions that highlanders marry their enemies. The Siane say, "They are our affinal relatives; with them we fight" (Salisbury 1962:25). Enga informants report, "We marry those whom we fight" (Meggitt 1958:278). In an extensive study of Enga warfare, Meggitt (1977:42) supports these assertions by reporting quite strong correlations between rates of intergroup marriage and killing.

While there is little doubt that there is a strong association between marriage and warfare, it is not clear at all that they are causally related in any direct fashion, i.e., warfare causing marriage or marriage causing warfare. It is highly unlikely that warfare causes marriage. Researchers have noted the difficulty in arranging marriages between hostile groups. It is similarly unlikely that marriage causes warfare (although exceptions can certainly be pointed out). While disputes may arise between bride and groom or their families, the relations are generally highly valued and long term. The association between marriage and warfare can be reduced to two separate relationships. First, highlanders most frequently marry their neighbors. Second, highlanders most frequently go to war with their neighbors. This is because in the highlands, where travel is restricted and relations are multiplex, neighbors are the parties most likely to be involved in a dispute. Thus propinquity is causally related to both marriage and warfare; the positive correlation between marriage and warfare is spurious. Indeed, the essence of the argument made here is that if other variables could be "controlled" the association between warfare and marriage would in fact be negative.

The notion that there is no direct (as opposed to inverse) causal relationship between warfare and marriage is critical. Warfare results from precipitating disputes in the absence of sufficiently powerful third party mechanisms and other constraints which control the dispute. One dimension of constraint stems from marriage links.

In her paper "Enemies and Affines," Paula Brown (1964) carefully describes the relevant social relations among the central Simbu. During wedding ceremonies speeches proclaim that the groups of the bride and groom (consisting of subclansmen, some clansmen, kin, and affines) should remain on friendly terms and exchange visits and food. The marriage creates individual ties and obligations outside the clan which, while not institutionalized, are not wholly voluntary. At various stages in the life cycle payments are obligatory. Given the widely documented emphasis on transaction in highlands social relations, it is important to note that whenever a formal food presentation occurs between clans, the donors and recipients are related to one another through marriage. Extratribal relatives play an important role in conflict situations.

> The prevailing hostility between neighboring tribes gives extratribal relatives a special complex role. Men try not to injure their close kin and affines in any conflict between their agnatic group and the group of their relatives, but they may not attempt to prevent or stop hostilities. In any dealings between neighboring tribes, men with connections in both take a leading part; their political sphere of action encompasses both. When interme-

diaries and peacemakers are required these men are active (Brown 1964:348).

Thus, in Central Simbu, affines played some role in attempting to prevent warfare and were important in restoring peace. No amount of oral history data will tell us how many wars did not occur due to efforts made through these channels. Nor can such data tell us how many wars were shorter or less intense than they would have been had there been fewer cross-cutting ties. The importance of cross-cutting ties is recognized among the densely populated Enga.

> Even while or after two men or groups fight over an issue, others may intervene to urge negotiation and compromise. . . . Whether, however, noncombatants initiate some kind of conciliation or simply stand by and watch the fighting spread depends on a complex set of conditions . . . relevant factors . . . include, for instance, the importance traditionally ascribed to the object in contention (is it a pig or a sweet potato garden?), the number of antagonists, the kinship, affinal, or exchange connections among some or all of them, and between them and interested noncombatants (Meggitt:12).

Moreover, the frequency of intergroup marriage is related to the expansion or containment of a dispute. That is, the more intermarriage the greater the chance that disputes will be handled without violence or that the violence can be contained.

> Especially within the tribe, the supporters of each party include men with affines on the other side, most of whom are on good terms with their in-laws and have no wish to offend them. In such cases some men stay out of the fight while others, while participating, avoid meeting their affines in combat. This may serve to confine interclan conflict. Between tribes, similar serious disputes can more easily lead to fighting because fewer men have close ties which restrain them from supporting their fellow tribesmen (Brown 1964:352).

In sum, while there is an apparent correlation between marriage and warfare, marriage, in fact, establishes a social relationship which acts primarily as a constraint upon the expansion of a dispute. Second, as

Table 1   MARRIAGE TIES BY TIME PERIOD

	Before Contact		After Contact	
	N	%	N	%
Between tribes	85	75%	30	40%
Within tribes	29	25%	44	60%
Total	114	100%	74	100%

chi squared = 21.86 1 df

$p < 0.001$ (one tail)

phi = .341

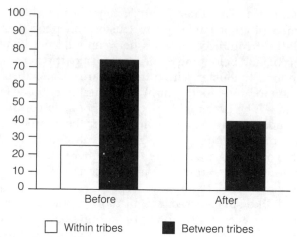

Figure 1
Percentage of Marriage Ties

Meggitt suggests, it is not merely the marriage ties between the two groups, but also between them and their allies, i.e., the web of affinal relations. Third, the frequency of marriage, or density of the web, is related to efficacy of conflict management processes.

CHANGING PATTERN OF INTERTRIBAL MARRIAGE

A null hypothesis that the proportion of intertribal marriages has gone up or remained the same can be rejected ($p < 0.001$) on the basis of the data shown in Table 1. Thus, we tend to believe, based upon these data, that there has in fact been an overall decline in intertribal marriage.

The data reveal a statistically significant change in the marriage pattern in the anticipated direction. Figure 1 describes the proportion of marriage ties within and between tribes, before and after Western influence. Comparing the intertribal (between) and intratribal (within) marriage rates in the precontact sample (labeled before), we see that intertribal marriage was nearly three times as frequent as intratribal marriage. Of the 114 marriage ties recorded in the precontact sample, 85 (75 percent) were between members of different tribes while only 29 (25 percent) were within the tribe. This allowed for a dense network of affinal ties between autonomous political groups. In the recent postcontact period (labeled after), in contrast, the number of intertribal marriages drops below the number of intratribal marriages. Of the 74 marriage ties in the postcontact sample, only 30 (40 percent) were between persons of different tribes while 44 (60 percent) were within the tribe. The intertribal marriage rate in the recent period is nearly half that of the precontact period.

The argument presented in this paper is that the dramatic reduction of intertribal marriage rates had significant implications for the structure of relations between politically autonomous tribal groups.

A Secondary Analysis

Sometimes it is possible to replicate one's findings by performing a secondary analysis on data collected by other researchers.

In 1964, Paula Brown published data on the marriage of some men in the Naregu tribe who live in the central Simbu near the capital of Kundiawa. Data for two clans are divided into previous generations (prior to 1930) and present generation. Brown's categories for marriage ties may be collapsed to match those used above.

What should we expect, a priori? Since Brown did not arrange the data to address this particular question, we expect some differences. Her temporal dichotomy is previous and present generation rather than before and after contact. Europeans did not reach this area until the mid-1930s and Brown's data are dichotomized at 1930. This means that precontact marriages are included in the present generation sample. Neither do Brown's data allow for a decade of transition. Based upon these differences in the data sets, we would expect the difference between the previous and present samples to be less extreme than the difference between the before and after sample in the Mul data (i.e., we expect a lower measure of association).

The data in Table 2 reveal a statistically significant change in the marriage pattern, although the association is lower (as we expected it would be) than in Mul. The between-tribe marriage rate (in the sample) dropped from 60 to 47 percent. This change was sufficient to draw Brown's attention. While the analysis fits our predictions, we cannot be certain that the change in marriage pattern observed by Paula Brown in central Simbu represents the same process occurring in

Table 2   MARRIAGES OF SOME MEN IN THE NAREGU TRIBE

	Pre-1930 (Before)		Post-1930 (After)	
	N	%	N	%
Between tribes	154	60%	130	47%
Within tribes	102	40%	144	53%
Total	256	100%	274	100%

chi squared = 8.597 1 df

$p < 0.005$ (one tail)

phi = .1272

Mul nearly twenty years later. Nevertheless, the analysis is intriguing. I think Brown was observing the initial stages of a process of change initiated by a reduction in the necessity for trade.[3]

TRADE AND MARRIAGE

Given the conventional wisdom that pacification would lead to greater intertribal contact and, therefore, an increase in the rate of intertribal marriage, it remains to be explained why the proportion of intertribal marriages decreased. In other words, what forces or situations affected the marriage pattern?

Interviews with young men of marriageable age and some of the oldest men in the community elicited two different perspectives. (Unfortunately, it was not possible for me, being a male, to maintain serious conversation with women on this topic.) Young men typically explained that they do not find wives from other areas because they are "tired"; they just do not have any desire to travel the long distances to visit women of other areas when there are women close at hand. This emic explanation is not particularly satisfactory from an anthropological perspective.

While the older men could not explain why the distribution of marriages in their younger days differed from that of more recent years, they were able to describe the ways young men and women met prospective spouses from other tribes prior to the coming of Europeans scarcely twenty years earlier. The old men reported that when they were young trade was very important. Salt, stone axes, bird of paradise feathers, shells of different kinds, pandanus oil, carpul fur, and the like were traded between tribes during trading expeditions. Figure 2 maps the trade network as described by the older residents of Mul.

When they were young, the old men reported, they would dress in their finest decorations and travel to the places described in Figure 2. The women at these places, they said, would see them arrayed in all their finery and want to marry them. Of course, the situation may not have been quite this straightforward.

These reports drew my attention to the link between intertribal marriage and trade for scarce necessary and luxury resources. What would be the effect of the introduction of European goods upon trade? And, could this affect marriage patterns?

According to the old men, pigs from Mul were traded south to the lower elevation, less densely populated areas in return for bird of paradise feathers and carpul fur (see Figure 2). Some of the fur and feathers were traded for cowrie shells with people from Sina. Cowries, in turn, were traded to the Gomgales for kina shells. Carpul fur and pandanus oil were traded to the

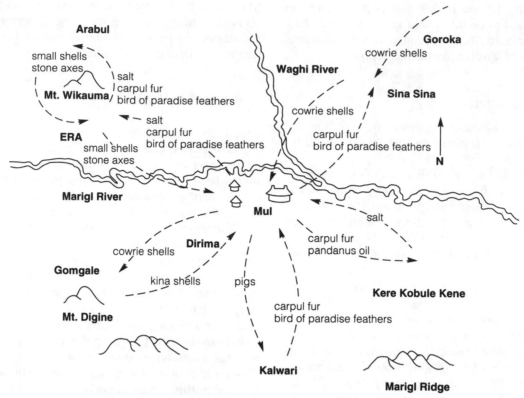

Figure 2
Traditional Exchange Network

east for salt. Finally, some of the fur and feathers obtained from the south and the salt obtained from the east were traded to the northeast for stone axes and small shells, which had in turn been brought in from even further off.

Enter the ubiquitous steel axe; exit the stone axe. No one in Mul today would use a stone axe. Indeed, it was difficult to find someone who recalled how to attach stone to handle. The effect was that the primary reason for trade between the peoples of Mul and Era (i.e., the need for stone axes) was eliminated and the Muls' need for fur, feathers, and salt was reduced (what may have begun to increase was a need for cash). Similarly, salt increasingly became more readily available. Nowadays it can be purchased at the store on the government station or in small trade stores which stock, for example, three bags of salt, two packs of cigarettes, a bit of rice, and two or three tins of mackerel. The availability of salt locally eliminates the need to trade for it and further reduces the need for fur. Thus, two of the five trade routes shown on Figure 2 become totally unnecessary and the usefulness of trade items from a third is reduced.

The elimination of the need to trade for necessary scarce resources allowed some trade relations to atrophy. I use the term *atrophy* since the process was probably one of gradual disuse of trade networks rather

than a catastrophic change. The remaining trade relations were reliant upon the need for luxury items such as shells and feathers. Scholars who have done long-term research in New Guinea have described the highlanders' declining interest in these decorative items.

With the introduction of Western goods and the reduction of trade, both the need and the opportunity for intermarriage declined. Intertribal marriage was functional in that it facilitated intergroup economic transactions. While there are a range of rights and obligations as well as affective ties which make marriage into neighboring groups preferable, more distant marriages have recognized importance. This same point was made by Roy Rappaport in his study of the Tsembaga Maring:

> While unions between men and women of a single local group are generally preferred, the Tsembaga recognize certain advantages in marriage to members of other local groups . . . unions with groups north of the Sambai River and south of the Bismarks strengthen trading relationships. Bird-of-paradise plumes and shell ornaments are still obtained from these groups and until the 1950s stone axes from the Jimi Valley were traded for salt manufactured in the Simbai Valley (1969:121).

An early paper on the Siani linked trade and marriage directly by focusing on the exchange of nonutilitarian valuables which occurred at marriage and at the rites of passage for children of the marriage (Salisbury 1956). Valuables were traded in from the coast about 70 miles to the northeast. Trading took the form of ceremonial gift exchange between affines. At the same time, Salisbury reports a statistically significant trend for Siane men to obtain wives from the south and west while their sisters marry into groups from the north and east (the direction from which valuables come).

Even more interesting for the present purpose is Salisbury's report on the affect of the introduction of European wealth goods. The European settlements nearest the Siane were in Goroka and Asaroka, 30 miles to the east and north. Groups nearest these (who were already closer than the Siane to coastal wealth) quickly became wealthy in shells, cloth, and other European goods. Salisbury reports that, as a result of this increased wealth, the movement of women in that direction become more pronounced. He also notes that "Neither the wealth difference nor the movement of women is recognized in Siane idealogy."

Thus, Salisbury clearly links marriage patterns to the need to obtain wealth not locally available, although no mention is made of utilitarian goods. While the initial response to "wealthy neighbors" is to increase "wife giving," it is easy to see that once wealth is more evenly (and locally) distributed this reason for marrying out will no longer be of major consequence.

Particularly in the many areas of the highlands where marriages were arranged by families with minimal, if any, consultation with the bride or groom, consideration of trade relations was likely to play a role in the selection of a spouse. Families had an interest in the establishment or maintenance of trade relations.

At the same time that the function of intertribal marriage for maintaining the economic system in terms of access to necessary resources was eliminated, the decline in trade itself reduced the opportunity to make marriage arrangements between non-adjacent groups. Generally speaking, opportunity for marriage is not random but may be structured by factors such as class, caste, religious affiliation, sorority membership, or political borders. Changes in this structure of opportunity may lead to observable changes in marriage patterns. In other words, a change in the visiting (or trading) pattern between autonomous political groups could affect the structure of opportunity. The importance of opportunity remains whether the individuals are free to choose their own mates or whether such choices are made for them.

In central Simbu elders choose a person's spouse for them and, although they can refuse, the bride and groom usually accept even though they may never have met. Brown (1969) reports that some groups do not intermarry because of the lack of opportunity to make arrangements.

Administrative policy and mission influence may have speeded the process. In some areas, such as South Fore or Manga, Australian patrol officers insisted (or at least strongly urged) that brides consent and that women have a right to choose a spouse. Nowadays in central Simbu more marriages are being initiated by the couples themselves. Choice in a mate is likely to further increase the importance of the structure of opportunity.

In sum, the argument here is that the replacement, by Western goods, of resources secured through trade reduced the economic need (function) for intergroup marriage and the opportunity to arrange such marriages. The effects of these changes were not felt immediately because of the extant relations between groups. Over time fewer and fewer intertribal marriages were arranged to replace those of the passing generation. The net effect was a gradual decay of the web of affinal and non-agnatic ties which cut across tribal boundaries.

CONCLUSION

Gordon (1989) has insightfully pointed out that there is very little sense in talking about or planning development if people live in fear of renewed tribal fighting. Moreover, he notes that this is a testing time for anthropologists "who find that their explanatory models are somewhat inadequate." Indeed, few of the explanations begin from a particular theoretical position nor even a unified conceptual model; there is little discussion of the mechanisms by which suggested "causes" result in the behavior being explained; and, little evidence is presented to test the explanations.

In this paper, I have employed a particular theoretic strategy, namely, cultural materialism, in which the efficacy of explanatory models are ranked: infrastructure, structure, and superstructure.

Prior to contact with the outside world, stone axe heads and salt were produced in local areas where these resources were available. Redistribution was accomplished through trade. One of the functions of intertribal marriage was the facilitation of trade between autonomous political groups. With the early introduction of Western goods, particularly steel axes and salt, local production was discontinued and marriage was no longer necessary to maintain these trade relations. As trade was discontinued, so declined the opportunity to make marriage arrangements between non-adjacent groups. Of course, existing marriage ties facilitated continued contact between groups, but probably less frequently, and there was no pragmatic reason for young people to marry others from distant areas. Particularly in the case of women, where such a marriage necessitated a move far from her natal family, there were distinct disadvantages. Thus, as older people died and fewer marriages were arranged between groups, the web of affinal and non-agnatic kin ties decayed. Intertribal marriages provided a linkage through which groups could communicate, and a mechanism and reason for containing conflict. With the decline in intergroup marriage over time, the likelihood of a dispute expanding into full-scale warfare increased.

This explanation began with infrastructural conditions (production) and showed how they were causally related to structural changes (trade relations) which in turn caused further structural changes (the web of kin ties), finally leading to changes in conflict behaviors. I have tried to explain each of the stages in this temporal process, i.e., the relationship between trade and marriage and the relationship between marriage and warfare.

Scientific hypotheses and models can be tested by examining predictions which can be deduced from them. The model which I have outlined predicts the unlikely occurrence that, with pacification and the ability to wander further afield without the threat of life and limb, intertribal marriage actually declined rather than rose as was thought would be the case. The hypothesis was tested on genealogical data collected in this research site as well as on data published earlier from a different area of the Simbu province. This is but a single case study and there is no statistical reason to extend the findings to other areas of the highlands. However, the inability to falsify the hypothesis in this case lends support to the general efficacy of the explanation.

NOTES

1. Financial support from the National Science Foundation (Grant No. BNS76-218 37) is gratefully acknowledged.
2. For a more extensive discussion of this period with special reference to the resurgence of fighting, see Brown 1982a and 1982b.

3. Paula Brown reports (pers. comm.) that recently many Simbu women are marrying outside the Simbu to men they had met in the district or on visits. She notes that there are, now, advantages for older men having a daughter married to a prestigious outsider. Naregu men who migrate probably also marry outsiders.

Such marriages further the process described here since, although they are extra-tribal, they do not link neighboring potential enemy groups.

REFERENCES

Brown, P. 1964. Enemies and Affines. *Ethnology* 3:335–356.

———. 1969. Marriage in Chimbu. *In* R. M. Glasse and M. Meggitt (eds.), *Pigs, Pearlshells and Women*, pp. 77–95. Englewood Cliffs, NJ: Prentice-Hall.

———. 1970. Chimbu Transactions. *Man* 5:99–117.

———. 1982a. Conflict in the New Guinea Highlands. *Journal of Conflict Resolution* 26:525–546.

———. 1982b. Chimbu Disorder: Tribal Fighting in Newly Independent Papua New Guinea. *Pacific Viewpoint* 22: 1–21.

Gordon, R. 1980. Rituals of Governance and the Breakdown of Law and Order in Papua New Guinea. Paper presented at the annual meeting of the American Anthropological Association. Washington, D.C.

———. 1983. The Decline of the Kiapdom and the Resurgence of "Tribal Fighting" in Enga. *Oceania* 53:205–223.

Howlett, D., et al. 1976. *Chimbu: Issues in Development*. Development Studies Centre Monograph No. 4 Canberra.

Koch, K. 1974. *The Anthropology of Warfare*. Addison-Wesley Module in Anthropology No. 52.

Meggitt, M. 1958. The Enga of the New Guinea Highlands. *Oceania* 28:253–330.

———. 1977. *Blood Is Their Argument: Warfare Among the Mae Enga Tribesmen of the New Guinea Highlands*. Palo Alto, CA: Mayfield.

Rappaport, R. 1969. Marriage Among the Maring. *In* R. M. Glasse and M. Meggitt (eds.), *Pigs, Pearlshells and Women*, pp. 117–137. Englewood Cliffs, NJ: Prentice-Hall.

Salisbury, R. F. 1956. Asymmetrical Marriage Systems. *American Anthropologist* 58:639–655.

———. 1962. *From Stone to Steel*. London: Cambridge University Press.

Standish, B. 1973. The Highlands. *New Guinea* 8:4–30.

Wormsley, W. 1982. *Tribal Fighting, Law and Order, and Socioeconomic Development in Enga, Papua New Guinea*. Paper presented at the meetings of the American Anthropological Association. Washington, D.C.

32

Flaming Crosses and Body Snatchers

David L. Kertzer

How do political organizations establish and legitimize the group identity of their people? How does the holder of a political position communicate the legitimacy of his or her use of power? In this selection, David Kertzer demonstrates the powerful role of rituals and symbols in political organizations.

Political ritual is not trivial fanfare or window dressing, but rather an important means for getting and maintaining power. Moreover, there are significant similarities surrounding this use of ritual across cultures and in diverse political systems. Kings, revolutionaries, presidents, and even the Ku Klux Klan use symbols and rituals to build their political organizations. Similarly, the internal political organization and status differences within a group are communicated through symbols.

This discussion of politics and symbols is a good example of how anthropologists emphasize the connection between different parts of a cultural system. The use of ritual is not limited to the expression of religious beliefs, and the world of political processes is not limited to rational decision making.

The connection among ritual, symbol, and politics not only exists in faraway societies; it also applies here in the United States. Yellow ribbons, flags, and parades for returning war heroes are obvious examples. The use of the American flag in political campaigns and the effort to make flag burning a criminal act through a constitutional amendment are others. People who are interested in political change use ritual as well, as in the case of protest rallies and civil rights marches. There are practical things to be learned here—if you want to be either a political organizer or an informed citizen.

As you read this selection, ask yourself the following questions:

☐ How are symbols and initiation rituals used to incorporate people into a social group?

☐ What does it mean if that group has secrets that cannot be shared with outsiders?

☐ Do political systems that centralize power and authority in a single office, like a king or dictator, have a greater need for political rituals than a democracy?

☐ Is the American flag a religious symbol?

☐ How can symbols create common emotional bonds among people in a political movement who are dispersed over a wide area?

The following terms discussed in this selection are included in the Glossary at the back of the book:

cultural values
institutions
rite of passage
ritual
socialization

status
symbol
taboo
totem

From *Ritual, Politics, and Power* by David L. Kertzer. Copyright © 1990 by Yale University Press.

With a half moon lighting their path, two thousand Georgians puffed their way to the treeless plateau on top of Stone Mountain. They had come in hopes of witnessing a dramatic ceremony, and they would not be disappointed. Up the side of the mountain came the Grand Dragon, in his rich green robe, leading seven hundred white-hooded figures, their sheets reaching the ground. Beyond them marched hundreds of other men, their uncovered heads and dark suits in stark contrast to the white masks and white robes that preceded them. The initiates marched in lock step, single file, each man's arms on the shoulders of the man in front, in a style recalling the old Georgia chain gangs. In the eerie light of the towering flaming cross—three hundred feet tall and two hundred wide—the initiates kneeled and bowed their heads before two white knights, one bearing a cross, the other an American flag. They repeated the oath by which Klansmen were made: "I most solemnly swear that I will forever keep sacredly secret the signs, words and grip and any and all other matters and knowledge of the klan. . . . I will die rather than divulge same, so help me God." It was May 9, 1946. The ceremonies had been postponed many times, leaders explained, because of the wartime shortage of sheets.[1]

No organization—whether Ku Klux Klan or General Motors—can exist without symbolic representation, for organizations can be "seen" only through their associated symbols. Indeed, people tend to think of organizations as physical units, part of the material world. Ritual is one of the important means by which these views of organizations are constructed and through which people are linked to them. Just how ritual accomplishes these tasks, especially how it contributes to the organizational life of politics, is the subject of this chapter.

BELONGING TO A POLITICAL ORGANIZATION

Since organizations themselves can only be represented symbolically, it follows that a person's allegiance to an organization can be expressed only through symbolism. I wear certain clothing, I say an oath, I sing a song, I cut my hair in a certain way, I address people with certain terms, and by doing so I consider myself and am considered by others to belong to a particular organization, whether it be the Boy Scouts, the Nazis, or the Kiwanis Club. Through such symbolism, in which ritual plays a major role, the relationships between individuals and organizations are objectified.

People make themselves, that is, they establish their own self-image, in part through their symbolic identification with these groupings. . . . By identifying with a larger group, the individual can assert his importance in a more effective and socially acceptable fashion than if he were to boast of his own virtues more directly. By praising such an organization, he is praising himself.

Organizations, in turn, do what they can to take advantage of this fact. In 1973, for example, the Soviet Communist Party, in an attempt to reinvigorate its membership, issued new membership cards. To inflate the significance of these slips of paper, they conducted a solemn ceremony in which card #1 was issued to Lenin and card #2 to Brezhnev. Lenin, unlike Babe Ruth, did not live long enough to see his jersey retired.[2]

If a person's identification with an organization can only be assured through symbolism, it follows that successful organizations depend on symbolic behavior. It is through such symbolism that people formulate their ideas about an organization. Some scholars have marveled at the fact that small children often make no distinction between the abstract organization and its symbolic representation. Thus, the flag does not simply stand for the country, but flag and country are thought of as the same thing. Yet, how different is it when they grow up and proclaim their willingness to die for the flag?

Such symbolic representations consist not only of inanimate objects such as flags, but also of individuals who symbolize the political unit. Recent attempts to establish new nations out of former colonial territories often involve just such creation of heroic political leaders, whose portraits adorn every wall, every coin, and every stamp. . . .

Not only does the individual come to feel a part of the political organization by adopting the symbols associated with it, but, just as importantly, he also comes to be recognized as a fellow member by others in the organization. Through symbols the individual is integrated into the organization and treated as a privileged member. This is seen most dramatically in rituals of membership induction, where incorporation into the group is often invested with powerful emotions. Why should the Ku Klux Klan bother with such elaborate rites as those I just described? A major goal, certainly, is to get the recruit to redefine his identity, to see himself as a Klansman with new loyalties and new priorities. A corollary organizational advantage of the rite is that it signals to other members that the recruit is now to be considered part of the group and treated accordingly. . . .

Even in organizations where membership is compulsory, such as the military, great emphasis may be placed on rituals of induction. In these situations, the major goal is to change the individual's definition of himself from his previous allegiances and roles to his new ones. The greater the transition, in general, the more elaborate the rites.

ORGANIZATIONAL DISTINCTIVENESS

In order to have members, or even adherents, an organization must have some way of representing itself, and it carves out a distinct identity through both mythic and ritual means. Organizations propagate myths regarding their origin and purpose, while members engage in symbolic practices that serve to mark them off from nonmembers. These myths often assert the group's superiority. Associated with these beliefs are rituals of purity and pollution, a system of taboos and other ritual observances that separate the members from the rest of the world. One effect of this organizational ritual is to make the group appear to other people as a solidarity unit. . . .

In its heyday in the 1920s, the Ku Klux Klan had millions of members. What defined the members was their participation in the rites and symbols of the organization. In Colorado in 1925, the KKK not only boasted a large male membership, but it also had thousands of women in its klaverns. In August of that year, ten thousand of these women, clad in white sheets, paraded through the streets of a Denver suburb, marching with military precision. But shortly thereafter, dissatisfied with the direction of the KKK, Minnie Love, the local commander, persuaded the majority of female members to drop the white sheets and wear Betsy Ross outfits instead. The organizational reaction was swift: the Imperial Commander suspended Love and revoked the charter of the Denver Klan.

An organization maintains its identity and its continuity through its symbolic representations. Since over time the people making up an organization, including its leaders, change, it is only through symbols that we think of the organization as being the same. Thus, it is crucial to organizations that they have a clear symbolic identity. Where a political leader has become an important symbol of organizational unity, the leader's death can threaten this unity. One solution is to keep the symbolism connected with the leader alive even after his demise. The temples containing the bodies of Lenin in Moscow and Mao in Beijing are among the more impressive examples of this political immortality, but similar examples can be found throughout history.

The symbols of organizational identity are important in all kinds of societies. Indeed, in nonliterate societies, where no written organizational charters exist, rituals are especially important. Among the Tallensi of West Africa, for example, the political system was organized around a system of clans and lineages. These clans and lineages were themselves defined in terms of common ritual practices: members of a lineage worshipped at a common ancestral shrine, separate from the members of all other lineages. Relationships among clans and lineages were made concrete through regular ritual celebrations in which each group had a specified place. Indeed, as with so many peoples, the very notion of being a Tallensi, one of "us," was defined by participation in common ritual. . . .

In New Guinea, where societies sometimes consist of but a few hundred people, there are graphic examples of this establishment of political identity through ritual. In the Strickland-Bosavi area, dotted by tiny indigenous polities, each distinguishes itself from the others on the basis of the male initiation rites it performs. From an outsider's perspective what is most striking is one similarity in these rites among the groups: they all believe that boys cannot become adults unless they are inseminated. What differs is the method of insemination found in the different societies: anal intercourse among the Kaluli, fellatio among the Etoro, and the smearing of semen on the initiates among the Onbabasulu. Each of the groups finds the customs of the other disgusting and, indeed, these sentiments not only reinforce notions of group allegiance, but can be whipped up to provoke hostilities among the groups.[3]

In modern states, written constitutions and other such documents are used as symbols of organizational distinctiveness, and mass media broadcast verbal symbols of organizational identity to all parts of the population. In nonliterate societies, the whole notion of a separate, distinguishable sphere of political life of specifically political organizations is generally absent. Politics occurs through societal mechanisms that are not themselves seen as political in nature. Primary among these are kinship systems and the organization of ritual, and both of these typically connect the temporal order with what can be called the supernatural realm.

For many people in nonstate societies, common ritual observances defined the boundaries of their polity. Just as the smaller political units—such as lineages and clans—were defined by a common set of ritual practices, from observance of certain taboos to worship at a certain shrine, what tied the larger society together was participation in a common set of rituals, often combined with an ideology of common descent from a founding ancestor. When such societies confronted European colonialists, the rituals that bound them together became a means for organizing politically on a larger scale than was previously known. Lacking formal political institutions, and under pressure to react in a more coordinated fashion to the perils posed by colonial expansion, these societies relied on key ritual specialists to lead their political and military response.

In centralized societies, where rites also play a major role in furnishing organizational distinctiveness, rulers who seek to distance their regimes from those of their predecessors must create new rites to replace the old. This was recognized many centuries ago when the T'ang dynasty arose in China on the embers of the vanquished Sui. Fu I, the Grand Astrologer of the new regime, urged the immediate creation of a new calendar, new color for court dress, new names for bureaucratic offices, new music, and new court rites. Indeed, the identification of a new regime with a new way of symbolizing time—evident in the creation of a new system for reckoning time—was found repeatedly not only in ancient China, but also in Rome from the emperors of old to Mussolini, and in France during the Revolution. By controlling time, rulers identified their political creation with the rhythms of nature.

More recently, the emancipation of European colonies has given rise to another round of attempts to replace the old political rites and symbols with new ones. Typical in this regard—but not in others—was the postwar experience in South Africa, where images of local heroes replaced British monarchs on stamps, coins, and paper currency. Awards such as the Cape of Good Hope Decoration replaced British honors like the Victoria Cross, and Settlers' Day and the Day of the Covenant replaced Empire Day and the Queen's Birthday. A new national flag and a new national anthem gave rise to further ritual change. A new political entity without new rites and symbols was inconceivable.

The importance of ritual in providing organizational distinctiveness is not limited to the societal level. The Monhegan Indians of New England, who have been struggling since the 1930s to maintain their own organization, provide a good example. As a result of European colonization and warfare, there was little left of traditional Monhegan society by the nineteenth century. In 1880, when the state legislature legally disbanded the tribe, observers assumed that the end of the Monhegans as a distinctive group was at hand. Yet Monhegan identity did not fade away. The effort to renew tribal identity began with the creation of a legally incorporated tribal organization in the 1930s, and from this a renaissance occurred.

The problem faced by the Monhegans was how to assert their distinctiveness in the face of a skeptical citizenry. For centuries, the Monhegans had intermarried with neighboring whites and blacks, so that they possessed no clear physical features that could mark them as Indians in terms of popular stereotype. Moreover, they no longer spoke their own language, and in all other respects they shared in the larger American culture in which they lived. As one Monhegan bitterly lamented, unless you rode to work on a horse and lived in a teepee, people would not believe you were an Indian. Somehow, a way had to be found to estab-

lish this identity. Yet there was a thin line between successfully asserting one's Indian identity and appearing ridiculous in neighbors' eyes.

The Monhegans solved this problem of organizational distinctiveness by stressing rites and symbols that identify them as Indians and as Monhegans. The most important of these rites is the annual powwow. Each year widespread publicity goes out to announce the event. The hosts invite Indians from other, better-established tribes to join with them and, before a large crowd of non-Indian neighbors and tourists, the Monhegans perform native dances, parade in Indian clothing, display Indian crafts, and recount their history.

The importance of these rites in carving out a distinctive organizational identity is poignantly reflected in the comments of the Monhegan chief at one of these powwows. Asked about the origin of the large headdress he was wearing, the chief immediately admitted that it was not Monhegan but of Plains Indian origin. He had ordered it through a Sears catalogue. With a resigned sigh, he explained that the public had come to expect such attire from Indian chiefs.

RELATING THE LOCAL TO THE NATIONAL

One problem that all large-scale organizations face is how to integrate local activity into the higher organizational level. The question might be put as follows: How can the actions of a group of villagers or townsmen be seen as an expression of national-level organizational life? Identification of the local with the national can take place only through the use of symbols that identify the one with the other.

This is why Minnie Love's switch from white sheets to Betsy Ross garb was so threatening to the Ku Klux Klan. What identified the action of a crowd of women parading through the streets of Denver with the action of a bunch of men in Chicago or Alabama was their use of a common symbolism, a common ritual. The common rites served not only to make these far-flung individuals feel part of a larger organization; they also made the public interpret the actions of the different groups of people as part of the same organization, the same political group. . . .

Just as ritual has been an important means of defining the boundaries of societies that lacked formal political institutions, so it has been important in coordinating the actions of different local groupings in such societies. A good example is provided in Bali, where coordination of the irrigation works was a supralocal task of great importance. Yet this was not accomplished through bureaucracy, but rather by a system of ritual obligations that regularly brought the scattered people together, facilitated the needed division of labor, and coordinated the timing of the distribution of water to the various fields.

But though many nonliterate societies made use of ritual to coordinate action beyond the local level, it was with the centralization of government that the problem of identifying local activities with higher-level political organizations became especially important. With the spread of the Roman Empire, problems of political integration arose that had never before been confronted on such a vast scale. What was it that made a town in Asia Minor part of the empire rather than an autonomous political unit? How were people encouraged to think of themselves as part of such a nebulous and distant concept as the Roman Empire, when all they actually saw were occasional soldiers and tax collectors, the latter often local residents themselves? Part of the solution was to construct monuments that served as perpetual reminders of imperial ties. Equally significant, popular participation in rites of allegiance became a regular feature of community life.

In many cases, rulers preferred to renew bonds of dependence through the more dramatic—and hence more effective—rites of royal entry. By staging large-scale rites in localities scattered throughout the realm, people were better able to identify with the power of the ruler, and, at the same time, the subservience of local authorities to the central ruler was made clear. . . .

This use of symbolism and ritual to relate local groups to national political movements is not by any means limited to official or governmental organizations. People seeking political change also express their relationships to the larger movement with which they identify by using symbol and ritual.

The Black Power movement in the United States in the 1960s shows just such use of common rites and symbols to create national unity. This case is especially interesting as an example of how far-flung, often uncoordinated, local activities can be formed into a national political entity in the absence of any national organization at all. What bound together these scattered local groups, and made their participants and the public see them as expressions of a common political force, was a system of symbols and rituals. This involved rallies, marches, demonstrations, and confrontations that incorporated such distinguishing features as stylized chants and songs, symbolic gestures, and clothing. By reacting at the same time and with the same rituals to events such as the assassination of Martin Luther King or the indictment of Huey Newton, these widely dispersed local groups further asserted their identity as part of a larger association. . . .

INVESTING AND DIVESTING POWER

Political organizations and, more generally, political systems require a division of labor. In all state societies this entails a hierarchy of status and power. In order to invest a person with authority over others, there must be an effective means for changing the way other people view that person, as well as for changing the person's conception of his right to impose his will on others. Authority, the belief that a person has the right to exercise influence over others' behavior, is itself an abstraction, and people can conceive of who has authority and who does not only through symbols and rituals. That the same person one moment has no such authority and at a subsequent moment acquires it must be represented through ritual performances. This is why formal ceremonies of induction are universal for public power holders in government. Through these rituals, a distinction is made between the individual and the role of authority with which he or she is being invested, but at the same time the individual becomes identified with the role. Ritual mobilizes societal authority for this investiture, while powerful symbols help make the general population emotionally receptive to the creation of such power over them.

. . . Ritual is used to constitute power, not just reflect power that already exists. This becomes most evident where authority is under attack. In 1485, the Tudors were struggling in England against their rivals' armies and it was not clear just who would win. The ritual coronation of Henry VII at Westminster in that year, and his subsequent marriage to Elizabeth, symbolically uniting the rival houses of York and Lancaster, were important parts of his victorious political campaign.

A more contemporary example is the simultaneous celebration at two different locations of the 1986 inauguration rites for the president of the Philippines. In one mass rite Ferdinand Marcos took the oath of office, while in another Corazon Aquino solemnly took the oath. Who thus became president of the Philippines? Although these rites were only one part of the political battle raging in Manila, their significance is clear if one considers what would have happened if Marcos had put off the ceremonies and Aquino had held hers on the appointed day. His already precarious position would have been further undermined.

The stability of hierarchical political systems, paradoxically, depends on the investment of authority in particular individuals at the same time that it depends on being able to replace them. This is a tricky proposition, especially where a ruler is proclaimed as the embodiment of the divine on earth. Religions may be able to wait millennia for a second coming, but more worldly political systems require speedier divine replacement. . . .

If assumption of political office is ritually marked, so are attempts to divest an officeholder of his authority. Having been previously ritually joined to the office, the individual must also be separated from his or her authority by further ritual. When the divesting of authority from a person is unscheduled, it is disruptive of the normal symbolic representation of the political order and violates the sacralization of power; at these times, especially powerful symbolism is likely to be employed. This ritual must fuse together strong emotions—often associated with the notion that the power holder has sinned against the community—with the idea that the individual who a moment ago could legitimately exercise power over them can do so no longer.

Just such ritualization was involved in the divesting of Richard Nixon's authority through the congressional hearings on Watergate. Nixon had not only been invested with the office of the presidency in an elaborate ritual display; he had for years been at the center of ceaseless ritualization that expressed and legitimated that authority. For five years, Nixon's every public appearance required a ceremonial entry, accompanied by the stirring chords of "Hail to the Chief." The hearings, with their symbolic drama, their use of highly charged political symbolism, and their emotional quality, provided an effective means for divesting Nixon of his authority. Had there been no such public ritual, had all the investigations been conducted privately, with a Congressional committee chairman releasing the final report, the political situation in the country would have been very different.

Such rites of degradation are by no means limited to divesting authority from current officeholders. They are also important in delegitimizing the authority associated with the symbolism of leaders of the past.

A good case of this is provided by the de-Stalinization campaign in the Soviet Union in the early 1960s, in the wake of Khrushchev's revelations about the crimes of the Stalin regime. In order to transform what had been a powerful symbol of political authority into a symbol of the abuse of authority, a variety of ritual changes were introduced. The leadership of the Soviet Union ordered that Stalin's body be removed from the mausoleum, thus putting an end to the mass daily pilgrimages honoring the former hero. Innumerable busts, statues, and portraits of Stalin were removed from public buildings and streets throughout the nation. Places named for Stalin, most notably the city of Stalingrad, were hastily renamed. With the dismantling of the ritual system centered on him, Stalin was posthumously divested of authority, and a blow was struck against those associated with him.

COMMUNICATION

For organizations to be effective they must have efficient means of internal and external communication, much of which takes place without ritual. But there is an element of ritual found in the communication of all organizations, and since much of what gets communicated is not new, the standardized, repetitive nature of ritual is an advantage. One of the most common uses of ritual within an organization is to socialize new members to the values and expectations that make up its culture.

Ritual is especially valuable to hierarchical organizations in communicating power relationships. Indeed, people can increase their power through the manipulation of ritual, just as they can lose power through ritual neglect or incompetence. This is most dramatically seen where power is most concentrated. Over two thousand years ago, for example, a Chinese peasant, Kao-tsu, rose to power and founded the Han dynasty. Since he had little background in such matters, one of his first acts as emperor was to abolish the court rituals, which he regarded as trivial. But the result of this move was that he was shown little respect by his followers in court, who disrupted court audiences through their drunken deportment. They traded loud insults and hacked on the wooden palace pillars with their swords. Disturbed and threatened by this lack of proper distance between himself and his followers, the emperor authorized a new ritual code. The change was dramatic. The emperor no longer walked into court but was borne in on a litter, with hundreds of banner-carrying officials announcing his arrival. All then rose and toasted him. He was now an emperor, no longer a peasant potentate.

Ritual communicates not only the authority of the head of the state or organization; it is also important in making claims to positions of political importance within that state. Ancient Rome affords a dramatic example, for the military leaders of this bellicose empire asserted their prestige and power through rites of triumphal entrance into the city. These entries were already well developed in Etruscan times. In the sixth century B.C., victorious generals donned purple togas and gold crowns, reddened their faces, and took up eagle-tipped scepters for their chariot-borne entries. The Roman authorities recognized the significance of these triumphal entries in establishing the powerful position of the celebrant, and the Senate sought to exercise control over them. Rules were thus enacted which set the criteria for such an honor. The general must have defeated a foreign enemy and killed at least five thousand men. Before authorizing such a ceremony, the Senate met the claimant outside the city to adjudicate his claim to the rite.

The impact of such ceremonies—a hundred were held in the one hundred fifty years from 220 to 70 B.C.—was great. Magistrates and senators led the long procession into the city, followed by trumpeters and carts bearing some of the spoils of war: arms, gold, silver, art, and other treasures. Paintings and models of the conquered lands followed, as well as the golden crowns presented to the general by the towns he had vanquished. A richly adorned white ox, soon to be sacrificed to Jupiter, was accompanied by priests carrying sacred vessels. Then trudged in the captives, in chains. Behind all these came the victorious general, who stood in his plush chariot amidst a rising screen of incense. Resplendently dressed, the general held a laurel branch in one hand and an eagle-topped scepter in the other. A slave held a golden crown over his head. Accompanied by his children, the general was followed by his officers on horseback or on foot. These, in turn, led the masses of exultant soldiers, who sang praises (or ribald rhymes) to their general. Once in Rome, captives were beheaded, strangled, or sacrificed. After the general had gone to the Capitol and put his laurel branch in the lap of the statue of Jupiter, he was feasted in the temple by the Senate. None of the participants or onlookers at such triumphal entries were likely to forget them.

Ritual is not only used to communicate that a person is to be exalted over others; it is also used to calibrate degrees of power within an organization, whether it be a Chinese empire or a New York law firm, and whether the symbolism involves the location of one's grave or the location of one's office. When the leaders of the Soviet Union gather on the Moscow reviewing stand as the troops pass by, their physical order relative to the central power holder symbolically represents and communicates their place in the hierarchy of authority and power. Yet this is not a new phenomenon: the use of space in rituals to communicate status can be traced back far through human history.

Transmission of messages through ritual dramatization is much more powerful than communication through verbal declaration. Moreover, in many situations, direct verbal expression of status differences is more likely to create overt conflict among those in lower ranks than is ritual expression of the same message. Such use of ritual is also especially important where there is a conflict between official norms regarding the hierarchy of power holders and the actual hierarchy of power relations.

This does not mean, however, that ritual expressions of status never lead to conflict. Officeholders are loathe to give up any of the ritual prerogatives of their position, lest it undermine their authority and power. More than one fist fight has broken out between participants at political rituals over their distance from the ruler. . . .

Ritual is employed to communicate power relations not just among the political elite, but between the powerful and the powerless as well. This occurs not only in the context of formal organizations, but also in defining political relations among people outside any formal context. In many peasant societies, for example, people depend on the protection offered by a patron, while the patron, in turn, depends for his own power and status on the number of "clients" he is able to accumulate. Though these patron-client relations are crucial to the political system, they have no formal organizational existence, nor any explicit legal basis. For the system to work there must be a means whereby people communicate their pledge of clientage to a particular patron and, likewise, a means by which the patron communicates his acceptance of that role vis-à-vis the prospective client. This does not take place through any written agreements, but by culturally standardized rituals.

In many cases these rites involve the offering of specified gifts by the client to the patron on certain ceremonial occasions, or the use of particular terms of address. When two men greet each other in rural Turkey, for example, they communicate their claim to equality by clasping hands, but one expresses his subservience to the other by taking the hand of the higher-status man, bowing, kissing it, and placing it to his forehead. Should the higher-status man not wish to have this dependent relationship publicly validated, he struggles to transform this ritual of subservience into the ritual of egalitarian greeting.

If ritual serves important communicative purposes within organizations or states, it is equally important for communication among organizations and among states. An organization's political position is often communicated more effectively, and more credibly, through ritual than through simple written platforms or oral addresses. It is in this light that the polemic between Italy's Socialist and Communist parties in October 1986 can be understood. A mass peace demonstration was to be held in Rome, with the Italian Communist Party prominent among the sponsors. The Socialists refused to get involved in the peace march, on the grounds that the Communists did not share the Socialists' even-handed approach to the problems of international aggression. And what was given as the primary evidence of the Communists' guile? The revealing fact, according to a prominent editorial in the Socialist Party newspaper, was that the Communists had never marched against the repression in Czechoslovakia or Poland, against the Russian tanks that rolled into Hungary, against the Soviet invasion of Afghanistan, or against the Vietnamese military role in

Cambodia. "We have seen them dissent and criticize, but never have they marched."[4] Here, the true indication of a political party's sympathies is to be found in its rituals, not in its public pronouncements.

The use of ritual for communication between states is, of course, highly developed in the world of international protocol. Should a ruler of another country arrive and certain rites not be performed—his national anthem played, his country's flag displayed with military honors alongside that of the hosts—serious international tensions can result. For example, in 1986, because of scheduling conflicts, Soviet leader Gorbachev was not met by Iceland's head of state on his arrival in Reykjavik for his meeting with President Reagan. Gorbachev was so incensed by this slight, which was blamed on the Soviet ambassador to Iceland, that, on his return to Moscow, he had the ambassador fired. . . .

It is not just deference that is communicated to visiting diplomats and heads of state through ritual. Indeed, such rites are often used to impress foreign powers with the strength and wealth of their host. Four centuries ago, in the mid-sixteenth century, Catherine de Medici . . . sponsored a series of magnificent court fêtes for foreign dignitaries; these were designed to disabuse them of the notion that her country was close to ruin. Catholics and Protestants may be at war with each other, the nation's purse bare, the king a mere inexperienced boy, but to admit to these conditions by scaling down or abandoning court rites would send an important signal of defeat to France's neighbors.

The role of ritual in impressing foreign political powers is also much in evidence in colonial administrations, where great emphasis was placed on ritual display as a means of communicating the authority and power of the rulers. This typically took the form of local ritual display of colonial superiority, but occasionally it involved bringing local indigenous rulers to the colonial homeland for a ritual lesson.

Such was the case in 1937 when Yeta, leader of Barotseland, left what was then Northern Rhodesia to attend the king's coronation in London. First Yeta went to meet Queen Mary. Taken through a large hall, he passed through huge doors to encounter the queen, standing in the middle of a cavernous room. When he subsequently encountered the king, Yeta got down on his knees before the monarch and gave the Barotse royal salute. The celebration of the coronation rites, though on a much more vast and opulent scale than he had ever witnessed, were not beyond his comprehension by any means, for such rites of rulers were as much part of politics in the states of Africa as they were in Europe.

Yeta was not the first African leader to visit British royalty in England, nor the first subject to a ritual lesson in the colonial hierarchy of power. Back in 1919, the Paramount Chief of Basutoland, in southern Africa, came to England for an audience with the king. When the chief asked permission to stop in Rome on his way back home, his English hosts refused. They feared that the potentially greater splendor of the Vatican's reception might lead the chief to conclude that the pope was more important than the king.

It would be difficult, though, to top the Aztecs in the use of ritual to intimidate the emissaries of other peoples. On special occasions, such as the dedication of a new temple, Aztec rulers invited kings and notables from neighboring societies to observe their rites, which always included human sacrifice. Since most of the sacrificial victims were war captives, it was not uncommon for the guests to witness the mass disembowelment of their own warriors. The message about the power of the Aztec state is best conveyed by contemporary descriptions of these rites, many of which have survived.

In the Aztec ceremonial system, the sacrifice of humans to the gods occupied a central place. Atop a long series of stone stairs stood the altar, before which a stone platform lay. One by one, the victims—many wailing as they climbed—were taken up the stairs. They were placed on the platform, facing the sky, with their backs painfully arched, and their hands and feet tied down. Using a flint knife, the officiant slit open the victim's taut chest and quickly cut out his heart. He then struck the heart against the altar, letting it drop on the ground, where it continued to beat. Meanwhile, the body was rolled down the steps, where it was recovered by the soldier who had originally captured the victim. The lucky soldier made off with the corpse, using it to prepare a feast for friends and relatives. Back on the altar, the priest smeared the blood on the lips of the stone depictions of the gods, thus nourishing them.

For rites of special state importance, held in the capital city, the ceremonies were on a spectacular scale, with long lines of victims waiting their turn to pay homage to the Aztec state. There, as on other major occasions, a high-ranking captive was kept for separate ritual purposes. The captive dignitary did not suffer the ignominy of having his body rolled down the altar stairs. Rather, he was flayed so that Montezuma, master of the Aztec empire, could wear his skin in a special dance. Should this ceremony not be sufficient to impress on the invited guests the power of the Aztec empire, subsequent tours of the long racks lined with thousands of skulls of previous sacrificial victims brought the point home. It would be difficult to find a more striking example of ritual overkill.

NOTES

1. Venemous descriptions of this KKK rite are found in *Life* magazine (27 May 1946): "The Ku Klux Klan tries a comeback," pp. 42–44, and *Time* (20 May 1946), p. 20. For the KKK oath, see the Committee on Un-American Activities (1967).

2. Lane, Christel. 1981. *The Rites of Rulers*. Cambridge: Cambridge University Press, p. 94. Another of the intended effects of this rite was undoubtedly to bolster the legitimacy of Brezhnev by associating him with Lenin.

3. Knauft, Bruce M. 1985. Ritual form and permutation in New Guinea: Implications of symbolic process for sociopolitical evolution. *American Ethnologist* 12: 321–40; and, Kelly, Raymond. 1977. *Etoro Social Structure*. Ann Arbor: University of Michigan Press.

4. Quoted in Vittorio Mimmi, "Sulla marcia della pace, nuova polemica Psi-Pci," *La Repubblica* (15 October 1986), p. 7.

33

Hallucinogenic Plants and Their Use in Traditional Societies

Wade Davis

In Western society drugs are used for either medicinal purposes or pleasure. These are the "good" and the "evil," the use and abuse of drugs. Our culture has defined those who use drugs for nonmedicinal purposes as deviant, and we have begun to view the use of drugs as a pathological condition unique in the annals of human history. Drug use is considered a major social problem. In Selection 5, an ethnography of "Crack Street," we saw the human dimension of that problem.

The use of drugs is widespread in traditional cultures around the world. However, in traditional societies hallucinogenic plants are used for religious purposes and in ritual settings. Throughout history, people have sought ways to see beyond the normal reality of everyday life. They have endured the risk of poison in experimenting with ways to prepare mind-altering substances. These substances may be smoked, chewed, eaten, sniffed, drunk, rubbed onto the skin or into cuts, or even taken as intoxicating enemas. They have taken these risks, not for pleasure or kicks, but for curing illnesses through magic, divining truth, peering into the future, and making contact with the spirit world. This is serious and important work for the people involved.

Another difference highlighted by the comparative study of drug use is the important effect of culture and context on the drug experience. Used in different settings, under different sets of expectations, the same drug may cause very different reactions, from nausea on the one hand to a religious experience on the other. Today we may find it odd that Native Americans (Amerindians) smoked tobacco to cause giddiness (one of the universal symptoms

of ecstasy) and to open the pathways through which shamans disassociated themselves from the normal state of awareness.

In light of America's drug problem, getting a broader historical and comparative vision of the role of drugs in society makes sense.

As you read this selection, ask yourself the following questions:

☐ *Were hallucinogenic plants discovered by chance?*

☐ *What is the relationship between medicinal drugs, psychotropic drugs, and poisons?*

☐ *What factors influence what an individual sees under the influence of hallucinogens?*

☐ *How do ritual and the role of the shamanistic leader create a different context for the use of hallucinogenic drugs in traditional and "modern" societies?*

☐ *Do drug users in our society have their own secular rituals?*

The following terms discussed in this selection are included in the Glossary at the back of the book:

Amerindian	psychoactive drug
decoction	rite of passage
hallucinogen	ritual
indigenous	sorcery

The passionate desire which leads man to flee from the monotony of everyday life has made him instinctively discover strange substances. He has done so, even where nature has been most niggardly in producing them and where the products seem very far from possessing the properties which would enable him to satisfy this desire.

Thus early in this century did Lewis Lewin, perhaps the preeminent pioneer in the study of psychoactive drugs, describe the primal search that led to man's discovery of hallucinogens. Strictly speaking, a hallucinogen is any chemical substance that distorts the senses and produces hallucinations—perceptions or experiences that depart dramatically from ordinary reality. Today we know these substances variously as psychotomimetics (psychosis mimickers), psychotaraxics (mind disturbers) and psychedelics (mind manifesters); dry terms which quite inadequately describe the remarkable effects they have on the human mind. These effects are varied but they frequently include a dreamlike state marked by dramatic alterations "in the sphere of experience, in the perception of reality, changes even of space and time and in consciousness of self. They invariably induce a series of visual hallucinations, often in kaleidoscopic movement, and usually in indescribably brilliant and rich colours, frequently accompanied by auditory and other hallucinations"—tactile, olfactory, and temporal. Indeed the effects are so unearthly, so unreal that most hallucinogenic plants early acquired a sacred place in indigenous cultures. In rare cases, they were worshipped as gods incarnate.

The pharmacological activity of the hallucinogens is due to a relatively small number of types of chemical compounds. While modern chemistry has been able in most cases successfully to duplicate these substances, or even manipulate their chemical structures to create novel synthetic forms, virtually all hallucinogens have their origins in plants. (One immediate exception that comes to mind is the New World toad, *Bufo marinus*, but the evidence that this animal was used for its psychoactive properties is far from complete.)

Within the plant kingdom the hallucinogens occur only among the evolutionarily advanced flowering plants and in one division—the fungi—of the more primitive spore bearers. Most hallucinogens are alkaloids, a family of perhaps 5,000 complex organic molecules that also account for the biological activity of most toxic and medicinal plants. These active compounds may be found in the various concentrations in different parts of the plant—roots, leaves, seeds, bark and/or flowers—and they may be absorbed by the human body in a number of ways, as is evident in the wide variety of folk preparations. Hallucinogens may be smoked or snuffed, swallowed fresh or dried, drunk in decoctions and infusions, absorbed directly through the skin, placed in wounds or administered as enemas.

To date about 120 hallucinogenic plants have been identified worldwide. On first glance, given that estimates of the total number of plant species range as high as 800,000, this appears to be a relatively small number. However, it grows in significance when compared to the total number of species used as food. Perhaps 3,000 species of plants have been regularly consumed by some people at some period of history, but today only 150 remain important enough to enter world commerce. Of these a mere 12–15, mostly domesticated cereals, keep us alive.

In exploring his ambient vegetation for hallucinogenic plants, man has shown extraordinary ingenuity, and in experimenting with them all the signs of pharmacological genius. He has also quite evidently taken great personal risks. Peyote (*Lophophora williamsii*), for example, has as many as 30 active constituents, mostly alkaloids, and is exceedingly bitter, not unlike most deadly poisonous plants. Yet the Huichol, Tarahumara and numerous other peoples of Mexico and the American Southwest discovered that sundried and eaten whole the cactus produces spectacular psychoactive effects.

With similar tenacity, the Mazatec of Oaxaca discovered amongst a mushroom flora that contained many deadly species as many as 10 that were hallucinogenic. These they believed had ridden to earth upon thunderbolts, and were reverently gathered at the time of the new moon. Elsewhere in Oaxaca, the seeds of the morning glory (*Rivea corymbosa*) were crushed and prepared as a decoction known at one time as ololiuqui—the sacred preparation of the Aztec, and one that we now realize contained alkaloids closely related to LSD, a potent synthetic hallucinogen. In Peru, the bitter mescaline-rich cactus *Trichocereus pachanoi* became the basis of the San Pedro curative cults of the northern Andes. Here the preferred form of administration is the decoction, a tea served up at the long nocturnal ceremonies during which time the patients' problems were diagnosed. At dawn they would be sent on the long pilgrimages high into the mountains to bathe in the healing waters of a number of sacred lakes.

Lowland South America has provided several exceedingly important and chemically fascinating hallucinogenic preparations, notably the intoxicating yopo (*Anadenanthera peregrina*) and ebene (*Virola calophylla*,

From *Cultural Survival* 9(4):2–5, 1985. Reprinted by permission of *Cultural Survival*.

V. calophylloidea, V. theiodora) snuffs of the upper Orinoco of Venezuela and adjacent Brazil and the ayahuasca-caapi-yagé complex (*Banisteriopsis caapi*) found commonly among the rainforest peoples of the Northwest Amazon. Yopo is prepared from the seeds of a tall forest tree which are roasted gently and then ground into a fine powder, which is then mixed with some alkaline substance, often the ashes of certain leaves. Ebene is prepared from the blood red resin of certain trees in the nutmeg family. Preparations vary but frequently the bark is stripped from the tree and slowly heated to allow the resin to collect in a small earthenware pot where it is boiled down into a thick paste, which in turn is sundried and powdered along with the leaves of other plants. Ayahuasca comes from the rasped bark of a forest liana which is carefully heated in water, again with a number of admixture plants, until a thick decoction is obtained. All three products are violently hallucinogenic and it is of some significance that they all contain a number of subsidiary plants that, in ways not yet fully understood, intensify or lengthen the psychoactive effects of the principal ingredients. This is an important feature of many folk preparations and it is due in part to the fact that different chemical compounds in relatively small concentrations may effectively potentiate each other, producing powerful synergistic effects—a biochemical version of the whole being greater than the sum of its parts. The awareness of these properties is evidence of the impressive chemical and botanical knowledge of the traditional peoples.

In the Old World may be found some of the most novel means of administering hallucinogens. In southern Africa, the Bushmen of Dobe, Botswana, absorb the active constituents of the plant kwashi (*Pancratium trianthum*) by incising the scalp and rubbing the juice of an onion-like bulb into the open wound. The fly agaric (*Amanita muscaria*), a psychoactive mushroom used in Siberia, may be toasted on a fire or made into a decoction with reindeer milk and wild blueberries. In this rare instance the active principals pass through the body unaltered, and the psychoactive urine of the intoxicated individual may be consumed by the others. Certain European hallucinogens—notably the solanaceous belladonna (*Atropa belladonna*), henbane (*Hyoscyamus niger*), mandrake (*Mandragora officinarum*) and datura (*Datura metel*)—are topically active; that is the active principals are absorbed through the skin. We now know, for example, that much of the behavior associated with the medieval witches is as readily attributable to these drugs as to any spiritual communion with the diabolic. The witches commonly rubbed their bodies with hallucinogenic ointments. A particularly efficient means of self-administering the drug for women is through the moist tissue of the vagina; the witches broomstick or staff was considered the most effective applicator. Our own popular image of the haggard woman on a broomstick comes from the medieval belief that the witches rode their staffs each midnight to the sabbat, the orgiastic assembly of demons and sorcerers. In fact, it now appears that this journey was not through space but across the hallucinatory landscape of their minds.

There is in the worldwide distribution of the hallucinogenic plants a pronounced and significant discrepancy that has only inadequately been accounted for but which serves to illustrate a critical feature of their role in traditional societies. Of the 120 or more such plants found to date, over 100 are native to the Americas; the Old World has contributed a mere 15–20 species. How might this be explained? To be sure it is in part an artifact of the emphasis of academic research. A good many of these plants have entered the literature due to the efforts of Professor R. E. Schultes and his colleagues at the Harvard Botanical Museum and elsewhere, and their interest has predominantly been in the New World. Yet were the hallucinogenic plants a dominant feature of traditional cultures in Africa and Eurasia, surely they would have shown up in the extensive ethnographic literature and in the journals of traders and missionaries. With few notable exceptions, they don't. Nor is this discrepancy due to floristic peculiarities. The rainforests of West Africa and Southeast Asia, in particular, are exceedingly rich and diverse. Moreover, the peoples of these regions have most successfully explored them for pharmacologically active compounds for use both as medicines and poisons. In fact, as much as any other material trait the manipulation of toxic plants remains a consistent theme throughout sub-Saharan African cultures. The Amerindians, for their part, were certainly no strangers to plant toxins which they commonly exploited as fish, arrow and dart poisons. Yet it is a singular fact that while the peoples of Africa consistently used these toxic preparations on each other, the Amerindian almost never did. And while the Amerindian successfully explored his forest for hallucinogens, the African did not. This suggests the critical fact that the use of any pharmacologically active plant—remembering that the difference between hallucinogen, medicine and poison is often a matter of dosage—is firmly rooted in culture. If the peoples of Africa did not explore their environment for psychoactive drugs, surely it is because they felt no need to. In many Amerindian societies the use of plant hallucinogens lies at the very heart of traditional life.

To begin to understand the role that these powerful plants play in these societies, however, it is essential to place the drugs themselves in proper context. For one, the pharmacologically active components do not produce uniform effects. On the contrary, any psychoactive drug has within it a completely ambivalent potential for good or evil, order or chaos. Pharmacologically it induces a certain condition, but that condition is mere raw material to be worked by particular cultural or psychological forces and expectations. This is what our own medical experts call the "set and setting" of any drug experience. *Set* in these terms is the individual's expectation of what the drug will do to him; *setting* is the environment —both physical and social—in which the drug is taken. This may be illustrated by an example from our own country. In the northwest rainforests of Oregon are a native species of hallucinogenic mushrooms. Those who go out into the forest deliberately intending to ingest these mushrooms generally experience a pleasant intoxication. Those who inadvertently consume them while foraging for edible mushrooms invariably end up in the poison unit of the nearest hospital. The mushroom itself has not changed.

Similarly the hallucinogenic plants consumed by the Amerindian induce a powerful but neutral stimulation of the imagination; they create a template, as it were, upon which cultural beliefs and forces may be amplified a thousand times. What the individual sees in the visions is dependent not on the drug but on other factors—the mood and setting of the group, the physical and mental states of the participants, his own expectations based on a rich repository of tribal lore and, above all in Indian societies, the authority, knowledge and experience of the leader of the ceremony. The role of this figure—be it man or woman, shaman, curandero, paye, maestro or brujo—is pivotal. It is he who places the protective cloak of ritual about the participants. It is he who tackles the bombardment of visual and auditory stimuli and gives them order. It is he who must interpret a complex body of belief, reading the power in leaves and the meaning in stones, who must skillfully balance the forces of the universe and guide the play of the winds. The ceremonial use of hallucinogenic plants by the Amerindian is (most often) a collective journey into the unconscious. It is not necessarily, and in fact rarely is, a pleasant or an easy journey. It is wondrous and it may be terrifying. But above all it is purposeful.

The Amerindian enters the realm of the hallucinogenic visions not out of boredom, or to relieve an individual's restless anxiety, but rather to fulfill some collective need of the group. In the Amazon, for example, hallucinogens are taken to divine the future, track the paths of enemies, ensure the fidelity of women, diagnose and treat diseases. The Huichol in Mexico eat their peyote at the completion of long arduous pilgrimages in order that they may experience in life the journey of the soul of the dead to the underworld. The Amahuaca Indians of Peru drink yage that the nature of the forest animals and plants may be revealed to their apprentices. In eastern North America during puberty rites, the Algonquin confined adolescents to a longhouse for two weeks and fed them a beverage based in part on datura. During the extended intoxication and subsequent amnesia—a pharmacological feature of this drug—the young boys forgot what it was to be a child so that they might learn what it meant to be a man. But whatever the ostensible purpose of the hallucinogenic journey, the Amerindian imbibes his plants in a highly structured manner that places a ritualistic framework of order around their use. Moreover the experience is explicitly sought for positive ends. It is not a means of escaping from an uncertain existence; rather it is perceived as a means of contribution to the welfare of all one's people.

34

The Doctor's White Coat:
The Image of the Physician in Modern America

Dan Blumhagen

Symbolic communication is an important characteristic of our species. What people wear provides others with a symbolic statement of who they are—that is, of their status and role. This selection by an anthropologist-physician presents a historical and symbolic analysis of the "costume" worn by medical doctors.

Symbols are central to both sacred and secular rituals because they have meaning; they are things that stand for something else. In the analysis of cultural symbols, anthropologists can uncover layers of meaning, so that a single symbolic behavior can communicate a rich and complex set of ideas.

Most of the time, people are unaware of the symbols being communicated in their ritual behavior. However, anthropologists believe that symbolic analysis can lead us to deeper understandings of the belief systems of other people. Like all aspects of culture, symbol systems change through time. As such, the anthropologist can use history to show how a particular object or behavior came to be associated with particular meanings.

In this selection, the author traces the social history of medicine in the United States by examining the white coat as a symbol. Such symbols are also employed in our pre-sentation of self to others, and, as we see in this article, in silently communicating messages about social relationships.

As you read this selection, ask yourself the following questions:

☐ *Why is the physician's coat white? Can you think of some impractical aspects of this cultural convention?*

☐ *Is the white coat simply a marker of an occupation, or are other cultural beliefs communicated through it?*

☐ *What taboos do we allow and expect a physician to violate?*

☐ *Does this symbolic analysis fit with your own experiences with physician-patient interactions?*

The following terms discussed in this selection are included in the Glossary at the back of the book:

cultural values
status
symbol
taboo

Reproduced, with permission, from: Dan Blumhagen, "The Doctor's White Coat: The Image of the Physician in Modern America." *Annals of Internal Medicine*, 91: 111–116, 1979.

All societies have healers who care for the sick.[1] The healer's interaction with a patient is often surrounded by a symbolic system that expresses the implicit cultural concepts of what "healing" means.[2] As changes occur in the social meanings attributed to healing, the symbols used to express those concepts also change. This paper will use the symbol-analysis approach, widely used in cultural anthropology, to examine the historical origins and the function of the symbol systems that surround American physicians and their patients. An understanding of how these were adopted first by the profession and then by the greater society will elucidate what it means to be a healer in American culture. This knowledge can be usefully applied to problematic patient consultations, as well as to understanding some of the conflicts that have arisen between the medical profession and society at large.

THE NATURE OF SYMBOL ANALYSIS

Most physicians are aware of the importance of symbol analysis in individual psychotherapy.[3] What is less widely appreciated is the application of a similar approach to understanding entire cultures. Anthropologists have found that symbols are often used as a way to express and reaffirm the fundamental belief systems that a society holds.[4] This is often done in ritualized events. Perhaps cultural symbols can be most usefully viewed as a form of communication, analogous to words in a natural language.[5] Like words, they can be used in social settings to define the shared interpretation of "what's really going on here," to direct each actor's behavior, and to express the dominance relationships that exist between the various individuals who are interacting. Since most symbol analyses have dealt with small-scale preliterate societies, there is no well-defined formula for doing such a study in a complex, literate society such as modern America. My approach here will be to look at doctor-patient interactions to determine what symbols may be used, then to examine historical data documenting how these came into use and the original meanings they bore. Finally, the use of these symbols in the medical setting will be compared with similar symbols used in other American rituals to develop the full spectrum of meaning that they communicate.

SYMBOLS OF THE PHYSICIAN

What, then, are the symbols surrounding physicians, and what do they mean? Table 1 shows how physicians are depicted in advertisements for medical journals and in newspaper comic strips. These sources were chosen because they represent stereotypes of the doctor as presented to the profession and to the public. They represent "all physicians in general" and do not merely reflect the idiosyncracies of a particular physician.

Table 1 shows that although there are some differences in the way physicians are depicted in medical and popular media, there appear to be four principal objects used to depict the doctor: the white coat, stethoscope, head mirror, and black bag. In this survey, there was only one physician depicted in a patient-care setting who did not have at least one of these items. The most frequent component of the image seems to be the white coat. Of 43 doctors pictured in patient-care settings (Table 1), 36 were wearing white. In the symbolism of white coats, the social concept of "what it means to be a physician" is summarized, intensified, and extended. Its importance as the symbol of physicians is seen in that when the advertising media—a reflection of the current social stereotype—wish to depict a person with the authority of a physician, he is usually shown wearing a white coat. Although professionals are reluctant to articulate the meanings they attribute to white coats, on occasion, under stress, such interpretations may be given.

The relationship between a physician and his patient is serious and purposeful, not social, casual or random. In this relation the patient unburdens himself or herself of a set of concerns regarding health matters and transfers them to the accepting physician. For a very long time it has been customary for individuals in society to dress rather formally when conducting serious business, and less formally when they are at leisure. The physician's dress should convey to even his most anxious patient a sense of seriousness of purpose that helps to provide reassurance and confidence that his or her complaints will be dealt with competently. True, the white coat is only a symbol of this attitude, but it also has the additional practical virtue of being identifiable, easily laundered, and more easily changed than street clothes if accidentally soiled. . . . Casual or slovenly dress is likely to convey, rightly or wrongly, casual or inattentive profes-

Table 1 DEPICTION OF PHYSICIANS IN MEDICAL AND LAY MEDIA

	Medical Journals	Newspaper Comics
Number	45	11
White coats	29	7
Stethoscopes	13	5
Head mirror	6	5
Black bag	0	5
No special identifiers	14	0

sional handling of their problem. Such a patient may respond in an inhibited manner, fail to volunteer information, refuse to carry out a recommended diagnostic or management program, fail to keep appointments, and be uncomfortable enough to seek help elsewhere. The rapport, so anxiously sought for with your patient, may be irretrievably lost.[6]

To fully understand how the white coat has achieved this position, we must look at the historical origins of white coats as the symbol of physicians. I have been able to identify three major origins for the white coat as it has been used until fairly recently: the operating room, the scientific, specifically microbiological, laboratory, and the hospital. Each adds a layer of meaning.

THE WHITE COAT IN THE OPERATING ROOM

Operating-room garb appears to have originated with the concept of aseptic surgery, which began in this country about 1889.[7] Photographs from that year in the Massachusetts General Hospital Archives show the surgeons and nurses (but not the anesthesiologist or observers in the balcony) wearing short-sleeved white coats over their street clothes. Masks and gloves had not yet come into use. The purpose of the coats in this setting appears to be twofold: to protect the patient from being contaminated by the physician, and to protect the physician from contamination by the patient during the procedure being performed. We will find that the white coat repeatedly serves to protect both the patient and the physician.

Another implication that surgery has for the public image of the physician is its incredible power to send a person into a deathlike state, open the previously inviolable body cavities, correct whatever was "wrong" and resurrect the patient, healed.

> I have said that the modern surgeon has become a popular hero. . . . One has only to glance through the month's illustrated magazines, or turn a few pages of the latest novel to find him in the act of revealing his demonical subtlety or demonstrating his incredible skill. The tall spare frame is capable on emergency of strength and endurance that would make Sandow stand aghast.[8]

White coats had not yet become symbolic of this heroism, but the newly developing film industry ground out a remarkable number of amplifications of this theme.[9] One such film, "Society Doctor," is described as being "played in spotless white. . . . and with an appropriate sense of glamor and nobility. . . . [The hero] persuades his best friend to operate on him, directing the work himself with the aid of mirrors."[10] In these quotations we see that the social image of the physician had become one of immense power and authority. These attributes were associated with the white clothing he wore.

Even though the operating room provided one of the earliest examples of doctors wearing white, and provides some of the basic cultural meaning, it does not appear to be the main source. Stahel's otherwise valuable article[11] confuses this point. With the goal of better aseptic technique, the white coats of 1889 rapidly became full-length gowns, and were referred to as such.[12] Aseptic surgery required that these gowns only be used in the operating room to avoid the risk of cross contamination. The back opening, a necessity for sterile technique, also made it impractical for other patient-care settings.[11] Additionally, the term "gown" in our culture usually refers to women's clothing, and thus is not suitable as a symbol for those who were "active, scientific men, virile, ambitious . . . upon whose shoulders the actual work of the institution will fall."[12]

White coats diverged from operating-room gowns. The step that took the garb of the scientific laboratory into a clinical setting appears to be the main source of our current white coats. The term "lab coat," the primary term used for the white coat, refers to this origin.

THE WHITE COAT IN THE LABORATORY

The representation of the physician as a scientist has a long history that culminated during the first decades of this century. In the middle of the 19th century, science had nearly destroyed the reputability of medicine by demonstrating that its cures were worthless, but it was unable to substitute more effective remedies. Medicine became simply one of a wide variety of healing cults and quackery.[13] Despite this inauspicious start, both the profession and public turned to science as the means by which healing would come. After all, the laboratories, whose inventions had transformed night into day, could transmit messages instantaneously, and had revolutionized transportation, were certainly the most important hope for the conquest of disease. Physicians were urged to present themselves as scientists. Cathell, whose book *The Physician Himself* went through many editions between 1882 and 1922, advised: "Show aesthetic cultivation in your office arrangement, and make it look fresh, neat, clean *and scientific*" [emphasis added].[14] Above all, one must avoid "forcing on everybody the conclusion that you are, after all, but an ordinary person."[14] By 1922, Cathell had become more emphatic in describing "*the office, the sanctuary—of an earnest, working scientific medical man . . .* " [emphasis in original] as the place where one will make "judicious and intelligent use of your scientific instruments of precision . . . to assist you in curing nervous and terrified people by increasing their confidence in your armamentarium and in your professional ability."[15] The authority of science is seen as validating the practice of medicine.

Demonstrations of the efficacy of modern science, such as the construction of the Panama Canal (1905), led to its public acceptance as the foundation of modern healing. An intense feeling of hope about the future of scientific medicine was expressed in cartoons. Other healing cults, particularly homeopathy and eclecticism, which had threatened the existence of scientific medicine only a few years earlier, withered away. Their schools closed or converted to biomedicine.

The medical profession rapidly consolidated its position as part of the scientific enterprise. Within a decade of the publication of the *Flexner Report* in 1910, medical education was restructured around laboratory science. The *content* of medicine changed. Textbooks were rewritten: Of all the books popular enough to go through multiple editions before the "progressive era," almost none were still being printed when it ended. (This was ascertained by a review of the books in the open stacks of the Countway Library. The most notable exceptions, of course, are *Gray's Anatomy* and Osler's *Textbook of Medicine* (1892), both of which are still being printed in revised editions. There were no technical or theoretical advances that would outdate the former, and the latter was written by one of the men who led medical education during this change.) Towards the end of this radical transformation of the profession of medicine, and as a reflection of it, physicians became stereotyped as scientists wearing white coats. The message of power and protection emerge: While wearing a white coat the physician is able to handle safely the deadly scourges that plague mankind and is able to render them innocuous. One result of this perception of power was that physician-scientists were granted tremendous authority. No mere individual desires or beliefs were allowed to stand in the way of the public's health as determined by medical laboratories.[16]

THE WHITE COAT IN THE HOSPITAL

The shift in locus of sick care from the home to the hospital was the third historical trend. The basis for this lay in the development of aseptic surgery and modern diagnostic and therapeutic techniques, which necessitated the use of personnel and resources that could not readily be taken to the patient's home. With the impact of the change in medical care, the image of the hospital changed from that of being a place where social outcasts died to being the only place where the sick could

be healed. The image changed from death to life. This was reflected in the change of the clothing of the healing staff. The black habits of the religious nursing orders, for example, became the white uniforms of the modern nursing profession.[17] Hornsby, then director of Michael Reese Hospital in Chicago, tells us in *The Modern Hospital* (12, pp. 543–5) that all people connected with the healing process (including patients and visitors) were to be dressed in white, whereas the *nonmedical* employees were to be given colored uniforms. White became associated with the *institutions* of healing, and it was within their halls that the use of white coats as the symbol of medicine was most pronounced. Physicians in private practice have never completely adopted their use.

This transition is most clearly indicated in the photographs of house staff that often accompany a hospital's annual report. These pictures show that during the period 1905–15 apprentice physicians exchanged their street clothes for white coats and pants. Hornsby indicates that this was not merely for the convenience of the hospital laundry; indeed, "Intern's white uniforms are difficult to launder, and should be done by hand."[12] In other words, there were compelling reasons for dressing interns in white that outweighed the economic disadvantages.

THE MEANING OF WHITENESS

Given the historical backdrop of the meaning of the white coat, what is added by the cultural conception of the meaning of whiteness? Originally, laboratory coats were tan and appear to have changed to white as they became associated with medicine. Why was not another, perhaps more functional, color adopted? Why were both the profession and the public so profoundly disturbed when Nobel Laureate Alexis Carrel wore *black gowns* in his laboratories and operating rooms at the fledgling Rockefeller Institute of Medicine?[18]

The significance of white as a symbol of life has already been mentioned. Since there are few celebrations of life in our society, this meaning is derived from its opposite color, black, which is clearly the color of death and mourning. The association with purity has also received comment. But this purity contains two strands of meaning: First is the concept of innocence. No shadow of malice, of intentional harm, can mar the white coat—the patient is safe in the hands of this powerful figure. Second is the purity of unaroused sexuality, particularly as this meaning is evoked in another ritual that uses the white bridal gown.

Closely allied to the concept of purity is the concept of superhuman power. The saying "cleanliness is next to godliness" originated long before the germ theory of disease! Whiteness as an attribute of superhuman power, at once irresistibly attractive and infinitely dangerous, is clearly expressed in Melville's *Moby Dick*[19] and, as has been shown, was explicitly applied to physicians. In religious symbols, Christ and the saints who have exercised their power over death and all other human frailties are robed in white (*Bible*, Revelations 7:9–17). But these are not merely powerful, they are supremely good.

A final meaning comes from the term *candor*, itself derived from the Latin *candidus* (white). This impartial truth-telling is often portrayed in statues of "justice," who is usually depicted wearing white.

If symbols affect behavior, the use of the white coat should affect how patients and physicians act. There appear to be two behavioral changes that have been mediated by the white coat: the physician's access to his patient's body, and the shift in the locus of the sick role from the home to an institution.

BODY AND SEXUAL TABOOS IN AMERICAN CULTURE

In many societies, the most powerful symbol systems are found in situations where strong social values appear to be challenged.[20] One of the strongest beliefs in our society is the inviolability of a person's physical body.[21, 22] There is even a legal term for the violation of a person's rights over his own body: battery. Merely touching another individual without that person's permission is to be at jeopardy of civil and criminal action.[23] The extent to which the physical examination is a serious breach of social custom has been clearly stated by Lief and Fox.[24]

> The amounts and occasions of bodily contact are carefully regulated in all societies, and very much so in ours. The kind of access to the body of the patient that a physician in our society has is a uniquely privileged one. Even in the course of a so-called routine physical examination, the physician is permitted to handle the patient's body in ways otherwise permitted to special intimates, and in the case of procedures such as rectal and vaginal examination in ways normally not even permitted to a sexual partner.

The physical body is not merely a threat to the person whose body is revealed, it is also considered to be dangerous to the one exposed to it. This is the basis of much of the American film rating system. Given these taboos, the perfunctory way that physicians are given permission to do the most intimate examination is remarkable.

The individual must stand before his doctor man to man, unclothed physically, mentally, and morally, revealing to him as he does to no other mortal, not even to his father confessor, the secrets of his most inmost soul; submitting his person to the most thorough scrutiny of the physician and to varied tests, physical, clinical, instrumental and what not, and without hesitation committing to his keeping the keys of the family skeleton closet.[25]

Physical examinations of apparently healthy people are a relatively recent phenomenon. Referring to the late 19th century, Duffy writes: "Physical diagnosis remained handicapped by the reluctance of patients, particularly females, to bare their skins to the probing, palpation or percussion of the physicians."[26] Rectal and pelvic examinations do not appear to have been frequently used. As late as 1927, Richard Cabot, a prominent *medical* educator, claimed that "it is not and should not be a part of the routine physical examination to examine the rectum."[27] Buttressed, however, by the successes of medicine in improving public health, a campaign was waged from 1922 to 1929 that promoted periodic physical examinations as a means of *improving the individual's* health.[28] These included pelvic and rectal examinations.

For this crusade to be successful, the cultural dangers of the physical contact had to be muted. A mechanism was needed that would reinterpret an ordinarily taboo activity into a socially acceptable, even desirable, one.[29] A set of symbols was needed to protect both the doctor and patient in this dangerous setting. The white coat, with its meanings of bilateral protections, purity, goodness, and unaroused sexuality, was ideally suited for the task. In the less-threatening situation where a male physician examined a man, the white coat was all that was needed: The patient was nude.[30] When the physician was a woman, however, a reciprocal symbolic dress was required, leading to the development of the examination gown. In one of the early descriptions of such a garment, the symbolic themes come out. Fisk[30] claims that this gown "gives the examinee a sense of protection and lessens the embarrassment." The disparate treatment of men and women can not be maintained, and soon men, too, were offered the protection of examination gowns.

The second behavioral change was a shift in the concept of where it was appropriate to act sick.[31] Previously, of course, illness had been a personal drama played in the bedroom, the most secluded, intimate, and protective area of the home. The physician could enter at the invitation of the family and be made privy to the physical and behavioral secrets contained therein without violating any social norms. Only those unfortunate persons who lacked a protective home sought care in an institution. It was only the "fallen women who enter hospitals,"[32] that is, only those people without anything worth concealing or without anyone to shield them. Symbols were required that would protect patients from the unwarranted intrusions that could occur in an institution and that would legitimize private behavior in a public place. The physician's white coat and the patient's examination gown met these needs perfectly.

These shared meanings direct patient and physician behavior in the following way: The physician is an active scientist, the patient is passive material; the physician prescribes, the patient complies; the physician is self-concealing, the patient is self-revealing. Clearly, as long as this social definition of the healing encounter exists, the physician will dominate the setting.

DEVELOPMENTS FROM 1930 TO 1960

The above set of symbols appears to have been fully functional by the early 1930s and remained largely intact until recently. There were minor changes, such as the adoption of blue or green garb in operating rooms when high-intensity lighting made the glare from white drapes unbearable, but these pastel shades did not conflict with the underlying value system as black or red, for example, would have.

Other practitioners found that some of the meanings communicated by the white coat were so overpowering that it interfered with their practice. Pediatricians and psychiatrists have discovered that this mark of authority has a tendency to overwhelm their patients, and they therefore tend to wear pastel coats or normal street clothes. As has been noted, many physicians, particularly those in private practice, did not adopt the white coat. Nonetheless, these trends did not affect the public image of what a physician should be. If anything, the beliefs were intensified, as is evidenced by the meteoric rise in the funding of medical research after World War II, which resulted in the National Institutes of Health and much of the rest of the academic medical enterprise.[33]

CURRENT TRENDS

During the past decade, however, much of this has changed. Physician-scientists who were once seen as validating medical practice no longer necessarily protect and heal patients, but may endanger them. A good example of this attitude is seen in the widespread laetrile movement, which is perceived as a direct assault on the biomedical establishment. Other social

symbols of authority are also being rejected. Hospitals are often accused of prolonging agony rather than renewing life. Body taboos do not seem to be as strong as they once were.

These social changes strike at the heart of the meanings communicated by white coats. No new consensus has developed that will define the nature of healing and give direction for patient behavior. This has had an effect on the use of both white coats and examination gowns.

The quote from Kriss[6] earlier in this paper that expounded the significance of white coats is the result of widespread student challenges of authority of this symbol. Debate over whether medical students should wear one still continues.[34] Voices from some of the countercultural movements recognize the implications of this symbolism and reject it. Some feminists, for example, "advise women to discard the drape by throwing it on the floor when the doctor enters. If he replaces it, throw it on the floor again."[35] This type of symbolic action tends to make physicians uncomfortable, for the rejection of symbols of established roles means that there is little guidance as to how they or their patients should act.

Cousins[36] comments on this redefinition of roles in the healing encounter when he claims that "the most important thing happening in American medicine today is not the discovery of magical new drugs but the new relationship that is emerging between physicians and patients."[36] The old model of the scientist-healer is rejected for a more humanistic relationship. He continues: "Traditionally the doctor is the authoritarian figure . . . the new relationship is more in the nature of a partnership." Note that the "traditional authoritarian figure" is, as has been documented here, a tradition that has only existed since the turn of the century. There were reasons for adopting that role at the time, there may be similar reasons for abandoning it now.

The dynamic relationship that exists between physicians and American culture is only beginning to be explored. As we learn more about the social meaning and function of healing, we will better understand some of the conflicts that we feel between society and the profession. This in turn may enable us to devise better institutional and individual means of meeting these needs. But even before that global understanding is reached, there may be benefits that accrue on a smaller scale. In all patient-physician encounters, careful consideration of the symbolic and other nonverbal communication may be important. In particularly unsettled interactions, painstaking, explicit discussion and negotiation on the exact role that the patient and the physician will take may be required for healing to occur.

REFERENCES

1. Landy, D. (ed.). 1977. *Culture, Disease and Healing: Studies in Medical Anthropology*, New York: Macmillan, 1.
2. Kleinman, A. M. 1975. The symbolic context of Chinese medicine: A comparative approach to the study of traditional medical and psychiatric forms of care in Chinese cultures. *Am J Chin Med*. 3:103–24.
3. Freud, S. 1900. *The Interpretation of Dreams*. New York: Macmillan.
4. Dolgin, J. L., Kemnitzer, D. S., Schneider, D. M. 1977. *Symbolic Anthropology: A Reader in the Study of Symbols and Meaning*. New York: Columbia University Press, 3–47.
5. Leach, E. 1976. *Culture and Communication: The Logic by Which Symbols Are Connected*. Cambridge: Cambridge University Press, 10.
6. Kriss, J. P. 1975. On white coats and other matters. *N. Engl J Med*. 292:1024–5.
7. Potter, R. A., ed. 1976. *Surgery in the United States*. The American College of Surgeons and the American Surgical Association, 17.
8. Whitby, C. J. 1912. *The Doctor and His Work*. London: Swift and Co., 23.
9. Spears, J. 1955. The doctor on the screen. *Films in Review*. 19 November 6:436–44.
10. *New York Times Film Review: 1913–1968: Volume 2, 1932–1938*. 1970. New York: New York Times, 1143.
11. Stahel, H. R. 1970. Der weisse Mantel in der Medizin. *Zürcher Medizingeschichtliche Abhandlungen*, 78:1–22.
12. Hornsby, J. A., Schmidt, R. E. 1913. *The Modern Hospital*. Philadelphia: W. B. Saunders, 543.
13. Shryock, R. H. 1947. *The Development of Modern Medicine*. New York: Alfred A. Knopf, Inc., 248–72.
14. Cathell, D. W. 1882. *The Physician Himself and What He Should Add to the Strictly Scientific*. Baltimore: Clishay and Barley, 10.
15. Cathell, D. W. 1922. *Book on the Physician Himself from Graduation to Old Age*. Emerson Hotel, Baltimore: Published by the author, 10.
16. Rosen, G. 1958. *A History of Public Health*. New York: MD Publications, 464–78.
17. Dietz, L. D. 1967. Lehozky, A. R. *History and Modern Nursing*. Philadelphia: F. A. Davis, 168–73.
18. Conner, G. W. 1964. *A History of the Rockefeller Institution*. New York: Rockefeller Foundation, 154.
19. Melville, H. 1930. *Moby Dick, or The White Whale*. New York: The Modern Library, 272–83.
20. Berger, P. L., Luckmann, T. 1966. *The Social Construction of Reality*. Garden City, New York: Doubleday and Co., 96.
21. Miner, H. 1975. Body ritual among the Nacirema. *In* J. P. Spradley and M. A. Rynkiewich (eds.), *The Nacirema*. Boston: Little, Brown and Co.
22. Glaser, B. G., Strauss, A. L. 1965. *Awareness of Dying*. Chicago: Aldine Publishing Co., 162.
23. Black, H. C. 1957. *Black's Law Dictionary*. St. Paul, Minnesota: West Publishing Co., 193.
24. Lief, H. I., Fox, R. C. 1963. Training for detached concern in medical students. *In* H. I. Lief, V. F. Lief, N. R. Lief, (eds.), *The Psychological Basis of Medical Practice*. New York: Harper and Row, 32.
25. Finney, J. M. T. 1923. *The Physician*. New York: Charles Scribner and Sons.
26. Duffy, J. 1976. *The Healers*. New York: McGraw-Hill, 232.
27. Cabot, R. C. 1927. *Physical Diagnosis*. New York: William Wood and Co., 435.
28. Rosen, G. 1975. *Preventive Medicine in the United States, 1900–1975*. New York: Science History Press, 59.
29. Emerson, J. P. 1970. Behavior in private places: sustaining definitions of reality in gynecological examinations. *In* H. P. Dreitzel, (ed.), *Recent Sociology: No. 2, Patterns of Communicative Behavior*. New York: Macmillan Publishing Co.
30. Fisk, E. L., Crawford, J. R. 1928. *How to Make the Periodic Physical Examination*. New York: Macmillan Publishing Co., 41.
31. Friedson, E. 1970. *Profession of Medicine*. New York: Harper and Row, 220.
32. Trousseau, A. 1882. *Clinical Medicine Letters*. Philadelphia: Blinkerston, 43.
33. Bordley, J. III, Harvey, A. M. 1976. *Two Centuries of American Medicine: 1776–1976*. Philadelphia: W. B. Saunders, 419.
34. McKinnon, J. A. 1977. Life in a short white coat. *New Physician*. November 26:24–30.
35. Dreifus, C. (ed.), *Seizing Our Bodies*. New York: Random House, 226.
36. Cousins, N. "A Better Rx for Patients." Los Angeles Times Syndicate; 2 April 1978. Syndicated editorial column.

35

The Integration of Modern and Traditional Health Sectors in Swaziland

Edward C. Green

All societies have medical systems, although it is sometimes difficult to distinguish between a medical system and a religious system. All medical systems include three parts: a theory of illness causation, a mechanism for diagnosis, and the prescription of appropriate therapy. Traditional healers are important figures in the rural communities of developing countries. They are people with special knowledge and skill who help members of their communities in times of need (usually for a fee, of course). Traditional healers must use symbols to encourage their patients' belief in their healing powers. In all cultures, there is a close connection between belief, ritual, and curing.

You might want to think about this symbolic dimension of medicine the next time you are in a waiting room waiting to see a doctor. But if you think that your wait is long, remember that in most other countries, modern biomedicine is both expensive and inaccessible because of severe shortages of biomedical doctors. In this selection, anthropologist Edward Green describes his work, which is aimed at helping to understand the problems of a shortage of health personnel and the possibility of incorporating traditional healers into Swaziland's health care delivery system.

Most developing nations are faced with the problem of becoming integrated into the world economy without getting consumed by it—that is, losing their national iden-

tity. The possibility of utilizing traditional healers in the improvement of health represents a solution to that bind. This type of blending of the "old" and the "new" can work to the advantage of both modern medicine and traditional medicine, but especially to the benefit of the people themselves.

As you read this selection, ask yourself the following questions:

☐ How did Dr. Green discover this project? How was it linked to the ethnographic method?

☐ Why did traditional healers think that their medicine was better?

☐ Why was the Ministry of Health interested in a survey of traditional healers?

☐ Did the cost of traditional health services surprise you? Why?

The following terms discussed in this selection are included in the Glossary at the back of the book:

biomedicine   medical anthropology
ethnographic methods   participant observation
ethnomedicine   qualitative methods
indigenous

Reprinted from *Anthropological Praxis*, edited by Robert M. Wulff and Shirley J. Fiske, 1987, by permission of Westview Press, Boulder, Colorado.

CLIENT AND PROBLEM

I went to Swaziland in March 1981 to serve as an anthropologist on the AID-funded Rural Water-Borne Disease Control Project. The project called for a knowledge, attitudes, and practices (KAP) survey on water and sanitation in Swaziland, and the survey was my primary responsibility as a member of a multidisciplinary project team of U.S. technical advisers. This article describes a major research and policy planning effort that developed serendipitously while I was involved in carrying out the KAP survey.

During the KAP survey I decided that getting to know and interview some traditional healers would be a good introduction to Swazi health-related beliefs and attitudes. My informal interviewing focused on diseases related to water and sanitation, but I also found myself discussing a variety of topics of interest to both healers and their patients. One finding with important implications was that most healers appeared interested in learning more about "modern medicine" (a shorthand term used here to denote Western allopathic biomedicine) and working cooperatively with doctors and nurses. Another was that healers regarded some diseases as distinctly African and therefore treatable only by African medicines and rituals, whereas they regarded others—a smaller number in fact—as new or foreign diseases more treatable by modern medicine. Swazi healers appeared to refer patients with the latter type of disease to modern clinics and hospitals. I discussed these findings with Swaziland Ministry of Health (MOH) officials in light of the World Health Organization recommendations that poorer nations try to find ways for indigenous healers to work cooperatively with modern health sector personnel. The health planning unit of the MOH was especially interested in developing some sort of working relationship with healers. This unit was particularly aware of human resources shortages in the modern health sector, having just concluded an assessment of health personnel. After discussions among health planners, the MOH director of medical services, and myself it was decided that the MOH should take preliminary steps toward fulfilling the WHO mandate, especially because traditional healers seemed to be especially numerous and influential in Swaziland.

In August 1982, the permanent secretary of the MOH formally asked my colleague Lydia Makhubu and myself to prepare a report on Swazi traditional healers. Makhubu was vice-chancellor of the University of Swaziland and a chemist who had been studying the properties of traditional medicines. Specifically, we were asked to provide an assessment of (1) human resources in the traditional health sector; (2) the areas and extent of cooperation possible be-

tween the traditional and modern health sectors, with special reference to the prevention and treatment of diarrheal diseases; (3) the extent to which alternative systems of health care had developed for the consumer; (4) customary law, modern legislation, and government policies regarding traditional healing and healers; (5) prospects for the development of a national traditional healers association, and a possible role for the MOH in promoting, monitoring, and liaising with such an association; and (6) the potential for the paraprofessional training of certain types of traditional healers.

PROCESS AND PLAYERS

Makhubu and I divided the tasks called for between ourselves. Makhubu reviewed her own research findings, checking on various points with her key informants, and consulted experts on Swazi law, customs, and traditions. I conducted a survey of healers to measure some of the apparent trends that had emerged through my earlier in-depth interviewing and participant-observation research. I also attempted to estimate the number of healers practicing in Swaziland. We felt that quantification was necessary because policymakers usually want statistics to back up the recommendations of researchers.

Between August 1982 and January 1983, my research assistants interviewed 144 traditional healers of all types (herbalists, diviner mediums, faithhealers). No adequate sampling frame of healers existed, and thus a random or probability sample was not feasible. However, roughly equal numbers of healers were interviewed in the four major geographic regions of Swaziland. Although the healer sample could have been more randomized by selecting only those healers who lived in randomly selected census enumeration areas, time and effort were saved by allowing interviewers to work primarily in areas where they had kinship ties or where they had interviewed during previous surveys. This approach also helped minimize suspicion and mistrust among the healers. In addition, a house-to-house census was conducted in four rural and four peri-urban communities in order to estimate the number of healers in Swaziland, along with certain of their characteristics. A total of 598 residential units in three geographic regions were covered in the census.

I decided that a precoded questionnaire that limited the range of responses would not be appropriate. My earlier interviews with Swazi healers suggested that at best, they would give stilted, formal, and stereotyped answers to a fixed interview schedule. On the other hand, if healers were approached properly, they would open up and offer rich information that went far beyond specific questions asked. This approach combined a sincere, interested, respectful attitude by the interviewer with a flexible, open-ended mode of questioning assisted by subtle probing techniques. The three Swazi interviewers chosen for the survey had worked on standard surveys before, but they had never done open-ended interviewing. I trained them in appropriate interview techniques as well as in taking shorthand notes and translating these into complete, detailed accounts of interviews.

I continued my participant-observation and in-depth interviews among some twenty healers I had come to know, while the interviewers carried out the fieldwork phase of the survey. The interviewers required little supervision in the field, but I carefully monitored the incoming data and discussed findings and their implications with the interviewers. Among the more important findings was that about 5,400 healers seemed to practice outside the modern health sector; in a country the size of Swaziland this number means one traditional healer for every 110 population. This figure compares to a physician/population ratio of about 1:10,000. Some 50 percent of the total number of healers were herbalists, 40 percent were diviner-healers, and 10 percent were Christian ("Zionist") faithhealers. About half the healers were female, and the vast majority of these were diviner-healers. Diviner-healers tend to be more prestigious than herbalists because ancestor spirits are believed to work directly through them.

The survey confirmed my earlier finding that nearly all types of illness were believed to be ultimately caused by sorcery or less frequently by loss of ancestral protection. However, many healers were prepared to accept the theory that illnesses might have more immediate causes about which doctors and nurses were knowledgeable. For example, a Swazi mother might accept the idea that her child will develop diarrhea if flies walk over the child's food; but she will also want to know how and why her enemies sent flies to harm her child.

We found that patients might seek treatment from both doctors and traditional healers for the same complaint. The doctor was considered capable of eliminating symptoms or treating the immediate cause of illness, and the healer was relied upon to explain the illness in culturally meaningful terms and to treat or eliminate its ultimate source. Clearly, a basis for cooperation already existed between the traditional and the modern health sector. In fact some 90 percent of healers surveyed claimed to routinely refer some of their patients to clinics—even though very few instances of referrals from clinics to healers were encountered.

Several survey questions showed that healers believed that their own rituals and medicines were superior to modern medicine in treating most diseases and that people relied on traditional medicines to ensure the sexual fidelity of a partner and to provide luck. A majority of healers said that modern medicine could better treat cholera, tuberculosis, heart disease, venereal disease, and bilharzia. In a separate question on cholera, 76 percent of healers said that they refer patients to clinics rather than try to treat a new disease that they do not understand (cholera first appeared in Swaziland in 1980).

The survey revealed that healers admired doctors for certain technical capabilities as well as for the medicines they possess. Most commonly cited were various surgical practices, blood transfusions, and use of X-ray machines. On the other hand, diviners felt that their ability to diagnose the ultimate causes of illness (thereby answering the "why" or "why me" questions of misfortune) and to perform the *femba* ceremony through which agents of illness are removed—both of which involve cultivated relationships with spirits—are as important skills as those that doctors possess. In fact, most of the healers interviewed either implied or explicitly stated their wish to be treated as equals by doctors.

The survey also sought to measure in some way the frequency of use of healing practices that seemed harmful. These included medicinal enemas used to prevent and treat several types of childhood diarrhea; induced vomiting to "clean out the chest" of tuberculosis patients; traditional vaccinations performed with an unclean razor; and use of powerful, mind-altering herbal medicines in treating madness. It was impossible to measure frequency of such practices with any accuracy, but all were employed. The use of enemas for children seemed sufficiently widespread that soon after the survey report was presented, the MOH asked me to conduct a study focusing specifically on beliefs and practices related to diarrheal diseases in Swaziland (Green 1985).

Since Makhubu and I were well aware of modern practitioners' strong negative bias toward traditional healers, we pointed out traditional healing practices that were probably beneficial to the patient—and perhaps to the patient's family and community as well. These included use of herbal medicines that seemed to be effective in various ways; the reduction of stress through ritual and through explanations reassuring to patient and family; and the removal of a patient from home to a therapeutic environment at the healer's homestead in which the patient can recover. We also pointed out that healers helped ease pressure on overburdened clinics by treating minor, self-limiting, psychosomatic, and certain other kinds of conditions in which traditional therapies are probably effective and appropriate.

Although it was difficult to obtain information on patient fees in the survey, I personally observed patients paying between $120 and $130 for treatment of a single condition such as *umtsebulo*, or soul loss. Healers were also earning about $140 for protecting (*kubetsela*) a homestead against mystical lightning strikes by enemies. A basic diagnostic fee of about $2 was standardized by a royal order-in-council in 1954, but healers earned an additional fee of between $10 to $20 to "open the bag" (*imvula sikhwama*) of medicines, which formalizes the beginning of any treatment.

Although Swaziland is a poor country, most people somehow find the money to pay the relatively high fees requested by traditional healers. These fees were even more remarkable because modern-sector clinic services at the time of the survey cost the equivalent of about $0.20 whatever the treatment entailed. My findings on healing fees helped explain why a recent attempt by the MOH to train healers as rural health motivators met with little success. These community health workers were being paid $20 per month. Several survey respondents were candid in remarking that healing is a lucrative and respectable profession and perhaps the best one to which women and those lacking formal education can aspire.

A system of registering healers began in Swaziland late in the British colonial period when the government recognized that doctors and nurses would not easily displace traditional healers and that the latter could not be completely ignored. Registration represented a first step toward recognition of healers and exercising a modicum of control over their activities. It also provided tax revenues. Since independence, the Swaziland government has continued to register and collect taxes from healers.

The survey showed that 82 percent of healers reported that they were currently registered, and 8 percent said that they had only recently qualified as healers and they intended to become registered. Even allowing for overreporting, the proportion of registered, tax-paying healers is higher than might be expected for a traditional African society. In addition, healers seemed to be favorably inclined toward registration. When healers were asked why they had registered, 30 percent commented that the police would support only registered healers in collecting overdue patient fees and that they would also protect healers against complaints of patients or their families. Other common remarks were that registration conferred legitimacy, respectability, and authority on healers, and it allowed them to travel and practice freely throughout Swaziland and neighboring countries.

Finally, the survey sought information on cooperation and paraprofessional training. An impressive (if slightly suspect) 98 percent of healers interviewed claimed they would like to achieve better cooperation between themselves and doctors and nurses. Ninety-one percent specifically expressed enthusiasm toward undergoing some sort of training in modern medicine. Most said that they wanted to improve their healing skills and to learn more about the treatments given in hospitals. However, several healers—most of them female—expressed concern that their lack of formal education would make communicating with doctors difficult.

In spite of the positive survey results, both Makhubu and I were aware that traditional healers were still suspicious about the motives of the MOH. And a great deal more suspicion and outright negative bias could be found in the modern health sector. Many local doctors preferred to pretend that healers did not exist, and some took the view that healers should be arrested for practicing medicine without a license. This bias resulted from a failure to understand the traditional healer's role in Swazi society, from the nature of formal (Western) medical education and professional socialization, from a certain amount of professional jealousy, from the "bad press" healers tended to receive by local, sensation-seeking media, and from the fact that healers engage in several practices deemed unacceptable by public health standards.

In view of the difficulties of developing a workable policy in an atmosphere of suspicion and mistrust, Makhubu and I recommended that the MOH proceed cautiously and not expect quick results. We suggested a policy of seeking cooperation rather than integration. Cooperation implies a better working relationship between the two health sectors by which appropriate referrals are routinely made between the sectors, certain traditional healing practices are improved or made safer, and the "cultural" or interpersonal sensitivity of modern health care workers is increased. The term "integration" implies a fundamental alteration of both healing systems and of the roles of the respective practitioners, although in reality only the traditional healer is expected to change. The danger here is that the traditional healer may become a second-rate paramedical worker and thereby cease to carry out his or her important function in the local community—a function with social, psychological, and spiritual as well as physical health dimensions. Such an outcome could be disruptive in multiple ways, including the undermining of a community's capacity to solve its own health problems.

We realized the importance of starting with an area of cooperation that would interest people in both health sectors and that was likely to succeed. We decided upon the treatment and prevention of childhood diarrheal diseases and the use of oral rehydration therapy (ORT) as an appropriate focus for an initial and experimental program of cooperation. The 1981 outbreak of cholera in southern Africa helped center attention on diarrheal diseases in both the government and the traditional sectors. By 1983 diarrheal diseases, especially those of childhood, had become a highest priority health concern of the MOH, and the widespread use of ORT was recognized as a technique that could significantly reduce morbidity and mortality from these diseases.

We believed that a program focused on diarrheal diseases and ORT would be of interest to traditional healers for several reasons: (1) Research indicated that healers would like to have a means by which they could prevent deaths from diarrheal diseases; (2) cholera had become a disease of high concern among healers as well as the general public, and most healers surveyed admitted they did not understand or try to treat cholera; (3) ORT is compatible with traditional treatments for diarrhea, i.e., herbal decoctions taken orally over a period of time; and (4) distribution of ORT packets to traditional healers would constitute an important gesture of trust and cooperation on the part of the government.

We recommended that the health education unit of the MOH be given the main responsibility for organizing and implementing a series of workshops designed to upgrade healers' skills in a few priority areas, most notably diarrheal diseases of childhood, and to sensitize modern health sector personnel to work more cooperatively with healers. Packets of oral rehydration salts (ORS) should be given to healers on a pilot basis, and subsequent evaluations would indicate if healers were mixing and administering the salts properly. If they were, then ORS distribution to healers could become a national program and other areas of potential cooperation could be explored.

RESULTS AND EVALUATION

As a result of the survey report, the MOH officially adopted a policy of seeking cooperation with traditional healers. Within a few months of receiving the health policy report, the MOH, through the health education unit, conducted three preliminary workshops designed to establish a dialogue between healers and modern health sector personnel. Topics focused on diarrheal diseases and administration of ORT, as well as on secondary topics such as immunization against childhood diseases, maternal/child health, breastfeeding, and nutrition.

The first regional workshop for healers, held in Motjane on June 1, 1983, was disappointing because only twelve healers turned up. The turnout was poor partly because of the failure to contact most healers in the area and partly because of the healers' mistrust regarding MOH motives. No diviner-healer wore the characteristic red-ochre hairstyle, the brightly colored cloths, the empowering medicine bags, or the beads that symbolize special relationships with certain spirits, indicating that the healers expected disapproval or even ridicule to be directed at them.

However, those who attended were well treated, and all present shared in an interesting exchange of views. Healers were treated as peers and colleagues. The nurses who attended the first workshop were health educators or public health nurses, and all were personally in favor of the new MOH policy. Their positive attitude toward the experiment in cooperation did not go unnoticed by the healers. The second and third regional workshops attracted more than 100 healers each, and the healers came in full traditional regalia. Part of the high turnout was due to the active support of an influential healer, Nhlavana Maseko, who had personally attended the late king of Swaziland. During 1983 Maseko was active in organizing a national association of traditional healers. Since the Green-Makhubu report had recommended that the MOH support the formation of such an association, the workshop organizers were happy to work with the emerging association leaders, especially because they offered a ready-made network for the dissemination of information about the workshops.

These first workshops in mid-1983 served the intended purpose of establishing a dialogue between healers and MOH personnel. Although critics of intersectoral cooperation could be found on both sides, good will and trust began to develop between those who attended the workshops. I witnessed genuine changes in the attitude of several MOH officials after they attended a workshop. Some of these had shared the view of many expatriate physicians in Swaziland that traditional healers are unprincipled charlatans. Others in the modern health sector seemed to drop their pose of contempt toward healers once the new MOH policy made it respectable to deal with healers.

My employment in the MOH ended in September 1983 when my already extended contract expired. I returned to the United States but returned to Swaziland from January 1984 to March 1985 as a personal services contractor for the AID mission. Although I primarily worked on other research and planning topics, I kept abreast of developments with traditional healers. One of these was the rapid growth of the Swaziland Traditional Healers Society (STHS) at both the national and district levels. Another was the continuation and growth of the MOH-sponsored training workshops for traditional healers. A U. S. health educator who joined the Rural Water-Borne Disease Control Project in 1983 became very active in promoting and implementing these workshops—probably too active in fact. There was a danger that the Swazi staff of the health education unit would feel that healer training was a U.S. project and not their own. However, as of late 1986, nearly two years after the departure of the last American from the health education unit, the unit was actively implementing workshops for traditional healers in all districts of Swaziland.

THE ANTHROPOLOGICAL DIFFERENCE

In retrospect I can assess the contribution of anthropology in the overall effort of formulating and implementing a new policy toward traditional healers. First, a body of anthropological literature on traditional healers helped me understand the complex belief systems and behavioral patterns of healers, the role and function of healers in their communities, the significance of ritual in curing, the sociological dimension of recruitment and membership in healing cults, and a host of other aspects of traditional healing.

John Janzen's recent comparative historical work (unpublished) on *ngoma* therapeutic cults in Africa helped me develop a wider and deeper perspective in my understanding of Swazi therapeutic cults. Likewise, I. M. Lewis's theoretical contributions on cults of affliction and the upward mobility of oppressed or marginal members of society (Lewis 1969, 1971) stimulated my insights into the cult of Swazi diviner-healers, even though the Swazi situation did not always fit Lewis's model. Lewis's ideas were especially useful in understanding the appeal of the diviner cult to Swazi women. Membership in this cult is the only traditional means by which Swazi women can achieve power and wealth (even though women can be born to this position) in a male-dominated society. Three other anthropologists, W. D. Hammond-Tooke, Harriet Ngubane, and Martin West, all with research experience among groups closely related to the Swazi, provided theoretical perspectives that guided my research and thinking: Hammond-Tooke on the sociology of witchcraft accusations, Ngubane on the support networks among Zulu diviner-healers, and West on Christian-Zionist faithhealers in Soweto.

It must be admitted, however, that the contribution of anthropological theory was indirect in my practical, policy-oriented work with traditional healers. The contribution of anthropological methods was more direct. I would not have been able to either advocate or undertake a survey of healers had I not gained in-depth information about traditional healing through standard anthropological methods. Furthermore, the healer survey design followed recognized anthropological procedures: a preliminary phase of in-depth interviewing and participant observation research, followed by a survey based on flexible, open-ended interviewing. And anthropology provided a framework for interpreting the resulting qualitative data, some of which were rather abstruse and arcane by the standards of other disciplines. Another direct contribution to my work came from the anthropologist D. M. Warren who has published about his experience in designing workshops for traditional healers in Ghana (Warren et al. 1981).

The contribution of an anthropological perspective and orientation cannot be overlooked. It was natural for me to regard traditional healers as fonts of wisdom and culture brokers par excellence and as respected health opinion leaders (rather than as quacks or charlatans) in their own communities. Yet the same cannot be said for those of other disciplines; otherwise someone would have begun mediating cooperation between the traditional and modern health sectors before I arrived in Swaziland.

REFERENCES

Green, E. 1985. Traditional Healers, Mothers and Childhood Diarrheal Disease in Swaziland: The Interface of Anthropology and Health Education. *Social Science and Medicine* 19(3):227–285.

Green, E. C., and L. Makhubu. 1984. Traditional Healers in Swaziland: Toward Improved Cooperation Between the Traditional and Modern Health Sectors. *Social Science and Medicine* 18(12):1071–1079.

Kuper, H. 1947. *An African Aristocracy, Rank Among the Swazi.* Oxford: Oxford University Press.

Lewis, I. M. 1969. Spirit Possession in Northern Somaliland. *In* J. Beattie and J. Middleton, eds., *Spirit Mediumship in Africa.* New York: Praeger, pp. 188–210.

———. 1971. *Ecstatic Religion. An Anthropological Study of Spirit Possession and Shamanism.* Middlesex: Penguin Books.

Marwick, B. A. 1940. *The Swazi.* London: Frank Cass.

Warren, D. M., G. S. Bova, M. A. Tregoning, and M. Kliewer. 1981. Ghanaian National Policy Toward Indigenous Healers: The Case of the Primary Health Training for the Indigenous Healers (PRHETIH) Programs. Paper presented at the annual meeting of the Society for Applied Anthropology, Edinburgh.

36

PROFILE OF AN ANTHROPOLOGIST

Anthropology and the World of Physicians

Thomas M. Johnson

In the previous selection, we saw an anthropologist active in efforts to have traditional medical practitioners cooperate with modern scientific medicine (biomedicine). The goal was to improve people's health in a Third World context. Medical anthropologists also work closer to home. Some analyze the culture of biomedicine as practiced in American hospitals, and some actually work within the system by trying to improve medical education for effective cross-cultural clinical care.

As a clinical faculty member in a medical school, Thomas Johnson not only helps train physicians but also is involved in patient care. In this selection, he describes his work in the hospital of the University of Alabama at Huntsville. As a true participant-observer, he offers many insights about the culture of biomedicine. Take, for instance, his comments about the meaning of time for clinicians. We are reminded not only of the cultural construction of time (see Selections 1 and 2) but also of the differences in the availability of time in tribal as opposed to modern societies (see Selection 20). Notice also how medical students have to be socialized (enculturated) into the culture of medicine.

As you read this selection, ask yourself the following questions:

☐ What are Thomas Johnson's goals in practicing his "specialized form of applied medical anthropology"?

☐ How did he gain acceptance in the world of clinicians?

☐ What is the difference between "explaining" and "understanding" in the clinical setting?

☐ What are some of the unspoken assumptions in the culture of biomedicine that can have a negative impact on clinical care?

The following terms discussed in this selection are included in the Glossary at the back of the book:

biomedicine
epistemology
ethos
medical anthropology
socialization
world view

Reprinted from *Anthropology Newsletter*, November and December 1991. Not for further reproduction.

Biomedicine has always fascinated me: the complex social organization of hospitals: the elaborate rituals and specialized language of practitioners; the poignancy of human emotions made exquisitely palpable in time of sickness; the powerful, even brutal molding of young people into physicians by the process of medical education. I have worked in medical settings for the past 25 years—from exploring every nook and cranny of a hospital as a maintenance worker/undergraduate sociology major, to discovering the existence of a specialty called medical anthropology that encouraged me to conduct ethnographic studies of hospital wards, indigent clinics and migrant farm worker health care as a graduate student. I learned about the power of medical education by immersing myself in the process—from cadaver dissection to bedside rounds—during dissertation research.

I concluded that the 1960s activist dreams I had about improving health care in this country could best be achieved by attempting to change the medical education process. Knowing that the most powerful professional socialization in medicine takes place in clinical settings rather than in the lecture hall, I became one of only a few nonphysician medical anthropologists whose primary teaching role has been in hospital wards and outpatient clinics. Ultimately, also I recognized that, for me at least, the immediacy of patient care was so rewarding that I completed another graduate degree in clinical psychology. With dual training and clinical credentials I consider almost everything I do—from leading a staff support group for nurses in a burn unit to being a psychotherapist—as a specialized type of applied medical anthropology.

With this background, I have spent most of the last fifteen years in clinical and teaching activities on the faculties of three medical schools and residency programs, although during that time I also taught for seven years in a graduate medical anthropology program. Currently, I am on the faculty of a family medicine residency program, in which I act as a consultant to residents and physician faculty in the care of their patients. I also give seminars and supervise residents in a required month-long clinical rotation in medical behavioral science.

Over the years, interacting with medical students and residents while interviewing a severely burned patient or a parent whose baby was stillborn an hour earlier not only has permitted me to influence medical practice, but has also allowed me to view with ever greater acuity the cultural contrasts between medicine and anthropology—differences in world views and epistemologies that must be understood to work successfully in medicine. My experiences suggest that any medical anthropologists desiring to work in biomedicine will have to struggle with these implicit, unspoken assumptions that characterize the culture of biomedicine. My purpose here is to present some of these distinctive features of biomedicine, particularly as they contrast with those of academic anthropology.

Most anthropologists recognize that culture can be defined in Kroeberian terms (as "acts, artifacts, beliefs, etc."), but it is also clear that culture is a phenomenon involving basic assumptions about the world. These assumptions, sometimes thought of as "core values," not only guide people in their activities, but also underlie group identity and serve boundary maintenance functions (defines who is "us" and who is "not us"). Because identity and boundary maintenance functions are a major feature of professionalization in complex cultures, many medical anthropologists may anticipate that being accepted by practitioners in a biomedical setting will be difficult. I have not experienced this to be true. In fact, I have found that physicians unconsciously divide the world moiety-like into two groups: practitioners and the public. Because *therapeutic activism* is a core value among practitioners, anyone willing to be even peripherally involved in the process of patient care will find acceptance. Anyone not involved in the therapeutic process is automatically relegated to the lay moiety.

Thus, although it is true that physicians may anticipate criticisms from a social scientist in their midst, once a medical anthropologist has demonstrated even a modicum of therapeutic activism, which initially involves passing what I call "ethnographic tests" (such as helping to remove an encrusted incisional drain without overt expressions of disgust, or enduring caustic and insensitive remarks about patients without becoming defensive), ready acceptance will follow. Such inevitable ethnographic tests are not unlike those in traditional cross-cultural fieldwork settings where anthropologists are expected to accept offers of certain indigenous foods or to witness rituals like clitoridectomy or infanticide without overt judgmentalism. As in any cross-cultural setting, it is axiomatic that learning "medicalese"—both informally through informants and by taking a course in medical terminology—is essential for effective participation.

My participation in biomedical settings has led me to see inevitable epistemological differences between anthropology and biomedicine. For example, among my biomedical colleagues there is an unspoken assumption that medical science is rational and objective. This ethos of *positivism* provides for a sense of certainty and control in the face of sickness. The touchstone of this view is "hard data": an emphasis on quantification, which predisposes physicians to value phenomena that can be reduced to numerical equivalents, such as blood pressure, serum amylase levels, and the like, but to be much more uncomfortable with phenomena such as anxiety or depression (unless, of course, these can be "measured" using psychological testing).

Thus, the very modes of acquiring knowledge in medical anthropology and biomedicine stand in sharp contrast. In biomedicine, diagnosis based on the core value of *affective neutrality*, is the *sine qua non* of inquiry. The term "diagnosis" literally means "to tell apart": not only to differentiate one disease from another, but also to separate those who are well or "in control" from those who are sick, which may effectively distance practitioners from patients. Of course, diagnosis is also a process that improves the confidence and reduces the anxiety of practitioners. Diagnosis emphasizes *explaining*, while knowledge acquisition in academic medical anthropology increasingly emphasizes *understanding*—bemoaning the decontextualization and disembodying of sickness and demanding that empathic attention be paid to the individual experiences and social contexts of people who are ill. Whenever I am asked to render a diagnosis, I debate with myself to clarify if the process will permit me to better understand and help the patient, or if it will distance me because I am feeling uncomfortable.

In actual treatment activities, this key difference in the way physicians and medical anthropologists are predisposed to gather and value data creates an inevitable tension within me. Although the anthropological predilection to immerse oneself in the lifeworld of patients is compelling, unless one is actively involved in the therapeutic process it is difficult to appreciate how *too much* understanding actually can be paralyzing. When agonizing clinical decisions have to be made, I have experienced how too much empathy can lead to overwhelming feelings of vulnerability and uncertainty. Nonetheless, I see how dangerous it can be to objectify patients so that, in my own clinical work, I constantly challenge myself to walk a tightrope between explaining and understanding—between distancing and empathy—recognizing always the liabilities of each.

While treatment decisions ostensibly are attempts to "control" the diseases to be treated, I have noticed an unconscious tendency for physicians to want to control patients themselves (the term "patient management" is common in biomedicine, and betrays this posture—I insist on the term "disease management," but recognize that this still involves a cooperative effort between physician and patient). When hospitalized and seriously ill, illusions of control of patients and their diseases are easier; in primary care outpatient settings, however, patient behavior is frustratingly difficult to predict, making attention to the psychosocial dimensions of patient care—the grist for a medical anthropologist's mill—essential.

I have discovered that work in biomedicine demands constant attention to other unspoken assumptions about the world, such as the *concept of time*, which is viewed differently in medical and academic anthropology settings. In the latter, time is one's own, and scholarship that results from working in relative isolation is expected and valued. Time is something that one can "control," as when a long-distance runner consciously sets an individual pace. In biomedicine, time is both a scarce commodity and a compelling force, in relation to which practitioners see themselves as out of control. In clinical settings one responds almost exclusively to demands from others, there is never enough time to meet all the demands, and it is impossible to predict when demands will be made. Although it seems trivial on the surface, one of the most frustrating aspects of working as an anthropologist in the biomedical world is seldom being able to enjoy conversations over meals, which invariably are eaten hurriedly for fear that one's beeper will go off at any moment.

Availability is another important core value in biomedical culture. Carrying a beeper is a symbolic statement that one is "always available": this is a powerful anxiety-allaying mechanism, reassuring all that help is always close when the inevitable emergencies occur. Although there are seldom emergencies demanding my involvement, I have found it imperative (albeit sometimes annoying) to adopt the "beeper mentality" that exists in biomedicine. Interestingly, my academic anthropology colleagues regularly questioned the presence of my beeper with derogatory suggestions that I was "playing doctor." The importance of availability in clinical settings is also symbolized in daily ritual activities in clinical settings: "making rounds" on patients starting at 7:00 AM, being "on call" at night, or working on holidays become rites of intensification that solidify group identity. I have found that I must be available to participate in such activities, even at onerous times, to remain an effective part of the group.

In individual physicians, the behavioral and attitudinal manifestations of therapeutic activism, positivism, affective neutrality, time pressure and expectations of availability are often expressed and/or perceived by outsiders as arrogance. Successful medical anthropologists must not be put off by such a posture in physician colleagues, but recognize it as a psychological defense against the uncertainties that attend patient care—something I truly believe most of my academic colleagues have never experienced (here, I recognize my own apparent arrogance!).

In truth, unspoken assumptions within biomedicine can and sometimes do have negative effects on clinical reasoning and decision making. Unless physicians can step back and examine these assumptions within biomedicine, there is very real likelihood that medical practice will become a compulsion to change patients, rather than an opportunity to help them. There is a danger that these unconscious assumptions of biomedicine will be a source of clinical distortion. Thus, in every patient care consultation, my goal is to get medical students and residents to understand themselves, and not simply help them explain their pa-tients' problems. My work is an attempt to help physicians become more genuine and flexible in their care of patients by better understanding the unconscious motivations and assumptions underlying their clinical activities.

37

Ritual in the Operating Room

Pearl Katz

Whether we recognize them or not, we are surrounded by rituals, only some of which are religious. Rituals provide a precise set of routine behaviors for performing certain tasks. Often they mark the beginning of some event (meals, sports) or stages in an ongoing process. Critical junctures in the life cycle, such as birth, adulthood, marriage, and death, are often marked by ritual. They may define a time or a place that is in some sense nonordinary and, as such, allows nonordinary behavior. Rituals produce cultural meaning by using symbols and symbolic behavior. We saw earlier how the Nacirema use ritual to express unconscious cultural ideas about the body and its tendency to degenerate.

The medical profession generally deals with the body rather than the soul. It cloaks itself with the most up-to-date scientific technologies. Most people would never associate medicine with something as "archaic" as ritual. Therefore, the following study of operating room procedure as ritual is particularly fascinating. Surprisingly, we find that ritual is an integral part of the efficient functioning of the operating room. As such, we wonder what other fields might be profitably analyzed from a ritual perspective, and, moreover, in what situations might we consciously introduce ritual to reduce risk and improve performance.

As you read this selection, ask yourself the following questions:

☐ What is the meaning of the term "ritual" as it is used in this selection?

☐ What are the similarities between the sacred and the profane, on the one hand, and the clean and the dirty, on the other?

☐ How do ritualized movements within the operating room maintain the separation of sterile and nonsterile people and objects?

☐ What are the three stages of operations, and what rituals are performed during each?

☐ As you come to understand the definition and function of rituals as described in this selection, can you identify other arenas—at home, at work, or at school—in which the ritualization of behavior functions in a fashion similar to that described here?

The following terms discussed in this selection are included in the Glossary at the back of the book:

pollution
ritual
symbols

From *Ethnology*, 1981. Reprinted by permission of *Ethnology*.

Ritual has been defined as standardized ceremonies in which expressive, symbolic, mystical, sacred, and nonrational behavior predominates over practical, technical, secular, rational, and scientific behavior, although anthropologists have acknowledged that rational, technical acts may occur as part of ritual behavior.

The analysis of ritual has assumed various forms. One is to investigate the meanings, types, and structures of the symbols used in rituals. Another is to examine the thought processes that occur in ritual, or how the actors believe in the effectiveness of the rituals, how the thoughts expressed in ritual reflect their social structure, and how thought processes in ritual compare with those in science. Another form of analysis of ritual focuses upon the structure and function of ritual in society. Van Gennup's pioneering work describes the ways in which rituals deal with movements of people through passages in time, place, and statuses, and distinctive phases. Gluckman shows how ritual may exaggerate the distinctions between different events enacted by the same people, and explained some means by which rituals masked conflicts by emphasizing solidarity. Douglas describes the ways in which rituals resolve anomaly by avoiding the dangers of pollution.

According to these studies of ritual, behavior in an operating room in a modern hospital would not be defined as ritual because it involves predominately technical, rational, and scientific activity. By relegating behavior in an operating room to a nonritual realm, the meanings of the symbols, movements, and thought processes they reveal are not likely to be subject to the same kinds of analyses as they would if they were termed ritual behavior. Even in Horton's provocative essay, in which he compares traditional and modern thought, traditional thought is conceived as magical, religious, and expressed in ritual; modern thought as secular, technical, and expressed in scientific activity. Although Horton emphasizes the similarities as well as the differences of these two kinds of thinking, he deliberately defines the two thinking styles as embedded in two separate and different contexts.

Recently, some anthropologists have acknowledged that secular ceremonies may be examined as rituals because they share the symbolic and communicative functions of rituals. In the same spirit this paper examines both ritual and science in one technical context, the hospital operating room. It describes behavior and thinking in the operating room in order to understand the functions of ritual in a scientific context. Specifically, it examines the functions and efficacy of sterility procedures.

Despite the elaborate rituals, and despite the rigorous application of advanced scientific knowledge in the operating room, infections do occur as a result of surgery. In the vast majority of cases the specific cause of these infections remains unknown. In the United States each year there are approximately two million postoperative infections, causing 79,000 deaths among surgical patients. This paper argues that the elaborate rituals and technical procedures of the modern hospital operating room, manifestly designed to prevent infection, better serve latent functions. Ritual actually contributes to the efficiency of a technical, goal-oriented, scientific activity, such as surgery, by permitting autonomy of action to the participants and enabling them to function in circumstances of ambiguity.

THE OPERATING ROOM

In most modern hospitals the surgical area is isolated from the rest of the hospital, and the operating room is further isolated from other parts of the surgical area. The surgical area may include dressing rooms, lounges, storage rooms, offices, and laboratories as well as operating rooms. Entrance to the surgical area is restricted to those people who are properly costumed and who are familiar with the rituals within. These include surgeons, anesthesiologists, pathologists, radiologists, operating room and recovery room nurses, student doctors, nurses, and ward orderlies who work in that area.[1] The major exception to these occupational roles is that of the surgical patient who, although costumed, is unfamiliar with the rituals. All of the people in the surgery area wear costumes which identify both their general role in the hospital, as well as denoting the specific areas within the surgical area which they are permitted to enter.

The restrictive entrance procedures and costume requirements contribute to the maintenance of cleanliness and prevention of contamination. Identification and separation of cleanliness and dirt are the most important concepts in the operating room. They govern the organization of the activities in surgery, the spatial organization of rooms and objects, the costumes worn, as well as most of the rituals.

The surgical area of University Hospital[2] has four parts: the periphery, outer, middle, and inner areas. Physical barriers separate these four areas. They function to prevent contamination from dirtier areas to cleaner ones. From outside to inside, these areas are differentiated according to increasing degrees of cleanliness. The periphery, the least clean area, includes the offices of the anesthesiologists, a small pathology laboratory for quick analyses of specimens, dressing rooms for men and women, and lounges for nurses and doctors. To enter the periphery area a person must wear a white jacket for identification as a member of the medical staff.

The outside area is separated from the periphery by a sliding door. Within the outer area, a nurse at the main desk can prevent the door from opening if an unauthorized person tries to enter. Entrance to the outer area is restricted to patients and to those medical personnel who wear blue or green costumes. The largest and most populated part of the outer area consists of an open corridor in which the daily operating schedule is posted and a blackboard indicating the current use of operating rooms. Patients awaiting surgery lie in narrow beds lined in a single row along one wall of the open corridor. A nurse, in charge of coordinating the timing and activities in each operating room, sits at an exposed desk in the outer area. She is in continual intercom communication with each operating room. The outer area also contains a large recovery room which houses patients immediately after their surgery is completed.

The middle area consists of three separate areas called "aseptic cores." Each aseptic core contains five doors. One of them links the outer area to the aseptic core. Each of the other four doors leads to an operating room. Each aseptic core contains a long sink, three sterilizing machines (autoclaves), and many carts and shelves containing surgical equipment, sheets, and towels. In order to enter an aseptic core, a person must wear a mask which covers the mouth and nose, coverings for shoes and for hair, and a blue or green outfit.

The innermost area contains the operating rooms and small laundry rooms. In each aseptic core there are four operating rooms and two laundry rooms. Each operating room contains three doors. One door adjoins the outer area and is used exclusively for the patient to enter and leave the operating room. A door with a small glass window connects the aseptic core to the operating room. This is used by the operating room staff. The third door leads to the laundry room which serves as a depository for contaminated clothing and instruments.

PREOPERATIVE RITUALS

One of the more important operating room rituals, scrubbing, takes place in the aseptic core before each operation begins. It is a procedure by which selected personnel wash their hands and lower arms according to rigidly prescribed timing and movements. The purpose of scrubbing is to remove as many bacteria as possible from the fingers, nails, hands, and arms to the elbows. The people who scrub are those who actually carry out, or directly assist in, the surgery; not everyone in the operating room scrubs. The surgeon, assistant surgeon(s), and the scrub nurse, participate in the scrubbing ritual. Medical students and other surgical assistants consider it an honor if they are asked to scrub with a surgeon.

Before a person begins scrubbing he checks the clock in order to time the seven-minute procedures. He turns on the water by pushing a button with his hip, and reaches for a package which contains a nail file, a brush and sponge which is saturated with an antiseptic solution. For two minutes he cleans under each of his nails with the nail file. For two-and-a-half minutes, he scrubs his fingers, hands and arms to his elbows, intermittently wetting the sponge and brush with running water. Using a circular motion he scrubs all of the surfaces of his fingers on one hand, his hand, and, finally, an arm to the elbow. After rinsing that arm thoroughly under running water, he repeats the procedure for two-and-a-half minutes on his second hand. After having scrubbed for seven minutes, he discards the sponge, brush, file, and paper and turns off the tap water by pressing a button on the sink with his hip.

After scrubbing, the surgeon and his assistant(s) enter the operating room by pushing the door with their hips. They hold their lower arms and hands in an upright position, away from the rest of their bodies. They are forbidden to allow their scrubbed hands and arms to come into contact with any object or person. The scrub nurse hands them a sterile towel to dry their hands. They dry each finger separately, and throw the towel into a container on the floor. The scrub nurse holds the outside, sterile part of a green gown for the surgeon and his assistant(s) to wear. They insert their hands through the sleeves, without allowing their hands to touch the outside of the gown. At this point, their hands, although scrubbed and clean, are not sterile. But the outside of the gown is sterile. After their arms pass through the sleeves, the scrub nurse holds their sterile gloves in place with the open side facing their hands. The surgeon, followed by his assistant, thrusts one hand at a time into each glove. They accomplish this in one quick movement, in which a hand is brought down from its upward position, thrust forward inside the glove and snapped in place over the sleeve. When only one glove is on, the surgeon is not permitted to adjust it with the other hand. However, when the second glove is on, he can adjust his glove and the sleeve of his gown and any other part of the front of the gown.

At this stage, the gown is not completely fastened. In order to fasten his gown, the surgeon unties a tie of his gown at waist level. Although this tie had been sterile, he hands it to the circulating nurse, who has not scrubbed. The circulating nurse brings the tie to the back of his gown. The back is a nonsterile area of the gown. The surgeon helps her reach the back by making a 360° turn, while she holds the tie. The circulating nurse secures this and two more ties to the back of the gown.

PRINCIPLES OF STERILITY AND CONTAMINATION

The rituals of scrubbing, gowning, and gloving suggest some basic principles underlaying most of the rituals in the operating room.

1. In the operating room, objects, or parts of objects and people, are classified either as sterile or nonsterile (S = sterile; NS = nonsterile);
   (a) Nonsterile objects are further classified as clean, dirty, or contaminated.
   (b) No part of the circulating nurse or the anesthesiologist is sterile.
   (c) Parts of the surgeon and the scrub nurse are sterile.

2. To remain sterile, sterile objects may only come into contact with other objects that are sterile (c = contact; > = remains, becomes, or is transformed into; therefore S c S > S).

3. To remain sterile, sterile objects may not come into contact with anything that is not sterile (~ = not; therefore, S ~ c NS > S).

4. Nonsterile objects may come into contact with other nonsterile objects, and both remain nonsterile (NS c NS > NS).

5. Sterile objects may be transformed into nonsterile by contact with objects which are nonsterile. This process is called contamination (S c NS > NS).

6. Contaminated objects can only be restored to sterility by either placing them in an autoclave for a specified period of time, or, in the case of a person's clothes, by discarding the contaminated clothes and replacing them with sterile clothes. If gloves become contaminated, rescrubbing for three minutes is required before replacing the gloves and the gown.

Before the operation begins, most sterile objects are either symbolized by the color green, or are in contact with an object colored green. Sterile instruments, for example, are placed upon a green towel which lies on a nonsterile tray. Although the green towel has been sterilized, it becomes contaminated at the bottom through contact with the nonsterile tray (S c NS > NS). The towel remains sterile at the top, however, and the sterile instruments laying on the top remain sterile (S c S > S).

The surgeon, his assistant(s), and the scrub nurse wear sterile gloves and a green or blue gown which is sterile in the front from the waist to the armpits. However, the gown is not sterile in the back nor above the armpits and below the waist in the front. That is why the surgeon unties the tie at the sterile side of his gown with his sterile gloves, and the circulating (nonsterile) nurse holds the tie without touching the surgeon's (sterile) gloves, and brings the tie toward the (nonsterile) back of the surgeon's gown. The sterile tie becomes contaminated when the circulating nurse's hand touches it. It remains contaminated because it is tied in the back of the surgeon's gown.

The potentials for manipulating the overhead light in the center of the operating room illustrate some principles of sterility and contamination. Before the operation begins, the scrub nurse places a sterile handle on the huge, movable, overhead light. This permits the light to be adjusted by the surgeon, his assistant(s), and the scrub nurse through contact with the sterile handle (S c S > S). The circulating nurse and anesthesiologist, however, are also able to manipulate the light by touching the nonsterile frame of the light (NS c NS > NS).

In order for a person to move to the other side of the person next to him, as the scrubbed members of the operating team stand next to the patient's table, a ritual must be enacted. The person making the move turns 360° in the direction of his move, allowing his back to face the back of his neighbor. This movement prevents his sterile front from coming into contact with his neighbor's nonsterile back (S ~ c NS > S). Instead, his nonsterile back only comes into contact with his neighbor's nonsterile back (NS c NS > NS).

Before the operation begins each member of the operating team is busily engaged in activities that are essentially similar for each operation. The surgeon and his assistant(s) gown and glove and check last-minute details about the forthcoming operation. The anesthesiologist checks his tools, his gas supply, and his respirator. He also prepares the instruments for monitoring the patient's vital functions, and prepares the patient for receiving anaesthesia. In the outer area, a nurse checks to insure that the patient is properly identified and his operative site is verified. She independently checks the preoperative instructions written by the surgeon with the administrative order written when the surgery was booked, and asks the surgeon to identify the proposed operation and the precise site of the operation. Finally, she asks the patient to identify his name and the site of the operation.

Within the operating room, the words, "clean," "dirty," "sterile," and "contaminated" assume different meanings according to different stages of the operation. Before the operation begins, the operating room is considered to be clean. Dirty objects have been removed or cleaned. Instruments and clothes which have been contaminated by the previous operation have been removed. Floors, walls, permanent fixtures, and furniture have been cleaned with antiseptic solution. The air in the operating room is continually cleaned during, and between, operations by a filter system.

Fields of sterility and cleanliness within the operating room are mapped out. Everyone in the operating room, with the exception of the patient, is knowledgeable about these fields. Some of the fields, such as that surrounding the patient, are invisible. Other fields are distinguished by the use of sterile paper sheets colored green. The sheets provide only a minimal material barrier against airborne bacteria yet serve as a symbolic shield separating fields of sterility and nonsterility. They are also used to isolate the operative area of the body from the rest of the patient's body. The sheets cover the entire body of the patient leaving a small opening for the operative area, or separate the head end of the patient from the rest of his body. The head end is considered nonsterile and is accessible to the anesthesiologist and his equipment, which are also nonsterile.

After the patient is rendered unconscious by the anesthesiologist, the scrub nurse applies an orange-brown antiseptic solution (Providine) onto the patient's skin. She pours the Providine liberally onto the skin, and distributes it with circular movements radiating outward from the center of the operative site. This action is repeated at least once, using a sterile sponge on a long holder which is discarded and replaced with each action. The sterile sponges become contaminated through contact with the patient's non-sterile skin (S c NS > NS). This action, which transforms the sterile sponge into a contaminated sponge, also transforms the dirty body area of the patient into a clean area. When this act is completed, sterile green paper towels are placed on the patient's body, exposing only his aseptic, painted, operative site.

Before the operation begins both nurses lay out and count all the sterile instruments and sponges that are likely to be used. The circulating nurse obtains articles from their nonsterile storage place. When the outside of sealed packages is nonsterile and contains sterile objects inside, the circulating nurse holds the outside of the package. She either thrusts the objects onto a green sterile towel, or asks the scrub nurse to grasp the sterile object by reaching down into the package and lifting the object upwards, with a straight, quick movement. These procedures are followed for each sterile needle, thread, or vial that is wrapped in a nonsterile wrapping in order to prevent contamination of sterile parts by the nonsterile parts of the same package. The two nurses also simultaneously count items that are laid out for use during surgery. The circulating nurse records the amounts of each item that is counted. Each item must be accounted for before the operation is completed, and the last count must concur with the total of the previous counts.

Different operations are classified according to the degree of sterility and contamination likely to be present. At University Hospital there are four categories of operations classified according to decreasing sterility: (1) clean; (2) clean contaminated; (3) contaminated; and (4) dirty. Eye operations, for example, are clean. Most gall bladder operations are clean contaminated. Duodenal operations are contaminated. Colonic operations are dirty. Intestinal operations are considered dirtier than many other operations because the contents of the intestines are highly contaminated with bacteria, requiring additional measurements for vigilance against contamination during the operation. Ritual during most operations is concerned with avoidance of contamination of the patient from the outside. Ritual in operations which are classified as contaminated or dirty are concerned, in addition, with contamination of the patient and the medical staff from inside the patient.

After the completion of dirty operations, the medical staff is required to discard all their outside garments before leaving the operating room. Since the unscrubbed members of the operating team wear only one set of clothing, before the operation they don an additional white, clean, nonsterile gown over their green or blue costume. After the operation is completed they discard the gown.

THE OPERATION

Although extensive variation exists among types of operations, as well as variations among the medical conditions of patients, there is, nevertheless, considerable similarity in the structure of all operations. Operations contain three distinct stages. Specific rituals are performed during these stages. Stage One consists of the incision, or opening. Stage Two consists of the excision and repair. Stage Three consists of the closure.[3]

The operation begins after the anaesthetized patient is draped, all sterilized instruments are counted and placed in orderly rows upon trays, and the nurses and doctors, wearing their appropriate costumes, are standing in their specified places. The anesthesiologist stands behind the green curtain at the head of the patient, outside of the sterile field. The surgeon stands next to the operative site, on one side of the patient. His assistant usually stands on the opposite side of the patient from that of the surgeon. The scrub nurse stands next to the surgeon, with the pole of an instrument tray between them. The instrument tray is suspended over the patient's body. The circulating nurse stands outside of the sterile field, near the outer part of the operating room.

Silence and tension prevail as the first stage of the operation begins. With a sterile scalpel, the surgeon makes the first incision through the layers of the patient's skin, then discards the scalpel in a sterile basin. He has transformed both the scalpel and the basin from sterile to nonsterile. The transformation takes place because the sterile scalpel touches the patient's nonsterile skin. (The patient's skin, although cleaned with an antiseptic, is not sterile.) The scalpel, which has become nonsterile (S c NS > NS), touches the sterile basin and contaminates the basin (NS c S > NS). The surgeon uses another sterile scalpel to cut through the remaining layers of fat, fascia, muscle, and, in an abdominal operation, the peritoneum. The same scalpel may be used for all the layers underlying the skin because, unlike the contaminated skin, these layers are considered to be sterile.

As the surgeon cuts, he or his assistant cauterizes or ties the severed blood vessels. The patient's blood is considered sterile once the operation has begun. Before the operation, however, the patient's blood is considered to be nonsterile. This was illustrated graphically at University Hospital before a particular emergency operation in which a patient was bleeding externally from an internal hemorrhage. The nurses complained about "the man who is dirtying our clean room!" However, once the operation on this man began, his blood was considered sterile. Sterile instruments which touched his blood during the operation remained sterile (S c S > S) until contaminated by touching something nonsterile.

The rituals enacted during the first stage of the operation involve the transformation of objects defined as sterile and nonsterile, at the same time that the appropriate instruments are made accessible and are being used to make the incisions. The beginning of the first stage, in which the first incision is made, introduces new definitions of sterile and nonsterile. For example, the patient's blood and internal organs, which had been considered nonsterile before the operation, are considered sterile once the operation begins. (The surgeon's blood, however, remains nonsterile.) The patient's skin, although cleansed with antiseptic before the operation, becomes nonsterile once the operation begins and the incision is made. The rituals also enforce the segregation of the sterile and nonsterile objects while the initial incisions are being made. The surgeon typically utters terse commands, usually stating the specific names of the instrument he needs. The

scrub nurse immediately places the requested instrument securely in the palm of the surgeon's hand. If the instrument remains clean, the surgeon returns it to the scrub nurse and the scrub nurse places it upon the sterile tray. If it becomes contaminated, as occurs to the skin scalpel after the first incision, the surgeon places it into a container which could only be handled by the circulating nurse.

As the technical tasks become routinized during the first stage of the operation, joking begins. Most of the joking at this stage revolves around the operative procedures which are to be carried out during the next stage: "I can't wait to get my hands on your gallbladder, Mr. Smith." "Okay, sports fans, we're going to have some action." The first stage of the operation ends when the first incision has been completed and the organs are exposed. The joking abruptly ends just as the second stage of the operation is about to begin.

The second stage of the operation consists either of repair, implantation or the isolation and excision of the organ, and the anastomosis. (An anastomosis is the connection of two parts of the body which are not normally connected.) This stage contains the greatest amount of tension of the entire operation, and adherence to ritual is strictly enforced. It begins with the identification and isolation of structures surrounding the organ to be excised. The surgeon identifies vessels, nerves, ducts, and connective tissues, carefully pulling them aside, and preserving, clamping, severing, or tying them. The surgeon utters abrupt, abbreviated commands for instruments to be passed by the scrub nurse, structures to be cut by the assistant(s), basins and materials to be readied by the circulating nurse, and the operating table to be adjusted by the anesthesiologist. These people respond to the surgeon's commands quickly, quietly, and efficiently. A delayed, or an incorrect, response may be met with noticeable disapproval from the others.

During the second stage of the operation many of the classifications of sterility differ from those of the first stage. In a cholecystectomy (gallbladder removal), for example, the gallbladder is considered to be nonsterile before the operation begins. Yet during the first and second stages the gallbladder is considered to be sterile, before it is severed. Once it is severed, however, although it is considered to be clean, it transforms to nonsterile. It is placed in a sterile container, but the container becomes contaminated by its contact with the nonsterile gallbladder (S c NS > NS). Because it is nonsterile after it has been removed, it can only be handled by a nonsterile person such as the circulating nurse. But, since the gallbladder is clean and must be examined, it must not be further contaminated from sources outside of the patient. To prevent further contamination, the circulating nurse wears a sterile glove over her nonsterile hand to examine the gallbladder and its contents. The gallbladder is not sterile, but it is not grossly contaminated. It is clean, but nonsterile. It is avoided by the sterile members of the team, yet only touched by the nonsterile members if they wear sterile gloves. The ritual surrounding its removal and examination is complex, and the removed organ is avoided by most members of the operating team because its classification is ambiguous.

Once the gallbladder has been removed, x-rays of its ducts (which remain inside the patient) are taken to determine if gallstones remain. A masked, gowned and lead-shielded radiologist enters the operating room with a large x-ray machine that is draped with green sterile sheets. The surgeon injects a radio-opaque dye into the ducts, and everyone, except the radiologist, leaves the room to avoid the invisible x-rays. When the x-rays have been taken, the radiologist and the machine exit, the staff enter, and the operation proceeds.

Although unexpected events may occur at any stage of the operation, they are more likely to occur at the second stage because this stage contains the greatest trauma to the patient's body. If a sudden hemorrhage or a cardiac arrest occurs, the rituals segregating sterile from nonsterile may be held in abeyance, and new rituals designed to control the unanticipated event take over. If, for example, hemorrhaging occurs, all efforts are dedicated to locating and stopping the source of the hemorrhage and replacing the blood that is lost. Even though immediate replacement of blood is required, rituals are enacted which delay the replacement, yet ensure accurate matching. The anesthesiologist and the circulating nurse independently check, recheck, record and announce the blood type, the number and date of the blood bank supply and the operating room request. They glue stickers onto the patient's record and onto the blood bank record. This complex ritual involves repetition, separation and matching records before the blood is transfused into the hemorrhaging patient.

If a patient's heart ceases beating, a prescribed ritual is enacted by a cardiac-arrest team, whose members enter the operating room with a mobile cart, and enact prescribed procedures to resuscitate the patient. Considerations of preserving the separation of sterility and nonsterility (including most of the rituals previously described) are ignored while this emergency ritual is enacted.

Tension remains high throughout the second stage of the operation. There is virtually no joking or small talk. As the remaining internal structures are repaired and restored in place, some of the tension is lifted, and the routinization of rituals continues. The second stage of the operation ends when all the adjustments to the internal organs are finished and only the suturing of the protective layers for the third stage remains.

The third stage of the operation begins with the final counting of the materials used in surgery. Both nurses engage in this ritual of counting. They simultaneously orally count all the remaining materials, including tools, needles, and sponges. The circulating nurse checks the oral count with her written tally of materials recorded at the beginning of the operation. When the circulating nurse has accounted for each item, she informs the surgeon that he may begin the closing.

The rituals enacted during this stage of the operation are similar to those enacted during the first stage. The surgeon, or his assistant(s), requests specific needles and sutures from the nurses. They sew the patient closed, layer by layer, beginning with the inside layer. Although careful suturing is an essential part of the operation, this stage is enacted in a comparatively casual manner. There is considerably less tension than there was during the second stage, and greater toleration for deviations from the rituals. Questions about the procedures are acknowledged and answered. Minor mistakes may be overlooked. If the surgeon touched his nonsterile mask with his sterile glove during this part of the operation, he would be less likely to reglove and regown than he would if the same incident had occurred during the second stage.

The silence of the second stage is replaced in the third stage by considerable talking, including jokes and small talk. Most of the joking revolves around events which occurred during the second stage and references are made to actual or potential danger during this stage. "I thought he'd never stop bleeding." "You almost choperated [sic] his spleen by mistake." "Well, I hope he has good term life insurance." Much of the small talk revolves around future activities of the medical staff. The subject of small talk rarely relates to the patient. It may involve the next operation, lunch plans, or sports results.

When the closure has been completed, the surgeon signals to the anesthesiologist to waken the patient. The staff members finish recording information, transport the patient to the recovery room, and prepare for the next case. The operation is finished.

DISCONTINUITY AND OPERATING ROOM RITUALS

The observed rituals help to establish the operating room as a separate place, discontinuous from its surroundings. They also help to establish and define categories of appropriate and inappropriate behavior. This includes indicating behavior categories and their limits.

The rituals in the operating room and the meanings of many of the words used there are exclusive to that setting. The observed rituals express beliefs and values which are exclusive to the operating room. The use of the words "clean," "dirty," "contaminated" in the operating room do not correspond to their use elsewhere. This indicates the existence of discontinuity between the operating room and the outside. Discontinuity between the operating room and the outside is also reflected in the restricted entrances, the specific costumes required for entrance, the special language used, the classification and segregation of objects into sterile and nonsterile, and the dispassionate emotional reactions to parts of the human body. A person can be prohibited from entering the operating room if he were not properly dressed, if he transgressed the rules for segregating sterile from nonsterile, and he did not behave in a dispassionate manner upon viewing or touching parts of the body.

The boundaries which separate the operating room from the outside contribute to a particular mental set for the participants, which enables them to participate in a dispassionate manner in activities they would ordinarily view with strong emotion. For example, in the operating room, they look dispassionately upon, and touch internal organs and their secretions, blood, pus, and feces. Outside of the operating room context, these same objects provoke emotions of embarrassment, fear, fascination and disgust in the same persons. Discontinuity was illustrated during a movie shown to the surgeons outside of the surgical area of the hospital. The film illustrated different techniques for draining and lancing pus-filled abscesses. The reactions observed for the surgeons watching this movie were unlike any reactions observed for the same surgeons while they drained abscesses in the operating room. They uttered comments and noises indicating their disgust. They looked away from the screen. Outside of the context of the operating room, with its rituals and its isolation, the same events are experienced differently. In the operating room a purulent lesion is mentally linked to the rituals that are enacted during the act of lancing. The image of the lesion is embedded in the entire operating room context, including the ritual prescriptions for managing that lesion and for organizing the behavior of others in the room. In contrast, outside of the operating room, the image of the lesion is embedded in images of everyday life. In that context, the reaction to the lesion is one of disgust. Outside of the operating room there are no rituals to diffuse their concentration. Moreover, sitting in a dark-

ened room, watching a movie, the viewers are forced to focus on the picture of the lesion. The only opportunity they have to diffuse their focus is to look away, or to make noises indicating their disgust. The operating room, with its focus upon precise rituals, permits diffusion of emotions and encourages discontinuity from everyday life.

The different stages of an operation express discontinuity of mental sets. For example, blood, internal organs, feces, and skin are classified differently during different stages of the operation, and some are different outside of the operating room. For each of the parts of the body—the patient's washed skin, gallbladder, colon, feces, blood, and the surgeon's blood—the greatest transformation of dirty and clean categories occurs before the first stage of the operation (incision) and between the second and third stage (the excision and closure). For example, the patient's blood is considered to be dirty outside of the operating room, yet is considered to be clean during the first and second stages of the operation. But during the third stage, blood is again classified as dirty. Similarly, the patient's skin, after having been thoroughly cleaned with antiseptic, is considered extremely clean outside of the operating room. However, once the operation begins, the patient's skin is classified as "dirty." It remains dirty for the first and second stages of the operation. Once closure takes place, during the third stage, the patient's skin is transformed again to "clean."

Rituals exaggerate the discontinuity in the operating room and they proclaim definite categories. An instrument is either sterile or nonsterile; it is never almost sterile or mostly sterile. A person is either scrubbed, gowned, and gloved, and, therefore, sterile, or he is not scrubbed, gowned, or gloved, and, therefore, not sterile. An operation is either in Stage One, Two, or Three, or it has not yet begun, or it has ended.

Rituals in the operating room are prescribed for four different kinds of situations: (1) passing through the three stages of surgery, (2) managing unanticipated events, such as cardiac arrest or sudden hemorrhaging, (3) matching information, such as blood types, operative sites or instrument counts, and (4) separating sterile from nonsterile objects. In each of these situations there exists a potential confusion about the appropriate classification of events. There is danger that objects and events can be confused or indistinct or there is danger of contact of forbidden categories: blood may not be properly matched; the wrong operative site may be selected; an instrument may remain in the patient's body; objects or events may not match or fit; or sterile objects may touch nonsterile ones. For those situations in which behavior categories are not clear, rituals clarify. In a recent textbook for operating room nurses, more than one hundred prescriptions for precise behavior are spelled out in which confusion existed about definitions of categories. At University Hospital, the head operating room nurse claimed that the rituals performed in the operating room "were introduced in response to actual mistakes, problems, conflicts that we had, when how to behave was not clearly spelled out." Rituals in the operating room not only indicate the categories which are potentially confusing, they also indicate the boundaries, or limits, for these categories. Through the use of rituals it is clear to all the participants when Stage One ends and Stage Two begins. It is clear to them which part of the surgeon's body is sterile (between the armpits and waist in front) and which part is not sterile (the remainder). Rituals, then, make salient, and even exaggerate, the boundaries of categories.

Rituals in the operating room have much in common with rituals in other contexts, sacred or secular. Rituals are enacted during periods of transition. In the operating room they are enacted during transitions of events or classifications of objects. Danger is perceived during these periods of transitions. Indeed, Van Gennep emphasizes the dangers which lie in transitional states because the classification of neither state is clear. When states are not clearly defined, ritual controls the danger. Similarly Douglas (1966) claims that pollution behavior takes place when categories are confused, or when accepted categories are not adhered to, as in anomaly.

Beyond the operating room, rituals also indicate categories and limits or boundaries for these categories. These include rituals which define passages— of time, seasons, stages of life, or passages through different lands—as well as rituals of pollution. Rituals proclaim that something is in one category and not in another. One is an adult, not a child. It is the rainy season, not the dry season. We are in the new land, not the old land. I belong to this kinship group now, not that group. Even the middle, liminal stage of ritual, which Turner describes as a kind of limbo, has limits. Although the middle state is neither incorporated into the first stage, nor reintegrated into the last stage, its boundaries are clearly recognized and known to all the participants.

In all societies rituals take place when categories are not clearly defined and when limits of categories are not known. Gluckman suggests, for example, that primitive societies have more rituals than modern societies because different roles are enacted with the same people in primitive societies. This may be understood as exaggerating the boundaries or limits of each of their roles, precisely because they are unclear. Indeed, ritual is found in modern secular society in those situations in which boundaries are unclear, not only during changes of status, such as marriages and

deaths, but also in situations such as entering or leaving a house, installing a political officer, and beginning a team sport.

The operating room observations suggest that through its elaborate, stylized behavioral prescriptions and obsession with detail, ritual exaggerates the boundaries between categories. Rituals create boundaries because boundaries have been transgressed or are unclear. When boundaries are not precisely defined, confusion may result about which category is operative at a particular time or place. The actors do not know to which situation to respond. Knowing the limits or boundaries gives shape and definition to the categories. Ritual by defining categories and prescribing specific behavior within these categories, creates boundaries. Moreover, when the boundaries are known, autonomy to function can increase.

AUTONOMY AND RITUAL

At first glance, it seems improbable that ritual, with its emphasis upon specific detailed prescriptions for behavior, may provide autonomy for its participants. To be sure, it is known that ritual exaggerates and often provides license for behavior which may be prohibited in everyday life. Studies by Katz suggest that autonomy increases when the limits of the system are known and implemented. On this basis one will expect that ritual, by indicating and clarifying boundaries of behavior categories—such as sterile/nonsterile or child/adult—increase the autonomy of the participants. Conversely, when the rituals have not been fully carried out—when a person is not clearly within the prescribed limits—there will be very little autonomy.

For example, when the surgeon enters the operating room after he has scrubbed, but before he has gowned and gloved, he is helpless. He has virtually no autonomy. His scrubbed, clean hands are not clearly classified as sterile, nor as contaminated (although strictly speaking, they are nonsterile). He has to exercise extreme caution lest his hands touch anything. If he touches a sterile object, that object becomes contaminated. If he touches a contaminated object, his hands become further contaminated, and he is required to rescrub. He is so helpless that he can do almost nothing. His hands are raised in a helpless position. He depends upon a nurse to give him a towel and to provide him with a gown and gloves. He is not able to put the gown on himself, nor to tie his gown once it is on. Even when he is gowned, he has no autonomy to touch anything. He cannot pull the sleeve of the gown from his hands. The nurse has to put his gloves on his hands for him. His classification of sterility is confusing because, being half sterile and half nonsterile, he does not clearly fit in either category. His autonomy is severely restricted. The autonomy of others interacting with him is also reduced. Only after he has completely scrubbed, gowned, and gloved, and become unequivocally sterile, does he attain his autonomy. He can move about within the sterile field and touch all sterile objects.

In the operating room, boundaries of categories are likely to become confused if a person is present who does not know the appropriate rituals. When this occurs, autonomy decreases, both for the uninitiated person, and for others who interact with him. On one occasion during surgery in University Hospital, the circulating nurse requested a scrubbed medical student to remove a sterile needle from the nonsterile wrapping which she held in her hand. Although the student knew that the wrapping was nonsterile and the needle was sterile, and he was familiar with many rituals, he did not know the precise ritual required for removing the needle. The ritual required him to grasp the needle between his forefinger and thumb, quickly thrust his fingers upwards, and place the needle upon the sterile tray. The circulating nurse was required to pull downward on the wrapping, discard the wrapping in a contaminated bag, and record the addition of that needle. Neither person had autonomy to deviate from this behavior.

The student succeeded in contaminating his glove and the needle by touching both with the nonsterile wrapping. A great deal of autonomy was lost through his failure to follow the prescribed ritual. The student had to reglove and regown. The circulating nurse had to aid him in regloving and regowning. The needle had to be discarded. Since the needle had contaminated the sterile green towel on the tray, the towel had to be replaced, the sterile contents of the tray removed from the contaminated towel and replaced on the sterile towel. In addition, the circulating nurse had mistakenly recorded the addition of that needle, and, near the end of the operation, it appeared that a needle was missing. All the people present searched for the needle, both inside and outside the patient. This activity delayed the completion of the operation until the circulating nurse realized the source of the mismatching. In this case, the autonomy of most of the staff was restricted because one person did not follow the ritual properly.

The surgical patient who is awake can reduce the autonomy of the operating team. The conscious patient has autonomy to express his fears and concerns about the operation. Most members of the medical staff in the operating room regard the waking patient as a hindrance to the smooth performance of preoperative rituals. The waking patient may restrict discus-

sions which are necessary for planning the strategy of the operation. Rendering the patient unconscious deprives the patient of all autonomy, while increasing the autonomy of the staff. The staff gains the autonomy to ignore the patient's psyche, to consider only the parts of his body relevant to the operative procedure, to joke about the patient and his expressions of fear, and to discuss subjects that have nothing to do with the operation. Although the patient loses autonomy, the staff gains autonomy.

It is well known to most laymen that irreverent behavior in the form of jokes and small talk occurs in the operating room. Jokes and small talk in the operating room represent autonomous behavior *par excellence*. They are autonomous because they are not a prescribed part of the operative procedure. They often express values which are antithetical to the serious and dangerous nature of the operation itself. Jokes differ from small talk in that jokes explicitly focus on events of surgery (whether real or imagined), whereas small talk revolves around events unrelated to surgery. Both jokes and small talk trivialize the solemnity, significance, discipline and danger that typically accompany surgery. Although the precise content of jokes and small talk in the operating room is unpredictable, their timing is. They are not expressed while transitions take place—when stages are crossed, transformations from sterile to nonsterile occur, or when mismatching or emergencies occur. During transitions danger is often perceived to be present. All attention becomes focused on the rituals which are enacted to restore the boundaries. Jokes and small talk are expressed during those periods in which categories—of stages, sterility, or matching—are clearly defined. They occur when ritual succeeds in restoring and bounding these categories, and activities are routinized. Once the boundaries have been restored by ritual, autonomy flourishes. When rituals are enacted routinely, the boundaries are defined and autonomy increased.

Jokes and small talk do not occur during periods of transition, when danger is present, although they express concern about these periods. Jokes are not expressed during the times that autonomy is most severely restricted, such as during the transitions. Autonomous behavior of joking and small talk occur after the transitions pass, after the tension subsides, after the rituals have been enacted in their carefully prescribed manner.

Most of the jokes focus on events which occur during transitional or dangerous periods. Jokes about organs to be severed do not occur during the dangerous period while the organ is being severed. Jokes about the incision do not occur while the incision is being made. Jokes about the incision only occur before or after the incision is made. When jokes touched on dangerous or transitional situations, they did so only after rituals had clearly indicated that the situation was over. Only then did the surgical staff make irreverent jokes about the most dangerous and vulnerable aspects of the operation. They made jokes in the crudest terms about internal organs, external appearances, sexual organs, the personality of the patient, or other members of the operating team. But they did not joke about the rituals themselves. The operating room staff treated the rituals with reverence and less questioning than other surgical activities.

Many anthropologists have tried to understand the simultaneous presence of both controlling and autonomous aspects of ritual. Van Gennup and later Firth emphasized the controlling and regulating function of ritual. Munn describes how ritual myths function as social control mechanisms by regulating states and bodily feelings. Turner describes the presence of elaborate autonomous improvisation within highly structured ritual. Leach suggests that stylization in secular ritual may be either "escetic, representing the intensification of formal restraint, or ecstatic, signifying the elimination of restraint." Gluckman describes license in rituals as reversals that express behavior outlawed in everyday life. Gluckman also recognizes that license is only permitted in ritual when the limits are known and agreed upon by the participants: "The acceptance of the established order as right and good, and even sacred, seems to allow unbridled license, very rituals of rebellion, for the order itself keeps this rebellion within bounds."

The rituals in the operating room, as well as those described by Gluckman, Leach, and Turner, suggest that the boundaries of behavior are not open to questioning. They are firm. However, within those boundaries there is a great deal of autonomy. In the operating room, the rituals themselves, as signposts indicating boundaries, are not open to question, nor to ridicule. However, within the boundaries considerable autonomy exists. There is autonomy to joke about everything, except the rituals. There is autonomy to question details about the rituals (e.g., how long to scrub), but virtually no autonomy to question the ritual itself (e.g., whether scrubbing was necessary).

CONCLUSION

In modern operating rooms rituals, as stylized, arbitrary, repetitive and exaggerated forms of behavior, occur as integral parts of surgical procedures. Most of the rituals in the operating room symbolize separation of areas containing micro-organisms from areas free of micro-organisms, or separation of realms of cleanliness (sterility, asepsis) from realms of pollution (nonsterility, sepsis, contamination).

Most rituals considered by anthropologists, especially those in sacred settings, express and communicate values, and are linked to institutions of everyday life. Such rituals are amenable to serious questioning of their major premises. It is different, however, with rituals in the hospital operating room. That setting is discontinuous with everyday life, and rituals there have no continuity with values or categories of thought outside of the medical setting. Inspection and introspection of their premises are thereby discouraged or overlooked, but nonetheless neglected. It is through the examination of rituals in extraordinary settings, whether in traditional or modern contexts, that we can become aware of some of the functions of rituals that, heretofore, have largely gone unrecognized in the anthropological literature. The study of the hospital operating room suggests that ritual defines categories and clarifies boundaries between important states by exaggerating the differences between them, doing so precisely where the boundaries normally are not clear and well-defined. It is then that rituals are enacted in order to avoid the confusion that may result when it is uncertain which categories are operative at a particular time.

By imposing exaggerated definitions upon categories, rituals also serve to increase the autonomy of the participants by providing them with an unambiguous understanding of precisely which categories are operative at a certain time. Without the boundaries provided by rituals, participants do not know to which situation to respond. When boundaries are known, autonomy is increased. Extreme license in ritual is an expression of this. In the operating room irreverent joking, as an example, is only possible after the ritual has succeeded in establishing a boundary between indistinct states. Autonomy is limited, and reverence and awe prevail during transitional states of ritual, when boundaries are not yet firm. When indistinct categories are ritually separated and given sharp definition, ambiguity of behavior is lowered and autonomy enhanced.

NOTES

1. Occasionally others, such as salesmen or filmmakers, are allowed in parts of the surgical area. I was allowed free access to all surgical areas at all times, which included scrubbing and standing next to the surgeons and patient during surgery.
2. University Hospital is a pseudonym for a hospital in North America affiliated with a medical school.
3. The stages are heuristic. I have not encountered surgeons nor surgery texts which describe three distinct stages.

38

AIDS as Human Suffering

Paul Farmer and Arthur Kleinman

Our environment is constantly changing, and the necessity of adapting to environmental change is a fundamental challenge for every species. Often, when people think of the "environment," they envision trees, mountains, water, and animals. Few people think of invisible life forms, like bacteria and viruses, as part of our environment—but they are. Disease organisms themselves are constantly changing, and the kinds of diseases that afflict a social group are largely determined by their ecology and culture.

In the last decade, humans have been faced by the challenge of a new virus (HIV) causing a lethal disease—acquired immune deficiency syndrome (AIDS)—that has spread throughout the world. In the United States we tend to think of AIDS as a disease that affects "risk groups" like gay men and intravenous drug users. But on a global basis, an estimated three quarters of AIDS sufferers contracted the HIV virus through heterosexual intercourse. In the United States, much of the public discussion about AIDS reflects moral judgments about people's lifestyles and places the blame for the disease on the sufferers. For people with AIDS, such cultural attitudes and stigmatization significantly compound their suffering.

In this selection, we see that social reactions to AIDS vary between cultures. The cross-cultural comparison of Robert and Anita, both dying from AIDS but in very different settings, has much to tell us about the cultures themselves. In this selection, two prominent medical anthropologists make the case that on a human plane the way that we think about AIDS and its victims compounds the suffering and tragedy of this epidemic.

In the history of this epidemic, anthropologists have played a role in describing and understanding the behavioral practices related to the transmission of the HIV virus. The biomedical challenge of AIDS is very large, but the challenge of coping with the human dimensions of AIDS is enormous, requiring both compassion and cross-cultural understanding.

As you read this selection, ask yourself the following questions:

☐ How might culture be a factor in the distribution of a disease (that is, in determining who gets the disease and who doesn't)?

☐ What are the main ways in which the deaths of Robert and Anita were different? How do those differences reflect cultural values?

☐ What are some practical suggestions for reducing the human suffering caused by AIDS?

☐ How is the cost of AIDS different between the United States and Third World countries?

The following terms discussed in this selection are included in the Glossary at the back of the book:

AIDS
cultural values
HIV
lexicon
medical anthropology
SIDA
stigma

"AIDS as Human Suffering" reprinted by permission of *Daedalus*, Journal of the American Academy of Arts and Sciences, from the issue entitled, "Living with AIDS," Spring 1989, Vol. 118, No. 2.

That the dominant discourse on AIDS at the close of the twentieth century is in the rational-technical language of disease control was certainly to be expected and even necessary. We anticipate hearing a great deal about the molecular biology of the virus, the clinical epidemiology of the disease's course, and the pharmacological engineering of effective treatments. Other of contemporary society's key idioms for describing life's troubles also express our reaction to AIDS: the political-economic talk of public-policy experts, the social-welfare jargon of the politicians and bureaucrats, and the latest psychological terminology of mental-health professionals. Beneath the action-oriented verbs and reassuringly new nouns of these experts' distancing terminology, the more earthy, emotional rumblings of the frightened, the accusatory, the hate-filled, and the confused members of the public are reminders that our response to AIDS emerges from deep and dividing forces in our experience and our culture.

AIDS AND HUMAN MEANINGS

Listen to the words of persons with AIDS and others affected by our society's reaction to the new syndrome:

- "I'm 42 years old. I have AIDS. I have no job. I do get $300 a month from social security and the state. I will soon receive $64 a month in food stamps. I am severely depressed. I cannot live on $300 a month. After $120 a month for rent and $120 a month for therapy, I am left with $60 for food and vitamins and other doctors and maybe acupuncture treatments and my share of utilities and oil and wood for heat. I'm sure I've forgotten several expenses like a movie once in a while and a newspaper and a book."[1]

- "I don't know what my life expectancy is going to be, but I certainly know the quality has improved. I know that not accepting the shame or the guilt or the stigma that people would throw on me has certainly extended my life expectancy. I know that being very up-front with my friends, and my family and coworkers, reduced a tremendous amount of stress, and I would encourage people to be very open with friends, and if they can't handle it, then that's their problem and they're going to have to cope with it."

- "Here we are at an international AIDS conference. Yesterday a woman came up to me and said, 'May I have two minutes of your time?' She said, 'I'm asking doctors how they feel about treating AIDS patients.' And I said, 'Well, actu-

ally I'm not a doctor. I'm an AIDS patient,' and as she was shaking hands, her hand whipped away, she took two steps backward, and the look of horror on her face was absolutely diabolical."

- "My wife and I have lived here [in the United States] for fifteen years, and we speak English well, and I do O.K. driving. But the hardest time I've had in all my life, harder than Haiti, was when people would refuse to get in my cab when they discovered I was from Haiti [and therefore in their minds, a potential carrier of HIV]. It got so we would pretend to be from somewhere else, which is the worst thing you can do, I think."

All illnesses are metaphors. They absorb and radiate the personalities and social conditions of those who experience symptoms and treatments. Only a few illnesses, however, carry such cultural salience that they become icons of the times. Like tuberculosis in *fin de siècle* Europe, like cancer in the first half of the American century, and like leprosy from Leviticus to the present, AIDS speaks of the menace and losses of the times. It marks the sick person, encasing the afflicted in an exoskeleton of peculiarly powerful meanings: the terror of a lingering and untimely death, the panic of contagion, the guilt of "self-earned" illness.

AIDS has offered a new idiom for old gripes. We have used it to blame others: gay men, drug addicts, inner-city ethnics, Haitians, Africans. And we in the United States have, in turn, been accused of spreading and even creating the virus that causes AIDS. The steady progression of persons with AIDS toward the grave, so often via the poor house, has assaulted the comforting idea that risk can be managed. The world turns out to be less controllable and more dangerous, life more fragile than our insurance and welfare models pretend. We have relegated the threat of having to endure irremediable pain and early death—indeed, the very image of suffering as the paramount reality of daily existence—to past periods in history and to other, poorer societies. Optimism has its place in the scale of American virtues; stoicism and resignation in the face of unremitting hardship—unnecessary character traits in a land of plenty—do not. Suffering had almost vanished from public and private images of our society.

Throughout history and across cultures, life-threatening disorders have provoked questions of control (What do we do?) and bafflement (Why me?). When bubonic plague depopulated fourteenth-century Europe by perhaps as many as half to three-fourths of the population, the black death was construed as a religious problem and a challenge to the moral authority as much or even more than as a public-health problem. In the late twentieth century, it is not surprising that great advances in scientific knowledge and technological intervention have created our chief responses to questions of control and bafflement. Yet bafflement is not driven away by the advance of scientific knowledge, for it points to another aspect of the experience of persons with AIDS that has not received the attention it warrants. It points to a concern that in other periods and in other cultures is at the very center of the societal reaction to dread disease, a concern that resonates with that which is most at stake in the human experience of AIDS even if it receives little attention in academic journals—namely, suffering.

A mortal disease forces questions of dread, of death, and of ultimate meaning to arise. Suffering is a culturally and personally distinctive form of affliction of the human spirit. If pain is distress of the body, suffering is distress of the person and of his or her family and friends. The affliction and death of persons with AIDS create master symbols of suffering; the ethical and emotional responses to AIDS are collective representations of how societies deal with suffering. The stories of sickness of people with AIDS are texts of suffering that we can scan for evidence of how cultures and communities and individuals elaborate the unique textures of personal experience out of the impersonal cellular invasion of viral RNA. Furthermore, these illness narratives point toward issues in the AIDS epidemic every bit as salient as control of the spread of infection and treatment of its biological effects.

Viewed from the perspective of suffering, AIDS must rank with smallpox, plague, and leprosy in its capacity to menace and hurt, to burden and spoil human experience, and to elicit questions about the nature of life and its significance. Suffering extends from those afflicted with AIDS to their families and intimates, to the practitioners and institutions who care for them, and to their neighborhoods and the rest of society, who feel threatened by perceived sources of the epidemic and who are thus affected profoundly yet differently by its consequences. If we minimize the significance of AIDS as human tragedy, we dehumanize people with AIDS as well as those engaged in the public-health and clinical response to the epidemic. Ultimately, we dehumanize us all.

ROBERT AND THE DIAGNOSTIC DILEMMA

It was in a large teaching hospital in Boston that we first met Robert, a forty-four-year-old man with AIDS.[2] Robert was not from Boston, but from Chicago, where he had already weathered several of the infections known to strike people with compromised immune

function. His most recent battle had been with an organism similar to that which causes tuberculosis but is usually harmless to those with intact immune systems. The infection and the many drugs used to treat it had left him debilitated and depressed, and he had come east to visit his sister and regain his strength. On his way home, he was prevented from boarding his plane "for medical reasons." Beset with fever, cough, and severe shortness of breath, Robert went that night to the teaching hospital's emergency ward. Aware of his condition and its prognosis, Robert hoped that the staff there would help him to "get into shape" for the flight back to Chicago.

The physicians in the emergency ward saw their task as straightforward: to identify the cause of Robert's symptoms and, if possible, to treat it. In contemporary medical practice, identifying the cause of respiratory distress in a patient with AIDS entails following what is often called an algorithm. An algorithm, in the culture of biomedicine, is a series of sequential choices, often represented diagrammatically, which helps physicians to make diagnoses and select treatments. In Robert's case, step one, a chest X-ray, suggested the opportunistic lung parasite *Pneumocystis* as a cause for his respiratory distress; step two, examination of his sputum, confirmed it. He was then transferred to a ward in order to begin treatment of his lung infection. Robert was given the drug of choice, but did not improve. His fever, in fact, rose and he seemed more ill than ever.

After a few days of decline, Robert was found to have trismus: his jaw was locked shut. Because he had previously had oral candidiasis ("thrush"), his trismus and neck pain were thought to suggest the spread of the fungal infection back down the throat and pharynx and into the esophagus—a far more serious process than thrush, which is usually controlled by antifungal agents. Because Robert was unable to open his mouth, the algorithm for documenting esophagitis could not be followed. And so a "GI consult"—Robert has already had several—was called. It was hoped that the gastroenterologists, specialists at passing tubes into both ends of the gastrointestinal tract, would be better able to evaluate the nature of Robert's trismus. Robert had jumped ahead to the point in the algorithm that called for "invasive studies." The trouble is that on the night of his admission he had already declined a similar procedure.

Robert's jaw remained shut. Although he was already emaciated from two years of battle, he refused a feeding tube. Patient refusal is never part of an algorithm, and so the team turned to a new kind of logic: Is Robert mentally competent to make such a decision? Is he suffering from AIDS dementia? He was, in the words of one of those treating him, "not with the program." Another member of the team suggested that Robert had "reached the end of the algorithm" but the others disagreed. More diagnostic studies were suggested: in addition to esophagoscopy with biopsy and culture, a CT scan of the neck and head, repeated blood cultures, even a neurological consult. When these studies were mentioned to the patient, his silent stare seemed to fill with anger and despair. Doctors glanced uncomfortably at each other over their pale blue masks. Their suspicions were soon confirmed. In a shaky but decipherable hand, Robert wrote a note: "I just want to be kept clean."

Robert got a good deal more than he asked for, including the feeding tube, the endoscopy, and the CT scan of the neck. He died within hours of the last of these procedures. His physicians felt that they could not have withheld care without having some idea of what was going on.

In the discourse of contemporary biomedicine, Robert's doctors had been confronted with "a diagnostic dilemma." They had not cast the scenario described above as a moral dilemma but had discussed it in rounds as "a compliance problem." This way of talking about the case brings into relief a number of issues in the contemporary United States—not just in the culture of biomedicine but in the larger culture as well. In anthropology, one of the preferred means of examining culturally salient issues is through ethnology: in this case, we shall compare Robert's death in Boston to death from AIDS in a radically different place.

ANITA AND A DECENT DEATH

The setting is now a small Haitian village. Consisting of fewer than a thousand persons, Do Kay is composed substantially of peasant farmers who were displaced some thirty years ago by Haiti's largest dam. By all the standard measures, Kay is now very poor; its older inhabitants often blame their poverty on the massive buttress dam a few miles away and note bitterly that it has brought them neither electricity nor water.

When the first author of this paper began working in Kay, in May of 1983, the word *SIDA*, meaning AIDS, was just beginning to make its way into the rural Haitian lexicon. Interest in the illness was almost universal less than three years later. It was about then that Anita's intractable cough was attributed to tuberculosis.

Questions about her illness often evoked long responses. She resisted our attempts to focus discussions. "Let me tell you the story from the beginning," she once said; "otherwise you will understand nothing at all."

As a little girl, Anita recalls, she was frightened by the arguments her parents would have in the dry seasons. When her mother began coughing, the family sold their livestock in order to buy "a consultation" with a distinguished doctor in the capital. Tuberculosis, he told them, and the family felt there was little they could do other than take irregular trips to Port-au-Prince and make equally irregular attempts to placate the gods who might protect the woman. Anita dropped out of school to help take care of her mother, who died shortly after the girl's thirteenth birthday.

It was very nearly the *coup de grâce* for her father, who became depressed and abusive. Anita, the oldest of five children, bore the brunt of his spleen. "One day, I'd just had it with his yelling. I took what money I could find, about $2, and left for the city. I didn't know where to go." Anita had the good fortune to find a family in need of a maid. The two women in the household had jobs in a U.S.-owned assembly plant; the husband of one ran a snack concession out of the house. Anita received a meal a day, a bit of dry floor to sleep on, and $10 per month for what sounded like incessant labor. She was not unhappy with the arrangement, which lasted until both women were fired for participating in "political meetings."

Anita wandered about for two days until she happened upon a kinswoman selling gum and candies near a downtown theater. She was, Anita related, "a sort of aunt." Anita could come and stay with her, the aunt said, as long as she could help pay the rent. And so Anita moved into Cité Simone, the sprawling slum on the northern fringes of the capital.

It was through the offices of her aunt that she met Vincent, one of the few men in the neighborhood with anything resembling a job: "He unloaded the whites' luggage at the airport." Vincent made a living from tourists' tips. In 1982, the year before Haiti became associated, in the North American press, with AIDS, the city of Port-au-Prince counted tourism as its chief industry. In the setting of an unemployment rate of greater than 60 percent, Vincent could command considerable respect. He turned his attention to Anita. "What could I do, really? He had a good job. My aunt thought I should go with him." Anita was not yet fifteen when she entered her first and only sexual union. Her lover set her up in a shack in the same neighborhood. Anita cooked and washed and waited for him.

When Vincent fell ill, Anita again became a nurse. It began insidiously, she recalls: night sweats, loss of appetite, swollen lymph nodes. Then came months of unpredictable and debilitating diarrhea. "We tried everything—doctors, charlatans, herbal remedies, injections, prayers." After a year of decline, she took Vincent to his hometown in the south of Haiti. There it was revealed that Vincent's illness was the result of malign magic: "It was one of the men at the airport who did this to him. The man wanted Vincent's job. He sent an AIDS death to him."

The voodoo priest who heard their story and deciphered the signs was straightforward. He told Anita and Vincent's family that the sick man's chances were slim, even with the appropriate interventions. There were, however, steps to be taken. He outlined them, and the family followed them, but still Vincent succumbed. "When he died, I felt spent. I couldn't get out of bed. I thought that his family would try to help me to get better, but they didn't. I knew I needed to go home."

She made it as far as Croix-des-Bouquets, a large market town at least two hours from Kay. There she collapsed, feverish and coughing, and was taken in by a woman who lived near the market. She stayed for a month, unable to walk, until her father came to take her back home. Five years had elapsed since she'd last seen him. Anita's father was by then a friendly but broken-down man with a leaking roof over his one-room, dirt-floor hut. It was no place for a sick woman, the villagers said, and Anita's godmother, honoring twenty-year-old vows, made room in her overcrowded but dry house.

Anita was diagnosed as having tuberculosis, and she responded to antituberculosis therapy. But six months after the initiation of treatment, she declined rapidly. Convinced that she was indeed taking her medications, we were concerned about AIDS, especially on hearing of the death of her lover. Anita's father was poised to sell his last bit of land in order to "buy more nourishing food for the child." It was imperative that the underlying cause of Anita's poor response to treatment be found. A laboratory test confirmed our suspicions.

Anita's father and godmother alone were apprised of the test results. When asked what she knew about AIDS, the godmother responded, "AIDS is an infectious disease that has no cure. You can get it from the blood of an infected person." For this reason, she said, she had nothing to fear in caring for Anita. Further, she was adamant that Anita not be told of her diagnosis— "That will only make her suffer more"—and skeptical about the value of the AIDS clinic in Port-au-Prince. "Why should we take her there?" asked Anita's godmother wearily. "She will not recover from this disease. She will have to endure the heat and humiliation of the clinic. She will not find a cool place to lie down. What she might find is a pill or an injection to make her feel more comfortable for a short time. I can do better than that."

And that is what Anita's godmother proceeded to do. She attempted to sit Anita up every day and encouraged her to drink a broth promised to "make her better." The godmother kept her as clean as possible,

consecrating the family's two sheets to her goddaughter. She gave Anita her pillow and stuffed a sack with rags for herself. The only thing she requested from us at the clinic was "a beautiful soft wool blanket that will not irritate the child's skin."

In one of several thoughtful interviews accorded us, Anita's godmother insisted that "for some people, a decent death is as important as a decent life. . . . The child has had a hard life; her life has always been difficult. It's important that she be washed of bitterness and regret before she dies." Anita was herself very philosophic in her last months. She seemed to know of her diagnosis. Although she never mentioned the word *SIDA*, she did speak of the resignation appropriate to "diseases from which you cannot escape." She stated, too, that she was "dying from the sickness that took Vincent," although she denied that she had been the victim of witchcraft—"I simply caught it from him."

Anita did not ask to be taken to a hospital, nor did her slow decline occasion any request for further diagnostic tests. What she most wanted was a radio—"for the news and the music"—and a lambswool blanket. She especially enjoyed the opportunity to "recount my life," and we were able to listen to her narrative until hours before her death.

AIDS IN CULTURAL CONTEXT

The way in which a person, a family, or a community responds to AIDS may reveal a great deal about core cultural values. Robert's story underlines our reliance on technological answers to moral and medical questions. "Americans love machines more than life itself," asserts author Philip Slater in a compelling analysis of middle-class North American culture. "Any challenge to the technological-over-social priority threatens to expose the fact that Americans have lost their manhood and their capacity to control their environment."[3] One of the less noticed but perhaps one of the farthest-reaching consequences of the AIDS epidemic has been the weakening of North America's traditional confidence in the ability of its experts to solve every kind of problem. In the words of one person with the disorder, "The terror of AIDS lies in the collapse of our faith in technology."[4]

This core cultural value is nowhere more evident than in contemporary tertiary medicine, which remains the locus of care for the vast majority of AIDS patients. Despite the uniformity of treatment outcome, despite the lack of proven efficacy of many diagnostic and therapeutic procedures, despite their high costs, it has been difficult for practitioners to limit their recourse to these interventions. "When you're at Disney

World," remarked one of Robert's physicians ironically, "you take all the rides."

Robert's illness raises issues that turn about questions of autonomy and accountability. The concept of autonomous individuals who are solely responsible for their fate, including their illness, is a powerful cultural premise in North American society. On the positive side, this concept supports concern for individual rights and respect for individual differences and achievement. A more ominous aspect of this core cultural orientation is that it often justifies blaming the victims. Illness is said to be the outcome of the free choice of high-risk behavior.

This has been especially true in the AIDS epidemic, which has reified an invidious distinction between "innocent victims"—infants and hemophiliacs—and, by implication, "the guilty"—persons with AIDS who are homosexuals or intravenous drug users. Robert's lonely and medicalized death is what so many North Americans fear: "He was terrified. He knew what AIDS meant. He knew what happens. Your friends desert you, your lover kicks you out into the street. You get fired, you get evicted from your apartment. You're a leper. You die alone."[5] The conflation of correlation and responsibility has the effect of making sufferers feel guilt and shame. The validity of their experience is contested. Suffering, once delegitimated, is complicated and even distorted; our response to the sufferer, blocked.

In contrast, in Haiti and in many African and Asian societies, where individual rights are often underemphasized and also frequently unprotected, and where the idea of personal accountability is less powerful than is the idea of the primacy of social relationships, blaming the victim is also a less frequent response to AIDS. Noticeably absent is the revulsion with which AIDS patients have been faced in the United States, in both clinical settings and in their communities. This striking difference cannot be ascribed to Haitian ignorance of modes of transmission. On the contrary, the Haitians we have interviewed have ideas of etiology and epidemiology that reflect the incursion of the "North American ideology" of AIDS—that the disease is caused by a virus and is somehow related to homosexuality and contaminated blood. These are subsumed, however, in properly Haitian beliefs about illness causation. Long before the advent of AIDS to Do Kay, we might have asked the following question: some fatal diseases are known to be caused by "microbes" but may also be "sent" by someone; is *SIDA* such a disease?

Differences in the responses of caregivers to Robert and Anita—such as whether to inform them of their diagnosis or undertake terminal care as a family or a community responsibility—also reflect the ego-

centered orientation in North American cities and the more sociocentric orientation in the Haitian village. An ironic twist is that it is in the impersonal therapeutic setting of North American healthcare institutions that concern for the patient's personhood is articulated. It is, however, a cool bioethical attention to abstract individual rights rather than a validation of humane responses to concrete existential needs. Perhaps this cultural logic—of medicine as technology, of individual autonomy as the most inviolable of rights, and so of individuals as responsible for most of the ills that befall them—helps us to understand how Robert's lonely death, so rich in all the technology applied to his last hours, could be so poor in all those supportive human virtues that resonate from the poverty-stricken village where Anita died among friends.

A core clinical task would seem to be helping patients to die a decent death. For all the millions of words spilled on the denial of death in our society and the various psychotechniques advertised to aid us to overcome this societal silence, AIDS testifies vividly that our secular public culture is simply unable to come to terms with mortality.

A final question might be asked in examining the stories of Robert and Anita: just how representative are they of the millions already exposed to HIV? As a middle-class, white gay male, Robert is thought by many to be a "typical victim of AIDS." But he is becoming increasingly less typical in the United States, where the epidemic is claiming more and more blacks and Hispanics, and Robert would not be sociologically representative of the typical AIDS patient in much of the rest of the world. In many Third World settings, sex differences in the epidemiology of HIV infection are unremarkable: in Haiti, for example, there is almost parity between the sexes. Most importantly, most people with AIDS are not middle-class and insured. All this points to the fact that the virus that causes AIDS might exact its greatest toll in the Third World.

AIDS IN GLOBAL CONTEXT

Although the pandemic appears to be most serious in North America and Europe, per capita rates reveal that fully seventeen of the twenty countries most affected by AIDS are in Africa or the Caribbean. Further, although there is heartening evidence that the epidemic is being more effectively addressed in the North American gay community, there is no indication that the spread of HIV has been curbed in the communities in which women like Anita struggle. Although early reports of high HIV seroprevalence were clearly based on faulty research, even recent and revised estimates remain grim: "In urban areas in some sub-Saharan countries, up to 25% of young adults are *already* HIV carriers, with rates among those reporting to clinics for sexually transmitted diseases passing 30%, and among female prostitutes up to 90%."[6] In other words, the countries most affected are precisely those that can least afford it.

These figures also remind us that AIDS has felled many like Anita—the poor, women of color, victims of many sorts of oppression and misfortune. Although heterosexual contact seems to be the means of spreading in many instances, not all who contract the disease are "promiscuous," a label that has often offended people in Africa, Haiti, and elsewhere. *Promiscuous* fails utterly to capture the dilemmas of millions like Anita. In an essay entitled "The Myth of African Promiscuity," one Kenyan scholar refers to the "'new poor': the massive pool of young women living in the most deprived conditions in shanty towns and slums across Africa, who are available for the promise of a meal, new clothes, or a few pounds."[7]

Equally problematic, and of course related, is the term *prostitute*. It is often used indiscriminately to refer to a broad spectrum of sexual activity. In North America, the label has been misused in investigations of HIV seroprevalence: "the category *prostitute* is taken as an undifferentiated 'risk group' rather than as an occupational category whose members should, for epidemiological purposes, be divided into IV drug users and nonusers—with significantly different rates of HIV infection—as other groups are."[8] A more historical view reminds us that prostitutes have often been victims of scapegoating and that there has long been more energy for investigation of the alleged moral shortcomings of sex workers than for the economic underpinnings of their work.

The implications of this sort of comparative exercise, which remains a cornerstone of social anthropology, are manifold. The differences speak directly to those who would apply imported models of prevention to rural Haiti or Africa or any other Third World setting. A substantial public-health literature, reflecting the fundamentally interventionist perspective of that discipline, is inarguably necessary in the midst of an epidemic without cure or promising treatment. The same must be true for the burgeoning biomedical literature on AIDS. But with what consequences have these disciplines ignored the issue of AIDS as suffering? Whether reduced to parasite-host interactions or to questions of shifting incidence and prevalence among risk groups, AIDS has meant suffering on a large scale, and this suffering is not captured in these expert discourses on the epidemic.

The meaning of suffering in this context is distinctive not only on account of different beliefs about illness and treatment responses but because of the brute reality of grinding poverty, high child and maternal mortality, routinized demoralization and oppression, and suffering as a central part of existence. The response to AIDS in such settings must deal with this wider context of human misery and its social sources. Surely it is unethical—in the broadest sense, if not in the narrow technical biomedical limits to the term—for international health experts to turn their backs on the suffering of people with AIDS in the Third World and to concentrate solely on the prevention of new cases.

DEALING WITH AIDS AS SUFFERING

To what practical suggestions does a view of AIDS as human suffering lead?

Suffering Compounded by Inappropriate Use of Resources

The majority of all medical-care costs for AIDS patients is generated by acute inpatient care. In many ways, however, infection with HIV is more like a chronic disease. Based on cases of transfusion-associated HIV transmission in the United States, the mean time between exposure to the virus and the development of AIDS is over eight years. This period may well be lengthened by drugs already available. And as the medical profession becomes more skilled at managing the AIDS condition, the average time of survival of patients with the full-blown syndrome will also be extended. For many with AIDS, outpatient treatment will be both more cost-effective and more humane. For the terminally ill, home or hospice care may be preferred to acute-care settings, especially for people who "just want to be kept clean." Helping patients to die a decent death was once an accepted aspect of the work of health professionals. It must be recognized and appropriately supported as a core clinical task in the care of persons with AIDS.

Not a small component of humane care for people with AIDS is soliciting their stories of sickness, listening to their narratives of the illness, so as to help them give meaning to their suffering. Restoring this seemingly forgotten healing skill will require a transformation in the work and training of practitioners and a reorganization of time and objectives in health-care delivery systems.

The practitioner should initiate informed negotiation with alternative lay perspectives on care and provide what amounts to brief medical psychotherapy for the threats and losses that make chronic illness so difficult to bear. But such a transformation in the provision of care will require a significant shift in the allocation of resources, including a commitment to funding psychosocial services as well as appropriate providers—visiting nurses, home health aides, physical and occupational therapists, general practitioners, and other members of teams specializing in long-term, outpatient care.

Suffering Magnified by Discrimination

In a recent study of the U.S. response to AIDS, the spread of HIV was compared to that of polio, another virus that struck young people, triggered public panic, and received regular attention in the popular media. "Although these parallels are strong," notes the author, "one difference is crucial: there was little early sympathy for victims of AIDS because those initially at risk—homosexual men, Haitian immigrants, and drug addicts—were not in the mainstream of society. In contrast, sympathy for polio patients was extensive."[9] This lack of sympathy is part of a spectrum that extends to hostility and even violence, and that has led to discrimination in housing, employment, insurance, and the granting of visas.[10] The victims of such discrimination have been not only people with AIDS or other manifestations of HIV infection but those thought to be in "risk groups."

In some cases, these prejudices are only slightly muted in clinical settings. In our own experience in U.S. hospitals, there is markedly more sympathy for those referred to as "the innocent victims"—patients with transfusion-associated AIDS and HIV-infected babies. At other times, irrational infection-control precautions do little more than heighten patients' feelings of rejection. Blame and recrimination are reactions to the diseases in rural Haiti as well—but there the finger is not often pointed at those with the disease.

Although the President's Commission on AIDS called for major coordinated efforts to address discrimination, what has been done has been desultory, unsystematic, and limited in reach. While legislation is crucial, so too is the development of public-education programs that address discrimination and suffering.

Suffering Augmented by Fear

Underlying at least some of the discrimination, spite, and other inappropriate responses to AIDS is fear. We refer not to the behavior-modifying fear of "the worried well" but to the more visceral fear that has played so prominent a role in the epidemic. It is fear that prompts someone to refuse to get into a taxi driven by a Haitian man; it is fear that leads a reporter to wrench her hand from that of a person with AIDS; it is fear that

underpins some calls for widespread HIV-antibody testing, and fear that has led some health professionals to react to patients in degrading fashion. The fact that so much of this fear is "irrational" has thus far had little bearing on its persistence.

Dissemination of even a few key facts—by people with AIDS, leaders of local communities, elected officials and other policy-makers, teachers, and health professionals—should help to assuage fear. HIV is transmitted through parenteral, mucous-membrane, or open-wound contact with contaminated blood or body fluids and not through casual contact. Although the risk of transmission of HIV to health-care professionals is not zero, it is extremely low, even after percutaneous exposure (studies show that, of more than 1,300 exposed health-care workers, only four seroconverted[11]).

Suffering Amplified by Social Death

In several memoirs published in North America, persons with AIDS have complained of the immediate social death their diagnosis has engendered. "For some of my friends and family, I was dead as soon as they heard I had AIDS," a community activist informed us. "That was over two years ago." Even asymptomatic but seropositive individuals, whose life expectancy is often better than that of persons with most cancers and many common cardiovascular disorders, have experienced this reaction. Many North Americans with AIDS have made it clear that they do not wish to be referred to as victims: "As a person with AIDS," writes Navarre, "I can attest to the sense of diminishment at seeing and hearing myself referred to as an AIDS victim, an AIDS sufferer, an AIDS case—as anything but what I am, a person with AIDS. I am a person with a condition. I am not that condition."[12]

It is nonetheless necessary to plan humane care for persons with a chronic and deadly disease—"without needlessly assaulting my denial," as a young man recently put it. The very notion of hospice care will need rethinking if its intended clients are a group of young and previously vigorous persons. Similarly, our cross-cultural research has shown us that preferred means of coping with a fatal disease are shaped by biography and culture. There are no set "stages" that someone with AIDS will go through, and there can be no standard professional response.

Suffering Generated by Inequities

AIDS is caused, we know, by a retrovirus. But we need not look to Haiti to see that inequities have sculpted the AIDS epidemic. The disease, it has been aptly noted, "moves along the fault lines of our society."[13] Of all infants born with AIDS in the United States, approximately 80 percent are black or Hispanic.[14] Most of these are the children of IV drug users, and attempts to stem the virus may force us to confront substance abuse in the context of our own society. For as Robert Gallo and Luc Montagnier assert, "efforts to control AIDS must be aimed in part at eradicating the conditions that give rise to drug addiction."[15]

There are inequities in the way we care for AIDS patients. In the hospital where Robert died, AZT—the sole agent with proven efficacy in treating HIV infection—is not on formulary. Patients needing the drug who are not in a research protocol have to send someone to the drugstore to buy it—if they happen to have the $10,000 per year AZT can cost or an insurance policy that covers these costs. Such factors may prove important in explaining the striking ethnic differences in average time of survival following diagnosis of AIDS. In one report it was noted that, "while the average lifespan of a white person after diagnosis is two years, the average minority person survives only 19 weeks."[16]

From rural Haiti, it is not the local disparities but rather the international inequities that are glaring. In poor countries, drugs like AZT are simply not available. As noted above, the AIDS pandemic is most severe in the countries that can least afford a disaster of these dimensions. A view of AIDS as human suffering forces us to lift our eyes from local settings to the true dimensions of this worldwide tragedy.

Compassionate involvement with persons who have AIDS may require listening carefully to their stories, whether narratives of suffering or simply attempts to recount their lives. Otherwise, as Anita pointed out, we may understand nothing at all.

NOTES

We thank Carla Fujimoto, Haun Saussy, and Barbara de Zalduondo for their thoughtful comments on this essay.

1. The first three of the four quotations cited here are the voices of persons with AIDS who attended the Third International Conference on AIDS, held in Washington, D.C. in June 1987. Their comments are published passim in 4 (1) (Winter/Spring 1988) of *New England Journal of Public Policy*. All subsequent unreferenced quotations are from tape-recorded interviews accorded the first author.

2. All informants' names are pseudonyms, as are "Do Kay" and "Ba Kay." Other geographical designations are as cited.

3. Philip Slater, *The Pursuit of Loneliness: American Culture at the Breaking Point* (Boston: Beacon Press, 1970), 49, 51.

4. Emmanuel Dreuilhe, *Mortal Embrace: Living with AIDS* (New York: Hill and Wang, 1988), 20.

5. George Whitmore, *Someone Was Here: Profiles in the AIDS Epidemic* (New York: New American Library, 1988), 26.

6. Renée Sabatier, *Blaming Others: Prejudice, Race, and Worldwide AIDS* (Philadelphia: New Society Publishers, 1988), 15.

7. Professor Aina, ibid., 80.

8. Jan Zita Grover, "AIDS: Keywords," in *AIDS: Cultural Analysis/Cultural Activism* (Cambridge: MIT Press, 1988), 25–26.

9. Sandra Panem, *The AIDS Bureaucracy* (Cambridge: Harvard University Press, 1988), 15.

10. See Sabatier for an overview of AIDS-related discrimination. As regards Haiti and Haitians, see Paul Farmer, "AIDS and Accusation: Haiti, Haitians, and the Geography of Blame," in *Cultural Aspects of AIDS: Anthropology and the Global Pandemic* (New York: Praeger, in press). The degree of antipathy is suggested by a recent *New York Times*–CBS News poll of 1,606 persons: "Only 36 percent of those interviewed said they had a lot or some sympathy for 'people who get AIDS from homosexual activity,' and 26 percent said they had a lot or some sympathy for 'people who get AIDS from sharing needles while using illegal drugs'" (*New York Times*, 14 October 1988, A12).

11. Infectious Diseases Society of America, 276.

12. Max Navarre, "Fighting the Victim Label," in *AIDS: Cultural Analysis/Cultural Activism* (Cambridge: MIT Press, 1988), 143.

13. Mary Catherine Bateson and Richard Goldsby, *Thinking AIDS: The Social Response to the Biological Threat* (Reading, Mass.: Addison-Wesley, 1988), 2.

14. Samuel Friedman, Jo Sotheran, Abu Abdul-Quadar, Beny Primm, Don Des Jarlais, Paula Kleinman, Conrad Mauge, Douglas Goldsmith, Wafaa El-Sadr, and Robert Maslansky, "The AIDS Epidemic among Blacks and Hispanics," *The Milbank Quarterly* 65, suppl. 2 (1987): 455–99.

15. Robert Gallo and Luc Montagnier, "AIDS in 1988," *Scientific American* 259 (4) (October 1988):48.

16. Sabatier, 19.

39

Advertising and Global Culture

Noreene Janus

Cultures have always undergone change, whether slow and evolutionary or rapid and revolutionary. Sometimes these changes make people's lives better and sometimes they make them worse, as was debated in Selection 16 on the agricultural revolution. Some social change is spontaneous and unplanned, while at other times change is the result of conscious efforts. Planned change can produce socially disastrous results or significant social benefits.

In this selection, Noreene Janus describes changes that are occurring on a global scale. The change agents—those creating the change—are transnational corporations and transnational advertising agencies. Through their efforts, Western goods and Western values are being introduced throughout the Third World, causing significant cultural transformations.

This selection raises the question of conflicting inalienable rights among the members of our "global village." Some people believe that transnational advertisers have the inalienable right to sell their products on a free market without worrying about the burden of long-term social consequences. Most Third World people feel they have the right to access to the world's consumer goods. But in doing so, are they aware of the long-term consequences that buying into the Western consumer model may have on the continuation of their cultural heritage? Some people think that Third World leaders should be warned of these consequences and have the opportunity to reject the consumer model by restricting advertising. The big question is whether Third World peoples are the beneficiaries or the victims of this global process of change.

As you read this selection, ask yourself the following questions:

☐ Are these global cultural changes spontaneous or planned? Who is responsible?

☐ What is the underlying value, the core, of transnational culture?

☐ What do you think is meant by "consumer democracy"?

☐ Do transnational advertisers seem to have their own culture, or set of values, about the legitimacy of their work?

☐ Do you think transnational advertisers have an inalienable right to advertise, or should restrictions be imposed on them?

The following terms discussed in this selection are included in the Glossary at the back of the book:

economy
social stratification
transnational culture
values

From *Cultural Survival* 7(2): 28–31. Reprinted with permission of *Cultural Survival*.

No one can travel to Africa, Asia, or Latin America and not be struck by the Western elements of urban life. The symbols of transnational culture—automobiles, advertising, supermarkets, shopping centers, hotels, fast food chains, credit cards, and Hollywood movies—give the feeling of being at home. Behind these tangible symbols are a corresponding set of values and attitudes about time, consumption, work relations, etc. Some believe global culture has resulted from gradual spontaneous processes that depended solely on technological innovations—increased international trade, global mass communications, jet travel. Recent studies show that the processes are anything but spontaneous; that they are the result of tremendous investments of time, energy and money by transnational corporations.

This "transnational culture" is a direct outcome of the internationalization of production and accumulation promoted through standardized development models and cultural forms.

The common theme of transnational culture is consumption. Advertising expresses this ideology of consumption in its most synthetic and visual form.

Advertisers rely on few themes: happiness, youth, success, status, luxury, fashion, and beauty. In advertising, social contradictions and class differences are masked and workplace conflicts are not shown. Advertising campaigns suggest that solutions to human problems are to be found in individual consumption, presented as an ideal outlet for mass energies . . . a socially acceptable form of action and participation which can be used to defuse potential political unrest. "Consumer democracy" is held out to the poor around the world as a substitute for political democracy. After all, as the advertising executive who transformed the U.S. Pepsi ad campaign "Join the Pepsi Generation" for use in Brazil as "Join the Pepsi Revolution" explains, most people have no other means to express their need for social change other than by changing brands and increasing their consumption.

Transnational advertising is one of the major reasons both for the spread of transnational culture and the breakdown of traditional cultures. Depicting the racy foreign lifestyles of a blond jetsetter in French or English, it associates Western products with modernity. That which is modern is good; that which is traditional is implicitly bad, impeding the march of progress. Transnational culture strives to eliminate local cultural variations. Barnett and Muller (1974:178) discuss the social impact of this process:

> What are the long range social effects of advertising on people who earn less than $200 a year? (Peasants, domestic workers, and laborers) learn of the outside world

through the images and slogans of advertising. One message that comes through clearly is that happiness, achievement, and being white have something to do with one another. In mestizo countries (sic) such as Mexico and Venezuela where most of the population still bear strong traces of their Indian origin, billboards depicting the good life for sale invariably feature blond, blue-eyed American-looking men and women. One effect of such "white is beautiful" advertising is to reinforce feelings of inferiority which are the essence of a politically immobilizing colonial mentality . . . The subtle message of the global advertiser in poor countries is "Neither you nor what you create are worth very much; *we will sell you a civilization*" (emphasis added).

But global culture is the incidental outcome of transnational marketing logic more than it is the result of a conscious strategy to subvert local cultures. It is marketing logic, for example, that created the "global advertising campaign," one single advertising message used in all countries where the product is made or distributed. This global campaign is both more efficient and less expensive for a firm. Thus, before the intensification of violence in rural Guatemala, for example, farmers gathered around the only television set in their village to watch an advertisement for Revlon perfume showing a blonde woman strolling down Fifth Avenue in New York—the same advertisement shown in the U.S. and other countries.

Transnational firms and global advertising agencies are clearly aware of the role of advertising in the creation of a new consumer culture in Third World countries. A top Israeli advertising executive says,

> Television antennas are gradually taking the place of the tom-tom drums across the vast stretches of Africa. Catchy jingles are replacing tribal calls in the Andes of Latin America. Spic-and-span supermarkets stand on the grounds where colorful wares of an Oriental Bazaar were once spread throughout Asia. Across vast continents hundreds of millions of people are awakening to the beat of modern times. Is the international advertiser fully aware of the magnitude of this slow but gigantic process? Is he alert to the development of these potential markets? Does he know how to use and apply the powerful tools of modern advertising to break into these vast areas of emerging consumers despite the barriers of illiteracy, tribal customs, religious prejudices and primitive beliefs? How great is the potential, and how promising are the prospects of the pioneer industrialist, marketer or advertiser who will venture into this vast Terra Incognita? [Tal, 1974].

Increasingly advertising campaigns are aimed at the vast numbers of poor in Third World countries. As one U.S. advertising executive observes about the Mexican consumer market, even poor families, when living together and pooling their incomes, can add up to a household income of more than $10,000 per year. He explains how they can become an important marketing target:

> The girls will need extra for cosmetics and clothes, but Jaime needs date money and, of course, something is going into the bank to send Carlito to the university. Once all day-to-day expenses have been covered there will come the big decisions that change lifestyles from month to month.
>
> First will probably be a TV set. Nobody can visit Latin America and not be shocked at the number of antennas on top of shacks. And once the TV set goes to work the Fernandez family is like a kid in a candy store. They are the audience that add up to five and one-half hours of viewing a day. They are pounded by some 450 commercials a week. They see all the beautiful people and all the beautiful things. And what they see, they want [Criswell, 27 October 1975].

Since an important characteristic of transnational culture is the speed and breadth with which it is transmitted, communications and information systems play an important role, permitting a message to be distributed globally through television series, news, magazines, comics, and films. The use of television to spread transnational culture is especially effective with illiterates. Grey Advertising International undertook a worldwide study of television to determine its usefulness as an advertising channel and reported that:

> Television is undisputedly the key communications development of our era. It has demonstrated its power to make the world a global village; to educate and inform; to shape the values, attitudes, and lifestyles of generations growing up with it. In countries where it operates as an unfettered commercial medium it has proven for many products the most potent of all consumer marketing weapons as well as a major influence in establishing corporate images and affecting public opinion on behalf of business [Grey Advertising International, 1977].

What do we know about the impact of transnational culture on Third World cultures? Personal observations are plentiful. Anyone who has heard children singing along with television commercials and introducing these themes into their daily games begins to see the impact. There are more extensive analyses as well. Pierre Thizier Seya studied the impact of transnational advertising on cultures in the Ivory Coast. He notes that transnational firms such as Colgate and Nestle have helped to replace traditional products—often cheaper and more effective—with industrialized toothpastes and infant formulas.

By consuming Coca-Cola, Nestle products, Marlboro, Maggi, Colgate or Revlon, Ivorians are not only fulfilling unnecessary needs but also progressively relinquishing their authentic world outlook in favor of the transnational way of life [Seya, 1982:17].

Advertising of skin-lightening products persuades the African women to be ashamed of their own color and try to be white.

> In trying to be as white as possible, that is to say, in becoming ashamed of their traditional being, the Ivorians are at the same time relinquishing one of the most powerful weapons at their disposal for safeguarding their dignity as human beings: their racial identity. And advertising is not neutral in such a state of affairs [Seya, 1982:18].

He also mentions that advertising is helping to change the Ivorian attitude toward aging, making women fear looking older and undermining the traditional respect for elders.

The consumption of soft drinks and hard liquor points to another social change. Traditionally drinks are consumed only in social settings, as evidenced by the large pot where they are stored. Yet, the advertising of Coca-Cola and Heinekens portrays drinking as an individual act rather than a collective one.

A study carried out in Venezuela explores the relationship between television content and children's attitudes. Santoro (1975) analyzed a week of television programming and interviewed 900 sixth grade children. The children were asked to invent a story by drawing the characters in a television screen and then to describe what they had drawn. The imaginary scenes were primarily stories about violence, crime, physical force, and competition, and the large majority of them depicted destructive actions motivated by greed. The "good" characters were primarily from the U.S., white, rich, of varied professions and English surnames. The "bad" characters were mostly from other countries including China and Germany, of black color, poor, workers or office personnel, and with English or Spanish surnames. Santoro concluded that these stereotypes held by children were largely the same ones to be found in typical Venezuelan television and advertising contents.

In another study carried out in Mexico by the National Consumer's Institute in 1981, more than 900 sixth grade children were quizzed on the contents of their textbooks and the contents of commercial television. They knew more about television personalities than about national heroes and recognized more trademarks for snacks, soft drinks, chewing gum and so on than national symbols such as the flag, a map of the country, the major party's symbol, etc. They knew much more about soap operas and action series than they did about episodes of Mexican history. The researchers concluded that advertising and the television medium are far more effective teachers than the public school system. If children are learning about consumption, soap operas and transnational symbols, their parents must be also.

In another research project, seven-year-old Mexican children from different economic backgrounds were interviewed to determine the role of the mass media—primarily television—as sources of information, the relationship established between children and television, and the degree to which the children have internalized transnational consumption patterns (Janus, 1982).

Children were shown pictures of the same man in three different settings—family, nature, and luxury possessions and asked to choose which of these three was the happiest. The question was meant to show the degree to which the children accept the fundamental assumption of advertising: consumption brings happiness. While slightly more than half of the children chose the family scene, poorer children were significantly more likely to associate the luxury possessions with happiness than the rich children.

In the same study, children were shown a series of industrial products along with the traditional products they had replaced: Tang and fresh orange juice, Wonder bread and traditional rolls, Nescafe and coffee beans. The question was designed to determine the degree to which these children actually thought of the industrialized product as the principal form of the food. Again, poor children more often answered that Nescafe *is* coffee, and Tang *is* orange juice.

Perhaps the most interesting result of the study concerns the ability of children to analyze consumption in terms of class. They were shown different categories of consumer products such as cigarettes and television sets, and asked which a rich person could buy and which a poor person could buy. Virtually every child showed an acute awareness of the different access to these products by class. They knew very well that a rich person could buy any or all of the products whereas the poor could buy only the cigarettes, the Coca-Cola, the snackfoods, and the lipstick.

These results, while very tentative, suggest that the impact of transnational culture is greater among the poor—the very people who cannot afford to buy the lifestyle it represents. The poor are more likely to associate consumption with happiness and feel that industrialized products are better than the locally made ones. But at the same time they are painfully aware that only the rich have access to the lifestyle portrayed.

This leads us to the most important questions. What political impact does the spread of transnational culture have on the poor for whom luxury lifestyles are not possible? How do they deal with the daily contradictions that this awareness implies? How much will they accept and how much will they reject? How can they maintain their own identities in the face of transnational culture?

REFERENCES

Barnett, R. and R. Muller, 1974. *Global Reach*. New York: Simon and Schuster.

Criswell, R. 1975. "Keeping up with the Fernandez." *Advertising Age*. October 27.

Grey Advertising International. 1977. "Survey of International Television." *Grey Matter*.

Instituto Nacional del Consumidor (INCO). 1981. *La Television y Los Niños: Conocimiento de la "Realidad Televisiva" vs. Conocimiento de la "Realidad Nacional."* Mexico City: INCO.

Janus, N. 1982. "Spiderman Drinks Tang: Television and Transnational Culture in Mexican Children." Mexico: Instituto Latinoamericano de Estudios Transnacionales (ILET).

Santoro, E. 1975. *La Television Venezolana y La Formacion de Estereotipos en el Niño*. Caracas: Universidad Central de Venezuela.

Seya, P. T. 1982. "Advertising as an Ideological Apparatus of Transnational Capitalism in the Ivory Coast." Mimeographed copy.

40

The Price of Progress

John H. Bodley

Anthropologists are not against progress: we do not want everyone to return to the "good old days" of our Paleolithic ancestors. On the other hand, the discoveries of cultural anthropologists have made us painfully aware of the human costs of unplanned social and economic change. Anthropologists do not want our society to plunge blindly into the future, unaware and unconcerned about how our present decisions will affect other people or future generations. Cultures are always changing, and the direction of that change is toward a single world system. As seen in the last selection on advertising, cultures change because a society's economy is pulled into the world economy. "Progress" is a label placed on cultural and economic change, but whether something represents "progress" or not depends on one's perspective.

In this selection, John Bodley reviews some of the unexpected consequences of economic development in terms of health, ecological change, quality of life, and relative deprivation. We have seen this same theme in previous selections on the invention of agriculture (Selection 16) and agricultural development (Selections 17 and 18). The benefits of economic development are not equally distributed within a developing society. In this selection, we see the relative costs and benefits of economic progress for some of the most marginalized people of the world—the tribal peoples who have been the traditional focus of cultural anthropology research. We believe that the problems detailed here should make our society think about the way cultural change can make people's lives worse; these are issues of social justice.

Anthropologists have been active in seeking solutions to the serious problems described in this selection. We have seen some examples of such work in this book. For example,

anthropologists have helped design effective solutions in reforestation (Selection 19), legal systems (Selection 30), and health care personnel shortages (Selection 35). But on the other hand, most anthropologists believe that tribal peoples have a right to lead their traditional lifestyles and not to be forced into change. In this regard an organization called Cultural Survival has been active in the international political arena in protecting the land and rights of native peoples.

As you read this selection, ask yourself the following questions:

☐ *What is meant by "quality of life"? Why might it increase or decrease for a population?*

☐ *What are the three ways in which economic development can change the distribution of disease?*

☐ *Why do people's diets change? Do people choose diets and behavior that are harmful to them?*

☐ *What is meant by relative deprivation? Can you think of other examples of this process?*

☐ *Are tribal peoples more vulnerable to the negative impact of social and economic change than larger industrial societies?*

The following terms discussed in this selection are included in the Glossary at the back of the book:

dental anthropology   *population pressure*
ecosystem   *relative deprivation*
ethnocentrism   *swidden*
nomadic band   *urbanization*

In aiming at progress . . . you must let no one suffer by too drastic a measure, nor pay too high a price in upheaval and devastation, for your innovation.

—Maunier, 1949:725

Until recently, government planners have always considered economic development and progress beneficial goals that all societies should want to strive toward. The social advantages of progress—as defined in terms of increased incomes, higher standards of living, greater security, and better health—are thought to be positive, *universal* goods, to be obtained at any price. Although one may argue that tribal peoples must sacrifice their traditional cultures to obtain these benefits, government planners generally feel that this is a small price to pay for such obvious advantages.

In earlier chapters, evidence was presented to demonstrate that autonomous tribal peoples have not *chosen* progress to enjoy its advantages, but that governments have *pushed* progress upon them to obtain tribal resources, not primarily to share with the tribal peoples the benefits of progress. It has also been shown that the price of forcing progress on unwilling recipients has involved the deaths of millions of tribal people, as well as their loss of land, political sovereignty, and the right to follow their own life style. This chapter does not attempt to further summarize that aspect of the cost of progress, but instead analyzes the specific effects of the participation of tribal peoples in the world-market economy. In direct opposition to the usual interpretation, it is argued here that the benefits of progress are often both illusory and detrimental to tribal peoples when they have not been allowed to control their own resources and define their relationship to the market economy.

PROGRESS AND THE QUALITY OF LIFE

One of the primary difficulties in assessing the benefits of progress and economic development for any culture is that of establishing a meaningful measure of both benefit and detriment. It is widely recognized that *standard of living*, which is the most frequently used measure of progress, is an intrinsically ethnocentric concept relying heavily upon indicators that lack universal cultural relevance. Such factors as GNP, per capita income, capital formation, employment rates, literacy, formal education, consumption of manufactured goods, number of doctors and hospital beds per thousand persons, and the amount of money spent on government welfare and health programs may be irrelevant measures of actual *quality* of life for autonomous or even semiautonomous tribal cultures. In

its 1954 report, the Trust Territory government indicated that since the Micronesian population was still largely satisfying its own needs within a cashless subsistence economy, "Money income is not a significant measure of living standards, production, or well-being in this area" (TTR, 1953:44). Unfortunately, within a short time the government began to rely on an enumeration of certain imported goods as indicators of a higher standard of living in the islands, even though many tradition-oriented islanders felt that these new goods symbolized a lowering of the quality of life.

A more useful measure of the benefits of progress might be based on a formula for evaluating cultures devised by Goldschmidt (1952:135). According to these less ethnocentric criteria, the important question to ask is: Does progress or economic development increase or decrease a given culture's ability to satisfy the physical and psychological needs of its population, or its stability? This question is a far more direct measure of quality of life than are the standard economic correlates of development, and it is universally relevant. Specific indication of this *standard* of living could be found for any society in the nutritional status and general physical and mental health of its population, the incidence of crime and delinquency, the demographic structure, family stability, and the society's relationship to its natural resource base. A society with high rates of malnutrition and crime, and one degrading its natural environment to the extent of threatening its continued existence, might be described as at a lower standard of living than is another society where these problems did not exist.

Careful examination of the data, which compare, on these specific points, the former condition of self-sufficient tribal peoples with their condition following their incorporation into the world-market economy, leads to the conclusion that their standard of living is *lowered*, not raised, by economic progress—and often to a dramatic degree. This is perhaps the most outstanding and inescapable fact to emerge from the years of research that anthropologists have devoted to the study of culture change and modernization. Despite the best intentions of those who have promoted change and improvement, all too often the results have been poverty, longer working hours, and much greater physical exertion, poor health, social disorder, discontent, discrimination, overpopulation, and environmental deterioration—combined with the destruction of the traditional culture.

DISEASES OF DEVELOPMENT

Perhaps it would be useful for public health specialists to start talking about a new category of diseases. . . . Such diseases could be called the "diseases of development" and would consist of those pathological conditions which are based on the usually unanticipated consequences of the implementation of development schemes [Hughes & Hunter, 1972:93].

Economic development increases the disease rate of affected peoples in at least three ways. First, to the extent that development is successful, it makes developed populations suddenly become vulnerable to all of the diseases suffered almost exclusively by "advanced" peoples. Among these are diabetes, obesity, hypertension, and a variety of circulatory problems. Second, development disturbs traditional environmental balances and may dramatically increase certain bacterial and parasite diseases. Finally, when development goals prove unattainable, an assortment of poverty diseases may appear in association with the crowded conditions of urban slums and the general breakdown in traditional socioeconomic systems.

Outstanding examples of the first situation can be seen in the Pacific, where some of the most successfully developed native peoples are found. In Micronesia, where development has progressed more rapidly than perhaps anywhere else, between 1958 and 1972 the population doubled, but the number of patients treated for heart disease in the local hospitals nearly tripled, mental disorder increased eightfold, and by 1972 hypertension and nutritional deficiencies began to make significant appearances for the first time (TTR, 1959, 1973, statistical tables).

Although some critics argue that the Micronesian figures simply represent better health monitoring due to economic progress, rigorously controlled data from Polynesia show a similar trend. The progressive acquisition of modern degenerative diseases was documented by an eight-member team of New Zealand medical specialists, anthropologists, and nutritionists, whose research was funded by the Medical Research Council of New Zealand and the World Health Organization. These researchers investigated the health status of a genetically related population at various points along a continuum of increasing cash income, modernizing diet, and urbanization. The extremes on this acculturation continuum were represented by the relatively traditional Pukapukans of the Cook Islands and the essentially Europeanized New Zealand Maori, while the busily developing Rarotongans, also of the Cook Islands, occupied the intermediate position. In 1971, after eight years of work, the team's preliminary findings were summarized by Dr. Ian Prior, cardiologist and leader of the research, as follows:

We are beginning to observe that the more an islander takes on the ways of the West, the more prone he is to succumb to our degenerative diseases. In fact, it does

not seem too much to say our evidence now shows that the farther the Pacific natives move from the quiet, carefree life of their ancestors, the closer they come to gout, diabetes, atherosclerosis, obesity, and hypertension [Prior, 1971:2].

In Pukapuka, where progress was limited by the island's small size and its isolated location some 480 kilometers from the nearest port, the annual per capita income was only about thirty-six dollars and the economy remained essentially at a subsistence level. Resources were limited and the area was visited by trading ships only three or four times a year; thus, there was little opportunity for intensive economic development. Predictably, the population of Pukapuka was characterized by relatively low levels of imported sugar and salt intake, and a presumably related low level of heart disease, high blood pressure, and diabetes. In Rarotonga, where economic success was introducing town life, imported food, and motorcycles, sugar and salt intakes nearly tripled, high blood pressure increased approximately ninefold, diabetes two- to threefold, and heart disease doubled for men and more than quadrupled for women, while the number of grossly obese women increased more than tenfold. Among the New Zealand Maori, sugar intake was nearly eight times that of the Pukapukans, gout in men was nearly double its rate on Pukapuka, and diabetes in men was more than fivefold higher, while heart disease in women had increased more than sixfold. The Maori were, in fact, dying of "European" diseases at a greater rate than was the average New Zealand European.

Government development policies designed to bring about changes in local hydrology, vegetation, and settlement patterns and to increase population mobility, and even programs aimed at reducing certain diseases, have frequently led to dramatic increases in disease rates because of the unforeseen effects of disturbing the preexisting order. Hughes and Hunter (1972) published an excellent survey of cases in which development led directly to increased disease rates in Africa. They concluded that hasty development intervention in relatively balanced local cultures and environments resulted in "a drastic deterioration in the social and economic conditions of life."

Traditional populations in general have presumably learned to live with the endemic pathogens of their environments, and in some cases they have evolved genetic adaptations to specific diseases, such as the sickle-cell trait, which provided an immunity to malaria. Unfortunately, however, outside intervention has entirely changed this picture. In the late 1960s, sleeping sickness suddenly increased in many areas of Africa and even spread to areas where it did not formerly occur, due to the building of new roads and migratory labor, both of which caused increased population movement. Large-scale relocation schemes, such as the Zande Scheme, had disastrous results when natives were moved from their traditional disease-free refuges into infected areas. Dams and irrigation developments inadvertently created ideal conditions for the rapid proliferation of snails carrying schistosomiasis (a liver fluke disease), and major epidemics suddenly occurred in areas where this disease had never before been a problem. DDT spraying programs have been temporarily successful in controlling malaria, but there is often a rebound effect that increases the problem when spraying is discontinued, and the malarial mosquitoes are continually evolving resistant strains.

Urbanization is one of the prime measures of development, but it is a mixed blessing for most former tribal peoples. Urban health standards are abysmally poor and generally worse than in rural areas for the detribalized individuals who have crowded into the towns and cities throughout Africa, Asia, and Latin America seeking wage employment out of new economic necessity. Infectious diseases related to crowding and poor sanitation are rampant in urban centers, while greatly increased stress and poor nutrition aggravate a variety of other health problems. Malnutrition and other diet-related conditions are, in fact, one of the characteristic hazards of progress faced by tribal peoples and are discussed in the following sections.

The Hazards of Dietary Change

The traditional diets of tribal peoples are admirably adapted to their nutritional needs and available food resources. Even though these diets may seem bizarre, absurd, and unpalatable to outsiders, they are unlikely to be improved by drastic modifications. Given the delicate balances and complexities involved in any subsistence system, change always involves risks, but for tribal people the effects of dietary change have been catastrophic.

Under normal conditions, food habits are remarkably resistant to change, and indeed people are unlikely to abandon their traditional diets voluntarily in favor of dependence on difficult-to-obtain exotic imports. In some cases it is true that imported foods may be identified with powerful outsiders and are therefore sought as symbols of greater prestige. This may lead to such absurdities as Amazonian Indians choosing to consume imported canned tunafish when abundant high-quality fish is available in their own rivers. Another example of this situation occurs in tribes where mothers prefer to feed their infants expensive and nutritionally inadequate canned milk from unsanitary, but *high status*, baby bottles. The high status of these

items is often promoted by clever traders and clever advertising campaigns.

Aside from these apparently voluntary changes, it appears that more often dietary changes are forced upon unwilling tribal peoples by circumstances beyond their control. In some areas, new food crops have been introduced by government decree, or as a consequence of forced relocation or other policies designed to end hunting, pastoralism, or shifting cultivation. Food habits have also been modified by massive disruption of the natural environment by outsiders—as when sheepherders transformed the Australian Aborigine's foraging territory or when European invaders destroyed the bison herds that were the primary element in the Plains Indians' subsistence patterns. Perhaps the most frequent cause of diet change occurs when formerly self-sufficient peoples find that wage labor, cash cropping, and other economic development activities that feed tribal resources into the world-market economy must inevitably divert time and energy away from the production of subsistence foods. Many developing peoples suddenly discover that, like it or not, they are unable to secure traditional foods and must spend their newly acquired cash on costly, and often nutritionally inferior, manufactured foods.

Overall, the available data seem to indicate that the dietary changes that are linked to involvement in the world-market economy have tended to *lower* rather than raise the nutritional levels of the affected tribal peoples. Specifically, the vitamin, mineral, and protein components of their diets are often drastically reduced and replaced by enormous increases in starch and carbohydrates, often in the form of white flour and refined sugar.

Any deterioration in the quality of a given population's diet is almost certain to be reflected in an increase in deficiency diseases and a general decline in health status. Indeed, as tribal peoples have shifted to a diet based on imported manufactured or processed foods, there has been a dramatic rise in malnutrition, a massive increase in dental problems, and a variety of other nutrition-related disorders. Nutritional physiology is so complex that even well-meaning dietary changes have had tragic consequences. In many areas of Southeast Asia, government-sponsored protein supplementation programs supplying milk to protein-deficient populations caused unexpected health problems and increased mortality. Officials failed to anticipate that in cultures where adults do not normally drink milk, the enzymes needed to digest it are no longer produced and milk *intolerance* results (Davis & Bolin, 1972). In Brazil, a similar milk distribution program caused an epidemic of permanent blindness by aggravating a preexisting vitamin A deficiency (Bunce, 1972).

Teeth and Progress

> There is nothing new in the observation that savages, or peoples living under primitive conditions, have, in general excellent teeth. . . . Nor is it news that most civilized populations possess wretched teeth which begin to decay almost before they have erupted completely, and that dental caries is likely to be accompanied by periodontal disease with further reaching complications [Hooton, 1945:xviii].

Anthropologists have long recognized that undisturbed tribal peoples are often in excellent physical condition. And it has often been noted specifically that dental caries and the other dental abnormalities that plague industrialized societies are absent or rare among tribal peoples who have retained their traditional diets. The fact that tribal food habits may contribute to the development of sound teeth, whereas modernized diets may do just the opposite, was illustrated as long ago as 1894 in an article in the *Journal of the Royal Anthropological Institute* that described the results of a comparison between the teeth of ten Sioux Indians and a comparable group of Londoners (Smith, 1894:109–116). The Indians were examined when they came to London as members of Buffalo Bill's Wild West Show and were found to be completely free of caries and in possession of all their teeth, even though half of the group were over thirty-nine years of age. Londoners' teeth were conspicuous for both their caries and their steady reduction in number with advancing age. The difference was attributed primarily to the wear and polishing caused by the traditional Indian diet of coarse food and the fact that they chewed their food longer, encouraged by the absence of tableware.

One of the most remarkable studies of the dental conditions of tribal peoples and the impact of dietary change was conducted in the 1930s by Weston Price (1945), an American dentist who was interested in determining what caused normal, healthy teeth. Between 1931 and 1936, Price systematically explored tribal areas throughout the world to locate and examine the most isolated peoples who were still living on traditional foods. His fieldwork covered Alaska, the Canadian Yukon, Hudson Bay, Vancouver Island, Florida, the Andes, the Amazon, Samoa, Tahiti, New Zealand, Australia, New Caledonia, Fiji, the Torres Strait, East Africa, and the Nile. The study demonstrated both the superior quality of aboriginal dentition and the devastation that occurs as modern diets are adopted. In nearly every area where traditional foods were still being eaten, Price found perfect teeth with normal dental arches and virtually no decay, whereas caries and abnormalities increased steadily as new diets were adopted. In many cases the change was sudden and striking. Among Eskimo groups subsisting entirely on

traditional food he found caries totally absent, whereas in groups eating a considerable quantity of store-bought food approximately 20 percent of their teeth were decayed. The figure rose to more than 30 percent with Eskimo groups subsisting almost exclusively on purchased or government-supplied food, and reached an incredible 48 percent among the Vancouver Island Indians. Unfortunately for many of these people, modern dental treatment did not accompany the new food, and their suffering was appalling. The loss of teeth was, of course, bad enough in itself, and it certainly undermined the population's resistance to many new diseases, including tuberculosis. But new foods were also accompanied by crowded, misplaced teeth, gum diseases, distortion of the face, and pinching of the nasal cavity. Abnormalities in the dental arch appeared in the new generation following the change in diet, while caries appeared almost immediately even in adults.

Price reported that in many areas the affected peoples were conscious of their own physical deterioration. At a mission school in Africa, the principal asked him to explain to the native schoolchildren why they were not physically as strong as children who had had no contact with schools. On an island in the Torres Strait the natives knew exactly what was causing their problems and resisted—almost to the point of bloodshed—government efforts to establish a store that would make imported food available. The government prevailed, however, and Price was able to establish a relationship between the length of time the government store had been established and the increasing incidences of caries among a population that showed an almost 100 percent immunity to them before the store had been opened.

In New Zealand, the Maori, who in their aboriginal state are often considered to have been among the healthiest, most perfectly developed of peoples, were found to have "advanced" the furthest. According to Price:

> Their modernization was demonstrated not only by the high incidence of dental caries but also by the fact 90 percent of the adults and 100 percent of the children had abnormalities of the dental arches [Price, 1945:206].

Malnutrition

Malnutrition, particularly in the form of protein deficiency, has become a critical problem for tribal peoples who must adopt new economic patterns. Population pressures, cash cropping, and government programs all have tended to encourage the replacement of traditional crops and other food sources that were rich in protein with substitutes high in calories but low in protein. In Africa, for example, protein-rich staples such as millet and sorghum are being replaced systematically by high-yielding manioc and plantains, which have insignificant amounts of protein. The problem is increased for cash croppers and wage laborers whose earnings are too low and unpredictable to allow purchase of adequate amounts of protein. In some rural areas, agricultural laborers have been forced systematically to deprive nonproductive members (principally children) of their households of their minimal nutritional requirements to satisfy the need of the productive members. This process has been documented in northeastern Brazil following the introduction of large-scale sisal plantations (Gross & Underwood, 1971). In urban centers the difficulties of obtaining nutritionally adequate diets are even more serious for tribal immigrants, because costs are higher and poor quality foods are more tempting.

One of the most tragic, and largely overlooked, aspects of chronic malnutrition is that it can lead to abnormally undersized brain development and apparently irreversible brain damage; it has been associated with various forms of mental impairment or retardation. Malnutrition has been linked clinically with mental retardation in both Africa and Latin America (see, for example, Mönckeberg, 1968), and this appears to be a worldwide phenomenon with serious implications (Montagu, 1972).

Optimistic supporters of progress will surely say that all of these new health problems are being overstressed and that the introduction of hospitals, clinics, and the other modern health institutions will overcome or at least compensate for all of these difficulties. However, it appears that uncontrolled population growth and economic impoverishment probably will keep most of these benefits out of reach for many tribal peoples, and the intervention of modern medicine has at least partly contributed to the problem in the first place.

The generalization that civilization frequently has a broad negative impact on tribal health has found broad empirical support (see especially Kroeger & Barbira-Freedman [1982] on Amazonia; Reinhard [1976] on the Arctic; and Wirsing [1985] globally), but these conclusions have not gone unchallenged. Some critics argue that tribal health was often poor before modernization, and they point specifically to tribals' low life expectancy and high infant mortality rates. Demographic statistics on tribal populations are often problematic because precise data are scarce, but they do show a less favorable profile than that enjoyed by many industrial societies. However, it should be remembered that our present life expectancy is a recent phenomenon that has been very costly in terms of medical research and technological advances. Further-

more, the benefits of our health system are not enjoyed equally by all members of our society. High infant mortality could be viewed as a relatively inexpensive and egalitarian tribal public health program that offered the reasonable expectation of a healthy and productive life for those surviving to age fifteen.

Some critics also suggest that certain tribal populations, such as the New Guinea highlanders, were "stunted" by nutritional deficiencies created by tribal culture and are "improved" by "acculturation" and cash cropping (Dennett & Connell, 1988). Although this argument does suggest that the health question requires careful evaluation, it does not invalidate the empirical generalizations already established. Nutritional deficiencies undoubtedly occurred in densely populated zones in the central New Guinea highlands. However, the specific case cited above may not be widely representative of other tribal groups even in New Guinea, and it does not address the facts of outside intrusion or the inequities inherent in the contemporary development process.

ECOCIDE

> "How is it," asked a herdsman . . . "how is it that these hills can no longer give pasture to my cattle? In my father's day they were green and cattle thrived there; today there is no grass and my cattle starve." As one looked one saw that what had once been a green hill had become a raw red rock [Jones, 1934].

Progress not only brings new threats to the health of tribal peoples, but it also imposes new strains on the ecosystems upon which they must depend for their ultimate survival. The introduction of new technology, increased consumption, lowered mortality, and the eradication of all traditional controls have combined to replace what for most tribal peoples was a relatively stable balance between population and natural resources, with a new system that is imbalanced. Economic development is forcing *ecocide* on peoples who were once careful stewards of their resources. There is already a trend toward widespread environmental deterioration in tribal areas, involving resource depletion, erosion, plant and animal extinction, and a disturbing series of other previously unforeseen changes.

After the initial depopulation suffered by most tribal peoples during their engulfment by frontiers of national expansion, most tribal populations began to experience rapid growth. Authorities generally attribute this growth to the introduction of modern medicine and new health measures and the termination of intertribal warfare, which lowered mortality rates, as well as to new technology, which increased food production. Certainly all of these factors played a part, but merely lowering mortality rates would not have produced the rapid population growth that most tribal areas have experienced if traditional birth-spacing mechanisms had not been eliminated at the same time. Regardless of which factors were most important, it is clear that all of the natural and cultural checks on population growth have suddenly been pushed aside by culture change, while tribal lands have been steadily reduced and consumption levels have risen. In many tribal areas, environmental deterioration due to overuse of resources has set in, and in other areas such deterioration is imminent as resources continue to dwindle relative to the expanding population and increased use. Of course, population expansion by tribal peoples may have positive political consequences, because where tribals can retain or regain their status as local majorities they may be in a more favorable position to defend their resources against intruders.

Swidden systems and pastoralism, both highly successful economic systems under traditional conditions, have proven particularly vulnerable to increased population pressures and outside efforts to raise productivity beyond its natural limits. Research in Amazonia demonstrates that population pressures and related resource depletion can be created indirectly by official policies that restrict swidden peoples to smaller territories. Resource depletion itself can then become a powerful means of forcing tribal people into participating in the world-market economy—thus leading to further resource depletion. For example, Bodley and Benson (1979) showed how the Shipibo Indians in Peru were forced to further deplete their forest resources by cash cropping in the forest area to replace the resources that had been destroyed earlier by the intensive cash cropping necessitated by the narrow confines of their reserve. In this case, a certain species of palm trees that had provided critical housing materials were destroyed by forest clearing and had to be replaced by costly purchased materials. Research by Gross (1979) and others showed similar processes at work among four tribal groups in central Brazil and demonstrated that the degree of market involvement increases directly with increases in resource depletion.

The settling of nomadic herders and the removal of prior controls on herd size have often led to serious overgrazing and erosion problems where these had not previously occurred. There are indications that the desertification problem in the Sahel region of Africa was aggravated by programs designed to settle nomads. The first sign of imbalance in a swidden system appears when the planting cycles are shortened to the point that garden plots are reused before sufficient forest regrowth can occur. If reclearing and planting continue in the same area, the natural pattern of forest succession may be disturbed irreversibly and the soil can be impaired permanently. An extensive tract of tropical rainforest in the lower Amazon of Brazil was reduced to a semiarid desert in just fifty years through such a process (Ackermann, 1964). The soils in the Azande area are also now seriously threatened with laterization and other problems as a result of the government-promoted cotton development scheme (McNeil, 1972).

The dangers of overdevelopment and the vulnerability of local resource systems have long been recognized by both anthropologists and tribal peoples themselves, but the pressures for change have been overwhelming. In 1948 the Maya villagers of Chan Kom complained to Redfield (1962) about the shortening of their swidden cycles, which they correctly attributed to increasing population pressures. Redfield told them, however, that they had no choice but to go "forward with technology" (Redfield, 1962:178). In Assam, swidden cycles were shortened from an average of twelve years to only two or three within just twenty years, and anthropologists warned that the limits of swiddening would soon be reached (Burling, 1963:311-312). In the Pacific, anthropologists warned of population pressures on limited resources as early as the 1930s (Keesing, 1941:64–65). These warnings seemed fully justified, considering the fact that the crowded Tikopians were prompted by population pressures on their tiny island to suggest that infanticide be legalized. The warnings have been dramatically reinforced since then by the doubling of Micronesia's population in just the fourteen years between 1958 and 1972, from 70,600 to 114,645, while consumption levels have soared. By 1985 Micronesia's population had reached 162,321.

The environmental hazards of economic development and rapid population growth have become generally recognized only since worldwide concerns over environmental issues began in the early 1970s. Unfortunately, there is as yet little indication that the leaders of the now developing nations are sufficiently concerned with environmental limitations. On the contrary governments are forcing tribal peoples into a self-reinforcing spiral of population growth and intensified resource exploitation, which may be stopped only by environmental disaster or the total impoverishment of the tribals.

The reality of ecocide certainly focuses attention on the fundamental contrasts between tribal and industrial systems in their use of natural resources. In many respects the entire "victims of progress" issue hinges on natural resources, who controls them, and how they are managed. Tribal peoples are victimized because they control resources that outsiders demand. The resources exist because tribals managed them conservatively. However, as with the issue of the health consequences of detribalization, some anthropologists minimize the adaptive achievements of tribal groups and seem unwilling to concede that ecocide might be a consequence of cultural change. Critics attack an exaggerated "noble savage" image of tribals living in perfect harmony with nature and having no visible impact on their surroundings. They then show that tribals do in fact modify the environment, and they conclude that there is no significant difference between how tribals and industrial societies treat their environments. For example, Charles Wagley declared that Brazilian Indians such as the Tapirape

> are not "natural men." They have human vices just as we do. . . . They do not live "in tune" with nature any more than I do; in fact, they can often be as destructive of their environment, within their limitations, as some civilized men. The Tapirape are not innocent or childlike in any way [Wagley, 1977:302].

Anthropologist Terry Rambo demonstrated that the Semang of the Malaysian rain forests have measurable impact on their environment. In his monograph *Primitive Polluters*, Rambo (1985) reported that the Semang live in smoke-filled houses. They sneeze and spread germs, breathe, and thus emit carbon dioxide. They clear small gardens, contributing "particulate matter" to the air and disturbing the local climate because cleared areas proved measurably warmer and drier than the shady forest. Rambo concluded that his research "demonstrated the essential functional similarity of the environmental interactions of primitive and civilized societies" (1985:78) in contrast to a "noble savage" view (Bodley, 1983) which, according to Rambo (1985:2), mistakenly "claims that traditional peoples almost always live in essential harmony with their environment."

This is surely a false issue. To stress, as I do, that tribals tend to manage their resources for sustained yield within relatively self-sufficient subsistence economies is not to make them either innocent children or natural men. Nor is it to deny that tribals "disrupt" their environment and may never be in absolute "balance" with nature.

The ecocide issue is perhaps most dramatically illustrated by two sets of satellite photos taken over the Brazilian rain forests of Rôndonia (Allard & McIntyre, 1988:780–781). Photos taken in 1973, when Rôndonia was still a tribal domain, show virtually unbroken rain forest. The 1987 satellite photos, taken after just fifteen years of highway construction and "development" by outsiders, show more than 20 percent of the forest destroyed. The surviving Indians were being concentrated by FUNAI (Brazil's national Indian foundation) into what would soon become mere islands of forest in

a ravaged landscape. It is irrelevant to quibble about whether tribals are noble, childlike, or innocent, or about the precise meaning of balance with nature, carrying capacity, or adaptation, to recognize that for the past 200 years rapid environmental deterioration on an unprecedented global scale has followed the wresting of control of vast areas of the world from tribal groups by resource-hungry industrial societies.

DEPRIVATION AND DISCRIMINATION

> Contact with European culture has given them a knowledge of great wealth, opportunity and privilege, but only very limited avenues by which to acquire these things [Crocombe, 1968].

Unwittingly, tribal peoples have had the burden of perpetual relative deprivation thrust upon them by acceptance—either by themselves or by the governments administering them—of the standards of socioeconomic progress set for them by industrial civilizations. By comparison with the material wealth of industrial societies, tribal societies become, by definition, impoverished. They are then forced to transform their cultures and work to achieve what many economists now acknowledge to be unattainable goals. Even though in many cases the modest GNP goals set by development planners for the developing nations during the "development decade" of the 1960s were often met, the results were hardly noticeable for most of the tribal people involved. Population growth, environmental limitations, inequitable distribution of wealth, and the continued rapid growth of the industrialized nations have all meant that both the absolute and the relative gap between the rich and poor in the world is steadily widening. The prospect that tribal peoples will actually be able to attain the levels of resource consumption to which they are being encouraged to aspire is remote indeed except for those few groups who have retained effective control over strategic mineral resources.

Tribal peoples feel deprivation not only when the economic goals they have been encouraged to seek fail to materialize, but also when they discover that they are powerless, second-class citizens who are discriminated against and exploited by the dominant society. At the same time, they are denied the satisfactions of their traditional cultures, because these have been sacrificed in the process of modernization. Under the impact of major economic change family life is disrupted, traditional social controls are often lost, and many indicators of social anomie such as alcoholism, crime, delinquency, suicide, emotional disorders, and despair may increase. The inevitable frustration resulting from this continual deprivation finds expression in the cargo cults, revitalization movements, and a variety of other political and religious movements that have been widespread among tribal peoples following their disruption by industrial civilization.

REFERENCES

Ackermann, F. L. 1964. *Geologia e Fisiografia da Região Bragantina, Estado do Pará*. Manaus, Brazil: Conselho Nacional de Pesquisas, Instituto Nacional de Pesquisas da Amazônia.

Allard, William Albert, and Loren McIntyre. 1988. Rôndonia's settlers invade Brazil's imperiled rain forest. *National Geographic* 174(6):772–799.

Bodley, John H. 1983. The World Bank tribal policy: Criticisms and recommendations. *Congressional Record*, serial no. 98-37, pp. 515–521. (Reprinted in Bodley, 1988.)

Bodley, John H., and Foley C. Benson. 1979. Cultural ecology of Amazonian palms. *Reports of Investigations*, no. 56. Pullman: Laboratory of Anthropology, Washington State University.

Bunce, George E. 1972. Aggravation of vitamin A deficiency following distribution of non-fortified skim milk: An example of nutrient interaction. In *The Careless Technology: Ecology and International Development*, ed. M. T. Farvar and John P. Milton, pp. 53–60. Garden City, N.Y.: Natural History Press.

Burling, Robbins. 1963. *Rengsanggri: Family and Kinship in a Garo Village*. Philadelphia: University of Pennsylvania Press.

Crocombe, Ron. 1968. Bougainville!: Copper, R. R. A. and secessionism. *New Guinea* 3(3):39–49.

Davis, A. E., and T. D. Bolin. 1972. Lactose intolerance in Southeast Asia. In *The Careless Technology: Ecology and International Development*, ed. M. T. Farvar and John P. Milton, pp. 61–68. Garden City, N.Y.: Natural History Press.

Dennett, Glenn, and John Connell. 1988. Acculturation and health in the highlands of Papua New Guinea. *Current Anthropology* 29(2):273–299.

Goldschmidt, Walter R. 1952. The interrelations between cultural factors and acquisition of new technical skills. In *The Progress of Underdeveloped Areas*, ed. Bert F. Hoselitz, pp. 135–151. Chicago: University of Chicago Press.

Gross, Daniel R., and Barbara A. Underwood. 1971. Technological change and caloric costs: Sisal agriculture. *American Anthropologist* 73(3):725–740.

Gross, Daniel R., et al. 1979. Ecology and acculturation among native peoples of Central Brazil. *Science* 206(4422):1043–1050.

Hooton, Earnest A. 1945. Introduction. In *Nutrition and Physical Degeneration: A Comparison of Primitive and Modern Diets and Their Effects* by Weston A. Price. Redlands, Calif.: The author.

Hughes, Charles C., and John M. Hunter. 1972. The role of technological development in promoting disease in Africa. In *The Careless Technology: Ecology and International Development*, ed. M. T. Farvar and John P. Milton, pp. 69–101. Garden City, N.Y.: Natural History Press.

Jones, J. D. Rheinallt. 1934. Economic condition of the urban native. In *Western Civilization and the Natives of South Africa*, ed. I. Schapera, pp. 159–192. London: George Routledge and Sons.

Keesing, Felix M. 1941. *The South Seas in the Modern World*. Institute of Pacific Relations International Research Series. New York: John Day.

Kroeger, Axel, and Françoise Barbira-Freedman. 1982. *Culture Change and Health: The Case of South American Rainforest Indians*. Frankfurt am Main: Verlag Peter Lang. (Reprinted in Bodley, 1988:221–236).

Maunier, René. 1949. *The Sociology of Colonies*. Vol. 2. London: Routledge and Kegan Paul.

McNeil, Mary. 1972. Lateritic soils in distinct tropical environments: Southern Sudan and Brazil. In *The Careless Technology: Ecology and International Development*, ed. M. T. Farvar and John P. Milton, pp. 591–608. Garden City, N.Y.: Natural History Press.

Mönckeberg, F. 1968. Mental retardation from malnutrition. *Journal of the American Medical Association* 206:30–31.

Montagu, Ashley. 1972. Sociogenic brain damage. *American Anthropologist* 74(5):1045–1061.

Price, Weston Andrew. 1945. *Nutrition and Physical Degeneration: A Comparison of Primitive and Modern Diets and Their Effects*. Redlands, Calif.: The author.

Prior, Ian A. M. 1971. The price of civilization. *Nutrition Today* 6(4):2–11.

Rambo, A. Terry. 1985. *Primitive Polluters: Semang Impact on the Malaysian Tropical Rain Forest Ecosystem*. Anthropological Papers no. 76, Museum of Anthropology, University of Michigan.

Redfield, Robert. 1962. *A Village That Chose Progress: Chan Kom Revisited*. Chicago: University of Chicago Press, Phoenix Books.

Reinhard, K. R. 1976. Resource exploitation and the health of western arctic man. In *Circumpolar Health: Proceedings of the Third International Symposium, Yellowknife, Northwest Territories*, ed. Roy J. Shephard and S. Itoh, pp. 617–627. Toronto: University of Toronto Press. (Reprinted in Bodley, 1988.)

Smith, Wilberforce. 1894. The teeth of ten Sioux Indians. *Journal of the Royal Anthropological Institute* 24:109–116.

TTR: *See under* United States.

United States, Department of State. 1955. *Seventh Annual Report to the United Nations on the Administration of the Trust Territory of the Pacific Islands* (July 1, 1953, to June 30, 1954).

———. 1959. *Eleventh Annual Report to the United Nations on the Administration of the Trust Territory of the Pacific Islands* (July 1, 1957, to June 30, 1958).

———. 1973. *Twenty-Fifth Annual Report to the United Nations on the Administration of the Trust Territory of the Pacific Islands* (July 1, 1971, to June 30, 1972).

Wagley, C. 1977. *Welcome of Tears: The Tapirape Indians of Central Brazil*. New York: Oxford University Press.

Wirsing, R. 1985. The health of traditional societies and the effects of acculturation. *Current Anthropology* 26:303–322.

Glossary

Affinal kin A kin relationship created by marriage.

Age grade A social category of people who fall within a particular, culturally distinguished age range; age grades often undergo life cycle rituals as a group.

Aggression A forceful action, sometimes involving physical violence, intended for social domination.

Agnatic Related through the male kinship line.

Agrarian Relating to agriculture.

Agricultural development Changes in agricultural production intended to improve the system by producing more harvest per unit of land.

AIDS Acquired Immune Deficiency Syndrome, a fatal disease caused by the human immunodeficiency virus (HIV) and usually transmitted through semen or blood.

Amerindian Native American populations.

Anthropology The systematic study of humans, including their biology and culture, both past and present.

Arable land Land suitable for cultivation.

Archaeology The field of anthropology concerned with cultural history; includes the systematic retrieval, identification, and study of the physical and cultural remains deposited in the earth.

Basic research Study directed toward gaining scientific knowledge primarily for its own sake.

Big men Political leaders in tribal societies whose status has been achieved and whose authority is limited.

Biological anthropology Subfield of anthropology that studies the biological nature of humans and includes primatology, paleoanthropology, population genetics, anthropomometry, and human biology.

Blood relatives A folk term referring to consanguineal kin, that is, kin related through birth.

Cadastral A government survey and record-keeping system for recording land ownership and property boundaries.

Canton A small territorial division of a country.

Caste A ranked group, sometimes linked to a particular occupation, with membership determined at birth and with marriage restricted to others within the group.

Ceremony Public events involving special symbols that signify important cultural values or beliefs.

Chiefdom A society more complex than a tribal society, characterized by social ranking, a redistributive economy, and a centralized political authority.

Civilization The culture of state level societies characterized by the following elements: (1) agriculture; (2) urban living; (3) a high degree of occupational specialization and differentiation; (4) social stratification; and (5) literacy.

Clan A kinship group whose members assume, but need not demonstrate, descent from a common ancestor.

Comparative framework An analytical approach in anthropology using the comparison of cultures across time and place.

Corporate culture The cultural characteristics of a workplace.

Correlation A statistical relationship between two variables.

Corvée A system of required labor; characteristic of ancient states.

Cro-magnon A term broadly referring to the first anatomically modern humans, from roughly 40,000 to 10,000 B.C.; named after a site in southwestern France.

Cross-cultural research The exploration of cultural variation by using ethnographic data from many societies.

Cross-cutting ties Affinal or trading relationships that serve to counteract the political isolation of social groups in tribal societies.

Cultural anthropology A field of anthropology emphasizing the study of the cultural diversity of contemporary societies, including their economies, sociopolitical systems, and belief systems.

Cultural evolution The process of invention, diffusion, and elaboration of the behavior that is learned and taught in groups and is transmitted from generation to generation; often used to refer to the development of social complexity.

Cultural materialism The idea, often associated with Marvin Harris, that cultural behaviors are best explained in relation to material constraints (including food-producing technology) to which humans are subjected.

Cultural relativism The principle that all cultural systems are inherently equal in value and, therefore, that each cultural item must be understood on its own terms.

Cultural reproduction The process by which cultural behaviors and beliefs are regenerated across generations or spread among people of the same generation; cultural construction creates reality.

Cultural values Ideas, beliefs, values, and attitudes learned as a member of a social group.

Culture Learned patterns of thought and behavior characteristic of a particular social group.

Culture area A largely outmoded idea that the world can be divided into a limited number of geographical regions, each defined by a certain set of cultural features that result from common ecological adaptation or history and are shared by all groups in the region.

Culture brokers Individuals, often anthropologists, who function as mediators or translators between members of two cultures.

Culture shock The experience of stress and confusion resulting from moving one culture to another; the removal or distortion of familiar cues and the substitution of strange cues.

Decoction The extraction of flavor by boiling.

Dental anthropology A specialization within biological anthropology; the study of the morphology of teeth across time and populations.

Diffusion A process of cultural change by which traits of one society are borrowed by another; the spread of cultural traits.

Domestication of plants and animals The invention of farming.

Dowry A payment or gift at the time of marriage from the bride's group to the groom's group; often

the bride or new couple have control of this compensation.

Economy The production, distribution, and consumption of resources, labor, and wealth within a society.

Ecosystem A community of plants and animals, including humans, within a physical environment, and the relationship of organisms to one another.

Egalitarian society A society that emphasizes the social equality of members and makes achieved statuses accessible to all adults.

Epidemic Higher-than-expected disease prevalence affecting individuals within a population at the same time.

Epidemiology The study of the incidence, distribution, and control of disease in a population.

Epistemology The study of the nature of knowledge and its limits.

Ergonomics Human engineering; an applied science concerned with the anthropometric characteristics of people in the design of technology for improved human-machine interaction and safety.

Ethnic groups A group of people within a larger society with a distinct cultural or historical identity; ethnicity is a common mechanism of social separation in complex, heterogeneous societies.

Ethnocentrism The assumption that one's own group's lifestyle, values, and patterns of adaptation are superior to all others.

Ethnographic methods The research techniques of cultural anthropology based on long-term participant observations, yielding a description of another culture.

Ethnography The intensive and systematic description of a particular society; ethnographic information is usually collected through the method of long-term participant-observation fieldwork.

Ethnology The study and explanation of cultural similarities and differences.

Ethos The world view of a particular society, including its distinctive character, sentiments, and values.

Evolutionary medicine An anthropological approach to disease, symptoms, and medical care based upon our evolutionary heritage.

Exogamous Relating to a custom that forbids members of a specific group from selecting a spouse from within that group.

Extended family A domestic unit created by the linking together of two or more nuclear families.

Fallow The period during which a unit of agricultural land is not cultivated so that nutrients can be restored to the soil.

Fieldwork The hallmark of research in cultural anthropology, it usually involves long-term residence with the people being studied.

Foraging Hunting and gathering; the original human economic system relying on the collection of natural plant and animal food sources.

Forensic anthropology Anthropological studies related to the introduction of evidence in court, most often involving the study of skeletal remains.

Fraternal polyandry An uncommon form of plural marriage in which a woman is married to two or more brothers at one time.

Gender The social classification of masculine or feminine.

Genealogy The systematic study of the consanguineal and affinal kin of a particular person, including his or her ancestors; a common method used in anthropological field studies.

Ghetto A subsection of a city in which members of a minority group live because of social, legal, or economic pressure.

Hallucinogen A substance that induces visions or auditory hallucinations in normal individuals.

HIV The human immunodeficiency virus that causes AIDS.

Holistic Refers to viewing the whole society as an integrated and interdependent system; an important characteristic of the anthropological approach to understanding humans.

Horticulture A plant cultivation system based upon relatively low energy input, like gardening by using only the hoe or digging stick; often involves use of the slash-and-burn technique.

Human universal A trait or behavior found in all human cultures.

Hunter-gatherers Peoples who subsist on the collection of naturally occurring plants and animals; food-foragers.

Hypothesis A tentative assumption or proposition about the relationship(s) between specific events or phenomena, tentatively set forth as a "target" to be tested.

Indigenous The original or native population of a particular region or environment.

Infanticide Killing a baby soon after birth.

Informant A member of a society who has established a working relationship with an anthropological fieldworker and who provides information about the culture; the subject of intensive interviewing.

Institutions Formal organizations within a society.

Intensive interviewing The ethnographic method of repeated interviews with a single informant.

Kinship A network of culturally recognized relationships among individuals, either through affinal or consanguineal ties.

Land concentration The degree to which land ownership is limited to a small number of people in a society.

Land tenure A system of land ownership and inheritance.

Levirate The practice by which a man is expected to marry the wife or wives of a deceased brother; commonly found in patrilineal descent systems.

Lexicon Vocabulary.

Lineage Refers to a kin group tracing common descent through one sex from a known ancestor.

Linguistic anthropology A subfield of anthropology entailing the study of language forms across space and time and their relation to culture and social behavior.

Linguistics The study of language, consisting of: (1) historical linguistics, which is concerned with the evolution of languages and language groups through time; (2) descriptive linguistics, which focuses on recording and analysis of the structures of languages; (3) sociolinguistics, the way in which speech patterns reflect social phenomena; and (4) ethnosemantics, the study of the connection between reality, thought, and language.

Literacy The ability to read; not possible for people who speak unwritten languages.

Longitudinal A research strategy that examines changes in a particular group over time.

Mana A supernatural force inhabiting objects or people.

Mediator The role of a disinterested third party in dispute settlement.

Medical anthropology The study of health and medical systems in a cross-cultural perspective; includes the study of biocultural adaptations to disease, ethnomedical systems, and cultural factors in health-seeking behavior.

Metalinguistics Elements of communication beyond verbal speech; includes the use of gesture, personal space, silence, and nonlinguistic sounds.

Moiety system A social system in which the entire group is divided into two kinship units, which are usually based on unilineal descent and exogamous.

Monogamy   Marriage between one man and one woman at a given time.

Moot   A public hearing or community assembly to decide local problems and administer justice.

Multiplex relationships   Complex social relations characterized by multiple patterns of interaction, for example by kinship, business, political party, ethnicity, and religion.

Neolithic   A stage in cultural evolution marked by the appearance of ground stone tools and, more importantly, the domestication of plants and animals, starting some 10,000 years ago.

Nomadic band   A food-foraging group that moves among a variety of campsites; a society without sedentary villages.

Nuclear family   A basic social grouping consisting of a husband and wife and their children, typical of societies with monogamous marriage with the family living at a distance from the parents of the husband and wife.

Origin myth   A story found in most cultures that explains the creation and population of the world.

Orthography   The way in which words in a particular language are written phonetically to include sounds (phonemes) not represented in our alphabet; anthropological linguists usually use the International Phonetic Alphabet (IPA).

Pacification   In tribal areas like New Guinea, the establishment by outside authorities of peace from blood-feud warfare.

Palaver   A discussion for purposes of dispute settlement, typically informal and following customary law.

Paleolithic   Old stone age; the archaeological period that includes the beginning of culture to the end of the Pleistocene glaciation.

Paleontology   The study of the fossils of ancient, usually extinct, animals and plants.

Paleopathology   The study of disease patterns in extinct populations, primarily through the examination of skeletal remains.

Participant observation   The primary research method of cultural anthropology, involving long-term observations conducted in natural settings.

Patriarchy   A form of social organization in which power and authority are vested in the males and in which descent is usually in the male line.

Patrilineal   Descent traced exclusively through the male line for purposes of group membership or inheritance.

Patrilocal   A postmarital residence rule by which a newlywed couple takes up permanent residence with or near the groom's father's family.

Peasants   Rural, agricultural populations of state-level societies who maintain parts of their traditional culture while they are tied into the wider economic system of the whole society through economic links of rent, taxes, and markets.

Polygyny   A common form of plural marriage in which one man is married to two or more women.

Population pressure   The situation of population growth in a limited geographical area causing a decline in food production and resources and sometimes triggering technological change.

Primogeniture   A rule of inheritance in which the homestead is passed down to the firstborn (male) child.

Psychoactive drugs   Chemicals that affect the mind or behavior and that may cause, among other things, hallucinations.

Qualitative methods   Research strategies that emphasize description, in-depth interviewing, and participant observation.

Quantitative methods   Research methods that translate behaviors or attitudes into reliable and valid numeric measures suitable for statistical analysis for hypothesis testing.

Reciprocal gift   A mechanism of establishing or reinforcing social ties between equals involving a "present," which is repaid at a later date.

Reforestation   To renew forest cover by seeding or planting.

Relative deprivation   A concept wherein individuals perceive that they are less well off only in relation to another group or to their own expectations.

Rite of passage   Religious rituals that mark important changes in individual status or social position at different points in the life cycle, such as birth, marriage, or death.

Ritual   A set of acts, usually involving religion or magic, following a sequence established by tradition.

Segmentary system   A hierarchy of more and more inclusive lineages; functions primarily in contexts of conflict between groups.

Self-sufficient   Refers to a characteristic of most prestate societies; the ability to maintain a viable economy and social system with minimal outside contact.

Sex roles Learned social activities and expectations made on the basis of gender.

Shaman A part-time religious practitioner typical of tribal societies who goes into trance to directly communicate with the spirit world for the benefit of the community.

SIDA The Spanish, French, Italian, and Haitian creole acronym for AIDS.

Single-interest relations A relationship based solely on one connection, such as landlord-tenant.

Slash-and-burn techniques Shifting form of cultivation (horticulture) with recurrent, alternate clearing and burning of vegetation and planting in the burnt fields; swidden.

Social class In state-level societies, a stratum in a social hierarchy based on differential group access to means of production and control over distribution; often endogamous.

Social control Practices that induce members of a society to conform to the expected behavior patterns of their culture; includes informal mechanisms, like gossip, legal systems, and punishment.

Social mobility The upward or downward movement of individuals or groups in a society characterized by social stratification.

Social networks An informal pattern of organization based on the complex web of social relations linking individuals; includes factors like kinship, friendship, economics, or political ties.

Social organization A culturally inherited system that orders social relations within social groups.

Social stratification An arrangement of statuses or groups within a society into a pattern of socially superior and inferior ranks; based on differential access to strategic resources.

Socialization The development, through the influence of parents and others, of patterns of thought and behavior in children that conform to beliefs and values of a particular culture.

Society A socially bounded, spacially contiguous group of people who interact in basic economic and political institutions and share a particular culture; societies retain relative stability across generations.

Sociocultural Refers to the complex combination of social and cultural factors.

Sociolinguistics A subfield of anthropological linguistics emphasizing the study of the social correlates to variations in speech patterns.

States A complex society characterized by urban centers, agricultural production, labor specialization, standing armies, permanent boundaries, taxation, centralized authority, public works, and laws designed to maintain the status quo.

Status Position in a social system that is characterized by certain rights, obligations, expected behaviors (roles), and certain social symbols.

Stigma Socially constructed shame or discredit.

Stratified societies A society in which groups experience structured inequality of access not only to power and prestige, but also to economically important resources.

Subculture The culture of a subgroup of a society that has its own distinctive ideas, beliefs, values, and world view.

Swidden Slash-and-burn horticulture.

Symbol A sign that consistently but arbitrarily represents an object or meaning; the basis of communication within a culture.

Taboo A supernaturally forbidden act as defined by a culture, violation of which can have severe negative consequences.

Time allocation study A quantitative anthropological method that identifies what people do and how much time they spend doing various activities; useful for cross-cultural comparison.

Totem A symbolic plant or animal associated with a social group (clan) used for identification and religious expression.

Transnational culture A pattern of cultural beliefs and behaviors characteristic of elites throughout the world and often spread through mass media.

Tribe A relatively small, usually horticultural, society organized on principles of kinship, characterized by little social stratification and no centralized political authority, and whose members share a culture and language.

Urban villages Small (usually segregated) communities of minorities or rural migrants located in cities.

Urbanization The worldwide process of the growth of cities at the expense of rural populations.

Usufruct rights The legal right of using land (or resources on land) which is not one's private property.

Values The ideals of a culture that are concerned with appropriate goals and behavior.

Walkabout A custom of Australian Aborigines involving a long circular journey to sacred places and a return to home.

World view The particular way in which a society constructs ideas of space, time, social relationship, and the meaning of life.

Index